MyEconLab® Provides the Power of Practice

Optimize your study time with **MyEconLab**, the online assessment and tutorial system. When you take a sample test online, **MyEconLab** gives you targeted feedback and a personalized Study Plan to identify the topics you need to review.

Study Plan

The Study Plan shows you the sections you should study next, gives easy access to practice problems, and provides you with an automatically generated quiz to prove mastery of the course material.

Unlimited Practice

As you work each exercise, instant feedback helps you understand and apply the concepts. Many Study Plan exercises contain algorithmically generated values to ensure that you get as much practice as you need.

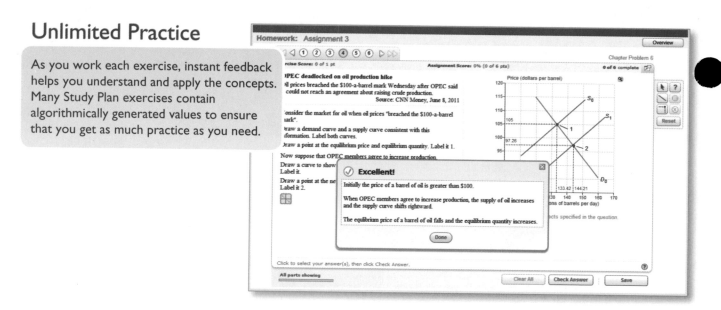

Learning Resources

Study Plan problems link to learning resources that further reinforce concepts you need to master.

- **Help Me Solve This** learning aids help you break down a problem much the same way as an instructor would do during office hours. Help Me Solve This is available for select problems.

- **eText links** are specific to the problem at hand so that related concepts are easy to review just when they are needed.

- A **graphing tool** enables you to build and manipulate graphs to better understand how concepts, numbers, and graphs connect.

MyEconLab®

Find out more at www.myeconlab.com

Real-Time Data Analysis Exercises

Up-to-date macro data is a great way to engage in and understand the usefulness of macro variables and their impact on the economy. Real-Time Data Analysis exercises communicate directly with the Federal Reserve Bank of St. Louis's FRED site, so every time FRED posts new data, students see new data.

End-of-chapter exercises accompanied by the Real-Time Data Analysis icon include Real-Time Data versions in **MyEconLab**.

Select in-text figures labeled **MyEconLab** Real-Time Data update in the electronic version of the text using FRED data.

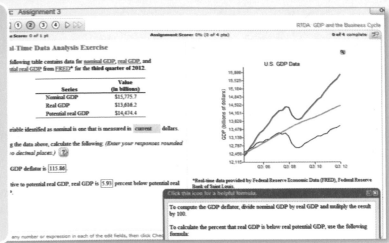

Current News Exercises

Posted weekly, we find the latest microeconomic and macroeconomic news stories, post them, and write auto-graded multi-part exercises that illustrate the economic way of thinking about the news.

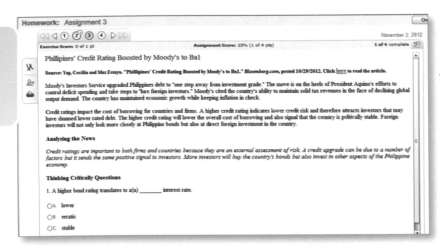

Interactive Homework Exercises

Participate in a fun and engaging activity that helps promote active learning and mastery of important economic concepts.

Pearson's experiments program is flexible and easy for instructors and students to use. For a complete list of available experiments, visit *www.myeconlab.com.*

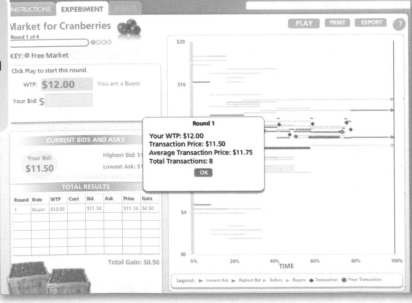

PEARSON Choices

Providing Options and Value in Economics

Money, Banking, and the Financial System

Second Edition

R. Glenn Hubbard
Columbia University

Anthony Patrick O'Brien
Lehigh University

PEARSON

Boston Columbus Indianapolis New York San Francisco Upper Saddle River
Amsterdam Cape Town Dubai London Madrid Milan Munich Paris Montreal Toronto
Delhi Mexico City São Paulo Sydney Hong Kong Seoul Singapore Taipei Tokyo

Dedication

For Constance, Raph, and Will
—R. Glenn Hubbard

**For Cindy, Matthew, Andrew,
and Daniel**
—Anthony Patrick O'Brien

Editor in Chief: Donna Battista
Executive Editor: David Alexander
AVP/Executive Development Editor: Lena Buonanno
VP/Director of Development: Stephen Deitmer
Senior Editorial Project Manager: Lindsey Sloan
Director of Marketing: Maggie Moylan
Executive Marketing Manager: Lori DeShazo
Managing Editor: Jeff Holcomb
Senior Production Project Manager: Kathryn Dinovo
Manufacturing Director: Evelyn Beaton
Senior Manufacturing Buyer: Carol Melville
Creative Director: Christy Mahon

Senior Art Director: Jonathan Boylan
Cover Illustration: Nikita Prokhorov
Manager, Rights and Permissions: Michael Joyce
Permissions Specialist, Project Manager: Samantha Graham
Executive Media Producer: Melissa Honig
Content Lead, MyEconLab: Noel Lotz
Full-Service Project Management: PreMedia Global
Composition: PreMedia Global
Printer/Binder: R. R. Donnelley/Jefferson City
Cover Printer: Lehigh-Phoenix Color/Hagerstown
Text Font: Minion Pro

Library of Congress Cataloging-in-Publication Data is available on request from the Library of Congress.

10 9 8 7 6 5 4 3 2 1

PEARSON

ISBN 10:   0-13-299491-7
ISBN 13: 978-0-13-299491-0

About the Authors

Glenn Hubbard, Professor, Researcher, and Policymaker

 R. Glenn Hubbard is the dean and Russell L. Carson Professor of Finance and Economics in the Graduate School of Business at Columbia University and professor of economics in Columbia's Faculty of Arts and Sciences. He is also a research associate of the National Bureau of Economic Research and a director of Automatic Data Processing, Black Rock Closed-End Funds, KKR Financial Corporation, and MetLife. He received a Ph.D. in economics from Harvard University in 1983. From 2001 to 2003, he served as chairman of the White House Council of Economic Advisers and chairman of the OECD Economy Policy Committee, and from 1991 to 1993, he was deputy assistant secretary of the U.S. Treasury Department. He currently serves as co-chair of the nonpartisan Committee on Capital Markets Regulation and the Corporate Boards Study Group. Hubbard's fields of specialization are public economics, financial markets and institutions, corporate finance, macroeconomics, industrial organization, and public policy. He is the author of more than 100 articles in leading journals, including *American Economic Review, Brookings Papers on Economic Activity, Journal of Finance, Journal of Financial Economics, Journal of Money, Credit, and Banking, Journal of Political Economy, Journal of Public Economics, Quarterly Journal of Economics, RAND Journal of Economics*, and *Review of Economics and Statistics*. His research has been supported by grants from the National Science Foundation, the National Bureau of Economic Research, and numerous private foundations.

Tony O'Brien, Award-Winning Professor and Researcher

 Anthony Patrick O'Brien is a professor of economics at Lehigh University. He received a Ph.D. from the University of California, Berkeley, in 1987. He has taught principles of economics for more than 15 years, in both large sections and small honors classes. He received the Lehigh University Award for Distinguished Teaching. He was formerly the director of the Diamond Center for Economic Education and was named a Dana Foundation Faculty Fellow and Lehigh Class of 1961 Professor of Economics. He has been a visiting professor at the University of California, Santa Barbara, and at Carnegie Mellon University. O'Brien's research has dealt with such issues as the evolution of the U.S. automobile industry, sources of U.S. economic competitiveness, the development of U.S. trade policy, the causes of the Great Depression, and the causes of black–white income differences. His research has been published in leading journals, including *American Economic Review, Quarterly Journal of Economics, Journal of Money, Credit, and Banking, Industrial Relations, Journal of Economic History, Explorations in Economic History*, and the *Journal of Policy History*. His research has been supported by grants from government agencies and private foundations. In addition to teaching and writing, O'Brien also serves on the editorial board of the *Journal of Socio-Economics*.

Brief Contents

Contents

Chapter 5   The Risk Structure and Term Structure of Interest Rates

124

Chapter 6   The Stock Market, Information, and Financial Market Efficiency   157

Chapter 7   Derivatives and Derivative Markets   190

Chapter 8   The Market for Foreign Exchange   224

Chapter 11   Investment Banks, Mutual Funds, Hedge Funds, and the Shadow Banking System   313

Chapter 12   Financial Crises and Financial Regulation   349

Chapter 13   The Federal Reserve and Central Banking   387

Chapter 14   The Federal Reserve's Balance Sheet and the Money Supply Process   415

Chapter 15   Monetary Policy   447

Chapter 16   The International Financial System and Monetary Policy
487

Chapter 17   Monetary Theory I: The Aggregate Demand and Aggregate Supply Model
519

Preface

Do You Think This Might Be Important?

It's customary for authors to begin textbooks by trying to convince readers that their subject is important—even exciting. Following the events of the financial crisis and recession of 2007–2009, we doubt anyone needs to be convinced that the study of money, banking, and financial markets is important. And it's exciting . . . maybe a little too exciting. Nothing comparable to the upheaval of 2007–2009 had happened in the financial system since the Great Depression of the 1930s. The financial crisis changed virtually every aspect of how money is borrowed and lent, how banks and other financial firms operate, and how policy-makers regulate the financial system. More than five years after the beginning of the crisis, there seems little doubt that its effects will linger for a very long time, just as did the effects of the Great Depression.

New to This Edition

We were gratified by the enthusiastic response of students and instructors who used the first edition. The response confirmed our view that a modern, relatively brief approach, paying close attention to recent developments in policy and theory, would find a receptive audience. In this second edition, we retain the approach of our first edition while making several changes to address feedback from instructors and students and also to reflect our own classroom experiences. Here is a summary of our key changes. Please see the pages that follow for details about these changes:

- Replaced 7 chapter-opening cases and updated retained cases
- Added 16 new *Making the Connection* features, including several that appeal to students' personal lives and decisions
- Added more than 40 new real-time data exercises that students can complete on MyEconLab
- Added 2 new *Solved Problems* features, and updated retained *Solved Problems*. Some *Solved Problems* also involve subjects that appeal to students' personal lives and decisions.
- Replaced or updated approximately one-half of the questions and problems at the end of each chapter
- Updated graphs and tables with the latest available data

New Chapter-Opening Cases

Each chapter-opening case provides a real-world context for learning, sparks students' interest in money and banking, and helps to unify the chapter. The second edition includes the following new chapter-opening cases:

- "Will Investors Lose Their Shirts in the Market for Treasury Bonds?" (Chapter 3, "Interest Rates and Rates of Return")
- "Are There Any Safe Investments?" (Chapter 4, "Determining Interest Rates")
- "Searching for Yield" (Chapter 5, "The Risk Structure and Term Structure of Interest Rates")
- "Using Financial Derivatives to Reduce Risk" (Chapter 7, "Derivatives and Derivative Markets")
- "Is Ben Bernanke Responsible for Japanese Firms Moving to the United States?" (Chapter 8, "The Market for Foreign Exchange")

- "Should You Crowd-Fund Your Startup?" (Chapter 9, "Transactions Costs, Asymmetric Information, and the Structure of the Financial System")
- "To Buy a House, You Need a Loan" (Chapter 10, "The Economics of Banking")

New Making the Connection *Features and Supporting Exercises at the End of Each Chapter*

Each chapter includes two or more *Making the Connection* features that provide real-world reinforcement of key concepts. Several of these *Making the Connection*s cover topics that apply directly to the personal lives and decisions that students make and include the subtitle of *In Your Interest*.

- "Microlending Aids U.S. Small Businesses" (Chapter 1, "Introducing Money and the Financial System")
- "What Do People Do with Their Savings?" (Chapter 1, "Introducing Money and the Financial System")
- "*In Your Interest*: Interest Rates and Student Loans" (Chapter 3, "Interest Rates and Rates of Return")
- "Why Are Bond Interest Rates So Low?" (Chapter 4, "Determining Interest Rates")
- "*In Your Interest*: Should You Invest in Junk Bonds?" (Chapter 5, "The Risk Structure and Term Structure of Interest Rates")
- "*In Your Interest*: Should You Invest in Emerging Markets?" (Chapter 8, "The Market for Foreign Exchange")
- "*In Your Interest*: Is It Safe to Invest Through Crowd-funding?" (Chapter 9, "Transactions Costs, Asymmetric Information, and the Structure of the Financial System")
- "*In Your Interest*: Corporations Are Issuing More Bonds; Should You Buy Them?" (Chapter 9, "Transactions Costs, Asymmetric Information, and the Structure of the Financial System")
- "*In Your Interest*: Your Bank's Message to You: 'Please Go Away!'" (Chapter 10, "The Economics of Banking")
- *In Your Interest*: "Is Your Neighborhood ATM About to Disappear?" (Chapter 10, "The Economics of Banking")
- "*In Your Interest*: Would You Invest in a Hedge Fund if You Could?" (Chapter 11, "Investment Banks, Mutual Funds, Hedge Funds, and the Shadow Banking System")
- "Greece Experiences a 'Bank Jog'" (Chapter 12, "Financial Crises and Financial Regulation")
- "The Consumer Financial Protection Bureau: The New Sheriff of Financial Town" (Chapter 12, "Financial Crises and Financial Regulation")
- "Fedspeak vs. Transparency" (Chapter 13, "The Federal Reserve and Central Banking")
- "*In Your Interest*: If You Were Greek, Would You Prefer the Euro or the Drachma?" (Chapter 16, "The International Financial System and Monetary Policy")
- "'Fracking' Transforms Energy Markets in the United States" (Chapter 17, "Monetary Theory I: The Aggregate Demand and Aggregate Supply Model")

Added More Than 40 New Real-Time Data Exercises That Students Can Complete on MyEconLab

MyEconLab is a powerful assessment and tutorial system that works hand-in-hand with *Money, Banking, and the Financial System*. MyEconLab includes comprehensive homework, quiz, test, and tutorial options, allowing instructors to manage all assessment needs in one program. Key innovations in the MyEconLab course for *Money, Banking, and the Financial System*, second edition, include the following:

- Real-time *Data Analysis Exercises*, marked with 🌐, allow students and instructors to use the absolute latest data from FRED, the online macroeconomic data bank from the Federal Reserve Bank of St. Louis. By completing the exercises, students become familiar with a key data source, learn how to locate data, and develop skills to interpret data.
- In the eText available in MyEconLab, select figures labeled MyEconLab Real-time data allow students to display a popup graph updated with real-time data from FRED.
- Current News Exercises, new to this edition of the MyEconLab course, provide a turn-key way to assign gradable news-based exercises in MyEconLab. Every week, Pearson scours the news, finds a current article appropriate for the money and banking course, creates an exercise around this news article, and then automatically adds it to MyEconLab. Assigning and grading current news-based exercises that deal with the latest money, banking, financial system events and policy issues has never been more convenient.

Other Changes

- New *Solved Problems*—Many students have great difficulty handling problems in applied economics. We help students overcome this hurdle by including worked-out problems in each chapter. The following *Solved Problems* are new to this edition:
  - *"In Your Interest:* How Do You Value a College Education?" (Chapter 3, "Interest Rates and Rates of Return"*)*
  - *"In Your Interest*: Should You Worry About Falling Bond Prices When the Inflation Rate Is Low?" (Chapter 4, "Determining Interest Rates")
- Replaced or updated approximately one-half of the questions and problems at the end of each chapter
- Updated graphs and tables with the latest available data

Our Approach

In this book, we provide extensive analysis of the financial events of the past few years. We believe these events are sufficiently important to be incorporated into the body of the text rather than just added as boxed features. In particular, we stress a lesson policymakers recently learned the hard way: What happens in the shadow banking system is as important to the economy as what happens in the commercial banking system.

We realize, however, that the details of the financial crisis and recession will eventually pass into history. What we strive to do in this text is not to add to the laundry list of facts that students must memorize. Instead, we present students with the underlying economic explanations of why the financial system is organized as it is and how the financial system is connected to the broader economy. We are gratified by the success of our principles of economics textbook, and we have employed a similar approach in this textbook: We provide students with a framework that allows them to apply the theory that they learn in the classroom to the practice of the real world. By learning this framework, students will understand not just the 2007–2009 financial crisis and other past events but also developments in the financial system during the years to come. To achieve this goal, we have built four advantages into this text:

1. A framework for understanding, evaluating, and predicting
2. A modern approach

3. Integration of international topics
4. A focus on the Federal Reserve

Framework of the Text: Understand, Evaluate, Predict

The framework underlying all discussions in this text has three levels. First, students learn to *understand* economic analysis. "Understanding" refers to students developing the economic intuition they need to organize concepts and facts. Second, students learn to *evaluate* current developments and the financial news. Here, we challenge students to use financial data and economic analysis to think critically about how to interpret current events. Finally, students learn to use economic analysis to *predict* likely changes in the economy and the financial system. Having just come through a period in which Federal Reserve officials, members of Congress, heads of Wall Street firms, and nearly everyone else failed to predict a huge financial crisis, the idea that we can prepare students to predict the future of the financial system may seem overly ambitious—to say the least. We admit, of course, that some important events are difficult to anticipate. But knowledge of the economic analysis we present in this book does make it possible to predict many aspects of how the financial system will evolve. For example, in Chapter 12, "Financial Crises and Financial Regulation," we discuss the ongoing cycle of financial crisis, regulatory response, financial innovation, and further regulatory response. The latest episode in this cycle was the passage in July 2010 of the Dodd-Frank *Wall Street Reform and Consumer Protection Act*. With our approach, students learn not just the new regulations contained in Dodd-Frank but, more importantly, the key lesson that over time innovations by financial firms are likely to supersede many of the provisions of Dodd-Frank. In other words, students will learn that the financial system is not static—it evolves over time in ways that can be understood using economic analysis.

A Modern Approach

Textbooks are funny things. Most contain a mixture of the current and the modern alongside the traditional. Material that is helpful to students is often presented along with material that is not so helpful or that is—frankly—counterproductive. We believe the ideal is to produce a textbook that is modern and incorporates the best of recent research on monetary policy and the financial system without chasing every fad in economics or finance. In writing this book, we have looked at the topics in the money and banking course with fresh eyes. We have pruned discussion of material that is less relevant to the modern financial system or no longer considered by most economists to be theoretically sound. We have also tried to be as direct as possible in informing students of what is and is not important in the financial system and policymaking as they exist today. For example, rather than include the traditional long discussion of the role of reserve requirements as a monetary policy tool, we provide a brief overview and note that the Federal Reserve has not changed reserve requirements since 1992. Similarly, it has been several decades since the Fed paid serious attention to targets for M1 and M2. Therefore, in Chapter 18, "Monetary Theory II: The *IS–MP* Model," we replace the *IS–LM* model—which assumes that the central bank targets the money stock, rather than an interest rate—with the *IS–MP* model, first suggested by David Romer more than 15 years ago. We believe that our modern approach improves the ability of students to make the connection between the text material and the economic and financial world they read about. (For those who do wish to cover the *IS–LM* model, we provide an appendix on that model at the end of Chapter 18.)

By cutting out-of-date material, we have achieved two important goals: (1) We provide a much briefer and more readable text, and (2) we have made room for discussion of essential topics, such as the "shadow banking system" of investment banks, hedge funds, and mutual funds, as well as the origins and consequences of financial crises. See Chapter 11, "Investment Banks, Mutual Funds, Hedge Funds, and the Shadow Banking System," and Chapter 12, "Financial Crises and Financial Regulation." Other texts either omit these topics or cover them only briefly.

We have both taught money and banking to undergraduate and graduate students for many years. We believe that the modern, real-world approach in our text will engage students in ways that no other text can.

Integration of International Topics

When the crisis in subprime mortgages began, Federal Reserve Chairman Ben Bernanke famously observed that it was unlikely to cause much damage to the U.S. housing market, much less the wider economy. (We discuss Bernanke's argument in Chapter 12, "Financial Crises and Financial Regulation," where we note that he was hardly alone in making such statements.) As it turned out, of course, the subprime crisis devastated not only the U.S. housing market but the U.S. financial system, the U.S. economy, and the economies of most of the developed world. That a problem in one part of one sector of one economy could cause a worldwide crisis is an indication that a textbook on money and banking must take seriously the linkages between the U.S. and other economies. Our text consists of only 18 chapters and is one of the briefest texts on the market. We achieved this brevity by carefully pruning many out-of-date and esoteric topics to focus on the essentials, which includes a careful exploration of international topics. We devote two full chapters to international topics: Chapter 8, "The Market for Foreign Exchange," and Chapter 16, "The International Financial System and Monetary Policy." In these chapters, we discuss such issues as the European sovereign debt crisis and the increased coordination of monetary policy actions among central banks. We realize, however, that, particularly in this course, what is essential to one instructor is optional to another. So, we have written the text in a way that allows instructors to skip one or both of the international chapters.

A Focus on the Federal Reserve

We can hardly claim to be unusual in focusing on the Federal Reserve in a money and banking textbook . . . but we do! Of course, all money and banking texts discuss the Fed, but generally not until near the end of the book—and the semester. Based on speaking to instructors in focus groups and based on our own teaching experience, we believe that this approach is a serious mistake. We have found that students often have trouble integrating the material in the money and banking course. To them, the course often seems a jumble of unrelated topics. Particularly in light of recent events, the role of the Fed can serve as a unifying theme for the course. Accordingly, we provide an introduction and overview of the Fed in Chapter 1, "Introducing Money and the Financial System," and in each subsequent chapter, we expand on the Fed's role in the financial system. So, by the time students read Chapter 13, "The Federal Reserve and Central Banking," where we discuss the details of the Fed's operation, students already have a good idea of the Fed's importance and its role in the system.

Special Features

We can summarize our objective in writing this textbook as follows: to produce a streamlined, modern discussion of the economics of the financial system and of the links between the financial system and the economy. To implement this objective, we have developed a number of special features. Some are similar to the features that have proven popular and effective aids to learning in our principles of economics textbook, while others were developed specifically for this book.

Key Issue and Question

Issue: During the financial crisis, the bond rating agencies were criticized for having given high ratings to securities that proved to be very risky.

Question: Should the government more closely regulate the credit rating agencies?

Answered on page 151

Answering the Key Question

Continued from page 124

At the beginning of this chapter, we asked:

"Should the government more closely regulate credit rating agencies?"

Like other policy questions we will encounter in this book, this question has no definitive answer. We have seen in this chapter that many investors rely on the credit rating agencies for important information on the default risk on bonds. During the financial crisis of 2007–2009, many bonds—particularly mortgage-backed securities—turned out to have much higher levels of default risk than the credit rating agencies had indicated. Some observers argued that the rating agencies had given those bonds inflated ratings because the agencies have a conflict of interest in being paid by the firms whose bond issues they rate. Other observers, though, argued that the ratings may have been accurate when given, but the creditworthiness of the bonds declined rapidly following the unexpected severity of the housing bust and the resulting financial crisis.

Key Issue–and–Question Approach

We believe that having a key issue and related key question in each chapter provides us with an opportunity to explain how the financial system works within the context of topics students read about online and in newspapers and discuss among themselves and with their families. In Chapter 1, "Introducing Money and the Financial System," we cover the key components of the financial system, introduce the Federal Reserve, and preview the important issues facing the financial system. At the end of Chapter 1, we present 17 key issues and questions that provide students with a roadmap for the rest of the book and help them to understand that learning the basic principles of money, banking, and the financial system will allow them to analyze intelligently the most important issues about the financial system and monetary policy. The goal here is not to make students memorize a catalog of facts. Instead, we use these key issues and questions to demonstrate that an economic analysis of the financial system is essential to understanding recent events. See pages 18–20 in Chapter 1 for a complete list of the issues and questions.

We start each subsequent chapter with a key issue and key question and end each of those chapters by using the concepts introduced in the chapter to answer the question.

Contemporary Opening Cases

Each chapter-opening case provides a real-world context for learning, sparks students' interest in money and banking, and helps to unify the chapter. For example, Chapter 11, "Investment Banks, Mutual Funds, Hedge Funds, and the Shadow Banking System," opens with a discussion of the rise of the shadow banking system in a case study entitled "When Is a Bank Not a Bank? When It's a Shadow Bank!" We revisit this topic throughout the chapter.

CHAPTER **11**

Investment Banks, Mutual Funds, Hedge Funds, and the Shadow Banking System

Learning Objectives

After studying this chapter, you should be able to:

11.1 Explain how investment banks operate (pages 314–327)

11.2 Distinguish between mutual funds and hedge funds and describe their roles in the financial system (pages 327–334)

11.3 Explain the roles that pension funds and insurance companies play in the financial system (pages 334–338)

11.4 Explain the connection between the shadow banking system and systemic risk (pages 339–342)

When Is A Bank Not A Bank? When It's A Shadow Bank!

What is a hedge fund? What is the difference between a commercial bank and an investment bank? At the beginning of the financial crisis of 2007–2009, most Americans would have been unable to answer these questions. Many members of Congress were in a

been deposited in banks, and they were using these funds to provide credit that banks had previously provided. These nonbanks were using newly developed financial securities that even long-time veterans of Wall Street often did not fully understand.

...d later became secretary of the ...a administration. A Federal ...s that by 2008, the shadow ...rown to be more than 50% larger ...anking system.

...isis worsened, two large investment ...nd Lehman Brothers—and ...—American International Group ...nter of the storm. Although many ...re also drawn into the crisis, 2007– ...irst time in U.S. history that a ma- ...not originated in the commercial ...ems with nonbanks made dealing ...fficult because U.S. policymaking and regulatory structures were based on the assumption

that commercial banks were the most important financial firms. In particular, the Federal Reserve System had been set up in 1913 to stabilize and regulate the commercial banking system.

Partly as a result of the financial crisis, the size of the shadow banking system has declined relative to the size of the commercial banking system, although shadow banking remains larger. Following the financial crisis, in 2010 Congress passed the Wall Street Reform and Consumer Protection Act, or the Dodd-Frank Act, which increased to some extent federal regulation of the shadow banking system. But a number of policymakers and economists continue to believe that shadow banking remains a source of instability in the financial system.

Sources: Zoltan Pozar, et al., "The Shadow Banking System," Federal Reserve Bank of New York, Staff Report No. 458, July 2010, Revised February 2012; Timothy F. Geithner, "Reducing Systemic Risk in a Dynamic Financial System," talk at The Economic Club of New York, June 9, 2008; and Paul McCulley, "Discussion," Federal Reserve Bank of Kansas City, *Housing, Housing Finance, and Monetary Policy*, 2007, p. 485.

Making the Connection Features

Each chapter includes two to four *Making the Connection* features that present real-world reinforcement of key concepts and help students learn how to interpret what they read on the Web and in newspapers. Most *Making the Connection* features use relevant, stimulating, and provocative news stories, many focused on pressing policy issues. Several of these *Making the Connections* cover topics that apply directly to the personal lives and decisions that students make and include the subtitle of *In Your Interest*.

Here are examples:

- "*In Your Interest*: Interest Rates and Student Loans" (Chapter 3, page 61)

- "*In Your Interest*: Interest Rates and Student Loans" (Chapter 3, page 61)

- "*In Your Interest*: How Much Volatility Should You Expect in the Stock Market?" (Chapter 7, page 210)

- "Has Securitization Increased Adverse Selection Problems in the Financial System?" (Chapter 9, page 263)

- "*In Your Interest*: Your Bank's Message to You: 'Please Go Away!'" (Chapter 10, page 291)

- "Did Moral Hazard Derail Investment Banks?" (Chapter 11, page 322)

- "Why Was the Severity of the 2007–2009 Recession So Difficult to Predict?" (Chapter 12, page 355)

Each *Making the Connection* has at least one supporting end-of-chapter problem to allow students to test their understanding of the topic discussed.

Making the Connection | In Your Interest

Interest Rates and Student Loans

With rising tuition costs, more students are taking out student loans, and the loans are for larger amounts. In 2012, the total amount of student loans outstanding passed $1 trillion for the first time—more than the total value of credit card debt. Student loan payments are often the largest item in the budgets of recent college graduates. Even future presidents are not immune. According to Michelle Obama: "In fact, when [Barack and I] were first married . . . our combined monthly student loan bills were actually higher than our mortgage."

There are three main types of student loans:

1. Subsidized student loans
2. Unsubsidized student loans
3. Private loans

In 2012, most undergraduate students were eligible to borrow up to $31,000 in federal student loans, with a maximum of $23,000 being subsidized loans. In 2012, subsidized federal student loans had a fixed interest rate of 3.4% and unsubsidized federal loans had an interest rate of 6.8%. Under the standard repayment plan, federal student loans are paid back over 10 years. Private student loans, obtained from banks, have a variety of interest rates and repayment times.

We can use the concepts of compounding and discounting to analyze some of the ... With a payback ... or many ... nber that ... make is a ... ears, you are paying down the $20,000 principal more slowly, so you are paying more in total interest over the life of your loan. With a 10-year payback period, your total interest payments are $7,619.28, while with a 30-year payback period, your total interest payments are nearly $27,000, or almost four times as high.

Being familiar with the interest rate concepts we are discussing in this chapter can help students and their parents as they decide how to finance a college education. Helpful loan calculators are available on the studentaid.ed.gov and bankrate.com Web sites.

Sources: Rachel Louise Ensign, "Time to Repay Student Loans," *Wall Street Journal*, September 15, 2012; Charlie Spiering, "At Princeton, Michelle Obama Complains about Her Student Loans," *Washington Examiner*, September 24, 2012; "Student Loans," *New York Times*, September 9, 2012; and studentaid.ed.gov.

See related problem 2.6 at the end of the chapter.

Solved Problem Features

Many students have great difficulty handling problems in applied economics. We help students overcome this hurdle by including worked-out problems in each chapter. Our goals are to keep students focused on the main ideas of each chapter and to give students a model of how to solve an economic problem by breaking it down step by step. Several of these *Solved Problems* cover topics that apply directly to the personal lives and decisions that students make and include the subtitle *In Your Interest*.

Additional exercises in the end-of-chapter *Problems and Applications* section are tied to every *Solved Problem*. Students can also complete related *Solved Problems* on www.myeconlab.com. (See page xxv of this preface for more on MyEconLab.)

Solved Problem 3.1A | In Your Interest

Using Compound Interest to Select a Bank CD

Suppose you are considering investing $1,000 in one of the following bank CDs:

- The first CD will pay an interest rate of 4% per year for three years

- The second CD will pay an interest rate of 10% the first year, 1% the second year, and 1% the third year

Which CD should you choose?

Solving the Problem

Step 1 Review the chapter material. This problem is about compound interest, so you may want to review the section "Compounding for More Than One Period" on page 52.

Step 2 Calculate the future valu... interest rate is the same ... years will be equal to the ... principal, multiplied by 1 ...

$1,00...

Step 3 Calculate the future valu... second CD, the interest r... different compounding fa...

$1,000 × (1 + 0.10...

Step 4 Decide which CD you should choose. You should choose the investment with the highest future value, so you should choose the first CD.

EXTRA CREDIT: Note that the average interest rate received across the three years is 4% for both CDs. When asked to guess the answer to this problem without first doing the calculations, many students choose the second CD. They reason that the high 10% interest rate received in the first year means that even though the interest rates in the second and third years are low, the second CD will end up with the higher future value. As the table below shows, although the first CD starts out well behind after the first year, it finishes the third year with the higher value. This example illustrates the sometimes surprising results of compounding.

	First CD	Second CD
After 1 year	$1,040.00	$1,100.00
After 2 years	1,081.60	1,111.00
After 3 years	1,124.86	1,122.11

See related problem 1.6 at the end of the chapter.

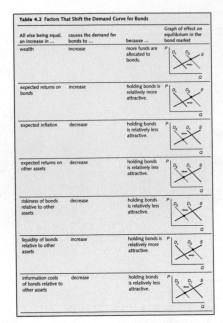

Table 4.2 Factors That Shift the Demand Curve for Bonds

All else being equal, an increase in ...	causes the demand for bonds to ...	because ...	Graph of effect on equilibrium in the bond market
wealth	increase	more funds are allocated to bonds.	
expected returns on bonds	increase	holding bonds is relatively more attractive.	
expected inflation	decrease	holding bonds is relatively less attractive.	
expected returns on other assets	decrease	holding bonds is relatively less attractive.	
riskiness of bonds relative to other assets	decrease	holding bonds is relatively less attractive.	
liquidity of bonds relative to other assets	increase	holding bonds is relatively more attractive.	
information costs of bonds relative to other assets	decrease	holding bonds is relatively less attractive.	

Graphs and Summary Tables

We use four devices to help students read and interpret graphs:

1. Detailed captions
2. Boxed notes
3. Color-coded curves
4. Summary tables with graphs

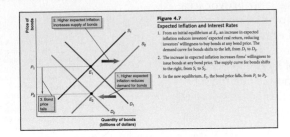

Figure 4.7
Expected Inflation and Interest Rates

1. From an initial equilibrium at E_1, an increase in expected inflation reduces investors' expected real return, reducing investors' willingness to buy bonds at any bond price. The demand curve for bonds shifts to the left, from D_1 to D_2.

2. The increase in expected inflation increases firms' willingness to issue bonds at any bond price. The supply curve for bonds shifts to the right, from S_1 to S_2.

3. In the new equilibrium, E_2, the bond price falls, from P_1 to P_2.

Key Terms and Problems

Key Terms

Bond rating, p. 126
Default risk (or credit risk), p. 126
Expectations theory, p. 140

Liquidity premium theory (or preferred habitat theory), p. 147
Municipal bonds, p. 132
Risk structure of interest rates, p. 125

Segmented markets theory, p. 146
Term premium, p. 147
Term structure of interest rates, p. 137

5.1 The Risk Structure of Interest Rates
Explain why bonds with the same maturity can have different interest rates.

Review Questions

1.1 Briefly explain why bonds that have the same maturities often do not have the same interest rates.

1.2 How is a bond's rating related to the bond issuer's creditworthiness?

1.3 How does the interest rate on an illiquid bond compare with the interest rate on a liquid bond? How does the interest rate on a bond with high information costs compare with the interest rate on a b

1.4 What

1.5 Comp
the fo
Hous
by the

Problems

1.6 Draw
show
lower
curve
befor

1.7 Acco

1.8 **[Related to the** Chapter Opener **on page 124]**
According to an article in the *New York Times*, in 2012, "everyone has piled into" the junk bond market. The article also observed, "The average yields on these bonds have dropped to 6.6 percent, hovering near a record low."

a. What are junk bonds?

b. Is there a connection between everyone

1.10 **[Related to the** Making the Connection **on page 129]**
According to an article in the *New York Times*, "It was the near universal agreement that potential conflicts were embedded in the [bond] ratings model." What is the bond ratings model? What potential conflicts are embedded in it?
Source: David Segal, "Debt Raters Avoid Overhaul After Crisis," *New York Times*, December 7, 2009.

1.11 Some economists have argued that one important role of rating a
agers of firms that i
funds raised in way
best interests of the
Why might the ma
ent goals than the
bonds? How does t
reduce this conflict
managers?

demand for Spanish government bonds was increasing or decreasing? Briefly explain.

b. Can we tell from the headline whether the prices of Spanish government bonds were increasing or decreasing? Briefly explain.

c. The article observes that Spain is "reaping the bitter harvest of a decade of ambitious and often unchecked spending on infrastructure and services." What does this observation have to do with the article's headline?

5.2 The Term Structure of Interest Rates
Explain why bonds with different maturities can have different interest rates.

Review Questions

2.1 How does the Treasury yield curve illustrate the term structure of interest rates?

2.2 What are three key facts about the term structure?

2.3 Briefly describe the three theories of the term structure.

Problems and Applications

2.4 Suppose that you want to invest for three years to earn the highest possible return. You have three options: (a) Roll over three one-year bonds, which pay interest rates of 8% in the first year, 11% in the second year, and 7% in the third year; (b) buy a two-year bond with a 10% interest rate

gives you the highest return by 2018: (a) Buy a four-year bond on January 1, 2014; (b) buy a three-year bond January 1, 2014, and a one-year bond January 1, 2017; (c) buy a two-year bond January 1, 2014, a one-year bond January 1, 2016, and another one-year bond January 1, 2017; or (d) buy a one-year bond January 1, 2014, and then additional one-year bonds on the first days of 2015, 2016, and 2017?

2.6 Suppose that the interest rate on a one-year Treasury bill is currently 1% and that investors expect that the interest rates on one-year Treasury bills over the next three years will be 2%, 3%, and 2%. Use the expectations theory to calculate the current interest rates on two-year, three-year, and four-year Treasury notes.

Review Questions and Problems and Applications—Grouped by Learning Objective to Improve Assessment

The end-of-chapter *Review Questions* and *Problems and Applications* are grouped under learning objectives. The goals of this organization are to make it easier for instructors to assign problems based on learning objectives, both in the book and in MyEconLab, and to help students efficiently review material that they find difficult. If students have difficulty with a particular learning objective, an instructor can easily identify which end-of-chapter questions and problems support that objective and assign them as homework or discuss them in class. Exercises in a chapter's *Problems and Applications* section are available in MyEconLab. Using MyEconLab, students can complete these and many other exercises online, get tutorial help, and receive instant feedback and assistance on exercises they answer incorrectly. Also, student learning will be enhanced by having the summary material and problems grouped together by learning objective, which will allow students to focus on the parts of the chapter they find most challenging. Each major section of the chapter, paired with a learning objective, has at least two review questions and three problems.

We include one or more end-of-chapter problems that test students' understanding of the content presented in each *Solved Problem*, *Making the Connection*, and chapter opener. Instructors can cover a feature in class and assign the corresponding problem for homework. The Test Item Files also include test questions that pertain to these special features.

Data Exercises

Each chapter ends with at least two *Data Exercises* that help students become familiar with a key data source, learn how to locate data, and develop skills to interpret data.

Real-time *Data Analysis Exercises*, marked with 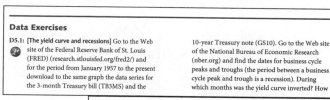, allow students and instructors to use the very latest data from FRED, the online macroeconomic data bank from the Federal Reserve Bank of St. Louis.

Data Exercises

D5.1: [The yield curve and recessions] Go to the Web site of the Federal Reserve Bank of St. Louis (FRED) (research.stlouisfed.org/fred2/) and for the period from January 1957 to the present download to the same graph the data series for the 3-month Treasury bill (TB3MS) and the 10-year Treasury note (GS10). Go to the Web site of the National Bureau of Economic Research (nber.org) and find the dates for business cycle peaks and troughs (the period between a business cycle peak and trough is a recession). During which months was the yield curve inverted? How many of these periods were followed within a year by a recession?

D5.2: [Predicting with the yield curve] Go to www.treasury.gov and find the page "Daily Treasury Yield Curve Rates." Briefly describe the current shape of the yield curve. Can you use the yield curve to draw any conclusion about what investors in the bond market expect will happen to the economy in the future? org/fred2/) and for the period from January 1997 to the present, download to the same graph the data series for the BofA Merrill Lynch US Corporate AAA Effective Yield (BAMLC0A1CAAAEY) and the BofA Merrill Lynch US High Yield CCC or Below Effective Yield (BAMLH0A3HYCEY). Describe how the difference between the yields on high-grade corporate bonds and on junk bonds have changed over this period.

Supplements

The authors and Pearson Education have worked together to integrate the text, print, and media resources to make teaching and learning easier.

MyEconLab

MyEconLab is a powerful assessment and tutorial system that works hand-in-hand with *Money, Banking, and the Financial System*, second edition. MyEconLab includes comprehensive homework, quiz, test, and tutorial options, allowing instructors to manage all assessment needs in one program. Key innovations in the MyEconLab course for *Money, Banking, and the Financial System*, second edition, include the following:

- Real-time *Data Analysis Exercises*, marked with 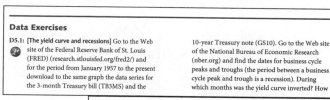, allow students and instructors to use the very latest data from FRED, the online macroeconomic data bank from the Federal Reserve Bank of St. Louis. By completing the exercises, students become familiar with a key data source, learn how to locate data, and develop skills to interpret data.

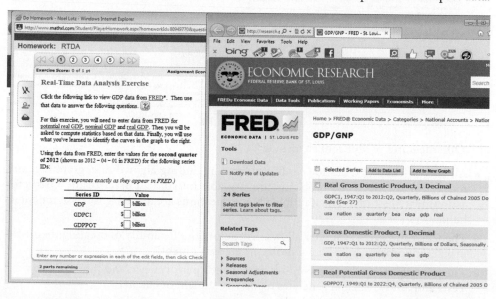

- In the eText available in MyEconLab, select figures labeled MyEconLab Real-time data allow students to display a popup graph updated with real-time data from FRED.

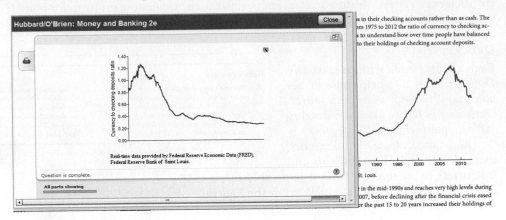

- Current News Exercises, new to this edition of the MyEconLab course, provide a turn-key way to assign gradable news-based exercises in MyEconLab. Each week, Pearson scours the news, finds a current article appropriate for the money and banking course, creates an exercise around this news article, and then automatically adds it to MyEconLab. Assigning and grading current news-based exercises that deal with the latest macro events and policy issues has never been more convenient.

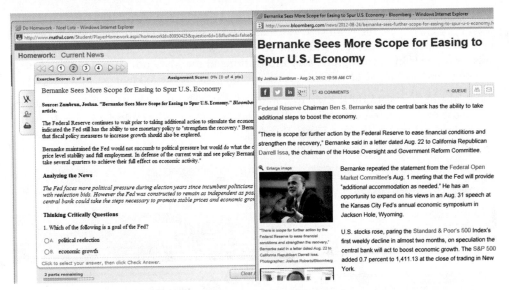

Other features of MyEconLab include:

- All end-of-chapter Questions and Problems, including algorithmic, graphing, and numerical questions and problems, are available for student practice and instructor assignment. Test Item File multiple-choice questions are available for assignment as homework.
- The Custom Exercise Builder allows instructors the flexibility of creating their own problems or modifying existing problems for assignment.
- The powerful Gradebook records each student's performance and time spent on the Tests and Study Plan and generates reports by student or chapter.

A more detailed walk-through of the student benefits and features of MyEconLab can be found at the beginning of this book. Visit **www.myeconlab.com** for more information on and an online demonstration of instructor and student features.

MyEconLab content has been created through the efforts of Melissa Honig, executive media producer, and Noel Lotz and Courtney Kamauf, content leads.

Access to MyEconLab can be bundled with your printed text or purchased directly with or without the full eText, at **www.myeconlab.com**.

Test Item File

William Seyfried of Rollins College prepared the *Test Item File*, which includes more than 1,500 multiple-choice and short-answer questions. Test questions are annotated with the following information:

- **Difficulty:** 1 for straight recall, 2 for some analysis, and 3 for complex analysis
- **Type:** Multiple-choice, short-answer, and essay
- **Topic:** The term or concept that the question supports
- **Learning objective:** The major sections of the main text and its end-of-chapter questions and problems are organized by learning objective. The Test Item File questions continue with this organization to make it easy for instructors to assign questions based on the objective they wish to emphasize.
- **Advanced Collegiate Schools of Business (AACSB) Assurance of Learning Standards:**
  Communication
  Ethical Reasoning
  Analytic Skills
  Use of Information Technology
  Multicultural and Diversity
  Reflective Thinking
- **Page number:** The page in the main text where the answer appears allows instructors to direct students to where supporting content appears.
- **Special features in the main book:** Chapter-opening story, the *Key Issue & Question*, *Solved Problem*, and *Making the Connection*.

The Test Item File is available for download from the Instructor's Resource Center (**www.pearsonhighered.com/hubbard**).

The multiple-choice questions in the Test Item File are also available in TestGen software for both Windows and Macintosh computers, and questions can be assigned via MyEconLab. The computerized TestGen package allows instructors to customize, save, and generate classroom tests. The TestGen program permits instructors to edit, add, or delete questions from the Test Item Files; analyze test results; and organize a database of tests and student results. This software allows for extensive flexibility and ease of use. It provides many options for organizing and displaying tests, along with search and sort features. The software and the Test Item Files can be downloaded from the Instructor's Resource Center (**www.pearsonhighered.com/hubbard**).

PowerPoint Lecture Presentation

Instructors can use the PowerPoint slides for class presentations, and students can use them for lecture preview or review. These slides include all the graphs, tables, and equations from the textbook. Student versions of the PowerPoint slides are available as PDF files. These files allow students to print the slides and bring them to class for note taking. Instructors can download these PowerPoint presentations from the Instructor's Resource Center (**www.pearsonhighered.com/hubbard**).

Blackboard and WebCT Course Content

Pearson Education offers fully customizable course content for the Blackboard and WebCT Course Management Systems.

CourseSmart for Instructors CourseSmart goes beyond traditional expectations, providing instant online access to the textbooks and course materials you need at a lower cost to students. And, even as students save money, you can save time and hassle with a digital textbook that allows you to search the most relevant content at the very moment you need it. Whether it's evaluating textbooks or creating lecture notes to help students with difficult concepts, CourseSmart can make life a little easier. See how when you visit **www. coursesmart.com/instructors**.

CourseSmart for Students CourseSmart goes beyond traditional expectations, providing instant, online access to the textbooks and course materials students need at lower cost. Students can also search, highlight, and take notes anywhere, at any time. See all the benefits to students at **www.coursesmart.com/students**.

Accuracy Checkers, Class Testers, and Reviewers

The guidance and recommendations of the following instructors helped us to revise the content and features of this text. While we could not incorporate every suggestion from every reviewer, we carefully considered each piece of advice we received. We are grateful for the hard work that went into their reviews and truly believe that their feedback was indispensable in revising this text. We appreciate their assistance in making this the best text it could be; they have helped teach a new generation of students about the exciting world of money and banking.

Special thanks to Edward Scahill of the University of Scranton for preparing some of the *Making the Connection* features. We also extend special thanks to Bob Gillette of the University of Kentucky for his extraordinary work accuracy checking these chapters in page proof format and playing a critical role in improving the quality of the final product.

Mohammed Akacem, Metropolitan State College of Denver
Maharukh Bhiladwalla, New York University
Tina A. Carter, Tallahassee Community College
Darian Chin, California State University–Los Angeles
Dennis Farley, Trinity Washington University
Amanda S. Freeman, Kansas State University

Robert Gillette, University of Kentucky
Anthony Gyapong, Pennsylvania State University–Abington
Sungkyu Kwak, Washburn University
Raoul Minetti, Michigan State University
Hilde E. Patron-Boenheim, University of West Georgia
Andrew Prevost, Ohio University
Edward Scahill, University of Scranton
Heather L.R. Tierney, University of California, San Diego

First Edition Accuracy Checkers, Class Testers, and Reviewers

Special thanks to Ed Scahill of the University of Scranton for preparing the *An Inside Look* news feature in the first edition. Nathan Perry of Mesa State College and Robert Gillette of the University of Kentucky helped the authors prepare the end-of-chapter problems.

We are also grateful to Robert Gillette of the University of Kentucky, Duane Graddy of Middle Tennessee State University, Lee Stone of the State University of New York at Geneseo, and their students for class-testing manuscript versions and providing us with guidance on improving the chapters.

First Edition Accuracy Checkers

In a long and relatively complicated manuscript, accuracy checking is of critical importance. Our thanks go to a dedicated group who provided thorough accuracy checking of both the manuscript and page proof chapters. Special thanks to Timothy Yeager of the University of Arkansas for both commenting on and checking the accuracy of all 18 chapters of the manuscript.

Clare Battista, California Polytechnic State University–San Luis Obispo

Howard Bodenhorn, Clemson University

Lee A. Craig, North Carolina State University

Anthony Gyapong, Pennsylvania State University

Robert Gillette, University of Kentucky

Woodrow W. Hughes, Jr., Converse College

Andrew Prevost, Ohio University

Ellis W. Tallman, Oberlin College

Timothy Yeager, University of Arkansas

First Edition Reviewers and Focus Group Participants

We also appreciate the thoughtful comments of our reviewers and focus group participants. They brought home to us once again that there are many ways to teach a money and banking class. We hope that we have written a text with sufficient flexibility to meet the needs of most instructors. We carefully read and considered every comment and suggestion we received and incorporated many of them into the text. We believe that our text has been greatly improved as a result of the reviewing process.

Mohammed Akacem, Metropolitan State College of Denver

Stefania Albanesi, Columbia University

Giuliana Andreopoulos-Campanelli, William Paterson University

Mohammad Ashraf, University of North Carolina–Pembroke

Cynthia Bansak, St. Lawrence University

Clare Battista, California Polytechnic State University–San Luis Obispo

Natalia Boliari, Manhattan College

Oscar Brookins, Northeastern University

Michael Carew, Baruch College

Tina Carter, Florida State University

Darian Chin, California State University–Los Angeles

Chi-Young Choi, University of Texas at Arlington

Julie Dahlquist, University of Texas at San Antonio

Peggy Dalton, Frostburg State University

H. Evren Damar, State University of New York–Brockport

Ranjit Dighe, State University of New York College–Oswego

Carter Doyle, Georgia State University

Mark Eschenfelder, Robert Morris University

Robert Eyler, Sonoma State University

Bill Ford, Middle Tennessee State University

Amanda Freeman, Kansas State University

Joseph Friedman, Temple University

Marc Fusaro, Arkansas Tech University

Soma Ghosh, Albright College

Mark J. Gibson, Washington State University

Anthony Gyapong, Pennsylvania State University

Denise Hazlett, Whitman College

Scott Hein, Texas Tech University

Tahereh Hojjat, DeSales University

Woodrow W. Hughes, Jr., Converse College

Aaron Jackson, Bentley University

Christian Jensen, University of South Carolina

Eungmin Kang, St. Cloud State University

Leonie Karkoviata, University of Houston

Hugo M. Kaufmann, Queens College, City University of New York

Randall Kesselring, Arkansas State University

Ann Marie Klingenhagen, DePaul University

Sungkyu Kwak, Washburn University

John Lapp, North Carolina State University

Robert J. Martel, University of Connecticut

Don Mathews, College of Coastal Georgia

James McCague, University of North Florida

Christopher McHugh, Tufts University

Doug McMillin, Louisiana State University

Carrie Meyer, George Mason University

Jason E. Murasko, University of Houston–Clear Lake

Theodore Muzio, St. John's University

Nick Noble, Miami University

Hilde Patron, University of West Georgia

Douglas Pearce, North Carolina State University

Robert Pennington, University of Central Florida

Dennis Placone, Clemson University

Stephen Pollard, California State University–Los Angeles

Andrew Prevost, Ohio University

Maria Hamideh Ramjerdi, William Paterson University

Luis E. Rivera, Dowling College

Joseph T. Salerno, Pace University

Eugene J. Sherman, Baruch College

Leonie Stone, State University of New York–Geneseo

Ellis W. Tallman, Oberlin College

Richard Trainer, State University of New York–Nassau

Raúl Velázquez, Manhattan College

John Wagner, Westfield State College

Christopher Westley, Jacksonville State University

Shu Wu, The University of Kansas

David Zalewski, Providence College

A Word of Thanks

We benefited greatly from the dedication and professionalism of the Pearson Economics team. Executive Editor David Alexander's energy and support were indispensable. David shares our view that the time has come for a new approach to the money and banking textbook. Just as importantly, he provided words of encouragement whenever our energy flagged. Executive Development Editor Lena Buonanno worked tirelessly to ensure that this text was as good as it could be and to coordinate the many moving parts involved in a project of this complexity. We remain astonished at the amount of time, energy, and unfailing good humor she brought to this project. Without Lena, this book would not have been possible.

Director of Key Markets David Theisen provided valuable insight into the changing needs of money and banking instructors. We have worked with Executive Marketing Manager Lori DeShazo on all three of our books, and we continue to be amazed at her energy and creativity in promoting the field of economics. We also appreciate the input of Steve Deitmer, Director of Development. Lindsey Sloan managed the supplement package that accompanies the text. Emily Brodeur managed the review program. Kathryn Dinovo and Jonathan Boylan turned our manuscript pages into a beautiful published book. Tammy Haskins and Nancy Kincade went above and beyond the call of duty to carefully incorporate all the changes we requested while ensuring consistency and accuracy. We are grateful for their flexibility and the care they took in preparing the text.

Fernando Quijano of Dickinson State University created the graphs, ensuring a consistent style. He also diligently accuracy checked the graphs in two rounds of page proofs. We received excellent and speedy research assistance on the first edition from Andrey Zagorchev. We thank Pam Smith, Elena Zeller, and Jennifer Brailsford for their careful proofreading of two rounds of page proofs. We extend our special thanks to Wilhelmina Sanford of Columbia Business School, whose speedy and accurate typing of multiple drafts is much appreciated.

A good part of the burden of a project of this magnitude is borne by our families, and we appreciate their patience, support, and encouragement.

CHAPTER 1

Introducing Money and the Financial System

Learning Objectives

After studying this chapter, you should be able to:

1.1 Identify the key components of the financial system (pages 2–15)

1.2 Provide an overview of the financial crisis of 2007–2009 (pages 15–18)

1.3 Explain the key issues and questions the financial crisis raises (pages 18–20)

Is Prosperity Just Around the Corner?

In 2007, the United States entered what is likely to be the worst recession of your lifetime. Millions of people lost their jobs during the recession. Although the recession ended in June 2009, the recovery was weak and in late 2012, the unemployment rate was still very high at just below 8%. When the recession began, few economists or policymakers suspected that it would be so deep or that the recovery would be so slow.

The only comparable episode in the past 100 years was the Great Depression of the 1930s. In 1931, President Herbert Hoover famously announced, "Prosperity is just around the corner," even though nine more years of high unemployment lay ahead. During and after the recession of 2007–2009, some policymakers and economists made similarly incorrect predictions that prosperity would soon return. In the fall of 2012, there were some signs that the economic recovery was picking up steam and the unemployment rate was heading toward more normal levels. Even the most optimistic forecasters, however, believed it would take several more years for the economy to return to unemployment rates of 5% to 5.5%, which economists consider to be full employment.

Why was the recession of 2007–2009 so severe, and why was the recovery so weak? The simple answer is that unlike any other recession since the Great Depression of the 1930s, the recession of 2007–2009 had been accompanied by a financial crisis.

To understand why a financial crisis deepens a recession, think about how dependent farmers are on water. Large areas of southern Arizona and California's central valley have rich soils but receive very little rain. Without an elaborate irrigation system of reservoirs and canals, water would not flow to these areas, and farmers could not raise their vast crops of lettuce, asparagus, cotton, and more. The financial system is like an irrigation system, although it is money, not water, that flows through the financial system. During the economic crisis that began in 2007, the financial system was disrupted, and large sections of the U.S. economy were cut off from the flow of funds they needed to thrive. Just as cutting off the irrigation water in California's San Joaquin Valley would halt the production of crops, the financial crisis resulted in a devastating decline in production of goods and services throughout the economy.

Like engineers trying to repair a damaged irrigation canal to restore the flow of water, officials of the U.S. Treasury Department and the Federal Reserve (the Fed) took strong actions during the financial crisis to restore the flow of money through banks and financial markets to the firms and households that depend on it. Although some of these policies were controversial, most economists believe that some government intervention was necessary to pull the economy out of a deep recession.

Few households or firms escaped the fallout from the financial crisis and the recession it caused, so they came to realize the importance of the financial system. However, people also came to realize that the financial system had become very complex.

In this chapter, we provide an overview of the important components of the financial system and introduce key issues and questions that we will explore throughout the book.

1.1 Key Components of the Financial System

Learning Objective
Identify the key components of the financial system.

The purpose of this book is to provide you with the tools you need to understand the modern financial system. First, you should be familiar with the three major components of the financial system:

1. Financial assets
2. Financial institutions
3. The Federal Reserve and other financial regulators

As vendors in baseball parks like to yell: "You can't tell the players without a program." We will briefly consider each of these components now and then return to them in later chapters.

Financial Assets

Asset Anything of value owned by a person or a firm.

Financial asset An asset that represents a claim on someone else for a payment.

Security A financial asset that can be bought and sold in a financial market.

Financial market A place or channel for buying or selling stocks, bonds, and other securities.

An **asset** is anything of value owned by a person or a firm. A **financial asset** is a financial claim, which means that if you own a financial asset, you have a claim on someone else to pay you money. For instance, a bank checking account is a financial asset because it represents a claim you have against a bank to pay you an amount of money equal to the dollar value of your account. Economists divide financial assets into those that are *securities* and those that aren't. A **security** is *tradable*, which means that it can be bought and sold in a *financial market*. **Financial markets** are places or channels for buying and selling stocks, bonds, and other securities, such as the New York Stock Exchange. If you own a share of stock in Apple or Google, you own a security because you can sell that share in the stock market. If you have a checking account at Citibank or Wells Fargo, you can't sell it. So, your checking account is an asset but not a security.

In this book, we will discuss many financial assets. The following are five key categories of assets:

1. Money
2. Stocks
3. Bonds
4. Foreign exchange
5. Securitized loans

Money Although we typically think of "money" as coins and paper currency, even the narrowest government definition of *money* includes funds in checking accounts. In fact, economists have a very general definition of **money**: Anything that people are willing to accept in payment for goods and services or to pay off debts. The **money supply** is the total quantity of money in the economy. As we will see in Chapter 2, money plays an important role in the economy, and there is some debate about the best way to measure it.

Stocks Stocks, also called *equities*, are financial securities that represent partial ownership of a corporation. When you buy a share of Microsoft stock, you become a Microsoft *shareholder*, and you own part of the firm, although only a tiny part because Microsoft has issued millions of shares of stock. When a firm sells additional stock, it is doing the same thing that the owner of a small firm does when taking on a partner: increasing the funds available to the firm, its *financial capital*, in exchange for increasing the number of the firm's owners. As an owner of a share of stock in a corporation, you have a legal claim to a share of the corporation's assets and to a share of its profits, if there are any. Firms keep some of their profits as retained earnings and pay the remainder to shareholders in the form of **dividends**, which are payments corporations typically make every quarter.

Bonds When you buy a **bond** issued by a corporation or a government, you are lending the corporation or the government a fixed amount of money. The **interest rate** is the cost of borrowing funds (or the payment for lending funds), usually expressed as a percentage of the amount borrowed. For instance, if you borrow $1,000 from a friend and pay him back $1,100 a year later, the interest rate on the loan was $100/$1,000 = 0.10, or 10%. Bonds typically pay interest in fixed dollar amounts called *coupons*. When a bond *matures*, the seller of the bond repays the principal. For example, if you buy a $1,000 bond issued by IBM that has a coupon of $65 per year and a maturity of 30 years, IBM will pay you $65 per year for the next 30 years, at the end of which IBM will pay you the $1,000 principal. A bond that matures in one year or less is a *short-term bond*. A bond that matures in more than one year is a *long-term bond*. Bonds can be bought and sold in financial markets, so, bonds are securities just as stocks are.

Foreign Exchange Many goods and services purchased in a country are produced outside that country. Similarly, many investors buy financial assets issued by foreign governments and firms. To buy foreign goods and services or foreign assets, a domestic business or a domestic investor must first exchange domestic currency for foreign currency. For example, consumer electronics giant Best Buy exchanges U.S. dollars for Japanese yen when importing Sony televisions. **Foreign exchange** refers to units of foreign currency. The most important buyers and sellers of foreign exchange are large banks. Banks engage in foreign currency transactions on behalf of investors who want to buy foreign financial assets. Banks also engage in foreign currency transactions on behalf of firms that want to import or export goods and services or to invest in physical assets, such as factories, in foreign countries.

Securitized Loans If you don't have the cash to pay the full price of a car or a house, you can apply for a loan at a bank. Similarly, if a developer wants to build a new office building or shopping mall, the developer can also take out a loan with a bank. Until about 30 years ago, banks made loans with the intention of making profits by collecting interest

Money Anything that is generally accepted in payment for goods and services or to pay off debts.

Money supply The total quantity of money in the economy.

Stock Financial securities that represent partial ownership of a firm; also called *equities*.

Dividend A payment that a corporation makes to its shareholders.

Bond A financial security issued by a corporation or a government that represents a promise to repay a fixed amount of money.

Interest rate The cost of borrowing funds (or the payment for lending funds), usually expressed as a percentage of the amount borrowed.

Foreign exchange Units of foreign currency.

Securitization The process of converting loans and other financial assets that are not tradable into securities.

payments on a loan until the borrower paid off the loan. It wasn't possible to sell most loans in financial markets, so loans were financial assets but not securities. Then, the federal government and some financial firms created markets for many types of loans (see Chapter 11). Loans that banks could sell on financial markets became securities, so the process of converting loans into securities is known as **securitization**.

For example, a bank might grant a *mortgage*, which is a loan a borrower uses to buy a home, and sell it to a government-sponsored enterprise or a financial firm that will bundle the mortgage together with similar mortgages that other banks granted. This bundle of mortgages will form the basis of a new security called a *mortgage-backed security* that will function like a bond. Just as an investor can buy a bond from IBM, the investor can buy a mortgage-backed security from the government agency or financial firm. The bank that grants, or *originates*, the original mortgages will still collect the interest paid by the borrowers and send those interest payments to the government agency or financial firm to distribute to the investors who have bought the mortgage-backed security. The bank will receive fees for originating the loan and for collecting the loan payments from borrowers and distributing them to lenders.

Financial liability A financial claim owed by a person or a firm.

Note that what a saver views as a financial asset a borrower views as a *financial liability*. A **financial liability** is a financial claim owed by a person or a firm. For example, if you take out a car loan from a bank, the loan is an asset from the viewpoint of the bank because it represents your promise to make a certain payment to the bank every month until the loan is paid off. But the loan is a liability to you, the borrower, because you owe the bank the payments specified in the loan.

Financial Institutions

The financial system matches savers and borrowers through two channels: (1) Banks and other *financial intermediaries* and (2) *financial markets*. These two channels are distinguished by how funds flow from savers, or lenders, to borrowers and by the financial institutions involved.[1] Funds flow from lenders to borrowers indirectly through **financial intermediaries**, such as banks, or directly through financial markets, such as the New York Stock Exchange.

Financial intermediary A financial firm, such as a bank, that borrows funds from savers and lends them to borrowers.

If you get a loan from a bank to buy a car, economists refer to this flow of funds as *indirect finance*. The flow is indirect because the funds the bank lends to you come from people who have put money in checking or savings deposits in the bank; in that sense, the bank is not lending its own funds directly to you. On the other hand, if you buy stock that a firm has just issued, the flow of funds is *direct finance* because the funds are flowing directly from you to the firm.

Savers and borrowers can be households, firms, or governments, both domestic and foreign. Figure 1.1 shows that the financial system channels funds from savers to borrowers, and channels *returns* back to savers, both directly and indirectly. Savers receive

---

[1]Note that for convenience, we sometimes refer to households, firms, and governments that have funds they are willing to lend or invest as *lenders,* and we refer to households, firms, and governments that wish to use those funds as *borrowers*. These labels are not strictly accurate because the flow of funds does not always take the form of loans. For instance, investors who buy stock are buying part ownership in a firm, not lending money to the firm.

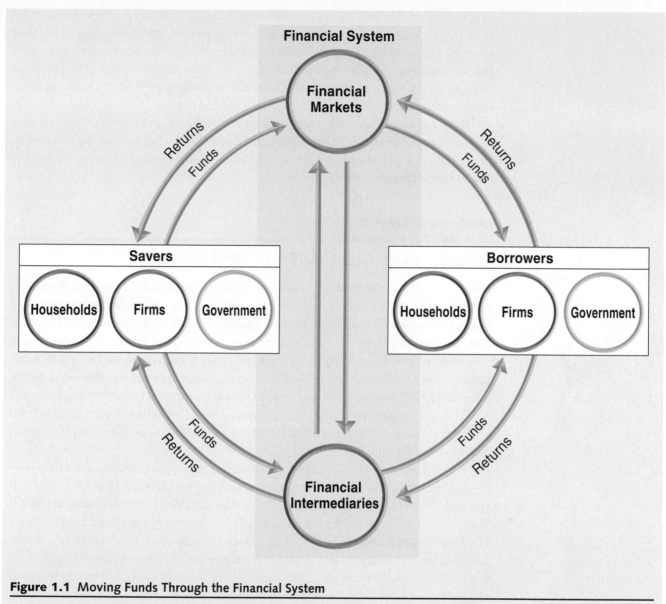

Figure 1.1 Moving Funds Through the Financial System

The financial system transfers funds from savers to borrowers. Borrowers transfer returns back to savers through the financial system. Savers and borrowers include domestic and foreign households, businesses, and governments.

their returns in various forms, including dividend payments on stock, coupon payments on bonds, and interest payments on loans.

Financial Intermediaries **Commercial banks** are the most important financial intermediaries. Commercial banks play a key role in the financial system by taking in deposits from households and firms and investing most of those deposits, either by making loans to households and firms or by buying securities, such as government bonds or securitized loans. Most households rely on borrowing money from banks when they purchase

Commercial bank A financial firm that serves as a financial intermediary by taking in deposits and using them to make loans.

"big-ticket items," such as cars or homes. Similarly, many firms rely on bank loans to meet their short-term needs for *credit*, such as funds to pay for inventories or to meet their payrolls. Many firms rely on bank loans to bridge the gap between the time they must pay for inventories or meet their payrolls and when they receive revenues from the sales of goods and services. Some firms also rely on bank loans to meet their long-term credit needs, such as funds they require to physically expand the firm.

In each chapter, the *Making the Connection* feature discusses a news story or another application related to the chapter material. Read the following *Making the Connection* for a discussion of how firms were affected by the decline in bank lending during the financial crisis that began in 2007.

Making the Connection

Microlending Aids U.S. Small Businesses

Low-income countries generally have poorly developed financial markets. Typically, these countries have no stock and bond markets and only weak banking systems. As a result, the owners of small firms in these countries have had to rely for funds on their own savings, the savings of relatives and friends, or a few local lenders who often charge very high interest rates. In recent years, some small firms have gained access to funds through *microlending* or *microfinance*. Microlending involves making small loans, often just a few hundred dollars or less, to people attempting to start or expand small businesses. The loans are made by a variety of groups, including pooled savings from a village, international aid agencies, or large financial firms, such as Citigroup, often operating through small local banks.

According to many economists, microlending has aided economic growth in low-income countries. Few economists saw microlending playing a role in the U.S. financial system because U.S. firms typically have access to bank loans. But the financial crisis of 2007–2009 greatly reduced the ability of small businesses to borrow from banks.

Large businesses can raise funds in financial markets by selling stocks and bonds, but small businesses don't have this option. Because it's costly for investors to gather information on small businesses, these businesses cannot sell stocks and bonds and must rely instead on loans from banks. Firms use bank loans for a variety of purposes, including to bridge the gap between when the firms must pay employees and suppliers and when they receive revenue from selling their products.

Over the past 20 years, the relationship between banks and small businesses has changed. At one time, government regulations kept many banks small. As a result, banks made most of their loans in a limited geographic area. In those circumstances, bank loan officers usually had extensive personal knowledge of the finances of most local businesses and used that knowledge to determine whether to grant loans. By the 2000s, changes in banking law meant that many small businesses were receiving loans from banks that operated on a regional, or even national, basis. These larger banks typically applied fixed guidelines for granting loans that left little room for the personal judgment traditionally exercised by loan officers of small banks. Such guidelines were both good news and bad news for small businesses. On the one hand, businesses that met the guidelines would receive loans even if aspects of their financial situation not covered by the guidelines made them riskier borrowers. On the other hand, businesses that failed to meet the guidelines might be turned down for loans even though they were very likely to be able to make their payments.

By the mid-2000s, though, many banks became convinced that it would be profitable to loosen their loan guidelines to make more borrowers eligible to receive credit. These banks believed that the larger number of borrowers who would *default* on their loans because of the looser guidelines would be more than offset by the payments received from the additional borrowers who would now qualify for loans. Unfortunately, during the financial crisis that began in mid-2007, the number of borrowers defaulting on loans turned out to be much higher than banks had predicted. Loan losses began rising in the spring of 2008, and by the end of 2009, they were four times greater than at the end of 2007.

In fact, the loan losses during 2007–2009 were by far the largest since the Great Depression of the 1930s. Partly as a result of these losses and partly because of pressure from government bank regulators, most banks tightened their loan guidelines, which made it much more difficult for households and businesses to qualify for loans. Between 2009 and 2010, business loans declined by about 40% before beginning to recover. Large U.S. banks have significantly reduced their small business lending, offering these businesses credit cards instead. Because the credit cards often have low credit limits, involve fees, and have high interest rates, many small businesses find credit cards much less desirable than loans.

Cut off from their normal source of funds, many small businesses had to resort to drastic measures, such as borrowing from pawnshops or borrowing from friends and family members, in order to survive. It was no surprise, then, when many economists argued during the crisis that the economy would not recover until banks increased their lending to small businesses.

In 2012, some small firms began to turn to lenders willing to make microloans similar to those seen in low-income countries. For example, Mohamed Diallo is a cab driver in New York City who needed a loan to buy a cab and go into business for himself. Unable to find a bank willing to lend him money, he was finally able to secure a $2,000 microloan from the Business Center for New Americans, a nonprofit organization. The U.S. Small Business Administration, a federal government agency, has provided funds to a number of microlenders across the country, in an attempt to increase lending to small businesses.

As the U.S. financial system has evolved since the financial crisis, a surprising change has been the increased importance of microlending to small businesses.

Sources: Joseph Adinolfi, "Mini Loans Feed Bigger Ambitions," *Wall Street Journal*, September 8, 2012; Ian Mount, "When Banks Won't Lend, There Are Alternatives, Though Often Expensive," *New York Times*, August 1, 2012; and Gary Fields, "People Pulling Up to Pawnshops Today Are Driving Cadillacs and BMWs," *Wall Street Journal*, December 30, 2008.

See related problem 1.8 at the end of the chapter.

Nonbank Financial Intermediaries Some financial intermediaries, such as *savings and loans*, *savings banks*, and *credit unions*, are legally distinct from banks, although these "nonbanks" operate in a very similar way by taking in deposits and making loans. Other financial intermediaries include investment banks, insurance companies, pension funds, mutual funds, and hedge funds. Although these institutions don't at first glance appear to be very similar to banks, they fulfill a similar function in the financial system by channeling funds from savers to borrowers.

Investment Banks   Investment banks, such as Goldman Sachs and Morgan Stanley, differ from commercial banks in that they do not take in deposits and rarely lend directly to households. Instead, they provide advice to firms issuing stocks and bonds or considering mergers with other firms. They also engage in *underwriting*, in which they guarantee a price to a firm issuing stocks or bonds and then make a profit by selling the stocks or bonds at a higher price. In the late 1990s, investment banks increased their importance as financial intermediaries by becoming heavily involved in the securitization of loans, particularly mortgage loans. Investment banks also began to engage in *proprietary trading*, which involves earning profits by buying and selling securities.

Insurance Companies   Insurance companies specialize in writing contracts to protect their policyholders from the risk of financial losses associated with particular events, such as automobile accidents or fires. Insurance companies collect *premiums* from policyholders, which the companies then invest to obtain the funds necessary to pay claims to policyholders and to cover their other costs. So, for instance, when you buy an automobile insurance policy, the insurance company may lend the premiums you pay to a hotel chain that needs funds to expand.

Pension Funds   For many people, saving for retirement is the most important form of saving. Pension funds invest contributions from workers and firms in stocks, bonds, and mortgages to earn the money necessary to pay pension benefit payments during workers' retirements. With about $13 trillion in assets in 2011, private and state and local government pension funds are an important source of demand for financial securities.

Portfolio A collection of assets, such as stocks and bonds.

Mutual Funds   A mutual fund, such as Fidelity Investment's Magellan Fund, obtains money by selling shares to investors. The mutual fund then invests the money in a **portfolio** of financial assets, such as stocks and bonds, typically charging a small management fee for its services. By buying shares in a mutual fund, savers reduce the costs they would incur if they were to buy many individual stocks and bonds. Small savers who have only enough money to buy a few individual stocks and bonds can also lower their investment risk by buying shares in a mutual fund because most mutual funds hold a large number of stocks and bonds. If a firm issuing a stock or a bond declares bankruptcy, causing the stock or bond to lose all of its value, the effect on a mutual fund's portfolio is likely to be small. The effect might be devastating, though, on a small investor who had invested most of his or her savings in the stock or bond. Because mutual funds are willing to buy back their shares at any time, they also provide savers with easy access to their money.

Hedge Funds   Hedge funds, such as Bridgewater run by Ray Dalio, are similar to mutual funds in that they accept money from investors and use the funds to buy a portfolio of assets. However, a hedge fund typically has no more than 99 investors, all of whom are wealthy individuals or institutions such as pension funds. Hedge funds typically make riskier investments than do mutual funds, and they charge investors much higher fees.

Financial Markets Financial markets are places or channels for buying and selling stocks, bonds, and other securities. Traditionally, financial markets have been physical places, such as the New York Stock Exchange, which is located on Wall Street in New York City, or the London Stock Exchange, which is located in Paternoster Square in London. On these exchanges, dealers would meet face-to-face to trade stocks and bonds. Today, most securities trading takes place electronically between dealers linked by computers and is called "over-the-counter" trading. *NASDAQ*, which originally stood for the *National Association of Securities Dealers Automated Quotation System*, is an over-the-counter market on which the stocks of many high-tech firms such as Apple and Intel are traded. Stocks and bonds sold in a particular market are "listed" on that market. For instance, General Electric is listed on the New York Stock Exchange, and Apple is listed on NASDAQ.

Economists make a distinction between *primary markets* and *secondary markets*. A **primary market** is a financial market in which stocks, bonds, and other securities are sold for the first time. An *initial public offering (IPO)* refers to when a company for the first time sells its stock in the primary market. For example, Facebook's IPO took place in May 2012. A **secondary market** is a financial market in which investors buy and sell already existing securities. For example, if you purchased Facebook stock in 2012 and sold it in 2013, that sale took place in the secondary market. Primary and secondary markets can be in the same physical—or virtual—place, as when an IPO takes place for a stock listed on the New York Stock Exchange or on NASDAQ.

Primary market A financial market in which stocks, bonds, and other securities are sold for the first time.

Secondary market A financial market in which investors buy and sell existing securities.

Making the Connection

What Do People Do with Their Savings?

If you're like most college students, your primary financial asset is your checking account. After you begin your career, though, you'll accumulate a variety of different assets. The Federal Reserve System publishes data on household holdings of financial assets that shows how households divide up their total financial wealth. The figure below compares households' holdings of financial assets in 1978 and 2012. Some assets, such as stocks and bonds, are supplied by financial markets. Other assets, such as bank deposits and mutual fund shares, are supplied by financial intermediaries.

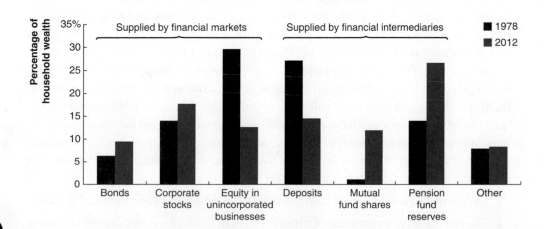

The figure shows some significant changes over the decades in how households hold their financial wealth. The categories of wealth held in assets supplied by financial markets show that households increased their holdings of bonds—including Treasury bonds, corporate bonds, and bonds issued by state and local governments—and stocks from about 22.5% of their total wealth in 1978 to about 27.5% in 2012. But households now have much less equity in unincorporated businesses. Unincorporated businesses include partnerships and sole proprietorships, which are businesses owned by a single person. The equity in these businesses represents the difference between what the businesses could be sold for minus their debts. This equity is a less important part of household wealth partly because many relatively large firms that were organized as partnerships in 1978 had become corporations by 2012.

The categories of wealth held in assets supplied by financial intermediaries show that households now hold a much smaller percentage of their wealth in bank deposits, including checking accounts, savings accounts, and certificates of deposit. Households hold much larger percentages of their wealth in mutual fund shares and as pension fund reserves, which represent the value of household claims on pension plans at private companies, state and local government pension plans, and the value of individual retirement accounts (IRAs). The increase in the value of household pensions is a result of substantial increases in pensions that state and local governments have promised their workers and an increase in the funds workers have deposited in IRAs and 401(k) plans offered by companies. The income workers deposit in IRAs and 401(k) accounts is not taxed until they withdraw the funds after they retire.

Source: Board of Governors of the Federal Reserve, *Flow of Funds Accounts of the United States*, various issues.

See related problem 1.9 at the end of the chapter.

The Federal Reserve and Other Financial Regulators

During the financial crisis of 2007–2009, many people looked around at failing banks, the frozen markets for some financial assets, and plummeting stock prices and asked: "Who's in charge here? Who runs the financial system?" In a sense, these are unusual questions to ask because the point of a market system is that no one individual or group is in charge. Consumers decide which goods and services they value the most, and firms compete to offer those goods and services at the lowest price. Few people think to ask: "Who's in charge of the frozen pizza market?" or "Who's in charge of the breakfast cereal market?" In most markets, the government plays a very limited role in deciding what gets produced, how it gets produced, what prices firms charge, or how firms operate. But policymakers in the United States and most other countries view the financial system as different from the markets for most goods and services. It is different because, when left largely alone, the financial system has experienced periods of instability that have led to economic recessions.

The federal government of the United States has several agencies that are devoted to regulating the financial system, including these:

- The Securities and Exchange Commission (SEC), which regulates financial markets
- The Federal Deposit Insurance Corporation (FDIC), which insures deposits in banks

- The Office of the Comptroller of the Currency, which regulates federally chartered banks
- The Federal Reserve System, which is the central bank of the United States

Although we will discuss all these federal agencies in this book, we will focus on the Federal Reserve System. Here we provide a brief overview of the Federal Reserve. We explore its operations in greater detail in later chapters.

What Is the Federal Reserve? The **Federal Reserve** (usually referred to as "the Fed") is the central bank of the United States. Congress established the Fed in 1913 to deal with problems in the banking system. As we have seen, the main business of banking is to take in deposits and to make loans. Banks can run into difficulties, though, because depositors have the right to withdraw their money at any time, while many of the loans banks grant to people buying cars or houses will not be repaid for years. As a result, if large numbers of depositors simultaneously demand their money back, banks may not have the funds necessary to satisfy the demand. One solution to this problem is for a country's central bank to act as a *lender of last resort* and make short-term loans that provide banks with funds to pay out to their depositors. Because Congress believed that the Fed had failed to carry out its duties as a lender of last resort during the Great Depression of the 1930s, it established the Federal Deposit Insurance Corporation (FDIC) in 1934. The FDIC insures deposits in banks up to a limit of $250,000 per account.

Federal Reserve The central bank of the United States; usually referred to as "the Fed."

What Does the Federal Reserve Do? The modern Fed has moved far beyond its original role as a lender of last resort. In particular, the Fed is now responsible for *monetary policy*. **Monetary policy** refers to the actions the Federal Reserve takes to manage the money supply and interest rates to pursue macroeconomic policy objectives. These policy objectives include high levels of employment, low rates of inflation, high rates of growth, and stability in the financial system. The Fed is run by the Board of Governors, which consists of seven members who are appointed by the president of the United States and confirmed by the U.S. Senate. One member of the Board of Governors is designated as chair. Currently, the chair is Ben Bernanke, who was first appointed by President George W. Bush in 2006 and then reappointed by President Barack Obama in 2010. The Federal Reserve System is divided into 12 districts, each of which has a District Bank, as shown in Figure 1.2. The Federal Open Market Committee (FOMC) is the main policymaking body of the Fed. The FOMC consists of the seven members of the Board of Governors, the president of the Federal Reserve Bank of New York, and four presidents from the other 11 Federal Reserve District Banks.

Monetary policy The actions the Federal Reserve takes to manage the money supply and interest rates to pursue macroeconomic policy objectives.

The FOMC meets in Washington, DC, eight times per year to discuss monetary policy. At these meetings, the FOMC decides on a target for a particularly important interest rate: the **federal funds rate**, which is the interest rate that banks charge each other on short-term loans.

Federal funds rate The interest rate that banks charge each other on short-term loans.

The Fed was heavily involved in the financial crisis of 2007–2009. Before providing a brief discussion of the financial crisis, we conclude our overview of the financial system by discussing the key services that the financial system provides.

What Does the Financial System Do?

In this book, we will do much more than just describe the financial system. We will also use the basic tools of economics to *analyze* how the system works. In your principles of economics class, you learned about these tools, including the model of demand

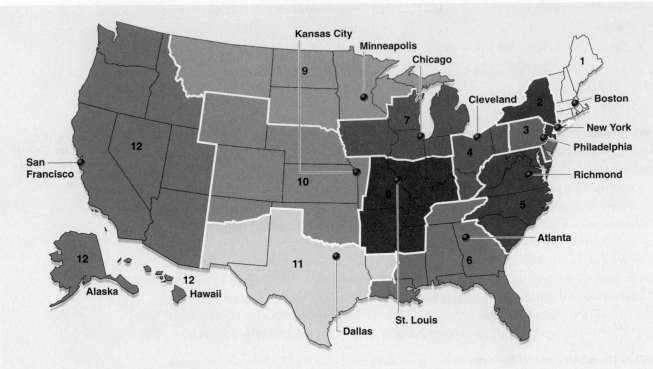

Figure 1.2 The Federal Reserve System

The Federal Reserve System is divided into 12 districts, each of which has a district bank identified by a purple dot in the figure. The federal government created the Federal Reserve System, but each regional Federal Reserve Bank is owned by the commercial banks within its district. Note that Hawaii and Alaska are included in the Twelfth Federal Reserve District.

Source: Board of Governors of the Federal Reserve System.

and supply and marginal analysis. You also learned the basic economic idea that firms compete to supply the goods and services that consumers most want. Therefore, it is important in discussing the financial system to consider the key services provided by the banks, insurance companies, mutual funds, stock brokers, and the other *financial services firms* that make up the financial system.

Economists believe there are three key services that the financial system provides to savers and borrowers: *risk sharing*, *liquidity*, and *information*. Financial services firms provide these services in different ways, which makes different financial assets and financial liabilities more or less attractive to individual savers and borrowers.

Risk Sharing *Risk* is the chance that the value of financial assets will change relative to what you expect. One advantage of using the financial system to match individual savers and borrowers is that it allows the sharing of risk. For example, if you buy a share of Apple stock for $200, that share may be worth $100 or $300 in one year's time, depending on how profitable Apple is. Most individual savers seek a steady return on their assets rather than erratic swings between high and low earnings. One way to improve the chances of a steady return is by holding a portfolio of assets. For example, you might hold some U.S.

savings bonds, some shares of stock, and some shares in a mutual fund. Although during any particular period one asset or set of assets may perform well and another not so well, overall the returns tend to average out. This splitting of wealth into many assets to reduce risk is known as **diversification**. The financial system provides **risk sharing** by allowing savers to hold many assets.

The ability of the financial system to provide risk sharing makes savers more willing to buy stocks, bonds, and other financial assets. This willingness, in turn, increases the ability of borrowers to raise funds in the financial system.

Liquidity The second service that the financial system offers savers and borrowers is **liquidity**, which is the ease with which an asset can be exchanged for money. Savers view the liquidity of financial assets as a benefit. When they need their assets for consumption or investment, they want to be able to sell them easily. More liquid assets can be quickly and easily exchanged for money, while less liquid—or *illiquid*—assets can be exchanged for money only after a delay or by incurring costs. For instance, if you want to buy groceries or clothes, you can easily use dollar bills or a debit card linked to your checking account. Selling your car, however, takes more time because personal property is illiquid. To sell your car, you may incur the costs of advertising or have to accept a relatively low price from a used car dealer. By holding financial claims on a factory—such as stocks or bonds issued by the firm that owns the factory—individual investors have more liquid savings than they would if they owned the machines in the factory. Investors could convert the stocks or bonds into money much more easily than they could convert a specialized machine into money.

In general, we can say that assets created by the financial system, such as stocks, bonds, or checking accounts, are more liquid than are physical assets, such as cars, machinery, or real estate. Similarly, if you lend $100,000 directly to a small business, you probably can't resell the loan, so your investment would be illiquid. If, however, you deposit the $100,000 in a bank, which then makes the loan to the business, your deposit is a much more liquid asset than the loan.

Financial markets and intermediaries help make financial assets more liquid. For instance, investors can easily sell their holdings of government securities and the stocks and bonds of large corporations, making those assets very liquid. As we noted earlier, during the past two decades, the financial system has increased the liquidity of many other assets besides stocks and bonds. The process of securitization has made it possible to buy and sell securities based on loans. As a result, mortgages and other loans have become more desirable assets for savers to hold. Savers are willing to accept lower interest rates on assets with greater liquidity, which reduces the costs of borrowing for many households and firms. One measure of the efficiency of the financial system is the extent to which it can transform illiquid assets into the liquid assets that savers want to buy.

Information A third service of the financial system is the collection and communication of **information**, or facts about borrowers and expectations of returns on financial assets. Your local bank is a warehouse of information. It collects information on borrowers to forecast their likelihood of repaying loans. Borrowers fill out detailed loan applications, and the bank's loan officers determine how well each borrower is doing financially. Because the bank specializes in collecting and processing information, its costs for

Diversification Splitting wealth among many different assets to reduce risk.

Risk sharing A service the financial system provides that allows savers to spread and transfer risk.

Liquidity The ease with which an asset can be exchanged for money.

Information Facts about borrowers and expectations of returns on financial assets.

information gathering are lower than yours would be if you tried to gather information about a pool of borrowers. The profits the bank earns on its loans are partly compensation for the bank's work in gathering information.

Financial markets convey information to both savers and borrowers by determining the prices of stocks, bonds, and other securities. When the price of your shares of Apple stock rises, you know that other investors must expect that Apple's profits will be higher. This information can help you decide whether to continue investing in Apple stock. Likewise, the managers of Apple can use the price of the firm's stock to determine how well investors think the firm is doing. For example, a major increase in Apple's stock price conveys investors' positive outlook for the firm. Apple may use this information in deciding whether to sell more stock or bonds to finance an expansion of the firm. The incorporation of available information into asset prices is an important feature of well-functioning financial markets.

In each chapter of this book, you will see the special feature *Solved Problem*. This feature will increase your understanding of the material by leading you through the steps of solving an applied problem in money, banking, and financial markets. After reading the problem, you can test your understanding by working the related problems that appear at the end of the chapter. You can also complete related Solved Problems on www.myeconlab.com and receive tutorial help.

Solved Problem 1.1

The Services Securitized Loans Provide

We noted earlier that securitized loans are an important new financial asset that has increased in importance during the past 20 years. Briefly discuss the extent to which securitized loans embody the key services of risk sharing, liquidity, and information. In your answer, be sure to explain what securitized loans are.

Solving the Problem

Step 1 Review the chapter material. This problem is about the services securitized loans provide, so you may want to review the sections "Financial Assets," which begins on page 2, and "What Does the Financial System Do?" which begins on page 11.

Step 2 Define securitized loans. Ordinary (non-securitized) loans cannot be resold after they have been granted by a bank or another lender. Therefore, non-securitized loans are financial assets but not financial securities. Securitized loans are loans that have been bundled with other loans and resold to investors. Therefore, securitized loans are both financial assets and financial securities.

Step 3 Explain whether securitized loans provide risk sharing, liquidity, and information. Securitized loans provide all three of these key services. For example, before mortgage loans were securitized, the risk that the borrower would default, or stop making payments on the loan, was borne by the bank or other lender. When a mortgage is bundled together with similar mortgages in mortgage-backed securities, the buyers of the securities jointly share the risk of a default. Because any individual mortgage represents only a small part of the value of the security in which it is included, the buyers of the securities will suffer only a small loss if a borrower defaults on that individual mortgage.

A loan that is not securitized is illiquid because it cannot be resold. A securitized loan can be resold and so has a secondary market, which makes it liquid. One reason individual investors are reluctant to make loans directly to firms or households is that they lack good information on the financial condition of the borrowers. When loans are securitized, investors can, in effect, make loans to households and firms by buying a securitized loan without needing to have direct information on the financial condition of the borrowers. In buying the securitized loan, investors are relying on the bank or other *loan originator* to have gathered the necessary information.

So, securitized loans provide all three key financial services: risk sharing, liquidity, and information.

See related problem 1.12 at the end of the chapter.

The Financial Crisis of 2007–2009

We can use the overview of the financial system in this chapter to briefly discuss the financial crisis of 2007–2009. A **financial crisis** is a significant disruption in the flow of funds from lenders to borrowers. Because the financial crisis has had far-reaching and lasting effects on the financial system, we will discuss it in later chapters as well.

Origins of the Financial Crisis

The origins of the financial crisis lie in large part in the housing bubble of 2000–2005. A **bubble** is an unsustainable increase in the price of a class of assets, such as stocks issued by high-tech companies, oil and other commodities, or houses. Figure 1.3 shows the growth of the housing bubble and its eventual implosion. Panel (a) shows new home sales in the United States, and panel (b) shows the Case-Shiller index, which measures changes in the prices of single-family homes. Panel (a) shows that new home sales rose by 60% between January 2000 and July 2005 and then fell by an astonishing 80% between July 2005 and July 2010. Panel (b) shows that home prices followed a similar pattern: They increased by nearly 90% between the beginning of 2000 and the beginning of 2006 and then declined more than 30% between the beginning of 2006 and the beginning of 2009.

Many economists believe that changes in the market for mortgages played a key role in the housing bubble. Mortgages were the first loans to be widely securitized. To promote home ownership, Congress created a secondary market in mortgages that made it easier for families to borrow money to buy houses. To reach this goal, Congress used two *government-sponsored enterprises (GSEs)*: the Federal National Mortgage Association ("Fannie Mae") and the Federal Home Loan Mortgage Corporation ("Freddie Mac"). Fannie Mae and Freddie Mac sell bonds to investors and use the funds to purchase mortgages from banks. By the 1990s, a large secondary market existed in mortgages, with funds flowing from investors through Fannie Mae and Freddie Mac to banks and, ultimately, to people borrowing money to buy houses.

1.2

Learning Objective
Provide an overview of the financial crisis of 2007–2009.

Financial crisis A significant disruption in the flow of funds from lenders to borrowers.

Bubble An unsustainable increase in the price of a class of assets.

MyEconLab Real-time data

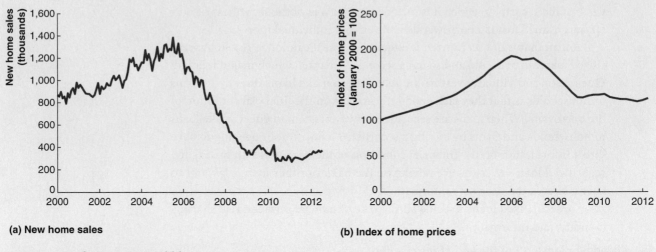

(a) New home sales

(b) Index of home prices

Figure 1.3 The Housing Bubble

Panel (a) shows that the housing bubble resulted in rapid increases in sales of new houses between 2000 and 2005, followed by sharp decreases in sales from early 2006 through early 2009 and then a slow revival.

Panel (b) shows that home prices followed a similar pattern to home sales.

Sources: U.S. Bureau of the Census; and S&P/Case-Shiller, standardandpoors.com.

By the 2000s, important changes had taken place in the mortgage market. First, investment banks became significant participants in the secondary market for mortgages. Investment banks began buying mortgages, bundling large numbers of them together as mortgage-backed securities, and reselling them to investors. Mortgage-backed securities proved very popular with investors because they often paid higher interest rates than other securities with comparable default risk. Second, by the height of the housing bubble in 2005 and early 2006, lenders had greatly loosened the standards for obtaining a mortgage loan. Traditionally, only borrowers who had good credit histories and who were willing to make a down payment equal to at least 20% of the value of the house they were buying would be able to receive a mortgage. By 2005, however, many mortgages were being issued to *subprime borrowers* with flawed credit histories. In addition, *Alt-A borrowers*, who stated—but did not document—their incomes, and borrowers who made very small down payments found it easier to take out loans. Lenders also created new types of *adjustable-rate mortgages* that allowed borrowers to pay a very low interest rate for the first few years of the mortgage and then pay a higher rate in later years. The chance that the borrowers using these nontraditional mortgages would default was higher than for borrowers using traditional mortgages. Why would borrowers take out mortgages on which they might have trouble making the payments, and why would lenders grant such mortgages? Both borrowers and lenders anticipated that housing prices would continue to rise, which would reduce the chance of borrowers defaulting on their mortgages and also make it easier for borrowers to convert to more traditional mortgages in the future.

Unfortunately, the decline in housing prices that began in 2006 led to rising defaults among subprime and Alt-A borrowers, borrowers with adjustable-rate mortgages, and borrowers who had made only small down payments. When borrowers began defaulting on mortgages, the value of many mortgage-backed securities declined sharply, and investors feared that they would lose money by purchasing them. Many commercial and investment banks owned mortgage-backed securities, and the decline in the value of the securities caused those banks to suffer heavy losses. By mid-2007, the decline in the value of mortgage-backed securities and the large losses suffered by commercial and investment banks began to cause turmoil in the financial system. Many investors refused to buy mortgage-backed securities, and some investors would buy only bonds issued by the U.S. Treasury. Banks began to restrict credit to all but the safest borrowers. The flow of funds from savers to borrowers, on which the economy depends, began to be greatly reduced.

Beginning in the spring of 2008, the Federal Reserve and the U.S. Department of the Treasury took unusual policy actions to deal with the results of the financial crisis and the recession that began in December 2007. Although the Fed had traditionally made loans only to commercial banks, in March 2008 it began making loans to some investment banks. Also in March, the Fed and the Treasury helped JPMorgan Chase acquire the investment bank Bear Stearns, which was in danger of failing. The Fed and Treasury were convinced that a failure by Bear Stearns had the potential of causing a financial panic, as many investors and financial firms would have stopped making short-term loans to other investment banks.

The Deepening Crisis and the Response of the Fed and Treasury

Some economists and policymakers criticized the decision by the Fed and the Treasury to help arrange the sale of Bear Stearns to JPMorgan Chase. The main concern was with the *moral hazard problem*, which is the possibility that managers of financial firms such as Bear Stearns might make riskier investments if they believe that the federal government will save them from bankruptcy. The Treasury and Fed acted in March 2008 to save Bear Stearns because they believed that the failure of a large financial firm could have wider economic repercussions. In September 2008, when the investment bank Lehman Brothers was near bankruptcy, the Fed and the Treasury were again concerned that the failure of the firm would endanger the flow of funds through the financial system.

The Fed and the Treasury allowed Lehman Brothers to go bankrupt, which it did on September 15, 2008. The adverse reaction in financial markets was stronger than the Fed and Treasury had expected, which led them to decide two days later to have the Fed provide an $85 billion loan to American International Group (AIG)—the largest insurance company in the United States—in exchange for an 80% ownership stake, effectively giving the federal government control of the company. However, the fallout from the Lehman Brothers bankruptcy had widespread repercussions, including a sharp decline in most types of lending. Finally, in October 2008, Congress passed the *Troubled Asset Relief Program (TARP)*, under which the Treasury provided funds to commercial banks in exchange for stock in those banks. Taking partial ownership of private commercial banks was an unprecedented action for the federal government. Many policies of the Fed and Treasury during the recession of 2007–2009 were controversial because they involved partial government ownership of financial firms, implicit guarantees to large financial firms that they would not be allowed to go bankrupt, and unprecedented intervention in financial markets. These actions by the Fed and the Treasury were meant to restore the flow of funds from savers to borrowers. Without an increase in the flow of funds to more normal levels, households would lack the credit they needed to buy houses, cars, and other consumer durables, and firms would lack the credit they needed to finance new investment in plant and equipment, or, in many cases, even to finance their inventories and meet their payrolls.

Most economists and policymakers believed the severity of the crisis justified the Fed's use of innovative policies, but many feared that the Fed's actions might reduce its independence. Traditionally, Fed chairmen have closely guarded the Fed's independence from the rest of the executive branch—including the Treasury Department—and from Congress. But during the financial crisis, the Fed worked closely with the Treasury in arranging to inject funds into the commercial banking system by taking partial owner-ship of some banks and in several other policy actions. Close collaboration between the Fed and the Treasury, were it to continue, raises the question of whether the Fed would be able to pursue policies independent from those of the administration in power.

1.3

Learning Objective

Explain the key issues and questions the financial crisis raises.

Key Issues and Questions About Money, Banking, and the Financial System

In this text, we will cover many different topics. Beginning in Chapter 2, we highlight one key issue and related question at the start of each chapter, and we end each chapter by using the analysis from the chapter to answer the question. Here are the issues and questions that provide a framework for the chapters that follow:

Chapter 2: Money and the Payments System

Issue: The Federal Reserve's actions during the financial crisis led to concerns about whether it could maintain its independence.

Question: Should a central bank be independent of the rest of the government?

Chapter 3: Interest Rates and Rates of Return

Issue: Some investment analysts argue that very low interest rates on some long-term bonds make them risky investments.

Question: Why do interest rates and the prices of financial securities move in opposite directions?

Chapter 4: Determining Interest Rates

Issue: Federal Reserve policies to combat the recession of 2007–2009 led some economists to predict that inflation would rise and make long-term bonds a poor investment.

Question: How do investors take into account expected inflation and other factors when making investment decisions?

Chapter 5: The Risk Structure and Term Structure of Interest Rates

Issue: During the financial crisis, the bond rating agencies were criticized for having given high ratings to securities that proved to be very risky.

Question: Should the government more closely regulate credit rating agencies?

Chapter 6: The Stock Market, Information, and Financial Market Efficiency

Issue: During the financial crisis, many small investors sold their stock investments, fearing that they had become too risky.

Question: Is the 2007–2009 financial crisis likely to have a long-lasting effect on the willingness of individuals to invest in the stock market?

Chapter 7: Derivatives and Derivative Markets

Issue: During the 2007–2009 financial crisis, some investors, economists, and policymakers argued that financial derivatives had contributed to the severity of the crisis.

Question: Are financial derivatives "weapons of financial mass destruction"?

Chapter 8: The Market for Foreign Exchange

Issue: Volatility in exchange rates during recent years has led some Japanese firms to relocate production to the United States and other countries.

Question: Why has the value of the dollar declined against other major currencies during the past 10 years?

Chapter 9: Transactions Costs, Asymmetric Information, and the Structure of the Financial System

Issue: Following the financial crisis, many firms complained that they were having difficulty borrowing funds to expand their operations.

Question: Why do firms rely more on loans and bonds than on stocks as a source of external finance?

Chapter 10: The Economics of Banking

Issue: During and immediately following the 2007–2009 financial crisis, there was a sharp increase in the number of bank failures.

Question: Is banking a particularly risky business? If so, what types of risks do banks face?

Chapter 11: Investment Banks, Mutual Funds, Hedge Funds, and the Shadow Banking System

Issue: During the 1990s and 2000s, the flow of funds from lenders to borrowers outside the banking system increased.

Question: Does the shadow banking system pose a threat to the stability of the U.S. financial system?

Chapter 12: Financial Crises and Financial Regulation

Issue: The financial crisis of 2007–2009 was the most severe since the Great Depression of the 1930s.

Question: Was the severity of the 2007–2009 recession due to the financial crisis?

Chapter 13: The Federal Reserve and Central Banking

Issue: Following the financial crisis, Congress debated whether to reduce the independence of the Federal Reserve.

Question: Should Congress and the president have greater authority over the Federal Reserve?

Chapter 14: The Federal Reserve's Balance Sheet and the Money Supply Process

Issue: Years after the end of the financial crisis, banks continued to hold record levels of reserves.

Question: Why did bank reserves increase rapidly during and after the financial crisis, and should policymakers be concerned about the increase?

Chapter 15: Monetary Policy

Issue: During the financial crisis, the Federal Reserve employed a series of new policy tools in an attempt to stabilize the financial system.

Question: Should price stability still be the most important policy goal of central banks?

Chapter 16: The International Financial System and Monetary Policy

Issue: The financial crisis led to controversy over the European Central Bank's monetary policy.

Question: Should European countries abandon using a common currency?

Chapter 17: Monetary Theory I: The Aggregate Demand and Aggregate Supply Model

Issue: During the recovery from the financial crisis, the unemployment rate remained stubbornly high.

Question: What explains the high unemployment rates during the economic expansion that began in 2009?

Chapter 18: Monetary Theory II: The *IS–MP* Model

Issue: By December 2008, the Federal Reserve had driven the target for the federal funds rate to near zero.

Question: In what circumstances is lowering the target for the federal funds rate unlikely to be effective in fighting a recession?

Key Terms and Problems

Key Terms

Asset, p. 2

Bond, p. 3

Bubble, p. 15

Commercial bank, p. 5

Diversification, p. 13

Dividend, p. 3

Federal funds rate, p. 11

Federal Reserve, p. 11

Financial asset, p. 2

Financial crisis, p. 15

Financial intermediary, p. 4

Financial liability, p. 4

Financial market, p. 2

Foreign exchange, p. 3

Information, p. 13

Interest rate, p. 3

Liquidity, p. 13

Monetary policy, p. 11

Money, p. 3

Money supply, p. 3

Portfolio, p. 8

Primary market, p. 9

Risk sharing, p. 13

Secondary market, p. 9

Securitization, p. 4

Security, p. 2

Stock, p. 3

1.1 Key Components of the Financial System
Identify the key components of the financial system.

Review Questions

1.1 Briefly define each of the five key financial assets. Is every financial asset also a financial security? Is it possible that what a saver would consider a financial asset a borrower would consider a financial liability?

1.2 What is the difference between direct finance and indirect finance? Which involves financial intermediaries, and which involves financial markets?

1.3 Briefly explain why the financial system is one of the most highly regulated sectors of the economy.

1.4 What is the Federal Reserve? Who appoints the members of the Federal Reserve's Board of Governors? How do the Fed's current responsibilities compare with its responsibilities when Congress created it?

1.5 Briefly describe the three key services that the financial system provides to savers.

Problems and Applications

1.6 A student remarks:

> When I pay my car insurance premiums, I never get that money back. My insurance premiums represent payments for a service I receive from the insurance company. When I deposit money in the bank, I can always withdraw the money later if I want to. So, my bank deposit represents a financial investment for me. Therefore, a bank is a financial intermediary, but an insurance company is not.

Briefly explain whether you agree with the student's argument.

1.7 [Related to the Chapter Opener **on page 1**] In a talk at the White House in December 2009, President Barack Obama argued, "Ultimately in this country we rise and fall together: banks and small businesses, consumers and large corporations." Why in this statement did the president single out banks? Aren't supermarkets, airlines, software companies, and many other businesses also important to the economy?

Source: Helene Cooper and Javier C. Hernandez, "Obama Tells Bankers That Lending Can Spur Economy," *New York Times*, December 14, 2009.

1.8 [Related to the Making the Connection **on page 6**] An article in the *New York Times* in mid-2012 noted, "with the economy still struggling and new regulations meant to eliminate bad lending, bank loans continue to lag."

a. What does the article mean by "bad lending"?

b. Which types of firms might find it harder to receive loans if banks reduce "bad lending"? Briefly explain.

c. What alternatives do the firms you identified in part (b) have for obtaining credit if they are unable to get bank loans?

Source: Ian Mount, "When Banks Won't Lend, There Are Alternatives, Though Often Expensive," *New York Times*, August 1, 2012.

1.9 [Related to the Making the Connection **on page 9**] Households have a much larger fraction of their savings in stocks than in bonds. Can you think of reasons why this is the case?

1.10 Typically, you will receive a very low interest rate on money you deposit in a bank. Interest rates on car loans and business loans are much higher. Why, then, do most people prefer putting their money in a bank to lending it directly to individuals or businesses?

1.11 Suppose financial intermediaries did not exist and only direct finance were possible. How would this affect the process of an individual buying a car or a house?

1.12 [Related to Solved Problem 1.1 **on page 14**] During the 2007–2009 recession, many people who had taken out mortgages to buy homes had trouble making the payments on their mortgages. Because housing prices were falling, the amount that people owed on their mortgages was greater than the price of their homes. Significant numbers of people defaulted on their mortgages. The following appeared in an article discussing this issue in the *Economist* magazine:

> Since foreclosures are costly for lenders as well as painful for borrowers, both sides could be better off by renegotiating a mortgage. The sticking-point, according to conventional wisdom, is securitization. When mortgages are sliced into numerous pieces it is far

harder to get lenders to agree on changing their terms.

Why might both lenders and borrowers be better off as a result of renegotiating a mortgage? How does securitization result in mortgages being "sliced into numerous pieces"? Why would securitization make renegotiating a loan more difficult? How would these difficulties affect the services that securitization provides to savers and borrowers?

Source: "Mortgage Mistakes," *Economist*, July 9, 2009.

1.2 The Financial Crisis of 2007–2009
Provide an overview of the financial crisis of 2007–2009.

Review Questions

2.1 What do economists mean by a "bubble"? Why do many economists believe that there was a housing bubble in the United States between 2000 and 2005?

2.2 By the 2000s, what significant changes had taken place in the mortgage market? What is a "subprime" borrower? What is an "Alt-A" borrower?

2.3 What problems did the decline in housing prices that began in 2006 cause for the financial system?

2.4 What actions did the Federal Reserve and Treasury take in dealing with the financial crisis? What is the moral hazard problem? How is it related to the Federal Reserve's and Treasury's actions?

Problems and Applications

2.5 Why is a bubble more likely to occur in the housing market than in the market for automobiles or the market for refrigerators?

2.6 Panel (b) of Figure 1.3 on page 16 shows the Case-Shiller price index of houses. Economists Karl Case of Wellesley College and Robert Shiller of Yale University developed this index. Many economists consider changes in the average price of houses in the United States to be difficult to measure. What challenges might exist in accurately measuring housing prices?

2.7 How does the creation of a secondary market in mortgages help to promote home ownership? Why might the federal government decide to intervene in the housing market to promote home ownership?

Data Exercises

D1.1: Go to the Web site of the Bureau of Economic Analysis (www.bea.gov) and use the data there to calculate the percentage change in GDP for each year from 2000 through 2009. Graph your data.

Do the movements in GDP correspond well to the movements in the Case-Shiller price index of houses shown in panel (b) of Figure 1.3 on page 16? Briefly explain.

CHAPTER 2

Money and the Payments System

Learning Objectives

After studying this chapter, you should be able to:

2.1 Analyze the inefficiencies of a barter system (pages 24–26)

2.2 Discuss the four key functions of money (pages 26–29)

2.3 Explain the role of the payments system in the economy (pages 29–32)

2.4 Explain how the U.S. money supply is measured (pages 32–35)

2.5 Use the quantity theory of money to analyze the relationship between money and prices in the long run (pages 36–43)

Who Hates the Federal Reserve?

The annual inflation rate in the United States has averaged 2.5% since 1994. What if it jumped to 10%? How would you be affected? If you have student loans, car loans, or other debt with a fixed interest rate, you would benefit from paying your debts back with dollars that were rapidly losing their value. A larger issue, though, is that such high inflation rates cause problems that can affect an entire economy. For example, the United States experienced high inflation rates during the late 1970s and early 1980s. The Federal Reserve responded vigorously to the high inflation rates. Partly due to the Fed's actions, the unemployment rate soared to 10.8% in November 1982, its highest level since the

Great Depression of the 1930s. So, if high inflation rates were to return, you might have difficulty finding a job or you could lose the job you have.

The Federal Reserve is widely blamed for having allowed inflation to increase during the 1970s. Since that time, avoiding another period of such high inflation has been a top priority of Federal Reserve officials and members of Congress. But in the view of some economists and policymakers, the actions the Fed took during the financial crisis of 2007–2009 had the potential to increase inflation significantly. In addition, some of the Fed's actions were far removed from its normal policies. Some economists and

Continued on next page

Key Issue and Question

Issue: The Federal Reserve's actions during the financial crisis led to concerns about whether it could maintain its independence.

Question: Should a central bank be independent of the rest of the government?

Answered on page 43

policymakers argued that in using these policies, the Fed was acting contrary to the basic idea embodied in the Federal Reserve Act of 1913: The Fed was granted substantial independence from Congress and the president, but in exchange would only engage in monetary policy, narrowly defined.

Following the financial crisis, several members of Congress introduced bills that would have sharply increased Congressional oversight of the Federal Reserve. During debate over the bills, Federal Reserve Chairman Ben Bernanke protested that if they became law, the bills would greatly reduce the independence of the Fed from the rest of the federal government. Bernanke argued that making the Fed less independent would actually increase the risk of high inflation. In the end, Bernanke's arguments were successful, and Congress did not pass any of the bills.

The struggle over central bank independence and its potential effect on inflation is not just a political issue in the United States. In the African country of Zimbabwe, the inflation rate during 2008 was an almost unimaginable 15 *billion* percent. The country's central bank began printing Zimbabwean dollar currency in denominations of $50 billion, then $100 billion, and then $100 trillion. The extraordinary inflation rates in Zimbabwe contributed to disastrous declines in production and employment. Finally, in 2009, in an attempt to rein in inflation, the Zimbabwean government decided to abandon its own currency entirely in favor of the U.S. dollar.

Is there a connection between the attempts of the U.S. Congress to reduce the independence of the Fed and the decision by the government of Zimbabwe to abandon using its own currency in a desperate attempt to rein in ruinous inflation? While it is highly unlikely that the United States will ever suffer from inflation rates like those Zimbabwe experienced, as we will see, most economists believe that there is a connection between how independent a country's central bank is and how much inflation the country experiences. This connection is one reason why government control of the money supply can be a heated political issue in many countries.

Sources: John Cochrane, "The Federal Reserve: From Central Bank to Central Planner," *Wall Street Journal*, August 31, 2012; and Luca Di Leo, "Bernanke Continues Fight Against More Fed Scrutiny," *Wall Street Journal*, May 26, 2010.

Because very high rates of inflation in a country almost always lead to declines in production and employment, the links between money, inflation, and the policies of a country's central bank are very important. In this chapter, we begin to explore these links, starting with a brief discussion of what money is and how it is measured. At the end of the chapter, we discuss the quantity theory of money, which shows the links between changes in the money supply and the inflation rate in the long run.

Do We Need Money?

2.1

Learning Objective
Analyze the inefficiencies of a barter system.

Money Anything that is generally accepted as payment for goods and services or in the settlement of debts.

Economists define **money** very broadly as *anything* that is generally accepted as payment for goods and services or in the settlement of debts. Do we need money? It may seem obvious that an economy needs money to operate, but think back to your introductory economics course. In the discussions of supply and demand, production, competition, and other microeconomic topics, money may not have been mentioned. Of course, there was an unstated understanding that money is involved in all the buying and selling. But the fact that you can tell the basic story of how a market system operates without mentioning money suggests that the services that money provides to households and firms are not always obvious.

Barter

Economies *can* function without money. In the early stages of an economy's development, individuals often exchange goods and services by trading output directly with each other. This type of exchange is called **barter**. For example, on the frontier in colonial America, a farmer whose cow died might trade several pigs to a neighboring farmer in exchange for one of the neighbor's cows. In principle, people in a barter economy could satisfy all their needs by trading for goods and services, in which case they would not need money. In practice, though, barter economies are inefficient.

There are four main sources of inefficiency in a barter economy. First, a buyer or seller must spend time and effort searching for trading partners. The first neighbor the farmer approaches may not want to trade a cow for pigs. In a barter system, each party to a trade must want what the other party has available to trade. That is, there must be a *double coincidence of wants*. Because of the time and effort spent searching for trading partners in a barter economy, the **transactions costs**, or the costs in time or other resources of making a trade or exchange, will be high. A second source of inefficiency is that under barter, each good has many prices. The farmer might be able to exchange three pigs for a cow, 10 bushels of wheat for a plow, or a table for a wagon. So, what is the price of a cow, a plow, or a wagon? The answer is that each good will have many prices—one for every other good it might be exchanged for. A cow will have a price in terms of pigs, a price in terms of wheat, a price in terms of wagons, and so forth. A barter economy with only 100 goods would have 4,950 prices; one with 10,000 goods would have 49,995,000 prices![1] A third source of inefficiency arises from a lack of standardization: All pigs and cows are not the same, so the price of cows in terms of pigs would have to specify the size and other characteristics of the animals. Finally, imagine the difficulty of accumulating wealth. The only way to do so in a barter system would be by accumulating stores of goods.

The Invention of Money

The inefficiencies of barter forced most people to be self-sufficient. On the frontier in colonial America, most people grew their own food, built their own homes, and made their own clothes and tools. Such economies have trouble growing because, in doing everything, an individual does some tasks well and does others poorly. To improve on barter, people had an incentive to identify a specific product that most people would generally accept in an exchange. In other words, they had a strong incentive to invent money. For example, in colonial times, animal skins were very useful in making clothing. The first governor of Tennessee received a salary of 1,000 deerskins per year, and the state's secretary of the treasury received 450 otter skins per year. A good used as money that also has value independent of its use as money is called **commodity money**. Historically, once a good became widely accepted as money, people who did not have an immediate use for it were still willing to accept it. A colonial farmer—or the governor of Tennessee—might not want a deerskin, but as long as he knew he could use it to buy other goods and services, he would be willing to accept it in exchange for what he had to sell.

Barter A system of exchange in which individuals trade goods and services directly for other goods and services.

Transactions costs The costs in time or other resources that parties incur in the process of agreeing and carrying out an exchange of goods and services.

Commodity money A good used as money that has value independent of its use as money.

---

[1]These calculations are based on the formula for determining how many prices we need with N goods—that is, the number of prices when there are N items: Number of prices $= N(N - 1)/2$.

What's Money? Ask a Taxi Driver!

Some years ago, one of the authors of this book learned a great lesson about money from Russian taxi drivers. In August 1989, as part of a group of American economists, he traveled to Moscow and Leningrad (now St. Petersburg) in what was then the Soviet Union to discuss with Soviet economists some economic problems both countries faced.

Taking taxis in Moscow to and from meetings and dinners was an ordeal. The author's hosts had given the U.S. economists rubles (Soviet currency at the time), but Russian merchants and taxi drivers discouraged payments in rubles. Taxi drivers quoted a bewildering array of fares in terms of U.S. dollars, German marks, or Japanese yen. And the fares varied from cab to cab.

When the author relayed this frustration to his wife, she explained that she had no difficulties with taxis. She paid the fare with Marlboro cigarettes instead of currency! The author used Marlboros the next day (no other brand worked as well) and was able to pay taxi drivers with great success. He found that the taxi drivers could easily convert all major currencies to Marlboro equivalents.

At least during that period, Marlboro cigarettes had displaced the official currency (rubles) as the money most widely used by Moscow taxi drivers.

See related problems 1.6 and 1.7 at the end of the chapter.

Specialization A system in which individuals produce the goods or services for which they have relatively the best ability.

Once a society invents money—as has happened many times and in many places around the world—transactions costs are greatly reduced, as are the other inefficiencies of barter. People can take advantage of **specialization**, producing the good or service for which they have relatively the best ability. Most people in modern economies are highly specialized. They do only one thing—work as an accountant, a teacher, or an engineer—and use the money they earn to buy everything else they need. By specializing, people are far more productive than they would be if they tried to produce all the goods and services they consume themselves. The high income levels in modern economies are based on the specialization that money makes possible.

So, the answer to the question "Do we need money?" is: "Yes, because money allows for specialization, higher productivity, and higher incomes."

2.2

Learning Objective

Discuss the four key functions of money.

The Key Functions of Money

Money serves four key functions in the economy:

1. It acts as a medium of exchange.
2. It is a unit of account.
3. It is a store of value.
4. It offers a standard of deferred payment.

Medium of Exchange

If you are a teacher or an accountant, you are paid money for your services. You then use that money to buy goods and services. You essentially exchange your teaching or accounting services for food, clothing, rent, and other goods and services. But unlike with barter, where goods and services are exchanged directly for other goods and services, the exchanges you participate in involve money. Money is providing the service of a **medium of exchange**. That is, money is the *medium* through which exchange takes place. Because, by definition, money is generally accepted as payment for goods and services or as payment for debts, you know that the money your employer pays you will be accepted at the stores where you purchase food, clothing, and other goods and services. In other words, you can specialize in producing teaching or accounting services without having to worry about directly producing the other goods and services you require to meet your needs, as you would in a barter economy.

Medium of exchange Something that is generally accepted as payment for goods and services; a function of money.

Unit of Account

Using a good as a medium of exchange provides another benefit: Instead of having to quote the price of a single good in terms of many other goods—as is the case with barter—each good has a single price quoted in terms of the medium of exchange. This function of money gives households and firms a **unit of account**, or a way of measuring value in the economy in terms of money. For instance, in the U.S. economy, each good or service has a price in terms of dollars.

Unit of account A way of measuring value in an economy in terms of money; a function of money.

Store of Value

Money allows value to be stored easily, thereby providing the service of a **store of value**. If you do not use all your accumulated dollars to buy goods and services today, you can hold the rest for future use. Note, though, that if prices in an economy rise rapidly over time, the amount of goods and services a given amount of money can purchase declines, and money's usefulness as a store of value is reduced.

Store of value The accumulation of wealth by holding dollars or other assets that can be used to buy goods and services in the future; a function of money.

Of course, money is only one of many *assets* that can be used to store value. In fact, any asset—shares of Apple stock, Treasury bonds, real estate, or Renoir paintings, for example—represents a store of value. Indeed, financial assets, such as stocks and bonds, offer an important benefit relative to holding money because they generally pay interest or offer the possibility of increasing in value. Other assets also have advantages relative to money because they provide services. For instance, a house provides its owner with a place to sleep. Why, then, does anyone bother to hold money? The answer is *liquidity*, or the ease with which an asset can be exchanged for money. Money itself is, of course, perfectly liquid, while you incur transactions costs when you exchange other assets for money. When you sell bonds or shares of stock, for example, you pay a fee, or commission, either online or to your broker. If you have to sell your house on short notice because you take a job in a different state, you will have to pay a commission to a real estate agent and probably have to accept a lower price to sell the house quickly. To avoid such transactions costs, people are willing to hold money as well as other assets, even though other assets offer a greater return as a store of value.

Standard of Deferred Payment

Money is also useful because of its ability to serve as a **standard of deferred payment**. Money can facilitate exchange at a *given point in time* by providing a medium of exchange and unit of account. Money can also facilitate exchange *over time* by providing a store of value and standard of deferred payment. For example, a furniture store may

Standard of deferred payment The characteristic of money by which it facilitates exchange over time; a function of money.

order 25 dining room tables from a furniture manufacture by promising to make full payment at an agreed price in 60 days.

Distinguishing Among Money, Income, and Wealth

Wealth The sum of the value of a person's assets minus the value of the person's liabilities.

It's important to keep straight the differences among *money*, *income*, and *wealth*. We often say that people in *Forbes* magazine's list of richest Americans have a lot of money. We don't really mean that they have a lot of paper currency in their pockets (or hidden away in their mansions or yachts); instead, we mean that they own valuable assets, such as stocks, bonds, or houses. Money, like other assets, is a component of **wealth**, which is the sum of the value of a person's assets minus the value of the person's liabilities. However, only if an asset serves as a medium of exchange can we call it *money*. A person's *income* is equal to his or her earnings over a period of time. So, a person typically has considerably less money than income or wealth.

What Can Serve as Money?

We noted earlier that any asset can be used as money, provided that it is generally accepted as payment. In practical terms, an asset is suitable to use as a medium of exchange if it is:

- *Acceptable* to (that is, usable by) most people
- *Standardized in terms of quality*, so that any two units are identical
- *Durable*, so that it does not quickly become too worn out to be usable
- *Valuable* relative to its weight, so that amounts large enough to be useful in trade can be easily transported
- *Divisible*, because prices of goods and services vary

U.S. paper currency—Federal Reserve Notes—meet all these criteria.

The Mystery of Fiat Money

Fiat money Money, such as paper currency, that has no value apart from its use as money

Legal tender The government designation that currency is accepted as payment of taxes and must be accepted by individuals and firms in payment of debts.

Notice that paper currency has no intrinsic value. You can use a $20 bill to buy goods and services, but beyond that, it has no value to you—except, perhaps, as a bookmark. The Federal Reserve issues the paper currency of the United States, but the Fed is under no obligation to redeem it for gold or any other commodity. Money, such as paper currency, that has no value apart from its use as money is called **fiat money**.

People accept paper currency in exchange for goods and services partly because the federal government has designated it to be **legal tender**, which means the government accepts paper currency in payment of taxes and requires that individuals and firms accept it in payment of debts. In reality, though, the more important reason paper currency circulates as a medium of exchange is the confidence of consumers and firms that if they accept paper currency, they will be able to pass it along to someone else when they need to buy goods and services. Basically, it is a case of self-fulfilling expectations: You value something as money only if you believe that others will accept it from you as payment. Our society's willingness to use green pieces of paper issued by the Federal Reserve System as money makes them an acceptable medium of exchange.

As we will see later in the chapter, if consumers and firms ever lose confidence that they will be able to pass along currency in buying goods and services, then the currency will cease to be a medium of exchange.

Making the Connection

Apple Didn't Want My Cash!

If Federal Reserve Notes are legal tender, doesn't that mean that everyone in the United States, including every business, has to accept paper money? The answer to this question is "no," as a woman in California found out when she went to an Apple store in Palo Alto and tried to buy an iPad using $600 in currency. Apple had just released the iPad and did not want to sell large numbers to people who were buying them to resell on eBay, Craigslist, or elsewhere. So, a customer wanting to buy an iPad had to pay either with a credit card or a debit card, which would make it easier for Apple to keep track of anyone attempting to buy more than the limit of two per customer.

Because Federal Reserve Notes are legal tender, creditors must accept them in payment of debts, and the government will accept them in payment of taxes. However, as this incident made clear, firms do not have to accept cash as payment for goods and services. As the U.S. Treasury Department explains on its Web site:

> There is . . . no Federal statute mandating that a private business, a person or an organization must accept currency or coins as payment for goods and/or services. . . . For example, a bus line may prohibit payment of fares in pennies or dollar bills. In addition, movie theaters, convenience stores and gas stations may refuse to accept large denomination currency (usually notes above $20) as a matter of policy.

The woman who tried to buy an iPad for cash was disabled and on a limited income, so the incident led to bad publicity for Apple. As a result, Apple decided to lift its ban on paying for iPads with cash, provided that the customer was willing to set up an Apple account at the time of purchase. In addition, Apple presented a free iPad to the customer who was originally turned down when she tried to pay with cash.

Sources: Michael Winter, "Apple Ends No-Cash Policy and California Woman Gets Free iPad," usatoday. com, May 20, 2010; and "FAQs: Currency," www.treasury.gov/resource-center/faqs/Currency/Pages/legal-tender.aspx.

See related problem 2.8 at the end of the chapter.

The Payments System

Money facilitates transactions in the economy. The mechanism for conducting such transactions is known as a **payments system**. The payments system has evolved over time from relying on payments made in gold and silver coins, to payments made with paper currency and checks written on deposits in banks, to payments made by electronic funds transfers.

The Transition from Commodity Money to Fiat Money

Historians disagree about precisely when people began using metallic coins. Evidence suggests that people in China were using metallic coins in the year 1000 B.C., and people in Greece were using them in the year 700 B.C. For centuries thereafter, buyers and sellers

2.3

Learning Objective

Explain the role of the payments system in the economy.

Payments system The mechanism for conducting transactions in the economy.

used coins minted from precious metals, such as gold, silver, and copper, as money. Gold and silver coins suffer from some drawbacks, however. For instance, from the days of the Roman Empire, to gain additional funds, governments would sometimes *debase* the currency, melting down coins and re-minting them with a greater amount of less valuable metals mixed in with the gold and silver. An economy's reliance on gold and silver coins alone makes for a cumbersome payments system. People had difficulty transporting large numbers of gold coins to settle transactions and also ran the risk of being robbed. To get around this problem, beginning around the year A.D. 1500 in Europe, governments and private firms—early banks—began to store gold coins in safe places and issue paper certificates. Anyone receiving a paper certificate could claim the equivalent amount of gold. As long as people had confidence that the gold was available if they demanded it, the paper certificates would circulate as a medium of exchange. In effect, paper currency had been invented.

In modern economies, the central bank, such as the Federal Reserve in the United States, issues paper currency. The modern U.S. payments system is a fiat money system because the Federal Reserve does not exchange paper currency for gold or any other commodity money. The Federal Reserve issues paper currency and holds deposits from banks and the federal government. Banks can use these deposits to settle transactions with one another. Today, the Fed has a legal monopoly on the right to issue currency. Although in the nineteenth century private banks issued their own currency, they can no longer do so.

The Importance of Checks

Paper money has drawbacks. For instance, it can be expensive to transport paper money to settle large commercial or financial transactions. Imagine going to buy a car with a suitcase full of dollar bills! Another major innovation in the payments system came in the early twentieth century, with the increasing use of *checks*. **Checks** are promises to pay on demand money deposited with a bank or other financial institution. They can be written for any amount, and using them is a convenient way to settle transactions.

Check A promise to pay on demand money deposited with a bank or other financial institution.

Settling transactions with checks does, however, require more steps than settling transactions with currency. Suppose that your roommate owes you $50. If she gives you $50 in cash, the transaction is settled. Suppose, however, that she writes you a check for $50. You first must take the check to your bank. Your bank, in turn, must present the check for payment to your roommate's bank, which must then collect the money from her account. Processing the enormous flow of checks in the United States costs the economy several billion dollars each year. There are also information costs to using checks—the time and effort required for the seller to verify whether the check writer (the buyer) has a sufficient amount of money in her checking account to cover the amount of the check. Accepting checks requires more trust on the part of the seller than does accepting dollar bills.

Electronic Funds and Electronic Cash

Breakthroughs in electronic telecommunication have improved the efficiency of the payments system, reducing the time needed for clearing checks and for transferring funds. Settling and clearing transactions now occur over *electronic funds transfer systems*, which are computerized payment-clearing devices such as *debit cards*, *Automated Clearing House (ACH)* transactions, *automated teller machines* (ATMs), and *e-money*.

Debit cards can be used like checks: Cash registers in supermarkets and retail stores are linked to bank computers, so when a customer uses a debit card to buy groceries or other products, his bank instantly credits the store's account with the amount and deducts it from his account. Such a system eliminates the problem of trust between the buyer and seller that is associated with checks because the bank computer authorizes the transaction.

ACH transactions include direct deposits of payroll checks into the checking accounts of workers and electronic payments on car loans and mortgages, where the payments are sent electronically from the payer's account and deposited in the lender's account. ACH transactions reduce the transactions costs associated with processing checks, reduce the likelihood of missed payments, and reduce the costs lenders incur in notifying borrowers of missed payments.

Forty years ago, ATMs did not exist, so to deposit or withdraw money from your checking account, you needed to fill out a deposit or withdrawal slip and wait in line at a bank teller's window. Adding to the inconvenience was the fact that many banks were open only between the hours of 10 A.M. and 3 P.M. Today, ATMs allow you to carry out the same transactions at your bank whenever it is most convenient for you. Moreover, ATMs are connected to networks (such as Cirrus) so you can withdraw cash from the ATMs of banks other than your own.

The boundaries of electronic funds transfers have expanded to include **e-money**, or electronic money, which is digital cash people use to buy goods and services over the Internet. A consumer purchases e-money from an Internet bank, which transfers the money to a merchant's computer when the consumer makes a purchase. The best-known form of e-money is the PayPal service, which is owned by eBay, the online auction site. An individual or a firm can set up a PayPal account by transferring funds from a checking account or credit card. As long as sellers are willing to accept funds transferred from a buyer's PayPal (or other e-money) account, e-money functions as if it were conventional, government-issued money. The central bank does not control e-money, though, so it is essentially a private payments system. PayPal was originally developed to make payments for online auctions easier, but in recent years, PayPal and other e-money providers have attempted to expand to capture a greater share of the payments made online.

The developments in e-money are exciting and lead some commentators to predict a "cashless society." A Federal Reserve study found that noncash payments continue to increase as a fraction of all payments, and electronic payments now make up more than two-thirds of all noncash payments. Not surprisingly, the number of checks written has been dropping by more than 2 billion per year. In reality, though, an entirely cashless (or checkless) society is unlikely for two key reasons. First, the infrastructure for an e-payments system is expensive to build. Second, many households and firms worry about protecting their privacy in an electronic system that is subject to computer hackers. While the flow of paper in the payments system is likely to continue to shrink, it is unlikely to disappear.

The efficiency of the payments system, which increases as the cost of settling transactions decreases, is important for the economy. Suppose that the banking system broke down, and all transactions—commercial and financial—had to be carried out in

E-money Digital cash people use to buy goods and services over the Internet; short for electronic money.

cash. You would have to carry large amounts of cash to finance all your purchases and would incur additional costs for protecting your cash from theft. No bank credit would be possible, which would prevent the financial system from performing its key role of matching savers and borrowers. Disruptions in the payments system increase the cost of trade and credit. Many economists, for example, blame problems in the banking system for the severity of the Great Depression of the 1930s. The efficient functioning of the economy's payments system is a significant public policy concern, so governments typically establish safeguards to protect it.

Measuring the Money Supply

2.4

Learning Objective
Explain how the U.S. money supply is measured.

Households, firms, and policymakers are all interested in measuring money because, as we will see, changes in the quantity of money are associated with changes in interest rates, prices, production, and employment. If the only function of money was to serve as a medium of exchange, then we might want to include in the money supply only currency, checking account deposits, and traveler's checks because households and firms can easily use these assets to buy goods and services.

But including just these three assets would result in too narrow a measure of the money supply in the real world. Households and firms can use many other assets as mediums of exchange, even though they are not as liquid as cash or a checking account deposit. For example, you can easily convert your savings account at a bank into cash. Likewise, if you own shares in a money market mutual fund—which is a mutual fund that invests exclusively in short-term bonds, such as Treasury bills—you can write checks against the value of your shares. So, we may want to consider assets such as savings accounts and money market mutual fund shares part of the medium of exchange.

Measuring Monetary Aggregates

As part of its responsibility to regulate the quantity of money in the United States, the Federal Reserve currently publishes data on two different definitions of the money supply. Figure 2.1 illustrates these definitions—referred to as **monetary aggregates**.

Monetary aggregate A measure of the quantity of money that is broader than currency; M1 and M2 are monetary aggregates.

M1 A narrow definition of the money supply: The sum of currency in circulation, checking account deposits, and holdings of traveler's checks.

M1 Aggregate The narrow definition of the money supply is **M1**. As panel (a) in Figure 2.1 shows, M1 measures money as the traditional medium of exchange: currency, checking account deposits, and traveler's checks. Through the early 1980s, government regulations did not allow banks to pay interest on checking accounts, which made them close substitutes for currency. Since then, financial innovation in the banking industry and government deregulation in the 1970s, 1980s, and 1990s have made more types of accounts close substitutes for traditional bank checking accounts. These new accounts include checking accounts at savings institutions and credit unions, as well as interest-bearing checking accounts at commercial banks. Measures of M1 now include these other deposits against which checks may be written, along with non-interest-bearing checking account deposits called *demand deposits*, traveler's checks, and currency.

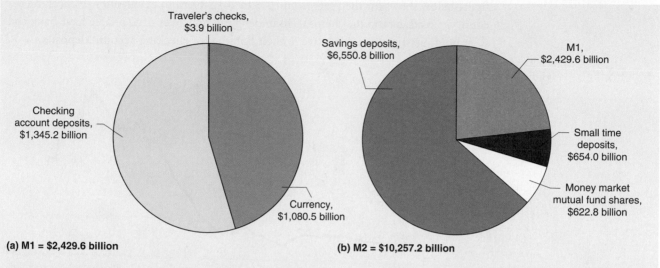

(a) M1 = $2,429.6 billion

(b) M2 = $10,257.2 billion

Figure 2.1 Measuring the Money Supply, October 2012

The Federal Reserve uses two different measures of the money supply: M1 and M2. M1 includes currency, checking account deposits, and traveler's checks. M2 includes all the assets in M1, as well as the additional assets shown in panel (b).

Note: In panel (b), savings deposits include money market deposit accounts.

Source: Board of Governors of the Federal Reserve System, *Federal Reserve Statistical Release, H6*, November 8, 2012.

M2 Aggregate M2 is a broader definition of the money supply than M1 and includes accounts that many households treat as short-term investments. These accounts can be converted into currency, although not as easily as the components of M1. As shown in panel (b) of Figure 2.1, in addition to the assets included in M1, M2 includes:

- Time deposits with a value of less than $100,000, primarily *certificates of deposits* in banks
- Savings accounts
- Money market deposit accounts at banks
- Noninstitutional money market mutual fund shares ("Noninstitutional" means that individual investors rather than institutional investors, such as pension funds, own the money market fund shares. Noninstitutional is also sometimes referred to as "retail.")

M2 A broader definition of the money supply: all the assets that are included in M1, as well as time deposits with a value of less than $100,000, savings accounts, money market deposit accounts, and noninstitutional money market mutual fund shares.

Making the Connection

Show Me the Money!

Panel (a) of Figure 2.1 shows that in October 2012, the total value of U.S. currency was $1,080.5 billion. The value for currency included in M1 is technically "currency outstanding," which includes all paper currency and coins outside the Federal Reserve, the Treasury, and the banking system. That total represents more than $3,400 for every person in the United States. Even given that firms hold some of the currency, $3,400 still seems like far more currency than the typical person holds. Most people keep the funds that they want to easily access in their checking accounts rather than as cash. The figure below shows for the years from 1975 to 2012 the ratio of currency to checking account deposits, a ratio that helps us to understand how over time people have balanced their holdings of currency relative to their holdings of checking account deposits.

MyEconLab Real-time data

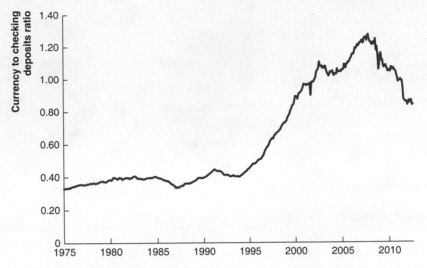

Source: Federal Reserve Bank of St. Louis.

Note that the ratio starts to rise in the mid-1990s and reaches very high levels during the financial crisis that began in 2007, before declining after the financial crisis eased during 2009. Why have people over the past 15 to 20 years increased their holdings of cash relative to their checking account balances? The Federal Reserve estimates that as much as two-thirds of the $1,080.5 billion in currency outstanding in October 2012 was held by individuals, firms, and governments outside the United States. During the 1990s, a number of economies in Asia, Latin America, and Eastern Europe experienced high rates of inflation or other problems with their currencies. In these countries, many individuals and firms switched to conducting transactions in U.S. dollars rather than in their domestic currencies. Even though the U.S. dollar is not legal tender in most other countries, it still can be used as a medium of exchange, as long as most households and firms are willing to accept it. Some countries, including Panama, El Salvador, and Ecuador, use the U.S. dollar as their official currency. As we saw in the chapter opener, in 2009, the government of Zimbabwe abandoned its own currency in favor of the dollar. Countries can use the U.S. dollar as their currency without the formal approval of the U.S. government.

Finally, note in the figure that demand for U.S. currency spiked in late 2008, during the worst period of the financial crisis, before declining again during 2009, as the crisis eased. Although some of this increase may have been due to consumers in the United States converting their checking accounts into currency because of fears of bank failures, most of the increase came once again from households and firms in other countries, who saw the dollar as a safe haven during a time when they doubted the stability of their own currencies.

Source: Federal Reserve Bank of New York, "The Money Supply," July 2008.

See related problem 4.9 at the end of the chapter.

Does It Matter Which Definition of the Money Supply We Use?

Which is the better measure of money: M1 or M2? If M1 and M2 move together closely enough, the Fed could use either of them to try to influence the economy's output, prices, or interest rates. If M1 and M2 do not move together, they may tell different stories about what is happening to the money supply.

Panel (a) of Figure 2.2 shows the levels of M1 and M2 from January 1960 through July 2012. Note that M2 grew much more over these years than did M1. This is not surprising because certificates of deposit, money market mutual fund shares, and other assets that are included only in M2 have grown much faster than have currency or checking accounts. Economists believe that *changes* in an economic variable are usually more important than are *levels* of the variable. For instance, as we make financial plans for the future, we are usually more interested in the *inflation rate*—which measures the percentage change in the price level—than we are in the current price level. If we believe that changes in the money supply cause inflation, then a graph like panel (b), showing growth rates M1 and M2, measured as percentage changes at an annual rate, provides more information than does the graph in panel (a).

Panel (b) in Figure 2.2 shows that growth rates of M1 and M2 were significantly different over the past 20 years. Overall, the growth rate of M2 was more stable than the growth of M1, which soared during the recessions of 1990–1991, 2001, and 2007–2009 and also had several periods of being negative. A negative growth rate means that the money supply measured by M1 actually declined during those periods. Given the difference in growth rates of M1 and M2, how do the Fed and private forecasters decide which measures to use to explain changes in other economic variables, such as the economy's total output, the price level, and interest rates? In fact, which measure of the money supply is best for forecasting remains an open question that Federal Reserve economists, academic economists, and private forecasters continue to research.

MyEconLab Real-time data

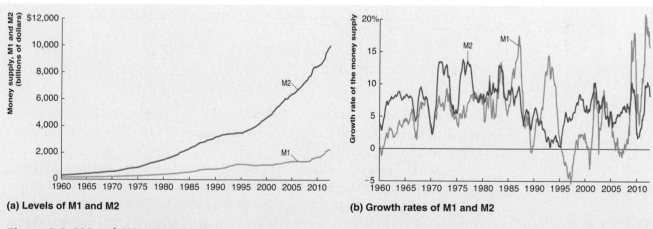

(a) Levels of M1 and M2

(b) Growth rates of M1 and M2

Figure 2.2 M1 and M2, 1960–2012

Panel (a) shows that since 1960 M2 has increased much more rapidly than has M1. Panel (b) uses quarterly data to show the annual growth rates of M1 and M2 since 1960. M1 has experienced much more instability than has M2.

Note: In panel (b), percentage changes are measured as the compound annual rate of change using quarterly data.

Source: Federal Reserve Bank of St. Louis.

2.5

Learning Objective

Use the quantity theory of money to analyze the relationship between money and prices in the long run.

The Quantity Theory of Money: A First Look at the Link Between Money and Prices

The relationship between increases in the money supply and increases in prices has been discussed by writers dating back at least as far as the Greek philosopher Aristotle in the fourth century B.C. During the sixteenth century, the Spanish conquest of Mexico and Peru resulted in huge quantities of gold and silver being exported to Europe, where they were minted into coins, greatly increasing the European money supply. Many writers noted that this increase in the money supply was followed by an increase in the price level and a corresponding loss of *purchasing power*, which is the ability of consumers to use money to acquire goods and services. In this section, we explore how economists continue to study this link between changes in the money supply and changes in the price level.

Irving Fisher and the Equation of Exchange

In the early twentieth century, Irving Fisher, an economist at Yale University, developed the quantity theory of money to make more explicit the relationship between the money supply and inflation. Fisher began his analysis by using the *equation of exchange*:

$$M \times V = P \times Y.$$

The equation states that the quantity of money, M, multiplied by the velocity of money, V, equals the price level, P, multiplied by the level of real GDP, Y. Recall that the price level measures the average level of the prices of goods and services in the economy. There are several measures of the price level. The measure that is most relevant here is the *GDP deflator*, which includes the prices of all goods and services included in GDP. If we multiply real GDP by the GDP deflator, we get nominal GDP, so the right side of the equation of exchange equals nominal GDP. Fisher defined the *velocity of money*— or, simply, *velocity*—as the number of times during a period of time each dollar in the money supply is spent on a good or a service that is included in GDP, or:

$$V = \frac{PY}{M}.$$

For example, in 2011, nominal GDP was \$15,075 billion and M1 was \$2,006 billion, so velocity in 2011 was \$15,075 billion/\$2,006 billion $=$ 7.5. This result tells us that during 2011, on average, each dollar of M1 was spent 7.5 times on goods or services included in GDP.

Because Fisher defined velocity to be equal to PY/M, we know that the equation of exchange must always be true. The left side *must* be equal to the right side. A theory is a statement about the world that might possibly be false. Therefore, the equation of exchange is not a theory. Fisher turned the equation of exchange into the **quantity theory of money**, by asserting that velocity is constant. Fisher argued that the average number of times a dollar is spent depends on how often people get paid, how often they go shopping, how often businesses send out bills, and other factors that change very slowly. Because this assertion about velocity may be true or false, the quantity theory of money is, in fact, a theory.

Quantity theory of money A theory about the connection between money and prices that assumes that the velocity of money is constant.

The Quantity Theory Explanation of Inflation

To investigate the effects of changes in the money supply on inflation, we need to re-write the equation of exchange from levels to percentage changes. We can do this by using a handy mathematical rule that states that an equation where variables are multiplied together is equal to an equation where the *percentage changes* of those variables are *added* together. So, we can rewrite the quantity equation as:

$$\% \text{ Change in } M + \% \text{ Change in } V = \% \text{ Change in } P + \% \text{ Change in } Y.$$

If Irving Fisher was correct that velocity is constant—say, it always equals 7.5—then the percentage change in velocity will be zero. Remember that the percentage change in the price level equals the inflation rate. Taking these two facts into account, we can rewrite the quantity equation one last time:

$$\text{Inflation rate} = \% \text{ Change in } M - \% \text{ Change in } Y.$$

This relationship gives us a useful way of thinking about the relationship between money and prices: Provided that velocity is constant, when the quantity of money increases faster than real GDP, there will be inflation. The greater the percentage change in the quantity of money, the greater the inflation rate. In the United States, the long-run rate of growth of real GDP has been about 3% per year. So, the quantity theory indicates that if the Federal Reserve allows the money supply to increase at a rate faster than this, the result will be inflation.

Solved Problem 2.5

The Relationship Between Money and Income

A student makes the following assertion: "It isn't possible for the total value of production to increase unless the money supply also increases. After all, how can the value of the goods and services being bought and sold increase unless there is more money available?" Explain whether you agree with this assertion.

Solving the Problem

Step 1 **Review the chapter material.** This problem is about the relationship between money growth and income growth, so you may want to review the section "Irving Fisher and the Equation of Exchange," which begins on page 36.

Step 2 **Explain whether output in an economy can grow without the money supply also growing.** The value of total production is measured by nominal GDP, or in symbols PY. PY is the right side of the equation of exchange, so for it to increase, the left side—MV—must also increase. The student is asserting that nominal GDP cannot increase unless the money supply increases, but the equation of exchange shows us that nominal GDP could increase with the money supply remaining constant, provided that V increases. In other words, the total amount of spending in the economy as represented by nominal GDP could increase, even if the total number of dollars remains constant, provided that the average number of times those dollars are spent—V—increases.

EXTRA CREDIT: Remember the distinction between money and income. As you learned in your introductory economics course, at the level of the economy as a whole, total production is equal to total income, or GDP = National income. (Although, technically, we need to subtract depreciation from GDP to arrive at national income, this distinction does not matter for most macroeconomic issues.) But the value of GDP or national income is much greater than the value of the money supply. In the United States, the value of GDP is typically about seven to eight times as large as the value of the M1 measure of the money supply.

See related problem 5.6 at the end of the chapter.

How Accurate Are Forecasts of Inflation Based on the Quantity Theory?

Note that the accuracy of the quantity theory depends on whether the key assumption that velocity is constant is correct. If velocity is not constant, then there may not be a tight link between increases in the money supply and increases in the price level. For example, an increase in the quantity of money might be offset by a decline in velocity, leaving the price level unaffected. As it turns out, velocity can move erratically in the short run, so we would not expect the quantity equation to provide good short-run forecasts of inflation. Over the long run, however, there is a strong link between changes in the money supply and inflation. Panel (a) of Figure 2.3 shows the relationship between the

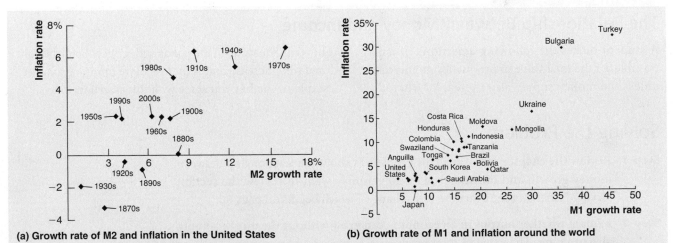

(a) Growth rate of M2 and inflation in the United States

(b) Growth rate of M1 and inflation around the world

Figure 2.3 The Relationship Between Money Growth and Inflation over Time and Around the World

Panel (a) shows the relationship between the growth rate of M2 and the inflation rate for the United States from the 1870s to the 2000s. Panel (b) shows the relationship between the growth rate of M1 and inflation for 36 countries during the 1995–2011 period. In both panels, high money growth rates are associated with higher inflation rates.

Sources: Panel (a): for 1870s to 1960s, Milton Friedman and Anna J. Schwartz, *Monetary Trends in the United States and United Kingdom:*

Their Relation to Income, Prices, and Interest Rates, 1867–1975, Chicago: University of Chicago Press, 1982, Table 4.8; for the 1970s to 2000s: Federal Reserve Board of Governors and U.S. Bureau of Economic Analysis; panel (b): International Monetary Fund, *International Financial Statistics.*

growth of the M2 measure of the money supply and the inflation rate by decade in the United States. (We use M2 here because data on M2 are available for a longer period of time than for M1.) Because of variations in the rate of growth of real GDP and in velocity, there is not an exact relationship between the growth rate of M2 and the inflation rate. But there is a clear pattern: Decades with higher growth rates in the money supply were also decades with higher inflation rates. In other words, most of the variation in inflation rates across decades can be explained by variation in the rates of growth of the money supply.

Panel (b) provides further evidence consistent with the quantity theory by looking at rates of growth of the money supply and rates of inflation across countries for the period from 1995 to 2011. Although there is not an exact relationship between rates of growth of the money supply and rates of inflation across countries, panel (b) shows that countries where the money supply grew rapidly tended to have high inflation rates, while countries where the money supply grew more slowly tended to have much lower inflation rates. Not included in panel (b) are data for the African country of Zimbabwe, which we mentioned at the beginning of the chapter. Between 1999 and 2008, the money supply in Zimbabwe grew by more than 7,500% per year. The result was an accelerating rate of inflation that eventually reached 15 *billion* percent during 2008. Zimbabwe was suffering from **hyperinflation**—that is, a rate of inflation that exceeds 50% per month. In the next section, we discuss the problems that hyperinflation can cause to a nation's economy.

Hyperinflation Extremely high rates of inflation, exceeding 50% per month.

The Hazards of Hyperinflation

Episodes of hyperinflation are rare. Some examples are the Confederate States of America during the last years of the Civil War, Germany during the early 1920s, Argentina during the 1990s, and, as we saw in the chapter opener, Zimbabwe during recent years. In these cases of extreme inflation, prices rise so rapidly that a given amount of money can purchase fewer and fewer goods and services each day. Eventually, if prices rise as rapidly as they did in Zimbabwe during 2008, anyone holding money for even a few hours finds that the money has lost most of its value before he or she can spend it. In those circumstances, households and firms may refuse to accept money at all, in which case money no longer functions as a medium of exchange. When economies don't use money, the specialization necessary to maintain high rates of productivity breaks down. For instance, during the German hyperinflation of the early 1920s, many workers abandoned their jobs because the money firms paid them lost its value before they had time to spend it. Not surprisingly, economic activity contracted sharply, and unemployment soared. The resulting economic hardships helped pave the way for the rise of Adolf Hitler and the Nazi Party.

What Causes Hyperinflation?

The quantity theory indicates that hyperinflation is caused by the money supply increasing far more rapidly than real output of goods and services. Once prices begin to rise rapidly enough that money loses a significant amount of its value, households and firms try to hold money for as brief a time as possible. In other words, velocity begins to rise as money changes hands at a faster and faster rate. In quantity theory terms, during a hyperinflation, both *M* and *V* on the left side of the equation increase rapidly. Because there are limits in the rate at which *Y* can grow, as a matter of arithmetic the inflation rate must soar.

Although the quantity theory can help us understand the arithmetic of *how* a hyperinflation occurs, it doesn't explain *why* it occurs. Central banks control the money supply and, so, have the means to avoid the economic disaster of a hyperinflation. Why, then, at times have some central banks allowed the money supply to increase at very rapid rates? The answer is that central banks are not always free to act independently of the rest of the government. The ultimate cause of hyperinflation is usually governments spending more than they collect in taxes, which results in government budget deficits. A budget deficit forces the government to borrow the difference between government spending and tax collections, usually by selling bonds. High-income countries, such as the United States, Germany, and Canada, can sell government bonds to private investors because those investors are confident that governments can make the interest payments. But private investors are often unwilling to buy bonds issued by developing countries, such as Zimbabwe, because they doubt that those governments will make the payments due on the bonds.

Governments that can't sell bonds to private investors will often sell them to their central banks. In paying for the bonds, the central bank increases the country's money supply. This process is called *monetizing the government's debt*, or, more casually, funding government spending by printing money.

Making the Connection

Deutsche Bank During the German Hyperinflation

Banks don't like inflation. Because banks lend out a lot of money, inflation means borrowers pay back those loans in dollars that have less purchasing power. Particularly if the rate of inflation turns out to be higher than the bank expected it to be when making the loans, inflation will reduce bank profits. During a hyperinflation, the problems for banks are magnified because any loans will be repaid in money that will have lost most or all of its value.

One of the most famous hyperinflations occurred in Germany during the early 1920s. In 1918, when Germany lost World War I, the Allies—the United States, Great Britain, France, and Italy—imposed payments called *reparations* on the new German government. After a few years, the German government fell far behind in its reparations payment. In January 1923, the French government sent troops into the German industrial area known as the Ruhr to try to collect the payments directly. German workers in the Ruhr went on strike, and the German government decided to support them by paying their salaries. The government obtained the funds by selling bonds to the Reichsbank, thereby increasing the money supply.

The resulting increase in the money supply was very large: The total number of marks—the German currency—in circulation rose from 115 million in January 1922 to 1.3 billion in January 1923 and then to 497 billion billion, or 497,000,000,000,000,000,000, in December 1923. Just as the quantity theory predicts, the result was a staggeringly high rate of inflation. The German price index that stood at 100 in 1914 and 1,440 in January 1922 rose to 126,160,000,000,000 in December 1923. The German mark became worthless. The German government ended the hyperinflation by (1) negotiating a new agreement with the Allies that reduced its reparations payments, (2) balancing the budget by reducing government expenditures and raising taxes, and (3) replacing the existing mark with a new mark. Each new mark was worth 1 trillion old marks. The German central bank was also limited to issuing a total of 3.2 billion new marks.

Deutsche Bank was the largest bank in Germany at the time of the hyperinflation, and it remains the largest today. The hyperinflation put enormous strain on the bank. Because German currency was losing value so quickly, households and firms wanted their transactions processed as rapidly as possible. To handle these transactions, the bank had to increase its employees by six times compared with pre–World War I levels. Households and firms were anxious to borrow money to meet their own soaring expenses, and they expected to be able to pay back loans using money that had lost most of its purchasing power. According to one economic historian, the demand for loans increased "geometrically from day to day." Because most of these loans would have been unprofitable to the bank, the bank's managers ordered its branches to sharply reduce the number of loans granted. Eventually, as German currency became nearly worthless, Deutsche Bank would make loans only to borrowers who would repay them in either foreign currencies or commodities, such as coal or wheat.

Despite the intense financial strains on the bank, Deutsche Bank emerged from the hyperinflation in a stronger competitive position in Germany. The bank's managers believed that with the value of currency and financial investments rapidly disappearing, they would be better off acquiring other banks because they would be acquiring land and buildings that would be likely to retain their value. This strategy turned out to be shrewd. When the hyperinflation ended in 1924 and the German economy resumed growing, Deutsche Bank was in an excellent position to profit from that growth.

Sources: Thomas Sargent, "The End of Four Big Hyperinflations," in *Rational Expectations and Inflation*, New York: Harper & Row, 1986; and David A. Moss, "The Deutsche Bank," in Thomas K. McCraw, *Creating Modern Capitalism*, Cambridge, MA: Harvard University Press, 1997.

See related problems 5.10 and 5.11 at the end of the chapter.

Should Central Banks Be Independent?

In the modern economy, hyperinflations occur primarily in developing countries when their central banks are forced to create so much money to fund government spending that the inflation rate soars. But central banks in high-income countries may also come under political pressure to buy government bonds to help fund government budget deficits. The more independent a central bank is of the rest of the government, the more it can resist political pressures to increase the money supply, and the lower the country's inflation rate is likely to be.

In a classic study, Alberto Alesina and Lawrence Summers of Harvard University tested the link between the degree of independence of a country's central bank and the country's inflation rate for 16 high-income countries during the years 1955–1988. Figure 2.4 shows the results. Countries with highly independent central banks, such as

Figure 2.4

The Relationship Between Central Bank Independence and the Inflation Rate

For 16 high-income countries, the greater the degree of central bank independence, the lower the inflation rate. Central bank independence is measured by an index ranging from 1 (minimum independence) to 4 (maximum independence).

Source: Alberto Alesina and Lawrence H. Summers, "Central Bank Independence and Macroeconomic Performance: Some Comparative Evidence," *Journal of Money, Credit and Banking*, Vol. 25, No. 2, May 1993, pp. 151–162. Copyright 1993 by Ohio State University Press (Journals). Reproduced with permission of Ohio State University Press via Copyright Clearance Center.

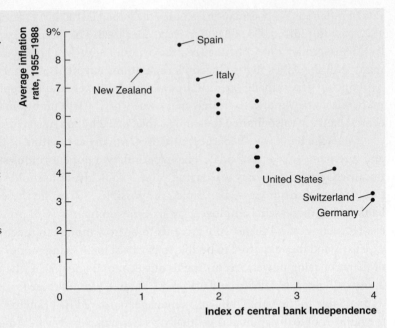

the United States, Switzerland, and Germany, had lower inflation rates than did countries whose central banks had little independence, such as New Zealand, Italy, and Spain. In recent years, New Zealand and Canada have granted their banks more independence, at least partly to better fight inflation.

It appears likely that the independence of the Federal Reserve helps to explain the relatively low inflation rates in the United States during the past 20 years. But the actions of the Fed during the 2007–2009 recession led many members of Congress to argue that the Fed's independence should be reduced. Some members had been long-time critics of the Fed and believed that in a democracy, monetary policy should be set by Congress and the president of the United States and implemented by officials who must directly answer to the president. Under existing law, the Federal Reserve operates independently because it is run by the seven-member Board of Governors who serve 14-year terms and are appointed by the president but cannot be replaced by the president or Congress unless they resign or their terms expire. Because the members of the Board of Governors do not run for election, they are not accountable for their actions to the ultimate authorities in a democracy—the voters. Other members of Congress objected to the actions of the Fed during the recession because they believed the actions exceeded the authority granted to the Fed under federal law. Some members were particularly concerned that the Fed had brought about increases in the money supply and bank reserves that threatened higher inflation rates in the future.

During 2010, Congress debated a financial reform bill. Although some early proposals would have significantly curtailed the Fed's independence, when the Wall Street Reform and Consumer Protection Act, or the Dodd-Frank Act, was passed in July 2010, the Fed was actually given enhanced authority. The act gave the Fed additional power to regulate financial firms other than commercial banks and the Fed was given a key role on a new Financial Stability Council, which was charged with ensuring that there would not be another financial crisis of the magnitude of 2007–2009. Passage of the Dodd-Frank Act, though, seems unlikely to end the debate among policymakers over whether the Fed's independence should be reduced.

Answering the Key Question

Continued from page 23

At the beginning of this chapter, we asked:

"Should a central bank be independent of the rest of the government?"

We have seen that policymakers disagree on the answer to this question. The degree of independence that a country grants to its central bank is ultimately a political question. We have also seen, though, that most economists believe that an independent central bank helps to control inflation.

Key Terms and Problems

Key Terms

Barter, p. 25
Check, p. 30
Commodity money, p. 25
E-money, p. 31
Fiat money, p. 28
Hyperinflation, p. 39
Legal tender, p. 28

M1, p. 32
M2, p. 33
Medium of exchange, p. 27
Monetary aggregate, p. 32
Money, p. 24
Payments system, p. 29
Quantity theory of money, p. 36

Specialization, p. 26
Standard of deferred payment, p. 27
Store of value, p. 27
Transactions cost, p. 25
Unit of account, p. 27
Wealth, p. 28

2.1 Do We Need Money?
Analyze the inefficiencies of a barter system.

Review Questions

1.1 What are the costs of a barter system?

1.2 Give two examples of commodity money.

1.3 What role does specialization play in an economy's standard of living?

Problems and Applications

1.4 Why might an individual find a $20 Federal Reserve Note to be more desirable as a form of money than a $20 gold coin? Which would the government find more desirable? Briefly explain.

1.5 What are the key differences between using a deerskin as money and using a dollar bill as money?

1.6 [Related to the Making the Connection **on page 26**] Should the packs of Marlboro cigarettes used to pay taxi drivers in Russia in the late 1980s be considered money? Briefly explain.

1.7 [Related to the Making the Connection **on page 26**] Following the end of World War II in 1945, the Reichsmark, the German currency, lost so much value that a barter economy developed. During this period, many Germans used U.S. cigarettes as currency. Why might people have used cigarettes, rather than another commodity, as currency in these circumstances?

MyEconLab Visit **www.myeconlab.com** to complete these exercises online and get instant feedback. Exercises that update with real-time data are marked with 🌐.

2.2   The Key Functions of Money
Discuss the four key functions of money.

Review Questions

2.1   What makes a dollar bill money? What makes a personal check money? Are there circumstances under which you would be reluctant to accept a dollar bill as money? A personal check?

2.2   Briefly describe each of the four main functions of money.

2.3   Is money the only store of value? If not, give some other examples of stores of value. Must money be a store of value to serve its function as a medium of exchange? Briefly explain.

2.4   What is the difference between commodity money and fiat money?

Problems and Applications

2.5   Suppose that you live in a simple farm economy where milk is accepted as the primary form of money. Discuss the difficulties with using milk as money in regard to:

  a. A medium of exchange

  b. A unit of account

  c. A store of value

  d. A standard of deferred payment

2.6   In 2009, the government of North Korea announced that it was replacing the existing currency with a new currency. The government would allow people to exchange only a limited amount of the old currency for the new currency. An article in the *Wall Street Journal* argued that the action amounted to seizing "most of its citizens' money and savings."

  a. Why would limiting the amount of old currency that could be exchanged for new currency result in the North Korean government's having seized its citizens' money and savings?

  b. How might people in North Korea act to reduce the impact of this government move?

Source: Evan Ramstad, "North Koreans Protest Currency Issue," *Wall Street Journal*, December 9, 2009.

2.7   Discuss whether your money, wealth, or income increases in each of the following situations:

  a. The value of your house increases.

  b. Your boss gives you a 10% raise.

  c. You take cash out of the bank and use it to buy an Apple iPad.

2.8   [Related to the Making the Connection **on page 29**] Suppose that Congress changes the law to require all firms to accept paper currency in exchange for whatever they are selling. Briefly discuss who would gain and who would lose from this legislation.

2.9   On January 1, 2002, Germany officially adopted the euro as its currency, and the deutsche mark stopped being legal tender. According to an article in the *Wall Street Journal*, even 10 years later many Germans continued using the deutsche mark, and many stores in Germany continued to accept it. Briefly explain how it is possible for people to continue to use a currency when the government that issued it has replaced it with another currency.

Source: Vanessa Fuhrmans, "Who Needs the Euro When You Can Pay with Deutsche Marks?" *Wall Street Journal*, July 18, 2012.

2.3   The Payments System
Explain the role of the payments system in the economy.

Review Questions

3.1   If there were a decrease in the efficiency of the payments system, what would be the cost to the economy?

3.2   Why did governments begin issuing paper currency?

3.3   Is the United States likely to become a "cashless society"? Briefly explain.

MyEconLab   Visit **www.myeconlab.com** to complete these exercises online and get instant feedback. Exercises that update with real-time data are marked with 🕭 .

Problems and Applications

3.4 Suppose that an economy in 10,000 B.C. used a rare stone as its money. Suppose also that the number of stones declined over time as stones were accidentally destroyed or used as weapons. What would have happened to the value of the stones over time? What would the consequences likely have been if someone had discovered a large quantity of new stones?

3.5 One historian has given the following description of the economy of the Roman Empire in the third century under the emperor Diocletian:

> The coinage had become so debased as to be virtually worthless. Diocletian's attempt to reissue good gold and silver coins failed because there simply was not enough gold and silver available to restore confidence in the currency.... Diocletian finally accepted the ruin of the money economy and revised the tax system so that it was based on payments in kind. The soldiers too came to be paid in kind.

a. What does it mean to say that the coinage had become debased?

b. Why would government officials need to restore confidence in the coins before people would use them as money?

c. What are "in kind" payments? How might moving from a system of payments being made in gold and silver coins to a system of payments being made in kind affect the economy of the empire?

Source: Ralph W. Mathisen, "Diocletian," *An Online Encyclopedia of Roman Emperors*, www.roman-emperors. org/dioclet.htm. Reprinted with permission from Professor Ralph W. Mathisen.

3.6 Suppose that debit cards, ATMs, ACH transactions, and other forms of electronic funds transfers did not exist. How would this change the way you shop and pay bills? How would transactions costs in the economy be affected?

3.7 In late 2009, Amazon introduced PayPhrase, an electronic payments system intended to compete with PayPal. Less than three years later, in early 2012, Amazon discontinued the program. PayPal is by far the largest electronic payments system. What problems might competitors encounter in trying to set up a competing system?

2.4 | Measuring the Money Supply
Explain how the U.S. money supply is measured.

Review Questions

4.1 Are the assets included in M1 more or less liquid than the assets included in M2? Briefly explain.

4.2 Since 1975, which measure of the money supply has grown more rapidly, M1 or M2? Briefly explain why. Has the growth of M1 been more or less stable than the growth rate of M2?

Problems and Applications

4.3 Define *liquidity*. Rank the following assets in terms of liquidity, from most to least liquid: money market mutual fund, savings account, corporate stock, dollar bill, house, gold bar, checking account.

4.4 Explain whether each of the following is included in only M1, only M2, or both M1 and M2:

a. Traveler's checks

b. Savings deposits

c. Certificates of deposit

d. Checking account deposits

4.5 Suppose you withdraw $1,000 from your checking account and use the funds to buy a certificate of deposit at your bank. What is the immediate effect of these actions on M1 and M2?

4.6 Why aren't credit cards included in M1 or M2?

MyEconLab Visit **www.myeconlab.com** to complete these exercises online and get instant feedback. Exercises that update with real-time data are marked with ⓌⓌ.

4.7 In a report, investment analyst Ned Davis referred to gold as "real money." Is gold used as money in the United States? What point was Davis making?

Source: E. S. Browning, "Adjusted for Inflation, Bad Run Looks Worse," *Wall Street Journal*, December 27, 2009.

4.8 Why might households and firms in a foreign country prefer to use U.S. dollars rather than their own country's currency in making transactions? What advantages or disadvantages do foreign governments experience because of the U.S. dollar being used rather than the domestic currency?

4.9 [**Related to the** Making the Connection **on page 33**] Explain whether you agree with the following statement:

> The Federal Reserve believes that two-thirds of the currency included in M1 is actually outside the United States. If this is correct, then M1 should be redefined to exclude that part of currency that is outside the United States. Otherwise, M1 provides a misleading measure of the amount of money available for U.S. households and firms to spend on goods and services in the United States.

2.5 | ## The Quantity Theory of Money: A First Look at the Link Between Money and Prices

Use the quantity theory of money to analyze the relationship between money and prices in the long run.

Review Questions

5.1 Is the equation of exchange a theory? Briefly explain.

5.2 What does the quantity theory indicate is the cause of inflation?

5.3 What is the cause of hyperinflation?

5.4 Briefly discuss the pros and cons of a central bank being independent of the rest of the government.

Problems and Applications

5.5 If during 2013 the money supply increases by 4%, the inflation rate is 2%, and the growth of real GDP is 3%, what must have happened to the value of velocity during 2013?

5.6 [**Related to** Solved Problem 2.5 **on page 37**] A student makes the following statement: "If the money supply in a country increases, then the level of total production in that country must also increase." Briefly explain whether you agree with this statement.

5.7 During the late nineteenth century, the United States experienced a period of sustained *deflation*, or a falling price level. Explain in terms of the quantity theory of money how a deflation is possible. Is it necessary for the quantity of money to decline for deflation to occur?

5.8 How does a high rate of inflation affect the value of money? How does it affect the usefulness of money as a medium of exchange?

5.9 An article in the *Economist* magazine observes: "One big reason to tie money to a commodity standard would be to limit its growth in order to protect against runaway inflation."

a. What is a "commodity standard"? What commodity did the United States and other countries at one time tie their money to?

b. Why would tying money to a commodity standard limit the growth of the money supply? Would doing so limit inflation?

Source: "On Gold and Golden Ages," *Economist*, September 11, 2012.

5.10 [**Related to the** Making the Connection **on page 40**] When the German government succeeded in ending the hyperinflation in 1924, was this better news for borrowers or for lenders? Briefly explain.

5.11 [**Related to the** Making the Connection **on page 40**] In 1919, the British economist John Maynard Keynes wrote the well-known book *The Economic Consequences of the Peace*, in which he argued that the reparations for World War I that Germany was being forced to pay to the United States, France, Italy, and the United Kingdom would have devastating consequences: "But who can say how much is endurable, or in what direction men will seek at last to escape from their misfortunes?" What is the connection between the war reparations that Germany was forced to pay and the later hyperinflation? Why might a hyperinflation lead to political unrest?

Source: John Maynard Keynes, *The Economic Consequences of the Peace*, New York: Harcourt, Brace and Howe, 1920, p. 251.

5.12 [**Related to the** Chapter Opener **on page 23**] Prior to 2009, Zimbabwe experienced several years of declining real GDP. According to an article in the *Wall Street Journal*, "After Zimbabwe abandoned its currency in favor of the greenback, the economy grew at an annual rate of 6% in 2009 and 9% in 2010."

  a. Why would Zimbabwe abandon its own currency to begin using U.S. dollars ("greenbacks")?

  b. Why would using the U.S. dollar as its currency have enabled the economy of Zimbabwe to resume growing?

  c. What potential problems could using U.S. dollars rather than its own currency pose for the Zimbabwean government?

Source: Patrick McGroarty, "Hanging On to Dollars in Zimbabwe," *Wall Street Journal*, March 26, 2012.

5.13 What does the statistical evidence show about the link between the growth rate of the money supply and the inflation rate in the long run? Is the link between the growth rate of the money supply and the inflation rate stronger in the short run or in the long run?

5.14 In late 2009, Federal Reserve Chairman Ben Bernanke wrote the following in a column published in the *Washington Post*:

> [Proposals in Congress to reduce the independence of the Fed] are very much out of step with the global consensus on the appropriate role of central banks, and they would seriously impair the prospects for economic and financial stability in the United States. . . . Our ability to take [monetary policy] actions without engendering sharp increases in inflation depends heavily on our credibility and independence from short-term political pressures.

Why would reducing the independence of the Fed "impair the prospects for economic and financial stability in the United States"? What does Bernanke mean by "short-term political pressures"? Why would the Fed's not being independent of short-term political pressures lead to "sharp increases in inflation"?

Source: Ben Bernanke, "The Right Reform for the Fed," *Washington Post*, November 29, 2009.

Data Exercises

D2.1: [**The components of M1**] Go to the web site of the Federal Reserve Bank of St. Louis (FRED) (research.stlouisfed.org/fred2/) and find the most recent values for the M1 Money Stock (M1), the Currency Component of M1 (CURRENCY), Total Checkable Deposits (TCD), and Travelers Checks Outstanding (WTCSL). Which of the components of M1 is the largest? Which is the smallest?

D2.2: [**The relationship between M1 and M2**] Go to the web site of the Federal Reserve Bank of St. Louis (FRED) (http://research.stlouisfed.org/fred2/)

MyEconLab Visit **www.myeconlab.com** to complete these exercises online and get instant feedback. Exercises that update with real-time data are marked with .

and find the most recent monthly values and values from the same month 5 years and 10 years earlier from FRED for the M1 Money Stock (M1SL) and the M2 Money Stock (M2SL).

a. Using these data, calculate M1 as a proportion of M2 for each of the years.

b. Explain whether this proportion has increased, decreased, or remained the same over time. Can you think of an explanation for any changes you observe?

D2.3: **[The equation of exchange]** Go to the web site of the Federal Reserve Bank of St. Louis (http://research.stlouisfed.org/fred2/) and find the most recent values and values for the same quarter in 1985 for nominal Gross Domestic Product (GDP), the Velocity of M1 Money Stock (M1V), and the Velocity of M2 Money Stock (M2V).

a. Using the data found above, compute the M1 money supply and the M2 money supply for both periods.

b. Describe how M1 velocity and M2 velocity differ in the two quarters.

D2.4: **[The relationship between changes in M2 and inflation]** Go to the St. Louis Fed's data site (FRED) (http://research.stlouisfed.org/fred2/) and, for January 1990 to the most recent available month, download and graph both the compounded annual rates of change of M2 (M2SL) and the rate of change of the CPI (CPIAUCSL). What relationship do you see between the two variables?

CHAPTER 3

Interest Rates and Rates of Return

Learning Objectives

After studying this chapter, you should be able to:

3.1 Explain how the interest rate links present value with future value (pages 50–58)

3.2 Distinguish among different debt instruments and understand how their prices are determined (pages 58–62)

3.3 Explain the relationship between the yield to maturity on a bond and its price (pages 62–67)

3.4 Understand the inverse relationship between bond prices and bond yields (pages 67–73)

3.5 Explain the difference between interest rates and rates of return (pages 73–75)

3.6 Explain the difference between nominal interest rates and real interest rates (pages 75–78)

Will Investors Lose Their Shirts in the Market for Treasury Bonds?

Want a safe investment? How about U.S. Treasury bonds? The Treasury issues bonds when it needs to borrow money to pay the federal government's bills. When you buy a bond, the Treasury will pay you interest every six months and pay you back the $1,000 face value of the bond when it matures. Unlike some local governments, corporations, or foreign governments that issue bonds, the U.S. government is almost certain to make the payments on these bonds. In other words, the *default risk* is effectively zero.

But in September 2012, many financial advisors believed Treasury bonds were too risky and therefore warned investors *not* to buy them. A contradiction? Not necessarily. At that time, 30-year Treasury bonds—bonds that would mature and pay the owner $1,000 in 30 years—had an interest rate of about 3%, which was much higher than the interest rate you would receive on a checking account or a savings account in a bank. But 3% was a historically low interest for 30-year Treasury bonds compared to the 15%

Continued on next page

Key Issue and Question

Issue: Some investment analysts argue that very low interest rates on some long-term bonds make them risky investments.

Question: Why do interest rates and the prices of financial securities move in opposite directions?

Answered on page 78

they had paid in 1981 or even the 5.25% they had paid in mid-2007. Why had the interest rate on Treasury bonds declined? As we will discuss in this chapter, interest rates are determined by the interaction between the interest rate borrowers, such as the U.S. Treasury, are willing to pay and the interest rate investors are willing to accept in exchange for lending their funds. One important factor that borrowers and investors take into account is the expected inflation rate. The higher the inflation rate, the lower the purchasing power of the dollars with which the borrower will repay the investor. When investors expect that future inflation rates will be high, they insist on being paid high interest rates on bonds.

One important reason 30-year Treasury bonds had such low interest rates in 2012 was that many investors expected that the inflation rate would remain 2% or less for years into the future. But some economists and investment advisors weren't so sure. During the financial crisis, the Federal Reserve had taken a number of steps that resulted in a large increase in the money supply. The quantity equation shows that in the long run, high rates of growth of the money supply lead to high

inflation rates. Federal Reserve Chairman Ben Bernanke argued the Fed would be able to avoid inflation as the economic expansion strengthened. But if Bernanke was wrong, inflation would increase and the Treasury would have to pay higher interest rates on newly issued bonds.

What happens if you buy a Treasury bond with an interest rate of 3%, when the Treasury begins selling Treasury bonds with interest rates of 5%? If you hold your bond all the way to maturity, you will continue receiving an interest rate of 3%. But what if you decide to sell the bond? Your bond pays only 3% interest, while the Treasury is selling new bonds that pay 5%. To find a buyer for your bond, you will have to cut its price to compensate the buyer for receiving the lower interest rate. In other words, you will have to accept a loss on your bond.

So, while it is true that in buying a Treasury bond, you do not face *default risk*, you will face *interest-rate risk*, which is the risk that the price of your bond will fluctuate in response to changes in market interest rates. If predictions of higher future inflation turn out to be accurate, many investors who owned bonds in 2012 stood to lose a substantial amount as the prices of their bonds declined.

In this chapter, we will begin exploring bonds and similar securities. Bonds play an important role in the financial system because they facilitate funds moving from savers to borrowers. A solid understanding of interest rates will help you make sense of bonds and nearly every other aspect of the financial system.

3.1

Learning Objective

Explain how the interest rate links present value with future value.

The Interest Rate, Present Value, and Future Value

During the Middle Ages in Europe, governments often banned lenders from charging interest on loans, partly because some people interpreted the Bible as prohibiting the practice and partly because most people believed that anyone with funds to spare should be willing to lend them to poorer friends and neighbors to purchase basic necessities, without charging interest on the loan. In modern economies, households and firms usually borrow money to finance spending on items such as houses and cars rather than on basic necessities. Perhaps as a result, charging interest on loans is no longer banned in most countries. Today, economists consider the interest rate to be the cost of credit.

Why Do Lenders Charge Interest on Loans?

If apple growers charged a zero price for apples, very few apples would be supplied. Similarly, if lenders, who are suppliers of credit, didn't charge interest on loans, there would be very little credit supplied. Recall from your introductory economics course the important idea of *opportunity cost*, which is the value of what you have to give up to engage in an activity. Just as the price of apples has to cover the opportunity cost of supplying apples, the interest rate has to cover the opportunity cost of supplying credit.

Consider the following situation: You make a $1,000 loan to a friend who promises to pay back the money in one year. There are three key facts you need to take into account when deciding how much interest to charge him:

1. By the time your friend pays you back, prices are likely to have risen, so you will be able to buy fewer goods and services than you could have if you had spent the money rather than lending it.
2. Your friend might not pay you back; in other words, he might *default* on the loan.
3. During the period of the loan, your friend has use of your money, and you don't. If he uses the money to buy a computer, he gets the use of the computer for a year, while you wait for him to pay you back. In other words, lending your money involves the opportunity cost of not being able to spend it on goods and services today.

So, we can think of the interest you charge on the loan as being the result of:

- Compensation for inflation
- Compensation for default risk—the chance that the borrower will not pay back the loan
- Compensation for the opportunity cost of waiting to spend your money

Notice two things about this list. First, even if lenders are convinced that there will be no inflation during the period of the loan and even if they believe there is no chance the borrower will default, lenders will still charge interest to compensate them for waiting for their money to be paid back. Second, these three factors vary from person to person and from loan to loan. For instance, during periods when lenders believe that inflation will be high, they will charge more interest. Lenders will also charge more interest to borrowers who seem more likely to default.

Most Financial Transactions Involve Payments in the Future

We are all familiar with interest rates that are charged on car loans or school loans and interest rates paid on assets such as certificates of deposit in banks. Actually, the interest rate is important to all aspects of the financial system because of the following key fact: *Most financial transactions involve payments in the future.* When you take out a car loan, you promise to make payments every month until the loan is paid off. When you buy a bond issued by General Electric, General Electric promises to pay you interest every year until the bond matures. We could go on to list many other similar financial transactions that also involve future payments. The fact that financial transactions involve payments in the future causes a problem: How is it possible to compare different transactions? For instance, suppose that you need to borrow $15,000 from your bank to buy a car. Consider two loans:

1. Loan A, which requires you to pay $366.19 per month for 48 months
2. Loan B, which requires you to pay $318.71 per month for 60 months

Which loan would you prefer? The interest rate provides a means of answering questions like this because it provides a *link between the financial present and the financial future*. In this case, even though Loan A has a higher monthly payment, it has a lower interest rate: The interest rate on Loan A is 8%, while the interest rate on Loan B is 10%. While the interest rate is not the only factor to consider when evaluating a loan, it is an important factor.

Two key ideas—compounding and discounting—can help us further explore how the interest rate provides a link between the financial present and the financial future, and can also help us understand how to calculate interest rates, like those on these two loans.

Compounding and Discounting

Future value The value at some future time of an investment made today.

Consider an example of compounding. Suppose that you deposit $1,000 in a one-year bank certificate of deposit (CD) that pays an interest rate of 5%. What will be the *future value* of this investment? **Future value** refers to the value at some future time of an investment made today. In one year, you will receive back your $1,000 *principal*—which is the amount invested (or borrowed)—and 5% interest on your $1,000, or:

$$\$1,000 + (\$1,000 \times 0.05) = \$1,050.$$

We can rewrite this compactly as:

$$\$1,000 \times (1 + 0.05) = \$1,050.$$

If:

$i = $ the interest rate
Principal $ = $ the amount of your investment (your original $1,000)
$FV = $ the future value (what your $1,000 will have grown to in one year),

then we can rewrite the expression as:

$$Principal \times (1 + i) = FV_1.$$

(Note that we add the subscript 1 to FV_1 to indicate that we are looking at the future value after *one* year.) This relationship is important because it states that we can calculate a future value in one year by multiplying the principal invested by 1 plus the interest rate.

Compounding for More than One Period Suppose that at the end of one year, you decide to reinvest in—or *roll over*—your CD for another year. If you reinvest your $1,050 for a second year, you will not only receive interest on your original investment of $1,000, you will also receive interest on the $50 in interest you earned the first year. The process of earning interest on interest as savings accumulate over time is called **compounding**. *Compound interest* is an important component of the total amount you earn on any investment.

Compounding The process of earning interest on interest, as savings accumulate over time.

We can calculate the future value after two years of your initial investment:

$$[\$1,000 \times (1 + 0.05)] \times (1 + 0.05) = \$1,102.50.$$

$$(\text{Amount you earned after one year}) \times (\text{Compounding during the second year})$$
$$= \text{Future value after two years}.$$

We can write this expression more compactly as:

$$\$1,000 \times (1 + 0.05)^2 = \$1,102.50,$$

or, in symbols, as:

$$Principal \times (1 + 0.05)^2 = FV_2.$$

We could continue to compound your initial $1,000 investment for as many years as you choose to roll over your CD. For instance, if you rolled it over for a third year at the same interest rate, at the end of the third year, you would have:

$$\$1,000 \times (1 + 0.05) \times (1 + 0.05) \times (1 + 0.05) = \$1,000 \times (1 + 0.05)^3 = \$1,157.63.$$

Note that the exponent on the compounding factor, $(1 + 0.05)$, equals the number of years over which the compounding takes place.

It's useful to generalize our result: If you invest $1,000 for n years, where n can be any number of years, at an interest rate of 5%, then at the end of n years, you will have:

$$\$1,000 \times (1 + 0.05)^n,$$

or, in symbols:

$$Principal \times (1 + i)^n = FV_n.$$

Solved Problem 3.1A   In Your Interest

Using Compound Interest to Select a Bank CD

Suppose you are considering investing $1,000 in one of the following bank CDs:

- The first CD will pay an interest rate of 4% per year for three years

- The second CD will pay an interest rate of 10% the first year, 1% the second year, and 1% the third year

Which CD should you choose?

Solving the Problem

Step 1 Review the chapter material. This problem is about compound interest, so you may want to review the section "Compounding for More Than One Period" on page 52.

Step 2 Calculate the future value of your investment with the first CD. Because the interest rate is the same each year for the first CD, the future value in three years will be equal to the present value of $1,000, which is the amount of your principal, multiplied by 1 plus the interest rate raised to the third power, or:

$$\$1,000 \times (1 + 0.04)^3 = \$1,124.86.$$

Step 3 Calculate the future value of your investment with the second CD. For the second CD, the interest rate is not the same each year. So, you need to use a different compounding factor for each year:

$$\$1,000 \times (1 + 0.10) \times (1 + 0.01) \times (1 + 0.01) = \$1,122.11.$$

Step 4 Decide which CD you should choose. You should choose the investment with the highest future value, so you should choose the first CD.

EXTRA CREDIT: Note that the average interest rate received across the three years is 4% for both CDs. When asked to guess the answer to this problem without first doing the calculations, many students choose the second CD. They reason that the high 10% interest rate received in the first year means that even though the interest rates in the second and third years are low, the second CD will end up with the higher future value. As the table below shows, although the first CD starts out well behind after the first year, it finishes the third year with the higher value. This example illustrates the sometimes surprising results of compounding.

	First CD	Second CD
After 1 year	$1,040.00	$1,100.00
After 2 years	1,081.60	1,111.00
After 3 years	1,124.86	1,122.11

See related problem 1.6 at the end of the chapter.

An Example of Discounting We have just used the interest rate to link the financial future with the financial present by starting with a dollar amount in the present and seeing what the amount will grow to in the future as a result of compounding. We can reverse the process and use the interest rate to calculate the *present value* of funds to be received in the future. The **present value** is the value today of funds to be received in the future. A key point is this: *Funds in the future are worth less than funds in the present, so funds in the future have to be reduced, or discounted, to find their present value.* The **time value of money** refers to the way that the value of a payment changes depending on when the payment is received. Why are funds in the future worth less than funds in the present? For the same three reasons that lenders charge interest on loans, as we noted earlier:

Present value The value today of funds that will be received in the future.

Time value of money The way that the value of a payment changes depending on when the payment is received.

1. Dollars in the future will usually buy less than dollars can today.
2. Dollars that are promised to be paid in the future may not actually be received.
3. There is an opportunity cost in waiting to receive a payment because you cannot get the benefits of the goods and services you could have bought if you had the money today.

Discounting The process of finding the present value of funds that will be received in the future.

To carry out **discounting**, we reverse the compounding process we just discussed. In our example, you are willing to part with your $1,000 for one year (by buying a one-year CD), provided that you receive $1,050 after one year. In other words, $1,000 in present value is the equivalent of $1,050 in future value to be received in one year. We could reverse the story and ask: How much would you be willing to pay the bank today if it promised to pay you $1,050 in one year? The answer, of course, is $1,000. Looked at this way, for you, $1,050 to be received in one year has a present value of $1,000.

From this perspective, compounding and discounting are equivalent processes. We can summarize this result (where PV = present value):

Compounding: $\$1,000 \times (1 + 0.05) = \$1,050$; or $PV \times (1 + i) = FV_1$.

Discounting: $\$1,000 = \dfrac{\$1,050}{(1 + 0.05)}$; or $PV = \dfrac{FV_1}{(1 + i)}$.

Note that while $(1 + i)$ is the compounding factor, which we use to calculate the future value of money we invest today, $1/(1 + i)$ is the discount factor, which we use to calculate the present value of money to be received in the future.

We can generalize this result for any number of periods:

Compounding: $PV \times (1 + i)^n = FV_n$.

Discounting: $PV = \dfrac{FV_n}{(1 + i)^n}$.

Some Important Points About Discounting We will use the idea of discounting future payments many times in this book, so it is important to understand the following four important points:

1. *Present value is sometimes called "present discounted value."* This terminology emphasizes that in converting dollars received in the future into their equivalent value in dollars today, we are discounting, or reducing, the value of the future dollars.

2. *The further in the future a payment is to be received, the smaller its present value.* We can see that this point is true by examining the discounting formula:

   $$PV = FV/(1 + i)^n.$$

   The larger the value of n, the larger the value of the denominator in the fraction and the smaller the present value.

3. *The higher the interest rate we use to discount future payments, the smaller the present value of the payments.* Once again, we can see that this point is true by examining the discounting formula:

   $$PV = FV/(1 + i)^n.$$

   Because the interest rate appears in the denominator of the fraction, the larger the interest rate, the smaller the present value. From an economic perspective, if you require a higher interest rate before you are willing to lend your money, you are saying that a larger number of dollars in the future is worth as much to you as a dollar today. That is the equivalent of saying that each dollar in the future is worth less to you today than if the interest rate were lower.

   We can illustrate the second and third points by using Table 3.1. The rows in the table show that for any given interest rate, the further in the future a payment is received, the smaller its present value. For example, at an interest rate of 5%, a $1,000 payment you receive in one year has a present value of $952.38, but the present value

Table 3.1 Time, the Interest Rate, and the Present Value of a Payment

	Present value of a $1,000 payment to be received in ...			
Interest rate	1 year	5 years	15 years	30 years
1%	$990.10	$951.47	$861.35	$741.92
2%	980.39	905.73	743.01	552.07
5%	952.38	783.53	481.02	231.38
10%	909.09	620.92	239.39	57.31
20%	833.33	401.88	64.91	4.21

drops to only $231.38 if you receive the payment in 30 years. The columns show that for any given number of years in the future you will receive a payment, the higher the interest rate is, the smaller the payment's present value will be. For example, a $1,000 payment you receive in 15 years has a present value of $861.35 when discounted at an interest rate of 1%, but the payment is worth only $64.91 when discounted at an interest rate of 20%. Note that a $1,000 payment you will receive in 30 years has a present value of only $4.21 when discounted at an interest rate of 20%.

4. *The present value of a series of future payments is simply the sum of the discounted value of each individual payment.* For example, what would the promise to pay you $1,000 in one year and another $1,000 in five years be worth to you? If we assume an interest rate of 10%, Table 3.1 shows that the present value of the payment you will receive in one year is $909.09 and the present value of the payment you will receive in five years is $620.92. So, the present value of the promise to make both these payments is equal to $909.09 + $620.92 = $1,530.01.

A Brief Word on Notation This book will *always* enter interest rates in numerical calculations as decimals. For instance, 5% will be 0.05, *not* 5. Failing to follow this rule will, obviously, result in your calculations being inaccurate—it makes a big difference whether you multiply (or divide) by 0.05 or by 5! This caution is so important that we gave it its own little section.

Solved Problem 3.1B   **In Your Interest**

How Do You Value a College Education?

According to the Census Bureau's Current Population Survey, at age 22, the typical college graduate makes about $7,200 more per year than does the typical high school graduate who has not attended college. The earnings gap between high school graduates and college graduates grows until about age 42.

Consider the following data on the gap between earnings by college graduates and high school graduates (for the sake of simplicity, suppose that the additional income received by a college graduate is all received at the end of the year):

Age 22: $7,200

Age 23: $7,200

Age 24: $7,300

Age 25: $7,300

a. Considering just ages 22 to 25, what is the present value of a college education? Assume an interest rate of 5%.

b. Suppose you are 18 years old and considering whether to enter the labor force by taking a job immediately after graduating from high school or to attend college and enter the labor force

at age 22. Briefly explain how you might calculate the present value for you of a college education. (Hint: Are there costs you would need to take into account?)

Source: Christopher Avery and Sarah Turner, "Student Loans: Do College Students Borrow Too Much, or Not Enough?" *Journal of Economic Perspectives*, Vol.26, No. 1, Winter 2012, pp. 165–192.

Solving the Problem

Step 1 Review the chapter material. This problem is about discounting future payments, so you may want to review the section "Some Important Points About Discounting," which begins on page 55.

Step 2 Answer part (a) by using the data given to calculate the present value of a college education for these years. Point 4 in the section "Some Important Points about Discounting" is: *The present value of a series of future payments is simply the sum of the discounted value of each individual payment.* You can consider the annual earnings gap between college graduates and high school graduates as being, in effect, a payment a college graduate receives. Therefore, the calculation of the present value of a college education for these years is (remembering to enter the interest rate as a decimal):

$$PV = \frac{\$7,200}{1 + 0.05} + \frac{\$7,200}{(1 + 0.05)^2} + \frac{\$7,300}{(1 + 0.05)^3} + \frac{\$7,300}{(1 + 0.05)^4} = \$25,699.50.$$

Step 3 Answer part (b) by considering how you might calculate the present value for you of a college education. The first step would be to extend the present value calculation you did in part (a) through normal retirement age of 67. But to better tailor the calculation to your circumstance, you would need to take into account the following points:

1. You incur explicit costs by attending college, including the costs of tuition, books, and so on. You should take these costs into account to calculate the *net present value*—that is, the present value after taking into account costs— of a college education. Because these costs will be incurred over the next few years, their present value will be significant.

2. By attending college, assuming that you can't also work full time, you incur the opportunity cost of the wages you could have earned had you directly entered the labor market. These costs also have a high present value because they are incurred close to the present.

3. Finally, rather than use in your present value calculation the gap between the average income of college graduates and the average income of high school graduates, you should use the gap between the average income of the occupation you intend to enter and the income of the job you might accept directly out of high school.

See related problems 1.7 and 1.8 at the end of the chapter.

Discounting and the Prices of Financial Assets

Most financial assets, such as loans, stocks, and bonds, are basically promises by the borrower to make certain payments to the lender in the future. Discounting lets us compare financial assets by giving us a means of determining the present value of payments to be received at different times in the future. In particular, discounting gives us a way of determining the prices of financial assets. To see this point, think about why an investor would want to buy a financial asset, such as a stock or a bond. Presumably, investors buy financial assets to receive payments from the sellers of the assets. What are those payments worth to the buyer? The payments are worth their present value. By adding up the present values of all the payments, we have the dollar amount that a buyer will pay for the asset. In other words, we have determined the asset's price.

Debt Instruments and Their Prices

Our conclusion at the end of the last section is a key fact about the financial system, so it is worth restating: *The price of a financial asset is equal to the present value of the payments to be received from owning it.* We can apply this key fact to an important class of financial assets called *debt instruments.* **Debt instruments** (also called **credit market instruments** or **fixed-income assets**) include loans granted by banks and bonds issued by corporations and governments. Stocks are not debt instruments but **equities** that represent part ownership in the firms that issue them. Debt instruments can vary in their terms, but they are all IOUs, or promises by the borrower both to pay interest and repay principal to the lender. Debt instruments take different forms because lenders and borrowers have different needs.

Loans, Bonds, and the Timing of Payments

There are four basic categories of debt instruments:

1. Simple loans
2. Discount bonds
3. Coupon bonds
4. Fixed-payment loans

We can use these four categories to identify the variations in the timing of payments that borrowers make to lenders. We know that these variations will affect the present values and, therefore, the prices of the debt instruments. In addition to describing each type of debt instrument, we represent the payments on a loan or bond on a *timeline* to make it easier to measure the inflows and outflows of funds.

Simple Loan With a **simple loan**, the borrower receives from the lender an amount of funds called the *principal* and agrees to repay the lender the principal plus interest on a specific date when the loan matures. The most common simple loan is a short-term business loan—called a *commercial and industrial loan*—from a bank. For example, suppose that the Bank of America makes a one-year simple loan of $10,000 at an interest rate of 10% to Nate's Nurseries. We can illustrate this transaction on a *timeline* to show the payment of interest and principal by the borrower to the lender.

3.2

Learning Objective

Distinguish among different debt instruments and understand how their prices are determined.

Debt instruments (also known as **credit market instruments** or **fixed-income assets**) Methods of financing debt, including simple loans, discount bonds, coupon bonds, and fixed payment loans.

Equity A claim to part ownership of a firm; common stock issued by a corporation.

Simple loan A debt instrument in which the borrower receives from the lender an amount called the principal and agrees to repay the lender the principal plus interest on a specific date when the loan matures.

After one year, Nate's would repay the principal plus interest: $10,000 + ($10,000 × 0.10), or $11,000. On a timeline, the lender views the transaction as follows:

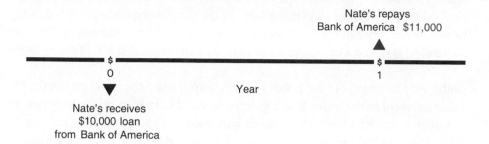

Discount Bond As with a simple loan, a borrower also repays a **discount bond** in a single payment. In this case, however, the borrower pays the lender an amount called the *face value* (or par value) at maturity but receives less than the face value initially. The interest paid on the loan is the difference between the amount repaid and the amount borrowed. Suppose that Nate's Nurseries issues a one-year discount bond and receives $9,091, repaying the $10,000 face value to the buyer of the bond after one year. So, the timeline for Nate's Nurseries discount bond is:

Discount bond A debt instrument in which the borrower repays the amount of the loan in a single payment at maturity but receives less than the face value of the bond initially.

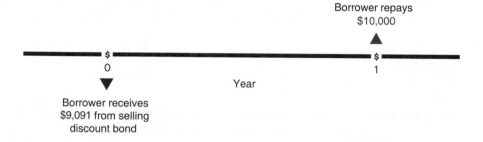

The lender receives interest of $10,000 − $9,091 = $909 for the year. Therefore, the interest rate is $909/$9,091 = 0.10, or 10%. The most common types of discount bonds are U.S. savings bonds, U.S. Treasury bills, and zero-coupon bonds.

Coupon Bonds Although they share the word "bond," *coupon bonds* are quite different from discount bonds. Borrowers issuing **coupon bonds** make interest payments in the form of coupons at regular intervals, typically semiannually or annually, and repay the face value at maturity. The U.S. Treasury, state and local governments, and large corporations all issue coupon bonds. Because of the importance of coupon bonds in the financial system, you should be familiar with the following terminology related to them:

Coupon bond A debt instrument that requires multiple payments of interest on a regular basis, such as semiannually or annually, and a payment of the face value at maturity.

- *Face value*, or *par value*. The amount to be repaid by the bond issuer (the borrower) at maturity. The face value of the typical coupon bond is $1,000.
- *Coupon*. The annual fixed dollar amount of interest paid by the issuer of the bond to the buyer.
- *Coupon rate*. The value of the coupon expressed as a percentage of the par value of the bond. For example, if a bond has an annual coupon of $50 and a face value of $1,000, its coupon rate is $50/$1,000 = 0.05, or 5%.

- *Current yield.* As we will see later in this chapter, after a coupon bond has been issued, it will often be resold many times in financial markets. As a result of this buying and selling, the bond's price may on a particular day be higher or lower than its $1,000 face value. The current yield is the value of the coupon expressed as a percentage of the current price of the bond. For example, if a bond has a coupon of $50, a par value of $1,000, and a current price of $900, its current yield is $50/$900 = 0.056, or 5.6%.
- *Maturity.* The length of time before the bond expires and the issuer makes the face value payment to the buyer. Many government and corporate bonds have maturities of 30 years, which means the issuer will make coupon payments each year for 30 years before making one last payment of the face value at the end of the thirtieth year. For example, if IBM issued a $1,000 30-year bond with a coupon rate of 10%, it would pay $100 per year for 30 years and a final payment of $1,000 at the end of 30 years. The timeline on the IBM coupon bond is:

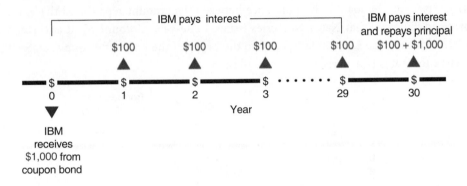

Fixed-Payment Loan With a **fixed-payment loan**, the borrower makes periodic payments (monthly, quarterly, or annually) to the lender. The payments are of equal amounts and include *both* interest and principal. Therefore, at maturity, the borrower has completely repaid the loan, and there is no lump-sum payment of principal. Common fixed-payment loans are home mortgages, student loans, and car loans. For example, if you are repaying a $10,000 10-year student loan with a 9% interest rate, your monthly payment is approximately $127. The timeline of payments is:

Fixed-payment loan
A debt instrument that requires the borrower to make regular periodic payments of principal and interest to the lender.

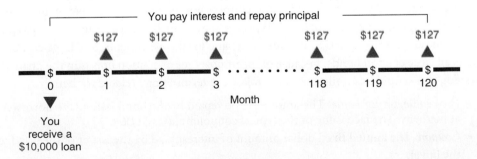

Fixed-payment loans are popular with households because as long as the household makes all the payments, the loan is completely paid off, and there is no large final payment to worry about, as with a simple loan. Fixed-payment loans also have the benefit to lenders that borrowers repay some principal with each loan payment, which reduces the chances of a borrower defaulting on the entire amount of the principal.

Although most debt instruments fall into these four categories, the changing needs of savers and borrowers have spurred the creation of new instruments having characteristics of more than one category.

Interest Rates and Student Loans

With rising tuition costs, more students are taking out student loans, and the loans are for larger amounts. In 2012, the total amount of student loans outstanding passed $1 trillion for the first time—more than the total value of credit card debt. Student loan payments are often the largest item in the budgets of recent college graduates. Even future presidents are not immune. According to Michelle Obama: "In fact, when [Barack and I] were first married . . . our combined monthly student loan bills were actually higher than our mortgage."

There are three main types of student loans:

1. Subsidized student loans
2. Unsubsidized student loans
3. Private loans

In 2012, most undergraduate students were eligible to borrow up to $31,000 in federal student loans, with a maximum of $23,000 being subsidized loans. In 2012, subsidized federal student loans had a fixed interest rate of 3.4% and unsubsidized federal loans had an interest rate of 6.8%. Under the standard repayment plan, federal student loans are paid back over 10 years. Private student loans, obtained from banks, have a variety of interest rates and repayment times.

We can use the concepts of compounding and discounting to analyze some of the loan options students face:

1. *What are the consequences of not making interest payments while you are in college?* With an unsubsidized student loan, you are responsible for paying the interest on your loan while you are in college, but you usually have the option of postponing paying the interest until you graduate. However, the unpaid interest accumulates and is added to the principal of your loan. To take a simplified example, if you have a $20,000 student loan at a 6.8% interest rate, you would have paid a total of $4,624 in interest during your four years in college. After you graduate, your loan total would then be $24,624, which means the monthly payment during your 10-year payback period would rise from $230.16 to $283.37, and you would end up paying $1,750 more in total interest payments. Students' financial circumstances vary tremendously, of course, so postponing making interest payments may be appealing to one student but not to another.

2. *What are the consequences of extending your payback period from 10 years to 30 years?* Although the standard payback period for a federal student loan is 10 years, many students are able to extend the period to as long as 30 years. Suppose,

once again, you have a $20,000 student loan with a 6.8% interest rate. With a 10-year payback period, your monthly payment is $230.16. With a 30-year payback period, the payment drops to $130.39, a more manageable payment for many students who have other bills to cover with their first paychecks. But remember that fixed-payment loans are amortized, which means that each payment you make is a mixture of interest and principal. By extending the payback period for 20 years, you are paying down the $20,000 principal more slowly, so you are paying more in total interest over the life of your loan. With a 10-year payback period, your total interest payments are $7,619.28, while with a 30-year payback period, your total interest payments are nearly $27,000, or almost four times as high.

Being familiar with the interest rate concepts we are discussing in this chapter can help students and their parents as they decide how to finance a college education. Helpful loan calculators are available on the studentaid.ed.gov and bankrate.com Web sites.

Sources: Rachel Louise Ensign, "Time to Repay Student Loans," *Wall Street Journal*, September 15, 2012; Charlie Spiering, "At Princeton, Michelle Obama Complains about Her Student Loans," *Washington Examiner*, September 24, 2012; "Student Loans," *New York Times*, September 9, 2012; and studentaid.ed.gov.

See related problem 2.6 at the end of the chapter.

3.3

Learning Objective

Explain the relationship between the yield to maturity on a bond and its price.

Bond Prices and Yield to Maturity

We have already seen that the price of a bond—or any other financial security—should equal the present value of the payments the owner receives from the bond. We can apply this concept to determine the price of a coupon bond.

Bond Prices

Consider a five-year coupon bond with a coupon rate of 6% and a face value of $1,000. The coupon rate of 6% tells us that the seller of the bond will pay the buyer of the bond $60 per year for five years, as well as make a final payment of $1,000 at the end of the fifth year. (Note that, in practice, coupons are typically paid twice per year, so a 6% bond will pay $30 after six months and another $30 at the end of the year. For simplicity, we will assume throughout this book that any payments made on a security are received at the end of a year.) Therefore, the expression for the price, P, of the bond is the sum of the present values of the six payments the investor will receive:

$$P = \frac{\$60}{(1+i)} + \frac{\$60}{(1+i)^2} + \frac{\$60}{(1+i)^3} + \frac{\$60}{(1+i)^4} + \frac{\$60}{(1+i)^5} + \frac{\$1,000}{(1+i)^5}.$$

We can use this reasoning to arrive at the following general expression for a bond that makes coupon payments, C, has a face value, FV, and matures in n years:

$$P = \frac{C}{(1+i)} + \frac{C}{(1+i)^2} + \frac{C}{(1+i)^3} + \cdots \frac{C}{(1+i)^n} + \frac{FV}{(1+i)^n}.$$

The dots (ellipsis) indicate that we have omitted the terms representing the years between the third year and the nth year—which could be the tenth, twentieth, thirtieth, or other, year.

Yield to Maturity

To use the expression for the price of a bond, we need to know the future payments to be received and the interest rate. Often, we know the price of a bond and the future payments, but we don't always know the interest rate. Suppose you face a decision like the following. Which is a better investment?

1. A three-year, $1,000 face value coupon bond with a price of $1,050 and a coupon rate of 8%
2. A two-year, $1,000 face value coupon bond with a price of $980 and a coupon rate of 6%

One important factor in making a choice between these two investments is determining the interest rate you will receive on each. Because we know the prices and the payments for the two bonds, we can use the present value calculation to find the interest rate on each investment:

$$\text{Bond 1: } \$1,050 = \frac{\$80}{(1 + i)} + \frac{\$80}{(1 + i)^2} + \frac{\$80}{(1 + i)^3} + \frac{\$1,000}{(1 + i)^3}.$$

Using a financial calculator, an online calculator, or a spreadsheet program, we can solve this equation for i. The solution for Bond 1 is $i = 0.061$, or 6.1%.

$$\text{Bond 2: } \$980 = \frac{\$60}{(1 + i)} + \frac{\$60}{(1 + i)^2} + \frac{\$1,000}{(1 + i)^2}.$$

For this bond, the solution for Bond 2 is $i = 0.071$, or 7.1%.

These calculations show us that even though Bond 1 may appear to be a better investment because it has a higher coupon rate than Bond 2, Bond 1's higher price means that it has a significantly lower interest rate than Bond 2. So, if you wanted to earn the highest interest rate on your investment, you would choose Bond 2.

The interest rate we have just calculated is called the **yield to maturity**, which equates the present value of the payments from an asset with the asset's price today. The yield to maturity is based on the concept of present value and is the interest rate measure that economists, firms, and investors use most often. In fact, it is important to note that unless they indicate otherwise, *whenever economists or investors refer to the interest rate on a financial asset, the interest rate they mean is the yield to maturity.* Calculating yields to maturity for alternative investments allows investors to compare different types of debt instruments.

Keep in mind the close relationship between discounting and compounding. We just calculated the yield to maturity by using a discounting formula. We can also think of the yield to maturity in terms of compounding. To do so, we need to ask, "If I pay a price, P, today for a bond with a particular set of future payments, what is the interest rate at which I could invest P and get the same set of future payments?" For example,

Yield to maturity The interest rate that makes the present value of the payments from an asset equal to the asset's price today.

instead of calculating the present value of the payments to be received on a 30-year Treasury bond, we can calculate the interest rate at which the money paid for the bond could be invested for 30 years to get the same present value.

Yields to Maturity on Other Debt Instruments

We saw in Section 3.2 that there are four categories of debt instruments. And we have calculated the yield to maturity on a coupon bond. Now we can calculate the yield to maturity on each of the other three types of debt instruments.

Simple Loans Calculating the yield to maturity on a simple loan is straightforward. We need to find the interest rate that makes the lender indifferent between having the amount of the loan today or the final payment at maturity. Consider again the $10,000 loan to Nate's Nurseries. The loan requires payment of the $10,000 principal plus $1,000 in interest one year from now. We calculate the yield to maturity as follows:

$$\text{Value today} = \text{Present value of future payments}$$

$$\$10,000 = \frac{\$10,000 + \$1,000}{(1 + i)},$$

from which we can solve for i:

$$i = \frac{\$11,000 - \$10,000}{\$10,000} = 0.10, \text{ or } 10\%.$$

Note that the yield to maturity, 10%, is the same as the simple interest rate. From this example, we can come to the general conclusion that, for a simple loan, the yield to maturity and the interest rate specified on the loan are the same.

Discount Bonds Calculating the yield to maturity on a discount bond is similar to calculating the yield to maturity on a simple loan. For example, suppose that Nate's Nurseries issues a $10,000 one-year discount bond. We can use the same equation to find the yield to maturity on the discount bond that we did in the case of a simple loan. If Nate's Nurseries receives $9,200 today from selling the bond, we can calculate the yield to maturity by setting the present value of the future payment equal to the value today, or $9,200 = \$10,000/(1 + i)$. Solving for i gives us:

$$i = \frac{\$10,000 - \$9,200}{\$9,200} = 0.087, \text{ or } 8.7\%.$$

From this example, we can write a general equation for a *one-year* discount bond that sells for price, P, with face value, FV. The yield to maturity is:

$$i = \frac{FV - P}{P}.$$

Fixed-Payment Loans Calculating the yield to maturity on a fixed-payment loan is similar to calculating the yield to maturity on a coupon bond. Recall that fixed-payment loans require periodic payments that combine interest and principal, but there is no face value payment at maturity. Suppose that Nate's Nurseries borrows $100,000 to buy a new warehouse by taking out a mortgage loan from a bank. Nate's has to make annual payments of $12,731. After making the payments for 20 years, Nate's will have paid off the $100,000 principal of the loan. Because the loan's value today is $100,000, the yield to maturity can be calculated as the interest rate that solves the equation:

Value today = Present value of payments

$$\$100{,}000 = \frac{\$12{,}731}{(1+i)} + \frac{\$12{,}731}{(1+i)^2} + \ldots + \frac{\$12{,}731}{(1+i)^{20}}.$$

Using a financial calculator, an online calculator, or a spreadsheet program, we can solve this equation to find that $i = 0.112$, or 11.2%. In general, for a fixed-payment loan with fixed payments, FP, and a maturity of n years, the equation is:

$$\text{Loan value} = \frac{FP}{(1+i)} + \frac{FP}{(1+i)^2} + \ldots + \frac{FP}{(1+i)^n}.$$

To summarize, if i is the yield to maturity on a fixed-payment loan, the amount of the loan today equals the present value of the loan payments discounted at rate i.

Perpetuities Perpetuities are a special case of coupon bonds. A perpetuity pays a fixed coupon, but unlike a regular coupon bond, a perpetuity does not mature. The main example of a perpetuity is the *consol*, which was at one time issued by the British government, although it has not issued new perpetuities in decades. Existing consols with a coupon rate of 2.5% are still traded in financial markets. You may think that computing the yield to maturity on a perpetuity is difficult because the coupons are paid forever. Actually, however, the relationship between the price, coupon, and yield to maturity is simple. If your algebra skills are sharp, see if you can derive this equation from the equation for a coupon bond that pays an infinite number of coupons:[1]

$$P = \frac{C}{i}.$$

So, a perpetuity with a coupon of $25 and a price of $500 has a yield to maturity of $i = \$25/\$500 = 0.05$, or 5%.

---

[1]Here is the derivation: The price of a consol equals the present value of the infinite series of coupon payments the buyer will receive: $P = \frac{C}{1+i} + \frac{C}{(1+i)^2} + \frac{C}{(1+i)^3} + \frac{C}{(1+i)^4} + \ldots$ The rules of algebra tell us that an infinite series of the form $1 + x + x^2 + x^3 + x^4 + \ldots$ is equal to $\frac{1}{1-x}$, provided that x is less than 1. In this case, $\frac{1}{1+i}$ is less than 1, so we have the following expression for the price of a consol: $P = C \times \left[\frac{1}{1 - \left(\frac{1}{1+i}\right)} - 1 \right]$. This expression simplifies to $P = \frac{C}{i}$, as given in the text.

Solved Problem 3.3

Finding the Yield to Maturity for Different Types of Debt Instruments

For each of the following situations, write the equation that you would use to calculate the yield to maturity. You do not have to solve the equations for i; just write the appropriate equation.

a. A simple loan for $500,000 that requires a payment of $700,000 in four years.

b. A discount bond with a price of $9,000, which has a face value of $10,000 and matures in one year.

c. A corporate bond with a face value of $1,000, a price of $975, a coupon rate of 10%, and a maturity of five years.

d. A student loan of $2,500, which requires payments of $315 per year for 25 years. The payments start in two years.

Solving the Problem

Step 1 Review the chapter material. This problem is about calculating yields to maturity for different debt instruments, so you may want to review the section "Bond Prices and Yield to Maturity," which begins on page 62.

Step 2 Write an equation for the yield to maturity on the debt instrument in (a). For a simple loan, the yield to maturity is the interest rate that results in the present value of the loan payment being equal to the amount of the loan. So, the correct equation is:

$$\$500,000 = \frac{\$700,000}{(1 + i)^4}.$$

Step 3 Write an equation for the yield to maturity on the debt instrument in (b). For a discount bond, the yield to maturity is the interest rate that results in the present value of the bond's face value being equal to the bond's price. So, the correct equation is:

$$\$9,000 = \frac{\$10,000}{(1 + i)}, \text{ or, } i = \frac{\$10,000 - \$9,000}{\$9,000}.$$

Step 4 Write an equation for the yield to maturity on the debt instrument in (c). For a coupon bond, such as a long-term corporate bond, the yield to maturity is the interest rate that results in the present value of the payments the buyer receives being equal to the bond's price. Remember that a bond with a coupon rate of 10% pays an annual coupon of $100. So, the correct equation is:

$$\$975 = \frac{\$100}{(1 + i)} + \frac{\$100}{(1 + i)^2} + \frac{\$100}{(1 + i)^3} + \frac{\$100}{(1 + i)^4} + \frac{\$100}{(1 + i)^5} + \frac{\$1,000}{(1 + i)^5}.$$

Step 5 Write an equation for the yield to maturity on the debt instrument in (d). For a fixed-payment loan, the yield to maturity is the interest rate that results in the present value of the loan payments being equal to the amount of the loan.

Note that in this case, there is no payment due at the end of the first year, so the typical first term in the expression is omitted. Therefore, the correct equation is:

$$\$2,500 = \frac{\$315}{(1 + i)^2} + \frac{\$315}{(1 + i)^3} + \ldots + \frac{\$315}{(1 + i)^{26}}.$$

See related problem 3.6 at the end of the chapter.

The Inverse Relationship Between Bond Prices and Bond Yields

3.4

Learning Objective

Understand the inverse relationship between bond prices and bond yields.

Coupon bonds issued by governments and by large corporations typically have maturities of 30 years. During those 30 years, investors are likely to buy and sell the bonds many times in the *secondary market*. Once a bond is sold the first time, the corporation or government issuing the bond is not directly involved in any of the later transactions. For instance, suppose that you pay $1,000 for a bond issued by the Ford Motor Company. Assume that the bond has a face value of $1,000 and a coupon rate of 8%. Whenever the price of a bond is equal to its face value, the bond's yield to maturity will be equal to its coupon rate. Presumably, you purchased the bond because you believed that 8% was a good interest rate to receive on your investment. If at some point you decide to sell your bond, the transaction is between you and the person buying your bond. Ford is not involved except for being informed that it should send future coupon payments to the new owner of the bond and not to you.

What Happens to Bond Prices When Interest Rates Change?

Suppose that one year after you purchased your bond, Ford issues more 30-year bonds, but these new bonds have coupon rates of 10% rather than 8%. Ford, like other corporations, varies the coupon rates on the bonds it sells based on conditions in the bond market. Ideally, corporations would like to borrow money at the lowest interest rate possible. But lenders—in this case, bond buyers—in some circumstances increase the interest rates they require to lend their funds. For instance, if bond buyers believe that future inflation will be higher than they had previously expected, they will require a higher interest rate before buying a bond. And if bond buyers believe that Ford is at a greater risk of defaulting on its bonds, they will also require a higher interest rate.

What effect will Ford's issuing new bonds with higher coupons have on your bond? First, note that once a firm issues a bond, its coupon rate does not change. So, even though Ford is paying buyers of its new bonds $100 per year, you are stuck receiving only $80 per year. If you decide to sell your bond, what price will you receive? Your bond clearly has a drawback to potential buyers—it pays a coupon of only $80, while newly issued Ford bonds pay coupons of $100. So, no investor would be willing to pay $1,000 for your 8% bond when he or she can pay $1,000 and receive a 10% bond from Ford. How much less than $1,000 will other investors be willing to pay you? We can answer the question by remembering the fundamental idea that the price of a financial security is equal to the present value of the payments to be received from owning the security. To calculate the price, we need to know what yield to maturity to use. When you purchased your bond, the yield to maturity was 8%. But conditions in the bond market have changed, and Ford has had to offer a 10% yield to maturity to attract buyers for its new bonds. If you want to sell your bond, it has to compete in the secondary market with the new 10% bonds, so 10% is the correct yield to maturity to use to calculate the new price of your bond.

In calculating the price of your bond (using a financial calculator, an online calculator, or a spreadsheet), keep in mind that the buyer of your bond will receive 29, rather than 30, coupon payments because one year has passed:

$$\$812.61 = \frac{\$80}{(1 + 0.10)} + \frac{\$80}{(1 + 0.10)^2} + \frac{\$80}{(1 + 0.10)^3} + \ldots + \frac{\$80}{(1 + 0.10)^{29}} + \frac{\$1,000}{(1 + 0.10)^{29}}.$$

It may seem odd that your bond, which has a face value of $1,000 if held to maturity, would have a market price of only $812.61. Keep in mind, though, that you or a new owner of the bond will not receive the $1,000 face value for 29 years. The present value of that $1,000 payment discounted at a 10% interest rate is only $63.04.

Capital gain An increase in the market price of an asset.

If the price of an asset increases, it is called a **capital gain**. If the price of the asset declines, it is called a **capital loss**. In our example, you will have suffered a capital loss of $1,000 − $812.61 = $187.39.

Capital loss A decrease in the market price of an asset.

Making the Connection

Banks Take a Bath on Mortgage-Backed Bonds

Banks play a key role in the financial system. While large firms are able to sell stocks and bonds to investors, small and midsize firms rely on bank loans for the funds they need to operate and expand. Households also rely heavily on banks for the credit they need to buy houses, cars, furniture, and other large purchases. Banks cut back on lending during the financial crisis, and this deepened the recession of 2007–2009.

Why did banks reduce lending during those years? The inverse relationship between interest rates and bond prices can help us answer this question. First, remember that the basis of commercial banking is to take in deposits from households and firms and invest the funds. Granting loans and buying bonds are the most important investments that banks make. During the housing boom of the early and mid-2000s, banks granted many residential mortgages to borrowers who had flawed credit histories and who in previous years would not have qualified for loans. Banks also granted many residential mortgages to borrowers who made small or no down payments. As we noted in Chapter 1, many of these mortgages were securitized, meaning they were pooled and turned into debt instruments known as *mortgage-backed securities*, and then sold to investors. Many mortgage-backed securities are similar to long-term bonds in that they pay regular interest based on the payments borrowers make on the underlying mortgages.

During the height of the housing boom, some banks invested heavily in mortgage-backed securities because their yields were higher than the yields on other investments with similar levels of default risk—or so the banks thought. When housing prices started to decline during 2006, borrowers began to default on their mortgages. As borrowers stopped paying on their mortgages, owners of mortgage-backed securities received lower payments than they expected. In the secondary market for mortgage-backed securities, buyers—when they could be found at all—were willing to buy the securities only if the securities had much higher yields to compensate for the higher levels of default risk. Higher yields on these securities meant lower prices. By 2008, the prices of many mortgage-backed securities had declined by 50% or more.

By early 2009, U.S. commercial banks had suffered losses on their investments of about $1 trillion. Beginning in 2010, these losses were somewhat reduced as the housing market stabilized and the prices of some mortgage-backed securities rose. Nevertheless, these heavy losses forced some banks to close. Other banks were saved by injections of funds from the federal government under the Troubled Asset Relief Program (TARP). Surviving banks became much more cautious in making new loans. Banks had relearned the lesson that soaring interest rates can have a devastating effect on investors who hold existing debt instruments.

See related problem 4.9 at the end of the chapter.

If you own a long-term coupon bond, it is clearly not good news when interest rates rise. But what if interest rates fall? Suppose that one year after you bought a Ford bond with a coupon rate of 8%, Ford begins to issue new bonds with coupon rates of 6%. Ford may be able to sell bonds with a lower coupon rate because investors expect that inflation in the future will be lower than they had previously expected or because they believe that Ford is less likely to default on the bonds. Your bond is now attractive to investors because it has a higher coupon rate than newly issued bonds. If you decide to sell your bond, it will be competing in the secondary market with the new 6% bonds, so 6% is the correct yield to maturity to use in calculating the new market price of your bond:

$$\$1{,}271.81 = \frac{\$80}{(1 + 0.06)} + \frac{\$80}{(1 + .06)^2} + \frac{\$80}{(1 + 0.06)^3} + \cdots + \frac{\$80}{(1 + 0.06)^{29}} + \frac{\$1{,}000}{(1 + 0.06)^{29}}.$$

In this case, you will have a capital gain of $1,271.81 − $1,000 = $271.81.

Bond Prices and Yields to Maturity Move in Opposite Directions

These examples have demonstrated two very important points:

1. If interest rates on newly issued bonds rise, the prices of existing bonds will fall.
2. If interest rates on newly issued bonds fall, the prices of existing bonds will rise.

In other words, *yields to maturity and bond prices move in opposite directions*. This relationship must hold because in the bond price equation, the yield to maturity is in the denominator of each term. If the yield to maturity increases, the present values of the coupon payments and the face value payment must decline, causing the price of the bond to decline. The reverse is true when the yield to maturity decreases. The economic reasoning behind the inverse relationship between bond prices and yields to maturity is that if interest rates rise, existing bonds issued when interest rates were lower become less desirable to investors, and their prices fall. If interest rates fall, existing bonds become more desirable, and their prices rise.

Finally, notice that the inverse relationship between yields to maturity and bond prices should also hold for other debt instruments. The present value and, therefore, the price of any debt instrument should decline when market interest rates rise, and rise when market interest rates decline.

Secondary Markets, Arbitrage, and the Law of One Price

Let's consider the process by which bond prices and yields adjust to changes in market conditions. Buying and selling in the markets for bonds, stocks, and other financial assets is similar to buying and selling in markets for goods and services, with a couple of key differences. Today, most trading of financial services is done electronically, with buyers and sellers linked together via computer systems, so very little trading occurs face-to-face. And most trading takes place very quickly, with millions of dollars of stocks and bonds being traded every second that the markets are open. Large volumes of bonds and stocks are traded over very brief periods because many participants in financial markets are *traders* rather than investors.

An investor in a financial market typically plans to earn a return by receiving payments on the securities he or she buys. For example, an investor in Microsoft buys the stock to receive dividend payments from Microsoft and to profit from an increase in the price of the stock over time. Traders, however, often buy and sell securities hoping to make profits by taking advantage of small differences in the prices of similar securities.

For example, recall what happens to prices of existing 8% coupon bonds when market interest rates fall to 6%: The price of an existing 8% bond increases from $1,000 to $1,271.81. Once this price increase occurs, the yields to maturity on those bonds and on newly issued 6% coupon bonds are the same—6%—so the bonds are equally desirable to investors. If market interest rates remain the same, no further price changes should occur. But, what about during the period *before* the prices of the 8% coupon bonds have risen all the way to $1,271.81? Clearly, a trader who buys the 8% bonds during that period can make a profit by, say, buying the bonds at $1,260 and reselling them when their prices have risen all the way to $1,271.81. The process of buying and reselling securities to profit from price changes over a brief period of time is called **financial arbitrage**. The profits made from financial arbitrage are called *arbitrage profits*. In competing to buy securities where earning arbitrage profits is possible, traders force prices up to the level where arbitrage profits can no longer be earned. Prices of securities adjust very rapidly—often within seconds—to eliminate arbitrage profits because of the very large number of traders participating in financial markets and the speed of electronic trading. Economists conclude that the prices of financial securities at any given moment allow little or no opportunity for arbitrage profits. In other words, *the prices of securities should adjust so that investors receive the same yields on comparable securities*. In our example, the prices of comparable coupon bonds adjust so that bonds with 8% coupon rates have the same yield as bonds with 6% coupon rates.

This description of how prices of financial securities adjust is an example of a general economic principle called the *law of one price*, which states that identical products

Financial arbitrage The process of buying and selling securities to profit from price changes over a brief period of time.

should sell for the same price everywhere. The possibility of arbitrage profits explains the law of one price. For instance, if apples sell for $1.00 per pound in Minnesota and $1.50 per pound in Wisconsin, you could make an arbitrage profit by buying apples in Minnesota and reselling them in Wisconsin. As you and others took advantage of this opportunity, the price of apples in Minnesota would rise, and the price of apples in Wisconsin would fall. Leaving aside transportation costs, arbitrage should result in the price of apples being the same in the two states.

As you read this book, keep in mind that because of financial arbitrage, comparable securities should have the same yield, except during very brief periods of time.

Making the Connection   In Your Interest

How to Follow the Bond Market: Reading the Bond Tables

Whether you want to invest in bonds or just want to follow developments in the bond market, where can you go to get information? You can find daily updates on the prices and yields for Treasury bills, notes, and bonds on the *Wall Street Journal* Web site or on Yahoo! Finance (finance.yahoo.com). The corporate bond listings given here are from the Web site of the Financial Industry Regulatory Authority (FINRA). Data on corporate bonds can also be found on Yahoo! Finance.

Treasury Bonds and Notes

The table below contains data on five U.S. Treasury bonds and notes from among the many bonds and notes that were being traded on secondary markets on September 14, 2012. Treasury notes have maturities of 2 years to 10 years from their date of issue; Treasury bonds typically have a maturity of 30 years from their date of issue.

The first two columns tell you the maturity date and the coupon rate. Bond A, for example, has a maturity date of August 2015, and a coupon rate of 4.250%, so it pays $42.50 each year on its $1,000 face value.

MATURITY MONTH/YEAR		COUPON	BID	ASKED	CHG	ASK YLD
Aug	2015	4.250	111.2500	111.2813	–0.1016	0.350
Mar	2016	2.375	106.7344	106.7656	–0.1875	0.444
Aug	2016	3.000	109.6406	109.7031	–0.2969	0.517
Feb	2025	7.625	159.8359	159.9141	–1.9609	2.112
Aug	2029	6.125	149.0703	149.1484	–2.4766	2.533

Bond A — first row.

The next three columns refer to the bond's price. All prices are reported per $100 of face value. For Bond A, the first price listed, 111.250, means a price of $1,112.50 for this $1,000 face value bond. The *bid* price is the price you will receive from a government securities dealer if you sell the bond. The *asked* price is the price you must pay the dealer if you buy the bond. The difference between the asked price and the bid price (known as the *bid–asked spread*) is the profit margin for dealers. Bid–asked spreads are low in the government securities markets, indicating low transactions costs and a liquid and competitive market. The "CHG" column tells you by how much the bid price increased or decreased from the preceding trading day. For Bond A, from the previous day, the bid price fell by $0.1016 per $100 of face value, or $1.106 for this $1,000 face value bond.

The final column contains the yield to maturity, calculated using the asked price by the method we discussed for coupon bonds. The *Wall Street Journal* reports the yield using the asked price because readers are interested in the yield from the perspective of the investor. So, you can construct three interest rates from the information contained in the table: the yield to maturity just described, the coupon rate, and the current yield (equal to the coupon divided by the price: $42.50/$1,112.81, or 3.82% for Bond A). Note that the current yield of Bond A is well above the yield to maturity of 0.350%. This illustrates that the current yield is not a good substitute for the yield to maturity for instruments with a short time to maturity because it ignores the effect of expected capital gains or losses.

Treasury Bills

The table below shows information about U.S. Treasury bill yields. Recall that Treasury bills are discount bonds, and unlike Treasury bonds and notes, they do not pay coupons. Accordingly, they are identified only by their maturity date (first column). In the Treasury bill market, following a very old tradition, yields are quoted as yields on a discount basis (or discount yields) rather than as yields to maturity.[2] The Bid and Asked columns of Treasury notes and bonds quote prices, while the Bid and Asked columns for Treasury bills quote yields. The bid yield is the discount yield for investors who want to sell the bill to dealers. The asked yield is the discount yield for investors who want to buy the bill from dealers. The dealers' profit margin is the difference between the asked yield and the bid yield. In comparing investments in Treasury bills with investments in other bonds, investors find it useful to know the yield to maturity. So, the last column shows the yield to maturity (based on the asked price). Because short-term interest rates were very low in 2012, the asked yield on the first bill listed is only 0.081%.

MATURITY	BID	ASKED	CHG	ASK YLD
11/23/2012	0.085	0.080	0.0000	0.081
12/27/2012	0.110	0.100	0.0050	0.101
02/28/2013	0.120	0.115	0.0000	0.117
05/30/2013	0.140	0.135	0.0050	0.137

Note that in both previous tables, the yield to maturity rises the further away the maturity date is.

---

[2]The yield on a discount basis for a bond with face value FV and a purchase price P is
$[(FV - P)/FV] \times (360 / \text{Number of days to maturity})$.

New York Stock Exchange Corporation Bonds

The table below gives quotations for some of the corporate bonds that are most actively traded on the New York Stock Exchange. The first column tells you the name of the corporation issuing the bond—in the case of Bond B, the Goldman Sachs investment bank. The next column gives you the bond's symbol, GS.AEH. The third column gives you the coupon rate, 5.750%. The fourth column gives you the maturity, January 2022. The next column gives you the bond's rating from the three major bond rating agencies. The rating provides investors with information on the likelihood that the firm will default on the bond, with AAA being the highest rating, given to bonds with very little chance of default. The next three columns present the highest price the bond traded for that day, the lowest price, and the last price. So, the last time this Goldman Sachs bond was traded that day, it sold for a price of $1,152.60. The Change column shows the change in the price from the end of trading the previous day. The last column gives the yield to maturity (3.800%).

Issuer Name	Symbol	COUPON	MATURITY	Moody's/S&P /Fitch	High	Low	Last	Change	Yield%
Bank Amer Corp	BAC3832855	3.875%	Mar 2017	Baa2/A–/A	107.5920	107.1200	107.3160	0.2740	2.163
Goldman Sachs Group Inc	GS.AEH	5.750%	Jan 2022	A3/A–/A	116.4130	113.3918	115.2160	0.1830	3.800
Citigroup	C3715831	4.450%	Jan 2017	Baa2/A–/A	110.5531	108.5000	109.6940	1.2980	2.085
Wal-Mart Stores Inc	WMT.AB	5.625%	Apr 2041	Aa2/AA/AA	128.5330	127.1780	128.1060	–1.3100	3.971

Bond B —

See related problem 4.10 at the end of the chapter.

Interest Rates and Rates of Return

When you make an investment, you are most concerned with what you earn during a given period of time, often called a *holding period*. If you buy a coupon bond and hold it for one year, the **return** on your investment in the bond for that year consists of (1) the coupon payment received and (2) the change in the price of the bond, which will result in a capital gain or loss. Usually, you are most interested in measuring your return as a percentage of your investment, which is your **rate of return,** R.

For example, consider again your purchase for $1,000 of a Ford bond with a face value of $1,000 and a coupon rate of 8%. If at the end of the year following your purchase, the price of the bond increases to $1,271.81, then during that year, you will have received a coupon payment of $80 and had a capital gain of $271.81. So, your rate of return for the year will have been:

$$R = \frac{\text{Coupon} + \text{Capital gain}}{\text{Purchase price}} = \frac{\$80 + \$271.81}{\$1,000} = 0.352, \text{ or } 35.2\%.$$

3.5

Learning Objective

Explain the difference between interest rates and rates of return.

Return The total earnings from a security; for a bond during a holding period of one year, the coupon payment plus the change in the price of the bond.

Rate of return, R The return on a security as a percentage of the initial price; for a bond during a holding period of one year, the coupon payment plus the change in the price of a bond divided by the initial price.

If the price of your bond had declined to $812.61, then you would have received the $80 coupon payment but suffered a capital loss of $187.39. So, your rate of return for the year would have been negative:

$$R = \frac{\$80 - \$187.39}{\$1,000} = -0.107, \text{ or } -10.7\%.$$

A General Equation for the Rate of Return on a Bond

We can extend these examples to write a general equation for the rate of return on a coupon bond during a holding period of one year. First, recall that the *current yield* on a coupon bond is the coupon divided by the current price of the bond. The *rate of capital gain or loss* on a bond is the dollar amount of the capital gain or loss divided by the initial price. So, we have the following equation for the rate of return for a holding period of one year:

$$\text{Rate of return } = \text{ Current yield } + \text{ rate of capital gain.}$$

$$R = \frac{\text{Coupon}}{\text{Initial price}} + \frac{\text{Change in price}}{\text{Initial price}}.$$

Here are three important points about rates of return:

1. In calculating the rate of return, we will use the price at the beginning of the year to calculate the current yield.
2. You incur a capital gain or loss on a bond even if you do not sell the bond at the end of the year. If you sell the bond, you have a *realized capital gain or loss*. If you do not sell the bond, your gain or loss is *unrealized*. In either case, the price of your bond has increased or decreased and needs to be included when calculating the rate of return on your investment.
3. If you buy a coupon bond, neither the current yield nor the yield to maturity may be a good indicator of the rate of return you will receive as a result of holding the bond during a particular time period because they do not take into account your potential capital gain or capital loss.

Interest-Rate Risk and Maturity

Interest-rate risk The risk that the price of a financial asset will fluctuate in response to changes in market interest rates.

We have seen that holders of existing bonds suffer a capital loss when market interest rates rise. **Interest-rate risk** refers to the risk that the price of a financial asset will fluctuate in response to changes in market interest rates. But are all bonds equally subject to interest-rate risk? We might expect that bonds with fewer years to maturity will be less affected by a change in market interest rates than will bonds with more years to maturity. The economic reasoning is that the more years until a bond matures, the more years the buyer of the bond will potentially be receiving a below-market coupon rate, and, therefore, the lower the price a buyer would be willing to pay.

Table 3.2 shows that the arithmetic of bond prices bears out this reasoning. Assume that at the beginning of the year, you pay $1,000 for a $1,000 face value bond with a coupon rate of 6%. Assume that at the end of the year, the yield to maturity on similar bonds has risen to 10%. The table shows your rate of return, assuming that the

Table 3.2 The Effect of Maturity on Interest-Rate Risk During the First Year of Owning a Bond

Years to maturity	Current yield	Initial price	Price at the end of the year	Rate of capital gain or loss	Rate of return during the year
1	6%	$1,000	$1,000.00	0%	6.0%
2	6	1,000	963.64	−3.6	2.4
10	6	1,000	769.64	−23.0	−17.0
20	6	1,000	665.40	−33.5	−27.5
30	6	1,000	625.22	−37.5	−31.5
50	6	1,000	603.75	−39.6	−33.6

bond you purchased has different maturities. For instance, the top row shows that if you purchased a one-year bond, your rate of return is equal to the current yield of 6%. You held the one-year bond for one year and received the $1,000 face value at maturity, so the change in market interest rates did not affect you. The second row shows that if your bond initially has a maturity of two years, you will take a capital loss, so your rate of return is less than the current yield. Your two-year bond now has only one year until maturity, so its price is:

$$\$963.64 = \frac{\$60}{(1 + 0.10)} + \frac{\$1,000}{(1 + 0.10)}.$$

The remaining rows show that the longer the maturity of your bond, the lower (more negative) your return. With a maturity of 50 years, your rate of return for the first year of owning your bond will be −33.6.

How Much Interest-Rate Risk Do Investors in Treasury Bonds Face?

We saw at the beginning of the chapter that in late 2012, 30-year U.S. Treasury bonds had interest rates of 3%. Although these bonds had no default risk, as long-term bonds, they had significant interest-rate risk. For example, suppose that at the beginning of 2013, you purchased for $1,000 a 30-year Treasury bond with a face value of $1,000 and a coupon rate of 3%. If at the end of the year, the yield to maturity on Treasury bonds had risen to a more normal rate of 5%, the price of your bond would decline to $697.18. You would suffer a capital loss of −30.3% and a rate of return of −24.3%. If the yield to maturity rose to 6%, your rate of return would be −34.8%. Some safe investment!

Nominal Interest Rates Versus Real Interest Rates

To this point in the chapter, we have discussed only **nominal interest rates**. That is, the interest rates were not adjusted for changes in purchasing power caused by changes in the price level. In fact, inflation can reduce the purchasing power of returns on any investment. For example, suppose that you buy a $1,000 bond that pays you $50 in interest each year for 20 years. If the purchasing power of the dollars that you receive declines over time, you are, in effect, losing part of your interest income

Nominal interest rate
An interest rate that is not adjusted for changes in purchasing power.

3.6

Learning Objective
Explain the difference between nominal interest rates and real interest rates.

to inflation. In addition, inflation causes the purchasing power of the principal to decline. For example, if inflation is 5% per year, the purchasing power of the $1,000 principal falls by $50 each year.

Real interest rate An interest rate that is adjusted for changes in purchasing power.

Lenders and borrowers know that inflation reduces the purchasing power of interest income, so they base their investment decisions on interest rates adjusted for changes in purchasing power. Such adjusted interest rates are called **real interest rates**. Because lenders and borrowers don't know what the *actual* real interest rate will be during the period of a loan, they must make saving or investing decisions on the basis of what they *expect* the real interest rate to be. So, to estimate the expected real interest rate, savers and borrowers must decide what they expect the inflation rate to be. The expected real interest rate, r, equals the nominal interest rate, i, minus the expected rate of inflation, π^e, or:[3]

$$r = i - \pi^e.$$

Note that this equation also means that the nominal interest rate equals the expected real interest rate plus the expected inflation rate: $i = r + \pi^e$.

For example, suppose you take out a car loan from your local bank. You are willing to pay, and the bank is willing to accept, a real interest rate of 3%. Both you and the bank expect that the inflation rate will be 2%. Therefore, you and the bank agree on a nominal interest rate of 5% on the loan. What happens if the inflation rate turns out to be 4%, which is higher than you and the bank had expected? In that case, the *real interest rate* that you end up paying (and the bank ends up receiving) equals 5% − 4% = 1%, which is less than the expected real interest rate of 3%. Because the inflation rate turns out to be higher than you and the bank expected, you gain by paying a lower real interest rate, and the bank loses by receiving a lower real interest rate.

We can generalize by noting that the real interest rate equals the nominal interest rate minus the inflation rate. If the inflation rate is *greater* than the expected inflation rate, the real interest rate will be less than the expected real interest rate; in this case, borrowers will gain and lenders will lose. If the inflation rate is *less* than the expected inflation rate, the real interest rate will be greater than the expected real interest rate; in this case, borrowers will lose and lenders will gain. Table 3.3 summarizes the important relationship among nominal interest rates, expected real interest rates, and real interest rates.

For the economy as a whole, economists often measure the nominal interest rate as the interest rate on U.S. Treasury bills that mature in three months. In Figure 3.1, we show the nominal interest rate, the real interest rate, and the expected real interest rate for the period from the first quarter of 1982 through the first quarter of 2012. To calculate the real interest rate, we used the inflation rate as measured by percentage changes in the consumer price index. To calculate the expected real interest rate, we used the expected percentage change in the consumer price index as reported in a survey of professional forecasters conducted by the Federal Reserve Bank of Philadelphia.

---

[3]To fully account for the effect of changes in purchasing power on the nominal interest rate, we should use the equation $\frac{1 + i}{1 + \pi^e} = 1 + r$. Rearranging terms gives us $1 + i = 1 + r + \pi^e + r\pi^e$. Or, $r = i - \pi^e - r\pi^e$. This equation is the same as the one in the text except for the term $r\pi^e$. The value of this term is usually quite small. For example, if the real interest rate is 2% and the expected inflation rate is 3%, then $r\pi^e = 0.02 \times 0.03 = 0.0006$. So, as long as the inflation rate is relatively low, the equation for the real interest rate given in the text is a close approximation.

Table 3.3 The Relationship Among the Nominal Interest Rate, the Expected Real Interest Rate, and the Real Interest Rate

If the inflation rate is ...	the real interest rate will be ...	and borrowers will ...	and lenders will ...
greater than the expected inflation rate ...	less than the expected real interest rate ...	gain	lose.
less than the expected inflation rate ...	greater than the expected real interest rate ...	lose	gain.

Figure 3.1 shows that the nominal and real interest rates tend to rise and fall together. The figure also shows that the real interest rates and expected real interest rates follow each other closely, which is an indication that during most of this period, expectations of the inflation rate were fairly accurate. Note that in some periods, particularly after the beginning of the financial crisis in 2007, the real interest rate was negative. Why would investors buy Treasury bills if they expected to receive a negative real interest rate on their investments? The best explanation is that during the crisis, investors were afraid of the high default risk on many other investments. So, they were willing to receive a negative real interest rate on U.S. Treasury bills rather than risk losing money by investing in corporate bonds or other riskier securities. For years following the financial crisis, short-term interest rates remained very low—well below the inflation rate. Lacking good alternatives, many investors continued to purchase Treasury bills, even though they expected to receive a negative real interest rate. Finally, note that it is possible for the nominal interest rate to be lower than the real interest rate. For this outcome to occur, the inflation rate has to be negative, meaning that the price level is decreasing rather than increasing. A sustained decline in the price level is called **deflation**. The United States experienced a period of deflation during the first 10 months of 2009.

Deflation A sustained decline in the price level.

MyEconLab Real-time data

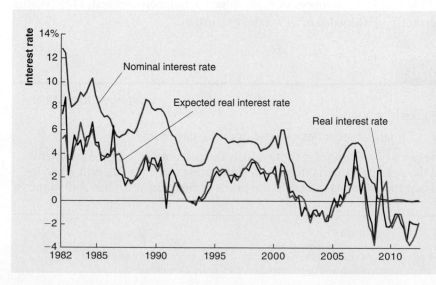

Figure 3.1

Nominal and Real Interest Rates, 1982–2012

In this figure, the nominal interest rate is the interest rate on three-month U.S. Treasury bills. The real interest rate is the nominal interest rate minus the inflation rate, as measured by changes in the consumer price index. The expected real interest rate is the nominal interest rate minus the expected rate of inflation as measured by a survey of professional forecasters. When the U.S. economy experienced deflation during 2009, the real interest rate was greater than the nominal interest rate.

Sources: Federal Reserve Bank of St. Louis; and Federal Reserve Bank of Philadelphia.

Figure 3.2

TIPS as a Percentage of All Treasury Securities

TIPS (Treasury Inflation-Protection Securities) were an increasing percentage of all U.S. Treasury securities until 2008. Value for 2012 is through June.

Source: U.S. Treasury, *Treasury Bulletin*, various issues.

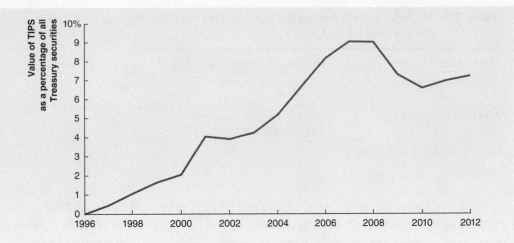

In January 1997, the U.S. Treasury started issuing *indexed bonds* to address investors' concerns about the effects of inflation on real interest rates. With these bonds, called TIPS (Treasury Inflation-Protection Securities), the Treasury increases the principal as the price level, as measured by the consumer price index, increases. The interest rate on TIPS remains fixed, but because it is applied to a principal amount that increases with inflation, the interest rate also increases with inflation. For example, suppose that when issued, a 10-year TIPS has a principal of $1,000 and an interest rate of 3%. If the inflation rate during the year is 2%, then the principal increases to $1,020. The 3% interest rate is applied to this larger principal amount, so an investor would actually receive $0.03 \times 1,020 = \$30.60$ in interest. Therefore, the actual interest rate the investor would have received on his or her original investment would be $30.60/$1,000 = 3.06\%$.[4] If the price level falls with deflation, the principal of a TIPS will decrease.

Figure 3.2 shows the value of TIPS as a percentage of the value of all U.S. Treasury securities. The share of TIPS in all Treasury securities increased steadily until 2008. During the following years, as investors' expectations of inflation declined, TIPS became a smaller percentage of the value of all Treasury securities.

Answering the Key Question

Continued from page 49

At the beginning of this chapter, we asked:

"Why do interest rates and the prices of financial securities move in opposite directions?"

We have seen in this chapter that the price of a financial security equals the present value of the payments an investor will receive from owning the security. When interest rates rise, present values fall, and when interest rates fall, present values rise. Therefore, interest rates and the prices of financial securities should move in opposite directions.

---

[4]Note that this calculation is somewhat simplified because the Treasury actually adjusts the TIPS principal for inflation each month and pays interest on TIPS every six months.

Key Terms and Problems

Key Terms

Capital gain, p. 68

Capital loss, p. 68

Compounding, p. 52

Coupon bond, p. 59

Credit market instruments, p. 58

Debt instruments, p. 58

Deflation, p. 77

Discount bond, p. 59

Discounting, p. 54

Equity, p. 58

Financial arbitrage, p. 70

Fixed-income assets, p. 58

Fixed-payment loan, p. 60

Future value, p. 52

Interest-rate risk, p. 74

Nominal interest rate, p. 75

Present value, p. 54

Rate of return, R, p. 73

Real interest rate, p. 76

Return, p. 73

Simple loan, p. 58

Time value of money, p. 54

Yield to maturity, p. 63

3.1 ## The Interest Rate, Present Value, and Future Value
Explain how the interest rate links present value with future value.

Review Questions

1.1 What are the main reasons that lenders charge interest on loans?

1.2 If you deposit $1,000 in a bank CD that pays interest of 3% per year, how much will you have after two years?

1.3 What is the present value of $1,200 to be received in one year if the interest rate is 10%?

1.4 How is the price of a financial asset related to the payments an investor receives from owning it?

Problems and Applications

1.5 Norman Jones, an economic historian at the University of Utah, has described the view of the ancient Greek philosopher Aristotle on interest:

> Aristotle defined money as a good that was consumed by use. Unlike houses and fields, which are not destroyed by use, money must be spent to be used. Therefore, as we cannot rent food, so we cannot rent money. Moreover, money does not reproduce. A house or a flock can produce new value by use, so it is not unreasonable to ask for a return on their use. Money, being barren, should not, therefore, be expected to produce excess value. Thus, interest is unnatural.

What did Aristotle mean in arguing that money is "barren"? Why would money being barren mean that lenders should not charge interest on loans? Do you agree with Aristotle's reasoning? Briefly explain.

Source: Norman Jones, "Usury," EH.Net Encyclopedia, edited by Robert Whaples, February 5, 2010, http://eh.net/encyclopedia/article/jones.usury.

1.6 **[Related to** Solved Problem 3.1A **on page 53]** Suppose that you are considering investing $1,000 in bank CDs.

a. First, you consider one of the following CDs:

- CD 1, which will pay an interest rate of 5% per year for three years
- CD 2, which will pay an interest rate of 8% the first year, 5% the second year, and 3% the third year

Which CD should you choose?

b. Would your answer to part (a) change if the second CD pays an interest rate of 1% the first two years and 10% in the third year? Briefly explain.

c. Now, suppose that in addition to the two CDs described in part (a), there is a third CD that pays an interest rate of 3% the first two years and an interest rate of 7% the third year.

How does the future value of this investment compare to the other two? Which is the best investment?

1.7 [Related to Solved Problem 3.1B **on page 56**] State and local governments typically offer their employees defined benefit pension plans. Under these plans, employees are promised a fixed monthly payment after they retire. A government's pension liability is the amount that it has committed to paying future retirees. An article in the *Economist* magazine notes that as interest rates fall, "the present value of future liabilities rises."

  a. What does the author mean by the "present value of future liabilities"?

  b. Why would a decline in interest rates increase the present value of a government's future pension liabilities?

Source: "Keeping It Real," *Economist*, June 30, 2012.

1.8 [Related to Solved Problem 3.1B **on page 56**] At the end of 2011, Jose Reyes signed a six-year contract to play shortstop for the Miami Marlins baseball team. (Reyes was later traded by the Marlins to the Toronto Blue Jays.) The contract was "backloaded," which means that Reyes would be paid much more in the later years of the contract than in the earlier years.

For example, the Marlins agreed to pay Reyes a salary of $10 million in 2012 but a salary of $22 million in 2015. In discussing why the Marlins preferred a backloaded contract, baseball writer Michael Jong argued that:

> Money in the future is obviously less valuable than money in the present. . . . If inflation goes up three percent a year in the next few seasons, that 2015 value of $22 million would really equate to $20 million . . . in today's money.

  a. Why is money in the future less valuable than money in the present? Is inflation the only reason?

  b. Assume for simplicity that Reyes receives his $22 million salary in a lump sum at the end of 2015. Assuming an interest rate of 3%, is the author correct that the present value of Reyes's salary was about $20 million at the beginning of 2012? Is 3% a good interest rate to use in calculating the present value of Reyes's salary if the inflation rate is expected to be 3%? What would be the present value of his 2015 salary at the beginning of 2012 using an interest rate of 10%?

Source: Michael Jong, "Jose Reyes Contract Heavily Backloaded," www.fishstripes.com, December 7, 2012.

3.2 **Debt Instruments and Their Prices**
Distinguish among different debt instruments and understand how their prices are determined.

Review Questions

2.1 What is the difference between a debt instrument and an equity?

2.2 What are the four basic categories of debt instruments? Which categories of debt instruments pay interest before the instrument matures? Which category of debt instrument pays back principal before the instrument matures?

Problems and Applications

2.3 Explain in which category of debt instrument the following belong:

  a. Car loan

  b. U.S. Treasury bond

  c. Three-month U.S. Treasury bill

  d. Mortgage loan

2.4 Why do consumers usually prefer fixed-payment loans to simple loans when buying cars and houses?

2.5 Suppose that Ford issues a coupon bond at a price of $1,000. Draw a timeline for the bond, assuming that it has the following characteristics:

- Coupon rate of 5%
- Par value of $1,000
- Maturity of 20 years

2.6 [Related to the Making the Connection **on page 61**] A student looking at the timeline for a student loan on page 60 of the text makes the following observation:

> The text states that the interest rate on the loan is 9%, but this calculation is obviously wrong. Each monthly payment is $127, so the student will be paying back $127 × 12 = $1,524 per year. Therefore, because the principal of the loan is $10,000, the interest rate must be $1,524/$10,000 = 0.1524, or 15.24%.

Briefly explain whether you agree with the student's reasoning.

3.3   Bond Prices and Yield to Maturity
Explain the relationship between the yield to maturity on a bond and its price.

Review Questions

3.1 Why is yield to maturity a better measure of the interest rate on a bond than is the coupon rate?

3.2 Write an expression that shows the relationship among:

  a. the price of a coupon bond, the coupon payments, the face value, and the yield to maturity.

  b. the amount borrowed on a simple loan, the required loan payment, and the yield to maturity.

  c. the price of a discount bond, the bond's face value, and the yield to maturity.

  d. the amount borrowed on a fixed-payment loan, the payments on the loan, and the yield to maturity.

Problems and Applications

3.3 Assume that the interest rate is 10%. Briefly explain whether you would prefer to receive (a) $75 one year from now, (b) $85 two years from now, or (c) $90 three years from now. Would your answer change if the interest rate is 20%?

3.4 Suppose that you are considering subscribing to *Economist Analyst Today* magazine. The magazine is advertising a one-year subscription for $60 or a two-year subscription for $115. You plan to keep getting the magazine for at least two years. The advertisement says that a two-year subscription saves you $5 compared to buying two successive one-year subscriptions. If the interest rate is 10%, should you subscribe for one year or for two years? (Assume that one year from now, a one-year subscription will still cost $60.)

3.5 Consider the case of a two-year discount bond—that is, a bond that pays no coupon and pays its face value after two years rather than one year. Suppose the face value of the bond is $1,000, and the price is $870. What is the bond's yield to maturity? (In this case, provide a numerical answer rather than just writing the appropriate equation.)

3.6 [Related to Solved Problem 3.3 **on page 66**] For each of the following situations, write the equation needed to calculate the yield to maturity. You do not have to solve the equations for i; just write the appropriate equations.

MyEconLab   Visit **www.myeconlab.com** to complete these exercises online and get instant feedback. Exercises that update with real-time data are marked with ⟨ᴡ⟩.

a. A simple loan for $350,000 that requires a payment of $475,000 in five years.

b. A discount bond with a price of $720 that has a face value of $1,000 and matures in five years.

c. A corporate bond with a face value of $1,000, a price of $950, a coupon rate of 8%, and a maturity of six years.

d. A student loan of $4,000 that requires payments of $275 per year for 20 years. The payments start in three years.

3.7 Consider a $1,000 face value bond that sells for an initial price of $450. It will pay no coupons for the first 10 years and will then pay a 6.25% coupon each year for the remaining 20 years. Write an equation that shows the relationship between the price of the bond, the coupon (in dollars), and the yield to maturity. You don't have to show every term in the expression but be sure to show enough terms to demonstrate that you understand the relationship.

3.8 Suppose that Ed Scahill owns a farm in a small town. In exchange for allowing a road to pass through his farmland, the town has agreed to pay Ed and future owners of the land $135 per year in perpetuity. Now, however, the town has offered, and he has accepted, a one-time payment of $1,125 in exchange for his giving up the right to receive the annual $135 payment. What implicit interest rate have Ed and the township used in arriving at this settlement?

3.9 Many retired people buy annuities. With an annuity, a saver pays an insurance company, such as Berkshire Hathaway Insurance Company or Northwestern Mutual Insurance Company, a lump-sum amount in return for the company's promise to pay a certain amount per year until the buyer dies. With an ordinary annuity, when the buyer dies, there is no final payment to his or her heirs. Suppose that at age 65, David Alexander pays $100,000 for an annuity that promises to pay him $10,000 per year for the remaining years of his life.

a. If David dies 20 years after buying the annuity, write an equation that would allow you to calculate the interest rate that David received on his annuity.

b. If David dies 40 years after buying the annuity, will the interest rate be higher or lower than if he dies after 20 years? Briefly explain.

3.4 **The Inverse Relationship Between Bond Prices and Bond Yields**
Understand the inverse relationship between bond prices and bond yields.

Review Questions

4.1 What does it mean to describe a bond as being bought and sold in a "secondary market"?

4.2 If you own a bond and market interest rates increase, will you experience a capital gain or a capital loss?

4.3 Briefly explain why yields to maturity and bond prices move in opposite directions.

4.4 What is the difference between an investor and a trader? What is financial arbitrage?

Problems and Applications

4.5 [Related to the Chapter Opener on page 49]
A student asks:

> If a coupon bond has a face value of $1,000, I don't understand why anyone who owns the bond would sell it for less than $1,000. After all, if the owner holds the bond to maturity, the owner knows he or she will receive $1,000, so why sell for less?

Answer the student's question.

4.6 Briefly explain whether you agree with the following statement:

> If interest rates rise, bonds become more attractive to investors, so bond prices will rise. Therefore, when interest rates rise, bond prices will also rise.

4.7 Consider the following information from September 15, 2012, for a coupon bond with a face value of $1,000 and a maturity date of September 15, 2014:

Coupon rate: 5.0%

Price: $955.11

Yield to maturity: 7.5%

a. What was the bond's current yield?

b. Why is the bond's yield to maturity greater than its coupon rate?

4.8 Ford Motor Company has issued bonds with a maturity date of November 1, 2046, that have a coupon rate of 7.40%, and it has issued coupon bonds with a maturity of February 15, 2047, that have a coupon rate of 9.80%. Why would Ford issue bonds with coupons of $74 and then a little more than a year later issue bonds with coupons of $98? Why didn't the company continue to issue bonds with the lower coupon?

4.9 [Related to the Making the Connection on page 68] An article in the *New York Times* discussing mortgage-backed bonds observed: "When demand for the bonds rises, which translates into lower interest rates on them, banks can offer homeowners lower interest rates on their underlying mortgages." Shouldn't increased demand for mortgage-backed bonds increase the interest rates on the bonds rather than lower them? Briefly explain.

Source: Nathaniel Popper, "Fed Action Spurs Broad Rally," *New York Times*, September 13, 2012.

4.10 [Related to the Making the Connection on page 71] Consider the following information on two U.S. Treasury bonds:

	Maturity	Coupon	Bid	Asked	Chg	Asked Yield
Bond A	2018 Nov 15	3.375	100:26	100:27	+ 1	2.26
Bond B	2018 Nov 15	4.750	101:29	101:30	+ 1	2.26

Briefly explain how two securities that have the same yield to maturity can have different prices.

4.11 Consider the following analysis:

> The rise and fall of a bond's price has a direct inverse relationship to its yield to maturity, or interest rate. As prices go up, the yield declines and vice versa. For example, a $1,000 bond might carry a stated annual yield, known as the coupon of 8%, meaning that it pays $80 a year to the bondholder. If that bond was bought for $870, the actual yield to maturity would be 9.2% ($80 annual interest on $870 of principal).

Do you agree with this analysis? Briefly explain.

3.5 **Interest Rates and Rates of Return**
Explain the difference between interest rates and rates of return.

Review Questions

5.1 What is the difference between the yield to maturity on a coupon bond and the rate of return on the bond?

5.2 Why does a bond with a longer maturity have greater interest-rate risk than a bond with a shorter maturity?

Problems and Applications

5.3 Suppose that for a price of $950, you purchase a 10-year Treasury bond that has a face value of $1,000 and a coupon rate of 4%. If you sell the bond one year later for $1,150, what was your rate of return for that one-year holding period?

5.4 In recent years, both Coca-Cola and Walt Disney have issued bonds with 100-year maturities. Why would any investor buy a bond with such a long maturity, given that the investor is unlikely to still be alive when the bond matures? If market interest rates were to rise, would these bonds be a particularly good or a particularly bad investment in comparison with an investment in a conventional 30-year bond?

Source: Richard Barley, "U.K. Century Bonds May Be a Stretch," *Wall Street Journal*, March 14, 2012.

5.5 Suppose that on January 1, 2013, you purchased a coupon bond with the following characteristics:

Face value: $1,000
Coupon rate: 8 3/8
Current yield: 7.5%
Maturity date: 2015

If the bond is selling for $850 on January 1, 2014, then what was your rate of return on this bond during the holding period of calendar year 2013?

5.6 Suppose that you just bought a four-year $1,000 coupon bond with a coupon rate of 6% when the market interest rate is 6%. One year later, the market interest rate falls to 4%. What rate of return did you earn on the bond during the year?

5.7 Suppose that you are considering investing in a four-year bond that has a face value of $1,000 and a coupon rate of 6%.

a. What is the price of the bond if the market interest rate on similar bonds is 6%? What is the bond's current yield?

b. Suppose that you purchase the bond, and the next day the market interest rate on similar bonds falls to 5%. What will the price of your bond be now? What will its current yield be?

c. Now suppose that one year has gone by since you bought the bond, and you have received the first coupon payment. How much would another investor now be willing to pay for the bond? What was your total return on the bond? If another investor had bought the bond a year ago for the amount that you calculated in (b), what would that investor's total return have been?

d. Now suppose that two years have gone by since you bought the bond and that you have received the first two coupon payments. At this point, the market interest rate on similar bonds unexpectedly rises to 10%. How much would another investor be willing to pay for your bond? What will the bond's current yield be over the next year? Suppose that another investor had bought the bond at the price you calculated in (c). What would that investor's total return have been over the past year?

3.6 **Nominal Interest Rates Versus Real Interest Rates**
Explain the difference between nominal interest rates and real interest rates.

Review Questions

6.1 What is the difference between the nominal interest rate on a loan and the real interest rate?

6.2 What is the difference between the real interest rate and the expected real interest rate?

6.3 What are TIPS? Why would an investor buy TIPS rather than conventional Treasury bonds?

Problems and Applications

6.4 Suppose you are about to borrow $15,000 for four years to buy a new car. Briefly explain which of these situations you would prefer to be in:

i. The interest rate on your loan is 10%, and you expect the annual inflation over the next four years to average 8%.

ii. The interest rate on your loan is 6%, and you expect the annual inflation rate over the next four years to average 2%.

6.5 When will the real interest rate differ from the expected real interest rate? Would this possible difference be of more concern to you if you were considering making a loan to be paid back in 1 year or a loan to be paid back in 10 years?

6.6 For several decades in the late nineteenth century, the price level in the United States declined. Was this likely to have helped or hurt U.S. farmers who borrowed money to buy land? Does your answer depend on whether the decline in the price level was expected or unexpected? Briefly explain.

6.7 Suppose that on January 1, 2013, the price of a one-year Treasury bill is $970.87. Investors expect that the inflation rate will be 2% during

2013, but at the end of the year, the inflation rate turns out to have been 1%. What are the nominal interest rate on the bill (measured as the yield to maturity), the expected real interest rate, and the real interest rate?

6.8 An article in the *New York Times* notes that "rising bond yields can … signal the threat of inflation." Briefly explain why, if investors expect inflation to be higher, the yields on bonds will rise.

Source: Nelson D. Schwartz, "Surprise Increase in Rates Is Credited to Signs of Recovery," *New York Times*, March 18, 2012.

Data Exercises

D3.1: [Compare interest rates on bonds of different maturities] Go to the Web site of the Federal Reserve Bank of St. Louis (FRED) (research.stlouisfed.org/fred2/) and download and graph the data series for the 3-month Treasury bill (TB3MS), the 10-year Treasury note (GS10), and the 30-year Treasury bond (GS30) for the period from January 1990 to the most recent month. (Notice that there is a period when the Treasury stopped selling 30-year bonds, so no data are available for these months.) During which periods is the gap between the 10-year note and the 30-year bond the greatest? During which periods is the gap between the 10-year note and the 3-month bill the greatest?

D3.2: [Calculate the real interest rate using a 1-year Treasury bill and the consumer price index] Go to the Web site of the Federal Reserve Bank of St. Louis (FRED) (research.stlouisfed.org/fred2/) and download the data for the 1-year Treasury bill (TB1YR) for the period from 1980 to the most recent month. Find the consumer price index for all urban consumers (CPIAUCSL) and then click on the link "Edit graph." In the pull-down menu for units, choose "Percentage change from year ago." Download the data. Subtract

your measure of inflation from the values for the 1-year Treasury bill and graph both the resulting real interest rate and the values for the nominal Treasury bill interest rate. During which periods is the gap between the nominal interest rate and the real interest rate the greatest?

D3.3: [Compare interest rates on TIPS and regular Treasury bonds] Go to the Web site of the Federal Reserve Bank of St. Louis (FRED) (research.stlouisfed.org/fred2/) and download and graph both the interest rate on the 10-year Treasury note (GS10) and the interest rate on the 10-year Treasury TIPS (FII10) for the period from January 2003 to the most recent month. What explains the difference between the two interest rates? When has the difference been the greatest?

D3.4: [Analyze real and nominal interest rates] Go to the Web site of the Federal Reserve Bank of St. Louis (FRED) (research.stlouisfed.org/fred2/) and download the most recent values for the following five variables: (1) the 30-Year Conventional Mortgage Rate (MORTG); (2) Moody's Seasoned Aaa Corporate Bond Yield (AAA); (3) the 3-Month Treasury Bill: Secondary Market Rate (TB3MS); (4) the 10-Year Treasury Constant Maturity Rate (GS10); and (5) the

University of Michigan's measure of expected inflation over the next 12 months (MICH).

a. Using these data, take the most recent expected inflation rate and compute the expected real interest rate for each of the nominal interest rates: the 30-Year Conventional Mortgage Rate, Moody's Seasoned Aaa Corporate Bond Yield, the 3-Month Treasury Bill: Secondary Market Rate, and the 10-Year Treasury Constant Maturity Rate.

b. Suppose the actual inflation rate is greater than the expected inflation rate. Will borrowers or lenders be made worse off? Briefly explain.

D3.5: **[Analyze bond prices and interest rates]** Go to the Web site of the Federal Reserve Bank of St. Louis (FRED) (research.stlouisfed.org/fred2/) and download the most recent values and values from the same month one year and two years earlier for the 1-Year Treasury Bill: Secondary Market Rate (TB1YR).

a. Suppose the 1-Year Treasury Bill has a face value of $1,000. Using the interest rates found above, calculate the price of a 1-Year Treasury Bill for each of the three months.

b. From the calculations you made in part (a), what can you conclude about the relationship between bond yields and bond prices?

CHAPTER 4

Determining Interest Rates

Learning Objectives

After studying this chapter, you should be able to:

4.1 Discuss the most important factors in building an investment portfolio (pages 88–95)

4.2 Use a demand and supply model to determine market interest rates for bonds (pages 95–105)

4.3 Use the bond market model to explain changes in interest rates (pages 105–110)

4.4 Use the loanable funds model to analyze the international capital market (pages 110–117)

Are There Any Safe Investments?

A newspaper article in 2012 included an interview with a Florida couple who had decided to "stuff their money in the mattress." That way, the husband said, "we can see the cash when we want." Although the reaction of this couple was extreme, many investors remained scarred by the volatility in the prices of stocks and bonds during and after the 2007–2009 financial crisis. The fall in stock prices between 2007 and 2009 had wiped out several trillion dollars in household wealth, leaving some people without enough money to retire or to pay for their children's college tuition. At the same time, interest rates on bank certificates of deposit (CDs) and other bank savings accounts had fallen to historically low levels. The interest rates were well below the inflation rate, which meant that the real interest rate on those deposits was negative.

To try to earn a higher interest rate, some investors purchased Treasury bonds or corporate bonds. But the interest rates on these bonds were also low. For example, between 1980 and 2009, the average interest rate on a 10-year U.S. Treasury note was 7.2%. In September 2012, it was only 1.9%. Similarly, between 1980 and 2009, the average interest rate on long-term bonds issued by large, financially sound corporations was 8.4%. In September 2012, it was only 1.7%. An increase in market interest rates causes prices of existing bonds to fall. So, if the interest rates on Treasury bonds or corporate bonds rose toward their historical averages, bond investors would suffer significant capital losses. Not surprisingly, many financial advisers warned investors that buying bonds could be risky.

Continued on next page

Key Issue and Question

Issue: Federal Reserve policies to combat the recession of 2007–2009 led some economists to predict that inflation would rise and make long-term bonds a poor investment.

Question: How do investors take into account expected inflation and other factors when making investment decisions?

Answered on page 118

Although the inflation rate in 2012 remained low, some economists were predicting that it might increase sharply in a few years. What would happen to bond prices if the inflation rate increased? Many investors were asking themselves this question as they decided which financial assets they should invest in. More generally, how should investors take into account expectations of inflation, as well as other factors, such as risk and information costs, when making investment decisions? We address these questions in this chapter.

Sources: Catherine Rampell, "As Low Rates Depress Savers, Governments Reap Benefits," *New York Times*, September 10, 2012.

In this chapter, we discuss how savers decide to allocate their wealth among alternative assets, such as stocks and bonds. We also further analyze the bond market and show that, as in other markets, the equilibrium price of bonds and the equilibrium interest rate depend on the demand and supply for bonds.

4.1

Learning Objective
Discuss the most important factors in building an investment portfolio.

How to Build an Investment Portfolio

As you proceed in your career and your income rises, you will begin to consider which financial assets you should invest in. You have many assets to choose from, ranging from basic checking and savings accounts in banks to stocks and bonds to complex financial securities. What principles should you follow as you build an investment *portfolio*? Recall that a portfolio is a collection of assets owned by an investor.

We begin by examining the objectives of the typical investor. You might expect that investors will attempt to earn the highest possible rate of return on their investments. But suppose you have the opportunity to invest $1,000 in an asset, such as a stock or bond, on which you expect a rate of return of 10%, but you also believe there is a significant chance of a return of −5%. Would you invest in that asset, or would you prefer to invest in an asset on which you expect a return of 5% and do not believe there is a chance of a negative return? Would it matter if you already have $1,000 in investments or if you already have $1,000,000 in investments? Would your answer be different if you were 60 years old rather than 20 years old?

The Determinants of Portfolio Choice

There are many ways to build an investment portfolio, depending on how an investor answers the questions we just asked. Even investors with the same income, wealth, and age will often have very different portfolios. Investors use the following *determinants of portfolio choice (or determinants of asset demand)* to evaluate different investment options:

1. The saver's *wealth*, or total amount of savings to be allocated among investments
2. The *expected rate of return* from an investment compared with the expected rates of return on other investments
3. The degree of *risk* in an investment compared with the degree of risk in other investments
4. The *liquidity* of an investment compared with the liquidity of other investments
5. The *cost of acquiring information* about an investment compared with the cost of acquiring information about other investments

We'll now consider each of these determinants.

Wealth Recall that income and wealth are different. *Income* is a person's earnings during a particular period, such as a year. Assets are anything of value, such as stocks and bonds, that a person owns. Liabilities are a person's loans or other debts. *Wealth* is the total value of assets a person owns, minus the total value of any liabilities that a person owes. As a person's wealth increases, we would expect the size of the person's financial portfolio to increase but not by proportionally increasing each individual asset. For instance, when you first graduate from college, you may not have much wealth, and the only financial asset you have may be $500 in a checking account. Once you have a job and your wealth begins to increase, the amount in your checking account may not increase very much, but you may purchase a bank certificate of deposit and some shares in a money market mutual fund. As your wealth continues to increase, you may begin to purchase individual stocks and bonds. In general, however, when we view financial markets as a whole, we can assume that an increase in wealth will increase the quantity demanded for most financial assets.

Expected Rate of Return Given your wealth, how do you decide which assets to add to your portfolio? You probably want to invest in assets with high rates of return. As we have seen, though, the rate of return for a particular holding period includes the rate of capital gain, which an investor can calculate only at the end of the period (see Chapter 3). Suppose that you are considering investing in an IBM 8% coupon bond that has a current price of $950. You know that you will receive a coupon payment of $80 during the year, but you do not know what the price of the IBM bond will be at the end of the year, so you cannot calculate your rate of return ahead of time. You can, though, make informed estimates of the price of the bond one year from now, so you can calculate an *expected rate of return* (which we simplify to **expected return**).

To keep the example simple, suppose you believe that at the end of the year, there are only two possibilities:

1. The IBM bond will have a price of $1,016.50, in which case you will have earned a capital gain of 7% and a rate of return of 8% + 7% = 15%
2. The IBM bond will have a price of $921.50, in which case you will have suffered a capital loss of −3% and will have a return of 8% − 3% = 5%.

The *probability* of an event occurring is the chance that the event will occur, expressed as a percentage. In this case, let's assume that you believe that the probability of either of the prices occurring is 50%. In general, we calculate the expected return on an investment by using this formula:

Expected return = [(Probability of event 1 occurring) × (Value of event 1)]
      + [(Probability of event 2 occurring) × (Value of event 2)].

This formula can be expanded to take into account as many events as the investor considers relevant. Applying the formula in this case, using decimals for the probabilities, gives us:

Expected return = (0.50 × 15%) + (0.50 × 5%) = 10%.

One way to think of expected returns is as long-run averages. That is, if you invested in this bond over a period of years, and your probabilities of the two possible returns occurring are correct, then in half of the years, you would receive a return of 15%, and in the other half you would receive a return of 5%. So, on average, your return would

Expected return The rate of return expected on an asset during a future period.

be 10%. Of course, this example is simplified because we assumed that there are only two possible returns, when in reality there are likely to be many possible returns. We also assumed that it is possible to assign exact probabilities for each return, when in practice that would often be difficult to do. Nevertheless, this example captures the basic idea that in making choices among financial assets, investors need to consider possible returns and the probability of those returns occurring.

Risk Now suppose that you are choosing between investing in the IBM bond just described and investing in a Ford bond that you believe will have a return of 12% with a probability of 50% or a return of 8% with a probability of 50%. The expected return on the Ford bond is:

$$(0.50 \times 12\%) + (0.50 \times 8\%) = 10\%,$$

or the same as for the IBM bond. Although the expected returns are the same, most investors would prefer the Ford bond because the IBM bond has greater risk. So far, we have mentioned default risk and interest-rate risk, but economists have a general definition of risk that includes these and other types of risk: **Risk** is the degree of uncertainty in the return on an asset. In particular, the greater the chance of receiving a return that is farther away from the asset's expected return, the greater the asset's risk. In the case of the two bonds, the IBM bond has greater risk because an investor could expect to receive returns that are either 5 percentage points higher or lower than the expected return, while an investor in the Ford bond could expect to receive returns that are only 2 percentage points higher or lower than the expected return. To provide a numerical measure of risk, economists measure the volatility of an asset's returns by calculating the standard deviation of an asset's actual returns over the years. If you have taken a course in statistics, recall that standard deviation is a measure of how dispersed a particular group of numbers is.[1]

Risk The degree of uncertainty in the return on an asset.

---

[1]We can use this example to show how to calculate the risk of investing in an asset as measured by the standard deviation of the returns on the asset. The first step in calculating the standard deviation is to find the deviation, or difference, between each return and the expected return on the bond. For example, for the IBM bond, the expected return equals 10% and the first return is 15%, so the difference from the expected return is 15% − 10% = 5%:

	Return 1	Deviation from the expected return	Return 2	Deviation from the expected return
IBM	15%	5%	5%	−5%
Ford	12%	2%	8%	−2

Next, we need to square the deviations of the returns and add them together, weighted by the probability of the returns occurring. The result is the variance of the returns:

	Return 1	Deviation squared	Return 2	Deviation squared	Weighted deviations squared (variance of the returns)
IBM	15%	25%	5%	25%	$(0.50 \times 25\%) + (0.50 \times 25\%) = 25\%$
Ford	12%	4%	8%	4%	$(0.50 \times 4\%) + (0.50 \times 4\%) = 4\%$

Finally, taking the square root of the variance gives us the standard deviation of the returns. Using this measure of risk, we find that the IBM bond is riskier than the Ford bond:

	Variance	Standard deviation
IBM	25%	5%
Ford	4%	2%

Most investors are *risk averse*, which means that in choosing between two assets with the same expected returns, they would choose the asset with the lower risk. Risk-averse investors will invest in an asset that has greater risk only if they are compensated by receiving a higher return. Because most investors are risk averse, in financial markets we observe a *trade-off between risk and return*. So, for example, assets such as bank CDs have low rates of return but also low risk, while assets such as shares of stock have high rates of return but also high risk. It makes sense that investors are usually risk averse because many individuals purchase financial assets as part of a savings plan to meet future expenses, such as buying a house, paying college tuition for their children, or having sufficient funds for retirement. They want to avoid having assets fall in value just when they need the funds.

Some investors are actually *risk loving*, which means they prefer to gamble by holding a risky asset with the possibility of maximizing returns. In our example, a risk-loving investor would be attracted to the IBM bond, with its 50% probability of a 15% return, even though the bond also has a 50% probability of a 5% return. Finally, some investors are *risk neutral*, which means they would make their investment decisions on the basis of expected returns, ignoring risk.

Making the Connection

Fear the Black Swan!

The table below provides data from 1926 to 2011 on four financial assets that are widely owned by investors. The "small" companies in the table are only small in the context of the U.S. stock market. In fact, they are fairly large, with the total value of their shares of stock being between $300 million and $2 billion. Investors are unwilling to buy stock from truly small companies, such as a local restaurant, because they lack sufficient information on the financial health of these companies. The "large" companies include Exxon Mobil, AT&T, and the other 500 firms included in the S&P 500, which is the most common average of the stock prices of firms valued at more than $10 billion. The average annual return is the simple average of the 86 yearly returns for each of the four assets during this period. Risk is measured as the volatility of the annual returns and is calculated as the standard deviation of each asset's annual returns during this period.

The data in the second and third columns of the table illustrate the trade-off between risk and return. Investors in stocks of small companies during these years experienced the highest average returns but also accepted the most risk. Investors in U.S. Treasury bills experienced the lowest average returns but also faced the least risk.

Financial asset	Average annual rate of return	Risk
Small company stocks	16.5%	32.5%
Large company stocks	11.8	20.3
Long-term corporate bonds	6.1	8.4
U.S. Treasury bills	3.6	3.1

Source: Morningstar/Ibbotson.

The conventional measure of risk used in the table gives us a good idea of the range within which returns typically fluctuate. Sometimes, though, returns occur that are far outside the usual range of returns. For instance, during 2008, at the height of the financial crisis, investors in large company stocks suffered a 37% *loss*. The probability of such a large loss was less than 5%. Stocks performed so poorly because the collapse of the housing market set off a financial crisis and the worst recession since the Great Depression of the 1930s. Nassim Nicholas Taleb, a professional investor and professor of economics at New York University, has popularized the term *black swan event* to refer to rare events that have a large effect on society or the economy. The name comes from the fact that until Europeans discovered black swans in Australia in 1697, they believed that all swans were white. So, a black swan event is surprising and contrary to previous experience. Some economists see the financial crisis as a black swan event because before it occurred, few believed it was possible.

Economists and investment professionals have begun to consider whether conventional measures of risk need to be revised in light of the financial crisis of 2007–2009. Some economists argue that when investors choose among assets, they need to consider both the range of likely returns *and* their losses if an unlikely event should occur. New measures of risk such as *expected shortfall* or *conditional expected risk* require sophisticated calculations but may allow investors to better gauge the risks their portfolios will be exposed to if an unlikely event occurs.

The financial crisis revealed that for the average investor, calculating risk when building a portfolio is more difficult than most investors used to think.

Sources: Nassim Nicholas Taleb, *The Black Swan: The Impact of the Highly Improbable*, 2nd ed., New York: Random House, 2010; and Peng Chen, "Is Modern Portfolio Theory Obsolete?" Morningstar.com, January 15, 2010.

See related problem 1.6 at the end of the chapter.

Liquidity Recall that *liquidity* is the ease with which an asset can be exchanged for money (see Chapter 2). Assets with greater liquidity help savers to smooth spending over time or to access funds for emergencies. For example, if you invest in certain assets to meet unanticipated medical expenses, you want to be able to sell those assets quickly if you need the money for an operation. The greater an asset's liquidity, the more desirable the asset is to investors. All else being equal, investors will accept a lower return on a more liquid asset than on a less liquid asset. Therefore, just as there is a trade-off between risk and return, there is a trade-off between liquidity and return. You are willing to accept a very low—possibly zero—interest rate on your checking account because you have immediate access to those funds.

The Cost of Acquiring Information Investors find assets more desirable if they don't have to spend much time or money acquiring information about them. For instance, information on bonds issued by the U.S. Treasury is easy to obtain. Every guide to investment explains that the federal government is very unlikely to default on its bonds, and investors can find the prices and yields on Treasury bonds in the *Wall Street Journal* or at a Web site such as Yahoo! Finance (finance.yahoo.com). If a new company issues bonds, however, investors must spend time and money collecting and analyzing information about the company before deciding to invest.

All else being equal, investors will accept a lower return on an asset that has lower costs of acquiring information. Therefore, just as there are trade-offs between risk and return and between liquidity and return, there is a trade-off between the cost of acquiring information and return.

We can summarize our discussion of the determinants of portfolio choice by noting that *desirable characteristics of a financial asset cause the quantity of the asset demanded by investors to increase, and undesirable characteristics of a financial asset cause the quantity of the asset demanded to decrease.* Table 4.1 summarizes the determinants of portfolio choice.

Diversification

It might appear that after weighing the attributes of different assets, an investor should end up with a portfolio composed of what he or she believes to be the one "best" asset. In fact, though, nearly all investors have multiple assets in their portfolios. They do so because the real world is full of uncertainty, and despite intensive analysis, an investor cannot be certain that an asset will perform as expected. To compensate for the inability to find a perfect asset, investors typically hold various types of assets, such as shares of stock issued by different firms. Dividing wealth among many different assets to reduce risk is called **diversification**.

Investors can take advantage of the fact that the returns on assets typically do not move together perfectly. For example, you may own shares of stock in Ford Motor Company and Apple. During a recession, the price of Ford's shares may fall as car sales decline, while the price of Apple's shares may rise if the firm introduces a popular new electronic product that consumers buy in large quantities, despite the recession. Similarly,

Diversification The division of wealth among many different assets to reduce risk.

Table 4.1 Determinants of Portfolio Choice

An increase in ...	causes the quantity demanded of the asset in the portfolio to ...	because ...
wealth	rise	investors have a greater stock of savings to allocate.
expected return on an asset relative to expected returns on other assets	rise	investors gain more from holding the asset.
risk (that is, the variability of returns)	fall	most investors are risk averse.
liquidity (that is, the ease with which an asset can be converted to cash)	rise	investors can easily convert the asset into cash to finance consumption.
information costs	fall	investors must spend more time and money acquiring and analyzing information on the asset and its returns.

the price of shares of the pharmaceutical firm Merck may fall if a new prescription drug unexpectedly fails to receive approval from the federal government, while the price of shares of Red Robin Gourmet Burgers may soar after the chain introduces a burger made of cauliflower and Brussels sprouts that becomes a sensation. So, the return on a diversified portfolio is more stable than are the returns on the individual assets that make up the portfolio.

Investors cannot eliminate risk entirely because assets share some common risk, called **market (or systematic) risk**. For example, economic recessions and economic expansions can decrease or increase returns on stocks as a whole. Few investments did well during the financial crisis of 2007–2009. Assets also carry their own unique risk called **idiosyncratic (or unsystematic) risk**. For example, the price of an individual stock can be affected by unpredictable events such as scientific discoveries, worker strikes, and unfavorable lawsuits that affect the profitability of the firm. Diversification can eliminate idiosyncratic risk but not systematic risk.

Market (or systematic) risk Risk that is common to all assets of a certain type, such as the increases and decreases in stocks resulting from the business cycle.

Idiosyncratic (or unsystematic) risk Risk that pertains to a particular asset rather than to the market as a whole, as when the price of a particular firm's stock fluctuates because of the success or failure of a new product.

Making the Connection   In Your Interest

How Much Risk Should You Tolerate in Your Portfolio?

Although all investments are risky—a point any saver who experienced the financial crisis of 2007–2009 knows too well!—you can take steps to understand and manage risk when building your portfolio. Financial planners encourage their clients to evaluate their financial situation and their willingness to bear risk in determining whether an investment is appropriate.

Your *time horizon* is one important factor when choosing the degree of risk to accept. Funds you are saving in order to buy a home in the next few years should probably be invested in low-risk assets, such as bank certificates of deposit, even though those assets will have low returns. If you are saving for a retirement that won't begin for several decades, you can take advantage of the long-term gains from riskier investments, such as shares of stock, without much concern for short-term variability in returns. As you approach retirement, you can then switch to a more conservative strategy to avoid losing a substantial portion of your savings.

The following two typical financial plans of younger and older savers differ in their time horizons and saving goals:

	Younger saver (younger than age 50)	Older saver (around age 60)
Timeline for needing funds	Wants to build the value of a financial portfolio over more than 10 years.	Has a financial portfolio at or near the amount the investor needs to retire.
Financial goal	Accumulate funds by earning high long-term returns.	Conserve existing funds to earn a return slightly above the inflation rate.
Portfolio plan	Build a financial portfolio based on maximizing expected returns, with only limited concern for the variability of returns.	Reduce risk by selecting safe assets to earn an expected return *after inflation* of about zero.

In assessing your saving plan, you need to consider the effects of inflation and taxes. Recall the important difference between real and nominal interest rates (see Chapter 3). In addition, the federal government taxes the returns from most investments, as do some state and local governments. Depending on the investment, your *real, after-tax return* may be considerably different from your nominal pretax return. Many investors choose to invest in stocks because they understand that over the long run, investing in safe assets, such as U.S. Treasury bills, may leave them with a very small real, after-tax return. (In the next chapter, we will look further at how differences in tax treatment can affect the returns on certain investments.)

Understanding how risk, inflation, and taxation affect your investments will help you reduce emotional reactions to market volatility and make better-informed investment decisions.

See related problem 1.7 at the end of the chapter.

Market Interest Rates and the Demand and Supply for Bonds

Learning Objective
Use a demand and supply model to determine market interest rates for bonds.

We can use the determinants of portfolio choice just discussed to show how the interaction of the demand and supply for bonds determines market interest rates. Although demand and supply analysis should be familiar from your introductory economics course, applying this analysis to the bond market involves a complication. Typically, we draw demand and supply graphs with the price of the good or service on the vertical axis. Although we are interested in the prices of bonds, we are also interested in their interest rates. Fortunately, we know that the price of a bond, P, and its yield to maturity, i, are linked by the equation showing the price of a bond with coupon payments C that has a face value FV and that matures in n years (see Chapter 3):

$$P = \frac{C}{(1 + i)} + \frac{C}{(1 + i)^2} + \frac{C}{(1 + i)^3} + \ldots + \frac{C}{(1 + i)^n} + \frac{FV}{(1 + i)^n}.$$

Because the coupon payment and the face value do not change, once we have determined the equilibrium price in the bond market, we have also determined the equilibrium interest rate. With this approach to showing how market interest rates are determined, sometimes called the *bond market approach*, we are considering the bond as the "good" being traded in the market. The bond market approach is most useful when considering how the factors affecting the demand and supply for bonds affect the interest rate. In Section 4.4, we will consider an alternative approach, called the *market for loanable funds approach*, that treats the funds being traded as the good. As in other areas of economics, which model we use depends on which aspects of a problem are most important in a particular situation.

A Demand and Supply Graph of the Bond Market
Figure 4.1 illustrates the market for bonds. For simplicity, let's assume that this is the market for a one-year discount bond that has a face value of $1,000 at maturity. The

Figure 4.1

The Market for Bonds

The equilibrium price of bonds is determined in the bond market. By determining the price of bonds, the bond market also determines the interest rate on bonds. In this case, a one-year discount bond with a face value of $1,000 has an equilibrium price of $960, which means it has an interest rate (*i*) of 4.2%. The equilibrium quantity of bonds is $500 billion.

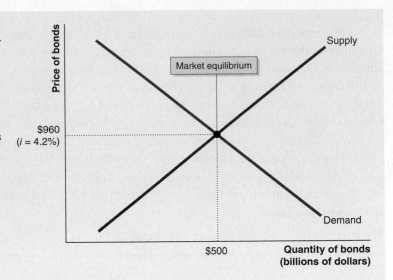

figure shows that the equilibrium price for this bond is $960, and the equilibrium quantity of bonds is $500 billion. Recall the formula for a one-year discount bond that sells for price *P* with face value *FV* (see Chapter 3):

$$i = \frac{FV - P}{P},$$

or, in this case:

$$i = \frac{\$1,000 - \$960}{\$960} = 0.042, \text{ or } 4.2\%.$$

As with markets for goods and services, we draw the demand and supply curves for bonds holding constant all factors that can affect demand and supply other than the price of bonds. The demand curve for bonds represents the relationship between the price of bonds and the quantity of bonds demanded by investors, holding constant all other factors. As the price of bonds increases, the interest rates on the bonds will fall, and the bonds will become less desirable to investors, so the quantity demanded will decline. Therefore, the demand curve for bonds is downward sloping, as shown in Figure 4.1.

Next, think about the supply curve for bonds. The supply curve represents the relationship between the price of bonds and the quantity of bonds supplied *by investors who own existing bonds and by firms that are considering issuing new bonds*. As the price of bonds increases, their interest rates will fall, and holders of existing bonds will be more willing to sell them. Some firms will also find it less expensive to finance projects by borrowing at the lower interest rate and will issue new bonds. For both of these reasons, the quantity of bonds supplied will increase.

As with markets for goods and services, if the bond market is currently in equilibrium, it will stay there, and if it is not in equilibrium, it will move to equilibrium. For example, in Figure 4.2, suppose that the price of bonds is currently $980, which

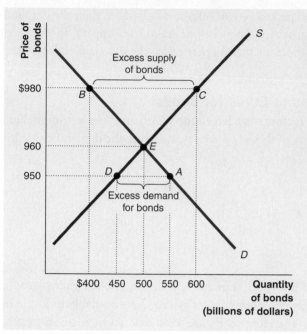

Figure 4.2

Equilibrium in Markets for Bonds

At the equilibrium price of bonds of $960, the quantity of bonds demanded by investors equals the quantity of bonds supplied by borrowers. At any price above $960, there is an excess supply of bonds, and the price of bonds will fall. At any price below $960, there is an excess demand for bonds, and the price of bonds will rise. The behavior of bond buyers and sellers pushes the price of bonds to the equilibrium of $960.

is above the equilibrium price of $960. At this higher price, the quantity demanded is $400 billion (point *B*), which is less than the equilibrium quantity demanded, while the quantity supplied is $600 billion (point *C*), which is greater than the equilibrium quantity supplied. The result is that there is an *excess supply of bonds* equal to $200 billion. Investors are buying all the bonds they want at the current price, but some sellers cannot find buyers. These sellers have an incentive to reduce the price they are willing to accept for bonds so that investors will buy their bonds. This downward pressure on bond prices will continue until the price has fallen to the equilibrium price of $960 (point *E*).

Now suppose that the price of bonds is $950, which is below the equilibrium price of $960. At this lower price, the quantity demanded is $550 billion (point *A*), which is greater than the equilibrium quantity demanded, while the quantity supplied is $450 billion (point *D*), which is less than the equilibrium quantity supplied. The result is that there is an *excess demand for bonds* equal to $100 billion. Investors and firms can sell all the bonds they want at the current price, but some buyers cannot find sellers. These buyers have an incentive to increase the price at which they are willing to buy bonds so that firms and other investors will be willing to sell bonds to them. This upward pressure on bond prices will continue until the price has risen to the equilibrium price of $960.

Explaining Changes in Equilibrium Interest Rates

In drawing the demand and supply curves for bonds in Figure 4.1, we held constant everything that could affect the willingness of investors to buy bonds—or firms and investors to sell bonds—except for the price of bonds. You may remember from your introductory economics course the distinction between a *change in the quantity de-manded* (or *the quantity supplied*) and a *change in demand* (or *supply*). If the price of bonds changes, we move along the demand (or supply) curve, but the curve does not shift, so we have a change in quantity demanded (or supplied). If any other relevant variable—such as wealth or the expected rate of inflation—changes, then the demand (or supply) curve shifts, and we have a change in demand (or supply). In the next sections, we review the most important factors that cause the demand curve or the supply curve for bonds to shift.

Factors That Shift the Demand Curve for Bonds

In Section 4.1, we discussed the factors that determine which assets investors include in their portfolios. A change in any of these five factors will cause the demand curve for bonds to shift:

1. Wealth
2. Expected return on bonds
3. Risk
4. Liquidity
5. Information costs

Wealth When the economy is growing, households will accumulate more wealth. The wealthier savers are, the larger the stock of savings they have available to invest in financial assets, including bonds. Therefore, as Figure 4.3 shows, an increase in wealth, holding all other factors constant, will shift the demand curve for bonds to the right, from D_1 to D_2, as savers are willing and able to buy more bonds at any given price. In the figure, as the demand curve for bonds shifts to the right, the equilibrium price of bonds rises from $960 to $980, and the equilibrium quantity of bonds increases from $500 billion to $600 billion. So, equilibrium in the bond market moves from point E_1 to point E_2. During a recession, as occurred during 2007–2009, households will experience declining wealth, and, holding all other factors constant, the demand curve for bonds will shift to the left, reducing both the equilibrium price and equilibrium quantity. In Figure 4.3, as the demand curve for bonds shifts to the left, from D_1 to D_3 the equilibrium price falls

Figure 4.3

Shifts in the Demand Curve for Bonds

An increase in wealth, holding all other factors constant, will shift the demand curve for bonds to the right. As the demand curve for bonds shifts to the right, the equilibrium price of bonds rises from $960 to $980, and the equilibrium quantity of bonds increases from $500 billion to $600 billion.

A decrease in wealth, holding all other factors constant, will shift the demand curve for bonds to the left, reducing both the equilibrium price and equilibrium quantity. As the demand curve for bonds shifts to the left, the equilibrium price falls from $960 to $940, and the equilibrium quantity of bonds decreases from $500 billion to $400 billion.

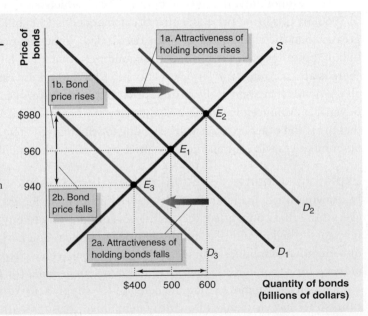

from \$960 to \$940, and the equilibrium quantity of bonds decreases from \$500 billion to \$400 billion. So, equilibrium in the bond market moves from point E_1 to point E_3.

Expected Return on Bonds If the expected return on bonds rises *relative to expected returns on other assets*, investors will increase their demand for bonds, and the demand curve for bonds will shift to the right. If the expected return on bonds falls relative to expected returns on other assets, the demand curve for bonds will shift to the left. Note that it is the expected return on bonds *relative* to the expected returns on other assets that causes the demand curve for bonds to shift. For instance, if the expected return on bonds remained unchanged, while investors decided that the return from investing in stocks would be higher than they had previously expected, the relative return on bonds would fall, and the demand curve for bonds would shift to the left.

The expected return on bonds is affected by the expected inflation rate. Because the expected real interest rate equals the nominal interest rate minus the expected inflation rate, an increase in the expected inflation rate reduces the expected real interest rate. Similarly, the expected real return on bonds equals the nominal return minus the expected inflation rate. An increase in the expected inflation rate reduces the expected real return on bonds, which will reduce the willingness of investors to buy bonds at any given price and shift the demand curve for bonds to the left. A decrease in the expected inflation rate will increase the expected real return on bonds, increasing the willingness of investors to buy bonds at any given price and shift the demand curve for bonds to the right.

Risk An increase in the riskiness of bonds *relative to the riskiness of other assets* decreases the willingness of investors to buy bonds and causes the demand curve for bonds to shift to the left. A decrease in the riskiness of bonds relative to the riskiness of other assets increases the willingness of investors to buy bonds and causes the demand curve for bonds to shift to the right. It is the perceived riskiness of bonds *relative* to other assets that matters. If the riskiness of bonds remains unchanged but investors decide that stocks are riskier than they had previously believed, the relative riskiness of bonds will decline, investors will increase their demand for bonds, and the demand curve for bonds will shift to the right. In fact, during late 2008 and early 2009, many investors believed that the riskiness of investing in stocks had increased. As a result, investors increased their demand for bonds, which drove up the equilibrium price of bonds and, therefore, drove down the equilibrium interest rate on bonds. The quantity of corporate bonds issued in the United States in 2009 soared to \$2.84 trillion, which was 38% more than in 2008.

Liquidity Investors value liquidity in an asset because an asset with greater liquidity can be sold more quickly and at a lower cost if the investor needs the funds to, say, buy a car or invest in another asset. If the liquidity of bonds increases, investors demand more bonds at any given price, and the demand curve for bonds shifts to the right. A decrease in the liquidity of bonds shifts the demand curve for bonds to the left. Once again, though, it is the relative liquidity of bonds that matters. For instance, online stock trading sites first appeared during the 1990s. These sites allowed investors to buy and sell stocks at a very low cost, so the liquidity of many stocks increased. The result was that the relative liquidity of bonds decreased, and the demand curve for bonds shifted to the left.

Information Costs The information costs investors must pay to evaluate assets affect their willingness to buy those assets. For instance, beginning in the 1990s, financial information began to be readily available on the Internet either for free or for a low price. Previously, an investor could find this information only by paying for a subscription to a newsletter or by spending hours in libraries, gathering data from annual reports and other records. Although the Internet helped to lower the information costs for both stocks and bonds, the effect appears to have been greater for bonds. Because stocks had been more widely discussed in the *Wall Street Journal* and other newspapers and magazines, while bonds had been less discussed, the effect of the Internet on the information available on bonds was greater. As a result of the lower information costs, the demand curve for bonds shifted to the right. During the financial crisis, many investors came to believe that for certain types of bonds—particularly mortgage-backed securities—they lacked sufficient information to gauge the likelihood that the bonds might default. Gathering sufficient information appeared to be very costly, if it were possible at all. As a result of these higher information costs, the demand curve for bonds shifted to the left.

Table 4.2 summarizes the most important factors that shift the demand curve for bonds.

Factors That Shift the Supply Curve for Bonds

Shifts in the supply curve for bonds result from changes in factors other than the price of bonds that affect either the willingness of investors who own bonds to sell them or the willingness of firms and governments to issue additional bonds. Four factors are most important in explaining shifts in the supply curve for bonds:

1. Expected pretax profitability of physical capital investment
2. Business taxes
3. Expected inflation
4. Government borrowing

Expected Pretax Profitability of Physical Capital Investment Most firms borrow funds to finance the purchase of real physical capital assets, such as factories and machine tools, that they expect to use over several years to produce goods and services. The more profitable firms expect investment in physical assets to be, the more funds firms want to borrow by issuing bonds. During the late 1990s, many firms came to believe that investing in Web sites that would allow them to make online sales to consumers would be very profitable. The result was a boom in investment in physical capital in the form of computers, servers, and other information technology, and an increase in bond sales.

Figure 4.4 shows how an increase in firms' expectations of the profitability of investment in physical capital will, holding all other factors constant, shift the supply curve for bonds to the right as firms issue more bonds at any given price. In the figure, as the supply curve for bonds shifts to the right, from S_1 to S_2, the equilibrium price of bonds falls from $960 to $940, and the equilibrium quantity of bonds increases from $500 billion to $575 billion. During a recession, firms often become pessimistic about the profits they could earn from investing in physical capital, with the result that, holding all other factors constant, the supply curve for bonds will shift to the left, increasing

Table 4.2 Factors That Shift the Demand Curve for Bonds

All else being equal, an increase in ...	causes the demand for bonds to ...	because ...	Graph of effect on equilibrium in the bond market
wealth	increase	more funds are allocated to bonds.	P, D_1, D_2, S, Q
expected returns on bonds	increase	holding bonds is relatively more attractive.	P, D_1, D_2, S, Q
expected inflation	decrease	holding bonds is relatively less attractive.	P, D_2, D_1, S, Q
expected returns on other assets	decrease	holding bonds is relatively less attractive.	P, D_2, D_1, S, Q
riskiness of bonds relative to other assets	decrease	holding bonds is relatively less attractive.	P, D_2, D_1, S, Q
liquidity of bonds relative to other assets	increase	holding bonds is relatively more attractive.	P, D_1, D_2, S, Q
information costs of bonds relative to other assets	decrease	holding bonds is relatively less attractive.	P, D_2, D_1, S, Q

Figure 4.4

Shifts in the Supply Curve of Bonds

An increase in firms' expectations of the profitability of investments in physical capital will, holding all other factors constant, shift the supply curve for bonds to the right as firms issue more bonds at any given price. As the supply curve for bonds shifts to the right, the equilibrium price of bonds falls from $960 to $940, and the equilibrium quantity of bonds increases from $500 billion to $575 billion.

If firms become pessimistic about the profits they could earn from investing in physical capital, then, holding all other factors constant, the supply curve for bonds will shift to the left. As the supply for bonds shifts to the left, the equilibrium price increases from $960 to $975, and the equilibrium quantity of bonds decreases from $500 billion to $400 billion.

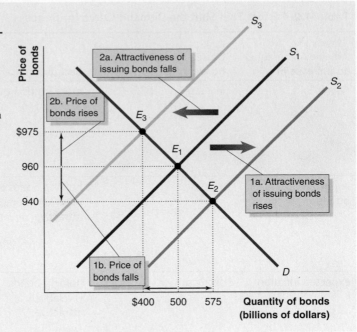

the equilibrium price of bonds, while decreasing the equilibrium quantity. In Figure 4.4, as the supply curve for bonds shifts to the left, from S_1 to S_3, the equilibrium price increases from $960 to $975, and the equilibrium quantity of bonds decreases from $500 billion to $400 billion.

Business Taxes Taxes on businesses also affect firms' expectations about future profitability because firms focus on the profits they have left after paying taxes. So, when business taxes are raised, the profits firms earn on new investment in physical capital decline, and firms issue fewer bonds. The result is that the supply curve for bonds will shift to the left. When the federal government cuts business taxes by enacting an investment tax credit, firms reduce their tax payments by a fraction of their spending on new physical capital. These lower taxes raise firms' profits on new investment projects, which leads firms to issue more bonds. So, the supply curve for bonds shifts to the right.

Expected Inflation We have seen that an increase in the expected rate of inflation reduces investors' demand for bonds by reducing the expected real interest rate that investors receive for any given *nominal* interest rate. From the point of view of a firm issuing a bond, a lower expected real interest rate is attractive because it means the firm pays less in real terms to borrow funds. So, an increase in the expected inflation rate results in the supply curve for bonds shifting to the right, as firms supply a greater quantity of bonds at every price. A decrease in the expected inflation rate results in the supply curve for bonds shifting to the left.

Government Borrowing So far, we have emphasized how the decisions of households and firms affect bond prices and interest rates. Decisions by governments can also affect

MyEconLab Real-time data

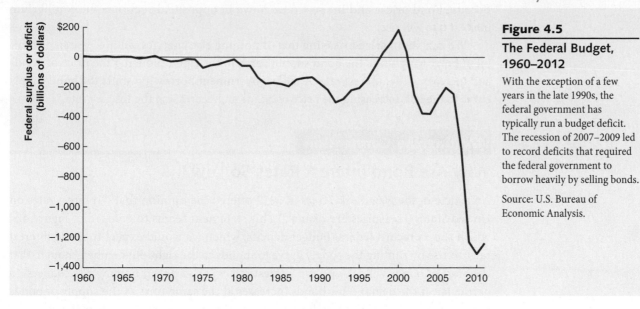

Figure 4.5

The Federal Budget, 1960–2012

With the exception of a few years in the late 1990s, the federal government has typically run a budget deficit. The recession of 2007–2009 led to record deficits that required the federal government to borrow heavily by selling bonds.

Source: U.S. Bureau of Economic Analysis.

bond prices and interest rates. For example, many economists believe that a series of large U.S. federal government budget deficits during the 1980s and early 1990s caused interest rates to be somewhat higher than they otherwise would have been.

When we talk about the "government sector" in the United States, we include not just the federal government but also state and local governments. The government sector is typically both a lender—as when the federal government makes loans to college students and small businesses—and a borrower. In recent years, the federal government has borrowed an enormous amount from U.S. and foreign investors as tax receipts have fallen far short of spending. The result has been large *federal budget deficits*. Figure 4.5 shows the federal budget deficit and surplus in the years since 1960. During most of these years, the federal budget has been in deficit, except for a few years in the late 1990s, when tax receipts exceeded government expenditures. The large deficits beginning in 2007 resulted, in part, from the severity of the 2007–2009 recession. When the economy enters a recession, tax receipts automatically decline as household incomes and business profits fall and the federal government automatically increases spending on unemployment insurance and other programs for the unemployed. The weakness of the economic recovery that began in 2009 meant that through 2012, the federal budget deficit remained very large. The severity of the recession also led to dramatic increases in spending and cuts in taxes by Congress and presidents George W. Bush and Barack Obama.

We can analyze the effect on the bond market of changes in the government's budget deficit or surplus. Suppose the federal government increases spending without increasing taxes. When the government finances the resulting deficit by issuing bonds, the supply curve for bonds will shift to the right. If we assume for now that households leave their saving unchanged in response to the government's increased borrowing, then the result of the government budget deficit, holding other factors constant, is to cause the equilibrium price of bonds to fall and the equilibrium quantity of bonds to rise. Because bond prices and interest rates move in opposite directions, the equilibrium interest rate will rise.

We can summarize by saying that, if nothing else changes, an increase in government borrowing shifts the bond supply curve to the right, reducing the price of bonds and increasing the interest rate. A fall in government borrowing shifts the bond supply curve to the left, increasing the price of bonds and decreasing the interest rate.

Making the Connection

Why Are Bond Interest Rates So Low?

An article in the *New York Times* in 2012 offered the opinion that: "Interest rates on United States Treasuries are dismal." This statement seems to contradict Figure 4.5, which shows record federal budget deficits, which we would expect to cause interest rates to rise by shifting the supply curve for bonds to the right. Remember, though, that the price of bonds will fall and the interest rate will rise *only if nothing else changes*. In particular, if the demand for bonds increases at the same time as the supply of bonds increases, then the price of bonds may actually rise, and the interest rate may fall.

The demand for bonds might increase when the government runs a deficit if households look ahead and conclude that at some point the government will have to raise taxes to pay off the bonds issued to finance the deficit. To prepare for those future higher tax payments, households may begin to increase their saving. This increased saving will shift the demand curve for bonds to the right at the same time that the supply curve for bonds shifts to the right because of the deficit. The effects of these two shifts on the interest rate might offset each other. In that case, the interest rate would not rise in response to the increase in government borrowing. However, studies by economists suggest that households do not increase their current saving by the full amount of an increase in the government budget deficit.

A much more important factor in shifting the demand curve for bonds to the right during 2012 was the low short-term interest rates that began during the financial crisis, in response to Fed policy, and continued during the following years. With interest rates on bank CDs and similar short-run assets pushed almost to zero, investors increased their demand for bonds, including those issued by the Treasury, by corporations, and by state and local governments. In addition, many investors switched from alternative investments, such as stocks, which they considered more risky following the financial crisis.

Although in 2012 interest rates on bonds remained very low, some economists and policymakers were convinced that if the federal government did not take steps to reduce the large budget deficits forecast for future years, interest rates on bonds would begin to increase to much higher levels.

Source: Peter Lattman, "Risk Builds as Junk Bonds Boom," *New York Times*, August 15, 2012.

See related problem 2.8 at the end of the chapter.

Table 4.3 summarizes the factors that shift the supply curve for bonds.

Table 4.3 Factors That Shift the Supply Curve for Bonds

All else being equal, an increase in ...	causes the supply of bonds to ...	because ...	Graph of effect on equilibrium in the bond market
expected profitability	increase	businesses borrow to finance profitable investments.	
business taxes	decrease	taxes reduce the profitability of investment.	
investment tax credits	increase	government tax credits lower the cost of investment, thereby increasing the profitability of investing.	
expected inflation	increase	at any given bond price, the real cost of borrowing falls.	
government borrowing	increase	more bonds are offered in the economy at any given interest rate.	

The Bond Market Model and Changes in Interest Rates

Movements in interest rates occur because of shifts in either the demand for bonds, the supply of bonds, or both. In this section, we consider two examples of using the bond market model to explain changes in interest rates:

1. The movement of interest rates over the *business cycle*, which refers to the alternating periods of economic expansion and economic recession experienced by the United States and most other economies

4.3

Learning Objective

Use the bond market model to explain changes in interest rates.

Figure 4.6

Interest Rate Changes in an Economic Downturn

1. From an initial equilibrium at E_1, an economic downturn reduces household wealth and decreases the demand for bonds at any bond price. The bond demand curve shifts to the left, from D_1 to D_2.

2. The fall in expected profitability reduces lenders' supply of bonds at any bond price. The bond supply curve shifts to the left, from S_1 to S_2.

3. In the new equilibrium, E_2, the bond price rises from P_1 to P_2.

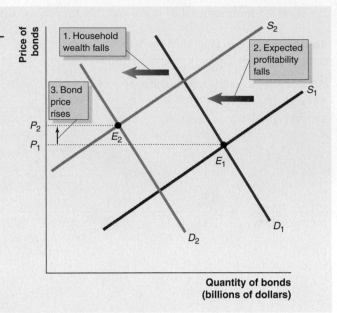

2. The *Fisher effect*, which describes the movement of interest rates in response to changes in the rate of inflation

In practice, many shifts in bond demand and bond supply occur simultaneously, and economists sometimes have difficulty determining how much each curve may have shifted.

Why Do Interest Rates Fall During Recessions?

We can illustrate changes in interest rates over the business cycle by using the bond market graph. At the beginning of an economic recession, households and firms expect that for a period of time, levels of production and employment will be lower than usual. Households will experience declining wealth, and firms will become more pessimistic about the future profitability of investing in physical capital. As Figure 4.6 shows, declining household wealth causes the demand curve for bonds to shift to the left, from D_1 to D_2, and firms' declining expectations of the profitability of investments in physical capital cause them to issue fewer bonds, which shifts the supply curve for bonds to the left, from S_1 to S_2. The figure shows that the equilibrium price of bonds rises, from P_1 to P_2. We know that an increase in the equilibrium price of bonds results in a decline in the equilibrium interest rate.

Notice that if during a recession the demand curve for bonds shifted to the left by more than the supply curve for bonds, the equilibrium price of bonds might fall and, therefore, the equilibrium interest rate might rise. Evidence from U.S. data indicates that interest rates typically fall during recessions (and rise during economic expansions), which suggests that across the business cycle, the supply curve for bonds shifts more than does the demand curve.

How Do Changes in Expected Inflation Affect Interest Rates? The Fisher Effect

Equilibrium in the bond market determines the price of bonds and the *nominal* interest rate. In fact, though, borrowers and lenders are interested in the *real* interest rate because they are concerned with the value of the payments they make or receive after adjusting for the effects of inflation. After the fact, we can compute the real interest rate by sub-tracting the inflation rate from the nominal interest rate. Because investors and firms don't know ahead of time what the inflation rate will be, they must form expectations of the inflation rate. Equilibrium in the bond market, then, should reflect the beliefs of borrowers and lenders about the *expected* real interest rate, which equals the nominal interest rate minus the *expected* inflation rate.

Irving Fisher, an economist at Yale University during the early twentieth century, argued that if equilibrium in the bond market indicated that lenders were willing to accept and borrowers were willing to pay a particular real interest rate, such as 3%, then any changes in expected inflation should cause changes in the nominal interest rate that would leave the real interest rate unchanged. For example, say that the current nominal interest rate is 5%, while the expected inflation rate is 2%. In that case, the expected real interest rate is 3%. Suppose now that investors and firms decide that the future inflation rate is likely to be 4%. Fisher argued that the result will be an increase in the nominal interest rate from 5% to 7%, which would leave the expected real interest rate unchanged, at 3%. Or, more generally, what is known as the **Fisher effect** states that *the nominal interest rate rises or falls point-for-point with changes in the expected inflation rate.*

Is the Fisher effect consistent with our understanding of how demand and supply adjust in the bond market? Figure 4.7 shows that it is. Suppose that initially participants in the bond market expect the inflation rate to be 2% and that the market is currently in equi-librium at E_1, determined by the intersection of D_1 and S_1. Now suppose that participants in the bond market come to believe that the future inflation rate will be 4%. As we have seen in the previous section, an increase in the expected inflation rate will cause the demand curve for bonds to shift to the left, from D_1 to D_2, because the expected real interest rate investors receive from owning bonds will fall for any given bond price. At the same time, an increase in the expected inflation rate will cause the supply curve to shift to the right, from S_1 to S_2, as the expected real interest rate firms pay on bonds will fall for any given bond price.

Fisher effect The assertion by Irving Fisher that the nominal interest rises or falls point-for-point with changes in the expected inflation rate.

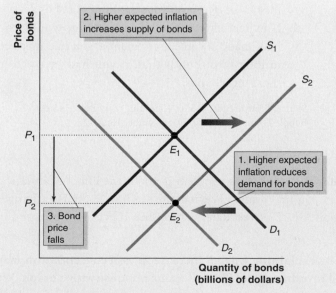

Figure 4.7

Expected Inflation and Interest Rates

1. From an initial equilibrium at E_1, an increase in expected inflation reduces investors' expected real return, reducing investors' willingness to buy bonds at any bond price. The demand curve for bonds shifts to the left, from D_1 to D_2.

2. The increase in expected inflation increases firms' willingness to issue bonds at any bond price. The supply curve for bonds shifts to the right, from S_1 to S_2.

3. In the new equilibrium, E_2, the bond price falls, from P_1 to P_2.

In response to the rise in expected inflation, both the demand curve and supply curve for bonds shift. In the new equilibrium, the price of bonds is lower, and, therefore, the nominal interest rate is higher. In the figure, the equilibrium quantity of bonds does not change because the nominal interest rate rises by an amount exactly equal to the change in expected inflation. In other words, the figure shows the Fisher effect working exactly. In practice, economists have found that various real-world frictions result in nominal interest rates not always increasing or decreasing by exactly the amount of a change in expected inflation. These real-world frictions include the payments brokers and dealers charge when buying and selling bonds for investors and the taxes investors must pay on some purchases and sales of bonds.

Even if it may not hold exactly, the Fisher effect alerts us to two important facts about the bond market:

1. Higher inflation rates result in higher nominal interest rates, and lower inflation rates result in lower nominal interest rates.
2. Changes in *expected* inflation can lead to changes in nominal interest rates before a change in *actual* inflation has occurred.

Solved Problem 4.3   **In Your Interest**

Should You Worry About Falling Bond Prices When the Inflation Rate Is Low?

A columnist in the *Wall Street Journal* offered the following opinion of the bond market in September 2012, when the inflation rate was about 2%: "Someone buying long-term bonds yielding 1.5% or 2%, and then seeing consumer price inflation of 4%, will be on the losing end of the bet."

a. Explain what will happen to the price of bonds if the expected inflation rate increases to 4% from 2%. Be sure to include in your answer a demand and supply graph of the bond market.

b. Suppose that you expect a greater increase in inflation than do other investors, but that you don't expect the increase to occur until 2015. Should you wait until 2015 to sell your bonds? Briefly explain.

c. The columnist also argued that long-term bonds would be a good investment only if "we get serious price deflation." Explain the effect on bond prices if investors decide that price deflation is likely to occur. How would an unexpected deflation affect the rate of return on your investment in bonds?

d. If expected inflation is increasing, would you have made a worse investment if you had invested in long-term bonds than if you had invested in short-term bonds?

Source: Brett Arends, "Bonds—Heading from Bull Market to Bubble?" *Wall Street Journal*, September 15, 2012.

Solving the Problem

Step 1 **Review the chapter material.** This problem is about the effect of inflation on bond prices, so you may want to review the section "How Do Changes in Expected Inflation Affect Interest Rates? The Fisher Effect," which begins on page 106.

Step 2 **Answer part (a) by explaining why an increase in expected inflation may make bonds a bad investment and illustrate your response with a graph.** We have seen in this chapter that an increase in expected inflation will affect both the demand curve and the supply curve for bonds. Your graph should show the demand curve for bonds shifting to the left, the supply curve shifting to the right, and a new equilibrium with a lower price. You will suffer capital losses if you hold bonds during a period when their prices fall.

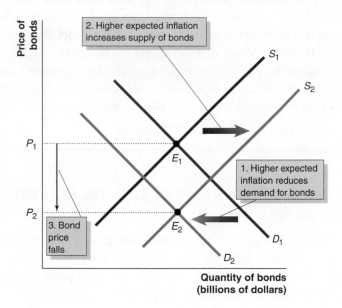

In the graph, the equilibrium price falls from P_1 to P_2, while the quantity of bonds remains unchanged, as in Figure 4.7 on page 107. Note that even if the pure Fisher effect does not hold, we know that the price of bonds will still be lower in the new equilibrium because the demand for bonds shifts to the left, and the supply of bonds shifts to the right, even if the sizes of the shifts may not be the same.

Step 3 **Answer part (b) by discussing the difference in the effects of actual and expected inflation on changes in bond prices.** *Changes* in bond prices result from *changes* in the expected rate of inflation. Current expectations of inflation are already reflected in the nominal interest rate and, therefore, in the price of bonds. For example, if buyers and sellers of bonds are willing to accept an expected real interest rate of 2%, then if the expected inflation rate is 1%, the nominal interest rate will be 3%. If buyers and sellers change their expectations, the nominal interest rate will adjust. So, if you believe that future inflation is going to be higher than other investors think, you would be wise to sell your bonds right away. Waiting for inflation to increase would mean waiting until the nominal interest rate had risen and bond prices had fallen. By then, it would be too late for you to avoid the capital losses on your bonds.

Step 4 **Answer part (c) by explaining the effect on the bond market of deflation unexpectedly occurring.** If investors come to expect deflation rather than inflation, then the expected inflation rate declines—that is, it becomes negative. The effect on the bond market is the reverse of the effect of an increase in expected inflation: The demand curve will shift to the right, and the supply curve will shift to the left. The result will be an increase in the price of bonds and a decline in the nominal interest rate. As a bond investor, you will experience a capital gain, so your rate of return will increase.

Step 5 **Answer part (d) by explaining why long-term bonds are a particularly bad investment if expected inflation increases.** An increase in expected inflation will increase the nominal interest rate on both short-term and long-term bonds. But we know that the longer the maturity of a bond, the greater the change in price as a result of a change in market interest rates (see Chapter 3). So, if expected inflation and nominal interest rates rise, your capital losses on long-term bonds will be greater than your capital losses on short-term bonds.

See related problem 3.5 at the end of the chapter.

4.4

Learning Objective

Use the loanable funds model to analyze the international capital market.

The Loanable Funds Model and the International Capital Market

In this chapter, we have analyzed the bond market from the point of view of the demand and supply for bonds. An equivalent approach focuses on *loanable funds*. In this approach, the borrower is the buyer because the borrower purchases the use of the funds. The lender is the seller because the lender provides the funds being borrowed. Although the two approaches are equivalent, the loanable funds approach is more useful when looking at the flow of funds between the U.S. and foreign financial markets. Table 4.4 summarizes the two views of the bond market.

The Demand and Supply for Loanable Funds

Figure 4.8 shows that the demand curve for bonds is equivalent to the supply curve for loanable funds. In the figure, we consider again the case of a one-year discount bond with a face value of $1,000. In panel (a), we show the demand curve for bonds, which is the same as the one we showed in Figure 4.1 on page 96 (although we have labeled it B^d rather than Demand), with the price of bonds on the vertical axis and the quantity of bonds on the horizontal axis. In panel (b), we show the supply curve for loanable funds, with the interest rate on the vertical axis and the quantity of loanable funds on the horizontal axis. Suppose in panel (a) that the price of the bond is initially $970, which

Table 4.4 Two Approaches to Analyzing the Bond Market

	Demand and supply for bonds approach	Demand and supply for loanable funds approach
What is the good?	The bond	The use of funds
Who is the buyer?	The investor (lender) who buys a bond	The firm (borrower) raising funds
Who is the seller?	The firm (borrower) who issues a bond	The investor (lender) supplying funds
What is the price?	The bond price	The interest rate

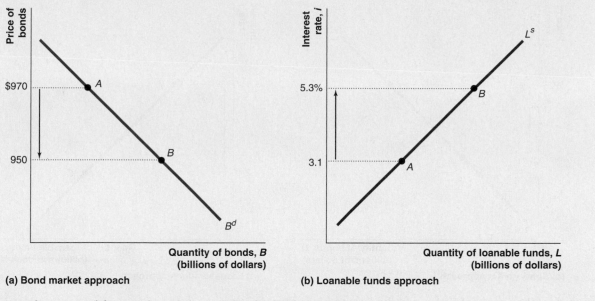

(a) Bond market approach

(b) Loanable funds approach

Figure 4.8 The Demand for Bonds and the Supply of Loanable Funds

In panel (a), the bond demand curve, B^d, shows a negative relationship between the quantity of bonds demanded by lenders and the price of bonds, all else being equal.

In panel (b), the supply curve for loanable funds, L^s, shows a positive relationship between the quantity of loanable funds supplied by lenders and the interest rate, all else being equal.

corresponds to point *A* on the demand curve for bonds. At that price, the bond will have an interest rate equal to ($1,000 − $970)/$970 = 0.031, or 3.1%, which we show as point *A* on the supply curve for loanable funds. Now suppose that the price of the bond declines to $950, which we show as point *B* on the demand curve for bonds. At this lower price, the bond will have a higher interest rate, equal to ($1,000 − $950)/$950 = 0.053, or 5.3%, which we show as point *B* on the supply curve for loanable funds. From the viewpoint of investors purchasing bonds—the bond market approach—the lower price increases the quantity of bonds demanded. Equivalently, from the viewpoint of investors providing loanable funds to borrowers—the loanable funds approach—the higher interest rate increases the quantity of loanable funds supplied.

Figure 4.9 shows that the supply curve for bonds is equivalent to the demand curve for loanable funds. In panel (a), we show the supply curve for bonds. In panel (b), we show the demand curve for loanable funds. Suppose in panel (a) that, once again, the price of the bond is initially $970, which corresponds to point *C* on the supply curve for bonds. At that price, we know that the bond will have an interest rate equal to 3.1%, which we show as point *C* on the demand curve for loanable funds. Now suppose that the price of the bond declines to $950, which we show as point *D* on the supply curve for bonds. At this lower price, the bond will have a higher interest rate, equal to 5.3%, which we show as point *D* on the demand curve for loanable funds. From the viewpoint of firms selling bonds—the bond market approach—the lower price decreases the quantity of bonds supplied. Equivalently, from the viewpoint of firms demanding loanable funds from borrowers—the loanable funds approach—the higher interest rate decreases the quantity of loanable funds demanded.

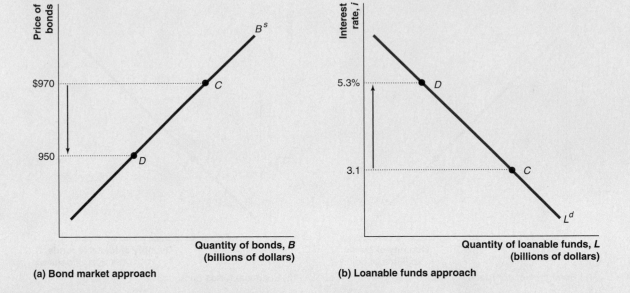

Figure 4.9 The Supply of Bonds and the Demand for Loanable Funds

In panel (a), the bond supply curve, B^s, shows a positive relationship between the quantity of bonds supplied by borrowers and the price of bonds, all else being equal.

In panel (b), the demand curve for loanable funds, L^d, shows a negative relationship between the quantity of loanable funds demanded by borrowers and the interest rate, all else being equal.

Equilibrium in the Bond Market from the Loanable Funds Perspective

Figure 4.10 shows equilibrium in the bond market using the loanable funds approach. Equilibrium occurs when the quantity of loanable funds demanded is equal to the quantity of loanable funds supplied. In the figure, we assume that the funds being traded are represented by a one-year discount bond with a face value of $1,000. The equilibrium interest rate is 4.2%, which is the interest rate on a one-year $1,000 bond with a price of $960. Notice that this analysis gives us the same interest rate as in Figure 4.1 on page 96, which reminds us that the demand and supply for bonds model and the demand and supply for loanable funds model are equivalent approaches.

Note that any of the factors that we listed on page 101 as causing the demand curve for bonds to shift will cause the supply curve for loanable funds to shift. Similarly, any of the factors that we listed on page 105 as causing the supply curve for bonds to shift will cause the demand curve for loanable funds to shift.

The International Capital Market and the Interest Rate

We have not directly taken into account how the foreign sector influences the domestic interest rate and the quantity of funds available in the domestic economy. In fact, foreign households, firms, and governments may want to lend funds to borrowers in the United States if the expected returns are higher than in other countries. Similarly, if opportunities are more profitable outside the United States, loanable funds will be drawn away from U.S. markets to investments abroad. The loanable funds approach

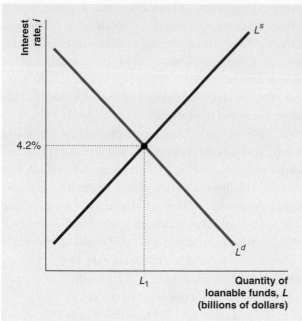

Figure 4.10

Equilibrium in the Market for Loanable Funds

At the equilibrium interest rate, the quantity of loanable funds supplied by lenders equals the quantity of loanable funds demanded by borrowers. At any interest rate below the equilibrium, there is an excess demand for loanable funds. At any interest rate above equilibrium, there is an excess supply of loanable funds. The behavior of lenders and borrowers pushes the interest rate to 4.2%.

provides a good framework for analyzing the interaction between U.S. and foreign bond markets. To keep matters simple, we assume that the interest rate is the expected real rate of interest—that is, the nominal interest rate minus the expected rate of inflation.

In a **closed economy**, households, firms, and governments do not borrow or lend internationally. In reality, nearly all economies are **open economies**, where *financial capital* (or loanable funds) is internationally mobile. Borrowing and lending take place in the *international capital market*, which is the capital market in which households, firms, and governments borrow and lend across national borders. The *world real interest rate*, r_w, is the interest rate that is determined in the international capital market. The quantity of loanable funds that is supplied in an open economy can be used to fund projects in the domestic economy or abroad. Decisions about the supply of or demand for loanable funds in small open economies, such as the economies of the Netherlands and Belgium, do not have much effect on the world real interest rate. However, shifts in the behavior of lenders and borrowers in large open economies, such as the economies of Germany and the United States, do affect the world real interest rate. In the following sections, we consider interest rate determination in each case.

Closed economy An economy in which households, firms, and governments do not borrow or lend internationally.

Open economy An economy in which households, firms, and governments borrow and lend internationally.

Small Open Economy

To this point, we have been implicitly assuming that we were analyzing a closed economy. In this type of economy, the equilibrium domestic interest rate is determined by the intersection of the demand curve and supply curve for loanable funds in the country, and we ignore the world interest rate. In an open economy, the world real interest rate is not determined by the intersection of the demand curve and supply curve of loanable funds in any one country; instead, it is determined in the international capital market.

Small open economy
An economy in which the quantity of loanable funds supplied or demanded is too small to affect the world real interest rate.

In the case of a **small open economy**, the quantity of loanable funds supplied or demanded is too small to affect the world real interest rate. So, a small open economy's domestic real interest rate equals the world real interest rate, as determined in the international capital market. For example, if the small country of Monaco, located in the south of France, had a large increase in domestic wealth, the resulting increase in loanable funds would have only a trivial effect on the total amount of loanable funds in the world and, therefore, a trivial effect on the world interest rate.

Why must the domestic interest rate in a small open economy equal the world interest rate? Suppose that the world real interest rate is 4%, but the domestic real interest rate in Monaco is 3%. A lender in Monaco would not accept an interest rate less than 4% because the lender could easily buy foreign bonds with a 4% interest rate. So, domestic borrowers would have to pay the world real interest rate of 4%, or they would be unable to borrow. Similarly, if the world real interest rate were 4%, but the domestic real interest rate in Monaco were 5%, borrowers in Monaco would borrow at the world rate of 4%. So, domestic lenders would have to lend at the world rate of 4%, or they would be unable to find anyone to lend to. This reasoning indicates why, for a small open economy, the domestic and world real interest rates must be the same.

Figure 4.11 shows the supply and demand curves for loanable funds for a small open economy. If the world real interest rate, (r_w), is 3%, the quantity of loanable funds supplied and demanded domestically are equal (point E), and the country neither lends nor borrows funds in the international capital market. Suppose instead that the world real interest rate is 5%. In this case, the quantity of loanable funds supplied domestically (point C) is greater than the quantity of funds demanded domestically (point B). What happens to the excess supply of loanable funds? They are loaned on the international

Figure 4.11

Determining the Real Interest Rate in a Small Open Economy

The domestic real interest rate in a small open economy is the world real interest rate, (r_w), which in this case is 3%.

If the world real interest rate is 5%, the quantity of loanable funds supplied domestically (point C) is greater than the quantity of loanable funds demanded domestically (point B). In this case, the country lends funds on the international capital market.

If the world real interest rate is 1%, the quantity of loanable funds supplied domestically (point D) is less than the quantity of loanable funds demanded domestically (point A). In this case, the country borrows funds on the international capital market.

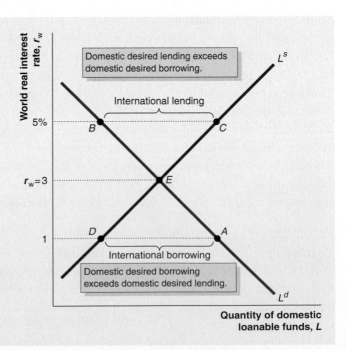

capital market at the world real interest rate of 5%. Because the country is small, the amount of funds it has to lend is small relative to the world market, so lenders in the country have no trouble finding borrowers in other countries.

Now suppose that the world real interest rate is 1%. As Figure 4.11 shows, the quantity of loanable funds demanded domestically (point A) now exceeds the quantity of funds supplied domestically (point D). How is this excess demand for funds satisfied? By borrowing on the international capital market. Because the country is small, the amount of funds it wants to borrow is small relative to the world market, so borrowers in the country have no trouble finding lenders in other countries.

We can summarize as follows: The real interest rate in a small open economy is the same as the interest rate in the international capital market. If the quantity of loanable funds supplied domestically exceeds the quantity of funds demanded domestically at that interest rate, the country invests some of its loanable funds abroad. If the quantity of loanable funds demanded domestically exceeds the quantity of funds supplied domestically at that interest rate, the country finances some of its domestic borrowing needs with funds from abroad.

Large Open Economy

Changes in the demand and supply of loanable funds in many countries—such as the United States, Japan, and Germany—are sufficiently large that they *do* affect the world real interest rate—the interest rate in the international capital market. Such countries are considered **large open economies**, which are economies large enough to affect the world real interest rate.

In the case of a large open economy, we cannot assume that the domestic real interest rate is equal to the world real interest rate. Recall that in a closed economy, the equilibrium interest rate equates the quantities of loanable funds supplied and demanded. Suppose we think of the world as two large open economies—the economy of the United States and the economy of the rest of the world. Then the real interest rate in the international capital market equates desired international lending (borrowing) by the United States with desired international borrowing (lending) by the rest of the world.

Figure 4.12 illustrates how interest rates are determined in a large open economy. The figure presents a loanable funds graph for the United States in panel (a) and a loanable funds graph for the rest of the world in panel (b). In panel (a), if the world real interest rate is 3%, the quantity of loanable funds demanded and supplied in the United States are both equal to $300 billion. However, we can see in panel (b) that at an interest rate of 3%, the quantity of loanable funds demanded in the rest of the world is $800 billion, while the quantity of loanable funds supplied is only $700 billion. This gap tells us that foreign borrowers want to borrow $100 billion more from international capital markets than is available. Foreign borrowers therefore have an incentive to offer lenders in the United States and in the rest of the world an interest rate greater than 3%.

The interest rate will rise until the excess supply of loanable funds from the United States equals the excess demand for loanable funds in the rest of the world. Figure 4.12 shows that this equality is reached when the real interest rate has risen to 4% and the excess supply of loanable funds in the United States and the excess demand for loanable funds in the rest of the world both are equal to $50 billion. In other words, at a 4% real interest rate,

Large open economy An economy in which changes in the demand and supply for loanable funds are large enough to affect the world real interest rate.

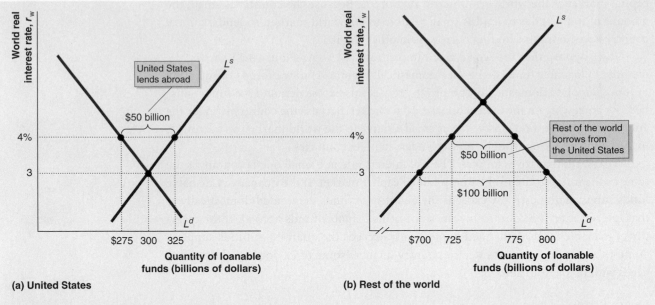

Figure 4.12 Determining the Real Interest Rate in a Large Open Economy

Saving and investment shifts in a large open economy can affect the world real interest rate. The world real interest rate adjusts to equalize desired international borrowing and desired international lending. At a world real interest rate of 4%, desired international lending by the domestic economy in panel (a) equals desired international borrowing by the rest of the world in panel (b).

desired international lending by the United States equals desired international borrowing by the rest of the world. Therefore, the international capital market is in equilibrium when the real interest rate in the United States and the rest of world equals 4%.

It's important to note that factors that cause the demand and supply of funds to shift in a large open economy will affect not just the interest rate in that economy but the world real interest rate as well.

Making the Connection

Did a Global "Saving Glut" Cause the U.S. Housing Boom?

The financial crisis of 2007–2009 was brought on by the bursting of a "bubble" in housing prices (see Chapter 1). One cause of the bubble was the increase in mortgage loans to subprime and Alt-A borrowers who prior to the 2000s would not have been able to find lenders willing to grant them mortgage loans. Some economists have argued, though, that unusually low interest rates on mortgage loans also played a role in the rapid increase in housing prices during the mid-2000s. Low interest rates increased the quantity of houses demanded, and, in particular, made it easier for investors who were speculating on future increases in house prices to buy multiple houses.

What explains the low interest rates during the 2000s? To help the U.S. economy recover from the 2001 recession, Federal Reserve policy reduced interest rates and kept them at very low levels through mid-2004. Some economists have argued that the Fed persisted in a low-interest-rate policy for too long a period, thereby fueling the housing boom. Federal Reserve Chairman Ben Bernanke has disagreed, arguing that global factors, rather than Fed policy, were most responsible for low interest rates during the early 2000s. In 2005, near the height of the housing bubble, Bernanke argued that "a significant increase in the global supply of saving—a global saving glut . . . helps to explain . . . the relatively low level of long-term interest rates in the world today." Bernanke argued that the saving glut was partly the result of high rates of saving in countries such as Japan, which had aging populations that increased their saving as they prepared for retirement. In addition, the level of global saving increased because beginning in the late 1990s, developing countries such as China and Korea increased their saving rates.

We can illustrate Bernanke's argument by using the loanable funds model for a large open economy. In the figure below, we start at equilibrium with the world real interest rate equal to 3%. In panel (a), at an interest rate of 3%, the United States is borrowing $200 billion from abroad. If the United States is borrowing $200 billion, then the rest of the world must be lending $200 billion, which is shown in panel (b). An increase in saving in the rest of the world—Bernanke's saving glut—shifts the supply curve of loanable funds to the right in panel (b). The real world interest rate begins to fall as the quantity of loanable funds that lenders in the rest of the world are willing to lend exceeds the quantity of loanable funds that borrowers in the United States are willing to borrow. The falling interest rate increases the quantity of funds demanded in the United States and decreases the quantity of funds supplied by the rest of the world. The real world interest rate declines to 1%, at which level the quantity of funds the United States borrows from abroad—$400 billion—once again equals the quantity of funds the rest of the world wishes to lend, and the international capital market is back in equilibrium.

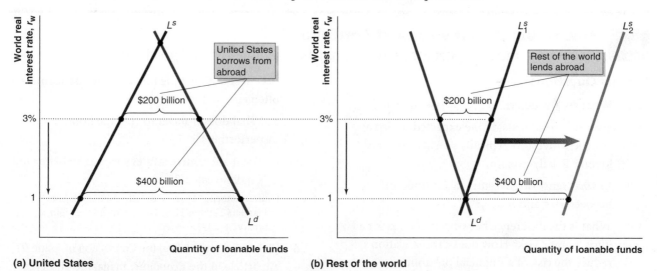

(a) United States   **(b) Rest of the world**

Some economists, notably John Taylor of Stanford University, have been skeptical of the argument that there was a significant increase in global saving during the 2000s. Taylor argues that Federal Reserve policy, rather than a global saving glut, fueled the housing bubble in the United States.

Sources: Ben S. Bernanke, "The Global Saving Glut and the U.S. Current Account Deficit," Homer Jones Lecture, April 14, 2005 (available at www.federalreserve.gov/boarddocs/speeches/2005/20050414/default.htm); and John B. Taylor, *Getting Off Track*, Stanford, CA: Hoover Institution Press, 2009.

See related problem 4.9 at the end of the chapter.

Answering the Key Question

Continued from page 87

At the beginning of this chapter, we asked:

"How do investors take into account expected inflation and other factors when making investment decisions?"

We have seen in this chapter that investors increase or decrease their demand for bonds as a result of changes in a number of factors. When expected inflation increases, investors reduce their demand for bonds because, for each nominal interest rate, the higher the inflation rate, the lower the real interest rate investors will receive. Increases in expected inflation lead to higher nominal interest rates and capital losses for investors who hold bonds in their portfolios.

Key Terms and Problems

Key Terms

Closed economy, p. 113

Diversification, p. 93

Expected return, p. 89

Fisher effect, p. 107

Idiosyncratic (or unsystematic) risk, p. 94

Large open economy, p. 115

Market (or systematic) risk, p. 94

Open economy, p. 113

Risk, p. 90

Small open economy, p. 114

4.1 ## How to Build an Investment Portfolio

Discuss the most important factors in building an investment portfolio.

Review Questions

1.1 What are the determinants of asset demand?

1.2 How do economists define expected return and risk? Are investors typically risk averse or risk loving? Briefly explain.

1.3 In what sense do investors face a trade-off between risk and return?

1.4 What is the difference between market risk and idiosyncratic risk? How does diversification reduce the risk of a financial portfolio?

Problems and Applications

1.5 An article in the *Wall Street Journal* observed that "investment pros" recommend that "individual investors spread their bets, pointing out those who bet the house on hot performers often end up losing."

a. What does it mean to "bet the house on hot performers"?

b. What alternative strategy would be better for small investors?

Source: Jonnelle Marte, "Diversification Loses Some Fans as Planners Tighten Their Focus," *Wall Street Journal*, February 21, 2012.

1.6 [**Related to the** Making the Connection **on page 91**] An article in the *Economist* magazine observes: "It is in the nature of black-swan-like events that they are near-impossible to predict." What are black swan events? Why are they nearly impossible to predict?

Source: "Not Up in the Air," *Economist*, April 20, 2010.

1.7 **[Related to the** Making the Connection **on page 94]** An article in the *Wall Street Journal* reported the advice that a financial planner offered to a young single male who had most of his savings invested in seven stocks: "Even if he doesn't plan to use the money soon, she thinks he should invest in something with less risk."

a. Why does the period of time before someone intends to use funds matter in deciding in which assets to invest the funds?

b. Why might investing all of your savings in seven stocks not be a good idea?

Source: Melissa Korn, "No Rent, No Mortgage," *Wall Street Journal*, September 10, 2012.

4.2 Market Interest Rates and the Demand and Supply for Bonds
Use a demand and supply model to determine market interest rates for bonds.

Review Questions

2.1 Why might the demand curve for bonds shift to the left? Why might the supply curve for bonds shift to the right?

2.2 Why does the supply curve for bonds slope up? Why does the demand curve for bonds slope down?

2.3 If the current price in the bond market is above the equilibrium price, explain how the bond market adjusts to equilibrium.

Problems and Applications

2.4 Briefly explain whether each of the following statements is true or false:

a. The higher the price of bonds, the greater the quantity of bonds demanded.

b. The lower the price of bonds, the smaller the quantity of bonds supplied.

c. As the wealth of investors increases, all else held constant, the interest rate on bonds should fall.

d. If investors start to believe that the U.S. government might default on its bonds, the interest rate on those bonds will fall.

2.5 For each of the following situations, explain whether the demand curve for bonds, the supply curve for bonds, or both would shift. Be sure to indicate whether the curve(s) would shift to the right or to the left.

a. The Federal Reserve publishes a forecast that the inflation rate will average 5% over the next five years. Previously, the Fed had been forecasting an inflation rate of 3%.

b. The economy experiences a period of rapid growth, with rising corporate profits.

c. The federal government runs a series of budget surpluses.

d. Investors believe that the level of risk in the stock market has declined.

e. The federal government imposes a tax of $10 per bond on bond sales and bond purchases.

2.6 Use a demand and supply graph for bonds to illustrate each of the following situations. Be sure that your graph shows any shifts in the demand or supply curves, the original equilibrium price and quantity, and the new equilibrium price and quantity. Also be sure to explain what is happening in your graphs.

a. The government runs a large deficit, holding everything else constant.

b. Households believe that future tax payments will be higher than current tax payments, so they increase their saving.

c. Both (a) and (b) occur.

2.7 Many economists assume that a boom in stock prices is a sign that profitable business opportunities are expected in the future. Use a demand and supply graph for bonds to show

---

the effect of a boom in stock prices on the equilibrium interest rate.

2.8 [Related to the Making the Connection **on page 104**] Writing in the *Wall Street Journal*, economists Jeremy Siegel and Jeremy Schwartz made the following prediction: "We believe that when investors awake from their depressed state, they will realize that they don't have to lend the U.S. government money for 10 years at a negative real yield."

a. By "negative real yield" did Siegel and Schwartz mean that the nominal interest rate on 10-year Treasury notes was negative? Briefly explain.

b. In 2012, why were investors willing to accept a negative real yield on 10-year Treasury notes?

Source: Jeremy J. Siegel and Jeremy Schwartz, "The Bond Bubble and the Case for Stocks," *Wall Street Journal*, August 22, 2012.

4.3 | ## The Bond Market Model and Changes in Interest Rates
Use the bond market model to explain changes in interest rates.

Review Questions

3.1 Briefly explain what typically happens to interest rates during a recession. Use a demand and supply graph for bonds to illustrate your answer.

3.2 How will the bond market adjust to an increase in the expected inflation rate? Use a demand and supply graph for bonds to illustrate your answer.

Problems and Applications

3.3 Explain what will happen to the equilibrium price and equilibrium quantity of bonds in each of the following situations. (If it is uncertain in which direction either the equilibrium price or equilibrium quantity will change, explain why.)

a. Wealth in the economy increases at the same time that Congress raises the corporate income tax.

b. The economy experiences a business cycle expansion.

c. The expected rate of inflation decreases.

d. The federal government runs a budget deficit.

3.4 In 2012, Spain had what the *Wall Street Journal* described as a "towering budget deficit." When the Spanish government had difficulty selling bonds to investors, the European Central Bank announced that it would begin buying these bonds. As a result, private investors increased their demand for Spanish bonds, and the interest rate on Spanish bonds fell from 5.75% to 3.87%.

Use a demand and supply graph for the bond market to illustrate why despite large government budget deficits, the interest rate on Spanish government bonds declined.

Source: Emese Bartha, Neelabh Chaturvedi, and Jonathan House, "Spain Clears Funding Hurdle with Bond Sale," *Wall Street Journal*, September 20, 2012.

3.5 [Related to the Solved Problem 4.3 **on page 108**] In 2012, an article in the *Economist* magazine recommended to investors that if economic growth and inflation remained low in the United States, the investors should buy bonds. But if inflation accelerated rapidly, investors should "buy commodities, especially gold."

a. Why would bonds be a good investment in a period of low growth and low inflation?

b. Why would bonds be a poor investment in a period of high inflation?

Source: "Ben Buys, Bulls Buoyant," *Economist*, September 22, 2012.

3.6 [Related to the Chapter Opener **on page 87**] An article in the *New York Times* in 2012 observed:

Older Americans and other savers are just unintended casualties of policies aimed at other economic targets, particularly the policy making it easier for consumers and companies to borrow.

a. What policies have made it easier for consumers and companies to borrow?

b. How have these policies made casualties of older Americans and other savers? Why would older Americans in particular be casualties?

Source: Catherine Rampell, "As Low Rates Depress Savers, Governments Reap Benefits," *New York Times*, September 10, 2012.

4.4 The Loanable Funds Model and the International Capital Market
Use the loanable funds model to analyze the international capital market.

Review Questions

4.1 Compare the bond market approach to the loanable funds approach by explaining the following for each approach.

a. What the good is

b. Who the buyer is

c. Who the seller is

d. What the price is

4.2 In the loanable funds model, why is the demand curve downward sloping? Why is the supply curve upward sloping?

4.3 When are economists most likely to use the bond market approach to analyze changes in interest rates? When are economists most likely to use the loanable funds approach?

Problems and Applications

4.4 The federal government in the United States has been running very large budget deficits.

a. Use the loanable funds approach to show the effect of the U.S. budget deficit on the world real interest rate, holding everything else constant.

b. Now suppose that households believe that deficits will be financed by higher taxes in the near future, and households increase their saving in anticipation of paying those higher taxes. Briefly explain how your analysis in part (a) will be affected.

4.5 Suppose that in a large open economy, the quantity of loanable funds supplied domestically is initially equal to the quantity of funds demanded domestically. Then an increase in business taxes discourages investment. Show how this change affects the quantity of loanable funds and the world real interest rate. Does the economy now borrow or lend internationally?

4.6 In a large open economy, how would each of the following events affect the equilibrium interest rate?

a. A natural disaster causes extensive damage to homes, bridges, and highways, leading to increased investment spending to repair the damaged infrastructure.

b. Taxes on businesses are expected to be increased in the future.

c. The World Cup soccer matches are being televised, and many people stay home to watch them rather than spending time shopping, thereby reducing consumption.

d. The government proposes a new tax on saving, based on the value of people's investments as of December 31 each year.

4.7 How would the following events affect the demand for loanable funds in the United States?

a. Many U.S. cities increase business taxes to help close their budget deficits.

b. Widespread use of tablet computers helps reduce business costs.

c. The government eliminates the tax deduction for interest that homeowners pay on mortgage loans.

4.8 An article in the *Economist* magazine in 2012 observed: "America can now borrow from the bond market at a cheaper rate than at any time in the history of the republic." Use the loanable funds model to analyze how this statement could be true even though the United States was running a large budget deficit in 2012.

Source: "To Strive, to Seek, to Find, and Not to Yield," *Economist*, June 30, 2012.

4.9 [Related to the Making the Connection **on page 116**] We have seen that Federal Reserve Chairman Ben Bernanke has argued that low interest rates in the United States during the mid-2000s were due to a global savings glut rather than to Federal Reserve policy. In an interview with Albert Hunt of Bloomberg Television, Alan Greenspan, who was Federal Reserve Chairman from August 1987 through January 2006, made a similar argument. Greenspan argued:

Behind the low level of long-term rates: a global savings glut as China, Russia and other emerging market economies earned more money on exports than they could easily invest.

a. Use two loanable funds graphs to illustrate Greenspan's argument that a global savings glut caused low interest rates in the United States. One graph should illustrate the situation in the United States, and the other graph should illustrate the situation in the rest of the world.

b. Why should a debate over the cause of low interest rates matter to Alan Greenspan?

Source: Rich Miller and Josh Zumbrun, "Greenspan Takes Issue with Yellen on Fed's Role in House Bubble," bloomberg. com, March 27, 2010.

Data Exercises

D4.1: [The bond market and recessions] Go to the web site of the Federal Reserve Bank of St. Louis (FRED) (research.stlouisfed.org/fred2/) and download and graph the data series for the 10-year U.S. Treasury note (GS10) from January 1954 until the most recent month available. Go to the Web site of the National Bureau of Economic Research (nber. org) and find the dates for business cycle peaks and troughs. (The period between a business cycle peak and trough is a recession.) Describe how the interest rate on the 10-year note moves just before, during, and just after a recession. Is the pattern the same across recessions?

D4.2: [Comparing movements in interest rates across countries] Go to the Web site of the Federal Reserve Bank of St. Louis (FRED) (research. stlouisfed.org/fred2/) and download to the same graph the following data series from January 1957 until the most recent available month: (1) the interest rate on the 20-year U.S. Treasury note (GS20) and (2) the interest rate for 20-year UK government securities (INTGSBGGM193N). During which periods has the interest rate on

long-term UK government bonds been higher than the interest rate on long-term U.S. government bonds? What has been the relationship between the two interest rates since 1995?

D4.3: [Analyzing saving and investment] Go to the web site of the Federal Reserve Bank of St. Louis (FRED) (research.stlouisfed.org/fred2/) and find the most recent values and the values from the same quarter three years earlier for Gross Private Saving (GPSAVE) and Gross Government Saving (GGSAVE).

a. Using these values, calculate the total gross saving in the economy for each period.

b. Draw a graph to show the loanable funds market in equilibrium. Explain which curve represents total gross saving.

c. On the graph drawn in part (b), show the effect on the loanable funds market from the change in total gross saving between the two periods in part (a).

D4.4: [Analyzing saving and investment] Go to the web site of the Federal Reserve Bank of St. Louis (FRED) (research.stlouisfed.org/fred2/) and find the most recent value and the value from the same quarter four years earlier for Gross Government Saving (GGSAVE).

a. Total gross saving in the economy is composed of gross private saving and gross government saving. What does gross government saving represent?

b. Using the values you found, explain whether the government budget was balanced, in a surplus, or in a deficit during these two quarters. From the first period to the most recent period, has government saving increased, decreased, or remained constant?

c. Draw a graph to show the loanable funds market in equilibrium. Assuming gross private saving remains constant and given your answer in part (b), show the effect on the loanable funds market. Explain what will happen to the level of investment in the economy.

D4.5: [Find data on expected inflation from bond yields]
 Go to the web site of the Federal Reserve Bank of St. Louis (FRED) (research.stlouisfed.org/fred2/) and find the most recent values and values from the same month five years earlier for the 10-Year Treasury Constant Maturity Rate (GS10), and the 10-Year Treasury Inflation-Indexed Security, Constant Maturity (FII10). Using these data, explain what has happened to expected inflation between these two periods.

CHAPTER 5

The Risk Structure and Term Structure of Interest Rates

Learning Objectives

After studying this chapter, you should be able to:

5.1 Explain why bonds with the same maturity can have different interest rates (pages 125–137)

5.2 Explain why bonds with different maturities can have different interest rates (pages 137–151)

Searching for Yield

Low interest rates are great if you are borrowing money but not so great if you are trying to live on interest received from bank certificates of deposit (CDs) or other bank savings accounts. In 2006, Citibank was advertising CDs with annual interest rates of 5%. In 2012, Citibank paid an annual interest rate of only 0.25% on a CD that would mature in one year. Even if you were willing to tie up your money by buying a five-year CD, you would receive an interest rate of just 0.75%.

Bank CDs and other savings accounts are only a small percentage of total household wealth. But many retired people rely on CDs and similar accounts for income because they are reluctant to invest in assets, such as stocks and bonds, whose prices may fall. Similarly, many young people saving for a wedding or to buy a car or a house see investing in CDs as a safe way to accumulate the funds. In 2012, savers owned $680 billion of bank CDs and $6,400 billion of other bank savings accounts. The difference in interest income received with an interest rate of 0.25% rather than an interest rate of 5% is more than $325 billion per year—a substantial amount for the people who rely on income from this source.

Why were interest rates so low? The recession of 2007–2009 was the worst since the Great Depression. In response to the recession, the Federal Reserve took steps to reduce short-term nominal interest rates nearly to zero. The Fed routinely reduces short-term interest rates when the economy enters a recession. But never before had the Fed driven interest rates so low or kept them at low levels for such a long time. In the fall of 2012, the Fed announced its intention to keep short-term interest rates near zero into 2015—or more than six years after the end of the recession. Fed Chairman Ben Bernanke was aware of the hardship low interest

Continued on next page

Key Issue and Question

Issue: During the financial crisis, the bond rating agencies were criticized for having given high ratings to securities that proved to be very risky.

Question: Should the government more closely regulate the credit rating agencies?

Answered on page 151

rates were inflicting on some savers but argued that the favorable effect that low interest rates would have on the economy more than offset this hardship:

> My colleagues and I are very much aware that holders of interest-bearing assets, such as certificates of deposit, are receiving very low returns. But low interest rates also support the value of many other assets that Americans own, such as homes and businesses large and small. Indeed, in general, healthy investment returns cannot be sustained in a weak economy, and of course it is difficult to save for retirement or other goals without the income from a job. Thus, while low interest rates do impose some costs, Americans will ultimately benefit most from the healthy and growing economy that low interest rates help promote.

Faced with such low interest rates on bank savings accounts, many investors searched for ways to earn more income from their savings. But to earn significantly higher interest rates, savers needed to consider buying either long-term bonds or bonds with relatively high default risk. So-called junk bonds, issued by corporations that financial analysts believe have significant default risk, attracted large numbers of investors searching for higher interest rates. In fact, demand for junk bonds was so great that by the fall of 2012, even interest rates on these bonds had reached record lows.

How should investors balance taking on additional risk as they search for higher interest rates? In this chapter, we explore the relationships among the many different interest rates in the economy to answer this question.

Sources: Board of Governors of the Federal Reserve System, "Transcript of Chairman Bernanke's Press Conference, September 13, 2012," September 13, 2012; Patrick McGee and Katy Burne, "Junk-Bond Yields Hit All-Time Low," *Wall Street Journal*, September 7, 2012; and Gretchen Morgenson, "0.2% Interest? You Bet We'll Complain," *New York Times*, March 3, 2012.

To this point, we have simplified our discussion of the bond market by assuming that there is a single type of bond and that the market for that bond determined the interest rate. That simplification was useful in letting us analyze the factors that affect the demand and supply for all bonds. In this chapter, we look more closely at the bond market by analyzing why interest rates on bonds differ and what causes interest rates to change over time.

We look first at the *risk structure of interest rates*, which explains differences in yields across bonds with the same maturity. Then we turn to the *term structure of interest rates*, which explains why bond yields vary according to their time to maturity. Economists use both types of analyses to forecast future movements in the yields on individual bonds as well as market interest rates.

The Risk Structure of Interest Rates

Why might bonds that have the same maturities—for example, all the bonds that will mature in 30 years—have different interest rates, or yields to maturity?

Bonds that have the same maturity may differ with respect to other characteristics that investors believe are important, such as risk, liquidity, information costs, and taxation. Bonds with more favorable characteristics have lower interest rates because investors are willing to accept lower expected returns on those bonds. Similarly, bonds with less favorable characteristics have higher interest rates because investors require higher expected returns on those bonds. Economists use the term **risk structure of interest rates** to describe the relationship among the interest rates on bonds that have different characteristics but the same maturities.

5.1

Learning Objective
Explain why bonds with the same maturity can have different interest rates.

Risk structure of interest rates The relationship among interest rates on bonds that have different characteristics but the same maturity.

Default Risk

Default risk (or credit risk) The risk that a bond issuer will fail to make payments of interest or principal.

Bonds differ with respect to **default risk** (sometimes called **credit risk**), which is the risk that a bond issuer will fail to make payments of interest or principal. For example, suppose that a bond issued by Ford Motor Company and a bond issued by cookie maker Mrs. Fields Famous Brands have the same maturity, but Mrs. Fields has a higher default risk. In this case, the Mrs. Fields bond will have a higher interest rate than the Ford bond.

Measuring Default Risk To determine the default risk on a bond, investors use U.S. Treasury bonds as a benchmark because they are considered to have zero default risk. We can assume that U.S. Treasury bonds have zero default risk because the U.S. government guarantees that it will make all principal and interest payments. Of course, like all other bonds, U.S. Treasury bonds are subject to interest-rate risk.

The *default risk premium* on a bond is the difference between the interest rate on the bond and the interest rate on a Treasury bond that has the same maturity. We can think of the default risk premium as being the additional yield that an investor requires for holding a bond with some default risk. For example, if you were willing to buy a 30-year Treasury bond with an interest rate of 3%, but you would buy a 30-year bond issued by IBM only if it had an interest rate of 5% because the IBM bond carries some default risk, then the default risk premium on the IBM bond is 5% − 3% = 2%.

Investors require a higher default risk premium the greater they believe the probability is that the bond's issuer will fail to make the payments on the bond. The cost of acquiring information on a bond issuer's *creditworthiness*, or ability to repay, can be high. As a result, many investors rely on *credit rating agencies*—such as Moody's Investors Service, Standard & Poor's Corporation, or Fitch Ratings—to provide them with information on the creditworthiness of corporations and governments that issue bonds. A **bond rating** is a single statistic that summarizes a rating agency's view of the issuer's likely ability to make the required payments on its bonds.

Bond rating A single statistic that summarizes a rating agency's view of the issuer's likely ability to make the required payments on its bonds.

Table 5.1 shows the ratings of the three largest credit rating agencies. The higher the rating, the lower the default risk. Bonds receiving one of the top four ratings are considered to be "investment grade," which means they have low to moderate levels of default risk. Bonds receiving one of the lower ratings are called "non-investment grade," "speculative," "high yield," or "junk bonds." These bonds have high levels of default risk. The rating agencies make their ratings publicly available and update them as the creditworthiness of issuers changes. For example, in 2011, Standard & Poor's cut its rating on long-term U.S. government debt from AAA to AA + because it believed that if the federal government continued to run very large annual budget deficits, the government would have to issue so many U.S. Treasury bonds that investors would begin to question the government's ability to continue to make the interest and principal payments on the bonds. In other words, Standard & Poor's no longer considered U.S. Treasury bonds to be free of default risk. In 2012, Moody's issued a warning that it might also lower its ratings of Treasury bonds if Congress and the president failed to arrive at an agreement that would reduce future budget deficits. Note that the rating agencies are offering *opinions*. Investors in financial markets may disagree with these opinions. In the case of Treasury bonds, investors did not seem any more worried about default risk after Standard & Poor's lowered its rating than they had been before.

Table 5.1 Interpreting Bond Ratings

	Moody's Investors Service	Standard & Poor's (S&P)	Fitch Ratings	Meaning of the ratings
Investment-grade bonds	Aaa	AAA	AAA	Highest credit quality
	Aa	AA	AA	Very high credit quality
	A	A	A	High credit quality
	Baa	BBB	BBB	Good credit quality
Non-investment-grade bonds	Ba	BB	BB	Speculative
	B	B	B	Highly speculative
	Caa	CCC	CCC	Substantial default risk
	Ca	CC	CC	Very high levels of default risk
	C	C	C	Exceptionally high levels of default risk
	—	D	D	Default

Note: The entries in the "Meaning of the ratings" column are slightly modified from those that Fitch uses. The other two rating agencies have similar descriptions. For each rating from Aa to Caa, Moody's adds a numerical modifier of 1, 2, or 3. The rating Aa1 is higher than the rating Aa2, and the rating Aa2 is higher than the rating Aa3. Similarly, Standard & Poor's and Fitch Ratings add a plus (+) or minus (−) sign. The rating AA + is higher than the rating AA, and the rating AA is higher than the rating AA −.

Sources: Moody's Investors Service, *Rating Symbols and Definitions*, September 2012; Fitch Ratings, *Definitions of Ratings and Other Forms of Opinion*, August 2012; and Standard & Poor's, *Standard and Poor's Ratings Definitions*, June 22, 2012.

Changes in Default Risk and in the Default Risk Premium How does a change in default risk affect the interest rate on a bond? If the rating agencies believe that a firm's ability to make payments on a bond has declined, they will give the bond a lower rating. If investors agree with the lower rating, they will demand a smaller quantity of the bond at any given price, so the demand curve for the bond will shift to the left. If the demand curve shifts to the left, the price of the bond will fall, and its yield will rise (see Chapter 4). For example, Bon-Ton Department Stores issued a bond that initially had an interest rate of 10.25%. But by September 2012, all three rating agencies had given the bond a non-investment-grade, or "junk," rating because they believed there was a significant probability that Bon-Ton would not make the remaining payments on the bond. As a result, the demand for the bond declined, and the price fell from $1,000 to

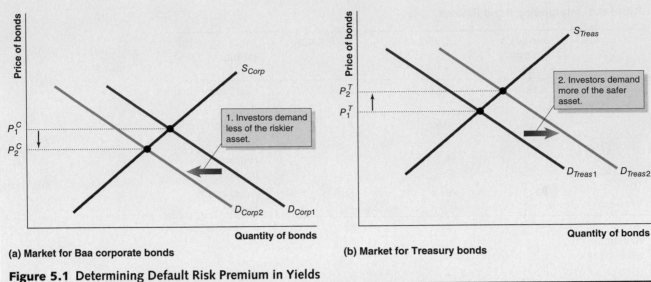

(a) Market for Baa corporate bonds

(b) Market for Treasury bonds

Figure 5.1 Determining Default Risk Premium in Yields

We can see the initial default risk premium by comparing yields associated with the prices P_1^T to P_1^C. Because the price of the safer U.S. Treasury bond is greater than that of the riskier corporate bond, we know that the yield on the corporate bond must be greater than the yield on the Treasury bond to compensate investors for bearing risk. As the default risk on corporate bonds increases, in panel (a), the demand for corporate bonds shifts to the left, from D_{Corp1} to D_{Corp2}. In panel (b), the demand for Treasury bonds shifts to the right, from D_{Treas1} to D_{Treas2}. The price of corporate bonds falls from P_1^C to P_2^C, and the price of Treasury bonds rises from P_1^T to P_2^T, so the yield on Treasury bonds falls relative to the yield on corporate bonds. Therefore, the default risk premium has increased.

$660. At such a low price, the bond's yield to maturity was 32.3%. Investors were requiring a great deal of extra return to compensate them for the high level of risk on the bond. In other words, the bond's default risk premium had soared.

Investors can decide that default risk has increased for a whole category of bonds. For instance, during recessions, the default risk on corporate bonds typically increases, which can cause a *flight to quality*. A flight to quality involves investors decreasing their demand for higher-risk bonds and increasing their demand for lower-risk bonds. Figure 5.1 illustrates this process. Panel (a) shows the market for Baa-rated corporate bonds. Typically during a recession, as corporate profits decline, investors conclude that the probability that firms will make their bond payments has decreased. As a result, the demand curve for Baa-rated corporate bonds shifts to the left, causing the equilibrium price to fall from P_1^C to P_2^C. Panel (b) shows that investor concerns about increasing default risk causes the demand curve for U.S. Treasury bonds to shift to the right. The equilibrium price increases from P_1^T to P_2^T. Because the price of corporate bonds is falling, the yield to maturity on corporate bonds is rising. And because the price of Treasury bonds is increasing, the yield on Treasury bonds is falling. Therefore, the size of the default risk premium is increasing.

Figure 5.2 shows the spread between the average interest rate on Baa-rated corporate bonds and the interest rate on Treasury bonds from January 1999 to August 2012. The two shaded areas show the recessions of 2001 and 2007–2009. For the 2001 recession, the figure shows a fairly typical pattern, with the spread rising from about 2 percentage

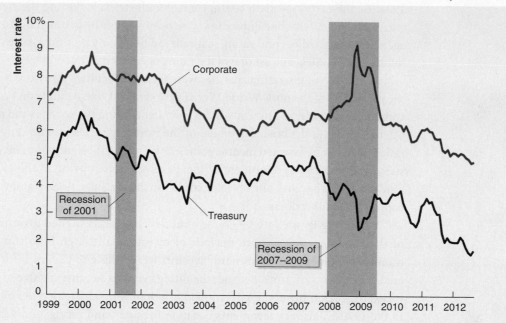

Figure 5.2 Rising Default Premiums During Recessions

The default premium typically rises during a recession. For the 2001 recession, the figure shows a fairly typical pattern, with the spread between the interest rate on corporate bonds and the interest rate on Treasury bonds rising from about 2 percentage points before the recession to more than 3 percentage points during the recession. For the 2007–2009 recession, the increase in the default risk premium was much larger. It rose from less than

2 percentage points before the recession began to more than 6 percentage points at the height of the financial crises in the fall of 2008.

Note: The corporate bond rate is for Baa-rated bonds. The Treasury bond rate is for 10-year Treasury notes.

Source: Federal Reserve Bank of St. Louis.

points before the recession to more than 3 percentage points during the recession. For the 2007–2009 recession, the figure shows that the increase in the default risk premium was much larger. The spread between the corporate bond and Treasury bond rates rose from less than 2 percentage points before the recession began to more than 6 percentage points at the height of the financial crisis in the fall of 2008, before falling back below 3 percentage points during the fall of 2009. As Figure 5.1 predicts, the increase in the risk premium was due to both the corporate bond rate increasing and the Treasury bond rate falling: The average interest rate on the Baa-rated corporate bonds rose from less than 6.5% in mid-2007 to nearly 9.5% in October 2008, while the interest rate on Treasury bonds fell from 5.0% in mid-2007 to less than 3.0% in late 2008.

Making the Connection

Do Credit Rating Agencies Have a Conflict of Interest?

The railroads in the nineteenth century were the first firms in the United States to issue large quantities of bonds. John Moody began the modern bond rating business by publishing *Moody's Analyses of Railroad Investments* in 1909. The firm that later became

Standard & Poor's began publishing ratings in 1916. Fitch Ratings began publishing in 1924. By the early twentieth century, many industries, including the steel, petroleum, chemical, and automobile industries, were raising funds by issuing bonds, and the rating agencies expanded beyond rating just railroad bonds. By that time, firms had difficulty selling bonds unless at least one of the rating agencies had rated them.

By the 1970s, the rating agencies were facing difficulties for two key reasons. First, the prosperity of the post–World War II period meant that defaults on bond issues were comparatively rare, so fewer investors were demanding the services the rating agencies offered. Second, the business model of the rating agencies was no longer viable. The rating agencies had earned income primarily by selling their ratings to investors through subscriptions. The development of inexpensive photocopying in the 1970s made this model difficult because one investor could purchase a subscription and then sell or give copies to nonsubscribers.

Beginning in the late 1970s, several developments turned around the fortunes of the rating agencies. First, periods of recession and high inflation increased the number of bond defaults, so more investors were willing to pay for information on the creditworthiness of firms. Second, the rating agencies became involved in rating bonds issued by foreign firms and governments, both of which increased in volume beginning in the 1970s. Third, governments began to include bond ratings in their regulation of banks, mutual funds, and other financial firms. For instance, many mutual funds are required to hold only highly rated bonds. Finally, the rating agencies began to charge the firms and governments—rather than investors—for their services.

The last change raised the question of whether rating agencies face a conflict of interest. Because firms issuing bonds can choose which of the agencies to hire to rate their bonds, the agencies may have an incentive to give higher ratings than might be justified in order to keep the firms' business. It became common for the agencies to provide bond issuers with "preview ratings" before the issuers agreed to hire the agencies. During the housing boom, investment banks issued many mortgage-backed bonds and other complex securities. When the housing market crashed, many of these securities plunged in value, despite having high ratings from the rating agencies. More than 90% of mortgage-backed securities issued during 2006 and 2007 that received AAA ratings later defaulted or were eventually given junk ratings. Some economists and policymakers believed the rating agencies provided the high ratings primarily to ensure that the firms would continue to hire them. Many of the mortgage-backed securities had complicated structures. Some reports indicated that analysts at the rating agencies were reluctant to push issuers of these securities for sufficient information to rate the securities accurately because the analysts were afraid that doing so might offend the issuers. Some investors, including the managers of a number of state government pension plans, sued the rating agencies on the grounds that they had not carried out their responsibility to investors to provide accurate ratings. Other economists and policymakers were less critical of the agencies, arguing that they could not have anticipated how severe the housing crisis would be or the extent to which the crisis would affect the values of mortgage-backed securities.

In 2010, Congress passed the Wall Street Reform and Consumer Protection Act, or Dodd-Frank Act, which included provisions that affected the regulation of credit rating agencies. A new Office of Credit Ratings was created within the Securities and Exchange Commission (SEC) to oversee the agencies. The act put new restrictions on conflicts of interest at the rating agencies, authorized investors to bring lawsuits if an agency could be shown to have failed to gather sufficient information to properly rate a security, and gave the SEC the authority to deregister an agency that had provided inaccurate ratings over time. Critics of the regulations argued that they had not gone far enough in limiting the conflicts of interest at the rating agencies. The ultimate effect of the new regulations, though, remained uncertain.

Sources: Edward Wyatt, "S.E.C Faults Credit Raters, but Doesn't Name Them," *New York Times*, September 30, 2011; Anusha Shrivastava, "Bond Sales? Don't Quote Us, Request Credit Firms," *Wall Street Journal*, July 21, 2010; David Segal, "Debt Raters Avoid Overhaul After Crisis," *New York Times*, December 8, 2009; and Richard Sylla, "An Historical Primer on the Business of Credit Rating," in Richard M. Levich et al., eds., *Ratings, Rating Agencies, and the Global Financial System*, Boston: Kluwer Academic Publishers, 2002.

See related problem 1.10 at the end of the chapter.

Liquidity and Information Costs

In addition to differences in default risk, differences in liquidity and information costs also lead to differences in interest rates. Because investors care about liquidity, they are willing to accept a lower interest rate on more liquid investments than on less liquid— or *illiquid*—investments, all other things being equal. So, investors expect to receive a higher return on an illiquid bond to compensate them for sacrificing liquidity.

Similarly, investors care about the costs of acquiring information on a bond. Spending time and money acquiring information on a bond reduces the bond's expected return. Not surprisingly, if two assets appear otherwise the same, an investor will prefer to hold the one with lower information costs. So, investors will accept a lower expected return on assets with lower costs for acquiring information than they will on a bond with higher costs for acquiring information.

An increase in a bond's liquidity or a decrease in the cost of acquiring information about the bond will increase the demand for the bond. In a bond market graph, the demand curve will shift to the right, increasing the bond's price and decreasing the bond's interest rate. Similarly, if a bond's liquidity declines or if the cost of acquiring information about the bond increases, the demand for the bond will decline. During the financial crisis of 2007–2009, many investors became reluctant to buy mortgage-backed bonds because homeowners were defaulting on many of the mortgages contained in the bonds. To make matters worse, investors came to realize that they did not fully understand these bonds and had difficulty finding information about the types of mortgages the bonds contained. We can illustrate this situation in a bond market graph by shifting the demand curve to the left, which will decrease the bond's price and increase the bond's interest rate.

Tax Treatment

Investors receive interest income in the form of coupon payments on bonds. Investors must include these coupons in their income when paying their taxes. The tax paid on the coupons differs, depending on who issued the bond. The tax also varies depending on where the investor lives. Investors care about the *after-tax return* on their investments—that is, the return the investors have left after paying their taxes. For example, consider two bonds each with $1,000 face values and 6% coupon rates, meaning they pay coupons of $60 per year. Suppose that on the first bond, issued by Ford, the investor has to pay a 40% tax on the coupon received. On the second bond, issued by the U.S. Treasury, the investor pays only a 25% tax on the coupon received. So, after paying taxes, the investor will have only $36 left from the $60 coupon on the Ford bond but $45 left on the Treasury bond. If the investor paid $1,000 for each bond, then, ignoring any capital gains or losses during the year, the investor will have received an after-tax return of $45/$1,000 = 0.045, or 4.5%, on the Treasury bond, but only $36/$1,000 = 0.036, or 3.6%, on the Ford bond. If the investor considered the risk, liquidity, and information costs of the two bonds to be the same, the investor would clearly prefer the higher after-tax return on the Treasury bond.

How the Tax Treatment of Bonds Differs We can consider three categories of bonds: corporate bonds, U.S. Treasury bonds, and **municipal bonds**, which are bonds issued by state and local governments. The coupons on corporate bonds can be subject to federal, state, and local taxes. The coupons on Treasury bonds are subject to federal tax but not to state or local taxes. The coupons on municipal bonds are typically not subject to federal, state, or local taxes. The tax situation for corporate bonds is somewhat complex because eight states have no state income tax. Some local governments also have no income tax, or they tax wage and salary income but not income from investments. Table 5.2 summarizes the tax situation for the three types of bonds.

Recall that bond investors can receive two types of income from owning bonds: (1) interest income from coupons and (2) capital gains (or losses) from price changes on the bonds. Interest income is taxed at the same rates as wage and salary income. In 2012, capital gains were taxed at a lower rate than interest income, although Congress was considering proposals to change this aspect of the tax code. Capital gains are also taxed only if they are *realized*, which means that the investor sells the bond for a higher price than he or she paid for it. *Unrealized* capital gains are not taxed. For instance, if you buy a bond for $800, and its price rises to $900, you have a taxable realized capital gain if you sell the bond; if you don't sell it, you have an unrealized gain, which is not taxed. Postponing the time when you pay capital gains tax has benefits because the further in the future you pay the tax, the lower the present value of the tax. Although interest income on municipal bonds is exempt from income tax, realized capital gains on these bonds are taxable.

Municipal bonds Bonds issued by state and local governments.

Table 5.2 Tax Treatment of Bond Coupon Payments

Type of bond	Taxed by state and local governments?	Taxed by the federal government?
Corporate bond	Taxed by most states and some cities	Yes
U.S. Treasury bond	No	Yes
Municipal bond	No	No

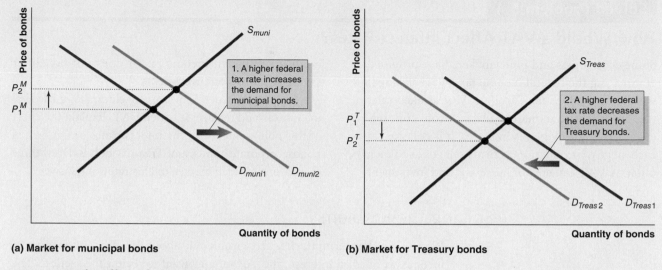

Figure 5.3 The Effect of Changes in Taxes on Bond Prices

If the federal income tax rate increases, tax-exempt municipal bonds will be more attractive to investors, and Treasury bonds will be less attractive. In panel (a), the demand curve for municipal bonds shifts to the right, from D_{Muni1} to D_{Muni2}, increasing the price from P_1^M to P_2^M and lowering the interest rate. In panel (b), the demand curve for Treasury bonds shifts to the left, from D_{Treas1} to D_{Treas2}, lowering the price from P_1^T to P_2^T and raising the interest rate.

The Effect of Tax Changes on Interest Rates We have seen that investors are interested in the after-tax return they receive on bonds and that tax rates on bonds differ according to the type of bond. So, a change in income tax rates will affect interest rates.

Figure 5.3 shows how a change in the federal income tax rate affects the interest rates on municipal bonds and Treasury bonds. We assume that initially the federal income tax rate is 35%. Panel (a) shows the market for municipal bonds, and panel (b) shows the market for Treasury bonds. The equilibrium price in panel (a), P_1^M, is higher than the equilibrium price in panel (b), P_1^T, which is the usual situation where the interest rate on municipal bonds is lower than the interest rate on Treasury bonds. Now suppose that the federal income tax rate rises to 45%. This higher tax rate will make the tax-exempt status of municipal bonds even more attractive to investors, and at the same time, it will reduce the after-tax return on Treasury bonds. In panel (a), the demand curve for municipal bonds shifts to the right, from D_{Muni1} to D_{Muni2}, increasing the price from P_1^M to P_2^M and lowering the interest rate. In panel (b), the demand curve for Treasury bonds shifts to the left, from D_{Treas1} to D_{Treas2}, lowering the price from P_1^T to P_2^T and raising the interest rate. If we assume that investors see the two bonds as having the same characteristics, other than the tax treatment of their coupons, then after the increase in the tax rate, the interest rates on the bonds should adjust until investors receive the same after-tax yield on both bonds. From this analysis, we can conclude that an increase in income tax rates will tend to raise the interest rate on Treasury bonds and lower the interest rate on municipal bonds.

Solved Problem 5.1

How Would a VAT Affect Interest Rates?

Some economists and policymakers have proposed eliminating the federal income tax and replacing it with a value-added tax (VAT). A VAT is like a sales tax, but rather than being collected from consumers when they buy goods in stores, it is collected at each stage of production as firms sell goods to each other. A VAT can encourage saving and investment because, unlike an income tax, it does not tax either saving or returns on investments.

Suppose the federal government eliminates the federal income tax and replaces it with a VAT. Explain the effect of this policy change on the interest rates on municipal bonds, corporate bonds, and Treasury bonds. Draw three graphs, one for each market, to illustrate your answer.

Solving the Problem

Step 1 **Review the chapter material.** This problem is about the effect of changes in income tax rates on interest rates, so you may want to review the section "The Effect of Tax Changes on Interest Rates" on page 133.

Step 2 **Analyze the effect of the tax policy change on the interest rate on municipal bonds.** As we have seen in this chapter, the coupons on municipal bonds are free from state, local, and federal taxes. Federal tax rates are much higher than state and local tax rates, so eliminating the federal income tax would greatly reduce the demand for municipal bonds. Your graph should look like the one below, with the demand curve for municipal bonds shifting to the left, from D_1 to D_2, causing the equilibrium price to fall from P_1^M to P_2^M. A fall in the price of municipal bonds means that the interest rate on the bonds has increased.

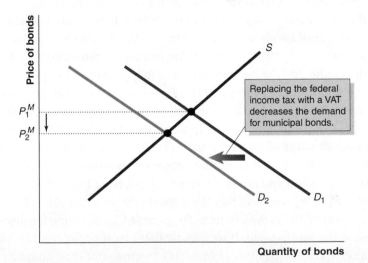

Step 3 **Analyze the effect of the tax policy change on the interest rate on corporate bonds.** The coupons on corporate bonds are taxed at the state, local, and federal levels. Eliminating the federal income tax will increase the demand for corporate bonds. Your graph should look like the one on the next page, with the demand curve for corporate bonds shifting to the right, from D_1 to D_2,

causing the equilibrium price to rise from P_1^C to P_2^C. A rise in the price of corporate bonds means that the interest rate on the bonds has decreased.

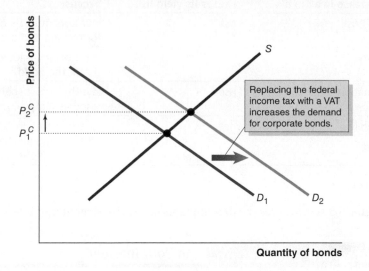

Step 4 **Analyze the effect of the tax policy change on the interest rate on Treasury bonds.** The coupons on Treasury bonds are taxed at the federal level but not at the state or local levels. Eliminating the federal income tax will increase the demand for Treasury bonds. Your graph should look like the one below, with the demand curve for Treasury bonds shifting to the right, from D_1 to D_2, causing the equilibrium price to rise from P_1^T to P_2^T. A rise in the price of Treasury bonds means that the interest rate on the bonds has decreased.

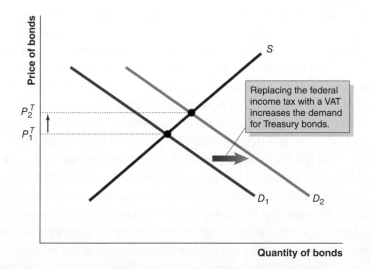

Step 5 **Summarize your findings.** Your graphs and analysis show that replacing the federal income tax with a VAT would increase the interest rate on municipal bonds and lower the interest rates on corporate bonds and Treasury bonds.

See related problem 1.13 at the end of the chapter.

Table 5.3 The Risk Structure of Interest Rates

An increase in a bond's ...	causes its yield to ...	because ...
default risk	rise	investors must be compensated for bearing additional risk.
liquidity	fall	investors incur lower costs in selling the bond.
information costs	rise	investors must spend more resources to evaluate the bond.
tax liability	rise	investors care about after-tax returns and must be compensated for paying higher taxes.

Table 5.3 summarizes the determinants of the risk structure of interest rates.

Making the Connection | In Your Interest

Should You Invest in Junk Bonds?

As we saw in the chapter opener, as interest rates on banks CDs and other safe assets plunged to record lows in 2012, investors searched for ways to earn higher interest rates. Many investors had been scared away from the stock market by the erratic price movements that began with the financial crisis. Paradoxically, though, many individual investors moved into the even more risky market for junk bonds, attracted by the relatively high interest rates.

Junk bonds is the popular name for corporate bonds the rating agencies have given a lower than investment grade rating (for example, a rating of Ba or below from Moody's). At one time, corporations were unable to sell bonds unless the bonds received an investment grade rating. As a result, all junk bonds were "fallen angels," a Wall Street term for a bond that was issued with an investment grade rating but was later downgraded, after the issuing corporation experienced financial problems. This situation changed in the late 1970s, after Michael Milken, a bond salesman at the investment bank Drexel Burnham Lambert, discovered academic research published by economist W. Bradock Hickman in his book *Corporate Bond Quality and Investor Experience*. Hickman had written this book for the National Bureau of Economic Research. Hickman used historical data to show that if an investor purchased a diversified portfolio of junk bonds, the investor would receive a return that was much higher than if the investor had invested in U.S. Treasury bonds. The difference in returns was more than enough to compensate for the additional risk from investing in junk bonds rather than in Treasuries. In other words, the interest rates on the junk bonds were high enough that even though some bonds in the investor's portfolio might default, causing losses on those bonds, the return on the whole portfolio would still be high.

Milken made Hickman's research the basis for presentations he made to institutional investors, such as pension funds and mutual funds, advocating that they invest in junk bonds. Milken was so successful in increasing demand for junk bonds that, for the first time, firms were able to issue new bonds with less than investment grade ratings. Although some institutional investors were prohibited from buying junk bonds either by their charters or by government regulators, many institutional investors began to make junk bonds a part of their investment portfolios.

By 2012, many individual investors had become comfortable with investing in junk bonds, either by buying individual bonds or, more commonly, by buying mutual funds that invest in junk bonds. Investors had pushed the Barclays bank index of junk bond yields to its lowest level ever. This increased demand was great news for companies raising funds by issuing junk bonds. In September 2012, a record $46.6 billion in junk bonds were issued. Hertz, the rental car company, was able to sell $1.2 billion in bonds, even though it received a very low CCC rating from Standard & Poor's.

But should you have considered these bonds to be good investments? As the yields on junk bonds declined, many financial advisers began to doubt that investors were still receiving high enough yields to compensate them for the high risk of defaults on these bonds. One analyst was quoted as saying, "Now that yields have come [down] significantly, people are getting their heads out of the sand and looking at what the risks are." Ironically, many investors were financing their purchases of junk bonds by selling their investments in stocks. In the second quarter of 2012, investors pulled more than $45 billion from stock mutual funds, while adding more than $75 billion to their holdings of bond mutual funds. For individual investors, though, the stock market in 2012 appeared to offer a more favorable trade-off between risk and return.

Only time will tell whether the enthusiasm that many individual investors had developed for junk bonds will pay off for them. But many financial advisers questioned whether before investing in junk bonds individual investors were "looking before they leaped."

Sources: Patrick McGee and Katy Burne, "Junk-Bond Yields Hit All-Time Low," *Wall Street Journal*, September 7, 2012; Katy Burne, "'Junkiest' Debt Issuance Hits Post-Crisis High," *Wall Street Journal*, October 1, 2012; Tom Lauricella, "A Safer Junk Bond Strategy?" *Wall Street Journal*, October 3, 2012; and W. Braddock Hickman, *Corporate Bond Quality and Investor Experience*, Princeton, NJ: Princeton University Press, 1958.

See related problem 1.15 at the end of the chapter.

The Term Structure of Interest Rates

We have seen why bonds with the same maturity may have different interest rates. We now consider the **term structure of interest rates**, which is the relationship among the interest rates on bonds that are otherwise similar but that have different maturities. Theories of the term structure attempt to answer this question: Why should bonds that have the same default risk, liquidity, information cost, and taxation characteristics have different interest rates just because they have different maturities? It is easiest to hold constant these characteristics, other than maturity, for Treasury bonds. So, a common way to analyze the term structure is by looking at the *Treasury yield curve*, which is the relationship on a particular day among the interest rates on Treasury bonds with different maturities. (Remember that Treasury bonds with a maturity of 1 year or less are *bills*, those with a maturity of 2 years to 10 years are *notes*, and those with a maturity of more than 10 years are *bonds*. For simplicity, we often refer to all these securities as *bonds*.)

5.2

Learning Objective
Explain why bonds with different maturities can have different interest rates.

Term structure of interest rates The relationship among the interest rates on bonds that are otherwise similar but that have different maturities.

MyEconLab Real-time data

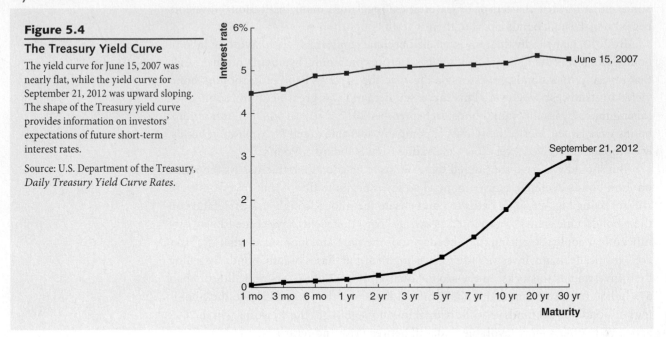

Figure 5.4

The Treasury Yield Curve

The yield curve for June 15, 2007 was nearly flat, while the yield curve for September 21, 2012 was upward sloping. The shape of the Treasury yield curve provides information on investors' expectations of future short-term interest rates.

Source: U.S. Department of the Treasury, *Daily Treasury Yield Curve Rates.*

Figure 5.4 graphs the Treasury yield curves for two days: June 15, 2007, before the start of the financial crisis of 2007–2009, and September 21, 2012. We can note a couple of important points about these two yield curves. First, the interest rates, or yields, on all maturities were much lower in 2012 than in 2007. For example, on June 15, 2007, the yield on the three-month Treasury bill was 4.56%, while on September 21, 2012, the yield was only 0.11%, or 11-hundredths of 1%. The very low yields in 2012 were due primarily to actions the Federal Reserve took to force down short-term interest rates to help deal with the financial crisis. Second, on both days, the yields on long-term bonds were higher than the yields on short-term bonds, although the difference was much greater in 2012 than in 2007. On September 21, 2012, although the yield on the three-month Treasury bill was only 0.11%, the yield on the 10-year Treasury note was 1.77%, and the yield on the 30-year Treasury bond was 2.95%.

This pattern of long-term rates being higher than short-term rates is typical. Figure 5.5 illustrates this pattern by showing that in the years since 1970, interest rates on 3-month Treasury bills—the blue line—have generally been lower than interest rates on 10-year Treasury notes—the red line. When short-term rates are lower than long-term rates, there is an *upward-sloping yield curve.* Close inspection of Figure 5.5, though, shows that there have been periods when the interest rate on the 3-month Treasury bill has been higher than the interest rate on the 10-year Treasury note. These are periods of *downward-sloping yield curves.* Because downward-sloping yield curves occur infrequently, they are also called *inverted yield curves.* Figure 5.5 also illustrates another important fact about the bond market: *Interest rates on bonds of different maturities tend to move together.* Note, for instance, that during the 1970s, interest rates on both

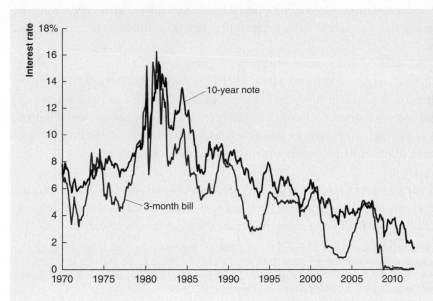

Figure 5.5

The Interest Rates on 3-Month Treasury Bills and 10-Year Treasury Notes, January 1970–August 2012

The figure shows that most of the time since 1970, the interest rate on the 3-month Treasury bills (indicated by the blue line) have been lower than the interest rate on the 10-year Treasury notes (indicated by the red line). During a few periods, though, the interest rate on the 3-month Treasury bill has been higher than the interest rate on the 10-year Treasury note.

Source: Federal Reserve Bank of St. Louis.

3-month Treasury bills and 10-year Treasury notes increased, reaching peaks in the early 1980s, after which they both declined. If we graphed bonds of other maturities, such as the 2-year Treasury note and the 30-year Treasury bond, we would observe the same pattern. In Figure 5.5, the difference between the rate on the 3-month Treasury bill and the rate on the 10-year Treasury note was largest during periods of recession when the Federal Reserve drove short-term rates to low levels.

Making the Connection

Negative Interest Rates on Treasury Bills?

Negative *real* interest rates happen frequently. For instance, during the third quarter of 2008, the nominal interest rate on the 3-month Treasury bill was 1.49%, while the inflation rate was 5.23%, so the real interest rate was 1.49% − 5.23% = −3.74%. But can the *nominal* interest rate ever be negative? You are probably thinking "no" because a negative nominal interest rate means that the *lender* is actually paying the *borrower* interest in return for borrowing the lender's money. What lender would ever do that?

During the Great Depression of the 1930s and again during the financial crisis of 2007–2009 and its aftermath, there were many investors who were happy to *pay* interest to the U.S. Treasury for brief periods in return for the Treasury borrowing their money. In other words, these investors were willing to accept negative interest rates on the Treasury bills they purchased by paying prices that were higher than the bills' face values. In both cases, investors were looking for safe havens at a time when virtually all other investments seemed very risky. Holding their funds in cash would require paying for secure storage. Because interest rates on other short-term investments, such as bank certificates of deposit or money market mutual fund shares, were also very low, investors were giving up relatively little to temporarily park their funds in default-risk free Treasury bills.

In the summer of 2012, both France and Germany sold short-term government bonds with negative interest rates. Like U.S. investors, European investors were looking for short-term investments without default risk at a time when bank deposits and money market accounts had interest rates barely above zero. Demand for short-term French and German bonds was also driven by fears that the governments of several other European countries, particularly Greece and Spain, might default on their debt.

For decades, negative interest rates on Treasury bills had seemed like a historical curiosity from the Great Depression. Their reappearance indicates the difficulty the world financial system has had in recovering from the recent financial crisis.

Sources: Emese Bartha, "France Joins Germany to Sell T-Bills at Negative Yield," *Wall Street Journal*, July 9, 2012; Deborah Lynn Blumberg, "Some Treasury Bill Rates Negative Again Friday," *Wall Street Journal*, November 20, 2009; and Daniel Kruger and Cordell Eddings, "Treasury Bills Trade at Negative Rates as Haven Demand Surges," Bloomberg.com, December 9, 2008.

See related problem 2.8 at the end of the chapter.

Explaining the Term Structure

Our discussion of Figures 5.4 and 5.5 indicates that any explanation of the term structure should be able to account for three important facts:

1. Interest rates on long-term bonds are usually higher than interest rates on short-term bonds.
2. Interest rates on short-term bonds are occasionally higher than interest rates on long-term bonds.
3. Interest rates on bonds of all maturities tend to rise and fall together.

Economists have three theories to explain these facts: *the expectations theory*, *the segmented markets theory*, and *the liquidity premium theory* or *preferred habitat theory*. As we will see, although the expectations theory best captures the logic of how the bond market operates, the liquidity premium theory, which combines elements of the other two theories, is the one most economists accept. In evaluating the theories, two criteria prove useful. First is logical consistency: Does the theory offer a model of the bond market that is consistent with what we know of investor behavior? Second is predictive power: How well does the theory explain actual data on yield curves? We consider each of the theories in turn.

The Expectations Theory of the Term Structure

The *expectations theory* provides the basis for understanding the term structure. The **expectations theory** holds that the interest rate on a long-term bond is an average of the interest rates investors expect on short-term bonds over the lifetime of the long-term bond. The theory views investors in the bond market as sharing the primary objective

Expectations theory A theory of the term structure of interest rates which holds that the interest rate on a long-term bond is an average of the interest rates investors expect on short-term bonds over the lifetime of the long-term bond.

of receiving the highest expected return on their bond investments. For a given holding period, the theory assumes that investors do not care about the maturities of the bonds they invest in. That is, if an investor intends to invest in the bond market for, say, 10 years, the investor will look for the highest return and will not be concerned about whether he or she receives that return by, for example, buying a 10-year bond at the beginning of the period and holding the bond until it matures or by buying a 5-year bond, holding it until it matures in 5 years, and then buying a second 5-year bond.

So, the two key assumptions of the expectations theory are:

1. Investors have the same investment objectives.
2. For a given holding period, investors view bonds of different maturities as being perfect substitutes for one another. That is, holding a 10-year bond for 10 years is the same to investors as holding a 5-year bond for 5 years and another 5-year bond for a second 5 years.

Neither of these assumptions is entirely accurate, so while the expectations theory provides important insight into the term structure, it is not a complete explanation. It is essential, though, to understand the expectations theory before moving on to a more complete explanation of the term structure, so let's consider an example of how the expectations theory works.

The Expectations Theory Applied in A Simple Example Suppose that you intend to invest $1,000 for two years and are considering one of two strategies:

1. *The buy-and-hold strategy.* With this strategy, you buy a two-year bond and hold it until maturity. We will assume that you buy a two-year discount bond. This simplification allows us to avoid having to deal with coupon payments, although the result would not change if we added that complication. The interest rate on the two-year bond is i_{2t}, where the subscript 2 refers to the maturity of the bond and the subscript t refers to the time period, with time t being the present. After two years, the $1,000 investment will have grown to $\$1,000(1 + i_{2t})(1 + i_{2t})$, which is just an application of the basic compounding formula (see Chapter 3).
2. *The rollover strategy.* With this strategy, you buy a one-year bond today and hold it until it matures in one year. At that time, you buy a second one-year bond, and you hold it until it matures at the end of the second year. Notice that with this strategy, you cannot be sure what interest rate you will receive on the one-year bond one year from now. Instead, you must rely on all the information you have about the bond market to form an *expectation* of what the interest rate on the one-year bond will be one year from now. The interest rate on the one-year bond today is i_{1t}, while the interest rate expected on the one-year bond one year from now (which is period $t + 1$) is i_{1t+1}^e. So, if you follow this strategy, after two years, you will expect your $1,000 investment to have grown to $1,000(1 + i_{1t})(1 + i_{1t+1}^e)$.

Under the assumptions of the expectations theory, the returns from the two strategies must be the same. To see why, remember that because of financial arbitrage, the prices of securities will adjust so that investors receive the same returns from holding comparable securities (see Chapter 3). According to the expectations theory, investors consider holding a two-year bond for two years or holding two one-year bonds for one year each as being comparable. Therefore, arbitrage should result in the returns from the two strategies being the same. So, your $1,000 should have grown to the same amount as a result of using either strategy, and we can write:

$$\$1,000\left(1 + i_{2t}\right)\left(1 + i_{2t}\right) = \$1,000\left(1 + i_{1t}\right)\left(1 + i_{1t+1}^{e}\right).$$

Multiplying out the expressions in the parentheses and then simplifying, we get:

$$2i_{2t} + i_{2t}^{2} = i_{1t} + i_{1t+1}^{e} + \left(i_{1t}\right)\left(i_{1t+1}^{e}\right).$$

We can simplify further by noting that i_{2t}^{2} on the left side of the equation and $\left(i_{1t}\right)\left(i_{1t+1}^{e}\right)$ on the right side of the equation are likely to be small numbers because they are each the product of two interest rates. For instance, if the interest rate on the two-year bond is 3%, then $i_{2t}^{2} = 0.03 \times 0.03 = 0.0009$, which is a small enough number that we can ignore it without significantly affecting the result. If we ignore i_{2t}^{2} and $\left(i_{1t}\right)\left(i_{1t+1}^{e}\right)$ and divide both sides of the equation by 2, we are left with:

$$i_{2t} = \frac{i_{1t} + i_{1t+1}^{e}}{2}.$$

This equation tells us that the interest rate on the two-year bond is the average of the interest rate on the one-year bond today and the expected interest rate on the one-year bond one year from now. For example, if the interest rate on the one-year bond today is 2% and the interest rate expected on the one-year bond one year from now is 4%, then the interest rate on the two-year bond today should be 3% ($= (2\% + 4\%)/2$).

The equality between the buy-and-hold strategy and the rollover strategy should be true for any number of periods. For instance, the interest rate on a 10-year bond should equal the average of the interest rates on the 10 one-year bonds during that 10-year period. So, we can say generally that the interest rate on an n-year bond—where n can be any number of years—is equal to:

$$i_{nt} = \frac{i_{1t} + i_{1t+1}^{e} + i_{1t+2}^{e} + i_{1t+3}^{e} + \ldots + i_{1t+(n-1)}^{e}}{n}.$$

Interpreting the Term Structure Using the Expectations Theory Notice that if the expectations theory is correct, the term structure provides us with information on what bond investors must expect to happen to short-term rates in the future. For example, if the interest rate on the one-year bond is 2% and the interest rate on the two-year bond is 3%, investors must be expecting that the interest rate on the one-year bond one year from now will be 4%. Otherwise, the average of the interest rates on the two one-year bonds would not equal the interest rate on the two-year bond.

Figure 5.6 shows three possible yield curves. We can use the expectations theory to interpret their slopes. Panel (a) shows an upward-sloping yield curve with the interest rate on the one-year bond equal to 2%, the interest rate on the two-year bond equal to 3%, and the interest rate on the three-year bond equal to 4%. The two-year rate is an average of the current one-year rate and the expected one-year rate one year from now:

$$3\% = \frac{2\% + \text{Expected one-year rate one year from now}}{2}.$$

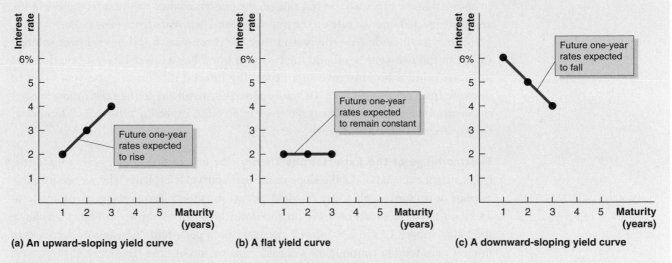

(a) An upward-sloping yield curve   **(b) A flat yield curve**   **(c) A downward-sloping yield curve**

Figure 5.6 Using the Yield Curve to Predict Interest Rates: The Expectations Theory

Under the expectations theory, the slope of the yield curve shows that future short-term interest rates are expected to (a) rise, (b) remain the same, or (c) fall relative to current levels.

So, the expected one-year rate one year from now equals $(2 \times 3\%) - 2\% = 4\%$.

Similarly, we can calculate the expected one-year rate two years from now using the expected one-year rate one year from now that we just calculated:

$$4\% = \frac{2\% + 4\% + \text{Expected one-year rate two years from now}}{3}.$$

So, the expected one-year rate two years from now $= (3 \times 4\%) - (2\% + 4\%) = 6\%$.

We can conclude that the reason that the three-year bond has a higher interest rate than the two-year bond and the two-year bond has a higher interest rate than the one-year bond is because investors expect the interest rate on the one-year bond to increase from 2% to 4% to 6%. Or, more generally, *according to the expectations theory, an upward-sloping yield curve is the result of investors expecting future short-term rates to be higher than the current short-term rate.*

Panel (b) of Figure 5.6 shows a flat yield curve, with the two-year and three-year bonds having the same interest rates as the one-year bond. Under the expectations theory, we can infer that investors must be expecting that the interest rate on the one-year bond will remain unchanged, at 2%. Or, more generally, *according to the expectations theory, a flat yield curve is the result of investors expecting future short-term rates to be the same as the current short-term rate.*

Finally, panel (c) of Figure 5.6 shows a downward-sloping yield curve with the interest rate on the one-year bond being 6%, the interest rate on the two-year bond being 5%, and the interest rate on the three-year bond being 4%. We can apply the same arithmetic we did in the case of the upward-sloping yield curve to calculate the expected interest rates on the one-year bond one year from now and two years from now. Doing so shows that the expected interest rate on the one-year bond one year from now is 4%, and the expected interest rate on the one-year bond two years from now is 2%.

We can conclude that the reason that the three-year bond has a lower interest rate than the two-year bond and the two-year bond has a lower interest rate than the one-year bond is because investors expect the interest rate on the one-year bond to decrease from 6% to 4% to 2%. Or, more generally, *according to the expectations theory, a downward-sloping yield curve is the result of investors expecting future short-term rates to be lower than the current short-term rate.*

Shortcomings of the Expectations Theory The expectations theory has an internally consistent explanation of the slope of the yield curve. It explains why we see upward-sloping, downward-sloping, and flat yield curves. The theory also explains why short-term and long-term rates tend to move up and down together, as shown in Figure 5.5. Since the 1940s, movements in U.S. interest rates have been persistent: Increases or decreases in interest rates tend to continue for a considerable period of time. Therefore, if short-term interest rates increase today, investors will expect future short-term rates to also be high, which, according to the expectations theory, will also lead to an increase in long-term rates.

The expectations theory, though, does a poor job of explaining the first of the important facts about the term structure that we listed on page 140: Interest rates on long-term bonds are usually higher than interest rates on short-term bonds. In other words, the yield curve is typically upward sloping. The expectations theory explains an upward-sloping yield curve as being the result of investors expecting future short-term rates to be higher than the current short-term rate. But if the yield curve is typically upward sloping, investors must be expecting short-term rates to rise most of the time. This explanation seems unlikely because at any particular time, short-term rates are about as likely to fall as to rise. We can conclude that the expectations theory is overlooking something important about the behavior of investors in the bond market.

Solved Problem 5.2A   **In Your Interest**

Can You Make Easy Money from the Term Structure?

The term *interest carry trade* refers to borrowing at a low short-term interest rate and using the borrowed funds to invest at a higher long-term interest rate.

  a. Would you use an interest-carry-trade strategy for your personal investments? Identify the difficulties with this strategy for an individual investor.

  b. If you were an investment adviser for an institutional investor, such as a pension fund or insurance company, would you advise that investor to use an interest-carry-trade strategy? Identify the difficulties with this strategy for an institutional investor.

  c. If the yield curve was inverted, or downward sloping, would an institutional investor still find an interest-carry-trade strategy to be possible? Briefly explain.

Solving the Problem

Step 1 **Review the chapter material.** This problem involves understanding the yield curve, so you may want to review the section "The Expectations Theory of the Term Structure," which begins on page 140.

Step 2 **Answer part (a) by explaining whether an individual investor can profitably engage in an interest carry trade.** The yield curve is typically upward sloping, so short-term interest rates are usually lower than long-term interest rates. Therefore, borrowing short term and investing the funds long term would seem to be a viable investment strategy. The average investor, though, would have difficulty using this strategy because the low short-term rates used in the yield curve—Treasury bill rates, for example—are well below the rates at which the typical investor can borrow from a bank or elsewhere. So, if you are an average investor, the gap between the rate at which you can borrow and the rate at which you could invest in Treasury bonds or other long-term bonds is likely to be small or even negative.

Step 3 **Consider the situation of an institutional investor to answer part (b).** Unlike individual investors, institutional investors, such as pension funds and insurance companies, can borrow at a low short-term rate and invest at a higher long-term rate because the risk that these investors will default is low, and lenders can easily acquire information about them. In carrying out this strategy, though, institutional investors face the risk that as they roll over their short-term loans, the interest rates on them may have risen. For example, if a pension fund borrows $10 million for 6 months at a 1% interest rate to invest in 10-year Treasury notes at a 3% interest rate, it runs the risk that at the end of 6 months, short-term interest rates will have risen above 1%, thereby narrowing the pension fund's profit. In fact, if the expectations theory is correct, the average of the expected short-term interest rates over the life of the long-term investment should be roughly equal to the interest rate on the long-term investment, which would wipe out any potential profits from the interest carry trade. Moreover, if interest rates rise more rapidly than expected, the price of the long-term investment will decline, and the investor will suffer a capital loss.

Step 4 **Answer part (c) by explaining whether the interest carry trade would still be possible if the yield curve were inverted.** If the yield curve were inverted, with long-term rates lower than short-term rates, an institutional investor could borrow long term and invest the funds at the higher short-term rates. In this case, the investor would be subject to *reinvestment risk*, or the risk that after the short-term investment has matured, the interest rate on new short-term investments will have declined. For example, an insurance company that borrows $10 million by issuing long-term bonds at 5% and invests the funds in 6-month Treasury bills at 7% may find that when the Treasury bills mature, the interest rate on new Treasury bills has fallen to 4%. In fact, once again, the expectations theory predicts that the average of the expected short-term interest rates over the life of the long-term loan should be roughly equal to the interest on the long-term loan, which would wipe out any potential profits from the interest carry trade.

We can conclude that the expectations theory indicates that the interest-carry-trade strategy is not ordinarily a road to riches.

See related problems 2.9 and 2.10 at the end of the chapter.

The Segmented Markets Theory of the Term Structure

Segmented markets theory A theory of the term structure of interest rates that holds that the interest rate on a bond of a particular maturity is determined only by the demand and supply for bonds of that maturity.

The **segmented markets theory** addresses the shortcomings of the expectations theory by making two related observations:

1. Investors in the bond market do not all have the same objectives.
2. Investors do not see bonds of different maturities as being perfect substitutes for each other.

These two observations imply that the markets for bonds of different maturities are separate, or *segmented*. Therefore, the interest rate on a bond of a particular maturity is determined only by the demand and supply for bonds of that maturity. The segmented markets theory recognizes that not all investors are the same. For instance, large firms often have significant amounts of cash on which they would like to earn interest but that they also want to have readily available. If you were managing this money for such a firm, you would probably put the funds in short-term Treasury bills rather than in longer-term Treasury notes or Treasury bonds, where the firm's money would be tied up for a period of years. Similarly, there are money market mutual funds that only buy Treasury bills, commercial paper, and other short-term assets and are not allowed by regulation to buy longer-term notes or bonds.

At the other end of the market, though, some investors who buy notes and bonds may buy few, if any, bills. For instance, insurance companies sell life insurance policies that require the companies to make payments when a policyholder dies. Actuaries who work for the companies can reliably estimate how much the company is likely to pay out during any particular year. The insurance companies use these estimates to buy bonds that will mature on a schedule that provides the funds needed to make payouts on the policies. If you were managing funds at an insurance company, you might be reluctant to invest in Treasury bills the funds that the company will need in 20 years to make expected payouts on its policies. Investing in bonds that mature in 20 years would be a better investment strategy than investing in Treasury bills.

The segmented markets theory indicates that investors who participate in the market for bonds of one maturity do not participate in markets for bonds of other maturities. Therefore, factors that affect the demand for Treasury bills or other short-term bonds have no effect on the demand for Treasury bonds or other long-term bonds.

In addition, the segmented markets theory indicates that investors do not view bonds of different maturities as being perfect substitutes for each other because long-term bonds have two shortcomings: (1) They are subject to greater interest-rate risk than short-term bonds, and (2) they are often less liquid than short-term bonds. As a result of these shortcomings, investors need to be compensated by receiving higher interest rates on long-term bonds than on short-term bonds. Economists who support the segmented markets theory also argue that investors who want to hold short-term bonds (for example, corporate money managers) outnumber investors who want to hold long-term bonds (for example, insurance companies). The result is that the prices of short-term bonds are driven up and their yields are driven down relative to those of long-term bonds.

The segmented markets theory, then, offers a plausible explanation of why the yield curve is typically upward sloping: There are more investors who are in the market for short-term bonds, causing their prices to be higher and their interest rates lower, and fewer investors are in the market for long-term bonds, causing their prices to be lower and their interest rates higher. In addition, investors who buy long-term bonds require a higher interest rate to compensate them for the additional interest-rate risk and lower liquidity of long-term bonds. So, the segmented markets theory does a good job of accounting for the first of our important facts about the term structure.

The segmented markets theory, though, has a serious shortcoming: It does not have a good explanation for the other two important facts about the term structure. The theory does not explain why short-term interest rates would ever be greater than long-term interest rates. In other words, why would the yield curve ever be downward sloping, even though we know that occasionally it is? If markets for bonds of different maturities truly are segmented (that is, completely independent of each other), it is difficult to understand the third important fact about the term structure: Interest rates of all maturities tend to rise and fall together.

The Liquidity Premium Theory

Neither the expectations theory nor the segmented markets theory provides a complete explanation of the term structure. Essentially, their shortcomings arise from the extreme position that each theory takes. Under the expectations theory, investors view bonds of different maturities as perfect substitutes for each other, while under the segmented markets theory, investors view bonds of different maturities as not being substitutes at all. The **liquidity premium theory** (or **preferred habitat theory**) of the term structure provides a more complete explanation by combining the insights of the other two theories while avoiding their extreme assumptions.

The liquidity premium theory holds that investors view bonds of different maturities as substitutes—but not perfect substitutes. Like the segmented markets theory, the liquidity premium theory assumes that investors prefer bonds with shorter maturities to bonds with longer maturities. Therefore, investors will not buy a long-term bond if it offers the same yield as a sequence of short-term bonds. Contrary to the segmented markets theory, however, investors will be willing to substitute a long-term bond for short-term bonds, provided that they receive a high enough interest rate on the long-term bond. The additional interest investors require in order to be willing to buy a long-term bond rather than a comparable sequence of short-term bonds is called a **term premium**. So, the liquidity premium theory holds that the interest rate on a long-term bond is an average of the interest rates investors expect on short-term bonds over the lifetime of the long-term bond, plus a term premium that increases in value the longer the maturity of the bond.

For example, suppose that the one-year bond currently has an interest rate of 2%, and the interest rate expected on the one-year bond one year from now is 4%. Would investors be just as happy buying a two-year bond with an interest rate of 3%? The two-year bond offers the same interest rate as the average interest rate expected on the two one-year bonds. But because investors *prefer* to buy one-year bonds, they must be given a higher interest rate—say 3.25%—as an incentive to buy the less desirable two-year bond. If investors were offered only 3% on the two-year bond, they would buy the one-year bond instead. The additional 0.25% that is needed to make investors see the two-year bond as being competitive with the one-year bonds is the term premium.

Liquidity premium theory (or preferred habitat theory) A theory of the term structure of interest rates that holds that the interest rate on a long-term bond is an average of the interest rates investors expect on short-term bonds over the lifetime of the long-term bond, plus a term premium that increases in value the longer the maturity of the bond.

Term premium The additional interest investors require in order to be willing to buy a long-term bond rather than a comparable sequence of short-term bonds.

The longer the maturity of a bond, the larger the term premium on the bond. So, a 5-year bond will have a larger term premium than will a 2-year bond, and a 20-year bond will have a larger term premium than will a 10-year bond. In effect, then, the liquidity premium theory adds a term premium to the expectations theory's equation linking the interest rate on a long-term bond to the interest rate on short-term bonds. For example, if i_{2t}^{TP} is the term premium on a 2-year bond, then the interest rate on a 2-year bond is:

$$i_{2t} = \frac{i_{1t} + i_{1t+1}^e}{2} + i_{2t}^{TP}.$$

Or, more generally, the interest rate on an n-period bond is equal to:

$$i_{nt} = \frac{i_{1t} + i_{1t+1}^e + i_{1t+2}^e + i_{1t+3}^e + \ \dots \ + i_{1t+(n-1)}^e}{n} + i_{nt}^{TP}.$$

Solved Problem 5.2B

Using the Liquidity Premium Theory to Calculate Expected Interest Rates

Use the data in the following table on Treasury securities of different maturities to solve this problem:

1 year	2 year	3 year
1.25%	2.00%	2.50%

Assume that the liquidity premium theory is correct. On this day, what did investors expect the interest rate to be on the one-year Treasury bill two years from that time if the term premium on a two-year Treasury note was 0.20% and the term premium on a three-year Treasury note was 0.40%?

Solving the Problem

Step 1 **Review the chapter material.** This problem is about calculating expected interest rates using the liquidity premium theory, so you may want to review the section "The Liquidity Premium Theory," which begins on page 147.

Step 2 **Use the liquidity premium equation that links the interest rate on a long-term bond to the interest rates on short-term bonds to calculate the interest rate that investors expected on the one-year Treasury bill in one year.** According to the liquidity premium theory, the interest rate on a two-year bond should equal the average of the interest rate on the current one-year bond and the interest rate expected on the one-year bond in one year, plus the term premium. The problem tells us that the term premium on a two-year Treasury note is 0.20%, so we can calculate the interest rate expected on the one-year bond one year in the future:

$$i_{2t} = 2.00\% = \frac{1.25\% + i_{1t+1}^e}{2} + 0.20\%,$$

or,

$$i_{1t+1}^e = 2.35\%.$$

Step 3 **Answer the problem by using the result from step 2 to calculate the interest rate investors expected on the one-year Treasury bill in two years.**

$$i_{3t} = 2.50\% = \frac{1.25\% + 2.35\% + i_{1t+2}^e}{3} + 0.40\%,$$

or,

$$i_{1t+2}^e = 2.70\%.$$

See related problem 2.11 at the end of the chapter.

Table 5.4 summarizes key aspects of the three theories of the term structure of interest rates.

Table 5.4 Theories of the Term Structure of Interest Rates

Theory	Assumptions	Predictions	What the theory explains
Expectations	Investors have the same investment objectives, and, for a given holding period, investors view bonds of different maturities as perfect substitutes for each other.	The interest rate on a long-term bond equals the average of the interest rates expected on the one-year bonds during this period.	Explains the slope of the yield curve and why interest rates on short-term and long-term bonds move together. Drawback: Does not explain why the yield curve is usually upward sloping.
Segmented markets	Investors in the bond market do not all have the same objectives, and investors do not see bonds of different maturities as being substitutes for each other.	Interest rates on bonds of different maturities are determined in separate markets.	Explains why the yield curve is usually upward sloping. Drawback: Does not explain why the yield curve should ever be downward sloping or why interest rates on bonds of different maturities should move together.
Liquidity premium	Investors view bonds of different maturities as substitutes for each other—but not as perfect substitutes.	The interest rate on an n-year bond equals the average of the interest rates expected on the n one-year bonds during these n years plus a term premium.	Explains all three important facts about the term structure.

Can the Term Structure Predict Recessions?

Investors, businesspeople, and policymakers can use information contained in the term structure of interest rates to forecast economic variables. Under the expectations and liquidity premium theories, the slope of the yield curve shows the short-term interest rates that bond market participants expect in the future. In addition, if fluctuations in expected real interest rates are small, the yield curve contains expectations of future inflation rates. To see why, suppose that you want to know the financial markets' prediction of the rate of inflation five years from now. If the real interest rate is expected to remain constant, you can interpret an upward-sloping yield curve to mean that inflation is expected to rise, leading investors to expect higher nominal interest rates in the future. To provide an accurate forecast of future inflation, you would also need to estimate the term premiums on long-term bonds. The Fed and many other financial market participants use the yield curve to forecast future inflation.

Economists and investors also look to the slope of the yield curve to predict the likelihood of a recession. Economists have focused attention on the *term spread*, which is the difference between the yield on the 10-year Treasury note and the yield on the 3-month Treasury bill. David C. Wheelock of the Federal Reserve Bank of St. Louis and Mark E. Wohar of the University of Nebraska, Omaha, have found that prior to every recession since 1953, the term spread has narrowed significantly. That is, the yield on the 10-year Treasury note has declined significantly relative to the yield on the 3-month Treasury bill. Wheelock and Wohar looked closely at what happened following periods when the yield curve was inverted, with short-term rates higher than long-term rates. With only one exception, every time the yield on the 3-month bill was higher than the yield on the 10-year note, a recession followed within a year. These results indicate that the slope of the yield curve is a useful tool in predicting recessions.[1]

We can see why the yield curve is useful in predicting recessions by examining several actual yield curves. Figure 5.7 shows three yield curves: one that slopes downward slightly, one that slopes upward slightly, and one that slopes upward steeply. If we apply the liquidity premium theory, these three yield curves—representing three particular days between 2007 and 2010—tell a story about financial markets' expectations about the economy.

The yield curve from February 2007 is slightly inverted, with the short-term rates being higher than the long-term rates. During 2006 and 2007, the Fed wanted to keep short-term rates relatively high to deal with increasing rates of inflation resulting from rising oil prices and the lingering effects of the housing boom. Investors, though, may have anticipated the economic recession that was to begin in December 2007. During recessions, interest rates typically fall, and short-term rates tend to fall more than long-term rates, as the Fed takes actions to lower rates in hopes of stimulating the economy. In this situation, the liquidity premium theory of the term structure predicts that long-term rates should be lower than short-term rates, making the yield curve inverted.

---

[1]David C. Wheelock and Mark E. Wohar, "Can the Term Spread Predict Output Growth and Recessions? A Survey of the Literature," *Federal Reserve Bank of St. Louis Review*, Vol. 91, No. 5, September/October 2009, pp. 419–440.

Figure 5.7

Interpreting the Yield Curve

Models of the term structure, such as the liquidity premium theory, help analysts use data on the Treasury yield curve to forecast the future path of the economy. The yield curve from February 2007 is inverted as investors anticipated that a recession was likely to cause future short-term rates to be lower than current short-term rates. The yield curve from January 2008 is characteristic of a normal yield curve under the liquidity premium theory. The sharply upward-sloping yield curve from February 2010 reflects the actions of the Federal Reserve to drive short-term rates to unusually low levels.

Source: U.S. Department of the Treasury.

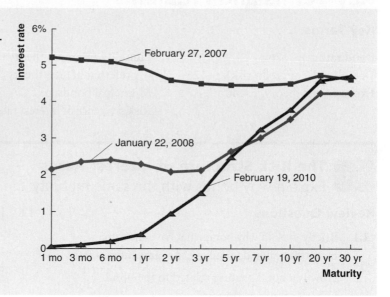

The upward slope in the yield curve during January 2008 is characteristic of a normal yield curve under the liquidity premium theory. By that time, the economy was two months into the recession. However, investors expected that, as economic activity increased in the future, the demand for credit would increase, causing interest rates to increase. In other words, investors expected future short-term rates to rise above then-current levels. Therefore, the yield curve was upward sloping.

The bottom yield curve is from February 2010, when the Fed had taken policy actions to drive short-term rates to extremely low levels. However, concerns about inflation and government budget deficits kept expected future short-term rates—and therefore current long-term rates—relatively high. The inflation fears added to the normal upward slope of the yield curve predicted by the liquidity premium theory, making the yield curve particularly steep.

Answering the Key Question

Continued from page 124

At the beginning of this chapter, we asked:

"Should the government more closely regulate credit rating agencies?"

Like other policy questions we will encounter in this book, this question has no definitive answer. We have seen in this chapter that many investors rely on the credit rating agencies for important information on the default risk on bonds. During the financial crisis of 2007–2009, many bonds—particularly mortgage-backed securities—turned out to have much higher levels of default risk than the credit rating agencies had indicated. Some observers argued that the rating agencies had given those bonds inflated ratings because the agencies have a conflict of interest in being paid by the firms whose bond issues they rate. Other observers, though, argued that the ratings may have been accurate when given, but the creditworthiness of the bonds declined rapidly following the unexpected severity of the housing bust and the resulting financial crisis.

Key Terms and Problems

Key Terms

Bond rating, p. 126
Default risk (or credit risk), p. 126
Expectations theory, p. 140

Liquidity premium theory (or
  preferred habitat theory), p. 147
Municipal bonds, p. 132
Risk structure of interest rates, p. 125

Segmented markets theory, p. 146
Term premium, p. 147
Term structure of interest rates,
  p. 137

5.1 The Risk Structure of Interest Rates

Explain why bonds with the same maturity can have different interest rates.

Review Questions

1.1 Briefly explain why bonds that have the same maturities often do not have the same interest rates.

1.2 How is a bond's rating related to the bond issuer's creditworthiness?

1.3 How does the interest rate on an illiquid bond compare with the interest rate on a liquid bond? How does the interest rate on a bond with high information costs compare with the interest rate on a bond with low information costs?

1.4 What are the two types of income an investor can earn on a bond? How is each taxed?

1.5 Compare the tax treatment of the coupons on the following bonds: a bond issued by the city of Houston, a bond issued by GE, and a bond issued by the U.S. Treasury.

Problems and Applications

1.6 Draw a demand and supply graph for bonds that shows the effect on a bond that has its rating lowered. Be sure to show the demand and supply curves and the equilibrium price of the bond before and after the rating is lowered.

1.7 According to Moody's, "Obligations rated Aaa are judged to be of the highest quality, with minimal credit risk."

   a. What "obligations" is Moody's referring to?

   b. What does Moody's mean by "credit risk"?

Source: Moody's Investors Service, *Moody's Rating Symbols and Definitions*, September 2012, p. 5.

1.8 [Related to the Chapter Opener on page 124]
 According to an article in the *New York Times*, in 2012, "everyone has piled into" the junk bond market. The article also observed, "The average yields on these bonds have dropped to 6.6 percent, hovering near a record low."

   a. What are junk bonds?

   b. Is there a connection between everyone having piled into the junk bond market and the yields on these bonds having fallen to a record low? Briefly explain.

Source: Peter Lattman, "Risk Builds as Junk Bonds Boom," *New York Times*, August 15, 2012.

1.9 In 2012, Anheuser-Busch In Bev NV, maker of Budweiser and other beers, sold debt of varying maturities. According to an article in the *Wall Street Journal*:

> The three-year notes priced with a risk premium of 0.50 percentage point over comparable Treasurys; the five-year notes at a spread of 0.80 percentage point to Treasurys; the 10-year notes at 1.05 percentage points over; and the 30-year bonds at a spread of 1.20 percentage points over Treasurys.

   a. What does the article mean by "comparable Treasurys"?

   b. What does the article mean by a "risk premium"?

c. Why does the risk premium increase the longer the maturity of Anheuser-Busch's debt?

Source: Katy Burne, "Budweiser Maker Has King-Sized Bond Deal on Tap," *Wall Street Journal*, July 11, 2012.

1.10 [Related to the Making the Connection **on page 129**] According to an article in the *New York Times*, "It was the near universal agreement that potential conflicts were embedded in the [bond] ratings model." What is the bond ratings model? What potential conflicts are embedded in it?

Source: David Segal, "Debt Raters Avoid Overhaul After Crisis," *New York Times*, December 7, 2009.

1.11 Some economists have argued that one important role of rating agencies is to keep the managers of firms that issue bonds from using the funds raised in ways that would not be in the best interests of the purchasers of the bonds. Why might the managers of firms have different goals than the investors who buy the firms' bonds? How does the existence of rating agencies reduce this conflict between investors and firm managers?

1.12 Beginning in 2009, Congress authorized "Build America Bonds," which states and cities could issue to build roads, bridges, and schools. Unlike with regular municipal bonds, however, the coupons on Build America Bonds are taxable. Would you expect the interest rates on these bonds to be higher or lower than the interest rates on comparable municipal bonds? Briefly explain.

1.13 [Related to Solved Problem 5.1 **on page 134**] Suppose a candidate who runs on a platform of "soak the rich" wins the 2016 presidential election. After being elected, he or she persuades Congress to raise the top marginal tax rate on the federal personal income tax to 65%. Use one graph to show the effect of this change in tax rates on the market for municipal bonds and another graph to show the effect on the market for U.S. Treasury bonds.

1.14 An article appeared in the *New York Times* in 2012 under the headline "Spanish Bond Yields Soar."

a. Can we tell from the headline whether the demand for Spanish government bonds was increasing or decreasing? Briefly explain.

b. Can we tell from the headline whether the prices of Spanish government bonds were increasing or decreasing? Briefly explain.

c. The article observes that Spain is "reaping the bitter harvest of a decade of ambitious and often unchecked spending on infrastructure and services." What does this observation have to do with the article's headline?

Source: Raphael Minder and Liz Alderman, "Spanish Bond Yields Soar," *New York Times*, July 23, 2012.

1.15 [Related to the Making the Connection **on page 136**] By 2012, actions by the Federal Reserve and other central banks had driven short-term interest rates close to zero. One portfolio manager was quoted as saying: "The market has heard … central bankers and has responded accordingly."

a. In what ways did individual investors respond to very low short-term interest rates?

b. If you owned a portfolio of long-term bonds in 2007, before the beginning of the financial crisis, would the return on your portfolio have been helped or hurt by the fall in interest rates? Briefly explain.

c. If you were a new investor who was just beginning to build an investment portfolio, would your investment opportunities have been helped or hurt by the decline in interest rates? Briefly explain.

Source: Patrick McGee and Katy Burne, "Junk-Bond Yields Hit All-Time Low," *Wall Street Journal*, September 7, 2012.

1.16 Suppose that, holding yield constant, investors are indifferent as to whether they hold bonds issued by the federal government or bonds issued by state and local governments (that is, they consider the bonds the same with respect to default risk, information costs, and liquidity). Suppose that state governments have issued perpetuities (or consols) with $75 coupons and that the federal government has also issued perpetuities with $75 coupons. If the state and federal perpetuities both have after-tax yields of 8%, what are their pretax yields? (Assume that the relevant federal income tax rate is 39.6%.)

5.2 The Term Structure of Interest Rates
Explain why bonds with different maturities can have different interest rates.

Review Questions

2.1 How does the Treasury yield curve illustrate the term structure of interest rates?

2.2 What are three key facts about the term structure?

2.3 Briefly describe the three theories of the term structure.

Problems and Applications

2.4 Suppose that you want to invest for three years to earn the highest possible return. You have three options: (a) Roll over three one-year bonds, which pay interest rates of 8% in the first year, 11% in the second year, and 7% in the third year; (b) buy a two-year bond with a 10% interest rate and then roll over the amount received when that bond matures into a one-year bond with an interest rate of 7%; or (c) buy a three-year bond with an interest rate of 8.5%. Assuming annual compounding, no coupon payments, and no cost of buying or selling bonds, which option should you choose?

2.5 Suppose that you have $1,000 to invest in the bond market on January 1, 2014. You could buy a one-year bond with an interest rate of 4%, a two-year bond with an interest rate of 5%, a three-year bond with an interest rate of 5.5%, or a four-year bond with an interest rate of 6%. You expect interest rates on one-year bonds in the future to be 6.5% on January 1, 2015, 7% on January 1, 2016, and 9% on January 1, 2017. You want to hold your investment until January 1, 2018. Which of the following investment alternatives gives you the highest return by 2018: (a) Buy a four-year bond on January 1, 2014; (b) buy a three-year bond January 1, 2014, and a one-year bond January 1, 2017; (c) buy a two-year bond January 1, 2014, a one-year bond January 1, 2016, and another one-year bond January 1, 2017; or (d) buy a one-year bond January 1, 2014, and then additional one-year bonds on the first days of 2015, 2016, and 2017?

2.6 Suppose that the interest rate on a one-year Treasury bill is currently 1% and that investors expect that the interest rates on one-year Treasury bills over the next three years will be 2%, 3%, and 2%. Use the expectations theory to calculate the current interest rates on two-year, three-year, and four-year Treasury notes.

2.7 A student says: "The interest rate on the one-year Treasury bill is currently 0.29%, while the interest rate on the 30-year Treasury bond is currently 3.10%. Why are any investors buying the Treasury bill when they can receive a much higher yield by buying the Treasury bond?" Provide an answer to the student's question.

2.8 [Related to the Making the Connection on page 139] What is the yield to maturity on a Treasury bill that matures one year from now, has a price of $1,010, and has a face value of $1,000? If the consumer price index is expected to decline during the year from 250 to 245, what is the expected real interest rate on the Treasury bill?

2.9 [Related to Solved Problem 5.2A on page 144] An anonymous billionaire investor was quoted in the *Wall Street Journal* as asking: "Has there ever been a carry trade that hasn't ended badly?" What is a carry trade? Why might it end badly?

Source: Robert Frank, "Where Billionaires Are Putting Their Money," *Wall Street Journal*, September 15, 2010.

2.10 [Related to Solved Problem 5.2A on page 144] Interest rates on U.S. Treasury bills are typically much lower than interest rates on U.S. Treasury notes and bonds. If the federal government wants to reduce the interest charges it pays when it borrows money, why doesn't the Treasury stop selling Treasury notes and bonds and sell only bills?

2.11 [Related to Solved Problem 5.2B on page 148] Use the data on Treasury securities in the following table to answer the following question:

1 year	2 year	3 year
0.75%	1.25%	2.00%

Assuming that the liquidity premium theory is correct, what did investors on this day expect the interest rate to be on the one-year Treasury bill two years from now if the term premium on a two-year Treasury note was 0.10% and the term premium on a three-year Treasury note was 0.25%?

2.12 In the spring of 2012, yields on Treasury securities increased. An article in the *Wall Street Journal* observed: "The immediate cause for the lift was the Federal Reserve's more optimistic tenor" about the state of the economy. Why would the Federal Reserve becoming more optimistic about future economic growth cause yields on Treasury securities to increase?

Source: Justin Lahart, "A Yield Curveball for the Fed," *Wall Street Journal*, March 14, 2012.

2.13 In 2012, an article in the *Wall Street Journal* had the headline "As Corporate-Bond Yields Sink, Risks for Investors Rise." Is the biggest risk of holding long-term corporate bonds at low interest rates the risk that the corporations will default? Or is there another type of risk that investors should be more worried about?

Source: Matt Wirz, "As Corporate-Bond Yields Sink, Risks for Investors Rise," *Wall Street Journal*, August 14, 2012.

2.14 The following is from an article in the *Wall Street Journal*, describing events in the market for Treasury securities that day: "Treasurys prices were mixed, with the shorter end of the curve rising and longer-dated Treasurys falling in price." On one graph, draw two Treasury yield curves, one showing the situation on that day (as described in the sentence) and one showing the situation on the day before. Label one curve "today" and the other curve "previous day." Be sure to label both axes of your yield curve graph.

Source: *Wall Street Journal*, February 22, 2008.

2.15 In 2012, an article in the *Wall Street Journal* contained the following observation: "The fact that Spanish short-term yields are shooting higher than long-term yields is a particularly bad sign." Why might this development in the market for Spanish government bonds indicate that investors feared that the Spanish economy would enter a recession?

Source: Matt Phillips, "Flatliners: Spanish Yield Curve Flattening Hard!" *Wall Street Journal*, July 23, 2012.

Data Exercises

D5.1: [The yield curve and recessions] Go to the Web site of the Federal Reserve Bank of St. Louis (FRED) (research.stlouisfed.org/fred2/) and for the period from January 1957 to the present download to the same graph the data series for the 3-month Treasury bill (TB3MS) and the 10-year Treasury note (GS10). Go to the Web site of the National Bureau of Economic Research (nber.org) and find the dates for business cycle peaks and troughs (the period between a business cycle peak and trough is a recession). During which months was the yield curve inverted? How many of these periods were followed within a year by a recession?

D5.2: [Predicting with the yield curve] Go to www.treasury.gov and find the page "Daily Treasury Yield Curve Rates." Briefly describe the current shape of the yield curve. Can you use the yield curve to draw any conclusion about what investors in the bond market expect will happen to the economy in the future?

D5.3: [The spread between high-grade bonds and junk bonds] Go to the Web site of the Federal Reserve Bank of St. Louis (FRED) (research.stlouisfed.org/fred2/) and for the period from January 1997 to the present, download to the same graph the data series for the BofA Merrill Lynch US Corporate AAA Effective Yield (BAMLC0A1CAAAEY) and the BofA Merrill Lynch US High Yield CCC or Below Effective Yield (BAMLH0A3HYCEY). Describe how the difference between the yields on high-grade corporate bonds and on junk bonds have changed over this period.

CHAPTER 6

The Stock Market, Information, and Financial Market Efficiency

Learning Objectives

After studying this chapter, you should be able to:

6.1 Understand the basic operations of the stock market (pages 158–164)

6.2 Explain how stock prices are determined (pages 164–170)

6.3 Explain the connection between the assumption of rational expectations and the efficient markets hypothesis (pages 170–177)

6.4 Discuss the actual efficiency of financial markets (pages 177–180)

6.5 Discuss the basic concepts of behavioral finance (pages 181–183)

Are You Willing to Invest in the Stock Market?

Everybody seems to love Apple. From the iPod to the iPhone to the iPad, the firm has released one hit product after another. But how good an investment has Apple been? Suppose your grandparents had given you 100 shares of Apple's stock in 1995. If you had held on to the shares through September 2012, what would have happened to your investment? As the following table shows, the dollar value of your 100 shares would have been 19 times greater in 2012 than it was in 1995. But the table also shows that you would have been in for a wild ride, with the value of your investment bouncing up and down like a yo-yo. But Apple is just one stock.

What if your stock market investment had been spread across a group of stocks?

Date	Price per share of Apple stock	Value of 100 shares of Apple stock
June 1995	$37	$3,700
July 1997	13	1,300
April 2000	132	13,200
December 2000	14	1,400
February 2005	91	9,100
November 2007	191	19,100
March 2009	85	8,500
September 2012	700	70,000

Continued on next page

Key Issue and Question

Issue: During the financial crisis, many small investors sold their stock investments, fearing that they had become too risky.

Question: Is the 2007–2009 financial crisis likely to have a long-lasting effect on the willingness of individuals to invest in the stock market?

Answered on page 183

The Dow Jones Industrial Average (often called "the Dow") is the best-known measure of the performance of the U.S. stock market. The Dow is an average of the stock prices of 30 large corporations. If you had invested in the Dow in 1995, your investment would have more than doubled by early 2000. Unfortunately, your investment would then have declined by more than 25% by early 2003. But, good news! Between early 2003 and the fall of 2007, your investment would have increased by more than 75% . . . before declining by more than 50% between the fall of 2007 and the spring of 2009 . . . and then bouncing back almost 50% by the end of 2009. So, your investment in the Dow would have been as unstable as your investment in just Apple.

Clearly, buying stocks is not for faint-hearted investors. But what explains the volatility of stock prices? More importantly, what role does the stock market play in the financial system and the economy? Although the stock market has always been volatile, the movements in stock prices during the past 15 years have been particularly large. The plunge in stock prices during the 2007–2009 financial crisis unnerved many investors, some of whom took all their savings out of the stock market and vowed never to return.

Following the tremendous decline in stock prices during the Great Depression of the 1930s, many investors permanently turned away from the stock market. Will investors have the same reaction to the stock market volatility of recent years? And if they do, what will be the consequences for the financial system and the economy?

The stock market is an important source of funds for large corporations. It is also where millions of individual investors save for large purchases or for retirement. Savers sometimes buy individual stocks, but more often their stock market investments are in mutual funds or pension funds. In this chapter, we discuss the stock market and look at the factors that determine stock prices.

Stocks and the Stock Market

6.1

Learning Objective

Understand the basic operations of the stock market.

As we saw in Chapter 1, by buying stock in a company, an investor becomes a partial owner of the company. As an owner, a stockholder, sometimes called a *shareholder*, has a legal claim on the firm's profits and on its *equity*, which is the difference between the value of the firm's assets and the value of its liabilities. Because ownership of a firm's stock represents partial ownership of a firm, stocks are sometimes referred to as *equities*. Bonds represent debt rather than equity. Most firms issue millions of shares of stock. For instance, by 2012, Apple had issued more than 900 million shares of stock. So, most shareholders own only a very small fraction of the firms they invest in.

People who are *sole proprietors*, which means that they are the sole owners of a firm, and people who own a firm with partners typically have unlimited liability for the firm's debts. The owners of these firms run the risk that if the firm goes bankrupt, anyone the firm owes money to can sue the owners for their personal assets. An investor who owns stock in a firm organized as a **corporation** is protected by *limited liability*. **Limited liability** is a legal provision that shields owners of a corporation from losing more than they have invested in the firm. If you bought $10,000 worth of stock in General Motors, that was the most you could lose when the firm went bankrupt in 2009. In the eyes of the law, a corporation is a legal "person," separate from its owners. Without the protection of limited liability, many investors would be reluctant to invest in firms whose key decisions are made by the firm's managers rather than by its stockholders.

Corporation A legal form of business that provides owners with protection from losing more than their investment if the business fails.

Limited liability A legal provision that shields owners of a corporation from losing more than they have invested in the firm.

Common Stock Versus Preferred Stock

There are two main categories of stock: common stock and preferred stock. Both represent partial ownership of a corporation, but they have some significant differences. A corporation is run by its *board of directors* who appoint the firm's top management, such as the chief executive officer (CEO), chief operating officer (COO), and chief financial officer (CFO). Common stockholders elect the members of the board of directors, but preferred stockholders are not eligible to vote in these elections.

Corporations distribute some of their profits to their stockholders by making payments called **dividends**, which are typically paid quarterly. *Preferred stockholders* receive a fixed dividend that is set when the corporation issues the stock. *Common stockholders* receive a dividend that fluctuates as the profitability of the corporation varies over time. Corporations suffering losses may decide to suspend paying dividends, but if the corporation does pay dividends, it must first pay the dividend promised to preferred stockholders before making any dividend payments to the common stockholders. If the corporation declares bankruptcy, its debt holders—investors and financial institutions that have bought the corporation's bonds or made loans to the corporation—are paid off first, and then the preferred stockholders are paid off. If any money remains, then the company pays the common stockholders.

The total market value of a firm's common and preferred stock is called the firm's *market capitalization*. For instance, in late 2012, the total value of Apple's outstanding stock—and, therefore, Apple's market capitalization—was about $550 billion, which was the largest among U.S. corporations.

Dividend A payment that a corporation makes to stockholders, typically on a quarterly basis.

How and Where Stocks Are Bought and Sold

Although there are more than 5 million corporations in the United States, only about 5,100 corporations are **publicly traded companies** that sell stock in the U.S. stock market. The remaining corporations, along with the millions of sole proprietorships and partnerships, are *private firms*, which means they do not issue stock that is bought and sold on the stock market.

Just as the "automobile market" refers to the many places where automobiles are bought and sold, the "stock market" refers to the many places where stocks are bought and sold. In the case of stocks, the "places" are both physical and virtual, as the electronic trading of stocks has become increasingly important. Still, when many people think of the U.S. stock market, they think of the New York Stock Exchange (NYSE) building, which is located on Wall Street in New York City. The NYSE is an example of a **stock exchange** where stocks are bought and sold face-to-face on a trading floor. Trading takes place every business day between the hours of 9:30 A.M. and 4:00 P.M. Many of the largest U.S. corporations, such as IBM, McDonald's, and Wal-Mart, are listed on the NYSE's Big Board. In recent years, much of the trading on the NYSE has been done electronically, although some trading still takes place on the floor of the exchange. Trading on the NASDAQ stock market, which is named for the National Association of Securities Dealers, is entirely electronic. The NASDAQ is an example of an **over-the-counter market**, in which *dealers* linked by computer buy and sell stocks. Dealers in an over-the-counter market attempt to match up the orders they receive from investors to buy and

Publicly traded company A corporation that sells stock in the U.S. stock market; only 5,100 of the 5 million U.S. corporations are publicly traded companies.

Stock exchange A physical location where stocks are bought and sold face-to-face on a trading floor.

Over-the-counter market A market in which financial securities are bought and sold by dealers linked by computer.

sell the stocks. Dealers maintain an inventory of the stocks they trade to help balance buy and sell orders.

Keep in mind the distinction between a primary market and a secondary market. In the stock market, just as in the bond market, most buying and selling is of existing stocks rather than newly issued stocks supplied by firms. So, for both stocks and bonds, the secondary market is much larger than the primary market.

Traditionally, an individual investor purchased stocks by establishing an account with a stockbroker, such as Merrill Lynch (now part of Bank of America). Brokers buy and sell stocks for investors in return for a payment known as a *commission*. Today, many investors buying individual stocks use online brokerage firms, such as E*TRADE or TD Ameritrade. Online brokers typically charge lower commissions than do traditional brokers, but they often do not provide investment advice and other services that traditional brokers offer. Many investors prefer to buy stock mutual funds rather than individual stocks. Because stock mutual funds, such as Fidelity Investment's Magellan Fund, hold many stocks in their portfolios, they provide investors with the benefits of diversification.

The 5,100 publicly traded U.S. corporations represent only about 10% of the firms listed on stock exchanges worldwide. Figure 6.1 shows the 10 largest global stock markets, listed by the total value of the shares traded. Although the NYSE remains the world's largest, foreign stock markets have been rapidly increasing in size. The shares of the largest foreign firms, such as Sony, Toyota, and Nokia, trade indirectly on the NYSE in the form of *American Depository Receipts*, which are receipts for shares of stock held in a foreign country. Some mutual funds, such as Vanguard's Global Equity Fund,

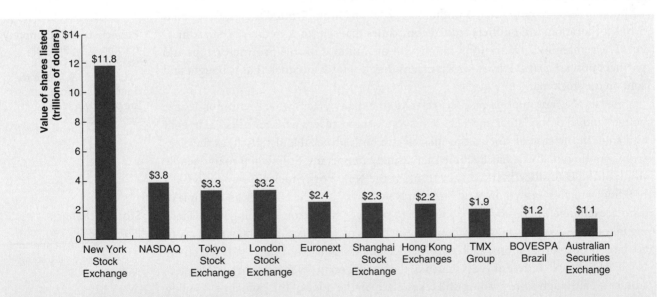

Figure 6.1 World Stock Exchanges, 2011

The New York Stock Exchange remains the largest stock exchange in the world, but other exchanges have been increasing in size. The exchanges are ranked on the basis of the total value of the shares traded on them.

Note: Although they operate independently, the New York Stock Exchange owns Euronext.

Source: www.world-exchanges.org.

also invest in the stock of foreign firms. It is possible to buy individual stocks listed on foreign stock exchanges by setting up an account with a local brokerage firm in the foreign country. Although at one time only the wealthy invested directly in foreign stock markets, today the Internet has made it much easier for the average investor to research foreign companies and to establish foreign brokerage accounts.

Measuring the Performance of the Stock Market

The overall performance of the stock market is measured using **stock market indexes**, which are averages of stock prices. The value of a stock market index is set equal to 100 in a particular year, called the *base year*. Because the stock market indexes are intended to show movements in prices over time rather than the actual dollar value of the underlying stocks, the year chosen for the base year is not important. The most widely followed stock indexes are the three that appear on the first page of the *Wall Street Journal*'s Web site: the Dow Jones Industrial Average, the S&P 500, and the NASDAQ Composite index. Although the Dow is an average of the prices of the stocks of just 30 large firms, including Coca-Cola, Microsoft, and Walt Disney, it is the most familiar index to many individual investors. The S&P 500 index includes the 30 stocks that are in the Dow as well as stocks issued by 470 other large companies, each of which has a market capitalization of at least $3.5 billion. A committee of the Standard & Poor's Company chooses the firms to represent the different industries in the U.S. economy. Because these firms are so large, the total value of their stocks represents 75% of the value of all publicly traded U.S. firms. The NASDAQ Composite index includes the 2,750 stocks that are traded in the NASDAQ over-the-counter market. Some firms in the NASDAQ Composite index, such as Microsoft and Intel, are also included in the Dow and in the S&P 500, but the NASDAQ includes stocks issued by many smaller technology firms that are not included in the other indexes.

> **Stock market index** An average of stock prices that is used to measure the overall performance of the stock market.

Although these three stock indexes are averages of the stock prices of different companies, Figure 6.2 shows that these indexes move broadly together. All three indexes

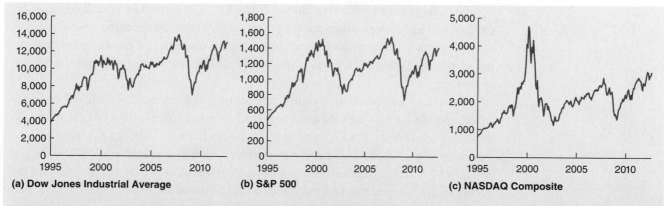

(a) Dow Jones Industrial Average

(b) S&P 500

(c) NASDAQ Composite

Figure 6.2 Fluctuations in the Stock Market, January 1995–August 2012

Investors can follow the performance of the U.S. stock market through stock market indexes, which are averages of stock prices. The most widely followed indexes are the Dow Jones Industrial Average, the S&P 500 index, and the NASDAQ Composite index. The graphs show that all three indexes follow roughly similar patterns, although the NASDAQ reached a peak in early 2000 that it has not come close to reaching again.

increased substantially in the late 1990s and reached peaks in early 2000. Much of the growth in stock prices during the late 1990s was fueled by the "dot-com boom," during which investors enthusiastically believed that many new online firms would become very profitable competing with traditional "brick and mortar" stores. Some dot-coms, such as Amazon.com, did succeed and become profitable, but many others, such as Pets.com, eToys.com, and Webvan.com, did not. Because the NASDAQ Composite index contained many more dot-com stocks than did the other two indexes, it soared to a particularly high peak in early 2000. As investors became convinced that many dot-coms would not become profitable, all three indexes declined sharply, although the decline in the NASDAQ was the most severe. The recession of 2001 also contributed to a general fall in stock prices.

The Dow and the S&P 500 recovered from the dot-com crash, reaching new all-time highs in the fall of 2007. The NASDAQ has yet to come close to regaining the high it reached in early 2000. The financial crisis and the recession that began in December 2007 caused all three indexes to decline sharply until the spring of 2009, when all three began to recover. In Wall Street jargon, an increase in stock prices of more than 20% is called a *bull market*, while a decline in stock prices of more than 20% is called a *bear market*. So, during the period covered by the graphs, the U.S. stock market experienced three bull markets and two bear markets.

Does the Performance of the Stock Market Matter to the Economy?

Figure 6.2 shows that the stock market goes through substantial swings. These swings affect the personal finances of investors who own stocks, but do the swings affect the broader economy? Fluctuations in stock prices can affect the economy by influencing the spending of households and firms. Rising stock prices can lead to increased spending, and falling stock prices can lead to decreased spending. Increases in spending can lead to increases in production and employment, while decreases in spending can lead to decreases in production and employment. The effect of changes in stock prices on spending occurs primarily through three channels.

First, large corporations use the stock market as an important source of funds for expansion. Higher stock prices make it easier for firms to fund spending on real physical investments such as factories and machinery, or on research and development, by issuing new stock. Lower stock prices make it more difficult for firms to finance this type of spending.

Second, stocks make up a significant portion of household wealth. When stock prices rise, so does household wealth, and when stock prices fall, so does household wealth. For example, the increase in stock prices between 1995 and 2000 increased wealth by $9 trillion, while the decline in stock prices between 2000 and 2002 wiped out $7 trillion in wealth. Similarly, the fall in stock prices between the fall of 2007 and the spring of 2009 wiped out $8.5 trillion in wealth. Households spend more when their wealth increases and less when their wealth decreases. So, fluctuations in stock prices can have a significant effect on the consumption spending of households.

Finally, the most important consequence of fluctuations in stock prices may be their effect on the expectations of consumers and firms. Significant declines in stock prices are typically followed by economic recessions. Consumers who are aware of this pattern may become more uncertain about their future incomes and jobs when they see a large fall in stock prices. Christina Romer, an economist at the University of California, Berkeley, and former chair of the Council of Economic Advisers in the Obama administration, has argued that the stock market crash of 1929 played an important role in causing the Great Depression of the 1930s. Romer argues that the crash increased uncertainty among consumers about their future incomes, which caused them to significantly reduce spending on consumer durables, such as automobiles, furniture, and appliances. These spending declines led to production and employment declines in the affected industries, which worsened the economic downturn that had already begun. By increasing uncertainty, fluctuations in stock prices can also cause firms to postpone spending on physical capital, such as equipment and factories.

Making the Connection | In Your Interest

Should You Invest in the U.S. Stock Market?

The financial crisis of 2007–2009 dealt the U.S. stock market a heavy blow. From its peak above 14,000 in October 2007, the Dow dropped to about 6,500 in March 2009, a decline of nearly 54%. The S&P 500 index and the NASDAQ Composite index suffered similar declines. Not surprisingly, many small investors headed for the stock market exits. Between the third quarter of 2008 and the first quarter of 2009, households redeemed, or sold back to the issuing company, $835 billion more in stock mutual fund shares than they purchased. The value of the mutual funds held by households declined by almost $2 *trillion* during this period.

As the Dow began to recover in 2009, some individual investors returned to the stock market, but many did not. In 2012, an article in the *Wall Street Journal* observed, "Many investors are paralyzed by this environment, which is unlike anything they have seen in their adult lives. As a result, they're hunkering down in cash and super-safe government bonds." There were bear markets in 2000–2002 and 2007–2009, so the period of 1999 to 2009 was a poor one for stock market investors. Is it possible that this 10-year period of poor performance has permanently soured individual investors on the U.S. stock market?

Economic research indicates that investors' willingness to participate in the stock market is affected by the returns they have experienced during their lives. The worst bear market in U.S. history occurred from 1929 to 1932, when the Dow declined by 89%, and even decades later, investors who lived through that period were reluctant to invest in the stock market. The impression that the market is not a level playing field may further reduce the participation of individual investors in the stock market. A poll in 2010 showed that while 24% of those polled had little or no faith in their local banks, 67% had little or no faith in Wall Street.

As a young investor, should you stay out of the stock market? The answer is that if you do, you may not meet your long-term investment goals because the long-run average annual return on investments in the stock market is far higher than the annual returns on investments in Treasury bills or bank certificates of deposit (CDs) (see Chapter 4). Suppose that you start investing by saving $100 per month beginning at age 22.

The table below shows how much you would accumulate at age 45 and at the normal retirement age of 67 if you save by buying bank CDs, U.S. Treasury bills, and stock.

Results of Investing $100 per Month Beginning at Age 22

	CDs (at 2.5%)	Treasury bills (at 4.0%)	Stocks (at 12.0%)
At age 45	$37,565	$45,862	$164,607
At age 67	$99,985	$151,550	$2,167,024
At age 67, after inflation	$54,100	$77,253	$887,240

No one can forecast exactly what the returns to these investments may be in the decades ahead, but we have chosen reasonable estimates based on past returns. Bank CDs are a very safe investment that cautious investors trust, but the second row shows that at age 45, you will have accumulated much less than if you had taken on slightly more risk by investing in Treasury bills or considerably more risk by investing in stocks, perhaps by buying a diversified stock mutual fund such as the Vanguard Index 500 fund. The longer your time horizon, the greater the gap between the investments becomes. By retirement age of 67, investing in stocks will leave you with more than 20 times the amount you would have accumulated from bank CDs.

The results in the first two rows of the table represent nominal returns, uncorrected for inflation. The final row shows how much you would accumulate in dollars that have the same purchasing power as they did when you were 22, assuming that inflation averages 2.5% per year. Once again, the gap between what you would accumulate by investing in CDs versus investing in stocks is very large: $54,100 versus $887,240.

An important issue for the U.S. financial system in the coming years is whether young investors whose experience with the stock market has been largely negative will be less willing than older investors to participate in the stock market. Economists debate the possible consequences for market efficiency if the share of stock market trading carried out by individual investors continues to shrink relative to the share carried out by institutional investors such as pension funds and hedge funds.

Note: The calculations in the table assume an initial deposit of $100 and that the annual interest rates are compounded monthly.

Sources: Tom Lauricella, "'Retro' Investing—Look Back to Get Ahead," *Wall Street Journal*, February 19, 2012; Ulrike Malmendier and Stefan Nagel, "Depression Babies: Do Macroeconomic Experiences Affect Risk-Taking?" *Quarterly Journal of Economics*, Vol. 126, No. 1, February 2011, pp. 373–416; Luigi Guiso, Paola Sapienza, and Luigi Zingales, "Trusting the Stock Market," *Journal of Finance*, Vol. 63, No. 6, December 2008, pp. 2557–2600; and Zogby Interactive, "Voter Confidence in Big Banks, Corporations, and Wall Street Even Lower Than That of Government," zogby.com, February 18, 2010.

See related problem 1.8 at the end of the chapter.

6.2

Learning Objective

Explain how stock prices are determined.

How Stock Prices Are Determined

We have seen that stock indexes fluctuate, but what determines the prices of the individual stocks that make up those indexes? Recall a key fact about financial markets: *The price of a financial asset is equal to the present value of the payments to be received from owning it* (see Chapter 3). We have applied this rule to the prices of bonds, but the rule holds equally true for stocks, as we will see in the following sections.

Investing in Stock for One Year

Individual investors do not purchase stock in an attempt to control the firms whose stock they buy; they leave that to the firms' managers, supervised by their boards of directors. Instead, investors view purchases of stock as a financial investment on which they hope to receive a high rate of return. Suppose you intend to invest in Microsoft stock for one year. During the year, you expect to receive a dividend, and at the end of the year you can, if you choose, sell the stock for its market price at that time. Firms pay dividends quarterly, but for the sake of simplicity, we will assume that they make a single payment of dividends at the end of the year. Suppose you expect that Microsoft will pay a dividend of $0.60 per share and that the price of Microsoft stock at the end of the year will be $32 per share. To the investor, the value of the stock equals the present value of these two dollar amounts, which are the *cash flows* from owning the stock.

We have seen how investors in the bond market use an interest rate to discount future payments in calculating the present value of a bond (see Chapter 3). Similarly, you need to use a discount rate to calculate the present value of the cash flows from the stock. Rather than use the interest rate on, say, bank CDs to discount the cash flows, it makes sense for you to use a rate that represents your expected return on alternative investments of comparable risk to investing in shares of Microsoft. Taking the viewpoint of investors, economists refer to this rate as the **required return on equities, r_E.** From the viewpoint of firms, this is the rate of return they need to pay to attract investors, so it is called the *equity cost of capital*. The required return on equities and the equity cost of capital are the same rate—just looked at from the differing perspectives of investors and firms.

We can think of the required return on equities as the sum of a risk-free interest rate—usually measured as the return on Treasury bills—and a risk premium that reflects that investments in stocks are riskier than investments in Treasury bills. The risk premium included in the required return on equities is called the *equity premium* because it represents the additional return investors must receive in order to invest in stocks (equities) rather than Treasury bills. The equity premium for an individual stock, such as Microsoft, has two components. One component represents the *systematic risk* that results from general price fluctuations in the stock market that affect all stocks, such as the decline in stock prices during the financial crisis of 2007–2009. The other component is *unsystematic*, or *idiosyncratic*, risk that results from movements in the price of that particular stock that are not caused by general fluctuations in the stock market. An example of unsystematic risk would be the price of Microsoft's stock falling because a new version of Windows has poor sales.

Suppose that taking these factors into account, you require a 10% return in order to be willing to invest in Microsoft. In this case, to you, the present value of the two dollar amounts—the expected dividend and the expected price of the stock at the end of the year—is:

$$\frac{\$0.60}{1 + 0.10} + \frac{\$32}{1 + 0.10} = \$29.64.$$

If the price of a share of Microsoft is currently less than $29.64, you should buy the stock because it is selling for less than the present value of the funds you will receive from owning the stock. If the price is greater than $29.64, you should not buy the stock.

Required return on equities, r_E The expected return necessary to compensate for the risk of investing in stocks.

If we take the perspective of investors as a group, rather than that of a single investor, then we would expect the price of a stock today, P_t, to equal the sum of the present values of the dividend expected to be paid at the end of the year, D^e_{t+1}, and the expected price of the stock at the end of the year, P^e_{t+1}, discounted by the market's required return on equities, r_E, or

$$P_t = \frac{D^e_{t+1}}{(1 + r_E)} + \frac{P^e_{t+1}}{(1 + r_E)}.$$

Note that we use the superscript e to indicate that investors do not know with certainty either the dividend the firm will pay or the price of the firm's stock at the end of the year.

The Rate of Return on a One-Year Investment in a Stock

For a holding period of one year, the rate of return on an investment in a bond equals the current yield on the bond plus the rate of capital gain on the bond. We can calculate the rate of return on an investment in a stock in a similar way. Just as the coupon divided by the current price is the current yield on a bond, the expected annual dividend divided by the current price is the **dividend yield** on a stock. The rate of capital gain on a stock is equal to the change in the price of the stock during the year divided by the price at the beginning of the year. So, the expected rate of return from investing in a stock equals the dividend yield plus the expected rate of capital gain:

Dividend yield The expected annual dividend divided by the current price of a stock.

$$\text{Rate of return} = \frac{\text{Expected annual dividend}}{\text{Initial price}} + \frac{\text{Expected change in price}}{\text{Initial price}},$$

Or,

$$R = \frac{D^e_{t+1}}{P_t} + \frac{(P^e_{t+1} - P_t)}{P_t}.$$

At the end of the year, you can calculate your actual rate of return by substituting the dividend actually received for the expected dividend and the actual price of the stock at the end of the year for the expected price. For example, suppose that you purchased a share of Microsoft for $30, Microsoft paid a dividend of $0.60, and the price of Microsoft at the end of the year was $33. Your rate of return for the year would be:

$$(\$0.60/\$30) + (\$33 - \$30)/\$30 = 0.02 + 0.10 = 0.12, \text{ or } 12\%.$$

Making the Connection   In Your Interest

How Should the Government Tax Your Investment in Stocks?

If you invest in stocks, you will receive dividends and capital gains on your investments, and you must report them as income on your tax return. Economists and policymakers debate the best way of taxing dividends and capital gains. Corporate profits are subject to the corporate profits tax, which companies pay before they distribute dividends to their stockholders. Because stockholders must pay individual income taxes on the dividends they receive, the result is a *double taxation of dividends*.

This double taxation has three important effects: First, because dividends are taxed at both the firm level and the individual level, the return investors receive from buying stocks is reduced, which reduces the incentive people have to save in the form of stock investments and increases the costs to firms of raising funds. Second, because profits that firms distribute to stockholders are taxed a second time, firms have an incentive to retain profits rather than to distribute them to stockholders. Retaining profits may be inefficient if firms are led to make investments that have lower returns than the investments stockholders would have made had they received dividends. Finally, because firms can deduct from their profits the interest payments they make on loans and bonds, the double taxation of dividends gives firms an incentive to take on what may be an excessive level of debt rather than issue stock.

Some economists have proposed eliminating the double taxation of dividends by integrating the corporate and individual income taxes. Under this plan, for tax purposes, firms would allocate all of their profits to their stockholders, even profits the firms don't distribute as dividends. The corporate income tax would be eliminated, and individuals would be responsible for paying all the taxes due on corporate profits. Although this plan would eliminate the problems with double taxation, it would require an extensive revision of the current tax system and has not attracted much support from policymakers.

Capital gains are taxed only when an investor sells an asset and realizes the gain. Some economists argue that taxing capital gains results in a *lock-in effect* because investors may be reluctant to sell stocks that have substantial capital gains. This reluctance is increased by the fact that investors have to pay taxes on their nominal gains without an adjustment for inflation. If many investors are locked in to their current portfolios, then the prices in those portfolios will be different than they would be in the absence of capital gains taxes, which may send misleading signals to investors and firms.

In 2003, Congress reduced from 35% to 15% both the tax on dividends and the tax on capital gains on stocks and other assets that investors held for at least one year. Because 15% is below the top individual tax rate of 35%, this rate cut reduced the inefficiencies resulting from the double taxation of dividends and the taxation of capital gains. Some policymakers have criticized the lower tax rate on dividends, however, for adversely affecting the distribution of after-tax income. For example, households at the very top of the income distribution earn three-quarters of their income from dividends and capital gains. So, the low tax rate on dividends and capital gains can reduce the tax rate high-income households pay relative to the tax rate paid by lower-income households, who may depend more heavily on wage income taxed at the regular rates. During 2012, President Barack Obama and Democratic leaders in Congress proposed raising the tax rate on dividends and capital gains to reduce what they perceived to be an inequity.

The trade-off between efficiency and equity is a recurring issue in economic policy. Policymakers must often balance the need to improve economic efficiency, which can increase incomes and growth, with the desire to distribute income more equally.

Sources: Jackie Calmes, "Obama Proposes Taxing Wealthiest Dividends," *New York Times*, February 13, 2012; and Robert Schroeder, "Democrats Paint Target on Wealthy over Capital Gains, *Wall Street Journal*, September 20, 2012.

See related problem 2.10 at the end of the chapter.

The Fundamental Value of Stock

Now consider the case of an investor who intends to invest in a stock for two years. We apply the logic we used in the case of the one-year investment to the case of a two-year investment: The price of the stock should be equal to the sum of the present values of the dividend payments the investor expects to receive during the two years plus the present value of the expected price of the stock at the end of two years:

$$P_t = \frac{D^e_{t+1}}{(1 + r_E)} + \frac{D^e_{t+2}}{(1 + r_E)^2} + \frac{P^e_{t+2}}{(1 + r_E)^2}.$$

We could continue to consider investments over more years, which would lead to similar equations, with the final expected price term being pushed further and further into the future. Ultimately, as we found when discussing bonds, the price of a share of stock should reflect the present value of all the payments to be received from owning the stock over however many periods. In fact, economists consider the *fundamental value* of a share of stock to be equal to the present value of all the dividends investors expect to receive into the indefinite future:

$$P_t = \frac{D^e_{t+1}}{(1 + r_E)} + \frac{D^e_{t+2}}{(1 + r_E)^2} + \frac{D^e_{t+3}}{(1 + r_E)^3} + \cdots,$$

where the ellipsis (. . .) indicates that the dividend payments continue forever. Because we are looking at an infinite stream of dividend payments, there is no longer a final price term, P^e, in the equation.

What about firms that pay no dividends, such as Facebook and Berkshire Hathaway, the company run by Warren Buffett, perhaps the best-known and most successful investor of recent decades? We can use this same equation to calculate the fundamental value of the firm, under the assumption that investors expect it to eventually start paying dividends. In that case, some of the initial expected dividend terms would be zero, and we would insert positive numbers starting in the year in which we expected the firm to begin paying dividends. Investors probably would not buy the stock of a firm that was never expected to pay dividends because in that case, investors would never expect to receive their proportionate share of the firm's profits.

The Gordon Growth Model

The equation given above for the fundamental value of a share of stock isn't too helpful to an investor trying to evaluate the price of a stock because it requires forecasting an infinite number of dividends. Fortunately, in 1959, Myron J. Gordon, then an economist at the Massachusetts Institute of Technology, developed a handy method of estimating the fundamental value of a stock. Gordon considered the case in which investors expect a firm's dividends to grow at a constant rate, g, which could be, say, 5%. In that case, each dividend term in the equation above would be 5% greater than the dividend received in the previous year. Using this assumption that dividends are expected to grow at a constant rate, Gordon developed an equation showing the relationship between the current price of the stock, the current dividend paid, the expected growth rate of dividends, and the required return on equities. This equation is called the **Gordon growth model**:

$$P_t = D_t \times \frac{(1 + g)}{(r_E - g)}.$$

Suppose that Microsoft is currently paying an annual dividend of $0.60 per share. The dividend is expected to grow at a constant rate of 7% per year, and the return investors require to invest in Microsoft is 10%. Then, the current price of a share of Microsoft stock should be:

$$\$0.60 \times \frac{(1 + 0.07)}{(0.10 - 0.07)} = \$21.40.$$

There are several points to notice about the Gordon growth model:

1. The model assumes that the growth rate of dividends is constant. This assumption may be unrealistic because investors might believe that dividends will grow in an uneven pattern. For instance, Microsoft's profits—and the dividends it pays—may grow more rapidly during the years following the introduction of a new version of Windows than during the following years. Nevertheless, the assumption of constant dividend growth is a useful approximation in analyzing stock prices.
2. To use the model, the required rate of return on the stock must be greater than the dividend growth rate. This is a reasonable condition because if a firm's dividends grow at a rate faster than the required return on equities, the firm will eventually become larger than the entire economy, which, of course, cannot happen.
3. Investors' expectations of the future profitability of firms and, therefore, their future dividends, are crucial in determining the prices of stocks.

> **Gordon growth model** A model that uses the current dividend paid, the expected growth rate of dividends, and the required return on equities to calculate the price of a stock.

Solved Problem 6.2

Using the Gordon Growth Model to Evaluate GE Stock

The Gordon growth model is a useful tool for calculating the price of a stock. Apply the model to the following two problems:

  a. If General Electric (GE) is currently paying an annual dividend of $0.40 per share, its dividend is expected to grow at a rate of 7% per year, and the return investors require to buy GE's stock is 10%, calculate the price per share for GE's stock.

  b. In September 2012, the price of IBM's stock was $207 per share. At the time, IBM was paying an annual dividend of $3.40 per share. If the return investors required to buy IBM's stock was 0.10, what growth rate in IBM's dividend must investors have been expecting?

Solving the Problem

Step 1 Review the chapter material. This problem is about using the Gordon growth model to calculate stock prices, so you may want to review the section "The Gordon Growth Model," which begins on page 168.

Step 2 **Calculate GE's stock price by applying the Gordon growth model equation to the numbers given in part (a).** The Gordon growth model equation is:

$$P_t = D_t \times \frac{(1 + g)}{(r_E - g)}.$$

Substituting the numbers given in the problem allows us to calculate the price of GE's stock:

$$\$0.40 \times \frac{(1 + 0.07)}{(0.10 - 0.07)} = \$14.27.$$

Step 3 **Calculate the expected growth rate of IBM's dividend by applying the Gordon growth model equation to the numbers given in part (b).** In this problem, we know the price of the stock but not the expected rate of dividend growth. To calculate the expected rate of dividend growth, we need to plug the numbers given into the Gordon growth equation and then solve for g:

$$\$207 = \$3.40 \times \frac{(1 + g)}{(0.10 - g)}$$

$$\$207 \times (0.10 - g) = \$3.40 \times (1 + g)$$

$$\$20.70 - \$207g = \$3.40 + \$3.40g$$

$$g = \frac{\$17.30}{\$210.40} = 0.082, \text{ or } 8.2\%.$$

Our calculation shows that investors must have been expecting IBM's dividend to grow at an annual rate of 8.2%.

See related problem 2.11 at the end of the chapter.

6.3

Learning Objective

Explain the connection between the assumption of rational expectations and the efficient markets hypothesis.

Rational Expectations and Efficient Markets

The Gordon growth model shows that investors' expectations of the future profitability of firms play a crucial role in determining stock prices. In fact, expectations play an important role throughout the economy because many transactions require participants to forecast the future. For instance, if you are considering taking out a mortgage loan in which you agree to pay a fixed interest rate of 5% for 30 years, you will need to forecast such things as:

- Your future income: Will you be able to afford the mortgage payments?
- The future inflation rate: What will be the real interest rate on the loan?
- The future of the neighborhood the house is in: Will the city extend a bus line to make it easier to travel downtown?

Adaptive Expectations Versus Rational Expectations

Economists have spent considerable time studying how people form expectations. Early studies of expectations focused on the use of information from the past. For example, some economists assumed that investors' expectations of the price of a firm's stock depended only on past prices of the stock. This approach is called **adaptive expectations**. Some stock analysts employ a version of adaptive expectations known as *technical analysis*. These analysts believe that certain patterns in the history of a stock's price are likely to be repeated, and, therefore, can be used to forecast future prices.

Today, most economists are critical of the adaptive expectations approach because it assumes that people ignore information that would be useful in making forecasts. For example, in the late 1970s, the rate of inflation increased each year from 1976 through 1980. Anyone forecasting inflation by looking only at its past values would have expected inflation to be *lower* than it turned out to be. The rate of inflation declined each year from 1980 through 1983. During this period, anyone forecasting inflation by looking only at its past values would have expected inflation to be *higher* than it actually was. Anyone taking into account additional information, such as Federal Reserve policy, movements in oil prices, or other factors that affect inflation rather than relying only on past values of inflation would have made a more accurate forecast.

In 1961, John Muth of Carnegie Mellon University proposed a new approach he labeled *rational expectations*. With **rational expectations**, people make forecasts using all available information. Muth argued that someone who did not use all available information would not be acting rationally. That is, the person would not be doing his or her best to achieve the goal of an accurate forecast. For example, in forecasting the price of a firm's stock, investors should use not just past prices of the stock but also any other information that is helpful in forecasting the future profitability of the firm, including the quality of the firm's management, new products the firm might be developing, and so on. If a sufficient number of investors and traders in the stock market have rational expectations, the market price of a stock should equal the best guess of the present value of expected future dividends, which, as we saw earlier, is the stock's *fundamental value*. Therefore, if market participants have rational expectations, they can assume that the stock prices they observe represent the fundamental values of those stocks.

To economists, if people have rational expectations, their expectations equal the optimal forecast (the best guess) of prices, using all information available to them. Although we are applying rational expectations to stocks, this concept applies to any financial security. If investors in the stock market have rational expectations, then the expectation of the future value of a stock should equal the optimal (best guess) price forecast. Of course, saying that investors have rational expectations is not the same as saying that they can foretell the future. In other words, the optimal forecast is optimal, but it may be wrong.

To state this concept more exactly, suppose that at the end of trading today on the stock market, P_{t+1}^e is the optimal forecast of the price of Apple's stock at the end of trading tomorrow. If P_{t+1} is the *actual* price of Apple's stock at the end of trading tomorrow, then it is very unlikely that we will see $P_{t+1}^e = P_{t+1}$. Why? Because tomorrow, investors and traders are likely to obtain additional information about Apple—perhaps sales of the iPad during the previous month are below what was forecast—that will change their view of the fundamental value of Apple's stock. So, there is likely to be a *forecast error*, which is the difference between the forecast price of Apple's stock and the actual price of Apple's stock. But no one can accurately forecast the size of that error because the error is caused by *new* information that is not available when the forecast is made. If the

Adaptive expectations
The assumption that people make forecasts of future values of a variable using only past values of the variable.

Rational expectations
The assumption that people make forecasts of future values of a variable using all available information; formally, the assumption that expectations equal optimal forecasts, using all available information.

information was available when the forecast is made, rational expectations tells us that it would have been incorporated into the forecast. To state the point more formally:

$$P_{t+1} - P_{t+1}^e = \text{Unforecastable error}_{t+1}.$$

So, when a forecast is made, we can be fairly sure that the forecast will turn out to be lower or higher than the actual value of the variable being forecast, but we have no way of telling how large the error will be or even whether it will be positive (that is, our forecast was too low) or negative (that is, our forecast was too high).

The Efficient Markets Hypothesis

Efficient markets hypothesis The application of rational expectations to financial markets; the hypothesis that the equilibrium price of a security is equal to its fundamental value.

As originally developed by John Muth, the concept of rational expectations applies whenever people are making forecasts. The application of rational expectations to financial markets is known as the **efficient markets hypothesis**. With respect to the stock market, the efficient markets hypothesis states that when investors and traders use all available information in forming expectations of future dividend payments, the equilibrium price of a stock equals the market's optimal forecast—the best forecast given available information—of the stock's fundamental value. How can we be sure that markets will operate as the efficient markets hypothesis predicts and that equilibrium prices will equal fundamental values?

An Example of the Efficient Markets Hypothesis Consider an example. Suppose that it is 10:14 Monday morning, and the price of Microsoft stock is $32.10 per share, the company is currently paying an annual dividend of $0.90 per share, and its dividend is expected to grow at a rate of 7% per year. At 10:15, Microsoft releases new sales information that indicates that sales of its latest version of Windows have been much higher than expected, and the firm expects higher sales to continue into the future. This news causes you and other investors to revise upward your forecast of the growth rate of Microsoft's annual dividend from 7% to 8%. At this higher growth rate and assuming an r_E of 10%, the present value of Microsoft's future dividends rises from $32.10 to $48.60. So, this new information causes you and other investors to buy shares of Microsoft. This increased demand will cause the price of Microsoft's shares to keep rising until they reach $48.60, which is the new fundamental value of the stock. Investors who have rational expectations can profit by buying or selling a stock when its market price is higher or lower than the optimal forecast of the stock's fundamental value. In this way, self-interested actions of informed traders cause available information to be incorporated into market prices.

Financial arbitrage The process of buying and selling securities to profit from price changes over a brief period of time.

Does the efficient markets hypothesis require that all investors and traders have rational expectations? Actually, it does not. The process of buying and reselling securities to profit from price changes over a brief period of time is called **financial arbitrage** (see Chapter 3). The profits made from financial arbitrage are called *arbitrage profits*. In competing to buy securities where earning arbitrage profits is possible, traders will force prices to the level where investors can no longer earn arbitrage profits. As long as there are some traders with rational expectations, the arbitrage profits provided by new information will give these traders the incentive to push stock prices to their fundamental values. For instance, in the example just discussed, once the new information on Microsoft becomes available, traders can earn arbitrage profits equal to $16.50 per share, or the difference between the old fundamental value and the new fundamental value. Competition among even a few well-informed traders will be enough to quickly drive the price up to its new fundamental value.

Although the efficient markets hypothesis indicates that the price of a share of stock is based on all available information, our Microsoft example shows that the prices of stocks will change day-to-day, hour-to-hour, and minute-to-minute. Stock prices constantly change as news that affects fundamental values becomes available. Note that anything that affects the willingness of investors to hold a stock or another financial asset affects the stock's fundamental value. Therefore, we would expect that if new information leads investors to change their opinions about the risk, liquidity, information costs, or tax treatment of the returns from owning a stock, the price of the stock will change because the r_E will change.

What About "Inside Information"? The efficient markets hypothesis assumes that publicly available information is incorporated into the prices of stocks. But what about information that is not publicly available? Suppose, for example, that the managers of a pharmaceutical firm receive word that an important new cancer drug has unexpectedly received government approval, but this information has not yet been publicly released. Or suppose that economists at the U.S. Bureau of Labor Statistics have finished calculating the previous month's inflation rate, which shows that inflation was much higher than investors had expected, but this information has also not yet been publicly released. Relevant information about a security that is not publicly available is called **inside information**. A strong version of the efficient markets hypothesis holds that even inside information is incorporated into stock prices. Many studies have shown, however, that it is possible to earn above-average returns by trading on the basis of inside information. For instance, the managers of the pharmaceutical firm could buy their company's stock and profit from the increase in the stock's price once the information on the drug's approval is released.

Inside information
Relevant information about a security that is not publicly available.

There is an important catch, though: Trading on inside information—known as *insider trading*—is illegal. Under U.S. securities laws, as enforced by the Securities and Exchange Commission (SEC), employees of a firm may not buy and sell the firm's stocks and bonds on the basis of information that is not publicly available. They also may not provide the information to others who would use it to buy and sell the firm's stocks and bonds. In 2012, a former Intel executive was among more than 20 people convicted of providing inside information about their firms to the manager of the Galleon hedge fund. The manager of the hedge fund was sentenced to 11 years in prison for having illegally earned $75 million trading stocks on the basis of inside information. Federal prosecutors called it the biggest insider trading case in history.

Are Stock Prices Predictable?

A key implication of the efficient markets hypothesis is that stock prices are not predictable. To see why, suppose that it is 4:00 P.M., stock trading has closed for the day, Apple stock has closed at a price of $675, and you are trying to forecast the price of Apple's stock at the close of trading tomorrow. What is your optimal forecast? The efficient markets hypothesis indicates that it is $675. In other words, the best forecast of the price

Random walk The unpredictable movements in the price of a security.

of a stock tomorrow is its price today. Why? Because the price today reflects all relevant information that is currently available. While the price of Apple's stock is unlikely to actually be $675 at the close of trading tomorrow, you have no information today that will allow you to forecast whether it will be higher or lower.

Rather than being predictable, stock prices follow a **random walk**, which means that on any given day, they are as likely to rise as to fall. We can certainly observe stocks that rise for a number of days in a row, but this does not contradict the idea that stock prices follow a random walk. Even though when we flip a coin, it is equally likely to come up heads or tails, we may still flip a number of heads or tails in a row.

Efficient Markets and Investment Strategies

Understanding the efficient markets hypothesis allows investors to formulate strategies for portfolio allocation as well as for trading and assessing the value of financial analysis. We consider these strategies in the following sections.

Portfolio Allocation As long as all investors have the same information, the efficient markets hypothesis predicts that the trading process will eliminate opportunities for above-average profits. In other words, you may be convinced that Apple will make very high profits from selling the iPad, but if every other investor also has this information, it is unlikely that investing in Apple will provide you with a return higher than you would receive by investing in another stock. Therefore, it is not a good strategy to risk your savings by buying only one stock. Instead, you should hold a diversified portfolio of assets. That way, news that may unfavorably affect the price of one stock can be offset by news that will favorably affect the price of another stock. If sales of the iPad are disappointing, the price of Apple's stock will fall, while if sales of a new veggie burger at McDonald's are higher than expected, the price of McDonald's stock will rise. Because we can't know ahead of time what will happen, it makes sense to hold a diversified portfolio of stocks and other assets.

Trading If prices reflect all available information, regularly buying and selling individual stocks is not a profitable strategy. Investors should not move funds repeatedly from one stock to another, or *churn* a portfolio, particularly because each sale or purchase incurs trading costs in the form of commissions. It is better to buy and hold a diversified portfolio over a long period of time.

Financial Analysts and Hot Tips Financial analysts, like those employed by Wall Street firms such as Bank of America Merrill Lynch and Goldman Sachs, fall into two broad categories: *technical analysts* who rely on patterns of past stock prices to predict future stock prices and *fundamental analysts* who rely on forecasting future profits of firms in order to forecast future stock prices. We have already mentioned that technical analysis relies on adaptive expectations. Economists believe that technical analysis is unlikely to be a successful strategy for forecasting stock prices because it neglects all the available information except for past stock prices.

Fundamental analysis seems more consistent with the rational expectations approach because it uses all available information. But is fundamental analysis likely to be a successful strategy for forecasting stock prices? Many financial analysts appear to think so because they use fundamental analysis to advise their clients about which stocks to buy. They also use fundamental analysis when recommending stocks on cable news programs or in interviews with financial newspapers. But the efficient markets hypothesis indicates that the stocks that financial analysts recommend are unlikely to outperform the market. Although analysts may be very good at identifying which firms have the best management, the most exciting new products, and the greatest capacity to earn profits in the future, other investors and traders also know all that information, and it is already incorporated into the prices of stocks.

Although it seems paradoxical, a firm that analysts and investors expect to be highly profitable in the future may be no better as an investment than a firm that they expect to be much less profitable. If investors require a 10% return to invest in the stock of either firm, the stock issued by the very profitable firm will have a much higher price than the stock issued by the less profitable firm. In fact, we know that the price of the more profitable firm's stock must be high enough and the price of the less profitable firm's stock must be low enough so that an investor would expect to earn 10% on either investment. The situation is the same as that in the bond market. If two bonds appear identical to investors in terms of risk, liquidity, information costs, and tax treatment, then competition among investors looking for the best investment will ensure that the two bonds have the same yield to maturity. If one bond has a coupon of $60 and the other bond has a coupon of $50, the bond with the higher coupon will also have a price high enough that it will have the same yield to maturity as the bond with the lower coupon.

Therefore, the efficient markets hypothesis indicates that the stock of a more profitable firm will not be a better investment than the stock of a less profitable firm.

What if You Invest in the Stock Market by Picking Stocks Randomly?

Burton Malkiel, an economist at Princeton University, has popularized the efficient markets hypothesis in his book *A Random Walk Down Wall Street*, which has sold more than 1 million copies and gone through multiple editions since it was first published in 1973. In an early edition of his book, Malkiel made the following observation about the efficient markets hypothesis: "Taken to its logical extreme the theory means that a blindfolded monkey throwing darts at a newspaper's financial pages could select a portfolio that would do just as well as one carefully selected by the experts."

In 1988, the *Wall Street Journal* decided to test Malkiel's assertion by running a contest. Every month (later changed to every six months), the newspaper asked four financial analysts to each choose one stock. Not having a blindfolded monkey available, the *Journal* used a reporter to throw a dart randomly at the stock listings taped to an office wall. (Malkiel was given the honor of throwing the first dart.) The *Journal* then compared the performance of the four stocks chosen by the analysts with the performance of the one stock chosen randomly.

After 14 years, the *Journal* ended the competition and announced the results. Overall, there had been 142 periods in which the analysts' picks were matched against the dartboard picks. The prices of the stocks the analysts picked outperformed the prices of the dartboard picks in 87 of the 142 periods. The *Journal* had apparently compiled evidence that, contrary to the efficient markets hypothesis, financial analysts could pick stocks better than a blindfolded monkey.

Malkiel argued, though, that results of the competition were deceiving. First, the *Journal* looked only at changes in the prices of the stocks, ignoring the dividends paid. But as we saw earlier in this chapter, the return an investor receives for holding stock consists of both the dividend yield and the rate of capital gain. The dividend yield for the analysts' picks was only 1.2%, while the dividend yield for the dartboard stocks was 2.3%. Second, the analysts also chose stocks with higher-than-average risk. Because there is a trade-off between risk and return in financial markets, part of the higher return from the analysts' stocks was compensation for their higher risk. Finally, there is evidence that the higher return for the analysts' picks was simply *due to the fact that the analysts had picked the stocks*. At that time, the *Wall Street Journal* had a circulation of more than 1.5 million copies, and many investors followed the dartboard competition. As some investors read about the analysts' picks, they became convinced that these were good stocks in which to invest. As investors increased their demand for these stocks, the prices of the stocks rose. The evidence that this effect was large comes from the fact that most of the increases in the prices of the analysts' stocks came within two days of the *Journal* article being printed. Taking these facts into account reversed the outcome of the contest, leaving the darts slightly ahead of the analysts.

As a group, Wall Street financial analysts are hardworking and knowledgeable, and they provide good information on the financial health of firms, on the competence of firms' managers, and on the likely success of new products. There is not much evidence, however, that they can be consistently successful in choosing the best individual stocks in which to invest.

Sources: Burton G. Malkiel, *A Random Walk Down Wall Street*, New York: W.W. Norton & Company, 2012 (first edition, 1973); and Georgette Jasen, "Journal's Dartboard Retires After 14 Years of Stock Picks," *Wall Street Journal*, April 18, 2002.

See related problem 3.9 at the end of the chapter.

Solved Problem 6.3   **In Your Interest**

Should You Pay Attention to the Advice of Investment Analysts?

Financial analysts typically advise investors to buy stocks whose prices they believe will increase rapidly and to sell stocks whose prices they believe will either fall or increase slowly. The following excerpt from an article by Bloomberg News describes how well stock market analysts succeeded in predicting prices during one year:

Shares of JDS Uniphase, the company with the most "sell" recommendations among analysts,

has been a more profitable investment this year than Microsoft, the company with the most "buys."

The article goes on to say, "Investors say JDS Uniphase is an example of Wall Street analysts basing recommendations on past events, rather than on earnings prospects and potential share gains." Briefly explain whether you agree with the analysis of these "investors."

Solving the Problem

Step 1 **Review the chapter material.** This problem is about whether we can expect financial analysts to successfully predict stock prices, so you may want to review the section "Are Stock Prices Predictable?" which begins on page 173.

Step 2 **Use your understanding of the efficient markets hypothesis to solve the problem.** From the point of view of the efficient markets hypothesis, it is not surprising that during that year, the price of JDS Uniphase's stock rose more than the price of Microsoft's stock. Although Microsoft may have had better managers and been more profitable than JDS Uniphase, Microsoft's stock price at the beginning of the year was correspondingly higher. At the beginning of the year, investors must have been expecting to get similar returns by investing in the stock of either firm. Which firm would turn out to be the better investment depended on events during the year that investors could not have foreseen at the beginning of the year. As it turned out, these unforeseen events were more favorable toward JDS Uniphase, so with hindsight, we can say that it was the better investment.

The analysis of the "investors," as quoted in the article, is not correct from the efficient markets point of view. The key point is not that analysts were "basing recommendations on past events, rather than on earnings prospects and potential share gains." Even if analysts based their forecasts on the firms' earning prospects, they would have been no more successful, because all the available information on the firms' earnings prospects was already incorporated into the firms' stock prices.

Source: Scott Lanman, "Analyst Ratings Based on Past Missing Mark," Bloomberg.com, September 23, 2003.

See related problem 3.11 at the end of the chapter.

Actual Efficiency in Financial Markets

Learning Objective
Discuss the actual efficiency of financial markets.

Many economists believe that movements in asset prices in most financial markets are consistent with the efficient markets hypothesis. For example, empirical work by Eugene Fama of the University of Chicago and other economists has provided support for the conclusion that changes in stock prices are not predictable.

Other analysts—especially active traders and people giving investment advice—are more skeptical about whether the stock market, in particular, is an efficient market. They point to three differences between the theoretical behavior of financial markets and their actual behavior that raise doubts about the validity of the efficient markets hypothesis:

1. Some analysts believe that *pricing anomalies* in the market allow investors to earn consistently above-average returns. According to the efficient markets hypothesis, those opportunities for above-average returns should not exist—or at least should not exist very often or for very long.

2. These analysts also point to evidence that some price changes are predictable using available information. According to the efficient markets hypothesis, investors should not be able to predict future price changes using information that is publicly available.

3. These analysts also argue that changes in stock prices sometimes appear to be larger than changes in the fundamental values of the stocks. According to the efficient markets hypothesis, prices of securities should reflect their fundamental value.

Pricing Anomalies

The efficient markets hypothesis holds that an investor will not consistently be able to earn above-average returns by buying and selling individual stocks or groups of stocks. However, some analysts believe they have identified *stock trading strategies* that can result in above-average returns. From the perspective of the efficient markets hypothesis, these trading strategies are *anomalies*, or outcomes not consistent with the hypothesis. Two anomalies that analysts and economists often discuss are the *small firm effect* and the *January effect*.

The small firm effect refers to the fact that over the long run, investment in small firms has yielded a higher return than has investment in large firms. During the years 1926–2011, an investment in the stock of small firms would have received an average annual return of 16.5%, while an investment in the stock of large firms would have received an average annual return of only 11.8%. The January effect refers to the fact that during some years, rates of return on stocks have been abnormally high during January.

Do pricing anomalies indicate a flaw in the efficient markets hypothesis? Opinions among economists vary, but many are skeptical that these anomalies are actually inconsistent with the efficient markets hypothesis, for several reasons:

- *Data mining.* It is always possible to search through the data and construct trading strategies that would have earned above-average returns—if only we had thought of them ahead of time! This is obvious when considering some frivolous trading strategies, such as the one incorporating the "NFC effect." Several Wall Street analysts discovered the NFC effect when they noticed that the stock market tended to rise during years in which a team from the National Football Conference (NFC) won the Super Bowl and to fall during years in which a team from the American Football Conference (AFC) won. Of course, this effect represents a chance correlation between unrelated events. And as a predictor of the stock market's performance, the NFC effect has done a poor job in recent years. For instance, in 2008, the NFC's New York Giants won the Super Bowl, but the Dow declined by more than 35%, while in 2009, the AFC's Pittsburgh Steelers won the Super Bowl, but the Dow rose 15%. More seriously, even if data mining could uncover a trading strategy that would earn above-average returns, once that strategy became widely known, it would be unlikely to still earn high returns. So, it's not surprising that once the January effect received substantial publicity in the 1980s, it largely disappeared.

- *Risk, liquidity, and information costs.* The efficient markets hypothesis does not predict that all stock investments should have the same expected rate of return. Instead, the hypothesis predicts that all stock investments should have the same return *after adjustment for differences in risk, liquidity, and information costs.* So, even though investments in small firm stocks have had a higher average annual rate of return than investments in large firm stocks, these investments have had much higher levels of risk. In addition, markets for many small firm stocks are less liquid and have higher information costs than the markets for large firm stocks. So, some economists argue that the higher returns on investments in small firm stocks actually are just compensating investors for accepting higher risk, lower liquidity, and higher information costs.

- *Trading costs and taxes.* Some stock trading strategies popularized in books, magazines, and newsletters are quite complex and require buying and selling many individual stocks or groups of stocks during the year. When calculating the returns from these strategies, the writers promoting them rarely take into account the costs of all the required buying and selling. Each time an investor buys or sells a stock, the investor has to pay a commission, and this cost should be subtracted from the investor's return on the strategy. In addition, when an investor sells a stock for a higher price than the investor bought it for, the investor incurs a taxable capital gain. Taxes paid also need to be taken into account when calculating the return. Taking into account trading costs and taxes eliminates the above-average returns supposedly earned using many trading strategies.

Mean Reversion

The efficient markets hypothesis holds that investors cannot predict changes in stock prices by using currently available information because only news can change prices and returns. The efficient markets hypothesis therefore is inconsistent with what is known as *mean reversion*, which is the tendency for stocks that have recently been earning high returns to experience low returns in the future and for stocks that have recently been earning low returns to earn high returns in the future. If this pattern is sufficiently widespread, an investor could earn above-average returns on his or her portfolio by buying stocks whose returns have recently been low and selling stocks whose returns have recently been high.

On the other hand, some investors have claimed they earned above-average returns by following a strategy known as *momentum investing* that is almost the opposite of mean reversion. Momentum investing is based on the idea that there can be persistence in stock movements, so that a stock that is increasing in price is somewhat more likely to rise than to fall, and a stock that is decreasing in price is somewhat more likely to fall than to rise. So, if you follow the Wall Street saying "the trend is your friend," it may be advisable to buy when stock prices are rising and sell when they are falling.

Although opinions among economists about mean reversion and momentum investing differ, careful studies indicate that in practice, trading strategies based on either idea have difficulty earning above-average returns in the long run, particularly when trading costs and taxes are taken into account.

Excess Volatility

The efficient markets hypothesis tells us that the price of an asset equals the market's best estimate of its fundamental value. Fluctuations in actual market prices therefore should be no greater than fluctuations in fundamental value. Robert Shiller of Yale University has estimated over a period of decades the fundamental value of the stocks included in the S&P 500. He has concluded that the actual fluctuations in the prices of these stocks have been much greater than the fluctuations in their fundamental values. Economists have debated the technical accuracy of Shiller's results because there are disagreements over estimates of stocks' fundamental value and other issues. Many economists believe, however, that Shiller's analysis does raise doubts as to whether the efficient markets hypothesis applies exactly to the stock market. In principle, Shiller's results could be used to earn above-average returns by, for instance, selling stocks when they are above their fundamental values and buying them when they are below their fundamental values. In practice, though, attempts to use this trading strategy have not been consistently able to produce above-average returns.

We can summarize by saying that evidence from empirical studies generally confirms that stock prices reflect available information. However, examination of pricing anomalies, mean reversion, and excess volatility in stock prices has generated debate over whether fluctuations in stock prices reflect only changes in fundamental values.

Making the Connection

Does the Financial Crisis of 2007–2009 Disprove the Efficient Markets Theory?

During the financial crisis of 2007–2009, the major stock indexes declined dramatically. Between October 2007 and March 2009, the Dow Jones Industrial Average declined by 54%, the S&P 500 declined by 57%, and the NASDAQ Composite index declined by 56%. The efficient markets hypothesis indicates that these price declines should represent declines in the fundamental values of these stocks. Is it plausible that the fundamental value of the firms included in these indexes had actually declined by more than 50%? After all, the firms had not been destroyed by the crisis. With a few exceptions, the firms still existed, and their factories, offices, research and development staffs, and other assets were largely intact.

The decline in stock prices, though, may have been consistent with substantial changes in the expectations of investors about both the future growth rate of dividends and the degree of risk involved in investing in stocks. When investors believe a category of investment has become riskier, they raise the expected return they require from that investment category. So, it seems likely that during the financial crisis, investors increased the required return on equities, r_E, and decreased the expected growth rate of dividends, g. The Gordon growth model indicates that an increase in r_E and a decrease in g will cause a decline in stock prices. So, a supporter of the efficient markets hypothesis would argue that the sharp decline in stock prices was caused by investors responding to new information on the increased riskiness of stocks and the lower future growth of dividends. Economists who are skeptical of the efficient markets hypothesis have argued, though, that the new information that became available to investors was not sufficient to account for the size of the decline in stock prices.

See related problem 4.6 at the end of the chapter.

Behavioral Finance

6.5

Learning Objective
Discuss the basic concepts of behavioral finance.

Over the past 20 years, some economists have argued that even if the efficient markets hypothesis is correct that trading strategies capable of delivering above-average returns are extremely rare, there is still a payoff to a better understanding of how investors make their decisions. *Behavioral economics* is the study of situations in which people make choices that do not appear to be economically rational. The new field of **behavioral finance** applies concepts from behavioral economics to understand how people make choices in financial markets.

Behavioral finance The application of concepts from behavioral economics to understand how people make choices in financial markets.

When economists say that consumers, firms, or investors are behaving "rationally," they mean that they are taking actions that are appropriate to reach their goals, given the information available to them. There are many situations, though, in which people do not appear to be acting rationally in this sense. Why might people not act rationally? The most obvious reason is that they may not realize that their actions are inconsistent with their goals. For instance, there is evidence that people are often unrealistic about their future behavior. Although some people have the goal of being thin, they may decide to eat chocolate cake today because they intend to follow a healthier diet in the future. Unfortunately, if they persist each day in eating cake, they never attain their goal of being thin. Similarly, some people continue smoking because they intend to give it up sometime in the future. But that time never comes, and they end up suffering the long-term health effects of smoking. In both of these cases, people's current behavior is inconsistent with their long-term goals.

Some firms have noticed that fewer than the expected number of employees enroll in voluntary retirement savings plans known as 401(k) plans. Although these employees have a long-run goal of saving enough to enjoy a comfortable retirement, in the short run, they spend the money they need to save to attain their goal. If, however, firms automatically enroll employees in these retirement plans, giving them the option to leave the plan if they choose to, most employees remain in the plans. To a fully rational employee, the decision about whether to save through a 401(k) plan should be independent of the minor amount of paperwork involved in either enrolling in a plan or leaving a plan in which the employer has enrolled the employee. In practice, though, automatically enrolling employees in a plan means that to leave the plan, the employees must confront the inconsistency between their short-run actions of spending too much and their long-run goal of a comfortable retirement. Rather than confront their inconsistency, most employees choose to remain in the plan.

Behavioral finance also helps to explain the popularity among some investors of technical analysis, which attempts to predict future stock prices on the basis of patterns in past prices. Studies indicate that when shown plots of stock prices generated by randomly choosing numbers, many people believe they see persistent patterns even though none actually exist. The results of these studies may explain why some investors believe they see useful patterns in plots of past stock prices even if the prices are actually following a random walk, as indicated by the efficient markets hypothesis.

Investors also show a reluctance to admit mistakes by selling their losing investments. Once a stock whose price has declined is sold, there is no denying that investing in the stock was a mistake. As long as an investor holds on to a losing stock, the investor can hope that eventually the price will recover, and the loser will turn into a winner, even though the chances are equally good that the stock will continue to decline. Studies have shown that investors are more likely to sell stocks that have shown a price increase—thereby, "locking in" their gains—than they are to sell stocks that have experienced a price decline. For tax purposes, this is the opposite of an efficient strategy because capital gains are taxed only if the stock is sold. So, it makes sense to postpone the sale of these stocks to the future, while receiving the immediate tax benefit of selling the stocks whose prices have declined.

Noise Trading and Bubbles

Studies in behavioral finance have provided evidence that many investors exhibit over-confidence in their ability to carry out an investment strategy. When asked to estimate their investment returns, many investors report a number that is far above the returns they have actually earned. One consequence of overconfidence can be *noise trading*, which involves investors overreacting to good or bad news. Noise trading can result from an investor's inflated view of his or her ability to understand the significance of a piece of news. For example, noise traders may aggressively sell shares of stock in a firm whose outlook is described unfavorably in the *Wall Street Journal* or *Fortune* magazine. Of course, the efficient markets hypothesis holds that information in a newspaper or magazine is readily available and will have been incorporated into the price of the stock long before the noise trader has even read the article. Nonetheless, the selling pressure from noise traders can force the stock price down by more than the decrease in its fundamental value.

Can't better-informed traders profit at the expense of noise traders? Doing so may be difficult because the increased price fluctuations due to noise traders may increase the risk in the market. After noise traders have overreacted, an investor who believes in the efficient markets hypothesis cannot be sure how long it will take a price to return to its fundamental value.

Noise trading can also lead to *herd behavior*. With herd behavior, relatively unin-formed investors imitate the behavior of other investors rather than attempting to trade on the basis of fundamental values. Investors imitating each other can help to fuel a spec-ulative *bubble*. In a **bubble**, the price of an asset rises above its fundamental value. Once a bubble begins, investors may buy assets not to hold them but to resell them quickly at a profit, even if the investors know that the prices are greater than the assets' fundamental values. With a bubble, the *greater fool theory* comes into play: An investor is not a fool to buy an overvalued asset as long as there is a greater fool to buy it later for a still higher price. During the stock market dot-com boom in the late 1990s, some investors knew that Pets.com and other Internet firms were unlikely to ever become profitable, but they bought these stocks anyway because they expected to be able to sell them for a higher price than they had paid. At some point, a bubble bursts as a significant number of in-vestors finally become concerned that prices are too far above their fundamental values and begin to sell stocks. As panel (c) of Figure 6.2 on page 161 shows, once the dot-com bubble popped, the prices of stocks in the NASDAQ index dropped very rapidly.

Bubble A situation in which the price of an asset rises well above the asset's fundamental value.

How Great a Challenge Is Behavioral Finance to the Efficient Markets Hypothesis?

If many participants in financial markets are noise traders and exhibit herd behavior, and if bubbles in asset prices are common, is the efficient markets hypothesis the best approach to analyzing these markets? Particularly after the wide swings in stock prices during and after the financial crisis, more economists have become skeptical about the accuracy of the efficient markets hypothesis. Research in behavioral finance questioning the extent to which investors in financial markets exhibit rational expectations has added to this skepticism. As we noted earlier, during bubbles, it may be difficult for better-informed investors to force prices back to their fundamental levels. Some investors who bet against dot-com stocks a year or two before their peaks suffered heavy losses even though the stocks were already far above their fundamental values—which in many cases was zero.

Although fewer economists now believe that investors can rely on asset prices to continually reflect fundamental values, many economists still believe that it is unlikely that investors can hope to earn above-average profits in the long run by following trading strategies. Ongoing research in behavioral finance attempts to reconcile the actual behavior of investors with the rational behavior economists have traditionally assumed prevails in financial markets.

Answering the Key Question

Continued from page 157

At the beginning of this chapter, we asked:

"Is the 2007–2009 financial crisis likely to have a long-lasting effect on the willingness of individual investors to invest in the stock market?"

We have seen that many investors suffered heavy losses during the financial crisis, with the stock market indexes declining by more than 50%. Although some individual investors returned to the market after stock prices began to rise in the spring of 2009, many did not. Even among investors who did return, continued market turbulence during the following years sent some back to the sidelines.

Academic research indicates that individual investors who have experienced bear markets will often be reluctant to invest in the stock market in later years. For example, the effects of the Great Depression of the 1930s on stock market investment may have persisted into the 1960s. So, it is quite possible that the financial crisis of 2007–2009 will have a long-lasting effect on individual investors.

Key Terms and Problems

Key Terms

Adaptive expectations, p. 171

Behavioral finance, p. 181

Bubble, p. 182

Corporation, p. 158

Dividend, p. 159

Dividend yield, p. 166

Efficient markets hypothesis, p. 172

Financial arbitrage, p. 172

Gordon growth model, p. 169

Inside information, p. 173

Limited liability, p. 158

Over-the-counter market, p. 159

Publicly traded company, p. 159

Random walk, p. 174

Rational expectations, p. 171

Required return on equities, r_E, p. 165

Stock exchange, p. 159

Stock market index, p. 161

6.1 Stocks and the Stock Market
Understand the basic operations of the stock market.

Review Questions

1.1 Why are stocks called "equities"? Are bonds also equities?

1.2 In what ways are dividends similar to coupons on bonds? In what ways are dividends different from coupons on bonds?

1.3 What is the difference between a stock exchange and an over-the-counter market? What are the three most important stock market indexes?

1.4 How do fluctuations in stock prices affect the economy?

Problems and Applications

1.5 A student makes the following observation: "The Dow Jones Industrial Average currently has a value of 13,500, while the S&P 500 has a value of 1,500. Therefore, the prices of the stocks in the DJIA are nine times as high as the prices of the stocks in the S&P 500." Briefly explain whether you agree with the student's reasoning.

1.6 A student remarks: "135,000,000 shares of General Electric were sold yesterday on the New York Stock Exchange, at an average price of $25 per share. That means General Electric just received over $3.4 billion from investors." Briefly explain whether you agree with the student's analysis.

1.7 An article in the *Wall Street Journal* notes that "investors tend to view [preferred stock] more like bonds than like [common] stock."

a. In what sense is preferred stock more like bonds than like common stock?

b. Many companies issue preferred stock with a provision that allows the company to buy back the preferred stock at its original price after five years. The article notes that this provision "can produce unexpected losses for investors." When would companies be likely to buy back their preferred shares? Why might these buybacks causes losses to investors?

Source: Ari I. Weinberg, "Playing 'Preferred' Shares," *Wall Street Journal*, September 7, 2012.

1.8 [Related to the Making the Connection on page 163] Ulrike Malmendier of the University of California, Berkeley, and Stefan Nagel of Stanford have shown that investors' willingness to participate in the stock market is affected by the returns they have experienced during their lives. Do you think that the explanation for this effect is entirely psychological? That is, do investors simply become afraid to invest in the stock market? Or, might there be other reasons individual investors purchase less stock following a bear market and more stock following a bull market?

Source: Ulrike Malmendier and Stefan Nagel, "Depression Babies: Do Macroeconomic Experiences Affect Risk-Taking?" *Quarterly Journal of Economics*, Vol. 126, No. 1, February 2011, pp. 373–416.

6.2 How Stock Prices Are Determined
Explain how stock prices are determined.

Review Questions

2.1 What is the relationship between the price of a financial asset and the payments investors will receive from owning that asset?

2.2 What is the relationship between the required return on equities and the equity cost of capital?

2.3 In words and symbols, write the two components of the rate of return on a stock investment for a holding period of one year.

2.4 What is the fundamental value of a share of stock?

2.5 Write the equation for the Gordon growth model. What key assumption does the Gordon growth model make?

Problems and Applications

2.6 Suppose that the price of Goldman Sachs stock is currently $142 per share. You expect that the firm will pay a dividend of $1.40 per share at the end of the year, at which time you expect that the stock will be selling for $160 per share. If you require a return of 8% to invest in this stock, should you buy it? Briefly explain.

2.7 At the beginning of the year, you buy a share of IBM stock for $120. If during the year you receive a dividend of $2.50 and IBM stock is selling for $130 at the end of year, what was your rate of return from investing in the stock?

2.8 A company is expected to pay a dividend per share of $20 per year forever. If investors require a 10% rate of return to invest in this stock, what is its price?

2.9 A friend has started a business selling software. The software is a great hit, and the firm quickly grows large enough to sell stock. Your friend's firm promises to pay a dividend of $5 per share every year for the next 50 years, at which point your friend intends to shut down the business. The firm's stock is currently selling for $75 per share. If you believe that the company really will pay dividends as stated and if you require a 10% rate of return to make this investment, should you buy the stock? Briefly explain.

2.10 [**Related to the** Making the Connection **on page 166**] A column in the *Wall Street Journal* observes that "while many people buy stocks in the hope of scoring profits down the road, dividends deliver cash right now." If stockholders desire dividends, why do some firms, such as Facebook, pay no dividends, while even those firms that do pay dividends often have dividend yields below 2%?
Source: Jason Zweig, "Why You Should Get a Bigger Slice of Earnings," *Wall Street Journal*, March 13, 2010.

2.11 [**Related to** Solved Problem 6.2 **on page 169**] Suppose that Coca-Cola is currently paying a dividend of $1.75 per share, the dividend is expected to grow at a rate of 5% per year, and the rate of return investors require to buy Coca-Cola's stock is 8%. Calculate the price per share for Coca-Cola's stock.

2.12 An article in the *Wall Street Journal* in 2012 described investors' behavior since 2000 as a "flight to safety" that has led to "a high equity risk premium."

a. What does "flight to safety" mean? In this situation, which types of assets are investors likely to be buying, and which are they likely to be selling?

b. Would an increase in the equity risk premium likely lead to higher stock prices or to lower stock prices? Briefly explain.

Source: Spencer Jakab, "Stocks Out of Fashion Amid More Bonding Upbeat Analysts Ignore Bumps in the Road," *Wall Street Journal*, July 1, 2012.

6.3 ## Rational Expectations and Efficient Markets
Explain the connection between the assumption of rational expectations and the efficient markets hypothesis.

Review Questions

3.1 What is the difference between adaptive expectations and rational expectations?

3.2 What is the relationship between rational expectations and the efficient markets hypothesis?

3.3 According to the efficient markets hypothesis, are stock prices predictable? What is a random walk?

Problems and Applications

3.4 Suppose that you buy an Apple iPad, you like it, and you think it will be a big seller. You expect that

Apple's profits will increase tremendously as a result of booming iPad sales. Should you buy Apple stock?

3.5 In 2012, the wireless company T-Mobile sold some of its cell towers to the Crown Castle company. When the agreement was announced, the stock price of Crown Castle declined. An article in the *Wall Street Journal* observed: "Analysts say investors likely priced in much of the deal during the runup to its announcement."

a. What does it mean to say that investors had "priced in" the deal before its announcement?

b. If the gains are priced in and you bought shares of Crown Castle on the basis of the profits you expect the company to earn from having bought some of T-Mobile's cell towers, would you be likely to earn above-average returns on your investment?

Source: Drew FitzGerald and Ben Fox Rubin, "T-Mobile USA to Sell Tower Rights to Crown Castle for $2.4 Billion," *Wall Street Journal*, September 28, 2012.

3.6 In 2010, Toyota recalled millions of automobiles to fix a potentially hazardous problem known as "sudden acceleration." Writing in the *Wall Street Journal*, James Stewart gave investors the following advice: "Toyota shares were over $90 as recently as Jan. 19. They closed Tuesday at $78.18, which strikes me as a modest decline under the circumstances. If I owned shares, I'd seize the chance to get out." Would a believer in the efficient markets theory be likely to follow Stewart's advice?

Source: James B. Stewart, "Toyota Recall Should Warn Investors Away," *Wall Street Journal*, February 3, 2010.

3.7 An article in the *Wall Street Journal* contained the following: "Burberry Group issued a surprise profit warning on Tuesday. . . . The announcement sent Burberry's stock down 21%."

a. What is the relationship between a firm's profits and its stock price?

b. If the decrease in Burberry's profits had not been a surprise, would the effect of the announcement on its stock price have been different? Briefly explain.

Source: Paul Sonne and Peter Evans, "Burberry Sends a Warning," *Wall Street Journal*, September 12, 2012.

3.8 Suppose that Apple's profits are expected to grow twice as fast as Microsoft's. Which firm's stock should be the better investment for you? Briefly explain.

3.9 [Related to the Making the Connection on page 175] Henry Blodget worked for Merrill Lynch during the dot-com boom. The New York attorney general accused Blodget of having praised Internet stocks in public and criticized the same stocks in private. In a negotiated settlement, Blodget declined to admit wrongdoing but accepted a ban from the securities industry for life. He has gone on to write extensively on financial matters, including the following advice:

> The problem for investors is that even though stock-picking usually hurts returns, it's extremely interesting and fun. If you are ever to wean yourself of this bad habit, therefore, the first step is to understand why it's so rarely successful.

What is "stock-picking"? Why does it usually hurt returns earned by investors? Why is it so rarely successful?

Source: Henry Blodget, "Stop Picking Stocks—Immediately," Slate.com, January 22, 2007.

3.10 The business writer Michael Lewis has quoted Michael Burry, a fund manager, as saying:

> I also immediately internalized the idea that no school could teach someone how to be a great investor. If that were true, it'd be the most popular school in the world, with an impossibly high tuition. So it must not be true.

Do you agree with Burry's reasoning? Briefly explain.

Source: Michael Lewis, *The Big Short: Inside the Doomsday Machine*, New York: W.W. Norton, 2010, p. 35.

3.11 [Related to Solved Problem 6.3 on page 176] An article in the *Wall Street Journal* noted that of the thousands of mutual funds investing in stocks or stocks and bonds, only 31 had managed to earn a higher rate of return than the S&P 500 in every year from 1999 through 2006.

a. Is it more likely that the people managing these 31 mutual funds were particularly good at choosing stocks that would increase in value or that they were particularly lucky?

b. Would your answer to part (a) change if you learned that only 14 of these 31 mutual funds had a higher return than the S&P 500 in 2007? Briefly explain.

Source: Jaclyne Badal, "Riding the Storm," *Wall Street Journal*, January 3, 2008.

3.12 [Related to the Chapter Opener on page 157] Many investors who bought stocks in 2000 and held them through 2010 found that they had received a negative real return on their investment over the 10-year period. Why would investors have invested in stocks during those years if they received a negative real return?

6.4 Actual Efficiency in Financial Markets

Discuss the actual efficiency of financial markets.

Review Questions

4.1 How might an investor use a pricing anomaly to earn above-average returns?

4.2 How might an investor use mean reversion or excess volatility to earn above-average returns?

4.3 Why are supporters of the efficient markets hypothesis unconvinced that differences between the theoretical and actual behavior of financial markets actually invalidate the hypothesis?

Problems and Applications

4.4 According to an article in the *Wall Street Journal*, "Cyclical sectors such as tech typically lead in the second year of a bull market, which is on track for the beginning of March."

a. What is a bull market?

b. If stocks issued by technology firms do in fact consistently outperform other stocks during the second year of a bull market, is this a pricing anomaly?

c. Is it likely that you would be able to earn above-average returns by buying tech stocks during the second year of a bull market?

Source: Jonathan Burton, "As Tech Stumbles, Some See an Opening," *Wall Street Journal*, February 23, 2010.

4.5 An article in the *Wall Street Journal* notes that since 1926, stock prices have gone up more in July than in any other month. Is this "July effect" a pricing anomaly? Will you be able to earn a greater-than-normal return on your stock market investments if you buy stock at the beginning of July every year and sell at the end of July? Briefly explain.

Source: Paul Vigna, "For Stocks, a Big Line in the Sand," *Wall Street Journal*, July 12, 2012.

4.6 [Related to the Making the Connection on page 180] A columnist in the *Economist* argues:

> The past ten years have dealt a series of blows to efficient-market theory. . . . In the late 1990s dot-com companies with no profits and barely any earnings were valued in billions of dollars; and in 2006 investors massively underestimated the risks in bundling together portfolios of American subprime mortgages.

a. Explain how the incidents this columnist discusses may be inconsistent with the efficient markets hypothesis.

b. Is it possible that these incidents might have occurred even though the efficient markets hypothesis is correct?

Source: Buttonwood, "The Grand Illusion," *Economist*, May 5, 2009.

4.7 Mutual funds that follow a "momentum trading" strategy are known on Wall Street as "momos." How might a mutual fund manager use a momentum trading strategy? Why might the fund manager expect to earn an above-average return?

4.8 Charles Dow was the original editor of the *Wall Street Journal*. He was the originator of "Dow

Theory," which holds that the prices of transportation stocks, such as Heartland Express, can predict changes in the price of industrial stocks, such as ExxonMobil.

a. An article in the *Wall Street Journal* refers to Dow Theory as the "granddaddy of technical analysis." Why would Dow Theory be considered technical analysis rather than fundamental analysis?

b. Would an investor be able to earn an above-average return on her stock investments by selling industrial stocks whenever she saw declines in transportation stocks and buying industrial stocks whenever she saw increases in transportation stocks? Briefly explain.

Source: Spencer Jakab, "Keep on Trucking Despite Dow Theory," *Wall Street Journal*, July 16, 2012.

6.5 Behavioral Finance

Discuss the basic concepts of behavioral finance.

Review Questions

5.1 How is behavioral finance related to behavioral economics?

5.2 What do economists mean when they describe investors as behaving rationally?

5.3 How can herd behavior lead to a bubble in a financial market?

Problems and Applications

5.4 Some mutual funds have started behavioral finance funds that attempt to use insights from behavioral finance in choosing stocks. According to an article in the *New York Times*:

> Emotions cause investors to misjudge the impact of events in systematic ways. . . . Identifying those patterns and trading against them, the [fund] managers say, allows them to enhance performance.

Is the strategy these fund managers are using consistent with the efficient markets hypothesis?

Source: Conrad de Aenlle, "When Emotions Move the Markets," *New York Times*, October 10, 2009.

5.5 Former Federal Reserve Chairman Alan Greenspan once argued that it is very difficult to identify bubbles until after they pop. What is a bubble, and why might bubbles be difficult to identify?

5.6 The British economist John Maynard Keynes once wrote that investors often do not rely on computing expected values when determining which investments to make:

> Most, probably, of our decisions to do something positive, the full consequences of which will be drawn out over many days to come, can only be taken as the result of animal spirits—a spontaneous urge to action rather than inaction—and not as the outcome of a weighted average of quantitative benefits multiplied by quantitative probabilities.

If it is true that investors rely on "animal spirits" rather than expected values when making investments, is the efficient markets hypothesis accurate? Briefly explain.

Source: John Maynard Keynes, *The General Theory of Employment, Interest, and Money*, London: Macmillan, 1936, p. 162.

5.7 Writing in *New York* magazine, Sheelah Kolhatkar asks an intriguing question:

> [The] investment-management company Vanguard released data showing that men were more likely than women to sell stocks at the bottom of the market. Could it be that the fairer sex is better able to ride the ups and downs of Wall Street without letting their emotions get in the way?

a. What is "the bottom of the market"?

b. Is selling stocks at the bottom of the market a good idea or a bad idea? Briefly explain.

c. If "a bad idea" is the answer to (b), is that behavior consistent with the efficient markets hypothesis? Briefly explain.

Source: Sheelah Kolhatkar, "What If Women Ran Wall Street?" *New York*, March 21, 2010.

5.8 When Facebook first began selling shares of stock to the public, the price for its initial public offering (IPO) was $38 per share. After a few days of trading, the price fell to $20 per share. An article in the *Wall Street Journal* quotes an investment analyst as explaining why demand for Facebook's IPO was initially so high but then collapsed: "The mass psychology of this IPO was that of a classic mania." Is this analyst's assessment consistent with behavioral finance? Briefly explain. Is it consistent with the efficient markets hypothesis? Briefly explain.

Source: Steven Russolillo, "Facebook Shares Tumble to Fresh IPO Lows," *Wall Street Journal*, May 29, 2012.

Data Exercises

D6.1: [The stock market and recessions] Go to the Web site of the Federal Reserve Bank of St. Louis (FRED) (research.stlouisfed.org/fred2/) and download and graph the data series for the S&P 500 stock index (SP500) from January 1957 until the most recent day available. Go to the Web site of the National Bureau of Economic Research (nber.org) and find the dates for business cycle peaks and troughs (the period between a business cycle peak and trough is a recession). Describe how stock prices move just before, during, and just after a recession. Is the pattern the same across recessions?

D6.2: [Testing the Dow Theory] Charles Dow was the original editor of the *Wall Street Journal*. He was the originator of "Dow Theory," which holds that the prices of transportation stocks, such as Heartland Express, can predict changes in the price of industrial stocks, such as ExxonMobil. Go to the Web site of the Federal Reserve Bank of St. Louis (FRED) (research.stlouisfed.org/fred2/) and download and plot on the same graph the data series for the Dow Jones Industrial Average (DJIA) and the Dow Jones Transportation Average (DJTA) from 1900 to the present. Explain whether the data in your graph support the Dow Theory.

D6.3: [Exploring dividends] Go to wsj.com and find the dividend per share for each of the following firms:

a. Microsoft

b. Apple

c. Coca-Cola

d. Facebook

To find the dividend per share, enter the company's name in the search box on the home page. Which pays the highest dividend? Which has the highest dividend yield? Which does not pay a dividend? Why might a firm not pay a dividend? Why would investors buy the stock of a firm that does not pay a dividend?

CHAPTER 7

Derivatives and Derivative Markets

Learning Objectives

After studying this chapter, you should be able to:

7.1 Explain what derivatives are and distinguish between using them to hedge and using them to speculate (pages 191–192)

7.2 Define forward contracts (pages 193–194)

7.3 Discuss how futures contracts can be used to hedge and to speculate (pages 194–202)

7.4 Distinguish between call options and put options and explain how they are used (pages 203–212)

7.5 Define swaps and explain how they can be used to reduce risk (pages 212–216)

Using Financial Derivatives to Reduce Risk

There are about 2.2 million farms in the United States. Suppose you own a farm and that wheat is your most important crop. Like other small businesses, you face the challenge of controlling costs while also maintaining equipment, paying suppliers, and hiring trustworthy employees. If you decide to expand, you will probably need to ask a bank for a loan. But unlike small businesses in other industries, you have an additional problem: You have no control over the price of the wheat you sell, and that price is volatile. In particular, between the time you plant your crop and the time you harvest it, the price of wheat may plunge, leaving you with heavy losses.

Derivatives provide you with a tool for reducing the risk you face from fluctuating wheat prices. Derivatives get their name from the fact that they are based on, or derived from, an underlying asset. These assets may be commodities, such as wheat or oil, or financial assets, such as stocks or bonds. In this case, you would be using *forward contracts* or *futures contracts* for wheat. Although forward and futures contracts differ in some respects, these contracts make it possible for you to agree today to deliver a specified amount of wheat on some future date. Such an agreement allows you to *hedge*, or reduce the risk you face in wheat farming.

Continued on next page

Key Issue and Question

Issue: During the 2007–2009 financial crisis, some investors, economists, and policymakers argued that financial derivatives had contributed to the severity of the crisis.

Question: Are financial derivatives "weapons of financial mass destruction"?

Answered on page 217

Although many U.S. businesses have used derivatives for decades, they were the subject of widespread debate during and after the financial crisis of 2007–2009. Warren Buffett is the chief executive officer of Berkshire Hathaway, which is headquartered in Buffett's hometown of Omaha, Nebraska. In 2012, *Fortune* magazine estimated his wealth at $44 billion, making him the third-richest person in the world. Buffett's many shrewd investments have earned him the nickname the "Oracle of Omaha," and investors closely read his annual letters to Berkshire Hathaway's shareholders. The popularity of these letters stems in part from Buffett's strongly stated opinions on the leading issues in financial markets. The letter for 2002 was no exception, with Buffett denouncing financial derivatives as "time bombs, both for the parties that deal in them and for the economic system." He concluded that "derivatives are financial weapons of mass destruction, carrying dangers that, while now latent, are potentially lethal." Despite Buffett's warnings, the markets for financial derivatives exploded in size between 2002 and 2007. When the financial crisis began in 2007, just as Buffett had warned, financial derivatives played an important role.

As we will see in this chapter, derivatives range from the relatively basic forward and futures contracts farmers often use to the extremely complex. (Buffett described some of the more complex derivatives as having been designed by "sometimes, so it seems, madmen.")

Despite Buffett's denunciations, derivatives play a useful role in the economy. Derivative markets offer investors risk sharing, liquidity, and information services that they would not be able to obtain elsewhere. As we will see, Buffett's criticisms were really aimed at how some of the more exotic derivative securities were used in the years leading up to the financial crisis.

Sources: Warren Buffet, "Chairman's Letter," in *Berkshire Hathaway, Inc. 2002 Annual Report*, February 21, 2003; and "The World's Billionaires," forbes.com.

We will discuss several types of derivative securities in this chapter: forward contracts, futures contracts, options contracts, and swaps. To understand why investors include derivatives in their portfolios, we describe the situations in which derivatives benefit the parties in a transaction, the obligations and benefits of each type of derivative, and the strategies investors use in buying and selling derivatives. Some derivatives are traded in markets, generating liquidity and information and providing common arrangements for settling transactions.

> **Derivative** An asset, such as a futures contract or an option contract, that derives its economic value from an underlying asset, such as a stock or a bond.

Derivatives, Hedging, and Speculating

Derivatives are financial securities that derive their economic value from an underlying asset, such as a stock or a bond. Most derivatives are intended to allow investors and firms to profit from price movements in the underlying asset. An important use of derivatives is to **hedge**, or reduce risk. For example, consider the situation of the managers responsible for producing Tropicana orange juice. Suppose the managers are worried that orange prices may rise in the future, thereby reducing the profits from selling orange juice. It is possible for Tropicana to hedge this risk by using a derivative that will increase in value if the price of oranges rises. That way, if the price of oranges does rise, Tropicana's losses when it buys higher-priced oranges will be offset by the increase in the value of the derivative. If the price of oranges falls, Tropicana will gain from a reduced cost of buying oranges but will suffer a loss on the value of the derivative.

> **7.1**
>
> **Learning Objective**
> Explain what derivatives are and distinguish between using them to hedge and using them to speculate.
>
> **Hedge** To take action to reduce risk by, for example, purchasing a derivative contract that will increase in value when another asset in an investor's portfolio decreases in value.

In this example, you may not see the net gain to Tropicana from using derivatives. Recall that economists measure risk on a financial investment as the degree of uncertainty in an asset's return (see Chapter 4). Similarly, a key risk in producing orange juice is that orange prices will fluctuate, thereby causing fluctuations in the profits Tropicana can earn from selling orange juice. Because derivatives reduce the uncertainty in orange juice profits, Tropicana finds them valuable. In other words, even though using derivatives reduces how much Tropicana benefits from a decrease in the price of oranges, it also reduces the losses from an increase in the price of oranges, so Tropicana benefits from a net reduction in risk.

Similarly, suppose that you buy 10-year Treasury notes, intending to sell them in 5 years to make a down payment on a house. You know that if interest rates rise, the market price of the notes will fall. You can hedge this risk by entering into a derivatives transaction that will earn a profit if interest rates rise. If interest rates fall rather than rise, you will benefit from the increase in the price of the notes. But you will suffer a loss on the derivatives transaction. Once again, though, you are willing to accept this trade-off because you gain a net reduction in risk.

In effect, derivatives can serve as a type of insurance against price changes in underlying assets. Insurance plays an important role in the economic system: If insurance is available on an economic activity, more of that activity will occur. For instance, if no fire insurance were available, many people would be afraid to own their own homes because of the heavy uninsured losses they would suffer in the event of a fire. The lower demand for housing would result in less residential construction. The availability of fire insurance increases the amount of residential construction. Similarly, if investors could not hedge the risk of financial investments, they would make fewer investments, and the flow of funds in the financial system would be reduced. Firms and households would have reduced access to funds, which would slow economic growth.

Speculate To place financial bets, as in buying or selling futures or option contracts, in an attempt to profit from movements in asset prices.

Derivatives can also be used to **speculate**, or place financial bets on movements in asset prices. For instance, suppose that your only connection with the orange business is to drink a glass of orange juice at breakfast every morning. However, your careful study of orange crop reports and long-range weather reports has convinced you that the price of oranges will rise in the future. A derivative that increases in value as orange prices rise gives you an opportunity to profit from your superior insight into the orange market. Of course, if your insight is wrong and orange prices fall, you will lose your bet.

Some investors and policymakers believe that speculation and speculators provide no benefit to financial markets. But, in fact, speculators help derivative markets operate by serving two useful purposes. First, hedgers are able to transfer risk to speculators. In derivatives markets, as in other markets, there must be two parties to a transaction. If a hedger sells a derivative security to a speculator, in purchasing the security, the speculator has accepted the transfer of risk from the hedger. Second, studies of derivatives markets have shown that speculators provide essential liquidity. That is, without speculators, there would not be a sufficient number of buyers and sellers for the markets to operate efficiently. As with other securities, investors are reluctant to hold derivative securities unless there is a market in which to easily sell them.

In the following sections, we look at the most important types of derivatives and the roles they play in the functioning of financial markets.

Forward Contracts

Firms, households, and investors often make plans that can be affected, for better or for worse, by changes in future prices. For instance, a farmer may plant wheat that will not be harvested for months. The farmer's profit or loss will depend on the price of wheat at the time the wheat is harvested. A bank may make you a four-year automobile loan with an interest rate of 5% that is profitable as long as the interest rate the bank pays on deposits stays at 2% or less. If the interest rate on deposits rises to 4%, the bank will lose money on the loan because it will not be able to cover all of its costs of making the loan.

Forward contracts give firms and investors an opportunity to hedge the risk on transactions that depend on future prices. Forward contracts make possible *forward transactions*, which are transactions agreed to in the present but settled in the future. Generally, forward contracts involve an agreement in the present to exchange a given amount of a *commodity*, such as wheat, oil, gold, or a financial asset, such as Treasury bills, at a particular date in the future for a set price. Forward contracts were first developed in agricultural markets. The supply of agricultural products depends on the weather and can therefore be subject to wide fluctuations. In addition, the demand for agricultural products is usually price inelastic. Recall from your principles of economics course that when demand is inelastic, fluctuations in supply cause large swings in equilibrium prices.

For example, suppose that you are a farmer who in May sows seed with the expectation of a yield of 10,000 bushels of wheat. The price at which you can sell the wheat you have available immediately is called the **spot price**. Suppose the spot price in May is $2.00 per bushel. You are concerned that when you harvest the wheat in August, the spot price will have fallen below $2.00, so you will receive less than $20,000 for your wheat. When General Mills buys wheat to make Wheaties and other breakfast cereals, it has the opposite concern: A manager at General Mills is concerned that in August the price of wheat will have risen above $2.00, thereby raising his cost of producing cereal. You and the General Mills manager can hedge against an adverse movement in the price of wheat by entering into a forward contract under which you commit to sell 10,000 bushels of wheat to General Mills at a price of $2.00 per bushel at a date in the future known as the **settlement date**, which is the date on which the contracted delivery must take place. Both parties to the contract have locked in today the price they will receive or pay in the future, on the settlement date.

Although forward contracts provide risk sharing, they have important drawbacks. Because forward contracts usually contain terms specific to the particular buyer and seller involved in a transaction, selling the contract is difficult because a buyer would have to accept the same terms. Therefore, forward contracts tend to be illiquid. In addition, forward contracts are subject to default risk because the buyer or the seller may be unable or unwilling to fulfill the contract. For instance, in the previous example, General Mills might have declared bankruptcy shortly after signing the contract and be unable to make the required payment to you. In this context, default risk is often called **counterparty risk**. The counterparty is the person or firm on the other side of the transaction. So, from the perspective of the seller, the buyer is the counterparty, and from the perspective of the buyer, the seller is the counterparty. Counterparty risk is

7.2

Learning Objective

Define forward contracts.

Forward contract An agreement to buy or sell an asset at an agreed-upon price at a future time.

Spot price The price at which a commodity or financial asset can be sold at the current date.

Settlement date The date on which the delivery of a commodity or financial asset specified in a forward contract must take place.

Counterparty risk The risk that the counterparty—the person or firm on the other side of the transaction—will default.

the risk that the buyer will not fulfill his or her obligation to the seller or that the seller will not fulfill his or her obligation to the buyer. As a result of counterparty risk, buyers and sellers of forward contracts will incur information costs when analyzing the creditworthiness of potential trading partners.

Futures Contracts

Futures contracts first evolved in commodity markets to keep the risk-sharing benefits of forward contracts while increasing liquidity and lowering risk and information costs. Futures contracts differ from forward contracts in several ways:

1. Futures contracts are traded on exchanges, such as the Chicago Board of Trade (CBOT) and the New York Mercantile Exchange (NYMEX).
2. Futures contracts typically specify a quantity of the underlying asset to be delivered but do not fix what the price will be on the settlement date when the asset is delivered. Instead, the price changes continually as contracts are bought and sold on the exchange.
3. Futures contracts are standardized in terms of the quantity of the underlying asset to be delivered and the settlement dates for the available contracts.

Because futures contracts are standardized according to the rules of the exchanges they trade on, they lack some of the flexibility of forward contracts. For instance, although buyers and sellers of forward contracts in wheat may choose any settlement date they want, the CBOT offers wheat futures contracts with only five settlement dates per year. But many investors and firms like futures contracts because they have less counterparty risk and lower information costs, as well as greater liquidity. Counterparty risk is reduced because the exchange serves as a *clearinghouse* (or *clearing corporation*) that matches up buyers and sellers, and the exchange—rather than the buyers and sellers—stands as the counterparty on each trade. For instance, someone buying a futures contract on the CBOT has the CBOT as a counterparty, which greatly reduces default risk. Having the exchange as a counterparty also reduces information costs because buyers and sellers of futures contracts do not have to devote resources to determining the creditworthiness of trading partners. Finally, the reduced risk and information costs, along with the standardization of contract terms, increase the willingness of investors to buy and sell futures contracts. The markets for many futures contracts are highly liquid, with large numbers of buyers and sellers.

Hedging with Commodity Futures

Suppose that you want to hedge against falling wheat prices by using futures contracts. You plant wheat in May, when the spot price of wheat is $2.00 per bushel, which is the price you could sell the wheat for at that time. You are afraid that when you harvest the wheat in August, the price will have fallen. The CBOT doesn't offer a wheat futures contracts with a settlement date in August, but it does offer one with a settlement date in September. Assume that the *futures price* in the contracts is $2.20. The futures price is $0.20 higher than the current spot price because buyers and sellers of futures contracts must be expecting that the spot price in September will be higher than the spot price in May.

7.3

Learning Objective

Discuss how futures contracts can be used to hedge and to speculate.

Futures contract A standardized contract to buy or sell a specified amount of a commodity or financial asset on a specific future date.

The buyers and sellers may base their expectation that the price of wheat will rise on information such as government crop reports and long-range weather forecasts.

Each wheat futures contract on the CBOT is standardized at 5,000 bushels, so to hedge against a price decline, you should sell two wheat futures contracts because you expect to harvest 10,000 bushels of wheat. To sell the contracts, you would need to use a registered futures broker who would be able to execute the trades for you on the CBOT. By selling wheat futures, you take a *short position* in the futures market. Someone has a **short position** if he or she has promised to sell or deliver the underlying asset. If a manager at General Mills who is worried about an increase in the future price of wheat buys the contract, he is taking the **long position** in the futures market, which means that he now has the right and obligation to buy or receive the underlying asset. Note that you are long in the spot market for wheat because you own wheat that you intend to sell after harvesting it, while the manager at General Mills is short in the spot market for wheat because he intends to buy wheat to carry out his breakfast cereal making operation. We can generalize this important point:

> *Hedging involves taking a short position in the futures market to offset a long position in the spot market or taking a long position in the futures market to offset a short position in the spot market.*

The price in a wheat futures contract changes in the course of each day's trading, as new information becomes available that is relevant to forecasting the future spot price of wheat on the settlement day. As the time to deliver approaches, the futures price comes closer to the spot price, eventually equaling the spot price on the settlement date. Why must the spot price equal the futures price on the settlement date? Because if there were a difference between the two prices, arbitrage profits would be possible. For instance, if the spot price of wheat were $2.00 on the settlement date of the futures contract but the futures prices were $2.20, an investor could buy wheat on the spot market and simultaneously sell futures contracts. The buyers of the futures contract would have to accept delivery of wheat at $2.20, which would allow the investor to make a risk-free profit of $0.20 per bushel of wheat. In practice, investors selling additional futures contracts would drive down the futures price until it equaled the spot price. Only then would arbitrage profits be eliminated.

To continue with our example, suppose that when you harvest your wheat in August, the futures price has fallen to $2.10 per bushel, while the spot price is $1.90. The futures price is higher than the spot price because traders in the futures market expect that the spot price of wheat will increase between August and September, when the futures contract expires. For simplicity, assume that you harvest and sell your wheat on that same day. To fulfill your futures market obligation, you can engage in either *settlement by delivery* or *settlement by offset*. Because you want to sell your wheat as soon as it is harvested in August, you will use settlement by offset, so rather than actually delivering wheat, you will close your position at the CBOT by buying two futures contracts, thereby offsetting the two contracts you sold in May. You sold the contracts for $22,000 (= $2.20 per bushel × 10,000 bushels). By buying them back for $21,000 (= $2.10 per bushel × 10,000 bushels), you earn a profit of $1,000 in the futures market. In the spot market, you sell your wheat for $19,000, thereby receiving

Short position In a futures contract, the right and obligation of the seller to sell or deliver the underlying asset on the specified future date.

Long position In a futures contract, the right and obligation of the buyer to receive or buy the underlying asset on the specified future date.

$1,000 less than you would have received at the May spot price. Because this $1,000 loss is offset by your $1,000 profit in the futures market, you have succeeded in hedging the risk of a price decline in the wheat market.

Notice that the manager at General Mills is in the reverse position. In settling his position in the futures market, he will sell two contracts at a futures price of $2.10 per bushel, thereby suffering a $1,000 loss—because the futures price when he bought the contracts in May was $2.20 per bushel. But he will buy wheat in the spot market for $1,000 less than he would have paid at the May spot price of $2.00 per bushel. If the spot price of wheat had risen rather than fallen, you would have lost money on your futures market position but earned a profit in the spot market, while the manager at General Mills would have earned a profit in the futures market but taken a loss in the spot market.

We can summarize the profits and losses of buyers and sellers of futures contracts:

Profit (or loss) to the buyer = Spot price at settlement − Futures price at purchase.
Profit (or loss) to seller = Futures price at purchase − Spot price at settlement.

Notice that the futures market is a *zero-sum game*, which means that if the seller makes a profit, the buyer must suffer a loss of exactly the same amount, and if the seller suffers a loss, the buyer will earn a profit of exactly the same amount. (To make sure you understand this point, review the example of the farmer and General Mills to check that whatever one gains the other loses.) Table 7.1 summarizes this example of using commodity futures contracts to hedge the risk of price fluctuations.

As we noted at the beginning of the chapter, it may appear at first that hedging with futures contracts serves no useful purpose because buyers and sellers can expect to lose on their futures positions about as often as they can expect to gain. In fact, given that there are costs involved in buying and selling futures contracts, you and the General Mills manager in our example may seem to have made yourselves worse off. Remember, though, that reducing the variance of returns, which using futures contracts does, reduces risk. Investors and firms are willing to pay for a reduction in risk, which is why they hedge by using futures contracts.

Table 7.1 Using Commodity Futures Contracts to Hedge

	Wheat farmer	Manager at General Mills
Concerned about . . .	lower wheat prices	higher wheat prices
Hedges risk by . . .	selling futures contracts	buying futures contracts
Position in futures market is . . .	short	long
Position in spot market is . . .	long	short
If wheat prices rise . . .	loses in the futures market but gains in the spot market	gains in the futures market but loses in the spot market
If wheat prices fall . . .	gains in the futures market but loses in the spot market	loses in the futures market but gains in the spot market

Making the Connection

Should Farmers Be Afraid of the Dodd-Frank Act?

Some policymakers and economists have argued that the use of derivatives contributed to the financial crisis of 2007–2009. In response to these concerns, in July 2010, Congress passed the Wall Street Reform and Consumer Protection Act, popularly known as Dodd-Frank, after its Congressional sponsors. Dodd-Frank contains some restrictions on trading in derivatives and requires that some derivatives that were previously traded over the counter be instead traded on exchanges. But there are still many unanswered questions about the act's regulation of derivatives, including the definition of key terms, whether restrictions apply to foreign affiliates of U.S. companies, and whether there would be exemptions from the act for small, non-financial companies, such as farms.

As we have seen, farmers use commodity futures frequently because weather and other factors cause wide fluctuations in the market prices of most crops. Although Dodd-Frank leaves futures trading on organized exchanges, such as the Chicago Board of Trade, largely unaffected, some farmers are worried because the bill gives the Commodity Futures Trading Commission (CFTC), the federal agency charged with regulating futures exchanges, the authority to write new rules. In particular, farmers are worried that they might have to post more collateral to trade futures, which would raise the costs of using these contracts to hedge risk. In addition, some farmers hedge risk by using forward contracts arranged for them by small community banks or special agriculture banks. The farmers worry that the CFTC will no longer allow these banks to offer forward contracts. Senator Saxby Chambliss of Georgia has argued against regulating derivatives trading by small banks in agricultural areas: "All of a sudden they are going to be treated like Goldman Sachs or those major firms on Wall Street."

Farmers breathed a sigh of relief in 2012, when the CFTC decided to exempt from the new regulations firms that use derivatives to hedge risk, including risk from fluctuations in commodity prices. The CFTC also decided to exempt cooperatives from the regulations. Rather than buy and sell forward or futures contracts as individuals firms, farmers often do so through cooperatives called farm credit associations, which will now be exempt from regulations.

The ultimate effect of Dodd-Frank on derivatives trading was still not entirely clear in 2012 because many of the regulations were only scheduled to take effect January 1, 2013.

Sources: Ben Protess, "Regulators Clarifying Timing of New Derivatives Rules," *New York Times*, September 5, 2012; Jamila Trindle, "CFTC Approves Key Derivatives Rules," *Wall Street Journal*, July 10, 2012; and Michael M. Phillips, "Finance Overhaul Casts Long Shadow on the Plains," *Wall Street Journal*, July 14, 2010.

See related problem 3.11 at the end of the chapter.

Speculating with Commodity Futures

We have given an example of firms—farmers and General Mills—that are involved in the market for wheat and want to use futures to reduce the risk in their business operations. Investors who are not connected with the wheat market can use wheat futures to speculate on the price of wheat. For instance, suppose that it is May, and after carefully studying all the information relevant to forecasting the future demand and supply for wheat, you conclude that in September the price of wheat will be $2.50 per bushel. If September wheat futures have a futures price of $2.20 per bushel, you stand to make a profit by buying them. Although, of course, you do not actually want to take delivery of the wheat in September, you stand to make a profit by settling your position by selling wheat futures at some point between May and the September settlement date. If you were convinced that the spot price of wheat were going to be lower in September than the current futures price, you could sell wheat futures with the intention of buying them back at the lower price on or before the settlement date.

Notice, though, that because you lack an offsetting position in the spot market, an adverse movement in wheat prices will cause you to take losses. For instance, if you buy wheat futures, but the price of wheat falls rather than rises, you will have to settle your position for a loss. Similarly, if you sell wheat futures and wheat prices rise, you will also have to settle your position for a loss.

As we noted at the beginning of the chapter, speculators play an important role in futures markets by adding needed liquidity. Without speculators, most futures markets would not have enough buyers or sellers to operate, thereby reducing the risk sharing available to hedgers.

Hedging and Speculating with Financial Futures

Futures contracts first appeared in commodity markets, such as the markets for wheat and oil, in the nineteenth century. Although trading in financial futures did not begin until 1972, today most futures traded are financial futures. Widely traded financial futures contracts include those for Treasury bills, notes, and bonds; stock indexes, such as the S&P 500 and the Dow Jones Industrial Average; and currencies, such as U.S. dollars, Japanese yen, euros, and British pounds. Financial futures contracts are regulated by exchange rules approved by the Commodity Futures Trading Commission (CFTC). The CFTC monitors potential price manipulation by traders on futures exchanges, as well as the conduct of the exchanges.

The process of hedging risk using financial futures is very similar to the process of hedging risk using commodity futures. Consider the following example of using financial futures to hedge interest-rate risk. Suppose you own Treasury notes but are concerned about being exposed to the risk of a decline in the price of the notes if market interest rates rise. Notice that you are in essentially the same situation as you were as a wheat farmer in our earlier example, in that you would like to hedge against a price decline. As when you were a wheat farmer, you are long in the spot market—you own Treasury notes. So to hedge the risk of a price decline, you should go short in the futures market by selling Treasury note futures contracts. If, as you feared, market interest rates rise and the price of your notes falls, the futures price will also fall. You can settle your futures position by buying futures contracts to offset your earlier sale. Because you buy the contracts for a lower price than you sold them for, you make a profit that offsets the losses caused by the falling price of your Treasury notes.

Who would want to be on the other side of this transaction? That is, who might be willing to buy the futures contracts you want to sell? Consider, for example, the manager of a company's pension fund who expects to receive contributions to the fund in six months.

Table 7.2 Using Financial Futures to Hedge Interest-Rate Risk

	Investor who owns Treasury notes	Pension fund manager who intends to buy Treasury notes in six months
Concerned about . . .	lower Treasury note prices (higher interest rates)	higher Treasury note prices (lower interest rates)
Hedges risk by . . .	selling futures contracts	buying futures contracts
Position in futures market . . .	short	long
Position in spot market . . .	long	short
If Treasury note prices rise (interest rates fall) . . .	loses in the futures market but gains in the spot market	gains in the futures market but loses in the spot market
If Treasury note prices fall (interest rates rise) . . .	gains in the futures market but loses in the spot market	loses in the futures market but gains in the spot market

The manager would like to invest the contributions in Treasury notes but may be afraid that the interest rate on the notes will have declined by then, reducing the return she would like to make on the investment. Worrying about a decline in the interest rate on Treasury notes is the same thing as worrying about an increase in their price, so the pension fund manager is like the manager at General Mills in our earlier example. The pension fund manager is short in the spot market for Treasury notes, so to hedge the risk of a price increase, she needs to go long in the futures market by buying Treasury futures contracts. If the interest rate on the Treasury notes falls and their price rises, the manager will be able to settle her Treasury futures position by selling futures contracts to offset her earlier purchase. Because she sells the contracts for a higher price than she bought them for, she makes a profit that offsets the lower returns she will receive when she buys the Treasury notes. Table 7.2 summarizes hedging with financial futures.

An investor who believes that he or she has superior insight into the likely path of future interest rates can use the futures market to speculate. For example, if you are convinced that in the future, interest rates on Treasury notes will be lower than indicated by the current price of Treasury futures, you could profit by buying Treasury futures. If you are correct, and future interest rates turn out to be lower than expected, the futures price will rise, and you can settle your position by selling Treasury futures contracts at a profit. If you wanted to speculate that future interest rates will be higher than expected, you could sell Treasury futures contracts.

Making the Connection **In Your Interest**

How to Follow the Futures Market: Reading the Financial Futures Listings

Investing in the futures market is typically best left to sophisticated investors, but following the futures market can help you understand developments in financial markets. Where can you go to get information? The *Wall Street Journal* reports online information on futures contracts each business day. You can also find data on the Web site of the CME group (www.cmegroup.com).

An example of a "quotation" on interest-rate futures on U.S. Treasury securities appears below. The quotation is from the end of trading on October 5, 2012, and is for five-year U.S. Treasury note futures traded on the Chicago Board of Trade (CBOT). The quotation is for a standardized contract of $100,000 in face value of notes paying a 6% coupon. The first column states the contract month and year for delivery. The delivery date for the contract in the first row is December 2012. The next five columns present price information: the Last price, which is the price of the last trade that day; the change (Chg) in price from the previous day; the Open price, or the price at which the first trade of the day took place; the High price for the day; and the Low price for the day. Two key points to note about the prices: (1) They are quoted per $100 of face value, and (2) the values after the apostrophe are thirty-secondths. For example, the Last price for the contract in the first row is $124 and 15/32 or $124.46875 per $100 of face value. There are 1,000 $100s of face value in a $100,000 contract. Therefore, the price of this contract is $124.46875 × 1,000 = $124,468.75. Because the price is above the face value of $100,000, we know that the yield to maturity on the contract must be less than the coupon rate of 6%.

Five-year U.S. Treasury note futures

Month	Last	Chg	Open	High	Low	Volume	OpenInt
Dec '12	124'15.0	− 0'05.7	124'20.0	124'21.2	124'13.5	406911	1437849
Mar '13	124'07.7	− 0'06.5	124'09.7	124'09.7	124'07.7	3	24
Jun '13	123'19.7	—	—	—	—	0	0
Sep '13	122'31.7	—	—	—	—	0	0
Dec '13	122'31.7	—	—	—	—	0	0

The Volume column tells you the number of contracts traded that day. In this case, 406,911 contracts of the December 2012 contract were traded. Open Interest (OpenInt) reports the volume of contracts outstanding—that is, not yet settled. For the December 2012 contract, open interest was 1,437,849 contracts. Note that on this day, no trading took place on the last three futures contracts listed. The prices in the table represent the last time the contracts were traded.

You can get useful information from these quotes. The interest-rate futures contracts tell you market participants' expectations of future interest rates. Note that futures prices are slightly lower for March 2013 than for December 2012, telling you that futures market investors expect long-term Treasury interest rates to rise slightly.

Although not shown here, you can also find interest-rate futures quotations for Treasury bonds and bills and foreign currencies. The financial futures listings also give you quotes on stock index futures, such as contracts on the S&P 500. Investors use stock index futures to anticipate broad stock market movements.

Sources of data: *Wall Street Journal,* October 5, 2012; and Chicago Board of Trade.

See related problem 3.12 at the end of the chapter.

Solved Problem 7.3   In Your Interest

How Can You Hedge an Investment in Treasury Notes When Interest Rates Are Low?

Following the financial crisis of 2007–2009, interest rates on Treasury bills, notes, and bonds and on many corporate and municipal bonds fell to very low levels. In 2012, many investors were still buying bonds despite their low yields, but an article in the *Wall Street Journal* warned about the possibility of a "nasty bear market in bonds."

a. What does a bear market in bonds mean?

b. What might cause a bear market in bonds?

c. How might you hedge the risk of investing in bonds?

Solving the Problem

Step 1 **Review the chapter material.** This problem is about hedging the risk of investing in bonds, so you may want to review the section "Hedging and Speculating with Financial Futures," which begins on page 198.

Step 2 **Answer part (a) by explaining what a bear market in bonds would be.** As we saw in discussing the stock market, a bear market refers to a price decline of at least 20%.

Step 3 **Answer part (b) by explaining what might cause a bear market in bonds.** A bear market in bonds could result from investors believing that the inflation rate might rise in the future. The Fisher effect tells us that a higher expected inflation rate will result in higher nominal interest rates. Higher nominal interest rates mean lower bond prices.

Step 4 **Answer part (c) by explaining how you can hedge the risk of investing in bonds.** We have seen that investors can use the futures market to hedge the risk of investing in bonds. Because, in this case, you would be worried about rising interest rates and falling bond prices, the appropriate hedge would be for you to sell futures contracts, such as those available on the CBOT for Treasury notes. By owning bonds, you are long in the spot market for bonds, so the appropriate hedge would be for you to go short in the futures market for bonds by selling futures contracts. As an individual investor, you can sell the contracts by using a registered futures broker who would place the sell order on the CBOT. Many stockbrokers are also futures brokers. Some brokers are so-called full-service brokers who offer trading advice and provide research support, as well as executing trades. Other brokers are discount brokers, who charge a lower commission to execute trades but do not typically offer advice. Individual investors will sometimes hedge the risk of investing in bonds by buying shares in mutual funds that invest in derivative contracts rather than by buying or selling the contracts themselves.

Source: Tom Lauricella, "Prospects for Stock and Bond Returns Are Dim," *Wall Street Journal*, September 22, 2012.

See related problem 3.13 at the end of the chapter.

Trading in the Futures Market

Margin requirement
In the futures market, the minimum deposit that an exchange requires from the buyer and seller of a financial asset; reduces default risk.

Marking to market In the futures market, a daily settlement in which the exchange transfers funds from a buyer's account to a seller's account or vice versa, depending on changes in the price of the contract.

As we have seen, buyers and sellers of futures contracts deal with an exchange rather than directly with each other, as would be the case with forward contracts. To reduce default risk, the exchange requires both the buyer and seller to place an initial deposit called a **margin requirement** into a *margin account*. For instance, on the CBOT, futures contracts for U.S. Treasury notes are standardized at a face value of $100,000 of notes, or the equivalent of 100 notes of $1,000 face value each. The CBOT requires that buyers and sellers of these contracts deposit a minimum of $1,100 for each contract into a margin account.

At the end of each trading day, the exchange carries out a daily settlement known as **marking to market**, in which, depending on the closing price of the contract, funds are transferred from the buyer's account to the seller's account or vice versa. For instance, suppose that you buy a Treasury note futures contract for a price of 100. From the *Making the Connection* on page 199, we know this price means that you paid $100,000 for the contract. Assume that you deposited just the minimum $1,100 required by the CBOT into your margin account, and the seller deposited the same amount into his or her account. The following day, at the end of trading in the market, the price of your contract has risen to 101, perhaps because new information has led traders to believe that interest rates will be lower in the future (and, therefore, Treasury note prices will be higher) than they had previously expected. Because the value of your contract has risen by $1,000, the exchange will transfer $1,000 from the seller's account to your account. The balance in the seller's account falls to $100. This amount is below the *maintenance margin*, which is sometimes less than the initial margin, but in the case of Treasury note futures contracts, it is also $1,100. The seller will be subject to a *margin call*, which is an order from the exchange for the seller to add enough funds to his or her account to reach the $1,100 maintenance margin. Because of margin requirements and marking to market, traders rarely default on futures contracts, which limits the exchange's exposure to losses.

Table 7.3 summarizes the activities of buyers and sellers in the futures market.

Table 7.3 Buyers and Sellers in the Futures Market

Buyer of a futures contract	Seller of a futures contract
Has the obligation to buy the underlying asset on the settlement date.	Has the obligation to deliver the underlying asset on the settlement date.
Can use buying a futures contract to hedge if the buyer is someone who intends to buy the underlying asset and wants to insure against the price rising.	Can use selling a futures contract to hedge if the seller is the owner of the underlying asset and wants to insure against the price falling.
Can use buying a futures contract to hedge if the buyer believes that the price of the underlying asset will rise.	Can use selling a futures contract to hedge if the seller believes that the price of the underlying asset will fall.

Options

Options are another type of derivative contract. As with futures contracts, options contracts allow investors and firms to hedge risk or to speculate. The buyer of an option has the right to buy or sell the underlying asset at a set price during a set period of time. A **call option** gives the buyer the right to buy the underlying asset at the **strike price** (or **exercise price**), at any time up to the option's *expiration date*. For instance, if you buy a call option on Apple with a strike price of $500 and an expiration date of July, you have the right to buy one share of Apple stock for $500 at any time up to the expiration date in July (typically the third Friday of the month).

A **put option** gives the buyer the right to sell the underlying asset at the strike price during a set period of time. For instance, if you buy a put option on Apple with a strike price of $500 and an expiration date of July, you have the right to sell one share of Apple stock for $500 at any time up to the expiration date in July. Note that the options being described here are *American options*, which an investor may exercise at any time up to the expiration date. An investor may exercise *European options* only on the expiration date. The price of an option contract is also called *the option premium*.

With futures contracts, buyers and sellers have symmetric rights and obligations. That is, the seller must deliver the underlying asset, and the buyer must take delivery at the futures price on the delivery date. In contrast, with options contracts, the buyer has rights, and the seller, called the *option writer*, has obligations. For example, if you buy a call option and exercise your right to buy the underlying asset, the seller of the call option has no choice but to fulfill the obligation to sell the asset. However, as the buyer of the call option, you have no obligation to exercise it and may choose, instead, to allow the option to expire, unexercised. Similarly, if you buy a put option and exercise your right to sell the underlying asset, the seller of the put option has no choice but to fulfill the obligation to buy the asset.

Options are traded both over the counter and on exchanges such as the Chicago Board Options Exchange (CBOE) and the New York Stock Exchange (NYSE). Options traded on exchanges are called *listed options*. Options contracts traded in the United States include options on individual stocks, stock index options, options on stock index futures contracts, options on interest-rate futures (such as futures contracts on U.S. Treasury notes), options on currencies, and options on currency futures (such as futures contracts on the Japanese yen, euro, Canadian dollar, and British pound). One important distinction between futures and options contracts is that when you purchase a futures contract, funds change hands daily as the contract is marked to market. With an options contract, however, funds change hands only when the option is exercised.

Why Would You Buy or Sell an Option?

Suppose that Apple stock has a current price of $600 per share, but you believe the price will rise to $650 at some point during the coming year. You could purchase shares of Apple and earn a profit if the price rises as you expect. There are two potential downsides to this strategy: Buying the shares outright will require a sizable investment, and if the price of Apple falls rather than rises, you will face a possibly substantial loss. As an alternative, you could buy call options that would allow you to buy Apple at

7.4

Learning Objective
Distinguish between call options and put options and explain how they are used.

Option A type of derivative contract in which the buyer has the right to buy or sell the underlying asset at a set price during a set period of time.

Call option A type of derivative contract that gives the buyer the right to buy the underlying asset at a set price during a set period of time.

Strike price (or exercise price) The price at which the buyer of an option has the right to buy or sell the underlying asset.

Put option A type of derivative contract that gives the buyer the right to sell the underlying asset at a set price during a set period of time.

a strike price of, say, $610. The price to buy the options will be much lower than the price to buy the underlying stock. In addition, if the price of Apple never rises above $610, you can allow the options to expire without exercising them, which limits your loss to the price of the options.

If Apple's stock is selling for $600 per share and you are convinced it will decline in price, you could engage in a *short sale*. With a short sale, you borrow the stock from your broker and sell it now, with the plan of buying it back—and repaying your broker—after the stock declines in price. If, however, the price of Apple rises rather than falls, you will lose money by having to buy back the stock—which is called "covering a short"—at a price that is higher than you sold it for. If the price of Apple soars, you may face a substantial loss in covering your short. If, on the other hand, you buy a put with a strike price of $590 per share you will profit from a decline in the price of Apple's stock, while if the price rises you can allow the option to expire and limit your loss to the price of the option.

Figure 7.1 illustrates the potential gains and losses from buying options on Apple stock. We assume that the buyer of the option pays a price for the option but does not incur any cost when buying or selling the underlying stock. We assume that the price a buyer pays to buy either the call option or the put option is $10 per share. Although the buyer of the option can exercise the option at any time, for simplicity we focus on how the payoff to owning the option varies with the price of the stock on the expiration date.[1] In panel (a), we illustrate the profit to buying a call option with a strike price of $610. When the price of Apple stock is between zero and $610 on the expiration date, the owner of the option will not exercise it and will suffer a loss equal to the $10 price of the option. As the price of Apple rises above $610 per share, the owner of the option will earn a positive amount from exercising it. For example, if the price is $615, the owner can exercise the option, buy a share of Apple from the seller of the option for the strike price of $610, sell the share in the market for $615, and make $5. Because the owner paid $10 for the option, he or she has a net loss of $5. If the price of Apple is $620, the owner will break even. For prices above $620, the owner earns a profit. For example, if the price of Apple is $650, the owner exercises the option, buys a share for $610, sells the share in the market for $650, and makes a profit of $30 (= $40 − $10). The higher the price of Apple stock rises, the greater the profit to the buyer of the call option.

In panel (b), we illustrate the profit to buying a put option with a strike price of $590. The owner of a put option earns a maximum profit when the price of Apple stock is zero.[2] The owner would buy a share of Apple for a price of zero, exercise the option, and sell the share to the seller of the put option for $590. Subtracting the $10 price of the option, the buyer of the option is left with a profit of $580. As the price of Apple stock rises, the payoff from owning the put option falls. At a price of $580, the owner of the put would just break even because the owner would make $10 from exercising the

---

[1]Alternatively, we can think of Figure 7.1 as illustrating the situation for the highest price—panel (a)—Apple stock reaches before the expiration date or the lowest price—panel (b).

[2]In reality, of course, a stock has a price of zero only if the firm is bankrupt. In that case, trading in the stock would stop. A more realistic case would be a low price that would still be high enough that trading in the stock takes place.

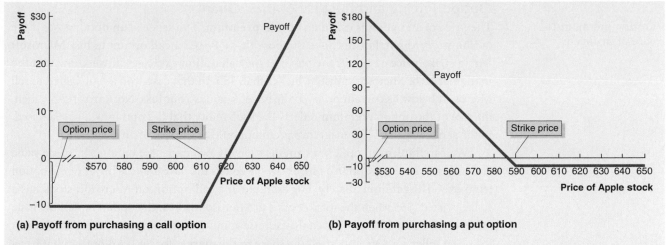

(a) Payoff from purchasing a call option **(b) Payoff from purchasing a put option**

Figure 7.1 Payoffs to Owning Options on Apple Stock

In panel (a), we illustrate the profit from buying a call option with a strike price of $610. When the price of Apple stock is between zero and $610, the owner of the option will not exercise it and will suffer a loss equal to the $10 price of the option. As the price of Apple rises above $610 per share, the owner of the option will earn a positive amount from exercising it. For prices above $620, the owner earns a profit.

In panel (b), we illustrate the profit from buying a put option with a strike price of $590. The owner of a put option earns a maximum profit when the price of Apple is zero. As the price of Apple stock rises, the payoff from owning the put option falls. At a price of $580, the owner of the put would just break even. For prices above the $590 strike price, the owner of the put option would not exercise it and would suffer a loss equal to the option price of $10.

option, which would just offset the $10 price of the option. For prices above the $590 strike price, the owner of the put option would not exercise it and would lose an amount equal to the option price of $10.

Table 7.4 summarizes the key features of basic call options and put options.

Table 7.4 Key Features of Basic Call Options and Put Options

	Call option	Put option
Buyer	Has the right to purchase the underlying option at the strike price on or before the expiration date	Has the right to sell the underlying asset at the strike price on or before the expiration date
Seller	Has the obligation to sell the underlying asset at the strike price if the buyer exercises the option	Has the obligation to buy the underlying asset at the strike price if the buyer exercises the option
Who would buy it?	An investor who wants to bet that the price of the underlying asset will increase	An investor who wants to bet that the price of the underlying asset will decrease
Who would sell it?	An investor who wants to bet that the price of the underlying asset will not increase	An investor who wants to bet that the price of the underlying asset will not decrease

Option Pricing and the Rise of the "Quants"

Option premium The price of an option.

The price of an option is called an **option premium**. The seller of an option loses if the option is exercised. For instance, suppose that you sell a call option to buy Microsoft with a strike price of $35. If the buyer of the call option exercises it, we know that the market price of Microsoft must be higher than $35. In that case, you are obligated to sell Microsoft below its current price, so the buyer's gain is your loss. Not surprisingly, then, the size of the option premium reflects the probability that the option will be exercised, in the same way that a car insurance premium reflects the risk of an accident.

We can think of an option premium as having two parts: the option's intrinsic value and its time value. An option's *intrinsic value* equals the payoff to the buyer of the option from exercising it immediately. For example, if a call option on Microsoft stock has a strike price of $35 when the market price of Microsoft is $40, the option has an intrinsic value of $5 because the buyer could exercise it immediately, buy a share of Microsoft from the seller for $35, and resell the share in the market for $40. An option that has a positive intrinsic value is said to be *in the money*. A call option is in the money if the market price of the underlying asset is greater than the strike price, and a put option is in the money if the market price of the underlying asset is less than the strike price. If the market price of the underlying asset is below the strike price, a call option is *out of the money*, or *underwater*. If the market price of the underlying asset is above the strike price, a put option is out of the money. If the market price equals the strike price, a call option or a put option is *at the money*. Notice that because a buyer does not have to exercise an option, an option's intrinsic value can never be less than zero.

In addition to its intrinsic value, an option premium has a *time value*, which is determined by how far away the expiration date is and by how volatile the stock price has been in the past. The further away the expiration date, the greater the chance that the intrinsic value of the option will increase. Suppose, for example, that the strike price on a call option on Microsoft is $35 and the current market price is $30. If the option expires tomorrow, the chance that the market price of Microsoft will rise above $35 is small. But if the option expires in six months, the chance is much greater. We can conclude that, all else being equal, *the further away in time an option's expiration date, the larger the option premium*. Similarly, if the volatility in the price of the underlying asset is small, the chance that the intrinsic value of the option may increase substantially because of a large price swing is small. But if the volatility in the price of the underlying asset is large, the chance is much greater. Therefore, all else being equal, *the greater the volatility in the price of the underlying asset, the larger the option premium*.

Calculating the intrinsic value of an option is straightforward, but it is more difficult to determine exactly how the option premium should be affected by the time until the option expires or by the volatility in the price of the underlying asset. It is so difficult that for many years, options were thinly traded—that is, investors seldom bought or sold them—because Wall Street firms and other professional investors were unsure how to price them. In 1973, a breakthrough occurred when Fischer Black and Myron Scholes, who were then economists at the University of Chicago, published an academic article in the *Journal of Political Economy* that used sophisticated mathematics to work out a formula for the optimal pricing of options. The Black-Scholes formula coincided with the establishment of the CBOE and led to an explosive growth in options trading.

The Black-Scholes formula had even wider significance because it demonstrated to Wall Street firms that sophisticated mathematical modeling could allow these firms to price complicated financial securities. The result was that Wall Street firms hired many people with advanced degrees in economics, finance, and mathematics to build mathematical models that the firms could use to price and evaluate new securities. These people became known as "rocket scientists," or "quants."

| Making the Connection | In Your Interest |

How to Follow the Options Market: Reading the Options Listings

As with futures, investing in options is typically best left to sophisticated investors, but following the options listings can help you understand what changes in futures prices of commodities and financial assets investors expect. Newspaper and online listings of options contracts contain many of the same measures as futures listings. However, there are some differences for individual options, depending on whether the underlying asset is a direct claim (for example, a bond or shares of stock) or a futures contract (for example, a stock index futures contract).

The quotations shown below are for options contracts on shares of Apple stock. The listing provides information on put options and call options with a strike price of $680.00 for October 4, 2012. On the previous day, the closing price for a share of Apple was $666.80. In fact, there are many put and call options available on Apple stock, with different strike prices; here we list just four. The first column gives the expiration date for the options. The second column gives the strike price. The next three columns give information on call options, and the last three columns give information on put options.

Call and Put Options for Apple (AAPL)

Underlying stock price: 666.80

Expiration	Strike	Call			Put		
		Last	Volume	Open Interest	Last	Volume	Open Interest
(1)	(2)	(3)	(4)	(5)	(6)	(7)	(8)
Oct	680.00	0.31	30097	15779	13.50	7869	3104
Nov	680.00	23.10	585	5436	37.40	202	4859
Jan	680.00	38.90	496	8894	51.60	60	3344
Apr	680.00	56.57	49	1265	71.30	11	393

Each of the two Last columns gives the last price the contract traded for on the previous day. For example, the October call option contract listed in the first row has a Last price of $0.31. Listed options contracts for stocks are for 100 shares of stock. So if you purchased the October call option contract, you would pay $0.31 \times 100 = \$31.00$. The Volume column provides information on how many contracts were traded that day, and the Open Interest column provides information on the number of contracts outstanding—that is, not yet exercised. Notice that the put options have higher prices than the call options with the same expiration date. These higher prices reflect the fact that because the strike price is above the underlying price, the put options are all *in the money*, while the call options are *out of the money*. Notice, also, that for both the call options and the put options, the further away the expiration date, the higher the price of the option.

Source of data: *Wall Street Journal*, October 5, 2012.

See related problem 4.8 at the end of the chapter.

| **Solved Problem 7.4** | **In Your Interest** |

Interpreting the Options Listings for Amazon.com

Use the following information on call and put options for Amazon.com to answer the questions. In your answers, ignore any costs connected with buying and selling options or the underlying stock apart from the prices of the options or stock.

Amazon (AMZN)						Underlying stock price: 260.47	
		Call			**Put**		
Expiration	Strike	Last	Volume	Open Interest	Last	Volume	Open Interest
Oct	245.00	16.50	164	2026	1.06	705	5073
Nov	245.00	22.05	45	144	6.80	81	574
Jan	245.00	26.50	114	1915	10.78	44	1051
Apr	245.00	33.00	3	68	18.65	10	107

a. Why are the call options selling for higher prices than the put options?
b. Why does the April call sell for a higher price than the October call?
c. Suppose you buy the April call. Briefly explain whether you would exercise that call immediately.
d. Suppose you buy the November call at the price listed and exercise it when the price of Amazon stock is $300. What will be your profit or loss? (Remember that each options contract is for 100 shares of stock.)
e. Suppose you buy the April put at the price listed, and the price of Amazon stock remains $260.47. What will be your profit or loss?

Solving the Problem

Step 1 **Review the chapter material.** This problem is about interpreting the listings for options, so you may want to review the section "Option Pricing and the Rise of the 'Quants'," which begins on page 206, and the *Making the Connection* "How to Follow the Options Market: Reading the Options Listings," which begins on page 207.

Step 2 **Answer part (a) by explaining why the call options are selling for higher prices than the put options.** Notice that the strike price of $245.00 is less than the price of the underlying stock, which is $260.47. So, the call options are all in the money because if you exercised one, you would be able to buy 100 shares of Amazon for $245.00 each from the seller of the call option, and then sell the shares in the market for $260.47 each, thereby making a profit of $15.47 (= $260.47 − $245.00) per share. The puts are all out of the money because you would not want to exercise your right to sell a share of Amazon for $245.00 to the seller of the put when you could sell a share in the market for $260.47. Therefore, the puts have zero intrinsic value and their prices are all lower than the prices for the calls.

Step 3 **Answer part (b) by explaining why the April call sells for a higher price than the October call.** The price of an option represents the option's *intrinsic value* plus its *time value*, which represents all other factors that affect the likelihood of the option's being exercised. The further away the expiration date, the greater the chance that the intrinsic value of the option will increase, and the higher the price of the option. Therefore, because the two call options have the same strike price, the April call will have a higher price than the October call.

Step 4 **Answer part (c) by explaining whether you would exercise the April call immediately.** If you purchased the April call, you would be able to buy Amazon for $245.00 per share from the seller of the call and sell the shares in the market for $260.47 per share, earning $15.47 per share. But the price of the call is $33.00, so you would not buy the call to exercise it immediately. You would buy the call only if you expected that before the expiration date of the call, the price of Amazon would rise sufficiently that the intrinsic value of the call would be greater than $33.00.

Step 5 **Answer part (d) by calculating your profit or loss from buying the November call and exercising it when the price of Amazon stock is $300.** If you exercise the November call, which has a strike price of $245.00, when the price of Amazon stock is $300, you will earn $55.00 minus the option price of $22.05, for a profit of $32.95. There are 100 shares in the option contract, so your total profit equals $32.95 × 100 = $3,295.00.

Step 6 **Answer part (e) by calculating your profit or loss from buying the April put if the price of Amazon remains at $260.47.** If the price of Amazon remains at $260.47, the April put will remain out of the money. Therefore, you will not exercise it, instead taking a loss equal to the option's price of $18.65 per share. Your total loss will be $18.65 × 100 = $1,865.00

See related problem 4.8 at the end of the chapter.

Using Options to Manage Risk

Firms, banks, and individual investors can use options, as well as futures, to hedge the risk from fluctuations in commodity or stock prices, interest rates, and foreign currency exchange rates. Options have the disadvantage of being more expensive than futures. But options have the important advantage that an investor who buys options will not suffer a loss if prices move in the opposite direction of that being hedged against. For instance, we saw earlier that if you own Treasury notes and want to hedge against a decline in their price, you can sell Treasury note futures. But what if prices of Treasury notes increase? In this case, you have a gain on your holdings of Treasury notes, but you suffer a loss on your futures position. You have hedged your risk, but you cannot profit from an increase in prices of Treasury notes.

Instead of *selling* Treasury futures, you can hedge by *buying* Treasury put options. If prices of Treasury notes fall, you can exercise your puts and sell at the strike price, thereby minimizing your losses. If prices of Treasury notes rise, you can allow your puts to expire without exercising them, thereby keeping most of the gains from the price rise. Because options contracts guard against a negative outcome while still allowing profits from a positive outcome, they are more like insurance than are futures contracts. This insurance aspect of options is why options prices are called options premiums. (The payments a buyer of an insurance policy makes to an insurance company are called premiums.)

When choosing between hedging with options and hedging with futures, a firm or an investor has to trade off the generally higher cost of using options against the extra insurance benefit that options provide. As an options buyer, you assume less risk than with a futures contract because the maximum loss you can incur is the option premium. Note, though, that the options *seller* does not have a limit on his or her losses. For instance, if Treasury note prices fall to very low levels, the seller of a put option is still obligated to buy at the strike price, even if it is far above the current market price.

Many hedgers buy options, not on the underlying financial asset but on a futures contract derived from that asset. For instance, in the previous example, rather than hedging against a decline in Treasury note prices by buying a put option on Treasury notes, you could buy a put option on Treasury note futures. Buying and selling *futures options* has several advantages over buying and selling options on the underlying assets. Futures contracts on Treasury notes and Treasury bonds are exchange-traded securities and, therefore, are more liquid than Treasury notes and bonds because the notes and bonds generally have to be traded through dealers. Similarly, the prices of futures contracts are readily available to investors on exchanges, while investors have to obtain the prices of Treasury notes and bonds from dealers.

Making the Connection   In Your Interest

How Much Volatility Should You Expect in the Stock Market?

You may be reluctant to invest in the stock market because of the volatility of stock prices. The larger the swings in an asset's price, the greater the risk to you as an investor. Is it possible to measure the degree of volatility that investors expect in the future? Such a measure might give you a way of comparing investing in stocks with investing in other financial assets.

One way to construct such a measure is by using the prices of options. In 1993, Robert E. Whaley, now of Vanderbilt University, noted that the prices of options on stock market indexes—such as the S&P 500—implicitly include a measure of investors' expectations of future market volatility. The measure of volatility is implicit, rather than explicit, because an option's price includes the option's intrinsic value plus other factors, including volatility, that affect the likelihood of an investor exercising the option. Whaley suggested a method to isolate the part of the option's price that represents investors' forecast of volatility.

The Chicago Board Options Exchange (CBOE) constructed the Market Volatility Index, called the VIX, using the prices of put and call options on the S&P 500 index. The VIX quickly became the most widely used measure of expected volatility in the U.S. stock market over the following 30 days. Many people refer to the VIX as the "fear gauge" because when investors expect volatility in stock prices to increase, they increase their demand for options, thereby driving up their prices and increasing the value of the VIX. The following graph shows movements in the VIX from January 2004 to October 2012:

MyEconLab Real-time data

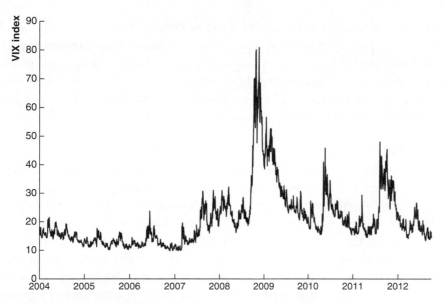

Source: Federal Reserve Bank of St. Louis.

Through the middle of 2007, the VIX generally had a value between 10 and 20, meaning that investors were expecting that during the next 30 days, the S&P 500 would rise or fall by 10% to 20% at an annual rate. Then, as the financial crisis began in 2007, the VIX began to increase, reaching record levels of 80 in October and November 2008, following the bankruptcy of the Lehman Brothers investment bank. The rise in the VIX was driven by investors bidding up the prices of options as they attempted to hedge their stock market investments in the face of expected increases in volatility. The VIX did not fall back below 20 until December 2009. It rose sharply again in May 2010 and again in the fall of 2011, as the market experienced another period of volatility. The volatility during 2010 and 2011 was tied to concerns about the possibility that financial problems in Europe might spill over into U.S. markets.

In March 2004, the CBOE began trading futures on the VIX, and in February 2006, it began trading VIX options. An investor who wanted to hedge against an increase in volatility in the market would buy VIX futures. Similarly, a speculator who wanted to bet on an increase in market volatility would buy VIX futures. A speculator who wanted to bet on a decrease in market volatility would sell VIX futures.

The VIX index provides a handy tool for gauging how much volatility investors are anticipating in the market and for hedging against that volatility.

Sources: Robert E. Whaley, "Understanding the VIX," *Journal of Portfolio Management*," Vol. 35, No. 3, Spring 2009, pp. 98–105; Robert E. Whaley, "Derivatives on Market Volatility: Hedging Tools Long Overdue," *Journal of Derivatives*, Vol. 1, Fall 1993, pp. 71–84; and Associated Press, "Wall Street's Fear Gauge Sinks to 2-Year Low," *New York Times*, March 23, 2010.

See related problem 4.12 at the end of the chapter.

Swaps

7.5

Learning Objective

Define swaps and explain how they can be used to reduce risk.

Swap An agreement between two or more counterparties to exchange sets of cash flows over some future period.

Interest-rate swap A contract under which counterparties agree to swap interest payments over a specified period on a fixed dollar amount, called the *notional principal*.

Although the standardization of futures and options contracts promotes liquidity, these contracts cannot be adjusted to meet the specific needs of investors and firms. This problem spurred the growth of *swap contracts*, or swaps. A **swap** is an agreement between two or more counterparties to exchange—or swap—sets of cash flows over some future period. In that sense, a swap resembles a futures contract, but as a private agreement between counterparties, its terms are flexible.

Interest-Rate Swaps

Consider a basic, or "plain vanilla," **interest-rate swap**, a contract under which the counterparties agree to swap interest payments over a specified period of time on a fixed dollar amount, called the *notional principal*. The notional principal is used as a base for calculations but is not an amount actually transferred between the counterparties. For example, suppose that Wells Fargo bank and IBM agree on a swap lasting five years and based on a notional principal of $10 million. IBM agrees to pay Wells Fargo an interest rate of 6% per year for five years on the $10 million. In return, Wells Fargo agrees to pay IBM a variable or floating interest rate. With interest-rate swaps, the floating interest rate is often based on the rate at which international banks lend to each other. This rate is known as *LIBOR*, which stands for London Interbank Offered Rate. Suppose that under the negotiated terms of the swap, the floating interest rate is set at a rate equal to the LIBOR plus 4%. Figure 7.2 summarizes the payments in the swap transaction.

If the first payment is based on a LIBOR of 3%, IBM owes Wells Fargo $600,000 (= $10,000,000 × 0.06), and Wells Fargo owes IBM $700,000 (= $10,000,000 × (0.03 + 0.04)). Netting the two payments, Wells Fargo pays $100,000 to IBM. Generally, parties exchange only the net payment.

Why might firms and financial institutions participate in interest-rate swaps? One motivation is transferring interest-rate risk to parties that are more willing to bear it. In our example, IBM is exposed to more interest-rate risk after the swap but is willing to bear the risk in anticipation of a return. On the first payment, IBM receives $100,000 more from Wells Fargo than it pays. Or, perhaps a bank that has a lot of floating-rate assets, such as adjustable-rate mortgages, might want to engage in an interest-rate swap with a bank that has a lot of fixed-rate mortgages. Banks and other firms often have good business reasons for acquiring floating-rate or fixed-rate assets. Swaps allow them

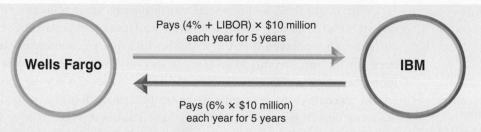

Figure 7.2 Payments in a Swap Transaction

Wells Fargo and IBM agree on a swap lasting five years and based on a notional principal of $10 million. IBM agrees to pay Wells Fargo an interest rate of 6% per year for five years on the $10 million. In return, Wells Fargo agrees to pay IBM a floating interest rate. In this example, IBM owes Wells Fargo $600,000 ($10,000,000 × 0.06), and Wells Fargo owes IBM $700,000 ($10,000,000 × (0.03 + 0.04)). Netting the two payments, Wells Fargo pays $100,000 to IBM. Generally, parties exchange only the net payment.

to retain those assets while changing the mix of fixed and floating payments that they receive. In addition, as already noted, swaps are more flexible than futures or options because they can be custom-tailored to meet the needs of counterparties. Swaps also offer more privacy than exchange trading, and swaps are subject to relatively little government regulation. Finally, swaps can be written for long periods, even as long as 20 years. As a result, they offer longer-term hedging than is possible with financial futures and options, which typically settle or expire in a year or less.

However, unlike with futures and exchange-traded options, with swaps, counterparties must be sure of the creditworthiness of their partners. This problem has led to the swaps market being dominated by large firms and financial institutions that have an easier time determining creditworthiness. In addition, swaps, like forward contracts, are not as liquid as futures and options. In fact, swaps are rarely resold.

The passage of the Dodd-Frank Act increased regulation of swaps. Starting in January 2013, financial firms that engage in more than $8 billion in swaps contracts per year must register with the Commodities Futures Trading Commission as "swap dealers." Swap dealers must trade swaps through a central clearinghouse. Data on trades would be publicly available and dealers would be required to deposit a fraction of the value of the swap contracts with the clearinghouse, as had long been the case when trading futures contracts.

Currency Swaps and Credit Swaps

In interest-rate swaps, counterparties exchange payments on fixed-rate and floating-rate debt. In a **currency swap**, counterparties agree to exchange principal amounts denominated in different currencies. For example, a French company might have euros and want to swap them for U.S. dollars. A U.S. company might have U.S. dollars and be willing to swap them for euros.

Currency swap A contract in which counterparties agree to exchange principal amounts denominated in different currencies.

A basic currency swap has three steps. First, the two parties exchange the principal amount in the two currencies. (Note the difference from the interest-rate swap, in which the counterparties deal in the same currency and typically exchange only the net interest amount, not the principal.) Second, the parties exchange periodic interest payments over the life of the agreement. Third, the parties exchange the principal amount again at the conclusion of the swap.

Why might firms and financial institutions participate in currency swaps? One reason is that firms may have a comparative advantage in borrowing in their domestic currency. They can then swap the proceeds with a foreign counterparty to obtain foreign currency for, say, investment projects. In this way, both parties may be able to borrow more cheaply than if they had borrowed directly in the currency they needed.

Credit swap A contract in which interest-rate payments are exchanged, with the intention of reducing default risk.

In a **credit swap**, interest-rate payments are exchanged, with the intention of reducing default risk, or credit risk, rather than interest-rate risk, as is the case with basic interest-rate swaps. For instance, a bank in Montana that makes many loans to firms that mine copper might engage in a credit swap with a bank in Kansas that makes many loans to wheat farmers. The Montana bank fears that if copper prices fall, some borrowers in that industry may default on their loans, while the Kansas bank fears that if wheat prices fall, some borrowers in that industry may default on their loans. The banks can reduce their risk by swapping payment streams on some of these loans. The alternative of the Montana bank diversifying its loan portfolio by making fewer loans to miners while making more loans to farmers may be difficult to carry out because many banks specialize in making loans to firms with which they have long-term relationships. The Kansas bank would face similar difficulties in diversifying its portfolio.

Credit Default Swaps

In the mid-1990s, Bankers Trust and the JPMorgan investment bank developed *credit default swaps*. The name is somewhat misleading because unlike the swaps we have discussed so far, **credit default swaps** are actually a type of insurance. During the financial crisis of 2007–2009, these swaps were most widely used in conjunction with mortgage-backed securities and collateralized debt obligations (CDOs), which are similar to mortgage-backed securities. The issuer of a credit default swap on a mortgage-backed security receives payments from the buyer in exchange for promising to make payments to the buyer if the security goes into default. For example, a buyer might purchase a credit default swap on a mortgage-backed security with a face value of $1,000 in exchange for paying the seller of the credit default swap $20 per year. If the issuer of the mortgage-backed security misses scheduled principal or interest payments and the bond defaults, its value will drop significantly. If the price of the bond drops to $300, the buyer of the credit default swap will receive $700 from the seller.

Credit default swap A derivative that requires the seller to make payments to the buyer if the price of the underlying security declines in value; in effect, a type of insurance.

By 2005, some investors became convinced that many of the subprime mortgages included in the mortgage-backed securities and collateralized debt obligations were likely to default and decided to speculate by buying credit default swaps on these securities. These investors were speculating, rather than insuring, because most of them did not own the underlying mortgage-backed securities on which they were buying credit default swaps. American International Group (AIG), the largest insurance company in the United States, issued large amounts of credit default swaps on mortgage-backed securities. In hindsight, AIG charged the buyers relatively small amounts compared to the actual risk. The volume of credit default swaps AIG issued left the firm vulnerable to a decline in the U.S. housing market because that would lead to defaults on the mortgages underlying the mortgage-backed securities the firm was insuring. AIG underestimated the extent of the risk it was taking on, apparently because it relied on the high ratings that S&P and Moody's gave to many of these securities. Like the ratings agencies, AIG's internal models did not account for the effects of a nationwide decline in home prices.

By September 2008, the prices of the securities on which AIG had written credit default swaps appeared to have declined substantially in value. There was some disagreement on this point between AIG and the buyers of the credit default swaps because by that time the underlying securities were no longer being actively traded, so it was difficult to determine their true prices. The buyers insisted that AIG post collateral so that the buyers could offset the counterparty risk that AIG posed and be sure of collecting the payments they believed they were owed because of price declines in the underlying securities. Because AIG lacked sufficient collateral, it was pushed to the brink of bankruptcy. The Treasury and the Federal Reserve decided that if AIG went bankrupt and defaulted on its obligations, including its obligations to make payments to holders of credit default swaps, the financial system would be severely disrupted. So, in exchange for the federal government receiving 80% ownership of the company, the Federal Reserve loaned AIG $85 billion. AIG's losses increased, however, and ultimately it received $182 billion in funds from the federal government. In late 2012, it appeared that through sales of subsidiaries and a rebound in the prices of some of its financial holdings, AIG might be able to eventually repay all of the funds it received from the federal government. The Treasury had sold the majority of its holdings in AIG and was left owning only about 16% of the firm's common stock.

The volume of credit default swaps from firms other than AIG also increased during the 2005–2006 period, even as the housing market began to decline. During the last months of the housing boom, the number of subprime mortgages being issued began to fall behind the demand for mortgage-backed securities and CDOs. Some commercial banks, investment banks, and other financial firms decided to place favorable bets on these securities by selling credit default swaps on them. Their reasoning was that the prices of the securities would remain high, so the firms would not have to pay anything to the buyers of the credit default swaps. The firms would earn a profit from the payments they would receive from the buyers. Unfortunately for these firms, the underlying securities plummeted in value, and the firms were liable for huge payments to the buyers of the credit default swaps.

A number of people in the financial community, as well as economists and policymakers, were concerned about the volume of credit default swaps outstanding. Because credit default swaps are traded over the counter rather than on exchanges, there are no reliable statistics on them. Credit default swaps were sold not just on securities but also on companies. It was very possible that multiple credit default swaps could have been sold on the same security or company. Therefore, a default on a security or a bankruptcy of a firm might lead to significant losses for the multiple firms that had sold credit default swaps on the security or firm. The heavy losses that AIG and other firms and investors suffered on credit default swaps deepened the financial crisis and led policymakers to consider imposing regulations on these derivatives.[3]

---

[3]An interesting and entertaining account of the development of credit default swaps during the financial crisis appears in Michael Lewis, *The Big Short: Inside the Doomsday Machine*, New York: W. W. Norton & Company, 2010. (Note that the book reproduces conversations with investors that involve substantial amounts of profanity.) An excellent source of information on collateralized debt obligations (CDOs) is an undergraduate senior thesis written at Harvard: Anna Katherine Barnett-Hart, "The Story of the CDO Market Meltdown," Harvard College, March 19, 2009.

Making the Connection

Are Derivatives "Financial Weapons of Mass Destruction"?

We have seen that derivatives can play an important role in the financial system, particularly by facilitating risk sharing. As noted in the chapter opener, though, billionaire investor Warren Buffett considers them to be "financial weapons of mass destruction." Note that Buffett is not referring to futures contracts and exchange-traded options of the types we have focused on in this chapter. Instead, he is referring to derivatives that are not traded on exchanges. These derivatives include forward contracts, non-listed option contracts, and credit default swaps.

Buffett has identified three problems with these derivatives:

1. These derivatives are *thinly traded*—that is, they are not often bought and sold—which makes them difficult to value. Lack of a market value makes it difficult to evaluate the financial health of either the buyers or the sellers. In addition, dealers in some of these options mark them to market using prices predicted by models rather than actual market prices, which may not exist. This practice means that the dealers add money to the accounts of either the buyers or sellers—whichever benefits from the price change—and subtract money from the accounts of the other. The side gaining from the increasing value of its derivatives can count the gain as earnings in its financial statements. Buffett argues that because the models used to estimate the price changes may be inaccurate, the increased earnings are likely inaccurate as well.

2. Many of these derivatives are not subject to significant government regulation, so firms may not put aside reserves to offset potential losses. AIG suffered from this problem: When the firm had to provide collateral to the buyers of its credit default swaps, it lacked sufficient funds and needed to borrow from the Federal Reserve and the Treasury.

3. These derivatives are not traded on exchanges, so they involve substantial counterparty risk. Recall that with exchange-traded derivatives, the exchange provides clearinghouse services and stands as the counterparty to both the buyer and the seller. By acting as counterparty to both sides, the exchange greatly reduces default risk. During the financial crisis, worries about counterparty risk resulted in trading on some derivatives markets drying up, as potential buyers worried about default risk. This problem was particularly severe after Lehman Brothers declared bankruptcy in October 2008, defaulting on many of its contracts.

Many economists and policymakers share Buffett's concerns. During 2010, Congress passed the Wall Street Reform and Consumer Protection Act, also called the Dodd-Frank Act, in response to the financial crisis. Under the act, many derivatives now must be bought and sold on exchanges. Economists are debating whether the decline in counterparty risk and the increase in transparency will be worth the loss of flexibility from standardizing these derivative contracts.

Source: The best source for Warren Buffet's views on derivatives is the "Chairman's Letter," in Berkshire Hathaway's *Annual Report* for the years 2002–2010.

See related problems 5.8 and 5.9 at the end of the chapter.

Answering the Key Question

Continued from page 190

At the beginning of this chapter, we asked:

"Are financial derivatives 'weapons of financial mass destruction'?"

We have seen that futures and exchange-traded options play an important role in the financial system and provide the key service of risk sharing. Warren Buffett has argued that some derivatives that are not exchange traded contributed significantly to the financial crisis. While not all derivatives are weapons of financial mass destruction, policymakers have enacted new regulations that are intended to ensure that use of some derivatives does not destabilize the financial system.

Key Terms and Problems

Key Terms

Call option, p. 203

Counterparty risk, p. 193

Credit default swap, p. 214

Credit swap, p. 214

Currency swap, p. 213

Derivative, p. 191

Forward contract, p. 193

Futures contract, p. 194

Hedge, p. 191

Interest-rate swap, p. 212

Long position, p. 195

Margin requirement, p. 202

Marking to market, p. 202

Option, p. 203

Option premium, p. 206

Put option, p. 203

Settlement date, p. 193

Short position, p. 195

Speculate, p. 192

Spot price, p. 193

Strike price (or exercise price), p. 203

Swap, p. 212

7.1 ### Derivatives, Hedging, and Speculating

Explain what derivatives are and distinguish between using them to hedge and using them to speculate.

Review Questions

1.1 Why do investors buy and sell derivatives rather than the underlying assets?

1.2 What is the difference between hedging and speculating?

Problems and Applications

1.3 Would derivatives markets be better off if the only people buying and selling derivatives contracts were hedgers? Briefly explain.

1.4 In each of the following situations, what risk do you face from price fluctuations? What would have to be true of a derivative security if the security were to help you to hedge this risk?

a. You are a corn farmer.

b. You are a manufacturer of cornbread.

c. You are buying Treasury bonds to finance your child's future college tuition.

 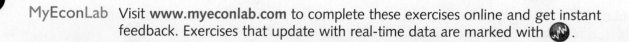

7.2 Forward Contracts
Define forward contracts.

Review Questions

2.1 What service do forward contracts provide in the financial system?

2.2 Why do forward contracts have counterparty risk?

Problems and Applications

2.3 Suppose that you are a wealthy investor. Although you have no connection with the oil industry, you are convinced from studying the determinants of demand and supply in the oil market that the price of oil will decline sharply in the future. How might you use forward contracts to profit from your forecast?

2.4 Suppose that oil prices decline by 50%. Which counterparty to a forward contract in oil has an incentive to default on the contract? Briefly explain.

7.3 Futures Contracts
Discuss how futures contracts can be used to hedge and to speculate.

Review Questions

3.1 What are the key differences between forward contracts and futures contracts? What is the difference between a commodity future and a financial future? Give two examples of each.

3.2 Is a firm likely to have a long position in both the spot market and the futures market? Briefly explain.

3.3 Give an example of speculating using commodity futures and speculating using financial futures.

Problems and Applications

3.4 Why did futures markets originate in agricultural markets? Would a farmer buy or sell futures contracts? What would a farmer hope to gain by doing so? Would General Mills buy or sell futures contracts in wheat? What would the company hope to gain by doing so?

3.5 According to an article in the *Wall Street Journal*, Canadian firms that import goods that are priced in U.S. dollars "buy futures contracts that guarantee that they can exchange Canadian dollars for U.S. [dollars] at fixed prices." Do you agree that a futures contract makes it possible to fix the price of the underlying asset?

Source: Phred Dvorak and Andy Georgiades, "Strong Loonie Sets Off a Retail Tiff," *Wall Street Journal*, May 19, 2010.

3.6 An article in the *Wall Street Journal* on the market for coffee futures noted that on that day, "traders began to close out bets that prices would rise, or liquidate their long positions."

a. What is a long position in the futures market?

b. Were the traders the article describes hedgers or speculators? Had they been buyers or sellers of coffee futures contracts? How would they have "liquidated" their positions?

Source: Alexandra Wexler and Leslie Josephs, "Coffee Rally Stalls, Sparking Selloff," *Wall Street Journal*, October 4, 2012.

3.7 An article in the *Wall Street Journal* noted that All Nippon Airways had "reduced its oil hedging to around 40% this fiscal year from 60% in the last fiscal year in a bid to capture the lower spot prices." Why would hedging against oil price increases reduce the ability of airlines to benefit from a decline in the spot price of oil? Your answer should include a definition of hedging.

Source: Joanne Chiu and Jeffrey Ng, "Oil Prices Fall but Airlines Not Benefiting," *Wall Street Journal*, June 15, 2012.

3.8 An article in the *Wall Street Journal* states, "Gasoline futures are falling, which could point to a drop in prices at the pump down the line."

  a. What does it means to say that "futures are falling"?

  b. Why might falling gasoline futures be an indication that retail gasoline prices might fall in the future?

  Source: Liam Pleven, "Gasoline Prices Pumped Down," *Wall Street Journal*, October 3, 2012.

3.9 Suppose that you are a wheat farmer. Answer the following questions.

  a. It is September, and you intend to have 50,000 bushels of wheat harvested and ready to sell in November. The current spot market price of wheat is $2.50 per bushel, and the current December futures price of wheat is $2.75 per bushel. Should you buy or sell wheat futures? If each wheat futures contract is for 5,000 bushels, how many contracts will you buy or sell, and how much will you spend or receive in buying or selling futures contracts?

  b. It is now November, and you sell 50,000 bushels of wheat at the spot price of $2.60 per bushel. If the futures price is $2.85 and you settle your position in the futures market, what was your gain or loss on your futures market position? Did you completely hedge your risk from price fluctuations in the wheat market? Give a numerical explanation.

3.10 An article in the *Wall Street Journal* discussing the nickel market contained the following:

  The sharp rise in nickel prices demonstrates how even a slight shift in demand and supply can roil tiny commodity markets like those for nickel, orange juice, and cocoa.

  a. What does the article mean by a market being "roiled"?

  b. Given this information about "tiny commodity markets," would it be more or less valuable for participants in these markets to have futures contracts available to them than it would be for participants in larger commodity markets, such as the market for oil?

  Source: Liam Pleven, "How the Nickel Rally Got Its Spark," *Wall Street Journal*, March 26, 2010.

3.11 [**Related to the** Making the Connection **on page 197**] An article in the *Wall Street Journal* discussed the fear that some farmers had that regulation of derivatives would make it harder for them to hedge risk. The article described the situation of a farmer who "uses derivatives to hedge the price he pays for feed and the price he gets for steers." How would this farmer use futures contracts to hedge these price risks?

  Source: Michael M. Phillips, "Finance Overhaul Casts Long Shadow on the Plains," *Wall Street Journal*, July 14, 2010.

3.12 [**Related to the** Making the Connection **on page 199**] Consider the listing below for 10-year Treasury note futures on the Chicago Board of Trade. One futures contract for Treasury notes = $100,000 face value of 10-year 6% notes.

  a. If today you bought two contracts expiring in December 2014, how much would you pay?

  b. What does the "OpenInt" on a futures contract mean? What is the OpenInt on the contract expiring in March 2015?

  c. If you were a speculator who expected interest rates to fall, would you buy or sell these futures contracts? Briefly explain.

Accompanies problem 3.12

Month	Last	Chg	Open	High	Low	Volume	OpenInt
Dec '14	**108'18.5**	**0'03.5**	108'13.0	108'21.0	108'06.5	564,322	2380328
Mar '15	**108'07.0**	**0'05.5**	108'00.0	108'05.0	107'26.0	4325	118728
Jun '15	**107'27.0**	**0'05.5**	107'27.0	107'27.0	107'21.5	2	19
Sep '15	**107'21.5**	**0'05.5**	107'21.5	107'21.5	107'21.5	0	0
Dec '15	**107'21.5**	**0'05.5**	107'21.5	107'21.5	107'21.5	0	0

d. Suppose you sell the December futures contract, and one day later, the Chicago Board of Trade informs you that it has credited funds to your margin account. What happened to interest rates during that day? Briefly explain.

3.13 [Related to Solved Problem 7.3 **on page 201**] Suppose that you are an investor who owns $10,000 in U.S. Treasury notes.

a. Will you be more worried about market interest rates rising or falling? Briefly explain.

b. How might you hedge against the risk you identified in part (a)?

3.14 According to an article in the *Economist* magazine:

> In 1958 American onion farmers, blaming speculators for the volatility of their crops' prices, lobbied a congressman from Michigan named Gerald Ford to ban trading in onion futures. Supported by the president-to-be, they got their way. Onion futures have been prohibited ever since.

Is it likely that banning trading futures contracts in onions reduced the volatility in onion prices? Are onion farmers as a group better off because of the ban?

Source: "Over the Counter, Out of Sight," *Economist*, November 12, 2009.

7.4 | **Options**
Distinguish between call options and put options and explain how they are used.

Review Questions

4.1 What is the difference between a call option and put option? What role does an option writer play?

4.2 How do the rights and obligations of options buyers and sellers differ from the rights and obligations of futures buyers and sellers?

4.3 What is an option premium? What is an option's intrinsic value? What other factors, besides intrinsic value, can affect the size of an option premium?

4.4 How can investors use options to manage risk?

Problems and Applications

4.5 An article in *Wall Street Journal* in the fall of 2012 quoted an options broker as saying: "The market is relatively strong with a good couple of months this summer, so put options are expensive as people try to protect gains."

a. What is a put option?

b. How would buying put options allow an investor to protect his or her gains made from an increase in stock prices?

Source: Kaitlyn Kiernan, "Traders Look Toward S&P 500 Records," *Wall Street Journal*, September 24, 2012.

4.6 An article on the stock market observes: "To protect profits, investors can buy put options, which act as insurance, while investors who want to add exposure to the market can buy call options."

a. How does buying a put option provide insurance against a fall in stock prices?

b. Compare the pros and cons of buying a put option versus selling stocks if you are worried that stock prices might decline.

c. What does "exposure" to the stock market mean? How does buying call options allow an investor to add exposure to the stock market to the investor's portfolio?

Source: Ben Levisohn, "How to Rock at Lower Volume," *Wall Street Journal*, August 31, 2012.

4.7 An article in the *Wall Street Journal* discussed put options on Facebook's stock. One put option had a strike price of $25. The article observed: "Puts are contracts that give the buyer the right to sell stock later for a set price. These particular bets maximize their profit if the stock trades at $25." Do you agree that as an investor you will maximize your investment in a put option with a strike price of $25 if the underlying stock has a market price of $25? Briefly explain.

Source: Kaitlyn Kiernan and Jonathan Cheng, "Investors Bet on Facebook Fall," *Wall Street Journal*, May 29, 2012.

4.8 [**Related to the** Making the Connection **on page 207 and** Solved Problem 7.4 **on page 208**] Use the following information on call and put options for Facebook to answer the questions.

		Call			Put		
Expiration	Strike	Last	Volume	Open Interest	Last	Volume	Open Interest
Oct	17.00	5.00	21	3064	0.02	13	14427
Nov	17.00	5.20	44	795	0.40	485	13098
Jan	17.00	5.50	1	691	0.55	231	7381
Apr	17.00	5.70	2	1409	1.15	69	7289
Oct	18.00	4.00	49	4762	0.07	154	22337
Nov	18.00	4.44	37	4047	0.50	4426	16197
Jan	18.00	4.50	10	943	0.80	409	13754
Apr	18.00	5.22	31	712	1.45	60	6659

Facebook — Underlying stock price: 21.95

a. What is the intrinsic value of the call option that expires in April and has a $17 strike price?

b. What is the intrinsic value of the put option that expires in January and has an $18 strike price?

c. Briefly explain why a call with an $18 strike price sells for less than a call with a $17 strike price (for all expiration dates), while a put with an $18 strike price sells for more than a put with a $17 strike price (for all expiration dates).

d. Suppose you buy the April call with a strike price of $18. If you exercise it when the price of Facebook is $25, what will be your profit or loss? (Remember that each options contract is for 100 shares of stock.)

e. Suppose you buy the April put with a strike price of $18 at the price listed, and the price of Facebook stock remains at $21.95. What will be your profit or loss?

4.9 An article in the *Wall Street Journal* observes: "When volatility is low, options are cheaper." Briefly explain the reasoning behind this observation.

Source: Ben Levisohn, "How to Rock at Lower Volume," *Wall Street Journal*, August 31, 2012.

4.10 An article in the *Wall Street Journal* noted that, "Options traders appeared to be taking a bullish approach to Target" because during the previous day they purchased 68,000 calls on the company's stock, but only 27,000 puts. What does a "bullish approach" mean? Why do the data on options purchases indicate that traders were taking a bullish approach?

Source: Tennille Tracy, "Retail Report Puts Target in Sights," *Wall Street Journal*, February 3, 2009.

4.11 Suppose that the Dow Jones Industrial Average is above the 13,000 level. If the Dow were to fall to 10,000, who would gain the most: investors who had bought call options, investors who had sold call options, investors who had bought put options, or investors who had sold put options? Who would be hurt the most?

4.12 [**Related to the** Making the Connection **on page 210**] The CBOE Web site quotes the CEO of an investment advisory firm as saying: "The VIX Index is an important and popular tool for measuring investor sentiment." Briefly explain in what sense the VIX is a measure of investor sentiment.

Source: www.cboe.com/micro/vix/introduction.aspx.

7.5 Swaps
Define swaps and explain how they can be used to reduce risk.

Review Questions

5.1 In what ways is a swap contract different from a futures contract?

5.2 In what ways is a credit swap different from an interest-rate swap?

5.3 How does a credit default swap differ from the other swap contracts discussed in this chapter? What difficulties did credit default swaps cause during the financial crisis of 2007–2009?

Problems and Applications

5.4 Suppose that you manage a bank that has made many loans at a fixed interest rate. You are worried that inflation might rise and the value of the loans will decline.

a. Why would an increase in inflation cause the value of your fixed-rate loans to decline?

b. How might you use swaps to reduce your risk?

5.5 A column in the *Wall Street Journal* observes: "Many regulators, politicians and academics consider credit default swaps to be insurance contracts." Briefly explain the reasoning behind this observation.

Source: Stuart M. Turnbull and Lee M. Wakeman, "Why Markets Need 'Naked' Credit Default Swaps," *Wall Street Journal*, September 11, 2012.

5.6 An article in the *Wall Street Journal* noted: "The cost of credit default swaps on Italian and Spanish government and corporate debt surged last week." What does an increase in the price of credit default swaps on Italian and Spanish government and corporate bonds indicate about the bonds? What likely happened to the yields on those bonds?

Source: Matt Wirz, "Summer's Over: Spain and Italy CDS Surge," *Wall Street Journal*, August 27, 2012.

5.7 [Related to the Chapter Opener **on page 190**] An article in the *Wall Street Journal* on proposals to change the regulations governing the trading of financial derivatives contained the following:

The SEC and the Commodity Futures Trading Commission are both seeking greater authority to police the over-the-counter market and hope new powers can help them reduce the risks that over-the counter trading may pose to the broader system.

a. What is the "over-the-counter market" for derivatives?

b. What does the article mean by "broader system"?

c. How might over-the-counter trading of derivatives result in risks to the broader system?

Source: Sarah N. Lynch, "Use of Derivatives by Funds Examined," *Wall Street Journal*, March 26, 2010.

5.8 [Related to the Making the Connection **on page 216**] In one of his annual letters to shareholders of Berkshire Hathaway, Warren Buffett wrote that trading derivatives has much more counterparty risk than does trading stocks or bonds because "a normal stock trade is completed in a few days with one party getting its cash, the other its securities. Counterparty risk therefore quickly disappears."

a. What is counterparty risk?

b. Why is counterparty risk greater for trading in derivatives than for trading in stocks and bonds?

Source: Warren Buffett, "Chairman's Letter," *Berkshire Hathaway Inc. 2008 Annual Report*, February 27, 2009.

5.9 [Related to the Making the Connection **on page 216**] In one of his annual letters to shareholders of Berkshire Hathaway, Warren Buffett wrote that "even experienced investors and analysts encounter major problems in analyzing the financial condition of firms that are heavily involved with derivatives contracts." Why might it be difficult for investors to analyze the financial condition of firms that are buying and selling large numbers of derivatives? Does it matter what type of derivatives the firms are buying and selling?

Source: Warren Buffett, "Chairman's Letter," *Berkshire Hathaway Inc. 2008 Annual Report*, February 27, 2009.

Data Exercises

D7.1: **[Comparing the volatility of one stock to the volatility of the whole market]** In addition to the VIX index based on S&P 500, there are VIX indexes available for some individual stocks. Go to the Web site of the Federal Reserve Bank of St. Louis (FRED) (research.stlouisfed.org/fred2/) and for the period from January 2010 to the present, download and plot on the same graph the data series for the VIX index (VIXCLS) and the VIX index for Apple's stock (VXAPLCLS). Which of the two series is the more volatile? Would you expect the relationship between the two series to change during a recession? Briefly explain.

D7.2: **[Options and market expectations]** Go to wsj.com and click on "Markets" and "Market Data Center." Under "U.S. Stocks" in the pull-down menu, click on "Listed Options Quotes." Find the data on call and put options for Facebook. Find the calls and puts with a strike price within $5 of Facebook's closing stock price. Is the volume of trading and the open interest greater for the puts or for the calls? Interpret these data with respect to market expectations for Facebook's stock price to rise or fall.

CHAPTER 8

The Market for Foreign Exchange

Learning Objectives

After studying this chapter, you should be able to:

8.1 Explain the difference between nominal and real exchange rates (pages 225–229)

8.2 Explain how markets for foreign exchange operate (pages 230–234)

8.3 Explain how exchange rates are determined in the long run (pages 234–238)

8.4 Use a demand and supply model to explain how exchange rates are determined in the short run (pages 238–246)

Is Ben Bernanke Responsible for Japanese Firms Moving to the United States?

In the modern global economy, people in the United States no longer find it surprising that foreign firms produce goods here. For example, Toyota and Honda have been assembling cars in the United States since the 1980s. There are many reasons firms produce goods in other countries, but a key one was highlighted in 2012 with respect to Japanese firms: the rising value of the Japanese yen against the U.S. dollar.

To buy goods, physical assets, or financial assets in other countries, people must first exchange currencies. When Apple buys components for the iPad from foreign suppliers, it must exchange U.S. dollars for foreign currency. A similar transaction takes place when the managers of Vanguard's European Stock Index mutual

fund buy shares of Nestlé, the Swiss company famous for its chocolate. The dollars that Vanguard has on deposit at a U.S. bank must be converted to bank deposits in Swiss francs. The *exchange rate* measures how much one currency is worth in terms of another currency. Because of the increased volume of purchases of goods, services, and financial assets across countries, policymakers at the world's central banks have become increasingly concerned about fluctuations in exchange rates.

The rising value of the yen was certainly a concern for Japanese policymakers in the years following the 2007–2009 financial crisis. Between mid-2007, when the financial crisis began, and mid-2012, the value of the yen had increased by over 35%. This increase imposed

Continued on next page

Key Issue and Question

Issue: Volatility in exchange rates during recent years has led some Japanese firms to relocate production to the United States and other countries.

Question: Why has the value of the dollar declined against other major currencies during the past 10 years?

Answered on page 247

a crippling burden on Japanese firms exporting to the United States because the firms received dollars when they sold their goods but had to use yen to pay their workers, their suppliers, and most of their other costs. A number of Japanese firms, including Toyota, Nissan, and Honda, decided that they needed to move production to the United States so that both their revenues and their costs would be in dollars. In 2012, Honda announced plans to eliminate exports of cars and trucks from Japan to North America, deciding to instead produce the vehicles in North America.

What explains the rise in the value of the yen against the dollar? During the past 20 years, as financial investment across borders has increased, investors have become more sensitive to differences in interest rates among countries. As the Federal Reserve drove U.S. interest rates to record low levels, many investors wanted to sell U.S financial assets to buy financial assets in other countries. As a result of investors selling dollars and buying other currencies, the value of the dollar declined against these currencies, including the yen.

Federal Reserve Chairman Ben Bernanke argued that the Fed had not intentionally lowered the exchange value of the U.S. dollar, but some economists and policymakers noted that the result of a weak dollar was to increase U.S. exports and reduce imports. Potentially, increased exports could help the U.S. economy's slow recovery from the 2007–2009 recession. Long gone are the days when the Federal Reserve could largely ignore how its policies affected the economies of other countries and ignore how financial and economic developments in other countries affected the U.S. economy.

Sources: Mike Ramsey, "Honda Bolsters Its Production in North America," *Wall Street Journal,* August 12, 2012; and Chester Dawson and Yoshio Takahasi, "Toyota's Profits Bounce Back," *Wall Street Journal*, August 3, 2012.

In this chapter, we analyze how exchange rates are determined and why they change over time. Exchange rates experience short-run fluctuations around long-run trends. Understanding these changes will show why economic developments in the United States, including movements in U.S. interest rates, can affect international financial markets and the broader global economy.

Exchange Rates and Trade

Today, markets for many goods, services, and financial assets are global. For example, both exports and imports have grown tremendously. In 2012, foreign consumers, firms, and governments purchased about 14% of the goods and services produced in the United States, while almost 18% of goods and services consumed in the United States were produced abroad. These percentages are more than twice what they were in the 1960s. When individuals or firms in the United States import or export goods or make investments in other countries, they need to convert dollars into foreign currencies. The **nominal exchange rate** is the price of one country's currency in terms of another country's currency. For example, in November 2012, 1 U.S. dollar could buy 82 Japanese yen or 13 Mexican pesos. The nominal exchange rate is usually referred to simply as the *exchange rate*.

Fluctuations in the exchange rate between the dollar and foreign currencies affect the prices that U.S. consumers pay for foreign imports. For instance, suppose that a Sony PlayStation 3 video game console has a price of ¥30,000 in Tokyo, and the exchange rate between the yen and the U.S. dollar is ¥100 = $1. Then, the dollar price of the PlayStation is $300 (= ¥30,000/(100 ¥/$)). If the exchange rate changes to ¥80 = $1, the dollar price of the PlayStation rises to $375 (= ¥30,000/(80 ¥/$)), even though the

8.1

Learning Objective

Explain the difference between nominal and real exchange rates.

Nominal exchange rate
The price of one currency in terms of another currency; also called the *exchange rate*.

yen price of the PlayStation in Tokyo stays the same. In this case, the yen has gained in value against the dollar because it takes fewer yen to buy a dollar.

An increase in value of one country's currency in exchange for another country's currency is called an **appreciation**. When the yen appreciates against the dollar, Japanese firms have more difficulty selling goods and services in the United States. In the same way, an appreciation of the yen against the dollar makes it easier for U.S. firms to sell goods and services in Japan. For instance, at an exchange rate of ¥100 = $1, a Hershey's candy bar that has a price of $1 in Philadelphia has a yen price of ¥100. But if the yen appreciates to ¥80 = $1, the candy bar has a yen price of only ¥80. Note that to say that the yen has experienced an *appreciation* against the dollar is equivalent to saying that the dollar has experienced a **depreciation**—or decrease in value—against the yen.

Appreciation An increase in the value of a currency in exchange for another currency.

Depreciation A decrease in the value of a currency in exchange for another currency.

Making the Connection

What's the Most Important Factor in Determining Sony's Profits?

Sony produces consumer electronics products, including game consoles, televisions, and Blu-ray disc players. In the long run, Sony's profitability depends on its ability to develop innovative new products, produce them at a low cost, and market them successfully to consumers. Sony has had many successes, as well as some missteps, such as its failure to realize that Apple's introduction of the iPod in 2001 would lead to a sharp decline in sales for Sony's once hugely popular Walkman portable CD player. In 2010, Sony was counting on the success of its new 3-D televisions to make it the market leader, but the company was disappointed when consumers were slow to adopt the new format and by 2012 sales were well under forecasts.

But what about in the short run, which is a period too brief for Sony to change its product line, build or close factories, or significantly expand or contract its workforce? In the short run, Sony's profits depend on the prices it charges relative to the prices its competitors charge for comparable products. But Sony lacks complete control over its prices because, although the company is based in Japan, it sells about 75% of its goods outside Japan. Fluctuations in the exchange rate between the yen and foreign currencies will affect the foreign currency prices of Sony's products. For instance, a rise in the value of the yen against the U.S. dollar raises the dollar price of the Play-Station 3, as well as Sony's Blu-ray players and televisions. Sony can, and sometimes does, hold constant the dollar price of its products in the United States, despite an increase in the value of the yen. For instance, the company held the retail price of the PlayStation 3 to around $299 for several years before cutting the price to $269, despite increases in the value of the yen during most of the period after 2009. Sony's profits on the PlayStation 3 declined because it received fewer yen in exchange for the $269 U.S. price, while the cost of producing the product in Japan—costs payable in yen—remained unaffected.

Sony was also hurt by the increase in the value of the yen versus the euro, which is the common currency used by most countries in Western Europe, because Europe accounts for about 20% of the firm's sales. The company estimated that an increase in the value of the yen from ¥105 = 1€ to ¥100 = 1€ would reduce the firm's profits by about ¥30 billion. Other Japanese firms are just as vulnerable to an appreciation of the yen. In 2012, Toyota, Honda, and Nissan estimated that for every 1¥ increase in the value of the yen versus the dollar, their combined profits declined by ¥67 billion. Given that the yen had increased in value from ¥122 = $1 in the summer of 2009 to ¥82 = $1 in the fall of 2012, the Japanese car companies were finding it very difficult to manufacture cars in Japan for sale in the United States.

Not surprisingly, the top managers of Japanese firms such as Sony, Toyota, and Honda continue to explore ways of cushioning the impact of fluctuations in the value of the yen on the profitability of their firms. As we saw in the chapter opener, Japanese car companies have decided to move significant production overseas, selling most of their domestic production in Japan where both revenue and costs are in yen.

Sources: Daisuke Wakabayashi, "Sony Loss Widens," *Wall Street Journal*, August 2, 2012; "Sony's Quarterly Profit Sinks, Hit by Weak Demand," *New York Times*, August 2, 2012; and Kenneth Maxwell, "Yen's Fall May Spring Profit Surge for Japan Firms," *Wall Street Journal*, February 23, 2012.

See related problem 1.7 at the end of the chapter.

Is It Dollars per Yen or Yen per Dollar?

Notice that there are two ways to express every exchange rate: (1) as units of foreign currency per unit of domestic currency or (2) as units of domestic currency per unit of foreign currency. For example, we can express the exchange rate between the U.S. dollar and the Japanese yen as ¥100 = $1 or as $0.01 = ¥1. The two expressions are mathematically equivalent, with one being the reciprocal of the other. Professional currency traders at banks and other financial institutions typically price, or "quote," exchange rates as units of domestic currency per unit of foreign currency, and these quotations are called *direct quotations*. *Indirect quotations* express exchange rates as units of foreign currency per unit of domestic currency.

In practice, there are certain conventions in reporting exchange rates in the financial news that are a mixture of direct and indirect quotations. For instance, the exchange rate between the U.S. dollar and the Japanese yen is almost always reported as yen per dollar, while the exchange rate between the euro and the dollar is reported as dollars per euro and the exchange rate between the British pound and the dollar is reported as dollars per pound. Many financial news outlets provide tables of currency "cross rates," such as the one shown in Figure 8.1, which provides both direct and indirect quotations for a day in October 2012. Reading across the rows, we have the direct quotations, while reading down the columns, we have the indirect quotations. For instance, the second entry in the U.S. row shows that the exchange rate on this day was $1.3034 per euro (€). The last entry in the U.S. dollar column shows that the exchange rate can also be expressed as €0.7672 per dollar.

Figure 8.2 shows fluctuations since 2000 in the exchange rates between the U.S. dollar and the yen, the Canadian dollar, and the euro. For consistency, in each case on the vertical axis we show the number of U.S. dollars necessary to buy one unit of the foreign currency. In showing the graphs this way, a larger value for the exchange rate

	U.S. dollar	Euro	Pound	Swiss franc	Peso	Yen	Canadian dollar
Canada	0.9785	1.2754	1.5786	1.0522	0.0765	0.0124	. . . . .
Japan	78.685	102.56	126.94	84.608	6.1490	. . . . .	80.414
Mexico	12.796	16.679	20.644	13.759	. . . . .	0.1626	13.077
Switzerland	0.9300	1.2122	1.5004	. . . . .	0.0727	0.0118	0.9504
UK	0.6199	0.8079	. . . . .	0.6665	0.0484	0.0079	0.6335
Euro	(0.7672)	. . . . .	1.2378	0.8250	0.0600	0.0098	0.7841
U.S.	. . . . .	(1.3034)	1.6133	1.0753	0.0782	0.0127	1.0220

Figure 8.1 Foreign-Exchange Cross Rates

Foreign-exchange rates can be expressed as either U.S. dollars per unit of foreign currency or as units of foreign currency per U.S. dollar. Reading across the rows, we have the direct quotations, while reading down the columns, we have the indirect quotations. For example, the second entry in the U.S. row shows that the exchange rate on this day was $1.3034 per

euro €. The last entry in the U.S. Dollar column shows that the exchange rate can also be expressed as €0.7672 per dollar.

Source: "Key Cross Currency Rates," *Wall Street Journal*, October 5, 2012.

represents a *depreciation* of the dollar and an *appreciation* of the other currency because more dollars are required to buy a unit of the foreign currency. Each graph shows a roughly similar pattern: a depreciation of the U.S. dollar through the early stages of the financial crisis in 2008, followed by a relatively short period of appreciation, and then a return to depreciation during the second half of 2009 and early 2010. The U.S. dollar appreciated against the euro in early 2010, as several European countries, including Greece, Spain, Portugal, and Ireland, experienced severe financial problems that made it possible that they might abandon the common euro currency. In section 8.3, we investigate the factors that lead to fluctuations in exchange rates.

MyEconLab Real-time data

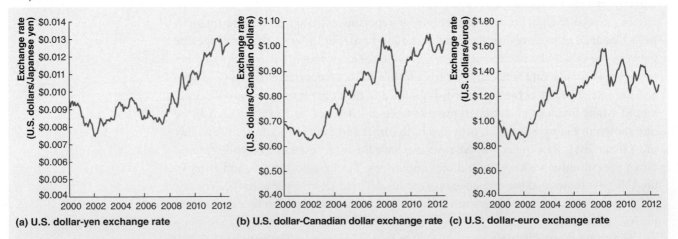

(a) U.S. dollar-yen exchange rate

(b) U.S. dollar-Canadian dollar exchange rate

(c) U.S. dollar-euro exchange rate

Figure 8.2 Fluctuations in Exchange Rates, 2000–2012

The panels show fluctuations in the exchange rates between the U.S. dollar and the yen, the Canadian dollar, and the euro. Because we are measuring the exchange rate on the vertical axis as dollars per unit of foreign

currency, an increase in the exchange rate represents a *depreciation* of the dollar and an *appreciation* of the other currency.

Source: Federal Reserve Bank of St. Louis.

Nominal Exchange Rates Versus Real Exchange Rates

Nominal exchange rates tell you how many yen or euros or Canadian dollars you will receive in exchange for a U.S. dollar, but they do not tell you how much of another country's goods and services you can buy with a U.S. dollar. When we are interested in the relative purchasing power of two countries' currencies, we use the **real exchange rate**, which measures the rate at which goods and services in one country can be exchanged for goods and services in another country. For simplicity, let's consider the real exchange rate using one particular product: the McDonald's Big Mac. Suppose we want to know the relative ability of U.S. dollars and British pounds to purchase Big Macs. Let's assume that a Big Mac in New York has a price of $4.50, a Big Mac in London has a price of £5.00, and the nominal exchange rate between the dollar and the pound is $1.25 = £1. We can convert the pound price of the London Big Mac into a dollar price by multiplying by the nominal exchange rate: £5.00 × $1.25/£ = $6.25. So, a U.S. Big Mac can exchange for only $4.50/$6.25 = 0.72 Big Macs in London.

> **Real exchange rate** The rate at which goods and services in one country can be exchanged for goods and services in another country.

We can summarize the previous calculation as an expression for the real exchange rate between the dollar and the pound in terms of Big Macs:

Real Big Mac exchange rate =

$$\frac{\text{Dollar price of Big Macs in New York}}{\text{Pound price of Big Macs in London} \times \text{Dollars per pound}}.$$
$$(\text{nominal exchange rate})$$

Of course, we don't have much interest in the real exchange rate in terms of a single product. But we can take the same approach to determine the real exchange rate between two currencies by substituting a consumer price index for each country in place of the price of a particular product. Recall that a consumer price index represents an average of the prices of all the goods and services purchased by a typical consumer and represents the *price level* in the country. Making this substitution gives us the following expression for the real exchange rate in terms of the nominal exchange rate and the price levels in each country:

Real exchange rate between the dollar and the pound =

$$\frac{\text{U.S. consumer price index}}{\text{British price index} \times \text{Dollars per pound exchange rate (nominal exchange rate)}}.$$

By rearranging terms and using symbols, we can write a more general equation showing the relationship between the nominal and real exchange rates:

$$e = E \times \left(\frac{P^{\text{Domestic}}}{P^{\text{Foreign}}}\right),$$

where:

E = nominal exchange rate, expressed as units of foreign currency per unit of domestic currency

e = real exchange rate

P^{Domestic} = domestic price level

P^{Foreign} = foreign price level

For example, if the real exchange rate between the British pound and the U.S. dollar were 2, this value would indicate that the average good or service produced in the United States can exchange for two of the average good or service in the United Kingdom.

8.2

Learning Objective

Explain how markets for foreign exchange operate.

Foreign-exchange market
An over-the-counter market where international currencies are traded.

Foreign-Exchange Markets

An individual consumer or investor can use exchange rates to convert one currency into another. If you go abroad, you have to convert U.S. dollars into Canadian dollars, Japanese yen, euros, British pounds, or other currencies. If the dollar rises in value relative to these currencies, you can buy more of other currencies during your travels, enabling you to enjoy a more expensive meal or bring back more souvenirs. Likewise, if you want to buy foreign stocks or bonds, you must convert U.S. dollars into the appropriate currency. Again, if the dollar appreciates, you can buy more Canadian, Japanese, or British stocks or bonds.

As with other prices, exchange rates are determined by the forces of demand and supply. Currencies are traded in **foreign-exchange markets** around the world. Traders in large commercial banks in North America, Europe, and Asia carry out the majority of the buying and selling of foreign exchange. Like the NASDAQ stock market, rather than being a physical place, the foreign-exchange market is an over-the-counter market consisting of dealers linked together by computers. The large commercial banks are called *market makers* because they are willing to buy and sell the major currencies at any time. Rather than enter the foreign-exchange market directly, most smaller banks and businesses pay a fee to a large commercial bank to carry out their foreign-exchange transactions. Typically, traders are buying and selling bank deposits denominated in currencies—rather than the currencies themselves. For instance, a currency trader at Bank of America may exchange euros for yen by trading euros held in an account owned by Bank of America in a Paris bank for yen held in an account owned by Deutsche Bank in a bank in Tokyo. Most foreign exchange trading takes place among commercial banks located in London, New York, and Tokyo, with secondary centers in Hong Kong, Singapore, and Zurich.

With daily trading in the trillions of dollars, the foreign-exchange market is the largest financial market in the world. In addition to commercial banks, major participants in the foreign-exchange market include investment portfolio managers and central banks, such as the Federal Reserve. Participants trade currencies such as the U.S. dollar, yen, pound, and euro around the clock. The busiest trading time is in the morning, U.S. east coast time, when the London and New York financial markets are both open for trading. But trading is always taking place somewhere. A currency trader in New York might receive a call in the middle of the night with news that leads him or her to buy or sell dollars or other currencies.

Forward and Futures Contracts in Foreign Exchange

Derivatives play an important role in the financial system (see Chapter 7). There are very active forward and futures markets in foreign exchange. In the foreign-exchange market, *spot market transactions* involve an exchange of currencies or bank deposits immediately (subject to a two-day settlement period) at the current exchange rate. In *forward transactions*, traders agree today to a *forward contract* to exchange currencies or bank deposits at a specific future date at an exchange rate known as the *forward rate*. *Futures contracts* in foreign exchange also exist. Futures contracts differ from forward contracts in several ways. While forward contracts are private agreements among traders to exchange any amount of currency on any future date, futures contracts are traded on exchanges, such as the Chicago Board of Trade (CBOT), and the quantity of currency being exchanged and the *settlement date* on which the exchange will take place are standardized. With forward contracts, the forward exchange rate is fixed at the time the contract is agreed to, while with futures contracts, the futures exchange rate changes continually as contracts are bought and sold on the exchange.

Counterparty risk refers to the risk that one party to the contract will default and fail to buy or sell the underlying asset. Counterparty risk is lower with futures contracts than with forward contracts because the exchange—rather than the buyers and sellers—stands as the counterparty on each trade. For instance, someone buying a futures contract on the CBOT has the CBOT as a counterparty, which reduces default risk. For many financial assets, the reduction in counterparty risk means more trading takes place in futures contracts than in forward contracts. This outcome does not hold for foreign exchange, however, because the bulk of the trading takes place among large banks whose traders ordinarily are confident that their trading partners will not default on forward contracts. Because banks like the flexibility of forward contracts, the amount of trading in forward contracts in foreign exchange is at least 10 times greater than the amount of trading in futures contracts.

Call and put options are available on foreign exchange. Recall that a call option gives the buyer the right to purchase the underlying asset at a set price, called the *strike price*, at any time until the option's expiration date. A put option gives the buyer the right to sell the underlying asset at the strike price.

Exchange-Rate Risk, Hedging, and Speculating

Exchange-rate risk is the risk that a firm will suffer losses because of fluctuations in exchange rates. A U.S. firm is subject to exchange-rate risk when it sells goods and services in a foreign country. Suppose, for example, that you work for Smucker's, a maker of jams, jellies, and other food products, headquartered in Orville, Ohio. Suppose Smucker's sells $300,000 worth of jams and jellies to a supermarket chain in England at a time when the exchange rate is $1.50 = £1. Smucker's agrees to ship the jams and jellies today, but—as is often the case—the English firm has 90 days to pay Smucker's the funds. Smucker's agrees that the English firm can pay in pounds, so Smucker's will receive a payment of £200,000 (= $300,000/$1.50/£) in 90 days. Smucker's is exposed to exchange-rate risk because if the pound falls in value relative to the dollar before the English supermarket chain makes its payment, Smucker's will receive less than $300,000. For instance, if in 90 days the exchange rate is $1.25 = £1, then Smucker's will be able to exchange the £200,000 it receives for only $250,000 (= £200,000 × $1.25/£).

As part of your job at Smucker's, you are responsible for reducing the firm's exposure to exchange-rate risk. You can *hedge*, or reduce, the exchange-rate risk Smucker's faces by entering into a forward contract—or, more likely, having the firm's bank carry out the forward transaction for a fee. With a forward contract, Smucker's would agree today to *sell* the £200,000 it will receive in 90 days for dollars at the current forward rate. If the current forward rate is the same as the spot rate of $1.50 = £1, then Smucker's will have completely hedged its risk, at the cost of the fee its bank charges. The forward rate will reflect what traders in the forward market expect the spot exchange rate between the dollar and pound to be in 90 days, so the forward rate may not equal the

Exchange-rate risk
The risk that a firm will suffer losses because of fluctuations in exchange rates.

current spot rate. Typically, though, the current spot rate and the 90-day forward rate are close together, allowing Smucker's to hedge most of the exchange-rate risk it faces.

Smucker's is hedging against the risk that the value of the pound will fall against the dollar. Suppose that Burberry, a British clothing manufacturer, sells £2 million of men's coats to Macy's, the U.S. department store chain. The current exchange rate is $1.50 = £1, and Burberry agrees to accept payment of $3.5 million (= £2 million × $1.50/£) in 90 days. Burberry is exposed to the risk that over the next 90 days the value of the pound will rise relative to the dollar, which would decrease the number of pounds it would receive in exchange for the $3.5 million payment it will receive from Macy's in 90 days. To hedge against this risk, Burberry can agree to *buy* pounds today at the current forward rate. Note that this is the opposite of the strategy Smucker's used: To hedge against a *fall* in the value of the pound, Smucker's *sells* pounds in the forward market; to hedge against a *rise* in the value of the pound, Burberry *buys* pounds in the forward market.

A hedger uses derivatives markets to reduce risk, while a *speculator* uses derivatives markets to place a bet on the future value of a currency. For example, if an investor becomes convinced that the future value of the euro will be lower than other people in the foreign-exchange market currently believe, the investor can sell euros in the forward market. If the value of euros does, in fact, fall, then the spot price of the euro in the future will be lower, which will allow the investor to fulfill the forward contract at a profit. Similarly, an investor who believes that the future value of the euro will be higher than other people in the foreign-exchange market currently believe can make a profit by buying euros in the forward market. Of course, in either case, if the value of the euro moves in the opposite direction to the one the investor expects, the investor will suffer losses on his or her forward position.

Firms and investors can also use options contracts to hedge or to speculate. For example, a firm concerned that the value of a currency will fall more than expected—such as Smucker's, in our previous example—could hedge against this risk by buying put options on the currency. That way, if the value of the currency falls below the strike price, the firm could exercise the option and sell at the (above-market) strike price. Similarly, a firm concerned that the value of a currency will rise more than expected—such as Burberry, in our previous example—could hedge against this risk by buying call options on the currency. If the value of the currency rose above the strike price, the firm could exercise the option and buy at the (below-market) strike price.

Options contracts have the advantage to hedgers that if the price moves in the opposite direction from the one being hedged against, the hedger can decline to exercise the option and instead can gain from the favorable price movement. For instance, suppose that Smucker's decided to purchase put options on the pound rather than sell pounds in the forward market. Smucker's would still have been protected against a fall in the value of the pound because it could exercise its put options, thereby selling pounds at an above-market price. But if the pound rises in value, Smucker's can allow the put options to expire without exercising them and profit from the additional dollars it receives when it exchanges the £200,000 from the English supermarket chain in 90 days. Although options appear to have an advantage over forward contracts in this respect, options prices (premiums) are higher than the fees incurred with forward contracts.

A speculator who believed that the value of a currency was likely to rise more than expected would buy calls, while a speculator who believed that the value of a currency was likely to fall more than expected would buy puts. If the value of the currency moves in the opposite direction to the one the speculator hopes, the speculator with an options contract doesn't have to exercise the option. So, the advantage of an options contract is that a speculator's losses are limited to whatever he or she paid for the option. But once again, the disadvantage of speculating with options contracts is that their prices are higher than those of forward contracts.

Can Speculators Drive Down the Value of a Currency?

Participants in the market for foreign exchange can be divided into two groups: (1) hedgers, who—like Smucker's and Burberry in our example—are motivated by the desire to reduce exchange-rate risk, and (2) speculators, who hope to profit from exchange rate movements. Currency speculators, like traders in stocks, bonds, and other financial assets, typically buy and sell a country's currency, hoping to make a profit over a short period of time. As we have seen, speculators serve a useful role by providing liquidity in financial markets. In order to hedge exchange-rate risk, firms need enough counterparties willing to be on the other side of the hedgers' buying or selling. Without speculators, many financial markets, including the foreign-exchange market would be significantly less liquid.

However, some policymakers blame speculators for driving down exchange rates to artificially low levels, thereby causing instability in foreign-exchange markets. For example, in 2010, a controversy erupted over whether the managers of hedge funds were conspiring to earn billions of dollars by driving down the price of the euro. Hedge funds are similar to mutual funds in that they accept money from investors and invest the funds in a portfolio of assets. Unlike mutual funds, hedge funds typically make relatively risky investments, and they have fewer than 100 investors, all of whom are either institutions, such as pension funds, or wealthy individuals. According to an article in the *Wall Street Journal*, the managers of four hedge funds met in New York City to discuss whether it would be profitable to use derivatives to bet that the value of the euro would fall. Present at the meeting were representatives of a fund run by George Soros, who had famously earned $1 billion in the early 1990s by placing bets against the value of the British pound.

At the time of the meeting, the exchange rate between the euro and the dollar was $1.35 = €1, having already fallen from $1.51 = €1 the previous December. Some hedge managers were convinced that during the next year, the value of the euro was likely to fall all the way to parity with the dollar, or $1 = €1. The hedge funds could profit from this fall by selling euros in the forward market, selling euros futures contracts, or buying put contracts on the euro. The hedge funds could make these investments by putting up only about 5% of the value of the investments in cash and borrowing the other 95%. This high degree of *leverage*—or use of borrowed money in the investment—would magnify the size of any return as a fraction of their actual cash investment. Because the payoff to such a large decline in the value of the euro was potentially enormous, some observers called it a "career trade," meaning that this one investment alone—should it actually pay off!—would make the hedge fund managers both very wealthy and very famous.

Although some government officials in the United States and Europe criticized the hedge funds, many economists were skeptical that the managers' actions could have much effect on the value of the euro. The total value of euros being bought and sold in global foreign-exchange markets is greater than $1.2 trillion *per day*. The four hedge fund managers present at the New York meeting were making long-term bets against the euro that amounted to only a few billion dollars. In any event, over the following two years, the euro–dollar exchange rate never dropped below $1.19 = €1, so anyone speculating on the value of the euro falling to parity had made a losing bet.

Government officials continue to complain about speculators. In the fall of 2012, for example, the value of the Iranian rial declined sharply against the U.S. dollar. Although the Iranian government had an official exchange rate of 12,260 rials = $1 dollar, private exchanges in Iran were exchanging rials for dollars at a rate of 33,500 rials = $1. The United States and other countries had imposed sanctions on Iran in an attempt to stop its government from developing nuclear weapons. As the value of the rial plunged, Iranians had to pay increasingly higher prices for the few imports that made it into the country. The Iranian government denounced currency speculators, who they blamed for the decline in the value of the rial. Once again, though, economists were skeptical that speculators were responsible for such a large movement in the exchange rate.

As we will see in the next section, the exchange rates among major currencies such as the euro and the dollar are determined by factors that a few speculators probably can't affect, however large their resources.

Sources: Benoit Faucon and Katie Martin, "Pressures Drive Iran's Currency to New Low," *Wall Street Journal*, October 1, 2012; Susan Pulliam, Kate Kelly, and Carrick Mollenkamp, "Hedge Funds Try 'Career Trade' Against Euro," *Wall Street Journal*, February 26, 2010; and Michael Casey, "Justice Regulators Fall for Conspiracy Theories," *Wall Street Journal*, March 3, 2010.

See related problems 2.4 and 2.5 at the end of the chapter.

8.3

Learning Objective

Explain how exchange rates are determined in the long run.

Exchange Rates in the Long Run

We have seen that fluctuations in exchange rates can affect the profitability of firms. We turn now to explaining why exchange rates fluctuate. We begin by examining how exchange rates are determined in the long run.

The Law of One Price and the Theory of Purchasing Power Parity

Law of one price The fundamental economic idea that identical products should sell for the same price everywhere.

Our analysis of what determines exchange rates in the long run begins with a fundamental economic idea called the **law of one price**, which states that identical products should sell for the same price everywhere. To see why the law of one price should hold, consider the following example: Suppose that an iPhone 5 with 32 GB of memory is selling for $299 in stores in Houston and for $199 in stores in Boston. Anyone who lives in Boston could buy iPhones for $199 and resell them for $299 in Houston, using eBay or Craigslist or by shipping them to someone they know in Houston, who could sell them in local flea markets. When similar securities have different yields, the opportunity for *arbitrage profits* causes prices of securities to change until similar securities have the same yields (see Chapter 3). Similarly, a gap in the prices of iPhones between Houston and Boston creates arbitrage profits that can be earned by buying cheap iPhones in Boston and re-selling them in Houston. If there is no limit to the number of $199 iPhones available in Boston, the process of arbitrage will continue until the increased supply of iPhones be-ing resold in Houston has driven the price there down to $199.

The law of one price holds not just for goods traded within one country but also for goods traded internationally. In the context of international trade, the law of one price is the basis for the **theory of purchasing power parity (PPP)**, which holds that exchange rates move to equalize the purchasing power of different currencies. In other words, in the long run, exchange rates should be at a level that makes it possible to buy the same amount of goods and services with the equivalent amount of any country's currency.

Theory of purchasing power parity (PPP) The theory that exchange rates move to equalize the purchasing power of different currencies.

Consider a simple example: If you can buy a 2-liter bottle of Dr. Pepper for $1.50 in New York City or £1 in London, then the theory of purchasing power parity states that the exchange rate between the dollar and the pound should be $1.50 = £1. If exchange rates are not at the values indicated by PPP, then arbitrage profits are possible. Suppose that you can buy a bottle of Dr. Pepper for $1.50 in New York or £1 in London, but the exchange rate between the dollar and the pound is $1 = £1. You could exchange $10 million for £10 million, buy 10 million bottles of Dr. Pepper in London, and ship them to New York, where you could sell them for $15 million. The result would be an arbitrage profit of $5 million (minus any shipping costs). If the dollar–pound exchange rate does not reflect purchasing power parity for many products—not just bottles of Dr. Pepper—you could repeat this process for many goods and become extremely wealthy. In practice, though, as you and others at-tempted to earn these arbitrage profits by exchanging dollars for pounds, the demand for pounds would increase, causing the pound's value in terms of dollars to rise until it reached the PPP exchange rate of $1.50 = £1. Once the exchange rate reflected the purchasing power of the two currencies, the opportunity for arbitrage profits would be eliminated. At the PPP exchange rate, 1 bottle of Dr. Pepper in the United States exchanges for 1 bottle of Dr. Pepper in London, so the real exchange rate equals 1.

The reasoning we have just gone through suggests that, in the long run, nominal exchange rates adjust to equalize the purchasing power of different currencies. That is, in the long run, the real exchange rate should equal 1. This theory should hold because, if it doesn't, then opportunities for arbitrage profits exist. In the long run, by buying and selling currencies in the foreign exchange market, individuals pursuing profit opportunities should cause the nominal exchange rate to adjust so that the real exchange rate equals 1, and purchasing power parity holds. Although this logic may seem convincing, it is actually flawed, as we will discuss in the next section.

PPP makes an important prediction about movements in exchange rates in the long run: If one country has a higher inflation rate than another country, the currency of the high-inflation country will depreciate relative to the currency of the low-inflation country. To see why, look again at the expression for the real exchange rate:

$$e = E \times \left(\frac{p^{\text{Domestic}}}{p^{\text{Foreign}}} \right).$$

We can use a handy mathematical rule that states that an equation where variables are multiplied together is approximately equal to an equation where percentage changes in those variables are added together. Similarly, we can approximate the division of two variables by subtracting their percentage changes. Remember that the percentage change in the price level is the same thing as the inflation rate.

If we let π^{Domestic} stand for the domestic inflation rate and π^{Foreign} stand for the foreign inflation rate, then we have:

$$\% \text{ change in } e = \% \text{ change in } E + \pi^{\text{Domestic}} - \pi^{\text{Foreign}}.$$

If the theory of purchasing power parity is correct, then in the long run e, the real exchange rate, equals 1. Therefore, the percentage change in the real exchange rate is zero, and we can rewrite the previous expression as:

$$\% \text{ change in } E = \pi^{\text{Foreign}} - \pi^{\text{Domestic}}.$$

This last equation tells us that the percentage change in the nominal exchange rate is equal to the difference between the foreign and domestic inflation rates. For example, if the inflation rate in the United Kingdom is higher than the inflation rate in the United States, we would expect the value of the dollar to increase relative to the value of the pound; that is, the nominal exchange rate would appreciate. In fact, this prediction of PPP theory is correct. In the long run, the value of the U.S. dollar has risen relative to the currencies of countries such as Mexico that have had higher inflation rates and fallen relative to the currencies of countries such as Japan that have had lower inflation rates.

Is PPP a Complete Theory of Exchange Rates?

Although the PPP theory generally makes correct predictions about movements in exchange rates in the long run, it has a much poorer track record in the short run. Three real-world complications keep purchasing power parity from being a complete explanation of exchange rates:

1. **Not all products can be traded internationally.** Where goods are traded internationally, arbitrage profits can be made whenever exchange rates do not reflect their PPP values. But more than half of the goods and services produced in most countries are not traded internationally. When goods are not traded internationally, arbitrage will not drive their prices to be the same. For example, suppose that the exchange rate is $1 = €1, but the price of having your shoes repaired is twice as high in Chicago as in Berlin. In this case, there is no way to buy up the lower-priced German service and resell it in the United States—and people in Chicago are not going to fly to Berlin just for that purpose. Because many goods and services are not traded internationally, exchange rates will not reflect exactly the relative purchasing power of currencies.

2. **Products are differentiated.** We expect the same product to sell for the same price around the world, but if two products are similar but not identical, their prices might be different. So, whereas oil, wheat, aluminum, and some other goods are essentially identical, automobiles, televisions, clothing, and many other goods are *differentiated*, so we would not expect them to have identical prices everywhere. In other words, for differentiated products, the law of one price doesn't hold.

3. **Governments impose barriers to trade.** The governments of most countries impose *tariffs* and *quotas* on imported goods. A **tariff** is a tax a government imposes on imports. A **quota** is a limit a government imposes on the quantity of a good that can be imported. The effect of both tariffs and quotas is to raise the domestic price of a good above the international price. For example, the U.S. government imposes a quota on imports of sugar. As a result, the U.S. price of sugar is typically two to three times the price of sugar in most other countries. Because of the quota, there is no legal way for someone to buy up low-priced foreign sugar and resell it in the United States. So, the law of one price doesn't hold for goods subject to tariffs and quotas.

> **Tariff** A tax a government imposes on imports.
>
> **Quota** A limit a government imposes on the quantity of a good that can be imported.

Solved Problem 8.3

Should Big Macs Have the Same Price Everywhere?

The *Economist* magazine tracks the prices of the McDonald's Big Mac hamburger in countries around the world. The following table shows the prices of Big Macs in the United States and in six other countries, along with the exchange rate between that country's currency and the U.S. dollar.

a. Explain whether the statistics in the table are consistent with the theory of purchasing power parity.

b. Explain whether your results in part (a) mean that arbitrage profits exist in the market for Big Macs.

Country	Big Mac price in domestic currency	Exchange rate (units of foreign currency per U.S. dollar)
United States	$4.33	—
Japan	320 yen	78.22
Mexico	37 pesos	13.69
Great Britain	2.69 pounds	0.65
China	15.65 yuan	6.39
Russia	75 rubles	32.77
Norway	43 kroner	6.09

Source: "The *Economist* Big Mac Index," *Economist*, July 26, 2012.

Solving the Problem

Step 1 Review the chapter material. This problem is about the theory of purchasing power parity, so you may want to review the sections "The Law of One Price and the Theory of Purchasing Power Parity," which begins on page 234, and "Is PPP a Complete Theory of Exchange Rates?," which begins on page 236.

Step 2 Answer part (a) by determining whether the theory of purchasing power parity applies to Big Macs. If purchasing power parity holds for Big Macs, then their price should be the same—$4.33—in every country when we use the exchange rate to convert the domestic currency price into dollars. For example, the price of the Big Mac in Japan is ¥320, so we can convert this price into dollars by dividing by the number of yen per dollar: ¥320/(¥78.22/$) = $4.09. We can use this procedure to construct a table like this one:

Country	Domestic currency price	Dollar price
Japan	320 yen	$4.09
Mexico	37 pesos	$2.70
Great Britain	2.69 pounds	$4.14
China	15.65 yuan	$2.45
Russia	75 rubles	$2.29
Norway	43 kroner	$7.06

The table shows that while the dollar prices of Big Macs in Japan and Great Britain are close to the U.S. price, the dollar prices of Big Macs in the other four countries are significantly different from the U.S. price. So, we can conclude that the law of one price and, therefore, the theory of purchasing power parity, does not hold for Big Macs.

Step 3 **Answer part (b) by explaining whether arbitrage profits exist in the market for Big Macs.** We expect the law of one price to hold because if it doesn't, arbitrage profits are possible. However, it is not possible to make arbitrage profits by buying low-price Big Macs in Beijing and shipping them to Seattle or by buying low-price Big Macs in Moscow and shipping them to London. The Big Macs would be a cold, soggy mess by the time they arrived at their destination. As we discussed in this section, one reason that the theory of purchasing power parity does not provide a complete explanation of exchange rates is that many goods—such as Big Macs—cannot be traded internationally.

See related problem 3.6 at the end of the chapter.

8.4

Learning Objective

Use a demand and supply model to explain how exchange rates are determined in the short run.

A Demand and Supply Model of Short-Run Movements in Exchange Rates

As we saw in Figure 8.2 on page 228, exchange rates fluctuate substantially. In fact, it is not unusual for exchange rates to fluctuate by several percentage points even during a single day. Because the purchasing power of currencies changes by only a tiny amount over the course of a few days, the size of short-run fluctuations in exchange rates is another indication that the theory of purchasing power parity cannot be a complete explanation of exchange rates.

A Demand and Supply Model of Exchange Rates

Economists use the model of demand and supply to analyze how market prices are determined. Because the exchange rate is the price of foreign currency in terms of domestic currency, we can analyze the most important factors affecting exchange rates in the short run by using demand and supply. Here we are considering a short period of time, and we are analyzing currencies in countries where annual inflation rates are low, so it is reasonable to assume that price levels are constant. We have already seen that the only factors that cause changes in the nominal exchange rate relative to the real exchange rate are the price levels in the two countries. Therefore, by assuming that price levels are constant, our model will determine *both* the equilibrium nominal exchange rate and the equilibrium real exchange rate.

The demand for U.S. dollars represents the demand by households and firms outside the United States for U.S. goods and U.S. financial assets. For example, a Japanese electronics store that wants to import Apple iPads has to exchange yen for dollars in order to pay for them. It seems logical that the quantity of dollars demanded will depend on the exchange rate. The lower the exchange rate, the cheaper it is to convert a foreign currency into dollars and the larger the quantity of dollars demanded. For example, more dollars will be demanded at an exchange rate of ¥80 = $1 than at ¥100 = $1. In Figure 8.3, we plot the exchange rate on the vertical axis. In this case, the exchange rate is yen per dollar, but we could have used the exchange rate between any two currencies. On the horizontal axis, we measure the quantity of dollars being exchanged for yen. The demand curve for dollars in exchange for yen is downward sloping because the quantity of dollars demanded will increase as the exchange rate declines and the yen price of U.S. goods and financial assets becomes relatively less expensive.

The supply of dollars in exchange for yen is determined by the willingness of households and firms that own dollars to exchange them for yen. U.S. households and firms want yen in exchange for dollars in order to purchase Japanese goods and Japanese financial assets. It seems logical that the quantity of dollars supplied will depend on the exchange rate. The more yen a U.S. household or firm receives per dollar, the cheaper the dollar price of Japanese goods and Japanese financial assets will be. So, the higher the exchange rate, the more yen households or firms will receive in exchange for dollars, and the larger the quantity of dollars supplied. In Figure 8.3, the supply curve of dollars in exchange for yen is upward sloping because the quantity of dollars supplied will increase as the exchange rate increases.

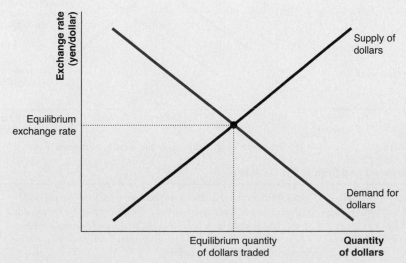

Figure 8.3

The Demand and Supply of Foreign Exchange

The lower the exchange rate, the cheaper it is to convert a foreign currency into dollars and the larger the quantity of dollars demanded. So, the demand curve for dollars in exchange for yen is downward sloping. The higher the exchange rate, the more yen households or firms will receive in exchange for dollars and the larger the quantity of dollars supplied. The supply curve of dollars in exchange for yen is upward sloping because the quantity of dollars supplied will increase as the exchange rate increases.

Shifts in the Demand and Supply for Foreign Exchange

With models of demand and supply, we assume that the demand and supply curves are drawn *holding constant all factors other than the exchange rate* that would affect the willingness of households and firms to demand or supply dollars. Changes in the exchange rate result in movements along the demand or supply curve—changes in the quantity of dollars demanded or supplied—but do not cause the demand or supply curve to shift. Changes in other factors cause the demand or supply curve to shift.

Anything that increases the willingness of Japanese households and firms to buy U.S. goods or U.S. assets will cause the demand curve for dollars to shift to the right. For example, panel (a) of Figure 8.4 illustrates the effect of Japanese consumers increasing their demand for tablet computers sold by U.S. firms. As Japanese retail stores increase their orders for these computers, they must increase their demand for dollars in exchange for yen. The figure shows that the demand curve for dollars shifts to the right, causing the equilibrium exchange rate to increase from ¥80 = $1 to ¥85 = $1 and the equilibrium quantity of dollars traded to increase from Dollars_1 to Dollars_2. Panel (b) illustrates the effect of U.S. consumers increasing their demand for Sony 3-D televisions. As U.S. retail stores increase their orders for these televisions, they must supply more dollars in exchange for yen. The figure shows that the supply curve for dollars in exchange for yen shifts to the right, causing the equilibrium exchange rate to decrease from ¥80 = $1 to ¥75 = $1 and the equilibrium quantity of dollars traded to increase from Dollars_1 to Dollars_2.

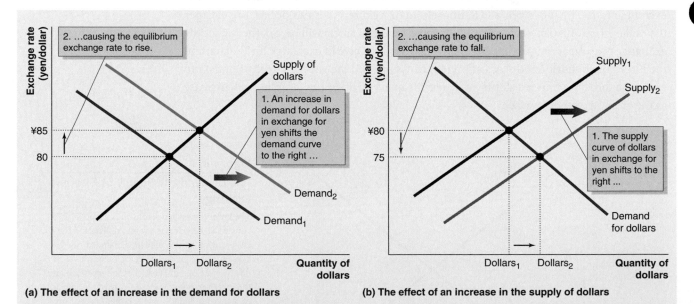

(a) The effect of an increase in the demand for dollars

(b) The effect of an increase in the supply of dollars

Figure 8.4 The Effect of Changes in the Demand and Supply for Dollars

Panel (a) illustrates the effect of an increase in the demand for dollars in exchange for yen. The demand curve for dollars shifts to the right, causing the equilibrium exchange rate to increase from ¥80 = $1 to ¥85 = $1 and the equilibrium quantity of dollars traded to increase from Dollars_1 to Dollars_2.

Panel (b) illustrates the effect of an increase in the supply of dollars in exchange for yen. The supply curve for dollars in exchange for yen shifts to the right, causing the equilibrium exchange rate to decrease from ¥80 = $1 to ¥75 = $1 and the equilibrium quantity of dollars traded to increase from Dollars_1 to Dollars_2.

Changes in interest rates are another important factor causing the demand curve and the supply curve for a currency to shift. For example, if interest rates in the United States rise relative to interest rates in other countries, the demand for U.S. dollars will increase as foreign investors exchange their currencies for dollars in order to purchase U.S. financial assets. The shift in the demand curve to the right results in a higher equilibrium exchange rate. As we discuss later, short-run fluctuations in exchange rates are driven much more by investors buying and selling currencies as they search across countries for the best investment opportunities than by the demand of households and firms for foreign goods and services.

The "Flight to Quality" During the Financial Crisis

The financial crisis of 2007–2009 caused the value of the dollar to soar for a brief period. One way to gauge the general value of one currency relative to other currencies is to calculate the *trade-weighted exchange rate*, which is an index number similar to the consumer price index. Just as the consumer price index weights individual prices by the share the product takes up in a household's budget, the trade-weighted exchange rate for the U.S. dollar weights each individual exchange rate by the share of that country's trade with the United States. Figure 8.5 shows movements in the trade-weighted exchange rate for the U.S. dollar between January 1995 and September 2012. The index is calculated so that the value for January 1997 is 100.

The increase in the value of the dollar during the late 1990s, as shown in Figure 8.5, was driven by strong demand from foreign investors for U.S. stocks and bonds, particularly U.S. Treasury securities. The increase in demand was not primarily due to higher U.S. interest rates but to problems in the international financial system. *Currency crises* in several East Asian countries, including South Korea, Thailand, Malaysia, and Indonesia, had resulted in sharp declines in the values of these currencies. When the currencies of Argentina and Russia also experienced sharp declines, many foreign investors engaged in a "flight to quality," in which they purchased assets denominated in U.S. dollars, particularly U.S. Treasury securities, because they appeared to be safe investments. These investors believed that there was only a small chance that the Treasury

MyEconLab Real-time data

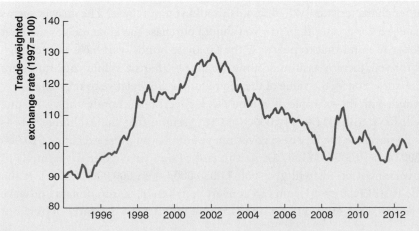

Figure 8.5

Movements in the Trade-Weighted Exchange Rate of the U.S. Dollar

The increase in the value of the dollar during the late 1990s, as shown in the figure, was driven by strong demand from foreign investors for U.S. stocks and bonds, particularly U.S. Treasury securities. Something similar happened during the financial crisis of 2007–2009: As many foreign investors sought a safe haven in U.S. Treasury securities, the demand for dollars increased.

Source: Federal Reserve Bank of St. Louis.

would default on its securities. The increased demand from foreign investors increased the value of the dollar.

Something similar happened during the financial crisis of 2007–2009. Although a recession had begun in the United States in December 2007, the recession did not begin in Europe until the spring of 2008. Only in the summer of 2008 did it become clear to many European investors that the banking systems in several countries were in serious trouble and that default risks even on government bonds might be rising. As many foreign investors sought a safe haven in U.S. Treasury securities, the demand for dollars increased. As Figure 8.5 shows, between July 2008 and March 2009, the value of the dollar increased by more than 20%. As the financial crisis eased during the summer and fall of 2009, many investors began selling dollars and shifting their investments out of U.S. Treasury securities. Between March 2009 and June 2010, the value of the dollar declined by about 10%, after which it fluctuated in a fairly narrow band through late 2012.

The Interest-Rate Parity Condition

On any given day in the foreign-exchange market, more than 95% of the demand for foreign exchange is the result of a desire by investors to buy foreign financial assets rather than a desire by households and firms to buy foreign goods and services. The tremendous demand for foreign exchange for purposes of financial investment reflects the importance of the increase in *international capital mobility* in recent decades. Policymakers in many countries have removed regulations that once hindered financial investments across national borders. The Internet allows investors in one country to easily access information about firms in other countries. The Internet also makes it easier for investors to contact financial firms, particularly brokerage firms, to make investments in foreign firms for them. In this section, we explore the implications of international capital mobility for the determination of exchange rates.

Suppose that you intend to invest $10,000 in one-year government bonds. Also suppose that one-year U.S. Treasury bills currently have an interest rate of 3%, while one-year Japanese government bonds currently have an interest rate of 5%. To keep the example simple, assume that you consider the two bonds to be identical except for their interest rates. That is, you believe they have the same default risk, liquidity, information costs, and other characteristics. Which bonds should you purchase? The answer seems obvious: Because 5% is greater than 3%, you should purchase the Japanese government bonds. But bear in mind that to purchase the Japanese bonds, you have to exchange your dollars for yen, thereby assuming some *exchange-rate risk*: While your funds are invested in Japanese bonds, the value of the yen might decline relative to the dollar.

To continue with the example, if you buy U.S. government bonds, then after one year, you will have \$10,300 (= \$10,000 × 1.03). Assume that the exchange rate is ¥100 = \$1. To purchase the Japanese government bonds, you must exchange \$10,000 for ¥1,000,000 (= \$10,000 × ¥100/\$). At the end of one year, your investment in Japanese government bonds will give you ¥1,050,000 (= ¥1,000,000 × 1.05). If the exchange rate is still ¥100 = \$1, you can convert your yen back into dollars and have \$10,500 (= ¥1,050,000/(¥100/\$)). So, the Japanese investment is clearly better. But what if during the year the value of the yen falls by 4%, to ¥104 = $1? (Note that this is the equivalent of the value of the dollar rising by 4%.) In this case, the ¥1,050,000 that you earn on your investment in the Japanese bond can be exchanged for only $10,096.15, and you would have been better off investing in U.S. bonds.

We assume that there are no arbitrage profits available in financial markets. Is this assumption consistent with a U.S. bond having a 3% interest rate, a Japanese bond having a 5% interest rate, and investors generally expecting a 4% depreciation in the yen (or, equivalently, a 4% appreciation of the dollar)? It is not consistent because investors would expect a much higher return on the U.S. investment than on the Japanese investment. This difference in returns would lead investors to buy U.S. government bonds, causing their prices to rise and their interest rates to fall, and it would lead investors to sell Japanese government bonds, causing their prices to fall and their interest rates to rise. By how much would the interest rate on the U.S. bond have to fall and the interest rate on the Japanese bond have to rise to eliminate the possibility of earning arbitrage profits? By enough so that *the difference between the two interest rates equals the expected change in the exchange rate between the yen and the dollar.*

For example, suppose that the interest rate on the U.S. bond fell to 2% and the interest rate on the Japanese bond rose to 6%, while the value of the yen was expected to decline by 4% relative to the dollar. Then you would receive either $10,200 from buying U.S. government bonds or ¥1,060,000/(¥104/$) = $10,192.30—nearly the same amount— from buying the Japanese government bond.[1]

The **interest-rate parity condition** holds that differences in interest rates on similar bonds in different countries reflect expectations of future changes in exchange rates. We can state this condition generally as:

Interest rate on domestic bond = Interest rate on foreign bond
                              − Expected appreciation of the domestic currency.

For instance, if the interest rate on a German government bond is 8% and the interest rate on an equivalent U.S. government bond is 6%, then the dollar must be expected to appreciate by 2% against the euro. The economic reasoning behind the interest-rate parity condition is the same as the economic reasoning behind the result that within a given country, rates of return on similar securities will be the same: If this result does not hold, then investors can make arbitrage profits. The interest-rate parity condition extends this result to global investments: If the expected return from owning a foreign asset—including expected changes in the exchange rate—isn't the same as the return from owning a domestic asset, then investors can make arbitrage profits because one asset or the other will be underpriced relative to its expected return.

Interest-rate parity condition The proposition that differences in interest rates on similar bonds in different countries reflect expectations of future changes in exchange rates.

---

[1]Why isn't the amount earned on the investment in the Japanese bond also equal to exactly $10,200? The answer is that the returns on the two investments will be equal only if the expected change in the exchange rate is slightly less than the difference between the two interest rates. So, the discussion in the text states a result that is only approximately correct. Stating the result exactly greatly increases the algebra, thereby making the main point more difficult to understand. For our purposes, the result stated in the text is a close approximation.

Does the interest-rate parity condition always hold? That is, can we be sure that differences in interest rates on similar bonds in different countries always reflect expectations of future changes in exchange rates? In practice, we can't be sure, for several reasons:

1. **Differences in default risk and liquidity.** There are always some differences that matter to investors between bonds in different countries. For instance, U.S. investors may consider that the default risk on German or Japanese government bonds, while low, is higher than on U.S. government bonds. Similarly, from the point of view of a U.S. investor, U.S. government bonds will be more liquid than will foreign government bonds. So, some of the differences we see between interest rates on bonds in different countries is compensating investors for differences in the characteristics of the bonds.

2. **Transactions costs.** Typically, the costs of purchasing foreign financial assets—the *transactions costs*—are higher than for domestic assets. For instance, foreign brokerage firms may charge higher commissions per share of a foreign firm's stock than would be charged on the stock of domestic firms by domestic brokerage firms or domestic online brokers.

3. **Exchange-rate risk.** The interest-rate parity condition, as we have stated it, does not take into account the exchange-rate risk from investing in a foreign asset. If you could receive 4% on a one-year Treasury bill in the United States or expect to earn 4% on a one-year German government bond, the investment in the German government bond comes with more risk because the value of the dollar may appreciate more than expected against the euro. Economists sometimes account for the additional risk of investing in a foreign asset by including a *currency premium* in the interest-rate parity equation:

Interest rate on the domestic bond $=$ Interest rate on the foreign bond
$-$ Expected appreciation of the domestic currency $-$ Currency premium.

For example, suppose that the interest rate on the one-year U.S. Treasury bill is 3%, the interest rate on the one-year German government bond is 5%, the expected appreciation of the dollar versus the euro is expected to be 1%, and U.S. investors require a 1% higher expected rate of return on a one-year euro-denominated investment relative to a one-year U.S. dollar-denominated investment to make the two investments equally attractive. Then we would have interest-rate parity: $3\% = 5\% - 1\% - 1\%$.

Solved Problem 8.4 **In Your Interest**

Can You Make Money Investing in Japanese Bonds?

Suppose you read the following investment advice: "One strategy for earning an above-average return is to borrow money in the United States at 3% and invest it in Japan in a comparable investment at 6%." Would you follow this strategy?

Solving the Problem

Step 1 **Review the chapter material**. This problem is about explaining differences in interest rates across countries, so you may want to review the section "The Interest-Rate Parity Condition," which begins on page 242.

Step 2 **Use the interest-rate parity condition to answer the question by explaining the relationship between expected changes in exchange rates and differences in interest rates across countries.** If the interest-rate parity condition holds, then a 3-percentage-point gap between the interest rate on a U.S. bond and the interest rate on a similar Japanese bond means that investors must be expecting that the value of the dollar will *appreciate* against the yen by 3%: 3% = 6% − 3%. Therefore, the expected return on a U.S. investment and a Japanese investment should be the same. If, as a U.S. investor, you borrow money at 3% in the United States and invest it at 6% in the Japan, you will not gain anything if the dollar appreciates by 3% because the true return on your Japanese investment will be 3% rather than 6%. In addition, you will be taking on exchange-rate risk because the dollar could appreciate by more than 3%.

See related problem 4.8 at the end of the chapter.

The interest-rate parity condition provides some insight into what happens to the exchange rate when a country's interest rate increases or decreases relative to interest rates in another country. For example, suppose that the interest rate on a one-year U.S. Treasury bill is currently 2%, the interest rate on a comparable French one-year government bond is 4%, and the dollar is expected to appreciate by 2% against the euro. If the Federal Reserve takes actions that lead to the Treasury bill rate increasing from 2% to 3%, we would expect that the demand for dollars will increase as investors in Europe attempt to exchange euros for dollars in order to invest in Treasury bills at the new higher interest rate. An increase in demand for dollars will cause the exchange rate to increase. In the new equilibrium, more euros will be required to buy a U.S. dollar.

This result of higher U.S. interest rates leading to a higher exchange rate is consistent with the interest-rate parity condition. If the exchange rate expected between the euro and the dollar one year from now remains the same, then an increase in the exchange rate now—the spot exchange rate—means that the rate of appreciation will be lower. In this example, an increase in the U.S. interest rate of 1%, with the French interest rate remaining unchanged, means that the expected rate of appreciation of the dollar will fall from 2% to 1%: 3% = 4% − 1%.

| Making the Connection | In Your Interest |

Should You Invest in Emerging Markets?

In response to stubbornly sluggish economic growth, in September 2012, Federal Reserve Chairman Ben Bernanke announced further monetary policy actions that would likely keep interest rates at record low levels for at least several more years.

While low interest rates are good news for borrowers, they offer meager returns for savers. With the economies of the world becoming more integrated over time, the choices for investors have expanded to include not only stocks and bonds of companies from high-income economies but also from "emerging markets." In the early 1980s, economists at the International Finance Corporation coined this term when referring to mutual funds that invested in companies located in developing countries. Since then, media sources have used *emerging markets* to refer to economies of countries, such as China and India, that beginning in the 1990s have experienced rapid rates of economic growth after making fundamental changes in their business environments.

The International Monetary Fund has estimated that emerging markets now account for about one-half of the world economy. With the United States struggling to recover from the 2007–2009 financial crisis and with Europe mired in an economic crisis of its own, many investors have viewed rapid growth in many developing countries as a good reason to diversify their portfolios with stocks and bonds of emerging-market companies. But rapid economic growth does not guarantee high returns on investment. One study found little correlation between long-term investment returns and growth in gross domestic product. The risk for investors hoping to profit from emerging markets was confirmed when stock markets in India, Brazil, and Russia performed poorly in 2011 before gaining over 20% in the first two months of 2012.

Although investors will continue to seek profits from emerging markets, analysts cite several reasons for caution. In rapidly growing economies, expectations of future growth are already reflected in stock prices. Some companies will experience higher-than-expected growth, but it is difficult to predict winners and losers in advance. And rapid growth typically results in a constant flow of new stocks that creates a "dilution effect," as financial investment is spread over an increasing number of stocks. One study estimates that the dilution effect in emerging markets can cost investors 10% annually, versus only 2% in the United States. Investors also pay fees to invest in funds that specialize in emerging market stocks that are higher than fees charged by more heavily traded funds.

Still, many investors are betting that long-run profits from stocks and bonds in emerging market stocks will ultimately make the risks worth it. Emerging-market analysts suggest two ways for investors to minimize these risks: (1) buy shares of a single international index fund that includes companies from both developed and emerging markets and (2) combine investments in a fund that includes emerging market stocks and bonds with more conventional investments.

Sources: Jon Hilsenrath, "How Bernanke Pulled the Fed His Way," *Wall Street Journal*, September 28, 2012; Tarun Khanna and Krishna G. Palepu, "How To Define Emerging Markets," *Forbes*, May 27, 2010; Brett Arends," Emerging Markets . . . It's a Jungle Out There," *Wall Street Journal*, March 17, 2012; and Walter Updegrave, "Emerging-Market Investing for the Long Haul," *CNNMoney*, September 13, 2012.

See related problem 4.9 at the end of the chapter.

Answering the Key Question

Continued from page 224

At the beginning of this chapter, we asked:

"Why has the value of the dollar declined against other major currencies during the past 10 years?"

We have seen that if foreign investors increase their demand for U.S. stocks and bonds, they will increase their demand for dollars in exchange for other currencies. An increase in the demand for dollars increases the exchange rate. During the peak of the financial crisis from the summer of 2008 to the fall of 2009, many foreign investors saw buying U.S. Treasuries as a safer investment than many alternatives. Over the longer run, though, somewhat higher inflation rates in the United States and lower interest rates have caused the value of the dollar to decline against most other major currencies.

Key Terms and Problems

Key Terms

Appreciation, p. 226

Depreciation, p. 226

Exchange-rate risk, p. 231

Foreign-exchange market, p. 230

Interest-rate parity condition, p. 243

Law of one price, p. 234

Nominal exchange rate, p. 225

Quota, p. 237

Real exchange rate, p. 229

Tariff, p. 237

Theory of purchasing power parity (PPP), p. 235

8.1 Exchange Rates and Trade
Explain the difference between nominal and real exchange rates.

Review Questions

1.1 What is the difference between the nominal exchange rate and the real exchange rate? When a newspaper article uses the term "the exchange rate," is the article typically referring to the nominal exchange rate or the real exchange rate?

1.2 What is the difference between a direct quotation of an exchange rate and an indirect quotation? If the exchange rate between the yen and the dollar changes from ¥80 = $1 to ¥90 = $1, has the yen appreciated or depreciated against the dollar? Has the dollar appreciated or depreciated against the yen?

1.3 Suppose that the euro falls in value relative to the dollar. What is the likely effect on European exports to the United States? What is the likely effect on U.S. exports to Europe?

Problems and Applications

1.4 A student makes the following observation:

> It currently takes 80 yen to buy 1 U.S. dollar, which shows that the United States must be a much wealthier country than Japan. But it takes more than 1 U.S. dollar to buy 1 British pound, which shows that Great Britain must be a wealthier country than the United States.

Briefly explain whether you agree with the student's reasoning.

1.5 If $2 buys £1 and €2.2 buys £1, how many euros are required to buy $1?

1.6 A student makes the following observation:

> This month the euro depreciated sharply against the U.S. dollar. That was good news

for attendance at Disneyland Paris and bad news for attendance at Walt Disney World in Orlando, Florida.

Briefly explain whether you agree with the student.

1.7 [Related to the Making the Connection **on page 226**] If the exchange rate between the yen and the dollar changes from ¥75 = $1 to ¥90 = $1, is this good news for Sony? Is it good news for U.S. consumers? Is it good news for U.S. firms that export to Japan? Is it good news for Japanese consumers?

1.8 [Related to the Chapter Opener **on page 224**] An article observes that the high value of the yen "is dealing crippling blows to the country's once all-important export machine." The article also observes, though, that "a high yen benefits Japan's rapidly expanding elderly population."

   a. Does a "high yen" mean that it takes more yen to exchange for one U.S. dollar or fewer yen?

   b. How does a high yen hurt Japanese exports?

   c. How might a high yen help the elderly population in Japan?

Source: Martin Fackler, "Strong Yen Is Dividing Generations in Japan," *New York Times*, July 31, 2012.

1.9 An editorial in the *Wall Street Journal* contains this statement: "The exchange rate is India's most important price."

   a. In what sense is the exchange rate a price?

   b. Why might the exchange rate be more important to a developing country such as India than to a high-income country such as the United States?

Source: "In Defense of the Rupee," *Wall Street Journal*, December 1, 2011.

1.10 Suppose that an Apple iPhone costs $200 in the United States, £65 in the United Kingdom, and ¥35,000 in Japan. If the exchange rates are $1.50 = £1 and ¥100 = $1, what are the real exchange rates between the dollar and the yen and the dollar and the pound?

8.2   Foreign-Exchange Markets
Explain how markets for foreign exchange operate.

Review Questions

2.1 What does it mean to describe the foreign-exchange market as an "over-the-counter market"?

2.2 What is the difference between a spot transaction and a forward transaction in the foreign-exchange market? What are the key differences between foreign-exchange forward contracts and foreign-exchange futures contracts? Why are forward contracts more widely used in the foreign-exchange market than are futures contracts?

2.3 How can exchange-rate risk be hedged using forward, futures, and options contracts? How might an investor use forward, futures, and options contracts to speculate on the future value of a currency?

Problems and Applications

2.4 [Related to the Making the Connection **on page 233**] Suppose you are convinced that the value of the Canadian dollar will rise relative to the U.S. dollar. What steps could you take to make a profit based on this conviction?

2.5 [Related to the Making the Connection **on page 233**] According to an article in the *Wall Street Journal*: "Fund managers tend to bid up options when they expect more erratic currency movements, and sell them when the outlook is calm."

   a. What does it mean to say that fund managers "bid up options"?

b. Why would fund managers be more likely to bid up options when they believe that exchange rates are likely to be erratic?

c. If this characterization of the actions of fund managers is correct, are they buying options primarily to hedge or primarily to speculate? Briefly explain.

Source: Matthew Walter, "Active Central Banks Crush Currency Volatility," *Wall Street Journal*, October 8, 2012.

2.6 Suppose that the U.S. firm Alcoa sells $2 million worth of aluminum to a British firm. If the exchange rate is currently $1.50 = £1 and the British firm will pay Alcoa £1,333,333.33 in 90 days, answer the following questions.

a. What exchange-rate risk does Alcoa face in this transaction?

b. In what alternative ways can Alcoa hedge this exchange-rate risk?

c. Give a specific example of how Alcoa could hedge this exchange-rate risk.

2.7 Suppose that Daimler AG, which manufacturers Mercedes-Benz automobiles, sells €5 million worth of automobiles to U.S. importers. Assuming that the current exchange rate is $1.22 = €1 and Daimler agrees to accept payment of $6.1 million in 90 days, answer the following questions.

a. What exchange-rate risk does Daimler face?

b. In what alternative ways can Daimler hedge this exchange-rate risk?

c. Give a specific example of how Daimler could hedge this exchange-rate risk.

2.8 Suppose that the U.S. firm Halliburton buys construction equipment from the Japanese firm Komatsu, at a price of ¥250 million. The equipment is to be delivered to the United States and paid for in one year. The current exchange rate is ¥100 = $1. The current interest rate on one-year U.S. Treasury bills is 6%, and the interest rate on one-year Japanese government bonds is 4%.

a. If Halliburton exchanges dollars for yen today and invests the yen in Japan for one year, how many dollars does it need to exchange today in order to have ¥250 million in one year?

b. If Halliburton enters a forward contract, agreeing to buy ¥250 million in one year at an exchange rate of ¥98 = $1, how many dollars does it need today if it plans to invest the dollars at the U.S. interest rate of 6%?

c. If Halliburton invests today at the U.S. interest rate of 6%, without entering into any other type of contract, does the firm know how many dollars it needs today to fulfill its equipment contract in one year? Briefly explain.

d. Which method(s) described in (a) through (c) provide(s) a hedge against exchange-rate risk? Which do(es) not? Which method is Halliburton likely to prefer?

e. What does the forward contract exchange rate have to be in (b) in order for the results in (a) and (b) to be equivalent?

8.3 Exchange Rates in the Long Run
Explain how exchange rates are determined in the long run.

Review Questions

3.1 How is the law of one price related to the theory of purchasing power parity (PPP)?

3.2 Is PPP a theory of exchange rate determination in the long run or in the short run?

3.3 According to the theory of purchasing power parity, if the inflation rate in Japan is lower than the inflation rate in Canada, what should happen to the exchange rate between the Japanese yen and the Canadian dollar in the long run?

Problems and Applications

3.4 According to a survey of professional foreign-exchange traders, the theory of purchasing power parity is considered to be "academic jargon." Why might foreign-exchange traders not find PPP to be useful as they trade currencies day-to-day?

Source: Cheung, Yin-Wong, and Menzie David Chinn, "Currency Traders and Exchange Rate Dynamics: A Survey of the U.S. Market," *Journal of International Money and Finance*, Vol. 20, No. 4, August 2001, pp. 439–471.

3.5 In a column in the *New York Times*, Uwe Reinhardt, an economist at Princeton, compared health care spending in Germany and the United States: "Total national health spending in Germany . . . amounted to $4,200 per capita in purchasing power parity, slightly more than half of American spending of $7,900." Did Reinhardt use the current exchange rate between the euro and the dollar to convert Germany's health care spending to euros? If not, why might doing so have been misleading?

Source: Uwe Reinhardt, "Social Insurance and Individual Freedom," *New York Times*, December 9, 2011.

3.6 [**Related to** Solved Problem 8.3 **on page 237**] The *Economist* magazine tracks the prices of the McDonald's Big Mac hamburger in countries around the world. The following table shows the price of Big Macs in the United States and in five other countries, along with the exchange rate between that country's currency and the U.S. dollar.

Country	Big Mac price in domestic currency	Exchange rate (units of foreign currency per U.S. dollar)
United States	$4.33	—
Brazil	10.08 reals	2.04
Israel	11.9 shekels	4.08
South Korea	3,700 won	1,151
Switzerland	6.5 Swiss francs	0.99
Venezuela	34 Bolivars	4.29

a. Explain whether the statistics in the table are consistent with the theory of purchasing power parity.

b. If the purchasing power parity theory allowed us to exactly determine exchange rates in the short run, what would be the exchange rate between the Brazilian real and the Israeli shekel?

Source: "The *Economist* Big Mac Index," *Economist*, July 26, 2012.

3.7 According to the theory of purchasing power parity, what should happen to the value of the U.S. dollar relative to the Mexican peso if each of the following occurs?

a. Over the next 10 years, the United States experiences an average annual inflation rate of 3%, while Mexico experiences an average annual inflation rate of 8%.

b. The United States puts quotas and tariffs on many imported goods.

c. The United States enters a period of deflation, while Mexico experiences inflation.

8.4 ## A Demand and Supply Model of Short-Run Movements in Exchange Rates
Use a demand and supply model to explain how exchange rates are determined in the short run.

Review Questions

4.1 Look again at Figure 8.3 on page 239 and answer the following questions.

a. Why is the demand curve for foreign exchange downward sloping?

b. Why is the supply curve for foreign exchange upward sloping?

c. Who would be interested in exchanging dollars for yen?

d. Who would be interested in exchanging yen for dollars?

4.2 How does the interest-rate parity condition account for differences in interest rates in different countries on similar bonds? What are the main reasons that interest-rate parity may not hold exactly?

Problems and Applications

4.3 Draw a graph of the demand and supply of U.S. dollars in exchange for Japanese yen to illustrate each of the following situations.

a. Sales of Apple iPhones and iPads soar in Japan.

b. The interest rate on one-year Japanese government bonds rises relative to the interest rate on one-year U.S. Treasury bills.

c. The Japanese government runs huge budget deficits, and investors believe that the government may default on its bonds.

4.4 According to an article in the *New York Times* in early 2012, "Bond yields have risen for countries like Brazil, Turkey and India, with investors preferring the safety of the dollar or yen." According to the article, an economist at the International Monetary Fund used the term "flight to safety" to describe the situation.

a. What is a "flight to safety"?

b. How would the flight to safety affect the exchange rate between the currencies of Brazil, Turkey, and India and the U.S. dollar and Japanese yen? Illustrate your answer with a demand and supply graph showing the market for U.S. dollars in exchange for Indian rupees.

Source: Annie Lowrey, "I.M.F. Seeks $500 Billion More to Lend as It Plans to Cut Growth Forecast," *New York Times*, January 18, 2012.

4.5 An article in the *Wall Street Journal* in 2012 noted that interest rates in Australia were higher than in the United States on comparable bonds. The article quoted a specialist on foreign exchange

at a bank as predicting the "Australian dollar will tumble" in value relative to the U.S. dollar. Explain the specialist's argument in terms of the interest-rate parity condition.

Source: Enda Curran, "Australian Dollar Set for Tumble as Perfect Storm Brews—HSBC," *Wall Street Journal*, September 11, 2012.

4.6 Suppose that the current exchange rate between the yen and the dollar is ¥100 = $1 and that the interest rate is 4% on a one-year bond in Japan and 3% on a comparable bond in the United States. According to the interest-rate parity condition, what do investors expect the exchange rate between the yen and the dollar to be in one year?

4.7 Suppose that the current exchange rate is €1.50 = £1, but it is expected to be €1.35 = £1 in one year. If the current interest rate on a one-year government bond in Germany is 4%, what does the interest-rate parity condition indicate the interest rate will be on a one-year government bond in the United Kingdom? Assume that there are no differences in risk, liquidity, taxation, or information costs between the bonds.

4.8 [Related to Solved Problem 8.4 on page 244] Borrowing at a low interest rate in one currency to lend at a higher interest rate in another currency is sometimes called a "carry trade." An article in the *New York Times* describes an investment strategy of this type: "A speculative carry trade in which investors borrowed euros at low interest rates to buy the higher-yielding Hungarian currency."

a. What does the article mean by the "higher-yielding Hungarian currency"?

b. Why does the article describe the strategy as speculative? Wouldn't investors be certain to make a profit by following this strategy? Briefly explain.

c. The article notes that the Hungarian currency, the forint, was "buoyed" by this strategy. Why would investors engaging in this carry trade cause an increase in the exchange value of the forint?

Source: Thomas Escritt, "Hungary's Struggle for a Competitive Edge," *New York Times*, October 30, 2011.

4.9 [Related to the Making the Connection on page 245] An article in the *Wall Street Journal* in 2012 noted: "Turkey's relatively strong economy and its attractive yields have kept emerging-market investors in the country."

a. What is an "emerging market"?

b. Why would investing in an emerging market have been particularly attractive to U.S. investors in 2012?

c. What risks are investors taking on by investing in an emerging market rather than in the United States?

Source: Erin McCarthy, "Emerging Market Currencies Weaker, South African Rand Drops Sharply," *Wall Street Journal*, October 5, 2012.

Data Exercises

D8.1: [Exchange rate movements] Go to the Web site of the Federal Reserve Bank of St. Louis (FRED) http://research.stlouisfed.org/fred2/) and download the most recent value and the value from the same month one year earlier from FRED for the U.S./Euro Foreign Exchange Rate (EXUSEU).

a. Using these values, compute the percentage change in the euro's value.

b. Explain whether the dollar appreciated or depreciated against the euro.

D8.2: [Exchange rate movements] Go to the Web site of the Federal Reserve Bank of St. Louis (FRED) (research.stlouisfed.org/fred2/) and download and plot the U.S. dollar-euro exchange rate (EXUSEU), the U.S. dollar-yen exchange rate (EXJPUS), and the U.S. dollar-Canadian dollar exchange rate (EXCAUS) for the period from 2001 to the present. Answer the following questions on the basis of your graphs.

a. In what year did the euro reach its highest value?

b. During the financial crisis of 2007–2009, did the yen appreciate or depreciate against the dollar? Briefly explain.

c. Against which currency did the U.S. dollar depreciate the most during this period?

D8.3: [Exchange rate movements] Go to the Web site of the Federal Reserve Bank of St. Louis Federal Reserve (FRED) (http://research.stlouisfed.org/fred2/) and download monthly data on the trade-weighted exchange rate for the U.S. dollar against major currencies (TWEXMMTH) from 1973 to the present.

a. What has been the long-term trend in the exchange value of the dollar? What effect should changes in the exchange rate during this period have had on U.S. net exports? Briefly explain.

b. What has been the trend in the exchange value of the dollar over the past year? What effect should changes in the exchange rate during the past year have had on U.S. net exports? Briefly explain.

D8.4: [Testing the theory of purchasing power parity] Go to the Web site of the Federal Reserve Bank of St. Louis Federal Reserve (FRED) (http://research.stlouisfed.org/fred2/) and download the most recent values from FRED for the Japan/U.S. Foreign Exchange Rate (DEXJPUS), China/U.S. Foreign Exchange Rate (DEXCHUS), and the Mexico/U.S. Foreign Exchange Rate (DEXMXUS).

a. Explain whether the exchange rates are quoted as U.S. dollars per unit of foreign currency or units of foreign currency per U.S. dollar.

b. Use the data to calculate the exchange rate between the Japanese yen and the U.S. dollar.

MyEconLab Visit **www.myeconlab.com** to complete these exercises online and get instant feedback. Exercises that update with real-time data are marked with .

c. Suppose a Big Mac sells for 300 yen in Japan, 14 yuan in China, and 34 pesos in Mexico. What is the price of a Big Mac in each country in terms of U.S. dollars?

d. Assuming no transportation costs, explain in which county you would want to purchase a Big Mac and in which country you would want to sell the same Big Mac in order to make the highest profit possible.

D8.5: **[Interest rates and exchange rates]** Go to the Web site of the Federal Reserve Bank of St. Louis (FRED) (research.stlouisfed.org/fred2/) and download and plot the difference between the interest rate on the U.S. 3-month Treasury bill (TB3MS) and the interest rate on Japanese government securities (INTGSBJPM193N) from 1990 to the present. Next, download the data for the yen–dollar exchange rate (EXJPUS). Describe the relationship between the two series.

Transactions Costs, Asymmetric Information, and the Structure of the Financial System

Learning Objectives

After studying this chapter, you should be able to:

9.1 Analyze the obstacles to matching savers and borrowers (pages 255–257)

9.2 Explain the problems that adverse selection and moral hazard pose for the financial system (pages 257–270)

9.3 Use economic analysis to explain the structure of the U.S. financial system (pages 270–274)

Should You Crowd-Fund Your Startup?

Great ideas for new businesses are fairly common: Opening a coffee shop in an underserved area, developing new applications for cell phones or tablets, or starting an innovative new web site to provide tutorial help to money and banking students. Locating the funding to actually start a new business is much more difficult. If you are like many entrepreneurs starting small businesses, you may have to rely for funds on your own savings or loans from family members and friends. You will probably have difficulty borrowing from a bank, unless you have good *collateral*, such as a home, that the bank can seize if you default on your loan. You might have an opportunity to borrow from a microlender (see page 6 of Chapter 1). But microlending is not widely available.

Soon, though, you may be able to obtain financing through *crowd-funding*, or raising small amounts of money from large numbers of people. Social networking has taken off in the past 10 years, with the popularity of Facebook and other sites. Some social networking sites, such as Kickstarter, have engaged in crowd-funding by raising money to finance creative projects, such as documentary films, video games, concerts, and similar efforts. A person who contributes to a project through Kickstarter or a similar site might receive a copy of the film or game but cannot receive ownership in the project. This prohibition on ownership is necessary because the federal government's security laws place strict limits on companies that raise money to make equity investments in startups. With an equity investment,

Continued on next page

Key Issue and Question

Issue: Following the financial crisis, many firms complained that they were having difficulty borrowing funds to expand their operations.

Question: Why do firms rely more on loans and bonds than on stocks as a source of external finance?

Answered on page 274

investors are buying part ownership of a firm in a way similar to buying the stock of a public corporation.

In 2012, Congress removed some of the restrictions on using crowd-funding to allow small investors to buy equity in startups as part of the Jumpstart Our Business Startups Act, or JOBS Act. Under previous regulations, when stock was sold to individual investors without the firm going through a formal initial public offering (IPO), the sale of the stock could not be publically advertised. In addition, only "qualified investors," with incomes of at least $200,000 per year and assets of at least $1 million, not counting the value of their houses, could purchase the stock. As this book is being published, the Securities and Exchange Commission (SEC) has not finished writing all the new regulations to implement the JOBS Act. But the SEC has allowed Web sites, such as CircleUp, to raise equity investment funds for startup businesses. Although in 2012 the number of investors in each startup was limited to a total of 200, one-quarter could be "unaccredited investors" who did not meet the requirements for being qualified investors. For example, Alison Bailey Vercruysse raised $500,000 on CircleUp to fund her startup, 18 Rabbits, which sells Bunny Bars made from Granola.

By 2013, the SEC was expected to further loosen restrictions on crowd-funding, making it possible for most small investors to buy equity in startups, although small investors were likely to be limited to investing no more than $10,000 in any one company. These developments are good news if you are an entrepreneur, but are they necessarily good news if you are a small investor? Some economists and policymakers worry that small investors may not fully understand the risks involved with crowd-funding. Traditionally, small investors have preferred to put their savings in banks or mutual funds to avoid the problem of *asymmetric information* in financial markets. Asymmetric information refers to a situation in which one party to an economic transaction has more information than the other party. In the case of crowd-funding, the startups raising funds are likely to know much more about how likely they are to be successful than are small investors. Investors frequently face very high transactions costs in gathering enough information to distinguish firms likely to be successful from those that aren't. As a result, small investors have traditionally relied on financial intermediaries such as banks and mutual funds rather than on making investments directly in firms.

If you are a small investor, you might be searching for ways to earn higher returns than those available on bank CDs or money market mutual funds. As crowd-funding sites become better known and regulations are relaxed, the sites may provide a way for you to earn high returns, or they may provide a way for you to suffer significant losses.

Sources: Eric Markowitz, "Start-ups to SEC: Move Faster on Crowdfunding," inc.com, September 13, 2012; Liz Gannes, "SEC Moves Forward on JOBS Act," allthingsd.com, August 29, 2012; and Ronald Barush, "Dealpolitik: SEC Proposes Rule which Could Have Huge Impact on IPO Dynamics, *Wall Street Journal*, August 31, 2012.

In this chapter, we analyze how factors such as asymmetric information and transactions costs explain the structure of the financial system. In particular, we look at what explains certain key facts about the financial system.

Obstacles to Matching Savers and Borrowers

Learning Objective

Analyze the obstacles to matching savers and borrowers.

Some people have funds to lend, and some people would like to borrow funds. Bringing together savers and borrowers is the role of the financial system. It would seem simple to bring together savers and borrowers to make a deal—lending money—that can benefit both. But, as we have already seen in previous chapters, the financial system can be complex. Why the complexity? We can begin to answer this question by considering obstacles that make it difficult for savers to find borrowers that they are willing to lend to and for borrowers to find savers who are willing to make loans.

The Problems Facing Small Investors

Suppose that you have saved $500 from working part time, and you want to invest it. Should you invest your money in stocks? A stockbroker will tell you that the commissions you must pay will be large relative to the size of your purchases because you are investing a small amount of money. This cost will be particularly high if you are attempting to diversify by buying a few shares each of different stocks. Should you turn instead to the bond market to buy, say, a bond issued by Microsoft? Unfortunately, with the bond having a face value of $1,000, you lack the money to buy even one bond.

Having had no luck with financial markets, you look for another way to invest your money. Conveniently, your roommate's cousin needs $500 to develop a new application (app) for the Apple iPad. He offers to pay you a 10% interest rate if you loan him your $500 for one year. But you don't know whether he is actually any good at writing apps. If his app fails, you suspect that he won't pay you back. Maybe you should seek out other borrowers and see what they would use your money for. Then you discover another problem: Your friend who is in law school tells you that to draw up a contract spelling out the terms of the loan—and what rights you would have if the borrower doesn't pay you back—would probably cost $300, which is more than half the money you have to invest. After hearing this news, you decide to forget about investing your $500. This is not just bad news for you but also for the app developer, who will face the same difficulty in trying to raise funds from other individual investors.

This example illustrates the concept of **transactions costs**, which are the costs of making a direct financial transaction, such as buying a stock or bond, or making a loan. In this example, the transactions costs would include the legal fees you would have to pay to draw up a contract with the borrower of your money and the time you spent trying to identify a profitable investment. This example also illustrates the concept of **information costs**, which are the costs that savers incur to determine the creditworthiness of borrowers and to monitor how they use the acquired funds. Because of transactions costs and information costs, savers receive a lower return on their investments and borrowers must pay more for the funds they borrow. As we have just seen, these costs can sometimes mean that funds are never lent or borrowed at all. Although transactions costs and information costs reduce the efficiency of the financial system, they also create a profit opportunity for individuals and firms that can reduce those costs.

Transactions costs The cost of a trade or a financial transaction; for example, the brokerage commission charged for buying or selling a financial asset.

Information costs The costs that savers incur to determine the creditworthiness of borrowers and to monitor how they use the funds acquired.

How Financial Intermediaries Reduce Transactions Costs

High transactions costs make individual savers unlikely to lend directly to borrowers. For the same reason, small to medium-sized firms that need to borrow money—or sell part ownership of the firm to raise funds—are unlikely to find individuals willing to invest in them. As a result, both small investors and small to medium-sized firms turn to financial intermediaries, such as commercial banks and mutual funds, to meet their financial needs. For example, many small investors buy shares in mutual funds such as Putnam Investment's Voyager Fund, which invests in a diversified portfolio of stocks and bonds. While an investor with just $500 to invest would find it difficult to buy a diversified portfolio without incurring substantial transactions costs, mutual funds provide diversification with low transactions costs. Similarly, an investor could purchase a certificate of deposit from a commercial bank. The commercial bank could then use the funds to make loans to household and business borrowers.

The Problems of Adverse Selection and Moral Hazard

How are banks, mutual funds, and other financial intermediaries able to reduce transactions costs sufficiently to meet the needs of savers and borrowers while still making a profit? Financial intermediaries take advantage of **economies of scale**, which refers to the reduction in average cost that results from an increase in the volume of a good or a service produced. For example, the fees dealers in Treasury bonds charge investors to purchase $1,000,000 worth of bonds are not much higher than the fees they charge to purchase $10,000 worth of bonds. By buying $500 worth of shares in a bond mutual fund that purchases millions of dollars' worth of bonds, an individual investor can take advantage of economies of scale.

Financial intermediaries can also take advantage of economies of scale in other ways. For example, because banks make many loans, they rely on standardized legal contracts, so the costs of writing the contracts are spread over many loans. Similarly, bank loan officers devote their time to evaluating and processing loans, and through this specialization, they are able to process loans efficiently, reducing the time required—and, therefore, the cost per loan. Financial intermediaries also take advantage of sophisticated computer systems that provide financial services, such as those automated teller machine networks provide.

To understand how financial intermediaries can also help reduce information costs, we need to consider the nature of information costs more closely. We do so in the next section.

The Problems of Adverse Selection and Moral Hazard

When savers lend to borrowers, a key consideration is the financial health of the borrower. Savers don't lend to borrowers who are unlikely to pay them back. Unfortunately for savers, borrowers in poor financial health have an incentive to disguise this fact. For example, a company selling bonds to investors may know that its sales are declining rapidly, and it is near bankruptcy, but the buyers of the bonds may lack this information. **Asymmetric information** describes the situation in which one party to an economic transaction has better information than does the other party. In financial transactions, typically the borrower has more information than does the lender.

Economists distinguish between two problems arising from asymmetric information:

1. **Adverse selection** is the problem investors experience in distinguishing low-risk borrowers from high-risk borrowers before making an investment.
2. **Moral hazard** is the problem investors experience in verifying that borrowers are using their funds as intended.

Sometimes, the costs arising from asymmetric information can be so great that an investor will lend only to borrowers who are transparently low risk, such as the federal government. However, more generally, there are practical solutions to the problems of asymmetric information, in which financial markets or financial intermediaries lower the cost of information needed to make investment decisions.

Adverse Selection

George Akerlof, of the University of California, Berkeley, was the first economist to analyze the problem of adverse selection. He did so in the context of the used car market. Akerlof was awarded the Nobel Prize in Economics in 2001 for his research

Economies of scale
The reduction in average cost that results from an increase in the volume of a good or service produced.

9.2

Learning Objective
Explain the problems that adverse selection and moral hazard pose for the financial system.

Asymmetric information
The situation in which one party to an economic transaction has better information than does the other party.

Adverse selection
The problem investors experience in distinguishing low-risk borrowers from high-risk borrowers before making an investment.

Moral hazard The risk that people will take actions after they have entered into a transaction that will make the other party worse off.

into the economics of information. Akerlof noted that the seller of a used car will always have more information on the true condition of a car than will a potential buyer. A "lemon," or a car that has been poorly maintained—by, for instance, not having its oil changed regularly—could have damage to its engine that even a trained auto mechanic might have difficulty detecting. The prices that potential buyers are willing to pay for used cars will reflect the buyers' lack of complete information on the true condition of the cars.

Consider a simple example: Suppose that the used car market consists only of individual buyers and sellers; that is, there are no used car dealers. Suppose that you are in the market for a used 2010 Honda Element and that while you and other buyers would be willing to pay $15,000 for a good, well-maintained car, you will only pay $7,000 for a lemon. Unfortunately, you cannot tell the lemons from the good cars, but you have read an online report that indicates that about 75% of used 2010 Elements are well maintained, while the other 25% are lemons. The *expected return* on an investment is calculated by adding up the probability of each event occurring multiplied by the value of each event (see Chapter 4). In this case, we can calculate the *expected value* to you of a 2010 Honda Element that you choose randomly from among those available for sale:

$$\text{Expected value} = (\text{Probability car is good}) \times (\text{Value if good})$$
$$+ (\text{Probability car is a lemon}) \times (\text{Value if a lemon}).$$

Or,

$$\text{Expected value} = (0.75 \times \$15,000) + (0.25 \times \$7,000) = \$13,000.$$

It seems reasonable for you to be willing to pay a price for a Honda Element equal to the expected value of $13,000. Unfortunately, you are likely to run into a major problem: From your perspective, given that you don't know whether any particular car offered for sale is a good car or a lemon, an offer of $13,000 seems reasonable. But the sellers *do* know whether they are selling good cars or lemons. To a seller of a good car, an offer of $13,000 is $2,000 below the true value of the car, and the seller will be reluctant to sell. But to a seller of a lemon, an offer of $13,000 is $6,000 *above* the value of the car, and the seller will be happy to sell. Because sellers of lemons take advantage of knowing more about the cars they are selling than buyers do, the used car market is subject to adverse selection: Most used cars offered for sale will be lemons. In other words, because of asymmetric information, the used car market has adversely selected the cars that will be offered for sale. Notice as well that the problem of adverse selection reduces the total quantity of used cars bought and sold in the market because few good cars are offered for sale. From Akerlof's analysis of adverse selection in the used car market, we can conclude that information problems reduce economic efficiency in a market.

There are aspects of the actual used car market that reduce—but don't eliminate—the degree of adverse selection when compared with a market composed only of individual buyers and sellers. To reduce the costs of adverse selection, car dealers act as intermediaries between buyers and sellers. To maintain their reputations with buyers, dealers are less willing to take advantage of private information about the quality of the used cars that they are selling than are individual sellers, who will probably sell at most a handful of used cars during their lifetimes. As a result, dealers sell both lemons and good cars at close to their true values. In addition, government regulations require that car dealers disclose information about the cars to consumers.

"Lemons Problems" in Financial Markets   How do adverse selection problems affect the ability of stock and bond markets to channel funds from savers to investors? First, consider the stock market. Take a simple example, similar to the one we just used for the automobile market. Suppose that there are good firms and bad, or lemon, firms. The firms are aware of whether they are good or lemons, but on the basis of available information, potential investors cannot tell the difference. The fundamental value of a share of stock should be equal to the present value of all the dividends an investor expects to receive into the indefinite future (see Chapter 6). Suppose that given your expectations of future dividends to be paid, you believe the value of the stock issued by a good firm is $50 per share but the value of stock issued by a lemon firm is only $5 per share. You are convinced from your reading of the *Wall Street Journal* and financial Web sites that 90% of firms offering stock for sale are good firms and 10% are lemon firms, but you lack the information to determine whether any particular firm is a good firm or a lemon firm.

You can use these assumptions to calculate the expected value to you of a share of stock issued by a randomly chosen firm among all the firms offering to sell stock:

$$\text{Expected value} = (0.90 \times \$50) + (0.10 \times \$5) = \$45.50.$$

So, you would be willing to pay $45.50 for a share of stock, but to a good firm, this price is below the fundamental value of the stock. To sell shares at that low a price would be to sell part ownership of the firm—which is what shares of stock represent—for less than its true value. Therefore, good firms will be reluctant to sell stock at this price. Lemon firms, though, will be very willing to sell stock at this price because it is well above the true value of their shares. As lemon firms take advantage of knowing more about the true value of their firms than investors do, the stock market, like the used car market, is subject to adverse selection.

One of the consequences of adverse selection in the stock market is that many small to medium-sized firms will be unable or unwilling to issue stock. These firms will be unable to find investors willing to buy their shares—because the investors will be afraid of buying stock in what may turn out to be a lemon firm—or the firms will be unwilling to sell shares for far below their fundamental value. As a result, in the United States, only about 5,100 firms are *publicly traded*, which means that they are able to sell stock on stock markets. These firms are large enough that investors can easily find information about their financial health from sources such as reports by Wall Street analysts and articles by financial journalists. This information helps investors overcome the adverse selection problem.

Adverse selection is present in the bond market as well. Just as investors are reluctant to buy the stock of firms when the investors are unsure whether the firms are good firms or lemons, they are also reluctant to lend money to firms by buying their bonds. Because the risk in lending to lemon firms is greater than the risk in lending to good firms, if investors had complete information on the financial health of every firm, they would be willing to lend money to good firms at a low interest rate and lend money to lemon firms at a high interest rate. Because of asymmetric information, though, investors are often reluctant to make any loans at high interest rates. Investors often reason that as interest rates on bonds rise, a larger fraction of the firms willing to pay the high interest rates are lemon firms. After all, the managers of a firm facing bankruptcy may be willing to pay very high interest rates to borrow funds that can be used to finance risky investments. If the investments do not succeed, the managers are no worse off than they were before: The firm will still be facing bankruptcy. Investors who bought the bonds, however, will be considerably worse off than if they had put their funds in a less risky investment. In other words, as interest rates rise, the creditworthiness of potential borrowers is likely to deteriorate, making the adverse selection problem worse. Because investors realize this problem, they are likely to reduce the number of loans they are willing to make rather than to raise interest rates to the level at which the quantity of funds demanded and supplied are equal. This restriction of lending is known as **credit rationing**. When lenders ration credit, firms—whether they are good firms or lemons—may have difficulty borrowing funds.

Credit rationing The restriction of credit by lenders such that borrowers cannot obtain the funds they desire at the given interest rate.

To summarize, in the market for used cars, adverse selection causes bad cars to push good cars from the market. In the stock market, adverse selection makes it difficult for any but the largest firms to sell stocks. And in the bond market, adverse selection leads to credit rationing.

Adverse selection is costly for the economy. When investors have difficulty obtaining information on good firms, the cost of raising funds for those firms increases. This situation forces many firms to grow primarily by investing *internal funds*, which are profits the firms have earned or funds raised from the owners of the firm. Since 1945, U.S. firms have raised more than two-thirds of the funds they need internally. Adverse selection problems are most likely to restrict opportunities for growth in younger firms in dynamic, emerging sectors of the economy, such as software and biotechnology because with these firms investors have particular difficulty in distinguishing the good firms from the lemons.

Attempts to Reduce Adverse Selection Financial market participants and the government have taken steps to try to reduce problems of adverse selection in financial markets. Following the great stock market crash of October 1929, it became clear that many firms selling stock on the New York Stock Exchange had not disclosed to investors crucial information on the firms' financial health or had actively misled investors about the firms' true condition. In response, in 1934 Congress established the Securities and Exchange Commission (SEC) to regulate the stock and bond markets. The SEC requires that publicly traded firms report their performance in financial statements, such as balance sheets and income statements, that the firms must prepare using standard accounting methods. In addition, firms must disclose *material information*, which is information that, if known, would likely affect the price of a firm's stock. The disclosure of information required by the SEC reduces the information costs of adverse selection, but it doesn't eliminate them for several reasons.

First, some good firms may be too young to have much information for potential investors to evaluate. Second, lemon firms will try to present the information in the best possible light so that investors will overvalue their securities. Third, there can be legitimate differences of opinion about how to report some items on income statements and balance sheets. For example, during the financial crisis of 2007–2009, many banks and other financial firms had on their balance sheets assets, such as loans and mortgage-backed securities, that had become illiquid. The markets for these assets "seized up," meaning that little or no buying and selling was occurring. In that situation, investors had difficulty discovering the true prices of the assets by reading these firms' balance sheets. Finally, the interpretation of whether information is material can be tricky. For example, some investors criticized Apple because the firm delayed reporting that CEO Steve Jobs had undergone a liver transplant in April 2009. Although representatives of Apple argued that Jobs's health problems were a private matter, some investors believe that the problems should have been more fully disclosed because they could have affected the future profitability of the firm and, therefore, its stock price.

Private firms have tried to reduce the costs of adverse selection by collecting information on firms and selling the information to investors. As long as the firms gathering information do a good job, savers purchasing it will be better able to judge the quality of borrowers, improving the efficiency of lending. Although investors must pay for the information, they can still benefit if it enables them to earn higher returns. Firms such as Moody's Investors Service, Standard & Poor's, Value Line, and Dun & Bradstreet specialize in collecting information from a variety of sources, including firms' income statements, balance sheets, and investment decisions, and selling the information to subscribers. Buyers include individual investors, libraries, and financial intermediaries. You can find some of these publications in your college library or online.

Private information-gathering firms can help minimize the cost of adverse selection, but they cannot eliminate it. Although only subscribers pay for the information collected, others can benefit without paying for it. Individuals who gain access to the information without paying for it are *free riders*. That is, they obtain the same benefits as those paying for the information, without incurring the costs. It is easy to photocopy and distribute the reports that private information-gathering firms prepare—or to scan them and post them on the Internet—so there may be many free riders for every paid subscriber. Because, in effect, private information-gathering firms end up providing their services to many investors for free, they are unable to collect as much information as they would if they didn't have to face the free-rider problem. In fact, in rating bonds, Moody's and Standard & Poor's were forced to shift from a business model that involved charging investors for information on the creditworthiness of firms issuing bonds to charging the issuing firms (see Chapter 5).

The Use of Collateral and Net Worth to Reduce Adverse Selection Problems The disclosure of information, either directly as a result of government regulation or indirectly as a result of the efforts of private information-gathering firms, does not eliminate adverse selection. As a result, lenders often rely on financial contracts that are designed to help reduce adverse selection problems. If the owners of a firm have invested little of their own money in their firm, they don't have much to lose if they default on bonds or fail to pay back loans. To make it more costly for firms to take advantage of their asymmetric information, lenders often require borrowers to pledge some of their assets as **collateral**,

Collateral Assets that a borrower pledges to a lender that the lender may seize if the borrower defaults on the loan.

which the lender claims if the borrower defaults. For example, a firm that owns a warehouse may have to pledge the warehouse as collateral when issuing a bond. If the firm fails to make the coupon payments on the bond, investors can seize the warehouse and sell it to cover their losses on the bond. Only very large, well-known firms, such as Microsoft and General Electric, are able to sell *debentures*, which are bonds issued without specific collateral.

Net worth The difference between the value of a firm's assets and the value of its liabilities.

    Net worth, which is the difference between the value of a firm's assets and the value of its liabilities, provides the same assurance to lenders as does collateral. When a firm's net worth is high, the firm's managers have more to lose by using borrowed money for high-risk investments. The managers of a firm with low net worth, on the other hand, have less to lose. Therefore, investors often reduce the chance of adverse selection by restricting their lending to high-net-worth firms.

    In the end, though, the cost of adverse selection makes it difficult for many firms to raise funds on financial markets. The costs of adverse selection are another reason, in addition to high transactions costs, many firms turn to financial intermediaries when they need external finance.

How Financial Intermediaries Reduce Adverse Selection Problems Financial intermediaries, particularly banks, specialize in gathering information about the default risk of borrowers. Banks know from long experience which characteristics of borrowers—both households and firms—are likely to be good predictors of default risk. Some of the information that banks rely on is widely available to any financial institution. This information includes credit reports and the FICO credit score, compiled by the firm now called FICO and formerly called Fair Isaac. But individual banks also have access to information on particular borrowers that is not generally available. The ability of banks to assess credit risks on the basis of private information about borrowers is called **relationship banking**. For example, a local bank may have been making loans to a local car dealership over a period of years, so the bank will have gathered information on the creditworthiness of the dealership that other potential lenders would have difficulty acquiring.

Relationship banking The ability of banks to assess credit risks on the basis of private information about borrowers.

    Banks raise funds from depositors, and, using their superior information on borrowers' creditworthiness, they lend the deposits to borrowers who represent good risks. Because banks are better able than individual savers to distinguish good borrowers from lemon borrowers, banks can earn a profit by charging a higher interest rate on loans than they pay to depositors. Depositors are willing to accept the low interest rate because they know that transactions costs and information problems make it difficult for them to lend their funds directly to borrowers.

    Banks can profit from their private information about borrowers because under relationship banking, they hold many of the loans they make. So, investors have a difficult time making a profit by observing which loans banks make and making similar loans. Banks can profit from gathering information on local businesses and households because it is difficult for other investors to compete with them for this loan business. The information advantage banks gain from relationship banking allows them to reduce the costs of adverse selection and helps explain the key role banks play in providing external financing to firms.

Making the Connection

Has Securitization Increased Adverse Selection Problems in the Financial System?

The financial crisis of 2007–2009 emphasized the important role that securitization had come to play in the economy. *Securitization* involves bundling loans, such as mortgages, into securities that can be sold on financial markets. Some economists believe that the increase in securitization over the past 15 years may have led to an increase in adverse selection. As we have seen, under relationship banking, banks have an incentive to acquire information about potential borrowers and to use that information to make loans to households and firms. With relationship banking, banks earn profits based on the difference between the interest rates they pay depositors and the interest rates they earn on loans, most of which they hold until maturity.

Securitization changes the focus of banks from relationship banking to the *originate-to-distribute* business model. With this model, banks still grant loans, but rather than hold them to maturity, banks either securitize the loans or sell them to other financial firms or to government agencies to be securitized. In either case, the banks hold the loans for a brief period rather than holding them to maturity. With the originate-to-distribute model, banks earn a profit from fees they receive from originating the loans and from fees they charge to process the loan payments that they receive from borrowers and pass on to the holders of the securities.

Some economists and policymakers argue that the originate-to-distribute model has reduced banks' incentive to distinguish between good borrowers and lemon borrowers. In other words, the model has reduced banks' incentive to reduce adverse selection. Once a loan has been securitized, if the borrower defaults, the owner of the security, rather than the bank that originated the loan, suffers most of the loss. In addition, some economists have argued that banks may use their information advantage to sell off the riskier loans while retaining the less risky loans for their own portfolios. It can be difficult for an investor purchasing securitized loans to evaluate the riskiness of loans included in the securities. Rating agencies, such as Moody's and Standard & Poor's, also have less information about the riskiness of the loans contained in the securities than do the banks that originated the loans. Securitization provides certain advantages to the financial system: It allows increased risk sharing, it increases liquidity in loan markets, it reduces the interest rates borrowers pay on loans, and it allows investors to diversify their investment portfolios. Securitization has the disadvantage that it may have inadvertently increased adverse selection problems.

Antje Berndt, of Carnegie Mellon University, and Anurag Gupta, of Case Western Reserve University, have studied the effects of the originate-to-distribute model on adverse selection. They examined loans banks made to corporations during the period from the beginning of 2000 through the end of 2004. They found that corporations whose bank loans ended up being securitized were significantly less profitable over the three-year period following the sale of their loans than were corporations whose bank loans were not sold or corporations that did not borrow funds from banks. Berndt and Gupta's results indicate that either banks were less careful in making loans that they intended to securitize or that they were more likely to sell loans that they had granted to less profitable firms.

In the Wall Street Reform and Consumer Protection Act, or Dodd-Frank Act, passed in July 2010, Congress addressed the possibility that securitization has increased adverse selection in the financial system. The bill requires banks and other financial firms that sell certain mortgage-backed securities and CDOs to retain at least 5% of the total securities issued, although there remained some questions about how the provisions would be administered. The debate over the effect of securitization is likely to continue.

Sources: Antje Berndt and Anurag Gupta, "Moral Hazard and Adverse Selection in the Originate-to-Distribute Model of Bank Credit," *Journal of Monetary Economics*, July 2009, Vol. 56, No. 5, pp. 725–743; and Dennis K. Berman, "Do Sold-off Corporate Loans Do Worse?" *Wall Street Journal*, November 19, 2008.

See related problem 2.11 at the end of the chapter.

Solved Problem 9.2

Why Do Banks Ration Credit to Small Businesses?

During the spring of 2010, an article in the *Economist* magazine made the following observations about bank lending in the United States:

Small business, the section of the economy that generates new jobs, is not getting access to credit. The National Federation of Independent Businesses says that the percentage of small business owners having access to credit fell 20% in the past year; only 38% of those applying for a new credit line received one.

a. Why would banks be unwilling to make loans to small businesses? If the banks believe some of the loans are risky, why wouldn't they just charge a higher interest rate to compensate for the risk?

b. Does it matter that the period involved here was shortly after the end of a deep recession?

Source: From "Buttonwood's Notebook," *Economist*, March 30, 2010.

Solving the Problem

Step 1 Review the chapter material. This problem is about adverse selection and credit rationing, so you may want to review the section "Adverse Selection," which begins on page 257.

Step 2 Answer part (a) by explaining how raising interest rates on loans can increase adverse selection problems for banks. We've seen that lenders can be reluctant to increase the interest rates they charge borrowers because high interest rates may attract less creditworthy borrowers. That is, higher interest rates may increase adverse selection. Although banks specialize in gathering information on borrowers, they still know less about the true financial state of borrowers than do the borrowers. A small business that is close to declaring bankruptcy may see a bank loan as a financial lifeline and be less concerned about having to pay a high interest rate than would a borrower in better financial health.

Step 3 **Answer part (b) by discussing whether it mattered that the period involved was near the end of a deep recession.** During the financial crisis, many banks engaged in *credit rationing*, limiting the number of loans they offered borrowers rather than increasing the interest rates they charged on loans. During any recession, the financial health of households and firms will deteriorate as workers lose their jobs and firms experience declining sales and profits. The result is that the number of lemon borrowers rises relative to the number of good borrowers. Banks, therefore, have to be more cautious in granting loans and will avoid actions—such as raising interest rates on loans—that are likely to increase their adverse selection problems.

See related problem 2.12 at the end of the chapter.

Moral Hazard

Even after a lender has gathered information on whether a borrower is a good borrower or a lemon borrower, the lender's information problems haven't ended. There is still a possibility that after a lender makes a loan to what appears to be a good borrower, the borrower will not use the funds as intended. This situation, known as *moral hazard*, is more likely to occur when the borrower has an incentive to conceal information or to act in a way that does not coincide with the lender's interests. Moral hazard arises because of asymmetric information: The borrower knows more than the lender does about how the borrowed funds will actually be used.

Moral Hazard in the Stock Market If you buy a firm's stock, you hope that the firm's management maximizes profits so that the value of your investment will increase. Unfortunately, monitoring whether the firm's management is actually maximizing profits is extremely difficult for an individual investor, which causes a significant moral hazard problem. When you buy stock Microsoft has newly issued, you can't tell whether the firm will spend your money wisely on research and development of a new version of Windows or fritter it away on gold faucets in the new executive restroom. The investment in research and development is likely to increase Microsoft's profits and your returns, while the gold faucets are not.

The organization of large, publicly traded corporations results in a *separation of ownership from control*. That is, legally, shareholders own the firm, but the firm is actually run by its top management—the chief executive officer (CEO), the chief operating officer (COO), the chief financial officer (CFO), and so on. In most large corporations, the top managers own only a small fraction of the firm's stock, typically less than 5%. Although the shareholders want the managers to run the firm so as to maximize the value of the shareholders' investment, the managers may have other objectives. Some top managers are accused of being "empire builders" who are interested in making the firm as large as possible through growth and the acquisition of other firms, even if the firm would be more profitable if it were smaller. Other top managers seem more concerned with using corporate jets and holding meetings in expensive vacation spots than with the firm's profits. Economists refer to the possibility that managers will pursue objectives different

Principal–agent problem
The moral hazard problem of managers (the agents) pursuing their own interests rather than those of shareholders (the principals).

from those of shareholders as a **principal–agent problem**. The shareholders, as owners of the firm, are the *principals*, while the top managers, who are hired to carry out the owner's wishes, are the *agents*.

Managers even have an incentive to underreport profits so that they can reduce the dividends they owe to shareholders and retain the use of the funds. Problems of underreporting are reduced to some extent because the SEC requires managers to issue financial statements prepared according to generally accepted accounting principles. Federal laws have made misreporting or stealing profits belonging to shareholders a federal offense, punishable by large fines or prison terms, or both. Spectacular cases of top managers misstating the true financial state of firms—including the Enron and WorldCom cases in the early 2000s—show that fines and prison terms have not been complete deterrents.

Investors elect boards of directors to represent them in controlling corporations. Unfortunately, boards of directors are not a full solution to the problem of moral hazard in stock investing. First, boards of directors typically meet infrequently—often only four times per year—and generally rely on information provided to them by top management. Even highly motivated and skeptical boards of directors cannot hope to know as much about the firm as do the top managers. Therefore, it is often difficult for members of a board of directors to decide whether managers are acting in the best interests of shareholders. Boards of directors cannot use profitability as the sole measure of the performance of top managers because factors other than the efforts of the managers determine a firm's profitability. For instance, a recession may cause a firm to suffer losses that managers could do nothing to avoid. Second, boards of directors are not always independent of top managers. Even though shareholders elect the members, many shareholders pay little attention to these elections, and CEOs can sometimes succeed in placing candidates favorable to them on the ballots. Some boards of directors include CEOs of other firms who are suppliers to the corporation. These board members may be reluctant to disagree with the CEO, for fear that he or she will retaliate by canceling their contracts. In recent years, the increased role of institutional investors, such as pension funds, in the election of boards of directors has helped to reduce moral hazard problems. For example, the California Public Employees' Retirement System (CalPERS) has a director of corporate governance who works to ensure that the pension fund invests in corporations that respect the interests of shareholders. Nevertheless, most economists believe that corporate boards of directors can reduce but not eliminate the moral hazard problem.

Finally, some boards of directors have attempted to reduce moral hazard by using *incentive contracts* to better align the goals of top managers with the goals of shareholders. With some incentive contracts, part of a manager's compensation is tied to the performance of the firm. For example, a CEO may receive his or her full compensation only if the firm meets certain profit targets. Other incentive contracts provide top managers with option contracts. The options allow the managers to buy the firm's stock at a price above the market price on the day when the options were granted. The options give managers an incentive to make the firm more profitable, which will raise the price of the firm's stock and make the options more valuable. Although incentive contracts can reduce moral hazard, they can at times also increase it by leading managers to make decisions that are not in the best interests of shareholders. For instance, if top managers have their compensation tied to the firm's profits, they may undertake risky investments that will increase the firm's short-term profits but jeopardize the firm's long-term prospects.

Some economists have argued that top managers at some financial firms made riskier investments than they otherwise would have during the financial crisis because some of their compensation depended on the short-run profits of their firms. Similar problems exist when boards of directors provide top managers with stock options. During the 2000s, top managers at several firms were caught backdating their stock options contracts. Rather than having the contracts reflect the price of the firm's stock on the day the options were granted, the managers manipulated the contracts to appear to have been granted on an earlier date, when the firm's stock price had been much lower. As a result, the managers were able to earn substantial sums from the options even if the firm's stock price had not increased from the date the options were actually granted. The SEC considers backdating fraud, so several executives who engaged in this practice were convicted and sent to prison.

Moral Hazard in the Bond Market There is less moral hazard in the bond market than in the stock market. When you buy a share of stock, you are relying on the firm's top management to maximize profits. Whether or not they do is difficult for both you and the board of directors to verify. However, when you buy a bond, you only need the firm's top management to make the coupon payments and a final face value payment when the bond matures. Whether the managers are maximizing profits doesn't concern you. In other words, the cost of monitoring the firm's management is much lower for an investor who is a bondholder than for an investor who is a stockholder.

Even though investors are subject to less moral hazard when buying bonds than when buying stocks, buying bonds isn't entirely free from this problem. Because a bond allows a firm to keep any profits that exceed the fixed payments due on the bond, the firm's managers have an incentive to assume more risk to earn these profits than is in the best interest of the bond investor. For example, suppose that you and other investors buy bonds issued by a software firm that has been successful in writing apps for the Apple iPhone and iPad. You expect that the firms will use the funds to develop new apps. Instead, the firm's management decides to use the funds on a much riskier venture—to develop a new tablet computer to compete with the iPad. In the likely event that the new tablet fails, the firm will be forced into bankruptcy and won't be able to make the payments it promised you.

A key way investors try to reduce moral hazard in bond markets is by writing *restrictive covenants* into bond contracts. **Restrictive covenants** either place limits on the uses of the funds the borrower receives or require that the borrower pay off the bond if the borrower's net worth drops below a certain level. As an example of the first type of restrictive covenant, a firm might be restricted to using the funds from a bond issue to buy a warehouse or factory building. The purpose of restrictive covenants of the second type is to keep a firm's managers from taking on too much risk. The managers know that if they suffer losses on risky investments, the firm's net worth might drop below the level that would trigger the covenant. Having to pay off a bond issue possibly years before it would mature may be difficult for the firm and might cause the board of directors to question the competence of the managers.

Restrictive covenant A clause in a bond contract that places limits on the uses of funds that a borrower receives.

Although restrictive covenants can reduce risk, they have the drawback of making bonds more complicated and possibly reducing their marketability on secondary markets. The cost of monitoring whether firms actually are complying with restrictive covenants further hampers a bond's marketability and liquidity. And restrictive covenants can't be detailed enough to protect lenders against every possible risky activity in which the borrower might engage.

How Financial Intermediaries Reduce Moral Hazard Problems Just as financial intermediaries play an important role in reducing the extent of adverse selection in the financial system, they also play an important role in reducing moral hazard. Commercial banks specialize in monitoring borrowers and have developed effective techniques for ensuring that the funds they loan are actually used for their intended purpose. For instance, when you take out a loan to buy a car, a bank will often provide the funds by giving you a check made out to the car dealer rather than to you. Similarly, if the owner of a pizza parlor takes out a loan to expand her business, the bank is likely to release the funds in stages, requiring proof that each phase of the construction has been completed. Bank loans often contain restrictive covenants. For example, if you take out a loan to buy a new car, the bank will require you to carry a minimum amount of insurance against theft or collision, and the insurance policy will usually be written so that both the bank's name and your name will appear on the check you receive from the insurance company following an accident. If you take out a mortgage loan to buy a house, you will have to carry insurance on the house, and you can't sell the house without first repaying your mortgage loan.

In some countries, banks have an additional tool for overcoming moral hazard when providing funds to firms. For instance, in Germany, a bank such as Deutsche Bank can buy stock in a firm and place its employees on the firm's board of directors. This step gives a bank greater access to information and makes monitoring the behavior of managers easier. In the United States, however, federal regulations bar banks from buying stock—that is, making *equity investments*—in nonfinancial firms.

Venture capital firm
A firm that raises equity capital from investors to invest in startup firms.

Other financial intermediaries have evolved to fill the gap in the financial system left by the ban on banks making equity investments in nonfinancial firms. **Venture capital firms**, such as Kleiner Perkins Caufield & Byers or Matrix, raise funds from investors and use the funds to make investments in small startup firms, often in high-technology industries. A venture capital firm frequently takes a large ownership stake in a startup firm, often placing its own employees on the board of directors or even having them serve as managers. These steps can reduce principal–agent problems because the venture capital firm has a greater ability to closely monitor the managers. The firm's managers are likely to be attentive to the wishes of a large investor because having a large investor sell its stake in the firm may make it difficult to raise funds from new investors. In addition, a venture capital firm avoids the free-rider problem when investing in a firm that is not publicly traded because other investors cannot copy the venture capital firm's investment strategy.

Private equity firm (or corporate restructuring firm) A firm that raises equity capital to acquire shares in other firms to reduce free-rider and moral hazard problems.

Venture capital firms target young firms. **Private equity firms** (or **corporate restructuring firms**), such as Blackstone or Kohlberg Kravis Roberts & Co. (KKR), become large investors in mature firms. Typically, they target firms where the managers appear not to be maximizing profits. By taking positions on the board of directors, they can monitor top managers and attempt to get them to follow new policies. In some cases, they will acquire a controlling interest in the firm and replace the top management. Private equity and corporate restructuring firms have helped to establish a *market for corporate control*, which can reduce moral hazard problems in the financial system by providing a means to remove top management that is failing to carry out the wishes of shareholders.

Making the Connection	In Your Interest

Is It Safe to Invest Through Crowd-funding?

As we saw in the chapter opener, passage of the JOBS Act in 2012 made it easier for startup firms to use crowd-funding. On crowd-funding sites, such as CircleUp, you will be able to invest up to $10,000 in equity shares in a startup firm. But should you? Does crowd-funding overcome the problems of transactions costs and asymmetric information that have traditionally kept many small investors from directly investing in firms?

As we saw earlier, prior to crowd-funding, if you wanted to invest $10,000 in a startup, you would likely incur substantial transactions costs locating a suitable firm and making sure that your investment was legally protected. By acting as financial intermediaries, crowd-funding sites are successful in reducing transactions costs for investors by identifying firms and by ensuring that the investors' funds are invested in accordance with federal securities laws.

It's less clear, however, whether crowd-funding sites can overcome information asymmetries. Crowd-funding sites typically screen firms that request permission to solicit investors on their site. In October 2012, for example, CircleUp required firms to have at least $1 million in revenue and accepted only 2% of the firms that applied to be listed. The track record of firms raising money on crowd-funding sites has been mixed, however. The Kickstarter site operated under the pre–JOBS Act rules, which did not allow investors to receive equity in the firms they were investing in. The firms typically promised only to provide the new product—or, sometimes, just a T-shirt—in return for investors' funds. Despite the limited return, by 2012 on Kickstarter, three million people had provided a total of $300 million to fund 30,000 projects. Unfortunately, a study by the Wharton School at the University of Pennsylvania found that 75% of design- or technology-related projects funded on the site had failed to meet their deadlines for finishing a product. It remains to be seen whether investors will have greater success under the new JOBS Act rules that allow them to make equity investments.

In addition, unlike venture capital firms, crowd-funding sites do not themselves invest in the startups that raise funds on their sites. So, the crowd-funding sites do not reduce the principal–agent problem through close monitoring of the startup's managers the way a venture capital firm does. Some economists and policymakers also worry that because the equity stakes investors are buying do not trade like the stocks of public corporations, the investments are illiquid. An investor who needs to quickly sell his or her equity investment is likely to have difficulty doing so.

Some policymakers are concerned that crowd-funding sites will be susceptible to fraud. The Arkansas securities commissioner was quoted as saying: "I'm terrified," and the president of the North American Securities Administrators Association, claimed that the result of the JOBS Act rules would be "more jobs for securities investigators."

If these potential problems can be overcome, crowd-funding can become an important source of funds to startup firms and a way for small investors to participate in the growth of these firms.

Sources: Mark Milian, "After Raising Money, Many Kickstarter Projects Fail to Deliver," *Bloomberg Businessweek*, August 21, 2012; "Many Scrappy Returns," *Economist*, November 19, 2011; and Jenna Wortham, "Success of Crowdfunding Puts Pressure on Entrepreneurs," *New York Times*, September 17, 2012.

See related problem 2.15 at the end of the chapter.

9.3

Learning Objective

Use economic analysis to explain the structure of the U.S. financial system.

Conclusions About the Structure of the U.S. Financial System

We have seen that transactions costs and information costs pose significant obstacles in the flow of funds from savers to borrowers. We have also seen how the financial system has adapted to minimize the effects of transactions costs and information costs. Note that the financial system is significantly different than it would be if transactions costs and asymmetric information problems didn't exist. A review of some key facts about the U.S. financial structure illustrates this point.

Figure 9.1 shows the most important sources of external funds to small to medium-sized firms during the years 2005–2011. These firms rely on loans of various types and on *trade credit*. Trade credit refers to the common situation where a firm ships goods ordered by another firm while agreeing to accept payment at a later date—typically after 30 to 90 days. For example, a home improvement store may receive a shipment of lawnmowers but have 60 days to pay the manufacturer for them. Figure 9.1 shows that mortgage loans are by far the most important source of external funds to these firms, with nonmortgage loans from banks being the next most important.

Figure 9.1

Sources of External Funds to Small to Medium-Sized Firms

Small and medium-sized businesses rely on loans—particularly mortgages—and trade credit as their major sources of external finance.

Note: Data are average annual totals for the period 2005–2011 and are for nonfinancial, noncorporate businesses.

Source: Board of Governors of the Federal Reserve System, *Flow of Funds Accounts of the United States*, September 20, 2012.

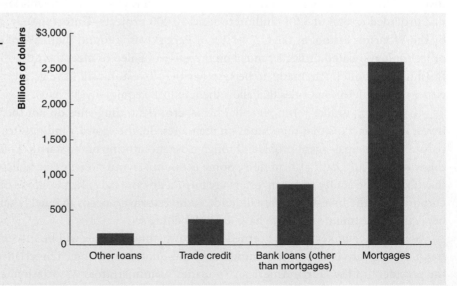

Figure 9.2 shows the external sources of funds to corporations. In the United States, corporations account for more than 80% of sales by all businesses, so their sources of funding are particularly important. Panel (a) displays sources of funds to corporations by the average values outstanding at the end of the year during the period 2005–2011. Panel (a) displays *stock values*—that is, the total values of these variables at a point in time. Because they are stock values, they reflect how corporations are meeting their current financing needs and also how they have met those needs in the past. For instance, the total value of bonds that corporations have outstanding includes some bonds that may have been issued decades in the past. Panel (b) shows *net* changes in these categories of funds. For instance, net new bond issues equals the difference between the value of new bonds corporations have issued during the year minus the value of bonds that have matured during the year and been paid off. Net new stock issues equals the difference between the value of new shares issued minus the value of shares that firms have repurchased from investors. The values in panel (b) are also annual averages for the period 2005–2011. Panel (a) in Figure 9.2 shows that the value of the stocks corporations have issued is much greater than the value of bonds or the value of loans, while panel (b) shows that bonds and loans were much more important sources of external financing for corporations during these years than were stocks.

We can use our discussion of transactions costs in Section 9.1, our discussion of information costs in Section 9.2, and the statistics in Figures 9.1 and 9.2 to discuss three key features of the financial system:

1. *Loans from financial intermediaries are the most important external source of funds for small to medium-sized firms.* As we have already noted, smaller businesses typically

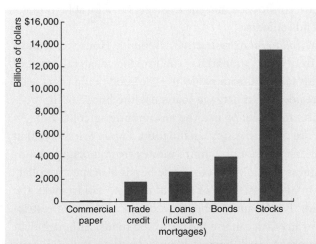

(a) Sources of corporate external funds, end-of-year values, 2005–2011

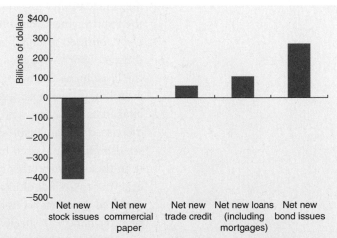

(b) Changes in sources of corporate external funds, 2005–2011

Figure 9.2 **External Sources of Funds to Corporations**

Panel (a) shows sources of funds to corporations, represented by the average values outstanding at the end of the year during the period 2005–2011. Panel (b) shows *net* changes in these categories. Panel (a) shows that the value of the stocks corporations have issued is much greater than the value of bonds or the value of loans, while panel (b) shows that bonds and loans were much more important sources of external financing for corporations during these years than were stocks.

Note: Data are for nonfarm, nonfinancial corporate businesses.

Source: Board of Governors of the Federal Reserve System, *Flow of Funds Accounts of the United States*, September 20, 2012.

have to meet most of their funding needs *internally*, from the owners' personal funds or from the profits the firms earn. Figure 9.1 on page 270 shows that loans are by far the most important *external* source of funds to smaller firms. Smaller firms cannot borrow directly from savers because transactions costs are too high when small savers attempt to make loans directly to businesses. Smaller firms cannot sell bonds or stocks because of the adverse selection and moral hazard problems that arise from asymmetric information. Because financial intermediaries—particularly commercial banks—can reduce both transactions costs and information costs, they are able to provide a channel by which funds can flow from savers to smaller firms.

2. *The stock market is a less important source of external funds to corporations than is the bond market.* What happens in the stock market each day is often the lead story in the financial news. The Web site of the *Wall Street Journal* prominently displays a box showing what is happening minute-by-minute to each of the major stock market indexes. Yet most of the trading on the stock market involves buying and selling existing shares of stock, not sales of new stock issues. Sales of new shares of stock are very small when compared with sales of existing shares of stock. As panel (b) of Figure 9.2 shows, in recent years, corporations have actually bought back from investors more stock than they have issued. Panel (b) also shows that loans and bonds are the most important categories of external credit to corporations. Why are corporations so much more likely to raise funds externally by selling bonds and by taking out loans—debt contracts—than by selling stock—equity? As we discussed earlier, moral hazard is less of a problem with debt contracts than with equity contracts. Investors who may doubt that the top managers of firms will actually maximize profits may still have confidence that the managers will be able to make the fixed payments due on bonds or loans.

3. *Debt contracts usually require collateral or restrictive covenants.* Households have difficulty borrowing money from banks unless they can provide collateral. Most of the large loans that households take out from banks use the good being purchased as collateral. For example, residential mortgage loans use the house being purchased as collateral, and automobile loans use the automobile as collateral. As discussed earlier, businesses are often in a similar situation. Figure 9.1 shows that small to medium-sized businesses raise much more money from mortgage loans than they do from other business loans. Many corporate bonds also specify collateral that the bondholders can take possession of should the firm fail to make the required payments on its bonds. Both loans and bonds also typically contain restrictive covenants that specify how the firm can use the borrowed funds. Although debt contracts are subject to less moral hazard than are equity contracts, they still have some potential exposure. The purpose of collateral and restrictive covenants is to reduce the amount of moral hazard involved with debt contracts.

Savers would like to receive the highest interest rate on their investments, and borrowers would like to pay the lowest interest rate. Transactions costs and information costs drive a wedge between savers and borrowers, lowering the interest rate savers receive and raising the interest rate borrowers must pay. By reducing transactions and information costs, financial intermediaries can offer savers higher interest rates, offer borrowers lower interest rates, and still earn a profit.

Commercial banks, investment banks, and other financial firms are continually searching for ways to earn a profit by expediting the flow of funds from savers to borrowers. Some of these ways involve developing new financial securities. During the financial crisis of 2007–2009, questions were raised about some of these securities and how they were traded.

Making the Connection   In Your Interest

Corporations Are Issuing More Bonds; Should You Buy Them?

Because the economy recovered very slowly from the recession of 2007–2009, the Federal Reserve took actions that resulted in interest rates on U.S. Treasury bonds falling to record low levels. As a result, investors searching for higher yields increased their demand for corporate bonds. This increased demand drove interest rates on corporate bonds also to record low levels, as shown in the figure below, which is an index of yields on investment grade corporate bonds prepared by Bank of America Merrill Lynch.

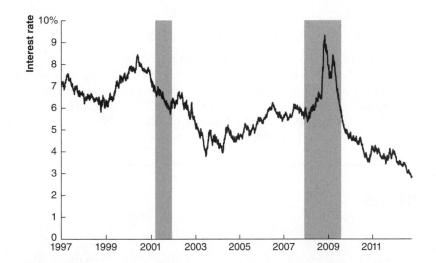

MyEconLab Real-time data

The dollar value of investment-grade 30-year corporate bonds issued in 2012 was also a record high. Some corporations, such as GE, that hadn't issued long-term bonds in several years decided to do so to take advantage of the low interest rates. One analyst with Moody's Investors Service was quoted as saying: "No treasurer or CFO [chief financial officer] wants to be the one treasurer or CFO who didn't get cheap long-term money when it was available."

Clearly, corporations are happy to sell bonds at such low interest rates, but as an investor, should you be happy to buy them? In October 2012, the average interest rate on investment-grade corporate bonds was just 2.83%, which was only about 1 percentage point above the expected inflation rate. While this interest rate was above the 1.72% interest rate on 10-year Treasury notes, the difference amounted to only a small default risk premium. The newly issued corporate bonds were primarily debentures, which means that the issuing corporations did not back them with any specific collateral.

In the event of the issuing corporation defaulting, bondholders would likely absorb significant losses. Although at the time the bonds were issued, ratings agencies gave them investment-grade ratings, there was ample time over 30 years for the financial health of the issuing firms to decline.

In addition, 30-year bonds have significant interest-rate risk. If interest rates on corporate bonds were to return to historically normal levels, investors who had purchased bonds in 2012 would suffer heavy losses. So, while 2012 was a great year for corporations to raise funds inexpensively by issuing long-term bonds, you would have been wise to proceed cautiously before investing in them.

Sources: Vipal Monga, "Companies Feast on Cheap Money," *Wall Street Journal*, October 8, 2012; and Federal Reserve Bank of St. Louis.

See related problem 3.7 at the end of the chapter.

Answering the Key Question

Continued from page 254

At the beginning of this chapter, we asked:

"Why do firms rely more on loans and bonds than on stocks as a source of external finance?"

We have seen that both the bond market and the stock market are subject to problems of moral hazard. In both cases, investors have to be concerned that once firms have received investment funds, they will not use them for their intended purpose. The problem of moral hazard is considerably less serious when an investor buys a firm's bonds than when the investor buys a firm's stock. As a result, investors are more willing to buy bonds than stock, which explains why bonds are a more important source of external finance for firms. Small to medium-sized firms are unable to issue either bonds or stock and must rely on bank loans as their main source of external finance.

Key Terms and Problems

Key Terms

Adverse selection, p. 257

Asymmetric information, p. 257

Collateral, p. 261

Credit rationing, p. 260

Economies of scale, p. 257

Information costs, p. 256

Moral hazard, p. 257

Net worth, p. 262

Principal–agent problem, p. 266

Private equity firm (or corporate restructuring firm), p. 268

Relationship banking, p. 262

Restrictive covenant, p. 267

Transactions costs, p. 256

Venture capital firm, p. 268

9.1 Obstacles to Matching Savers and Borrowers

Analyze the obstacles to matching savers and borrowers.

Review Questions

1.1 Why do savers with small amounts to invest rarely make loans directly to individuals or firms?

1.2 Why are financial intermediaries important to the financial system?

Problems and Applications

1.3 What advantages do financial intermediaries have relative to small savers in dealing with the transactions costs involved in making loans? If we lived in a world in which everyone was perfectly honest, would the difference in transactions costs between financial intermediaries and small savers disappear? Briefly explain.

1.4 How has the growth of the Internet affected the problem of transactions costs and information costs in the financial system?

1.5 Decades ago, many bank records were written by hand in ledgers. Were there significant economies of scale in keeping bank records under that system? How has the shift to keeping all records on computers affected economies of scale in banking?

9.2 The Problems of Adverse Selection and Moral Hazard

Explain the problems that adverse selection and moral hazard pose for the financial system.

Review Questions

2.1 What is the difference between moral hazard and adverse selection? Explain the "lemons problem." How does the lemons problem lead many firms to borrow from banks rather than from individual investors?

2.2 Why was the Securities and Exchange Commission (SEC) founded? What effect has the SEC had on the level of asymmetric information in the U.S. financial system?

2.3 How do banks and borrowers benefit from relationship banking?

2.4 How is the principal–agent problem related to the concept of moral hazard?

2.5 What is the difference between venture capital firms and private equity firms? What roles do they play in the financial system? In what ways do the activities of these firms differ from crowd-funding?

Problems and Applications

2.6 The author of a newspaper article providing advice to renters observed that "landlords will always know more than you do."

a. Do you agree with this statement? If so, what do landlords know that potential renters might not know?

b. If the statement is correct, what are the implications for the market for rental apartments?

c. In what ways is the market for rental apartments like the market for used cars? In what ways is it different?

Source: Marc Santora, "How to Be a Brainy Renter," *New York Times*, June 3, 2010.

2.7 At a used car lot, a nearly new car with only 2,000 miles on the odometer is selling for half the car's original price. The salesperson tells you that the car was "driven by a little old lady from Pasadena" who had it for two months and then decided that she "didn't like the color." The salesperson assures you that the car is in great shape and has had no major problems. What type of asymmetric information problem is present here? How can you get around the problem?

2.8 An article in the *Economist* magazine observes: "Insurance companies often suspect the only people who buy insurance are the ones most likely to collect."

a. What do economists call the problem being described in the article?

b. If insurance companies are correct in their suspicion, what are the consequences for the market for insurance?

Source: "The Money Talks," *Economist*, December 5, 2008.

2.9 **[Related to the** Chapter Opener **on page 254]**
An article in the *Economist* magazine on crowd-funding argued: "Start-ups are especially needy now, since many banks are loth to lend even to well-established companies."

  a. Why might banks be reluctant to lend to startups?

  b. Why might startups have an easier time obtaining equity investments from small investors through crowd-funding sites than obtaining loans from banks?

Source: "Many Scrappy Returns," *Economist*, November 19, 2011.

2.10 Brett Arends, a columnist for the *Wall Street Journal*, argues: "Today you should probably view [financial firms selling investments] the way you view someone selling a used car." How should you view someone selling a used car? Why might you want to view someone selling a financial investment the same way?

Source: Brett Arends, "Four Lessons from the Goldman Case," *Wall Street Journal*, May 2, 2010.

2.11 **[Related to the** Making the Connection **on page 263]**
Commercial real estate loans are mortgages that use apartment buildings, office buildings, or other commercial real estate as collateral. An article in the *New York Times* discussing the securitization of commercial real estate loans makes the following observation:

> The boom in commercial mortgage-backed securities in the middle of the last decade provided a lot of money for underwriters, enabled banks to earn fees from making and servicing bad loans and allowed property owners to withdraw large amounts of cash. The losers were the investors....

  a. What is securitization?

  b. Why would banks make bad commercial real estate loans? Don't banks lose money if these loans default?

  c. Why would investors buy securities that contain bad commercial real estate loans? Is it likely that the interest rates on these securities

were high enough to compensate investors for the additional risk involved with these securities? Briefly explain.

Source: Floyd Norris, "Commercial Mortgages Show How Bad It Got," *New York Times*, July 5, 2012.

2.12 **[Related to** Solved Problem 9.2 **on page 264]**
Yves Smith runs the popular financial blog nakedcapitalism.com. In one of his postings, he noted: "Amex [American Express] is offering very hefty balance reductions (20%) to business accounts who pay off balances early on credit line products that Amex has discontinued." Smith worried that Amex's offer would expose the credit card company to adverse selection. Briefly explain whether you agree.

Source: Yves Smith, "Credit Card Defaults Stabilizing?" nakedcapitalism.com, August 18, 2009.

2.13 Briefly explain in which of the following situations moral hazard is likely to be less of a problem.

  a. A manager is paid a flat salary of $150,000.

  b. A manager is paid a salary of $75,000 plus 10% of the firm's profits.

2.14 A news story reported that the former CEO of homebuilder KB Home was convicted "of four felony counts in a stock option backdating scam." The article goes on to note:

> A stock option allows an employee to purchase a company's stock at a preset price at a future date. [The KB Home CEO] retroactively tied the exercise price of his options to dates when the stock was selling for a low price.

  a. Why would a company use stock options as part of a top manager's compensation?

  b. What is the "exercise price" in an options contract? Why would this manager have wanted his options backdated?

  c. From the point of view of investors in KB Home, which information problem is involved here?

Source: Greg Risling, "Former KB Home CEO Convicted in Backdating Trial," Associated Press, April 21, 2010.

2.15 [Related to the Making the Connection **on page 269**] After a report appeared that many projects financed through crowd-funding site Kickstarter failed to meet their completion deadlines, an article in *Bloomberg Businessweek* noted: "The company says on its website that it doesn't vet or track whether projects fulfill their promises, though it encourages people to be skeptical." Crowd-funding sites typically take a percentage of the funds firms raise but do not make equity investments in the firms.

a. How do crowd-funding sites differ from venture capital firms?

b. Do crowd-funding sites reduce the transactions costs faced by small investors looking to make equity investments in startups? Do crowd-funding sites reduce asymmetric information problems faced by small investors? Briefly explain.

Source: Mark Milian, "After Raising Money, Many Kickstarter Projects Fail to Deliver," *Bloomberg Businessweek*, August 21, 2012.

9.3 **Conclusions About the Structure of the U.S. Financial System**
Use economic analysis to explain the structure of the U.S. financial system.

Review Questions

3.1 What is the most important source of funds for small to medium-sized firms? What is the most important source of *external* funds for small to medium-sized firms?

3.2 What is the most important method of debt financing for corporations?

3.3 List the three key features of the financial system and provide a brief explanation for each.

Problems and Applications

3.4 Consider the possibility of income insurance. With income insurance, if a person loses his job or doesn't get as big a raise as anticipated, he would be compensated under his insurance coverage. Why don't insurance companies offer income insurance of this type?

3.5 If everyone were perfectly honest, would there be a role for financial intermediaries?

3.6 Describe some of the information problems in the financial system that lead firms to rely more heavily on internal funds than external funds to finance their growth. Do these information problems imply that firms are able to spend less on expansion than is economically optimal? Briefly explain.

3.7 [Related to the Making the Connection **on page 273**] An article in the *Wall Street Journal* made the following comment on the surge in corporations selling long-term bonds in 2012: "For investors, the longer maturities provide better returns than shorter-term debt without the default worries associated with the high-yielding debt of some of Europe's troubled economies."

a. Are investment-grade corporate bonds free of default risk? Briefly explain.

b. Is default risk the only type of risk that investors in these bonds should be concerned about? Briefly explain.

Source: Vipal Monga, "Companies Feast on Cheap Money," *Wall Street Journal*, October 8, 2012.

3.8 *Wall Street Journal* columnist Brett Arends offered the opinion that "as a rule of thumb, the more complex a [financial] product is, the worse the deal." Do you agree? Why would a more complex financial product be likely to be a worse deal for an investor than a simpler product?

Source: Brett Arends, "Four Lessons from the Goldman Case," *Wall Street Journal*, May 2, 2010.

Data Exercises

D9.1: **[Comparing transactions fees]** Online brokerages generally charge transactions fees per trade. This means that a $5,000 stock purchase is charged the same fee as a $100 stock purchase. Go to the following online brokerages and compare their transactions fees: TD Ameritrade, E-TRADE, and ScottTrade. Which has the highest transactions fee? If you had $200 to invest, and if the expected return in the stock market is 5% over one year, does the transactions cost affect your decision to buy stock? (Remember that you get charged the transactions fee for both the buy transactions and sell transactions.)

D9.2: **[Recessions and the net worth of households]**
 Go to the Web site of the Federal Reserve Bank of St. Louis (FRED) (research.stlouisfed.org/fred2/) and download and graph the data series for the net worth of households (TNWBSHNO) from the first quarter of 1952 until the most recent quarter available. Go to the Web site of the National Bureau of Economic Research (nber.org) and find the dates for business cycle peaks and troughs (the period between a business cycle peak and trough is a recession).

a. What is household net worth?

b. Describe how household net worth changes just before, during, and just after a typical recession.

c. Why did household net worth decline by so much during the recession of 2007–2009? How might the decline in household net worth have affected the severity of the 2007–2009 recession?

D9.3: **[Recessions and the net worth of**
 corporations] Go to the Web site of the Federal Reserve Bank of St. Louis (FRED) (research. stlouisfed.org/fred2/) and download and graph the data series for the net worth of nonfinancial corporations (TNWMVBSNNCB) from the first quarter of 1952 until the most recent quarter available. Go to the Web site of the National Bureau of Economic Research (nber.org) and find the dates for business cycle peaks and troughs (the period between a business cycle peak and trough is a recession).

a. What is a nonfinancial corporation? Give two examples. What is corporate net worth?

b. Describe how corporate net worth changes just before, during, and just after a typical recession.

c. Why did corporate net worth decline by so much during the recession of 2007–2009? How might the decline in corporate net worth have affected the severity of the 2007–2009 recession?

CHAPTER 10

The Economics of Banking

Learning Objectives

After studying this chapter, you should be able to:

10.1 Understand bank balance sheets (pages 280–289)

10.2 Describe the basic operations of a commercial bank (pages 289–293)

10.3 Explain how banks manage risk (pages 293–299)

10.4 Explain the trends in the U.S. commercial banking industry (pages 299–307)

To Buy a House, You Need a Loan

If you are like the majority of people in the United States, you will buy a house some day. If you are a typical homebuyer, you are unlikely to have saved more than 20% of the purchase price of the house for a down payment, so you will have to borrow most of the money you need. In 2012, people planning to buy a home found themselves in what seemed to be a good position: Housing prices had fallen substantially from their highs at the peak of the housing bubble in 2005 and mortgage interest rates had hit record lows. Many potential homebuyers faced a problem, though: finding a bank willing to grant them a loan. Many homeowners who already had mortgage loans were also having trouble *refinancing*, or taking out new loans at lower interest rates, to replace their existing loans.

Obtaining a new mortgage loan or refinancing an existing loan was difficult in 2012 because of two developments in the housing market during previous years. First, during the housing boom of the mid-2000s, many banks and other mortgage lenders loosened their requirements for granting mortgage loans. In particular, so-called subprime borrowers, who may have previously missed payments on loans or otherwise had flawed credit histories, found that for the first time, they could easily obtain mortgage loans. People who could make less than the traditional 20% down payment were also able to obtain loans. Second, during the housing bubble, most banks securitized their mortgage loans by selling them to the Federal National Mortgage Association (Fannie Mae, or just Fannie) and the Federal Home Loan Mortgage Corporation (Freddie Mac, or just Freddie). Fannie Mae and

Continued on next page

Key Issue and Question

Issue: During and immediately following the 2007–2009 financial crisis, there was a sharp increase in the number of bank failures.

Question: Is banking a particularly risky business? If so, what types of risks do banks face?

Answered on page 307

Freddie Mac are government-sponsored enterprises that Congress established to help create a secondary market in mortgages. Fannie and Freddie bundled the loans they purchased from banks into mortgage-backed securities that were sold to investors. Because Fannie and Freddie guaranteed the securities against default, they suffered heavy losses when the housing bubble popped, housing prices sharply declined, and mortgage defaults soared.

To recover some of their losses, Fannie and Freddie began engaging in "put-backs," or requiring banks to repurchase defaulted mortgages that failed to meet certain requirements. Banks complained that Fannie and Freddie were making them buy back not just badly flawed mortgages but nearly every mortgage that had defaulted. As a result, banks began to grant mortgages only to applicants with nearly perfect credit histories and who were willing to make large down payments. As Treasury Secretary Timothy Geithner put it in testifying before Congress: "Mortgage credit is tighter than it should be. And the main reason is that banks … feel much more vulnerable now to what people call 'put-back.'"

The difficulty in obtaining mortgage loans or refinancing existing mortgages was a problem not just for the people directly involved but for the broader economy as well. Because the U.S. economy recovered very slowly from the 2007–2009 recession, the Federal Reserve had taken actions to drive down mortgage interest rates. The Fed's expectation was that lower interest rates would lead to increased demand for housing, helping to expand GDP and employment. In addition, people who refinanced their mortgages to lower interest rates would free up funds they could spend on other goods and services, thereby increasing demand. But the difficulty people had in finding new mortgage loans or in refinancing old ones meant that the Fed's policy was less effective than it might otherwise have been.

Problems in the mortgage market in 2012 highlighted again the crucial role that banks play in the financial system. Most people are unable to buy a house unless they can obtain a mortgage loan from a bank. Without a significant rebound in the housing market, most economists doubted that real GDP and employment would increase enough for the economy to fully recover from the 2007–2009 recession.

Sources: Nick Timiraos, "Burdened by Old Mortgages, Banks Are Slow to Lend Now," *Wall Street Journal*, October 3, 2012; Nick Timiraos, "Are Regulations to Blame for Tight Mortgage Credit?" *Wall Street Journal*, October 8, 2012; and Gretchen Morgenson, "0.2% Interest? You Bet We'll Complain," *New York Times*, March 3, 2012.

We know that banks are important to the efficient functioning of the financial system (see Chapter 9). In this chapter, we look more closely at how banks do business and how they earn profits. We then consider the problems banks face in managing risks. In recent years, banks have faced competition from other financial institutions that can offer savers and borrowers similar services but with lower risk. We conclude this chapter by describing some of the activities banks have undertaken in response to competition from other financial firms.

10.1

Learning Objective
Understand bank balance sheets.

The Basics of Commercial Banking: The Bank Balance Sheet

Commercial banking is a business. Banks fill a market need by providing a service, and they earn a profit by charging customers for that service. The key commercial banking activities are taking in deposits from savers and making loans to households and firms. To earn a profit, a bank needs to pay less for the funds it receives from depositors than it earns on the loans it makes. We begin our discussion of the business of banking by looking at a bank's *sources of funds*—primarily deposits—and *uses of funds*—primarily

Table 10.1 Consolidated Balance Sheet of U.S. Commercial Banks, October 2012

Assets (uses of funds)	(Percentage of total assets)	Liabilities + Bank capital (sources of funds)	(Percentage of total liabilities plus capital)
Reserves and other cash assets	7.9%	Deposits	73.3%
Securities	22.3	Checkable deposits	11.6
U.S. government and agency	15.8	Nontransaction deposits	61.7
State and local government and other securities	6.5	Small-denomination time deposits (CDs less than $100,000) plus savings deposits	55.1
Loans	59.9		
Commercial and industrial	11.1	Large-denomination time deposits (CDs greater than $100,000)	6.6
Real estate (including mortgages)	31.8		
Consumer	10.1	Borrowings	9.0
Interbank	0.9	From banks in the U.S.	0.9
Other loans	6.1	Other borrowings	8.1
Trading assets	1.5	Other liabilities	4.4
Other assets	8.4	Bank capital (or shareholders' equity)	13.3

Note: The data are for all domestically chartered commercial banks in the United States as of October 3, 2012.

Source: Federal Reserve Statistical Release H.8, October 12, 2012.

loans. A bank's sources and uses of funds are summarized on its **balance sheet**, which is a statement that shows an individual's or a firm's financial position on a particular day. Table 10.1 combines data from all the banks in the country into a consolidated balance sheet for the whole U.S. commercial banking system for October 2012. Normally, balance sheets show dollar values for each entry. For ease of interpretation, we have converted the dollar values to percentages. Table 10.1 shows the typical layout of a balance sheet, which is based on the following accounting equation:

$$\text{Assets} = \text{Liabilities} + \text{Shareholders' equity.}$$

An **asset** is something of value that an individual or a firm owns. A **liability** is something that an individual or a firm owes, or, in other words, a claim on an individual or a firm. *Shareholders' equity* is the difference between the value of a firm's assets and the value of its liabilities. Shareholders' equity represents the dollar amount the owners of the firm would be left with if the firm were to be closed, its assets sold, and its liabilities paid off. For a public firm, the owners are the shareholders. Shareholders' equity is also called the firm's *net worth*. In banking, shareholders' equity is usually called **bank capital**. Bank capital is the funds contributed by the shareholders through their purchases of the bank's stock plus the bank's accumulated, retained profits. The accounting equation above tells us that the left side of a firm's balance sheet must always have the same value as the right side. We can think of a bank's liabilities and its capital as the sources of its funds, and we can think of a bank's assets as the uses of its funds.

Balance sheet A statement that shows an individual's or a firm's financial position on a particular day.

Asset Something of value that an individual or a firm owns; in particular, a financial claim.

Liability Something that an individual or a firm owes, particularly a financial claim on an individual or a firm.

Bank capital The difference between the value of a bank's assets and the value of its liabilities; also called shareholders' equity.

Bank Liabilities

The most important bank liabilities are the funds a bank acquires from savers. The bank uses the funds to make investments or loans to borrowers. Bank deposits offer households and firms certain advantages over other ways in which they might hold their funds. For example, compared with holding cash, deposits offer greater safety against theft and may also pay interest. Compared with financial assets such as Treasury bills, deposits are more liquid. Deposits against which checks can be written offer a convenient way to make payments. Banks offer a variety of deposit accounts because savers have different needs. We next review the main types of deposit accounts.

Checkable deposits
Accounts against which depositors can write checks.

Checkable Deposits Banks offer savers **checkable deposits**, which are accounts against which depositors can write checks. Checkable deposits are also called *transaction deposits*. Checkable deposits come in different varieties, which are determined partly by banking regulations and partly by the desire of bank managers to tailor the checking accounts they offer to meet the needs of households and firms. Demand deposits and NOW (negotiable order of withdrawal) accounts are the most important categories of checkable deposits. *Demand deposits* are checkable deposits on which banks do not pay interest. NOW accounts are checking accounts that pay interest. Businesses often hold substantial balances in demand deposits, partly because U.S. banking regulations do not allow them to hold NOW accounts but also because demand deposits represent a liquid asset that can be accessed with very low transactions costs.

Banks must pay all checkable deposits on demand. In other words, a bank must exchange a depositor's check for cash immediately, provided that the depositor has at least the amount of the check on deposit. Finally, note that checkable deposits are liabilities to banks because banks have the obligation to pay the funds to depositors on demand. But checkable deposits are assets to households and firms because even though banks have physical possession of the funds, households and firms still own the funds. An accounting aside: It is important to grasp the idea that the same checking account can simultaneously be an asset to a household or firm and a liability to a bank. Understanding this point will help you to better follow some of the discussion later in this chapter.

Nontransaction Deposits Savers use only some of their deposits for day-to-day transactions. Banks offer *nontransaction deposits* for savers who are willing to sacrifice immediate access to their funds in exchange for higher interest payments. The most important types of nontransaction deposits are savings accounts, money market deposit accounts (MMDAs), and *time deposits*, or certificates of deposit (CDs). With savings accounts—which at one time were generally called *passbook accounts*—depositors must give the bank 30 days' notice for a withdrawal. In practice, though, banks usually waive this requirement, so most depositors expect to receive immediate access to the funds in their savings accounts. MMDAs are a hybrid of savings accounts and checking accounts in that they pay interest, but depositors can write only three checks per month against them.

Unlike savings deposits, CDs have specified maturities that typically range from a few months to several years. Banks penalize savers who withdraw funds prior to maturity by requiring the savers to forfeit part of the accrued interest. CDs are less liquid than savings accounts but pay depositors a higher rate of interest. There is an important difference between CDs of less than $100,000, which are called *small-denomination time deposits*, and CDs of $100,000 or more, which are called *large-denomination time deposits*. CDs worth $100,000 or more are *negotiable*, which means that investors can buy and sell them in secondary markets prior to maturity.

Households with limited funds to save often prefer checkable deposits and small-denomination time deposits because these deposits are covered by **federal deposit insurance**, which provides government guarantees for account balances of up to $250,000. Deposit insurance gives banks an edge over other financial intermediaries in acquiring funds from small savers because, for instance, money market mutual fund shares lack this government insurance.

Federal deposit insurance
A government guarantee of deposit account balances up to $250,000.

Borrowings Banks often have more opportunities to make loans than they can finance with funds they attract from depositors. To take advantage of these opportunities, banks raise funds by borrowing. A bank can earn a profit from this borrowing if the interest rate it pays to borrow funds is lower than the interest it earns by lending the funds to businesses and consumers. Borrowings include short-term loans in the *federal funds market*, loans from a bank's foreign branches or other subsidiaries or affiliates, repurchase agreements, and *discount loans* from the Federal Reserve System. The federal funds market is the market in which banks make short-term loans—often just overnight—to other banks. Although the name indicates that government money is involved, in fact, the loans in the federal funds market involve the banks' own funds. The interest rate on these interbank loans is called the *federal funds rate*.

With *repurchase agreements*—otherwise known as "repos," or RPs—banks sell securities, such as Treasury bills, and agree to repurchase them, typically the next day. Banks use repos to borrow funds from business firms or other banks, using the underlying securities as collateral. A firm or another bank that buys the securities earns interest without any significant loss of liquidity. Repos are typically between large banks or corporations, so the degree of *counterparty risk*, or the risk that the other party to the transaction will default on its obligation, was at one time considered to be small. But during the financial crisis, it became clear that even a large corporation might be quickly forced into bankruptcy, leaving the counterparties to its repos to suffer significant losses or a delay in accessing their funds, or both. For example, concern among the counterparties to the repos of the Lehman Brothers investment bank helped to force the firm into bankruptcy, worsening the financial crisis.

Making the Connection

The Rise and Fall and (Partial) Rise of the Checking Account

In 1960, plain-vanilla demand deposits, which pay no interest, made up more than half of commercial bank liabilities. The graph on the next page shows checkable deposits as a fraction of all bank liabilities for the period from January 1973 to September 2012. By 1973, checkable deposits made up less than one-third of bank liabilities, and by early 2008, they reached a low point of a little more than 6% of all bank liabilities. Then the financial crisis hit, and checkable deposits increased to about 11.5% of bank liabilities.

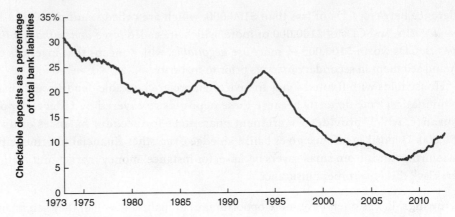

Sources: Federal Reserve Bank of St. Louis; and Board of Governors of the Federal Reserve System.

The decline in the popularity of checking accounts until the financial crisis may seem puzzling because, in some ways, these accounts became more attractive over time. In the 1960s and 1970s, the only checkable deposits available were demand deposits, which paid no interest. Interest-paying NOW accounts were authorized by changes in bank regulations that took effect in 1980. In addition, because there were no ATMs in those days, to withdraw money from your checking account, you needed to go to your bank, stand in line, and fill out a withdrawal slip. Banks were typically open only during "banker's hours" of 10 A.M. to 3 P.M. from Monday to Friday. If stores or restaurants declined to accept checks, consumers could not spend the funds in their accounts. Today, debit cards make it possible for consumers to access the funds in their checking accounts even when buying from a store that doesn't accept checks.

The improved services that checking accounts provide have been more than offset by alternative assets that offer higher interest rates. The chart below shows households' and firms' holdings of various short-term financial assets in September 2012. Note that the value of savings accounts and small time deposits (CDs of less than $100,000) is six times greater than the value of checkable deposits.

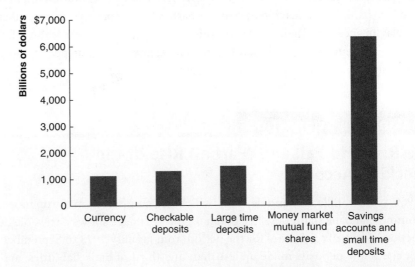

Sources: Federal Reserve Bank of St. Louis; and Board of Governors of the Federal Reserve System.

Households hold less in checking accounts relative to other financial assets than they once did, partly because households have become wealthier over time. With greater wealth, households have been better able to afford to hold assets, such as CDs, where their money is tied up for a while but on which they earn a higher rate of interest. Money market mutual funds, such as Vanguard's Prime Money Market Fund, which were first introduced in 1971, have also been popular. Like other mutual funds, money market mutual funds sell shares to investors and use the funds to buy financial assets. These funds buy only money market—or short-term—assets, such as Treasury bills and commercial paper issued by corporations. Money market mutual funds pay higher interest than bank deposit accounts, and they also allow for limited check writing, so they have been formidable competition for bank checking accounts.

The 2007–2009 financial crisis showed that checking accounts are still useful to households and firms, however. As the economic recession deepened, incomes declined and the perceived risk of investing in many financial assets increased, so checkable deposits as a fraction of all bank liabilities increased. Checking accounts provide a safe haven for households and small businesses because their funds are protected up to the $250,000 federal deposit insurance ceiling. In addition, the very low interest rates that persisted for more than three years after the end of the recession of 2007–2009 resulted in interest rates on CDs and money market mutual funds dropping to barely above zero. Many households moved their funds from CDs and money market mutual funds to checking accounts to take advantage of their greater liquidity without giving up much interest.

See related problem 1.5 at the end of the chapter.

Bank Assets

Banks acquire *bank assets* with the funds they receive from depositors, the funds they borrow, the funds they acquired initially from their shareholders, and the profits they retain from their operations. A bank's managers build a portfolio of assets that reflect both the demand for loans by the bank's customers and the bank's need to balance returns against risk, liquidity, and information costs. We now discuss the key bank assets.

Reserves and Other Cash Assets The most liquid asset that banks hold is **reserves**, which consist of **vault cash**—cash on hand in the bank (including ATMs) or in deposits at other banks—and deposits banks have with the Federal Reserve System. As authorized by Congress, the Fed mandates that banks hold a percentage of their demand deposits and NOW accounts (but not MMDAs) as **required reserves**. Reserves that banks hold over and above those that are required are called **excess reserves**. Banks had long complained that the Fed's failure to pay interest on the banks' reserve deposits amounted to a tax because, at least with respect to required reserves, banks earned no interest on funds they could otherwise have used to make loans or purchase securities. Congress responded in 2006 by authorizing the Fed to start paying interest on banks' required and excess reserve deposits beginning in October 2011. In October 2008, during the financial crisis, Congress authorized the Fed to begin paying interest immediately, which it did. The interest rate is very low—0.25% as of December 2012—and, of course, banks earn no

Reserves A bank asset consisting of vault cash plus bank deposits with the Federal Reserve.

Vault cash Cash on hand in a bank; includes currency in ATMs and deposits with other banks.

Required reserves Reserves the Fed requires banks to hold against demand deposit and NOW account balances.

Excess reserves Any reserves banks hold above those necessary to meet reserve requirements.

interest on vault cash. Until the financial crisis of 2007–2009, excess reserves had fallen to very low levels. But excess reserves can provide an important source of liquidity to banks, and during the financial crisis, bank holdings of excess reserves soared. In addition to the Fed's now paying interest on bank reserve accounts, as we saw in the chapter opener, during and immediately after the financial crisis, many banks were cautious about making loans, preferring to hold the funds as excess reserves instead.

Another important cash asset is claims banks have on other banks for uncollected funds, which is called *cash items in the process of collection*. Suppose your Aunt Tilly, who lives in Seattle, sends you a $100 check for your birthday. Aunt Tilly's check is written against her checking account in her bank in Seattle. If you deposit the check in your bank in Nashville, the check becomes a cash item in the process of collection. Eventually, your bank will collect the funds from the Seattle bank, and the cash item in the process of collection will be converted to reserves on your bank's balance sheet.

Small banks often maintain deposits at other banks to obtain foreign-exchange transactions, check collection, or other services. This function, called *correspondent banking*, has diminished in importance over the past 50 years, as the financial system has provided small banks with other ways to obtain these services.

Securities *Marketable securities* are liquid assets that banks trade in financial markets. Banks are allowed to hold securities issued by the U.S. Treasury and other government agencies, corporate bonds that received investment-grade ratings when they were first issued, and some limited amounts of municipal bonds, which are bonds issued by state and local governments. Because of their liquidity, bank holdings of U.S. Treasury securities are sometimes called *secondary reserves*. In the United States, commercial banks cannot invest checkable deposits in corporate bonds (although they may purchase them using other funds) or common stock. During the past decade, banks have increased their holdings of mortgage-backed securities. In 2012, mortgage-backed securities made up just over 50% of the securities that banks held. During the financial crisis of 2007–2009, the value of many mortgage-backed securities declined sharply, which caused many banks to suffer heavy losses and some banks to fail.

Loans The largest category of bank assets is loans. Loans are illiquid relative to marketable securities and entail greater default risk and higher information costs. As a result, the interest rates on loans are higher than those on marketable securities. Table 10.1 on page 281 shows that most bank loans fall into three categories:

1. Loans to businesses—called commercial and industrial, or C&I, loans
2. Consumer loans, made to households primarily to buy automobiles, furniture, and other goods
3. Real estate loans, which include mortgage loans and any other loans backed with real estate as collateral. Mortgage loans made to purchase homes are called *residential mortgages*, while mortgages made to purchase stores, offices, factories, and other commercial buildings are called *commercial mortgages*.

Figure 10.1 shows that the types of loans granted by banks have changed significantly since the early 1970s. Real estate loans have increased tremendously, growing from less than one-third of bank loans in 1973 to 60% of bank loans in 2012. C&I loans, which

MyEconLab Real-time data

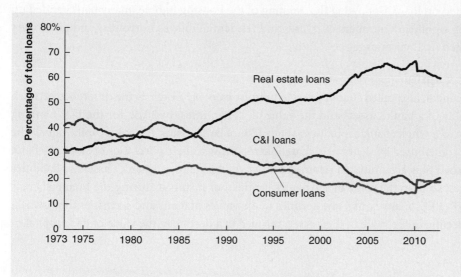

Figure 10.1

The Changing Mix of Bank Loans, 1973–2012

The types of loans granted by banks have changed significantly since the early 1970s. Real estate loans grew from less than one-third of bank loans in 1973 to 60% of bank loans in 2012. Commercial and industrial (C&I) loans fell from more than 40% of bank loans to less than 20%. Consumer loans fell from more than 27% of all loans to about 21%.

Note: The values are the shares of the total of C&I, consumer, and real estate loans at domestically chartered U.S. banks. Total loans do not include interbank loans or other loans.

Source: Federal Reserve Statistical Release H.8, October 12, 2012.

were the largest category of loans in 1973, have fallen from more than 40% of bank loans to less than 20%. Firms take out C&I loans either to finance long-term investments, such as purchases of machinery and equipment, or to meet short-term needs, such as financing inventories. Beginning in the late 1970s, some firms that had previously used C&I loans began to meet their long-term funding needs by instead issuing junk bonds, which are bonds that receive below-investment-grade ratings from the bond-rating agencies. Once a market for newly issued junk bonds developed in the late 1970s, many firms found the interest rates on these bonds to be lower than what they would have paid on C&I loans from banks. When the market for commercial paper developed in the 1980s, some firms that had been using short-term C&I loans from banks began issuing commercial paper instead.

The decline in the importance of C&I loans has fundamentally changed the nature of commercial banking. Traditionally, we could sum up commercial banking by saying that it consisted of taking in funds as checkable deposits and lending them to businesses. C&I loans were typically low-risk loans that banks could count on as the basis of their profits. Banks made C&I loans primarily to businesses on which they had gathered private information through long-term relationships. In addition, the loans were often well collateralized. Both of these factors reduced the chances that businesses would default on the loans. Banks usually did not face much competition in making the loans, which kept the interest rates on them relatively high. As the demand for C&I loans has declined, banks have been forced to turn to riskier uses of their funds, especially residential and commercial real estate lending. The bursting of the real estate bubble beginning in 2006 showed that replacing C&I loans with real estate loans had increased the degree of risk in a typical bank's loan portfolio.

Other Assets Other assets include banks' physical assets, such as computer equipment and buildings. This category also includes collateral received from borrowers who have defaulted on loans. Following the bursting of the housing bubble, many banks ended up owning significant numbers of houses and residential lots, as borrowers and developers defaulted on their mortgages.

Bank Capital

Bank capital, also called shareholders' equity, or *bank net worth*, is the difference between the value of a bank's assets and the value of its liabilities. In 2012, for the U.S. banking system as a whole, bank capital was about 13% of bank assets. A bank's capital equals the funds contributed by the bank's shareholders through their purchases of stock the bank has issued plus accumulated retained profits. As the value of a bank's assets or liabilities changes, so does the value of the bank's capital. For instance, during the financial crisis of 2007–2009, many banks saw declines in the values of loans and securities they owned. This decline in the value of their assets resulted in a decline in the value of their capital.

Solved Problem 10.1

Constructing a Bank Balance Sheet

The following entries are from the actual balance sheet of a U.S. bank:

Cash, including cash items in the process of collection	$121
Non-interest-bearing deposits	275
Deposits with the Federal Reserve	190
Commercial loans	253
Long-term bonds (issued by the bank)	439
Real estate loans	460
Commercial paper and other short-term borrowing	70
Consumer loans	187
Securities	311
Interest-bearing deposits	717
Buildings and equipment	16
Other assets	685
Other liabilities	491

Note: Values are in billions of dollars.

a. Use the entries to construct a balance sheet similar to the one in Table 10.1, with assets on the left side of the balance sheet and liabilities and bank capital on the right side.

b. The bank's capital is what percentage of its assets?

Solving the Problem

Step 1 **Review the chapter material.** This problem is about bank balance sheets, so you may want to review the section "The Basics of Commercial Banking: The Bank Balance Sheet," which begins on page 280.

Step 2 Answer part (a) by using the entries to construct the bank's balance sheet, remembering that bank capital is equal to the value of assets minus the value of liabilities.

Assets		Liabilities and bank capital	
Cash, including cash items in the process of collection	$121	Non-interest-bearing deposits	$275
Deposits with the Federal Reserve	190	Interest-bearing deposits	717
Commercial loans	253	Commercial paper and other short-term borrowing	70
Real estate loans	460	Long-term bonds	439
Consumer loans	187	Other liabilities	491
Securities	311	Total liabilities	1,992
Buildings and equipment	16	Bank capital	231
Other assets	685		
Total assets	$2,223	Total liabilities + bank capital	$2,223

Step 3 Answer part (b) by calculating the bank's capital as a percentage of its assets.

Total assets = $2,2223 billion

Bank capital = $231 billion

$$\text{Bank capital as a percentage of assets} = \frac{\$231 \text{ billion}}{\$2,223 \text{ billion}} = 0.104, \text{ or } 10.4\%$$

See related problem 1.7 at the end of the chapter.

The Basic Operations of a Commercial Bank

In this section, we look at how banks earn a profit by matching savers and borrowers. When a depositor puts money in a checking account and the bank uses the money to finance a loan, the bank has transformed a financial asset (a deposit) for a saver into a liability (a loan) for a borrower. Like other businesses, a bank takes inputs, adds value to them, and delivers outputs.

To analyze further the basics of bank operations, we will work with an accounting tool known as a **T-account**, which shows *changes* in balance sheet items that result from a particular transaction. To take a simple example, suppose you use $100 in cash to open a checking account at Wells Fargo. As a result, Wells Fargo acquires $100 in vault cash, which it lists as an asset and, according to banking regulations, counts as part of its reserves. Because you can go to a Wells Fargo branch or an ATM at any time and withdraw your deposit, Wells Fargo lists your $100 as a liability in the form of checkable deposits. We can use a T-account to illustrate the changes in Wells Fargo's balance sheet that result:

10.2

Learning Objective

Describe the basic operations of a commercial bank.

T-account An accounting tool used to show changes in balance sheet items.

WELLS FARGO

Assets		Liabilities	
Vault cash	+$100	Checkable deposits	+$100

Note that on Wells Fargo's balance sheet it will hold much larger amounts of vault cash and checkable deposits. The T-account shows only the changes in these items, not their levels.

What happens to the $100 that you deposited in Wells Fargo? By answering this question, we can see how banks earn profits. Suppose that Wells Fargo held no excess reserves before receiving your $100 deposit and that banking regulations require banks to hold 10% of their checkable deposits as reserves. Therefore, $10 of the $100 is required reserves and the other $90 is excess reserves. To show the difference between required reserves and excess reserves, we rewrite the amount that Wells Fargo holds as reserves as follows:

WELLS FARGO

Assets		Liabilities	
Required reserves	+$10	Checkable deposits	+$100
Excess reserves	+$90		

Reserves that a bank keeps as cash pay no interest, and those the bank keeps in deposits at the Fed pay a low rate of interest. In addition, checkable deposits generate expenses for the bank: The bank must pay interest to depositors and pay the costs of maintaining checking accounts, including record keeping and servicing ATMs. The bank, therefore, will want to use its excess reserves to make loans or buy securities to generate income. Suppose that Wells Fargo uses its excess reserves to buy Treasury bills worth $30 and make a loan worth $60. For simplicity, the units in this example are very small. (Thinking in thousands of dollars would be more realistic.) We can illustrate these transactions with the following T-account:

WELLS FARGO

Assets		Liabilities	
Reserves	+$10	Checkable deposits	+$100
Securities	+$30		
Loans	+$60		

Wells Fargo has used your $100 deposit to provide funds to the U.S. Treasury and to the person or business it granted the loan to. By using your deposit, the bank acquired interest-earning assets. If the interest Wells Fargo earns on these assets is greater than the interest the bank pays you on your deposit plus the other costs of servicing your deposit, then Wells Fargo will earn a profit on these transactions. The difference between the average interest rate banks receive on their assets and the average interest rate they pay on their liabilities is called the banks' *spread*.

To be successful, a bank must make prudent loans and investments so that it earns a high enough interest rate to cover its costs and to make a profit. This plan may sound simple, but it hasn't been easy for banks to earn profits in the past decade. As we have seen, many banks purchased mortgage-backed securities, whose value declined sharply following the bursting of the housing bubble. In addition, many banks, particularly community banks, provided substantial loans to commercial real estate developers. The severity of the 2007–2009 recession meant that a greater number of borrowers defaulted on their loans, forcing banks to take losses on those investments.

Making the Connection	In Your Interest

Your Bank's Message to You: "Please Go Away!"

Many people complain about the very low interest rates banks pay on checking accounts. Some checking accounts pay zero interest. You are letting the bank use the money in your checking account, and that's all the return you get? Actually, if you are like many bank customers, your bank may well be losing money on your checking account. It costs banks about $300 per year to process the checks, prepare checking account statements, and cover the other costs involved with a typical checking account. And that amount doesn't include the salaries of tellers or other costs of running bank branches.

How do banks expect to cover the costs of your checking account? Clearly not just from loaning out your money. Suppose you have $1,000 in your checking account, on which your bank is paying you no interest. Even if the bank can bundle your $1,000 with funds from other people's checking accounts to make a car loan at 6%, the bank has earned only $60 in interest on your deposit. Traditionally, banks have earned income from depositors in three other ways: (1) By collecting fees from stores when depositors use their debit cards for purchases, (2) by charging *overdraft fees* when depositors have insufficient funds in their accounts to cover the checks they write, and (3) by collecting fees when depositors take out loans or purchase mutual funds or other financial products. Income from the first two sources began to decline sharply as a result of new regulations authorized by the Wall Street Reform and Consumer Protection Act, or Dodd-Frank Act. These regulations put a cap on the amount that banks could charge merchants for debit card transactions. The cap was estimated to reduce bank revenues by $8 billion per year. In addition, limits were placed on overdraft fees, and in late 2012, the Consumer Financial Protection Bureau, which was established under the Dodd-Frank Act, indicated that it might place additional limits on these fees.

The new regulations meant that banks had to concentrate on the fees they could earn when depositors took out mortgage loans, bought mutual funds, or hired banks to manage their wealth. Low-to-moderate-income depositors, though, only infrequently take out mortgages, buy financial products, or hire anyone to manage their wealth. As a result, banks were losing money on the checking accounts held by these depositors. One industry analyst was quoted as saying: "Banks for a long time have been unable to charge enough to cover the cost of maintaining a checking account. The changes made by Congress certainly made it even harder." Jamie Dimon, CEO of JPMorgan Chase, estimated that half of Chase's depositors were unprofitable.

Banks have responded to the new environment in a number or ways. Some banks have closed branches in lower-income neighborhoods while opening additional branches in higher-income neighborhoods. Banks have increased their marketing of securities and financial advice to higher-income customers. Nearly all banks have raised minimum balance requirements for free checking accounts. Many banks have adopted a long-term strategy of trying to push low-income customers to transact most of their business through ATMs rather than by using tellers at bank branches.

Mark Williams of Boston University argues that: "The traditional banking model is fractured. Some lower-margin customers will have to go elsewhere to find the same level of service." It remains to be seen how the services banks offer customers will change as the banks fully adapt to the new regulations.

Sources: Robin Sidel, "'Free' Checking Costs More," *Wall Street Journal*, September 24, 2012; Aaron Elstein, "Chase Chief Loses Money on Nearly Half His Retail Customers," *Bloomberg News*, March 4, 2012; and Nelson D. Schwartz, "Got $100,000? Have a Cookie: Banks Try Luring the Top 10%," *New York Times*, March 10, 2012.

See related problem 2.7 at the end of the chapter.

Bank Capital and Bank Profits

As with any other business, a bank's profits are the difference between its revenues and its costs. A bank's revenues are earned primarily from interest on its securities and loans and from fees it charges for credit and debit cards, servicing deposit accounts, providing financial advice and wealth management services, originating and collecting payments on securitized loans, and carrying out foreign exchange transactions. A bank's costs are the interest it pays to its depositors, the interest it pays on loans or other debt, and its costs of providing its services. A bank's **net interest margin** is the difference between the interest it receives on its securities and loans and the interest it pays on deposits and debt, divided by the total value of its earning assets.[1] If we subtract the bank's cost of providing its services from the fees it receives, divide the result by the bank's total assets, and then add the bank's net interest margin, we have an expression for the bank's total profits earned per dollar of assets, which is called its **return on assets (ROA)**. ROA is usually measured in terms of *after-tax profit*, or the profit that remains after the bank has paid its taxes:

$$\text{ROA} = \frac{\text{After-tax profit}}{\text{Bank assets}}.$$

A bank's shareholders own the bank's capital and are interested in the profits the bank's managers are able to earn on their investment. So, shareholders often judge bank managers not on the basis of ROA but on the basis of **return on equity (ROE)**. Return on equity is after-tax profit per dollar of equity, or bank capital:

$$\text{ROE} = \frac{\text{After-tax profit}}{\text{Bank capital}}.$$

ROA and ROE are related by the ratio of a bank's assets to its capital:

$$\text{ROE} = \text{ROA} \times \frac{\text{Bank assets}}{\text{Bank capital}}.$$

At the end of September 2012, total assets of U.S. commercial banks were $12.9 trillion, and bank capital was $1.5 trillion, meaning that the ratio of assets to capital for the banking system as a whole was 8.6. If a bank earned 2% ROA and had a ratio of assets to capital of 8.6, then its ROE would be 17.2% ($= 2\% \times 8.6$). However, if the bank's ratio of assets to capital was 15, then its ROE would be 30%. In the mid-2000s, some financial firms had ratios of assets to capital as high as 35. For those firms, a

Net interest margin The difference between the interest a bank receives on its securities and loans and the interest it pays on deposits and debt, divided by the total value of its earning assets.

Return on assets (ROA) The ratio of the value of a bank's after-tax profit to the value of its assets.

Return on equity (ROE) The ratio of the value of a bank's after-tax profit to the value of its capital.

---

[1] Earning assets do not include assets, such as vault cash, on which a bank does not earn a return.

modest 2% ROA would translate to a whopping 70% ROE! We can conclude that *managers of banks and other financial firms may have an incentive to hold a high ratio of assets to capital.*

The ratio of assets to capital is one measure of *bank leverage*, the inverse of which (capital to assets) is called a bank's *leverage ratio*. **Leverage** is a measure of how much debt an investor assumes in making an investment. The ratio of assets to capital is a measure of **bank leverage** because banks take on debt by, for instance, accepting deposits to gain the funds to accumulate assets. A high ratio of assets to capital—high leverage—is a double-edged sword: Leverage can magnify relatively small ROAs into large ROEs, but it can do the same for losses. For example, suppose a bank suffers a 3% *loss* as a percentage of assets. With a ratio of assets to capital of 8.6, the result is a manageable −25.8% ROE. But if the bank's ratio of assets to capital were 35, the result would be a −105% ROE. In other words, a relatively small loss on the bank's assets would wipe out *all* of the bank's capital. We can conclude that high leverage increases the degree of risk financial firms are exposed to by magnifying swings in profits as measured by ROE.

Moral hazard can contribute to high bank leverage in two ways. First, bank managers are typically compensated at least partly on the basis of their ability to provide shareholders with a high ROE. Particularly if managers do not themselves own significant amounts of stock in the bank, they may have an incentive to take on more risk than shareholders would prefer. Second, federal deposit insurance has increased moral hazard by reducing the incentive depositors have to monitor the behavior of bank managers. Depositors with accounts below the deposit insurance limit do not suffer losses if their bank fails as a result of the bank's managers having taken on excessive risk. So, bank managers do not have to fear that becoming more highly leveraged will cause depositors to withdraw their funds.

To deal with the risk of banks becoming too highly leveraged, government regulations called *capital requirements* have placed limits on the value of the assets commercial banks can acquire relative to their capital (see Chapter 12). These same limits, however, have not been applied to other financial firms, such as investment banks. During the financial crisis of 2007–2009, high ratios of assets to capital at investment banks, such as Bear Stearns and Lehman Brothers, compounded their financial problems. Whether capital requirements will be extended beyond commercial banks to other financial firms is the subject of ongoing discussion among international financial regulators.

Managing Bank Risk

In addition to risks that banks may face from inadequate capital relative to their assets, banks face several other types of risk. In this section, we examine how banks deal with the following three types of risks: liquidity risk, credit risk, and interest-rate risk.

Managing Liquidity Risk

Liquidity risk refers to the possibility that a bank may not be able to meet its cash needs by selling assets or raising funds at a reasonable cost. For example, large deposit withdrawals might force a bank to sell relatively illiquid loans and possibly suffer losses on the sales. The challenge to banks in managing liquidity risk is to reduce their exposure

Leverage A measure of how much debt an investor assumes in making an investment.

Bank leverage The ratio of the value of a bank's assets to the value of its capital, the inverse of which (capital to assets) is called a bank's leverage ratio.

10.3

Learning Objective
Explain how banks manage risk.

Liquidity risk The possibility that a bank may not be able to meet its cash needs by selling assets or raising funds at a reasonable cost.

to risk without sacrificing too much profitability. For example, a bank can minimize liquidity risk by holding fewer loans and securities and more reserves. Such a strategy reduces the bank's profitability, however, because the bank earns no interest on vault cash and only a low interest rate on its reserve deposits with the Fed. So, rather than hold large amounts of excess reserves, banks typically reduce liquidity risk through strategies of *asset management* and *liquidity management*.

Banks can practice asset management by lending funds in the federal funds market, usually for one day at a time. Normally, banks can earn a higher interest rate by lending to other banks in the federal funds market than they can by keeping the funds on deposit with the Fed, although this typical situation was not true for several years following the financial crisis. A second option is to use *reverse repurchase agreements*, which involve a bank buying Treasury securities owned by a business or another bank while at the same time agreeing to sell the securities back at a later date, often the next morning. (With a repurchase agreement, the bank would sell the Treasury securities and agree to buy them back at a later date.) The reverse repurchase agreement acts, in effect, as a short-term loan from the bank to a business or other bank with the Treasury securities acting as collateral. Most banks use a combination of loans in the federal funds market and reverse repurchase agreements. Because the loans in the federal funds market and reverse repurchase agreements are very short term, the funds can be available to meet deposit withdrawals.

Banks can also meet a surge in deposit withdrawals by increasing their liabilities—borrowings—rather than by increasing their reserves. Liability management involves determining the best mix of borrowings needed to obtain the funds necessary to satisfy deposit withdrawals. Banks can borrow from other banks in the federal funds market, borrow from businesses or other banks using repurchase agreements, or borrow from the Fed by taking out *discount loans*.

Managing Credit Risk

Credit risk The risk that borrowers might default on their loans.

Credit risk is the risk that borrowers might default on their loans. Credit risk can arise because asymmetric information often results in the problems of *adverse selection* and *moral hazard* (see Chapter 9). Because borrowers know more about their financial health and their true plans for using borrowed money, banks may find themselves inadvertently lending to poor credit risks or to borrowers who intend to use borrowed funds for something other than their intended purpose. We next briefly consider the different methods banks can use to manage credit risk.

Diversification Investors—whether individuals or financial firms—can reduce their exposure to risk by diversifying their holdings (see Chapter 5). If banks lend too much to one borrower, to borrowers in one region, or to borrowers in one industry, they are exposed to greater risks from those loans. For example, a bank that had granted most of its loans to consumers and business in New Jersey would have likely suffered serious losses on those loans following Hurricane Sandy in 2012. By diversifying across borrowers, regions, and industries, banks can reduce their credit risk.

Credit-risk analysis The process that bank loan officers use to screen loan applicants.

Credit-Risk Analysis In performing **credit-risk analysis**, bank loan officers screen loan applicants to eliminate potentially bad risks and to obtain a pool of creditworthy borrowers. Individual borrowers usually must give loan officers information about their employment, income, and net worth. Business borrowers supply information about their current and projected profits and net worth. Banks often use *credit-scoring systems* to predict statistically whether a borrower is likely to default. For example, people who change jobs frequently are more likely to default than are people with more stable job histories. Loan officers collect information before granting a loan and also monitor the borrower during the term of the loan. Following the financial crisis, many banks tightened their lending procedures to reduce credit risk on loans, particularly mortgage loans. As we saw in the chapter opener, although this tightening may have helped banks reduce the risks they faced, it made it significantly harder for people to obtain mortgage loans.

Historically, loan rates to businesses were based on the **prime rate**, which was the interest rate charged on six-month loans to borrowers with the lowest expected default risk—so-called *high-quality borrowers*. Other loans carried interest rates greater than the prime rate, according to their credit risk. Higher-risk loans had higher interest rates. Today, however, banks charge most large to medium-sized businesses interest rates that reflect changing market interest rates instead of the stated prime rate, which is typically charged only to smaller borrowers.

Prime rate Formerly, the interest rate banks charged on six-month loans to high-quality borrowers; currently, an interest rate banks charge primarily to smaller borrowers.

Collateral To combat problems of adverse selection, banks generally require that a borrower put up collateral, or assets pledged to the bank in the event that the borrower defaults. For example, if you are an entrepreneur who needs a bank loan to start a new business, the bank will likely ask you to pledge some of your assets, such as your house, as collateral. In addition, the bank might require you to maintain a *compensating balance*, a required minimum amount that the business taking out the loan must maintain in a checking account with the lending bank.

Credit Rationing In some circumstances, banks minimize the costs of adverse selection and moral hazard through *credit rationing*. In **credit rationing**, a bank either grants a borrower's loan application but limits the size of the loan or simply declines to lend any amount to the borrower at the current interest rate. The first type of credit rationing occurs in response to possible moral hazard. Limiting the size of bank loans reduces costs of moral hazard by increasing the chance that the borrower will repay the loan to maintain a sound credit rating. Banks place credit limits on the MasterCard and Visa cards they issue for the same reason. With a credit limit of $2,500 on your credit card, you are likely to repay the bank so that you can borrow again in the future. If the bank were willing to give you a $2.5 million credit limit, you might be tempted to spend more money than you could repay. So, limiting the size of borrowers' loans to amounts less than borrowers demand at the current interest rate is both rational and profit maximizing for banks.

Credit rationing The restriction of credit by lenders with the result that borrowers cannot obtain all the funds they desire at the given interest rate.

The second type of credit rationing occurs in response to the adverse selection problem that arises when borrowers have little or no collateral to offer banks. What if a bank tries to raise the interest rate it charges to compensate itself for the higher default risk such borrowers represent? If the bank cannot distinguish the low-risk borrowers in this group from the high-risk borrowers, it runs the risk of having the low-risk borrowers drop out of the loan pool because of the high interest rate, leaving only the high-risk borrowers. So, keeping the interest rate at the lower level and denying loans altogether to some borrowers can be in the bank's best interest.

Monitoring and Restrictive Covenants To reduce the costs of moral hazard, banks monitor borrowers to make sure they don't use the funds borrowed to pursue unauthorized, risky activities. Banks keep track of whether borrowers are obeying *restrictive covenants*, or explicit provisions in the loan agreement that prohibit the borrower from engaging in certain activities. A business borrowing money to pay for new equipment might be explicitly barred from using the money to meet its payroll obligations or to finance inventories.

Long-Term Business Relationships The ability of banks to assess credit risks on the basis of private information on borrowers is called *relationship banking* (see Chapter 9). One of the best ways for a bank to gather information about a borrower's prospects or to monitor a borrower's activities is through a long-term business relationship with the borrower. By observing the borrower over time—through the borrower's checking account activity and loan repayments—the bank can significantly reduce problems of asymmetric information by reducing its information gathering and monitoring costs. Borrowers also gain from long-term relationships with banks. The customer can obtain credit at a lower interest rate or with fewer restrictions because the bank avoids costly information-gathering tasks.

Managing Interest-Rate Risk

Term	Definition
Interest-rate risk The effect of a change in market interest rates on a bank's profit or capital.	Banks experience **interest-rate risk** if changes in market interest rates cause bank profits or bank capital to fluctuate. The effect of a change in market interest rates on the value of a bank's assets and liabilities is similar to the effect of a change in interest rates on bond prices. That is, a rise in the market interest rate will lower the present value of a bank's assets and liabilities, and a fall in the market interest rate will raise the present value of a bank's assets and liabilities. The effect of a change in interest rates on a bank's profits depends in part on the extent to which the bank's assets and liabilities are *variable rate* or *fixed rate*. The interest rate on a variable-rate asset or liability changes at least once per year, while the interest rate on a fixed-rate asset or liability changes less often than once per year.

Table 10.2 shows the hypothetical balance sheet for Polktown National Bank. The table illustrates examples of fixed-rate and variable-rate assets and liabilities. If interest rates go up, Polktown will pay more interest on its $210 million in variable-rate liabilities while receiving more interest on only $150 million in variable-rate assets, so its profits will decline. Therefore, Polktown faces interest-rate risk.

The significant increase in the volatility of market interest rates during the 1980s caused heavy losses for banks and savings and loans that had made fixed-rate loans using funds from short-term, variable-rate deposits. For reasons we will explain in the next section, an increase in market interest rates also reduced the value of banks' assets relative to their liabilities, thereby reducing their capital and contributing to the increase in the failures of banks and savings and loans during the late 1980s.

Term	Definition
Gap analysis An analysis of the difference, or *gap*, between the dollar value of a bank's variable-rate assets and the dollar value of its variable-rate liabilities.	**Measuring Interest-Rate Risk: Gap Analysis and Duration Analysis** Bank managers use *gap analysis* and *duration analysis* to measure how vulnerable their banks are to interest-rate risk. **Gap analysis** looks at the difference, or *gap*, between the dollar value of a bank's variable-rate assets and the dollar value of its variable-rate liabilities. Most banks have negative gaps because their liabilities—mainly deposits—are more likely to have variable rates than

Table 10.2 Hypothetical Balance Sheet for Polktown National Bank

Polktown National Bank			
Assets		**Liabilities plus bank capital**	
Fixed-rate assets	$350 million	Fixed-rate liabilities	$250 million
Reserves		Checkable deposits	
Long-term marketable securities		Savings deposits	
Long-term loans		Long-term CDs	
Variable-rate assets	$150 million	Variable-rate liabilities	$210 million
Adjustable-rate loans		Short-term CDs	
Short-term securities		Federal funds	
		Bank capital	$ 40 million
Total assets	**$500 million**	**Total liabilities plus bank capital**	**$500 million**

are their assets—mainly loans and securities. For example, from Table 10.2, we can see that Polktown National Bank has a gap equal to $150 million $-$ $210 million $=$ $-$60 million. To simplify the analysis, suppose that the interest rates on all of Polktown's variable-rate assets and variable-rate liabilities increase by 2 percentage points over a one-year period. Then Polktown will earn $0.02 \times$ $150 million $=$ $3 million more on its assets but pay $0.02 \times$ $210 million $=$ $4.2 million more on its liabilities, so its profits will fall by $1.2 million. We can also calculate the fall in Polktown's profits directly by multiplying the change in the market interest rate by Polktown's gap: $0.02 \times$ $-$60 million $=$ $-$1.2 million. This simple gap analysis conveys the basics of how to calculate the vulnerability of a bank's profits to changes in market interest rates. In practice, though, a bank manager will conduct a more sophisticated analysis that takes into account the fact that different assets and liabilities are likely to experience different changes in interest rates.

In addition to affecting a bank's profits, changes in interest rates can affect a bank's capital by changing the value of the bank's assets and liabilities. We know that the longer the maturity of a financial asset, the larger the change in the asset's price as a result of a given change in interest rates. During the 1930s, Frederick Macaulay, an economist at the National Bureau of Economic Research, developed the concept of *duration* as a more precise measure than maturity of the sensitivity of a financial asset's price to changes in the interest rate.[2] The longer the duration of a particular bank asset or bank liability, the more the value of the asset or liability will change as a result of a change in market interest rates. **Duration analysis** measures how sensitive a bank's capital is to changes in market interest rates. A bank's *duration gap* is the difference between the

Duration analysis An analysis of how sensitive a bank's capital is to changes in market interest rates.

---

[2]For the mathematically minded, here is a more precise definition of duration: Duration is the weighted sum of the maturities of the payments from a financial asset, where the weights are equal to the present value of the payment divided by the present value of the asset. If we denote the present value of a payment at time t by PV_t, then the market value, MV, of an asset that matures in T periods is

$$MV = \sum_{t=1}^{T} PV_t, \text{ and the duration of the asset is } d = \sum_{t=1}^{T} t\left(\frac{PV_t}{MV}\right).$$

Table 10.3 Gap and Duration Analysis

Most banks have . . .	so an *increase* in market interest rates will . . .	and a *decrease* in market interest rates will . . .
a negative gap, and	*decrease* bank profits, and	*increase* bank profits, and
a positive duration gap,	*decrease* bank capital,	*increase* bank capital.

average duration of the bank's assets and the average duration of the bank's liabilities. If a bank has a positive duration gap, the duration of the bank's assets is greater than the duration of the bank's liabilities. In this case, an increase in market interest rates will reduce the value of the bank's assets more than the value of the bank's liabilities, which will decrease the bank's capital. Banks typically have positive duration gaps because their assets—mainly loans and securities—have longer durations than their liabilities—mainly deposits.

We summarize gap and duration analysis in Table 10.3. We can conclude that *falling* market interest rates are typically good news for banks because they will *increase* bank profits and the value of bank capital, while *rising* market interest rates are bad news for banks because they will *decrease* bank profits and the value of bank capital.

Reducing Interest-Rate Risk Bank managers can use a variety of strategies to reduce their exposure to interest-rate risk. Banks with negative gaps can make more adjustable-rate or *floating-rate* loans. That way, if market interest rates rise and banks must pay higher interest rates on deposits, they will also receive higher interest rates on their loans. Unfortunately for banks, many loan customers are reluctant to take out adjustable-rate loans because while the loans reduce the interest-rate risk banks face, they increase the interest-rate risk borrowers face. For example, if you buy a house using an adjustable-rate mortgage (ARM), your monthly payments will decline if market interest rates fall but rise if market interest rates rise. Many borrowers do not want to assume this interest-rate risk, so the great majority of residential mortgage loans are granted with fixed rates. Similarly, adjustable-rate car loans are rare. Fortunately for banks, they are able to sell many of their long-term loans as part of the securitization process that we have already discussed. In addition, many bank loans granted to businesses are short-term, variable-rate loans where the interest-rate risk is not very large.

Banks can use *interest-rate swaps* in which they agree to exchange, or swap, the payments from a fixed-rate loan for the payments on an adjustable-rate loan owned by a corporation or another financial firm (see Chapter 7). Swaps allow banks to satisfy the demands of their loan customers for fixed-rate loans while still reducing exposure to interest-rate risk. Banks can also use futures contracts and options contracts to help hedge interest-rate risk. Suppose, for example, that Polktown National Bank uses funds from variable-rate certificates of deposit (CDs) to make a long-term fixed-rate loan to a local auto parts factory. If interest rates rise, Polktown will have to pay higher interest rates on the CDs or lose the funds to another bank but will not receive an increase in interest payments on the fixed-rate loan. To reduce, or *hedge*, this interest-rate risk, Polktown could sell Treasury bill futures contracts. If market interest rates rise, the value of Treasury bill futures contracts will fall, which allows Polktown to earn a profit when it buys back the futures contracts to settle its position. This profit offsets the additional interest it will have to pay on the CDs. Polktown can undertake a similar hedge by using put options contracts on Treasury bills. (For a more complete discussion of futures and options contracts, see Chapter 7.)

Trends in the U.S. Commercial Banking Industry

The U.S. commercial banking industry has gone through tremendous changes over the years. In this section, we present a brief overview of the history of banking, as well as a look at important developments during the past 20 years, including the effects of the financial crisis of 2007–2009.

10.4
Learning Objective
Explain the trends in the U.S. commercial banking industry.

The Early History of U.S. Banking

For most of U.S. history, the overwhelming majority of banks have been small and have typically operated in limited geographical areas. After the failure of two early attempts to establish federally controlled banks with nationwide branches, for several decades all banks were *state banks*. This means that a bank had to obtain a charter—a legal document that allows a bank to operate—from the state government. The National Banking Act of 1863 made it possible for a bank to obtain a federal charter from the Office of the Comptroller of the Currency, which is part of the U.S. Treasury Department. Federally chartered banks are known as **national banks**. The United States currently has a **dual banking system** in which banks can be chartered either by state governments or by the federal government. The National Banking Acts of 1863 and 1864 also prohibited banks from using deposits to buy ownership of nonfinancial firms. This prohibition does not exist in some other countries, notably Germany and Japan.

National bank A federally chartered bank.

Dual banking system The system in the United States in which banks are chartered by either a state government or the federal government.

Bank Panics, the Federal Reserve, and the Federal Deposit Insurance Corporation

We have seen that banks can suffer from liquidity risk, which is driven by the possibility that depositors may collectively decide to withdraw more funds than the bank has immediately on hand. In the current banking system, this risk is relatively low because bank deposits are insured up to a limit of $250,000, which reduces the concern that depositors might otherwise have of losing their money in the event that their banks fail. In addition, the Federal Reserve plays the role of a *lender of last resort* by making discount loans to banks suffering from temporary liquidity problems. For most of the nineteenth and early twentieth centuries, however, neither federal deposit insurance nor the Federal Reserve existed. As a result, banks were subject to periodic *bank runs*, in which large numbers of depositors would decide that a bank might be in danger of failure and would simultaneously demand their deposits back. If a few banks were hit with runs, they might be able to satisfy depositors' demand for funds by borrowing from other banks. But if many banks simultaneously experienced runs, the result would be a *bank panic*, which often resulted in banks being unable to return depositors' money and having to temporarily close their doors. With households and firms cut off from their deposits and from access to credit, bank panics typically resulted in recessions. A particularly severe panic in 1907 finally convinced Congress that a central bank capable of serving as a lender of last resort was needed. Congress passed the Federal Reserve Act in December 1913, and the Federal Reserve System began operation in 1914.

Although the establishment of the Federal Reserve System put a temporary end to bank panics, they recurred in the early 1930s, during the Great Depression. Congress responded by setting up a system of federal deposit insurance run by the Federal Deposit Insurance Corporation (FDIC), which was established in 1934. All national banks were required to join the system, and state banks were given the option of joining. Today, about 99% of all depositors are fully insured, so most depositors have little incentive to withdraw their money and cause their bank to fail if there are questions about the bank's financial health. The FDIC generally handles bank failures in one of two ways: It closes the bank and pays off depositors, or it purchases and assumes control of the bank while finding another bank that is willing to purchase the failed bank. If the FDIC closes a bank, it pays off the insured depositors immediately, using the bank's assets. If those funds are insufficient, the FDIC makes up the difference from its insurance reserves, which come from assessments the FDIC levies on insured banks. After the FDIC has compensated insured depositors, any remaining funds are paid to uninsured depositors.

The FDIC prefers to keep failed banks open rather than close them. To keep a bank open, the FDIC will quickly find another bank that is willing to take over the failing bank—usually before the FDIC takes control of the failing bank. Another bank may be willing to take over the failing bank in order to enter a new geographical area or to gain access to the failed bank's deposit and loan customers. If the FDIC has to purchase and assume control of a failed bank, the FDIC typically incurs costs in the transition. Generally, it tries to find an acquiring bank to take on *all* of the failed bank's deposits. In that case, the FDIC subsidizes the acquisition by providing loans at low interest rates or by buying problem loans in the failed bank's portfolio. As Figure 10.2 shows, during the 2007–2009 financial crisis, the number of bank failures increased sharply, although failures did not reach the high levels seen during the savings and loan crisis of the late 1980s. (We discuss the savings and loan crisis in Chapter 12.) A number of failures

MyEconLab Real-time data

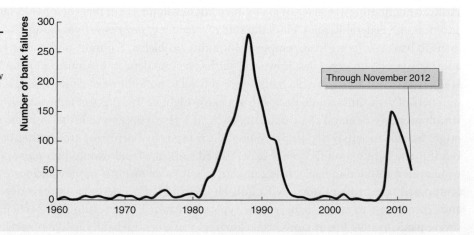

Figure 10.2

Commercial Bank Failures in the United States, 1960–2012

Bank failures in the United States were at low levels from 1960 until the savings and loan crisis of the mid-1980s. By the mid-1990s, bank failures had returned to low levels, where they remained until the beginning of the financial crisis in 2007.

Note: The total for 2012 is through November.

Source: Federal Deposit Insurance Corporation.

following the financial crisis were of large institutions, which required substantial expenditures by the FDIC.

The Rise of Nationwide Banking

A series of federal laws limited the ability of banks to operate in more than one state. The most recent of these was the McFadden Act, which Congress passed in 1927. In addition, most states were *unit banking states*, which means that they had regulations prohibiting banks from having more than one branch. Research by David Wheelock of the Federal Reserve Bank of St. Louis has shown that in 1900, of the 12,427 commercial banks in the United States, only 87 had any branches. By contrast, for many years, most other countries have had relatively few banks, each operating branches nationwide.

The U.S. system of many small, geographically limited banks was the result of political views that the power of banks should be limited by keeping them small and that the deposits banks received should be used only to fund loans in the local area. But most economists believe the U.S. system was inefficient because it failed to take full advantage of economies of scale in banking. *Economies of scale* refers to the reduction in average cost that results from an increase in volume (see Chapter 9). Larger banks are able to spread their fixed costs, such as the salaries of loan officers, computer systems, and the costs of operating bank buildings, over a larger volume of transactions. Keeping banks limited to a small geographical area was also inefficient because it exposed banks to greater credit risk by concentrating their loans in one area.

Over time, restrictions on the size and geographical scope of banking were gradually removed. After the mid-1970s, most states eliminated restrictions on branching within the state. In 1994, Congress passed the Riegle-Neal Interstate Banking and Branching Efficiency Act, which allowed for the phased removal of restrictions on interstate banking. The 1998 merger of NationsBank, based in North Carolina, and Bank of America, based in California, produced the first bank with branches on both coasts.

Rapid consolidation in the U.S. banking industry has resulted from these regulatory changes. While in 1975, there were 14,384 commercial banks in the United States, in 2012, there were only 6,222. This number is still much greater than in most other countries, so it seems likely that further consolidation will take place, and the number of banks will continue to dwindle. The decline in the number of banks understates the degree of consolidation in the U. S. banking industry. As Table 10.4 shows, the largest 10 banks have more than half of all deposits, with the top 3 banks having almost one-third.

During 2010, as Congress enacted changes in financial regulation, some members of the House and Senate suggested placing limits on the size of banks. They argued that when banks become too large, they acquire market power that enables them to pay lower interest rates to depositors and charge higher interest rates on loans. In addition, some economists and policymakers worried that large banks were "too big to fail," meaning that their failure would cause such financial disruption that the Federal Reserve, the FDIC, and the U.S. Treasury would be forced to take measures to keep them from bankruptcy however poorly they may have been managed. The Dodd-Frank Act of 2010 did not specifically limit bank size, although it did put some limits on the methods the FDIC and other federal regulators can use to save large banks that are at risk of failing (see Chapter 12). The debate over whether there should be regulatory limits on the size of banks continues.

Table 10.4 The 10 Largest U.S. Banks, 2012

Bank	Share of total deposits
JPMorgan Chase	12.0%
Bank of America	11.1
Wells Fargo Bank	9.9
Citigroup	9.7
U.S. Bancorp	2.5
Capital One	2.3
PNC	2.2
Bank of New York Mellon	2.1
TD Bank	1.8
State Street Bank	1.4
Total for top 10 banks	**54.9%**

Source: Federal Deposit Insurance Corporation; data are for the first quarter of 2012.

Expanding the Boundaries of Banking

The activities of banks have changed dramatically during the past five decades. Between 1960 and 2012, banks increased the amount of funds they raise from time deposits and negotiable CDs, and they increased their borrowings in the federal funds market and from repurchase agreements. Banks also reduced their reliance on C&I loans and on consumer loans, and they increased their reliance on real estate loans. In addition, banks have expanded into nontraditional lending activities and into activities where their revenue is generated from fees rather than from interest.

Off-Balance-Sheet Activities Banks have increasingly turned to generating *fee income* from *off-balance-sheet activities*. Traditional banking activity, such as taking in deposits and making loans, affects a bank's balance sheet because deposits appear on the balance sheet as liabilities, and loans appear as assets. **Off-balance-sheet activities** do not affect the bank's balance sheet because they do not increase either the bank's assets or its liabilities. For instance, when a bank buys and sells foreign exchange for customers, the bank charges the customers a fee for the service, but the foreign exchange does not appear on the bank's balance sheet. Banks also charge fees for *private banking* services to high-income households—those with a net worth of $1 million or more. Banks have come to rely on the following four off-balance-sheet activities to earn fee income:

1. *Standby letters of credit.* We have seen that during the 1970s and 1980s, banks lost some of their commercial lending business to the commercial paper market. As the commercial paper market developed, most buyers insisted that sellers provide a *standby letter of credit*. With a **standby letter of credit**, a bank promises to lend funds to the borrower—the seller of the commercial paper—to pay off its maturing commercial paper, if necessary. Banks generally charge a fee equal to 0.5% of the value of the commercial paper. Today, not only corporations but also state and

Off-balance-sheet activities Activities that do not affect a bank's balance sheet because they do not increase either the bank's assets or its liabilities.

Standby letter of credit A promise by a bank to lend funds, if necessary, to a seller of commercial paper at the time that the commercial paper matures.

local governments typically need standby letters of credit in order to sell commercial paper. Using standby letters of credit essentially splits the granting of credit into two parts: (1) credit-risk analysis through information gathering, and (2) actual lending. Banks can provide credit-risk analysis efficiently, while financial markets can provide the actual lending more inexpensively. Unlike conventional loans, standby letters of credit do not appear on bank balance sheets.

2. *Loan commitments.* In a **loan commitment**, a bank agrees to provide a borrower with a stated amount of funds during a specified period of time. Borrowers then have the option of deciding when or if they want to take the loan. Banks earn a fee for loan commitments. The fee is usually split into two parts: an *upfront fee* when the commitment is written and a *nonusage fee* on the unused portion of the loan. For loans that are actually made, the interest rate charged is a markup over a benchmark lending rate. Loan commitments fix the markup over the benchmark rate in advance but not the interest rate to be charged if the loan is made because the interest rate will vary with the benchmark rate. In addition, the bank's commitment to lend ceases if the borrower's financial condition deteriorates below a specified level.

> **Loan commitment** An agreement by a bank to provide a borrower with a stated amount of funds during a specified period of time.

3. *Loan sales.* We have already seen that *loan securitization* has been an important development in the U.S. financial system. With securitization, rather than holding the loans in their own portfolios, banks convert bundles of loans into securities that are sold directly to investors through financial markets. As part of the trend toward securitization since the 1980s, the market for bank loan sales in the United States grew from almost nothing to a substantial size. A **loan sale** is a financial contract in which a bank agrees to sell the expected future returns from an underlying bank loan to a third party. Loan sales are also called *secondary loan participations*. Formally, the loan contract is sold *without recourse*, which means that the bank provides no guarantee of the value of the loan sold and no insurance. Large banks sell loans primarily to domestic and foreign banks and to other financial institutions. Originally, banks sold only short-term, high-quality loans with low information-gathering and monitoring costs. Increasingly, however, banks are selling lesser-quality and longer-term loans. By selling loans, banks put their reputations on the line rather than their capital. A bank whose loans perform poorly is unlikely to remain a successful player in that market.

> **Loan sale** A financial contract in which a bank agrees to sell the expected future returns from an underlying bank loan to a third party.

4. *Trading activities.* Banks earn fees from trading in the multibillion-dollar markets for futures, options, and interest-rate swaps. Bank trading in these markets is primarily related to hedging the banks' own loan and securities portfolios or to hedging services provided for bank customers. But banks sometimes speculate in these markets by buying or selling, with the expectation that they can make a profit on changes in prices. Speculation, of course, carries the risk of losing money. The bank employees responsible for trading are often compensated on the basis of the profits they earn. So, a principal–agent problem can occur, with these employees taking on more risk—in the hope of earning higher profits and higher compensation—than the bank's top managers or its shareholders would prefer. During the financial crisis of 2007–2009, members of Congress became concerned that losses from trading in securities had worsened the financial situation at some banks. When Congress passed the Dodd-Frank Act in 2010, it included a provision based on a proposal

developed by former Federal Reserve Chairman Paul Volcker, who was serving as head of President Obama's economic recovery advisory board. Under the "Volcker Rule," banks have to give up trading for their own accounts, or they will no longer be eligible for financial support from the federal government should they need it in a future financial crisis.

Banks generate fee income from off-balance-sheet activities, but they also take on additional risk. To assess their exposure to risk in off-balance-sheet activities, banks have developed sophisticated computer models. One popular model, known as the *value-at-risk (VAR) approach*, uses statistical models to estimate the maximum losses a portfolio's value is likely to sustain over a particular time period—hence the name "value at risk." These models have been helpful to banks in assessing risk, but they proved to be far less than foolproof in shielding banks from heavy losses during the financial crisis of 2007–2009, mainly because they did not fully account for credit risk in trading assets.

Electronic Banking The development of inexpensive computer processing and the rise of the Internet have revolutionized how many banking transactions are handled. The first important development in electronic banking was the spread of automated teller machines (ATMs). ATMs for the first time allowed depositors regular access to their funds outside normal banking hours. Rather than having to arrive at a bank between 10 A.M. and 3 P.M., depositors could now withdraw money at 2 A.M. if they wanted to. ATMs were attractive to banks because once installed, the costs of running and maintaining them were far less than the costs of paying bank tellers. In addition, in states that restricted branch banking, ATMs were particularly appealing because they were not legally considered branches, so they allowed banks to extend their operations into areas where they could not have opened branches.

By the mid-1990s, *virtual banks* began to appear. These banks have no brick-and-mortar bank buildings but instead carry out all their banking activities online. Customers can open accounts, pay bills electronically, and have their paychecks directly deposited—all without paper. ING Direct, an online bank that is owned by Capital One, has more than 7.5 million depositors in the United States. By the mid-2000s, most traditional banks had also begun providing online services that allow depositors to easily pay some or all of their bills electronically rather than by paper check, typically without being charged a fee. Loan applications can also be made online, with the bulk of the approval process handled electronically; however, borrowers typically have to provide some paper documents as part of the process. Banks have also begun to clear the vast majority of checks electronically. Until a few years ago, if you deposited a check written against an account at another bank, your bank (or the Federal Reserve, which provided check-clearing services for banks) would have to physically send the check to the other bank in order to receive payment. Today, your bank is likely to clear the check by sending an electronic image of it to the other bank.

Virtual banking has played an increasing role in the banking industry, but brick-and-mortar bank branches continue to be built, and a majority of payments made using checking accounts still involve paper checks. The trend toward substituting electrons for paper in the banking industry seems clear, though.

Making the Connection	In Your Interest

Is Your Neighborhood ATM About to Disappear?

ATMs came into widespread use in the United States during the early 1970s and revolutionized banking. For the first time, customers could withdraw money and deposit checks without waiting in line for a teller during normal banking hours. Banks were also able to process more transactions with fewer employees, thereby increasing productivity. Some economists have argued that ATMs were the first important product of modern information technology because they appeared before personal computers became widely available. ATMs have continued to evolve over the years, and current ATMs can, among other things, accept deposits without an envelope and are equipped with scanners that are capable of detecting counterfeit currency.

As important as ATMs have been in banking for more than 40 years, is it possible that they are on their way out? There are conflicting influences on ATM usage. As we have seen, banks have responded to regulations that limit the fees they can charge merchants for processing debit cards and regulations limiting overdraft charges by increasing monthly charges on basic checking accounts and by reducing some services offered to lower-income customers. Some banks have closed branches in lower-income neighborhoods, forcing customers to either use ATMs or to travel further to use a branch. A few banks have even begun charging customers fees if they use a bank teller for transactions that could be handled by using an ATM. These developments have led to increased use of ATMs.

Other developments, however, are leading to reduced use of ATMs. For example, increased use of debit cards has reduced the demand for currency, thereby reducing the necessity of using ATMs. A possibly greater threat to ATMs, though, may come from smart phones and other mobile devices. New software, such as Apple's Passbook for its iPhone, makes it possible for consumers to pay for some goods using their phones. Industry analysts disagree about how likely consumers are to use this software, but it seems likely the software will further reduce the demand for currency. ATMs are much less costly to banks than are bank branches, but ATMs still have to be maintained, filled with cash, and have deposits picked up. It costs a bank about $1,100 per month to run an ATM at a branch and $1,700 per month to run one at a mall, a service station, or another location the bank doesn't own. As usage of ATMs has declined, some locations have ceased to be profitable. In 2012, Bank of America announced that it was eliminating more than 1,500 ATMs, primarily in malls and service stations.

Whether the ATM, once seen as a marvel of modern information technology, will go the way of the electric typewriter remains to be seen.

Sources: Robin Sidel, "Banks Join the Do-It-Yourself Craze," *Wall Street Journal*, May 15, 2012; Ann Carrns, "Whither the ATM?" *New York Times*, July 25, 2012; Rachel Swaby, "Safe, Smart, and … Fun? The Surprising Science of ATMs," gizmodo.com, March 22, 2012; and Hugh Son and Zachary Tracer, "BofA Yanks Most Teller Machines from Malls, Gas Stations," Bloomberg.com, July 23, 2012.

See related problem 4.9 at the end of the chapter.

The Financial Crisis, TARP, and Partial Government Ownership of Banks

Many of the subprime and Alt-A mortgage loans that banks granted during the financial crisis of 2007–2009 had been securitized and resold to investors. Banks held some of these securities as investments, and, as Figure 10.1 on page 287 shows, banks had also become dependent on making real estate loans. As the financial crisis unfolded, first residential real estate mortgages and then commercial real estate mortgages suffered higher default rates, causing securities based on both types of mortgages to decline in value. By mid-2008, housing prices in the 20 largest metropolitan areas had declined by more than 15%, and more than 6% of all mortgages—and 25% of subprime mortgages—were at least 30 days past due. The market for mortgage-backed securities froze, meaning that buying and selling of these securities largely stopped, making it very difficult to determine their market prices. These securities began to be called "toxic assets."

Evaluating the balance sheets of banks became difficult because neither investors nor banks themselves were sure of the true market value of these toxic assets. So, the true value of bank capital—or even whether a bank still had positive net worth—was difficult to determine. Beginning in August 2007, banks responded to their worsening balance sheets by tightening credit standards for consumer and commercial loans. The resulting *credit crunch* helped cause the recession that started in December 2007, as households and firms had increased difficulty funding their spending.

Troubled Asset Relief Program (TARP) A government program under which the U.S. Treasury purchased stock in hundreds of banks to increase the banks' capital.

In October 2008, to deal with the problems banks were facing, Congress passed the **Troubled Asset Relief Program (TARP)**. TARP provided the Treasury and the Fed with $700 billion in funding to help restore the market for mortgage-backed securities and other toxic assets in order to provide relief to financial firms that had trillions of dollars' worth of these assets on their balance sheets. Unfortunately, no good way of restoring a market for these assets was developed, so some of the funds were used instead for "capital injections" into banks. Under this program, called the Capital Purchase Program (CPP), the Treasury purchased stock in hundreds of banks, thereby increasing the banks' capital, just as any issuance of new stock would have done. Participating banks were required to pay the Treasury a yearly dividend equal to 5% of the value of the stock and to issue warrants that would allow the Treasury to purchase additional shares equal to 15% of the value of the Treasury's original investment. Although the Treasury stock purchases amounted to partial government ownership of hundreds of banks, the Treasury did not attempt to become involved in the management decisions of any of the banks. Table 10.5 shows the 10 largest Treasury investments under the program.

Some economists and policymakers criticized the TARP/CPP program as a "bailout" of banks or of Wall Street. Some economists argued that by providing funds to banks that had made bad loans and invested in risky assets, the Treasury was encouraging bad business decisions, thereby increasing the extent of moral hazard in the financial system. Fears were also raised that the managers of banks that had received Treasury investments might feel pressure to make lending and investment decisions on the basis of political, rather than business, concerns. Treasury and Fed officials feared that a surge in bank failures might plunge the U.S. economy into another Great Depression and argued that the program was justified, given the severity of the financial downturn. Criticism of the program lessened as the economy and banking system began to revive and many

Table 10.5 The 10 Banks Receiving the Largest Treasury Investments Under the TARP/CPP Program

Bank	Amount of Treasury investment
JPMorgan Chase	$25 billion
Citigroup Inc.	25 billion
Wells Fargo & Company	25 billion
Bank of America Corporation	10 billion
Goldman Sachs	10 billion
Morgan Stanley	10 billion
PNC Financial Services Group, Inc.	7.579 billion
U.S. Bancorp	6.599 billion
SunTrust Banks, Inc.	4.850 billion
Capital One Financial Corporation	3.555 billion

Source: www.financialstability.gov, "Monthly Report to Congress," September 2012.

banks bought back the Treasury's stock investment. During the period from October 1, 2008, through September 30, 2009, the Treasury had invested $245 billion in the CPP. By late 2012, $266 billion had been paid back or received as interest or dividends, leaving the program with a profit of $21 billion.

Answering the Key Question

Continued from page 279

Continued from page 279

At the beginning of this chapter, we asked:

"Is banking a particularly risky business? If so, what types of risks do banks face?"

In a market system, businesses of all types face risks, and many businesses fail. Economists and policymakers are particularly concerned about the risk and potential for failure that banks face because they play a vital role in the financial system. In this chapter, we have seen that the basic business of commercial banking—borrowing money short term from depositors and lending it long term to households and firms—entails several types of risks: liquidity risk, credit risk, and interest-rate risk.

Key Terms and Problems

Key Terms

Asset, p. 281

Balance sheet, p. 281

Bank capital, p. 281

Bank leverage, p. 293

Checkable deposits, p. 282

Credit rationing, p. 295

Credit risk, p. 294

Credit-risk analysis, p. 294

Dual banking system, p. 299

Duration analysis, p. 297

Excess reserves, p. 285

Federal deposit insurance, p. 283

Gap analysis, p. 296

Interest-rate risk, p. 296

Leverage, p. 293

Liability, p. 281

Liquidity risk, p. 293

Loan commitment, p. 303

Loan sale, p. 303

National bank, p. 299

Net interest margin, p. 292

Off-balance-sheet activities, p. 302

Prime rate, p. 295

Required reserves, p. 285

Reserves, p. 285
Return on assets (ROA), p. 292
Return on equity (ROE), p. 292

Standby letter of credit, p. 302
T-account, p. 289

Troubled Asset Relief Program
(TARP), p. 306
Vault cash, p. 285

10.1 The Basics of Commercial Banking: The Bank Balance Sheet
Understand bank balance sheets.

Review Questions

1.1 Write the key accounting equation on which balance sheets are based. What are the most important bank assets? What are the most important bank liabilities?

1.2 According to this chapter: "We can think of a bank's liabilities as the sources of its funds, and we can think of a bank's assets as the uses of its funds." Briefly explain what this statement means.

1.3 How have the types of loans banks make changed over time?

Problems and Applications

1.4 If commercial banks were allowed to purchase significant amounts of stock in the companies to which they make loans, would this increase or decrease the extent of moral hazard in the financial system? Briefly explain.

1.5 [Related to the Making the Connection on page 283] In 1960, federal regulations prohibited banks from paying interest on checking accounts. Today, banks are legally allowed to pay interest on checking accounts, yet the value of checking accounts has shrunk from more than 50% of commercial bank liabilities in 1960 to less than 12%. Because checking accounts now pay interest, shouldn't they have become more popular with households rather than less popular?

1.6 [Related to the Chapter Opener on page 279] An article in the *Wall Street Journal* in 2012 noted: "A battle over who gets stuck with tens of billions worth of bad housing loans made during the boom years explains why many Americans still can't get a mortgage."

a. Who was battling over bad housing loans? Why were they battling?

b. Why would a battle over bad loans made years ago reduce the number of new loans that banks were willing to make?

Source: Nick Timiraos, "Burdened by Old Mortgages, Banks Are Slow to Lend Now," *Wall Street Journal*, October 3, 2012.

1.7 [Related to Solved Problem 10.1 on page 288] The following entries (in millions of dollars) are from the balance sheet of Rivendell National Bank (RNB):

U.S. Treasury bills	$20
Demand deposits	40
Mortgage-backed securities	30
Loans from other banks	5
C&I loans	50
Discount loans	5
NOW accounts	40
Savings accounts	10
Reserve deposits with Federal Reserve	8
Cash items in the process of collection	5
Municipal bonds	5
Bank building	4

a. Use the entries to construct a balance sheet similar to the one in Table 10.1 on page 281, with assets on the left side of the balance sheet and liabilities and bank capital on the right side.

b. RNB's capital is what percentage of its assets?

1.8 A few years ago, Congress was considering having the federal government set up a "lending fund" for small banks. The U.S. Treasury would lend the funds to banks. The more of the funds

---

the banks loaned to small businesses, the lower the interest rate the Treasury would charge the banks on the loans. A member of Congress was asked to comment on whether the bill would be helpful to small businesses. Here is part of the member's response:

> The bank that's struggling to write down their commercial real estate assets is having to take a hit to capital, and this provides replacement capital on very, very favorable terms. So it deals with the left side of the balance sheet.

a. Would a loan from the Treasury be counted as part of a bank's capital?

b. Does a bank's capital appear on the left side of the bank's balance sheet?

Source: Robb Mandelbaum, "Can Government Help Small Businesses?" *New York Times*, July 29, 2010.

10.2 The Basic Operations of a Commercial Bank
Describe the basic operations of a commercial bank.

Review Questions

2.1 Use a T-account to show the effect on Bank of America's balance sheet of your depositing $50 in currency in your checking account.

2.2 What is the difference between a bank's return on assets (ROA) and its return on equity (ROE)? How are they related?

2.3 Why might the managers of a bank want the bank to be highly leveraged? Why might the bank's shareholders want the bank to be less highly leveraged?

Problems and Applications

2.4 Suppose that Bank of America sells $10 million in Treasury bills to PNC Bank. Use T-accounts to show the effect of this transaction on the balance sheet of each bank.

2.5 Suppose that Lena, who has an account at SunTrust Bank, writes a check for $100 to José, who has an account at National City Bank. Use T-accounts to show how the balance sheets of each bank will be affected after the check clears.

2.6 Suppose that National Bank of Guerneville (NBG) has $34 million in checkable deposits, Commonwealth Bank has $47 million in checkable deposits, and the required reserve ratio for checkable deposits is 10%. If NBG has $4 million in reserves, and Commonwealth has $5 million in reserves, how much in excess reserves does each bank have? Now suppose that a customer of NBG writes a check for $1 million to a real estate broker who deposits the check at Commonwealth. After the check clears, how much does each bank have in excess reserves?

2.7 [Related to the Making the Connection **on page 291**] An article in the *Wall Street Journal* noted that new federal banking regulations "mean only a 5 percent reduction in [bank] revenue ... from households with $500,000 in assets or more compared with a 35 percent decline ... from customers with balances of $5,000 or less."

a. What new banking regulations is the article referring to?

b. Why would these regulations have smaller effects on what banks earn from high-income customers than on what they earn from lower-income customers?

Source: Nelson D. Schwartz, "Got $100,000? Have a Cookie: Banks Try Luring the Top 10%," *New York Times*, March 10, 2012.

2.8 Suppose that the value of a bank's assets is $40 billion and the value of its liabilities is $36 billion. If the bank has a 2% ROA, then what is its ROE?

2.9 Suppose that First National Bank has $200 million in assets and $20 million in equity capital.

a. If First National has a 2% ROA, what is its ROE?

b. Suppose that First National's equity capital declines to $10 million, while its assets and ROA are unchanged. What is First National's ROE now?

2.10 An article in the *Wall Street Journal* argues that for investors to continue to see banks as good investments, the banks need an ROE of at least 12%. The average ROE for U.S. banks in 2012 was only 7%. The article states that ROE for U.S. banks has declined since the financial crisis in part because banks have "set aside more capital and reduced the debt they can take on to turbo-charge profits."

a. Why would banks have set aside more capital and reduced debt as a result of the financial crisis?

b. Why would increasing capital and reducing debt have reduced banks' ROE?

Source: Francesco Guerrera, "At Big Banks, ROE Woe," *Wall Street Journal*, October 15, 2012.

2.11 Suppose that you are considering investing in a bank that is earning a higher ROE than most other banks. You learn that the bank has $300 million in capital and $5 billion in assets. Would you become an investor in this bank? Briefly explain.

10.3 Managing Bank Risk
Explain how banks manage risk.

Review Questions

3.1 Discuss the steps banks take to manage liquidity risk, credit risk, and interest-rate risk.

3.2 What is the difference between gap analysis and duration analysis? What is the purpose of gap analysis, and what is the purpose of duration analysis?

Problems and Applications

3.3 Before 1933, there was no federal deposit insurance. Was the liquidity risk faced by banks during those years likely to have been larger or smaller than it is today? Briefly explain.

3.4 Does the existence of reserve requirements make it easier for banks to deal with bank runs? Briefly explain.

3.5 Briefly explain whether you agree with the following statements:

a. "A bank that expects interest rates to increase in the future will want to hold more rate-sensitive assets and fewer rate-sensitive liabilities."

b. "A bank that expects interest rates to decrease in the future will want the duration of its assets to be greater than the duration of its liabilities—a positive duration gap."

c. "If a bank manager expects interest rates to fall in the future, the manager should increase the duration of the bank's liabilities."

3.6 A Congresswoman introduces a bill to outlaw credit rationing by banks. The bill would require that every applicant be granted a loan, no matter how high the risk that the applicant would not pay back the loan. She defends the bill by arguing:

There is nothing in this bill that precludes banks from charging whatever interest rate they would like on their loans; they simply have to give a loan to everyone who applies. If the banks are smart, they will set their interest rates so that the expected return on each loan—after taking into account the probability that the applicant will default on the loan—is the same.

Evaluate the Congresswoman's argument and the likely effects of the bill on the banking system.

3.7 The following entries (in millions of dollars) are from the balance sheet of Rivendell National Bank (RNB):

U.S. Treasury bills	$20
Demand deposits	40
Mortgage-backed securities	30
Loans from other banks	5
C&I loans	50
Discount loans	5
NOW accounts	40
Savings accounts	10
Reserve deposits with Federal Reserve	8
Cash items in the process of collection	5
Municipal bonds	5
Bank building	4

If RNB's assets have an average duration of five years and its liabilities have an average duration of three years, what is RNB's duration gap?

10.4 Trends in the U.S. Commercial Banking Industry

Explain the trends in the U.S. commercial banking industry.

Review Questions

4.1 Why is the United States said to have a dual banking system?

4.2 Why was the FDIC established?

4.3 Why did nationwide banking come relatively late to the United States compared with other countries?

4.4 List four off-balance-sheet activities and briefly explain what they are.

4.5 What are the key developments in electronic banking?

4.6 When and why was TARP created?

Problems and Applications

4.7 Evaluate the following statement:

The United States has more than 6,000 banks, while Canada has only a few. Therefore, the U.S. banking industry must be more competitive than the Canadian banking industry.

4.8 In 2012, an article in the *Wall Street Journal* described how Amazon had begun making loans to the small businesses that sell on its site. Many of these businesses had previously been turned down for bank loans. An Amazon spokesman was quoted as saying: "Our goal is to solve a difficult problem for sellers."

a. Why might Amazon have been willing to make loans to small businesses that banks were not willing to make?

b. What would be the advantages and disadvantages to a small business of borrowing from Amazon rather than from a bank? What would be the advantages and disadvantages to Amazon of making the loan?

Source: Sarah E. Needleman and Greg Bensinger, "Small Businesses Are Finding an Unlikely Banker: Amazon," *Wall Street Journal*, October 4, 2012.

4.9 [Related to the Making the Connection on page 305] A bank analyst was quoted as saying: "There are very real expenses to owning and operating ATMs.... In the current environment, banks are unable to support the cost structure they have historically."

a. What does the analyst mean by "the current environment"?

b. What has happened to make some ATMs unprofitable?

c. Are the number of ATMs in the United States likely to increase or decrease over time? Briefly explain.

Source: Hugh Son and Zachary Tracer, "BofA Yanks Most Teller Machines from Malls, Gas Stations," *Bloomberg Businessweek*, July 23, 2012

4.10 The Capital Purchase Program carried out under TARP represented an attempt by the federal government to increase the capital of banks. Why would the federal government consider it important to increase bank capital? What might be some of the consequences of banks having insufficient capital?

4.11 A bank executive was quoted as arguing that: "TARP successfully stabilized not only the banking industry but a number of other industries as well." Why might stabilizing the banking industry have stabilized other industries?

Source: Jeffrey Sparshott, "Bank CEO: History Will Be Kind to TARP," *Wall Street Journal*, August 15, 2012.

Data Exercises

D10.1: [Movements in banks' net interest margins]
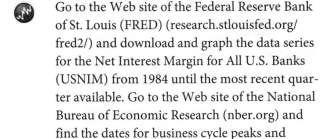
Go to the Web site of the Federal Reserve Bank of St. Louis (FRED) (research.stlouisfed.org/fred2/) and download and graph the data series for the Net Interest Margin for All U.S. Banks (USNIM) from 1984 until the most recent quarter available. Go to the Web site of the National Bureau of Economic Research (nber.org) and find the dates for business cycle peaks and troughs. (The period between a business cycle peak and trough is a recession.)

a. Describe how net interest margins move just before, during, and just after a recession.

b. Is there a long-term trend in net interest margins? What are the implications for bank profitability?

D10.2: [Nonperforming loans and recessions] Go to the Web site of the Federal Reserve Bank of St. Louis (FRED) (research.stlouisfed.org/fred2/) and download and graph the data series for Nonperforming Total Loans (NPTLTL) from January 1988 until the most recent quarter available. Go to the Web site of the National Bureau of Economic Research (nber.org) and find the dates for business cycle peaks and troughs. (The period between a business cycle peak and trough is a recession.)

a. Describe how nonperforming loans move just before, during, and just after a recession. Is the pattern the same across the three recessions in your data? Briefly explain.

b. Is there a long-term trend in nonperforming loans? What are the implications for bank profitability?

D10.3: [Long-term trend in the number of banks]
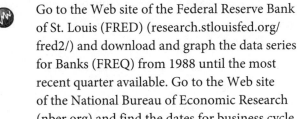
Go to the Web site of the Federal Reserve Bank of St. Louis (FRED) (research.stlouisfed.org/fred2/) and download and graph the data series for Banks (FREQ) from 1988 until the most recent quarter available. Go to the Web site of the National Bureau of Economic Research (nber.org) and find the dates for business cycle peaks and troughs. (The period between a business cycle peak and trough is a recession.)

a. Describe the trend in the number of banks in the United States during these years. Briefly discuss the factors that account for this trend.

b. Do your data indicate a significant effect of recessions on the number of banks in the United States? Briefly explain.

MyEconLab   Visit **www.myeconlab.com** to complete these exercises online and get instant feedback. Exercises that update with real-time data are marked with .

Investment Banks, Mutual Funds, Hedge Funds, and the Shadow Banking System

Learning Objectives

After studying this chapter, you should be able to:

11.1 Explain how investment banks operate (pages 314–327)

11.2 Distinguish between mutual funds and hedge funds and describe their roles in the financial system (pages 327–334)

11.3 Explain the roles that pension funds and insurance companies play in the financial system (pages 334–338)

11.4 Explain the connection between the shadow banking system and systemic risk (pages 339–342)

When Is A Bank Not A Bank? When It's A Shadow Bank!

What is a hedge fund? What is the difference between a commercial bank and an investment bank? At the beginning of the financial crisis of 2007–2009, most Americans would have been unable to answer these questions. Many members of Congress were in a similar situation. Most people were also unfamiliar with mortgage-backed securities (MBSs), collateralized debt obligations (CDOs), credit default swaps (CDSs), and other ingredients in the new alphabet soup of financial securities. The increasing familiarity of these new terms signaled that commercial banks no longer played the dominant role in routing funds from savers to borrowers. Instead, a variety of "nonbank" financial institutions were acquiring funds that had previously been deposited in banks, and they were using these funds to provide credit that banks had previously provided. These nonbanks were using newly developed financial securities that even long-time veterans of Wall Street often did not fully understand.

At a conference hosted by the Federal Reserve Bank of Kansas City in 2007, just as the financial crisis was beginning, Paul McCulley, a managing director of Pacific Investment Management Company (PIMCO), coined the label *shadow banking system* to describe the new role of nonbank financial firms. A year later, the term became well known after Timothy Geithner used it in a speech to the Economic Club of New York. Geithner was then the president of the Federal Reserve

Continued on next page

Key Issue and Question

Issue: During the 1990s and 2000s, the flow of funds from lenders to borrowers outside the banking system increased.

Question: Does the shadow banking system pose a threat to the stability of the U.S. financial system?

Answered on page 342

Bank of New York and later became secretary of the Treasury in the Obama administration. A Federal Reserve study indicates that by 2008, the shadow banking system had grown to be more than 50% larger than the commercial banking system.

As the financial crisis worsened, two large investment banks—Bear Stearns and Lehman Brothers—and an insurance company—American International Group (AIG)—were at the center of the storm. Although many commercial banks were also drawn into the crisis, 2007–2009 represented the first time in U.S. history that a major financial crisis had not originated in the commercial banking system. Problems with nonbanks made dealing with the crisis more difficult because U.S. policymaking and regulatory structures were based on the assumption that commercial banks were the most important financial firms. In particular, the Federal Reserve System had been set up in 1913 to stabilize and regulate the commercial banking system.

Partly as a result of the financial crisis, the size of the shadow banking system has declined relative to the size of the commercial banking system, although shadow banking remains larger. Following the financial crisis, in 2010 Congress passed the Wall Street Reform and Consumer Protection Act, or the Dodd-Frank Act, which increased to some extent federal regulation of the shadow banking system. But a number of policymakers and economists continue to believe that shadow banking remains a source of instability in the financial system.

Sources: Zoltan Pozar, et al., "The Shadow Banking System," Federal Reserve Bank of New York, Staff Report No. 458, July 2010, Revised February 2012; Timothy F. Geithner, "Reducing Systemic Risk in a Dynamic Financial System," talk at The Economic Club of New York, June 9, 2008; and Paul McCulley, "Discussion," Federal Reserve Bank of Kansas City, *Housing, Housing Finance, and Monetary Policy*, 2007, p. 485.

In this chapter, we describe the different types of firms that make up the shadow banking system, explore why this system developed, and discuss whether it poses a threat to financial stability.

11.1 Investment Banking

Learning Objective

Explain how investment banks operate.

When most people think of "Wall Street" or "Wall Street firms," they think of investment banks. Firms such as Goldman Sachs, Merrill Lynch, and JPMorgan have been familiar names from the business news. During the 2000s, the fabulous financial rewards some of their employees earned inspired many undergraduates to pursue careers on Wall Street. In this section, we discuss the basics of investment banking and how it has changed over time.

What Is an Investment Bank?

The basis of commercial banking is taking in deposits and making loans. In contrast, **investment banking** is mainly concerned with the following activities:

Investment banking
Financial activities that involve underwriting new security issues and providing advice on mergers and acquisitions.

1. Providing advice on issuing new securities
2. Underwriting new securities
3. Providing advice and financing for mergers and acquisitions
4. Financial engineering, including risk management
5. Research
6. Proprietary trading

The first three activities are central to investment banking. The remaining three activities have emerged more recently. We now briefly consider each of these activities.

Providing Advice On New Security Issues Microsoft is good at producing software, Campbell's is good at producing soup, and Coca-Cola is good at producing soft drinks. None of these firms, though, is good at knowing the ins and outs of financial markets. Firms usually turn to investment banks for advice on how to raise funds by issuing stock or bonds or by taking out loans. Investment banks have information about the current willingness of investors to buy different types of securities and on the prices investors are likely to require. This information would be difficult for firms to gather for themselves, but it is essential if they are to raise funds at a low cost.

Underwriting New Security Issues One way for investment bankers to earn income is by *underwriting* firms' sales of new stocks or bonds to the public. In **underwriting**, investment banks typically guarantee a price to the issuing firm, sell the issue in financial markets or directly to investors at a higher price, and keep the difference, known as the *spread*. On average, investment banks earn 6% to 8% of the total dollar amount raised for an **initial public offering (IPO)**, which represents the first time a firm sells stock to the public. An investment bank typically earns 2% to 4% of the dollar amount raised in a *secondary offering* (or *seasoned offering*), which represents security sales by a firm that has sold securities previously. Fees for bond offerings are usually substantially lower: 0.375% for investment grade bonds and 1% to 2% for non-investment grade, or junk bonds.

In return for the spread, the investment bank promises to use its "best effort" to resell the securities being underwritten. In a few cases, the investment bank will buy the securities outright, thereby taking on the *principal risk* that it may have misjudged the state of the market and may have to sell securities for a lower price than it had guaranteed to the issuing firm. The investment bank also agrees to make a secondary market in the securities. Doing so provides "support" for the IPO price. The support is only temporary, though, as the Facebook IPO in 2012 showed. Morgan Stanley, the lead underwriter of the IPO, purchased shares on the first day the stock was available for sale to ensure that the IPO price of $38 per share was maintained. On the following trading days, Morgan Stanley was no longer buying shares, and the price of Facebook stock quickly dropped well below the IPO price.

While a single investment bank may underwrite a relatively small issue of stocks or bonds, groups of investment banks called **syndicates** underwrite large issues. Thirty-three banks participated in underwriting Facebook's IPO, which raised $18.4 billion for the firm in 2012. In a syndicated sale, the lead investment bank acts as a manager and keeps part of the spread, and the remainder of the spread is divided among the syndicate members and brokerage firms that sell the issue to the public. Once a firm has chosen the investment bank that will underwrite its securities, the bank carries out a *due diligence process*, during which it researches the firm's value. The investment bank then prepares a *prospectus*, which the Securities and Exchange Commission (SEC) requires of every firm before allowing it to sell securities to the public. The prospectus should contain all information about the firm that a potential investor would find relevant to making a decision to buy the firm's stocks or bonds, including the firm's profitability and net worth, as well as risks faced by the firm, such as pending lawsuits. The investment bank then conducts a "road show," with visits to institutional investors, such as mutual funds, pension funds, and university endowment funds, that might be

Underwriting An activity in which an investment bank guarantees to the issuing corporation the price of a new security and then resells the security for a profit.

Initial public offering (IPO) The first time a firm sells stock to the public.

Syndicate A group of investment banks that jointly underwrite a security issue.

interested in buying the security issue. Finally, the investment bank sets a price for the stock that it estimates will equate the quantity of securities being sold with the quantity that investors will demand.

Underwriting can lower information costs between lenders and borrowers because investment banks put their reputations behind the firms they underwrite. Investors typically have confidence that the underwriting investment bank has gathered sufficient information on the issuing firm during the due diligence process that the investors can purchase the firm's securities without incurring excessive risk. During the financial crisis of 2007–2009, this investor confidence was shaken when investment banks underwrote mortgage-backed securities that turned out to be very poor investments.

Providing Advice and Financing for Mergers and Acquisitions Larger firms often expand by acquiring or merging with other firms. A small firm may decide that the fastest way to expand is to be acquired by another firm. For example, in 2006, the online video company YouTube was concerned that it lacked the financial resources to deal with legal issues arising from people uploading copyrighted material to its site. In addition to expanding the site, YouTube's management needed software that it could not develop on its own. YouTube considered being acquired by Microsoft and Yahoo, among other firms, before finally deciding to sell itself to Google for $1.65 billion.

Investment banks are very active in mergers and acquisitions (M&A). They advise both buyers—the "buy side mandate"—and sellers—the "sell side mandate." Typically, investment banks take the initiative in contacting firms about potential purchases, sales, or mergers. When advising a firm seeking to be acquired, investment banks attempt to find an acquiring firm willing to pay significantly more than the *market value* of the firm, which is the total value of the firm's outstanding shares. In a typical acquisition, the acquiring firm will pay a premium of 25% to 30% above the market value for the acquired firm. Investment banks can estimate the value of firms, lead negotiations, and prepare acquisition bids. An investment bank provides a *fairness opinion* to an acquired firm's board of directors, indicating that a proposed offer is fair. An acquiring firm may need to raise funds, through issuing stocks or bonds, or by taking out loans, in order to make the acquisition. As part of the advising process, an investment bank helps to arrange for this financing. Advising on M&A is particularly profitable for investment banks because, unlike with underwriting and most other investment banking activities, an investment bank does not have to invest its own capital. The only significant costs to advising on M&A are the salaries of the bankers involved in the deal and reserves to be used in the case of litigation.

In addition to giving advice on mergers and acquisitions, investment banks advise firms on their *capital structure*, which is the mix of stocks and bonds the firm uses to raise funds. With the very low interest rates on corporate bonds following the financial crisis, some investment banks advised client firms to issue bonds and use the funds to repurchase the firm's stock, particularly if the stock was selling for a low price. Investment banks can also provide advice on the size of the dividend a firm should pay on its stock.

Financial Engineering, Including Risk Management Investment banks have played a major role in designing new securities, a process called *financial engineering*. Financial engineering typically involves developing new financial securities or investment strategies, using sophisticated mathematical models developed by people with advanced degrees in economics, finance, and mathematics. These people have become known as "rocket scientists," or "quants." Derivative securities are the result of financial engineering (see Chapter 7). As we have seen, firms can use derivatives to *hedge*, or reduce, risk. For example, an airline can use futures contracts in oil to reduce the risk that a sharp increase in oil prices will reduce the airline's profits. Just as most firms lack the knowledge of financial markets to properly assess the best way to raise funds by selling stocks and bonds, most firms also need advice on how best to hedge risk using derivatives contracts. Investment banks supply this knowledge by constructing risk management strategies for firms in return for a fee.

During and after the financial crisis, some policymakers and economists criticized investment banks because they believed the banks had financially engineered securities, particularly those based on mortgages, that were overly complex and whose riskiness was difficult to gauge. Most of these new securities were not well suited to hedging risk. It became clear that many senior managers at commercial and investment banks had not fully understood the newly created derivative products, including collateralized debt obligations (CDOs) and credit default swap (CDS) contracts, that they were buying, selling, and recommending to clients. These managers greatly underestimated the risk that the prices of these derivatives might fall if housing prices declined and homeowners began to default on their mortgages. The managers of investment banks often relied on the high ratings given to the securities by the rating agencies, Moody's, Standard & Poor's, and Fitch. As it turned out, the analysts at the rating agencies also didn't understand some of these securities and failed to accurately gauge their risk.

Research Investment banks conduct several types of research. Banks assign research analysts to large firms, such as Apple or General Electric, and to industries, such as the automobile or oil industries. These analysts gather publicly available information on firms and sometimes visit a firm's facilities and interview its managers. The investment bank uses some of the research material compiled to identify merger or acquisition targets for clients, and it makes some research material public through the financial media as "research notes." Research analysts often provide advice to investors to "buy," "sell," or "hold" particular stocks. In recent years, some analysts have used the terms *overweight* for a stock they recommend and *underweight* for a stock they do not recommend. The opinions of senior analysts at large investment banks can have a significant effect on the market. For example, a research note from a senior analyst that is unexpectedly negative about a particular firm can cause the price of the firm's stock to fall.

Some analysts specialize in offering opinions on the current state of the financial markets, sometimes minute by minute during the hours that the markets are open. These opinions can provide useful information for the investment bank's *trading desks*, where traders buy and sell securities. Analysts also engage in economic research, writing reports on economic trends and providing forecasts of macroeconomic variables, such as gross domestic product, the inflation rate, employment, and various interest rates. William Dudley, currently the president of the Federal Reserve Bank of New York, holds a PhD in economics from the University of California, Berkeley, and was head of economic research at Goldman Sachs for many years.

Proprietary Trading The two core investment banking activities are providing advice on and underwriting new security issues and providing advice on mergers and acquisitions. Traditionally, making investments in securities, commercial real estate, or other assets was a minor part of the operations of most investment banks. Beginning in the 1990s, however, *proprietary trading*, or buying and selling securities and other assets for a bank's own account rather than for clients, became a major part of the operations and an important source of profits for many investment banks.

Proprietary trading exposes banks to *interest-rate risk*, *credit risk*, and *funding risk*. If investment banks hold long-term securities, such as U.S. Treasury bonds or many mortgage-backed securities, the banks are exposed to the risk of an increase in market interest rates that will cause the prices of their long-term securities to decline. During the financial crisis, though, it became clear that investment banks also faced credit risk from proprietary trading. *Credit risk* is the risk that borrowers might default on their loans. The credit risk on mortgage-backed securities—particularly those that consisted of subprime or Alt-A mortgage loans—was much higher than the investment banks or the credit rating agencies had expected. During the mid-2000s, investment banks originated hundreds of billions of dollars of mortgage-backed securities. They retained some of these securities during the underwriting process and also because they believed that they would be good investments. Beginning in 2007, the market prices of many of these securities began to decline, and by 2008, the markets for these securities had seized up or frozen, making them difficult to sell. The result was significant losses for some investment banks.

The problems investment banks faced during the financial crisis were made worse because they had used short-term borrowed funds to finance their purchases of long-term securities. *Funding risk* is the risk that an investor who uses short-term borrowing to make long-term investments will be unable to renew the short-term borrowing. If lenders—typically, other financial firms—making short-term loans to investment banks require that the loans be repaid rather than renewing them or rolling them over, investment banks have to sell their long-term securities to repay the loans. During the financial crisis, many of the long-term securities investment banks had invested in declined in value, leaving the investment banks unable to pay off the short-term loans they had received from lenders. Using borrowed funds also increases leverage. We will further discuss both funding risk and leverage in the next section.

"Repo Financing," Leverage, and Funding Risk in Investment Banking

We can consider further the funding risk investment banks face. Commercial banks finance their investments primarily from deposits. Investment banks do not take in deposits, so they must finance their investments in other ways. One source of funds is the investment bank's capital, which consists of funds from shareholders plus profits the bank has retained over the years. Another source of funds is short-term borrowing. Prior to the 1990s, most investment banks were organized as partnerships, and they did relatively little proprietary trading, concentrating instead on the traditional investment banking activities of underwriting and providing advice on mergers and acquisitions. The banks financed these activities largely from the partners' capital, or equity. During the 1990s and 2000s, however, most large investment banks converted from partnerships to publicly traded corporations, and proprietary trading became a more important source of profits.

Investment banks borrowed to finance their investments in securities and their direct loans to firms, including mortgage loans to developers of commercial real estate. Financing investments by borrowing rather than by using capital, or equity, increases a bank's *leverage*. Using leverage in investing is a double-edged sword: Profits from the investment are increased, but so are losses. Recall that the ratio of a bank's assets to its capital is its *leverage ratio*. Because a bank's *return on equity* (*ROE*) equals its *return on assets* (*ROA*) multiplied by its leverage ratio, the higher the leverage ratio, the greater the ROE for a given ROA. But the relationship holds whether the ROA is positive or negative.

Solved Problem 11.1

The Perils of Leverage

Suppose that an investment bank is buying $10 million in long-term mortgage-backed securities. Consider three possible ways that the bank might finance its investment:

1. The bank finances the investment entirely out of its equity.
2. The bank finances the investment by borrowing $7.5 million and using $2.5 million of its equity.
3. The bank finances the investment by borrowing $9.5 million and using $0.5 million of its equity.
   a. Calculate the bank's leverage ratio for each of these three ways of financing the investment.

b. For each of these ways of financing the investment, calculate the return on its equity investment that the bank receives, assuming that:
   i. The value of the mortgage-backed securities increases by 5% during the year after they are purchased.
   ii. The value of the mortgage-backed securities decreases by 5% during the year after they are purchased.

For simplicity, ignore the interest the bank receives from the securities, the interest it pays on funds it borrows to finance the purchase of the securities, and any taxes the bank must pay.

Solving the Problem

Step 1 **Review the chapter material.** This problem is about the interaction of leverage and risk, so you may want to review the section "'Repo Financing,' Leverage, and Funding Risk in Investment Banking," which begins on page 318.

Step 2 **Answer part (a) by calculating the leverage ratio for each way of financing the investment.** The leverage ratio equals the value of assets divided by the value of equity. In this case, the value of the assets is a constant $10 million, but the bank is investing different amounts of its own funds—different amounts of equity—with the three different ways of financing its investments. If the bank uses financing method 1, it uses $10 million of its own funds; if it uses financing method 2, it uses $2.5 million of its own funds; and if it uses financing method 3, it uses $0.5 million of its own funds. Therefore, its leverage ratios are:

$$1. \frac{\$10,000,000}{\$10,000,000} = 1.$$

$$2. \frac{\$10,000,000}{\$2,500,000} = 4.$$

$$3. \frac{\$10,000,000}{\$500,000} = 20.$$

Step 3 **Answer the first part of part (b) by calculating the bank's return on its equity investment for each of the three ways of financing the investment.** In each case, the bank experiences a gain of $500,000 from the increase in the prices of the mortgage-backed securities. Because the amount of equity the bank invests differs with the three methods of financing, the bank's returns also differ:

$$1. \frac{\$500,000}{\$10,000,000} = 0.05, \text{ or } 5\%.$$

$$2. \frac{\$500,000}{\$2,500,000} = 0.20, \text{ or } 20\%.$$

$$3. \frac{\$500,000}{\$500,000} = 1.00, \text{ or } 100\%.$$

Step 4 **Answer the second part of part (b) by calculating the return for each of the three ways of financing the investment.** In this case, the investment bank suffers a loss of $500,000 from the fall in the prices of the mortgage-backed securities. Therefore, the bank's returns are:

$$1. \frac{-\$500,000}{\$10,000,000} = -0.05, \text{ or } -5\%.$$

$$2. \frac{-\$500,000}{\$2,500,000} = -0.20, \text{ or } -20\%.$$

$$3. \frac{-\$500,000}{\$500,000} = -1.00, \text{ or } -100\%.$$

These results show that the more highly leveraged the bank's investment—that is, the more the bank relies on borrowing rather than on investing its own equity—the greater the potential profit *and* the greater the potential loss. As we will see, even the highest leverage ratio in this problem—20—is well below the leverage ratios of the large investment banks in the years leading up to the financial crisis!

See related problem 1.8 at the end of the chapter.

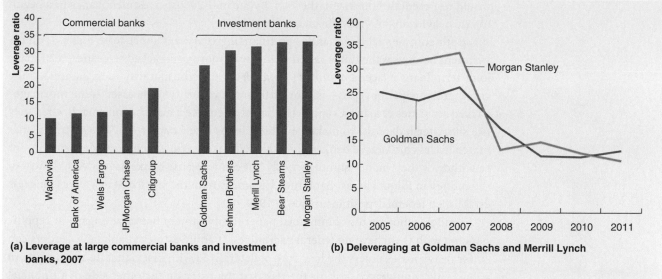

(a) Leverage at large commercial banks and investment banks, 2007

(b) Deleveraging at Goldman Sachs and Merrill Lynch

Figure 11.1 Leverage in Investment Banks

Panel (a) shows that at the start of the financial crisis in 2007, large investment banks were more highly leveraged than were large commercial banks.

Panel (b) shows that after 2008, Goldman Sachs and Morgan Stanley reduced their leverage ratios, or deleveraged.

Sources: Company annual reports and annual balance sheets, as reported on wsj.com.

Federal banking regulations put limits on the size of a commercial bank's leverage ratio (see Chapter 12). These regulations did not, however, apply to investment banks. As a result, during the 2000s, as investment banks increased their investments financed with borrowed funds, their leverage ratios rose well above those of large commercial banks. Panel (a) of Figure 11.1 shows leverage ratios for five large commercial banks and five large investment banks in 2007, as the financial crisis began. As a group, the investment banks were significantly more highly leveraged than the commercial banks. As we will discuss in the next section, by the end of 2008, Goldman Sachs and Morgan Stanley were the only large investment banks that remained independent. As panel (b) of Figure 11.1 shows, after 2008, Goldman Sachs and Morgan Stanley reduced their leverage ratios to levels more consistent with those of commercial banks. This process of reducing leverage is called *deleveraging*.

In addition to being highly leveraged, investment banks were vulnerable to funding risk because of how they financed their investments. Investment banks borrowed primarily by either issuing commercial paper or by using *repurchase agreements*. Repurchase agreements, or *repos*, are short-term loans backed by collateral. For example, an investment bank might borrow money by selling Treasury bills to another bank or a pension fund, and at the same time the investment bank would agree to buy the Treasury bills back at a slightly higher price either the next day or within a few days. The difference between the price of the Treasury bills when sold and when repurchased would represent the interest on the loan. By the mid-2000s, investment banks had begun to rely heavily on this "repo financing."[1]

Both commercial paper and repo financing represent short-term loans. If an investment bank uses the funds raised to invest in mortgage-backed securities or to make long-term loans it faces a *maturity mismatch* because the maturity of its liabilities—the commercial paper or repos—is shorter than the maturity of its assets—the mortgage-backed securities or loans. Commercial banks often face a maturity mismatch when they use short-term deposits to make long-term loans (see Chapter 10). The maturity mismatch leaves commercial banks vulnerable to bank runs in which many depositors want to withdraw their money simultaneously but can't because banks have invested most of the money in illiquid loans. Bank runs became rare in the United States after Congress established federal deposit insurance in 1934.

Lenders who buy the commercial paper of investment banks or engage in repo financing with them have no federal guarantees. If an investment bank fails, lenders can suffer heavy losses unless the loans are collateralized with assets that do not decline in value. This *counterparty risk*, or the risk that the party on the other side of a financial transaction will not fulfill its obligations, played an important role in the financial crisis of 2007–2009. As investment banks suffered heavy losses on mortgage-backed securities, the funding risk they had undertaken became clear as lenders refused to buy the banks' commercial paper or enter into repo financing agreements with them. Several large investment banks, particularly Bear Stearns and Lehman Brothers, suffered severe financial difficulties because they had financed illiquid, long-term assets with short-term borrowing. As Jamie Dimon, the chairman and CEO of JPMorgan Chase, has put it: "There is one financial commandment that cannot be violated: Do not borrow short to invest long—particularly against illiquid, long-term assets."[2] Unfortunately, in the years leading up to the financial crisis, a number of investment banks violated this commandment.

Making the Connection

Did Moral Hazard Derail Investment Banks?

Until the early 1980s, all the large investment banks were partnerships. The funds the banks used to finance their operations came primarily from the partners' own equity in the firm. If a bank made profits, the partners shared them, and if the bank suffered losses, those were shared as well. The financial writer Roger Lowenstein has described the situation at the Salomon Brothers investment bank in the late 1970s, as the partners worried about an investment that had not been going well:

> The firm's capital account used to be scribbled in a little book, left outside the office of a partner named Allan Fine, and each afternoon the partners would nervously tiptoe over to Fine's to see how much they had lost.

---

[1]The Lehman Brothers investment bank went bankrupt in 2008. A report released by a court-appointed bankruptcy examiner in 2010 indicated that the investment bank had accounted for some of its repos as sales rather than loans, as is typically done, in order to reduce both the assets and debt reported on its balance sheet, thereby reducing how leveraged the bank would appear to investors.

[2]James Dimon, "Letter to Shareholders," March 10, 2008, in JPMorgan Chase's Annual Report, 2007, p. 12.

In 1981, Salomon Brothers was the first of the large investment banks to "go public" by converting from a partnership to a corporation. By the time of the financial crisis, all the large investment banks had become publicly traded corporations. With corporations, there is a separation of ownership from control because although the shareholders own the firm, the top management actually controls it (see Chapter 9). The moral hazard involved can result in a principal–agent problem, as the top managers may take actions that are not in the best interest of the shareholders.

One way to reduce moral hazard is for shareholders to monitor the behavior of top managers. But in the early 2000s, investment banks moved away from traditional activities such as underwriting and giving advice on mergers and acquisitions and toward trading in complex financial securities, such as collateralized debt obligations (CDOs) and credit default swap (CDS) contracts. Shareholders and boards of directors often did not understand these activities or their risks and therefore could not effectively monitor the firms' managers. Some commentators and policymakers have argued that as a result, investment banks took on more risk during the housing boom by increasing their leverage and buying what turned out to be risky mortgage-backed securities. They did so because top managers would not bear the consequences of heavy losses to the extent that they would have had the firms remained partnerships. Michael Lewis, who worked for several years as a bond salesman at Salomon Brothers and later became a financial author, has argued:

> No investment bank owned by its employees would have leveraged itself 35 to 1 or bought and held $50 billion in mezzanine CDOs. I doubt any partnership would have sought to game the rating agencies . . . or even allow mezzanine CDOs to be sold to its customers. The hope for short-term gain would not have justified the long-term hit.

Other commentators are skeptical of this argument. Many top managers of investment banks suffered significant losses during the financial crisis, which suggests that the moral hazard problem may not have been severe. At both Bear Stearns and Lehman Brothers, two of the most highly leveraged investment banks, most managers owned significant amounts of company stock. As the stock in these companies lost nearly all of its value during the financial crisis, the personal fortunes of many of the firms' managers dwindled. Richard Fuld, the chairman and CEO of Lehman Brothers at the time of its bankruptcy, suffered losses of about $930 million from the decline in the value of his Lehman Brothers stock.

The debate over why investment banks became more highly leveraged and took on more risk in the years before the financial crisis is likely to continue.

Sources: Michael Lewis, "The End," *Portfolio*, December 2008; Roger Lowenstein, *When Genius Failed: The Rise and Fall of Long-Term Capital Management*, New York: Random House, 2000, p. 4; and Aaron Lucchetti, "Lehman, Bear Executives Cashed Out Big," *Wall Street Journal*, November 22, 2009.

See related problem 1.9 at the end of the chapter.

The Investment Banking Industry

Prior to the Great Depression of the 1930s, the federal government allowed financial firms to engage in both commercial banking and investment banking. During the

Depression, a financial panic occurred that involved a collapse in stock prices and the failure of more than 9,000 banks. As part of a series of laws intended to restructure the financial system, Congress passed the Glass-Steagall Act in 1933 to legally separate investment banking from commercial banking. Congress saw investment banking as inherently more risky than commercial banking. The great stock market crash of October 1929 had resulted in heavy losses from underwriting because investment banks were forced to sell securities for lower prices than they had guaranteed to the issuing firms. The Glass-Steagall Act also contained provisions for a system of federal deposit insurance. A majority in Congress believed that if the federal government was going to insure deposits, it should not allow banks to use the deposits to engage in what it saw as risky investment banking activities.

Following the passage of the Glass-Steagall Act, many larger banks had to separate into independent commercial and investment banks. Many banks saw their commercial banking activities as more profitable than their investment banking activities and so spun off their investment banking activities into separate firms. For example, JPMorgan, then a commercial bank, spun off Morgan Stanley, an investment bank, and First National Bank of Boston spun off First Boston Corporation, which became an independent investment bank. As the decades passed and the disorderly conditions of the banking industry in the early 1930s faded from memory, economists and policymakers began to rethink the rationale for the Glass-Steagall Act. In principle, the Glass-Steagall Act was designed to protect people with deposits in commercial banks from risky investment activities by banks. In practice, however, some economists argued that the act had protected the investment banking industry from competition, which enabled it to earn larger profits than the commercial banking industry. As a result, firms were forced to pay more for issuing securities than they would have if competition from commercial banks had been allowed. By the 1990s, sentiment in Congress was gradually shifting toward repeal of the Glass-Steagall Act. Finally, in 1999, the Gramm-Leach-Bliley (or Financial Services Modernization) Act repealed the Glass-Steagall Act. The Gramm-Leach-Bliley Act authorized new financial holding companies, which would permit securities and insurance firms to own commercial banks. The act also allowed commercial banks to participate in securities, insurance, and real estate activities. During the financial crisis of 2007–2009, some economists and policymakers argued that repeal of the Glass-Steagall Act had been a mistake. They argued that, just as during the 1930s, risky investment banking activity had damaged commercial banks and put government-insured deposits at risk.

Following the repeal of the Glass-Steagall Act, the investment banking industry underwent significant changes. The largest investment banks, known as "bulge bracket" firms, were of two types: Some, such as JPMorgan, Citigroup, and Credit Suisse, were part of larger financial firms with extensive commercial banking activity. Others, such as Goldman Sachs, Morgan Stanley, Lehman Brothers, Bear Stearns, and Merrill Lynch, were standalone investment banks that engaged in no significant commercial banking activity. Large commercial banks, such as Bank of America, UBS, Wachovia, and Deutsche Bank also had investment banking affiliates. Finally, smaller or regional investment banks, known as "boutiques," such as the Blackstone Group, Piper Jaffray, Lazard, Raymond James, and Perella Weinberg, also played a significant role in the industry.

Where Did All the Investment Banks Go?

The financial crisis of 2007–2009 had a profound effect on the investment banking industry. Firms that held significant amounts of mortgage-backed securities suffered heavy losses as the prices of those securities plummeted. The standalone investment banks had difficulty weathering the crisis, in part because they relied on short-term borrowing from institutional investors and from other financial firms to fund their long-term investments. As the crisis deepened, borrowing money short term became difficult, and these firms were forced to sell assets, often at low prices. In addition, because they were not commercial banks, they could not borrow by taking out discount loans from the Federal Reserve to meet temporary liquidity problems. In March 2008, Bear Stearns was on the edge of bankruptcy and sold itself at a very low price to JPMorgan Chase. In September 2008, Lehman Brothers filed for bankruptcy. Shortly thereafter, Merrill Lynch sold itself to Bank of America. In October, the only two remaining large standalone investment banks, Goldman Sachs and Morgan Stanley, petitioned the Federal Reserve to allow them to become *financial holding companies*, which are regulated by the Federal Reserve and eligible for discount loans through their bank subsidiaries. As financial holding companies, Goldman Sachs and Morgan Stanley could both borrow from the Fed and, following Congress's passage of the Troubled Asset Relief Program (TARP) in October 2008, be eligible for injections of capital from the U.S. Treasury purchasing their stock.

Some commentators labeled the effect of the financial crisis on investment banks as "the end of Wall Street" because large standalone investment banks had long been seen as the most important financial firms in the stock and bond markets. Table 11.1

Table 11.1 The Fate of Large Investment Banks

Year	Investment bank	Fate of the bank
1988	First Boston	Bought by Credit Suisse
1997	Salomon Brothers	Bought by Travelers
2000	Donaldson, Lufkin, & Jenrette	Bought by Credit Suisse
	JPMorgan	Bought by Chase
	PaineWebber	Bought by UBS
2007	A.G. Edwards	Bought by Wachovia
2008	Bear Stearns	Bought by JPMorgan Chase
	Goldman Sachs	Became a financial holding company
	Lehman Brothers	Failed
	Merrill Lynch	Bought by Bank of America
	Morgan Stanley	Became a financial holding company

Notes: Credit Suisse is a bank headquartered in Zurich, Switzerland; Travelers is an insurance company headquartered in Hartford, Connecticut; UBS (originally the Union Bank of Switzerland) is a bank headquartered in Zurich, Switzerland; Chase is the Chase Manhattan Bank, headquartered in New York City, and is currently named JPMorgan Chase; and Wachovia is a bank headquartered in Charlotte, North Carolina, that subsequently merged with Wells Fargo Bank.

Source: Tabular adaptation of p. 80 ("The End of the Line") from Dave Kansas, *The Wall Street Guide to the End of the Wall Street as We Know It*, New York: Collins Business, 2009.

shows the fates over the past 25 years of 11 large investment banks. Although the structure of the industry has changed, the activities of investment banking—underwriting, providing advice on mergers and acquisitions, and so on—continue at subsidiaries of financial holding companies, at affiliates of commercial banks, and at boutique investment banks.

Making the Connection   In Your Interest

So, You Want to Be an Investment Banker?

Over the past 20 years, investment banking has been one of the most richly rewarded professions in the world. Top executives at investment banks such as Goldman Sachs, Morgan Stanley, and JPMorgan have earned tens of millions of dollars in salary and bonuses in recent years. This pay has been controversial. Some political commentators argue that the economic contribution from underwriting and providing advice on mergers and acquisitions is not worth the compensation these executives receive. Some critics lament that the high compensation is luring too many of the country's "best and brightest" to investment banking and away from what they see as more productive pursuits in industry, the sciences, and professions such as law, medicine, and teaching. Criticism of the top managers of investment banks increased as the financial crisis unfolded, and some policymakers and economists argued that investment banks had helped bring on the crisis by promoting mortgage-backed securities. As we have seen, following the financial crisis, none of the larger investment banks survived as standalone firms engaged only in investment banking.

But investment banking activity continues. The investment banking arms of commercial banks remain very active in underwriting and providing advice on mergers and acquisitions. Many boutique and regional investment banks continue to thrive, and Goldman Sachs and Morgan Stanley, although now technically financial holding companies, operate largely as they did before the crisis. Goldman Sachs, which had made a profit of $17.6 billion in 2007, swung to a loss of $1.3 billion in 2008 during the worst of the crisis but was back to a profit of $19.8 billion in 2009 and remained profitable through 2012. Lloyd Blankfein, Goldman's CEO, earned $16.2 million in salary and bonus in 2012 (which was actually much lower than the $68.6 million he earned in 2007, before the financial crisis), and the average salary and bonus of the firm's 32,600 employees during 2012 was $336,442, although this compensation was down from $498,000 in 2009. Goldman's compensation was near the average for investment bank employees. So, a career in investment banking is still appealing to many new college graduates, even if the number of positions available has been significantly reduced since 2007.

New college graduates hired by investment banks will sometimes take so-called "back-office" jobs in which they provide clerical or technical support for the firms' operations. Entry-level hires in investment banking proper are usually called *analysts*. These positions famously require workweeks of 80 hours or more. The day-to-day responsibilities of analysts include researching industries and firms, making presentations to the bank's clients, gathering and analyzing data, helping in the due diligence process for IPOs, drafting financial documents, and participating in "deal teams" for mergers and acquisitions. Investment banks typically have an "up or out" approach to their analysts: After two to three years, the bank either promotes an analyst to the position of associate or asks him or her to leave the firm. New hires with MBAs, rather than just undergraduate degrees, are sometimes hired directly as associates. The higher rungs on the investment banking job ladder are typically titled vice president, director, and managing director.

Changes to financial regulations enacted by Congress in the Dodd-Frank Act of 2010 had the potential to reduce the compensation investment bankers earn. Whether these changes would also reduce the allure of investment banking to many young college graduates remains to be seen.

Sources: Brett Philbin, "Goldman Sachs Compensation per Employee Climbs 15%," *Wall Street Journal*, October 16, 2012; and "Key Facts" and "Annual Earnings" for Goldman Sachs Group, Inc., on wsj.com.

See related problem 1.10 at the end of the chapter.

Investment Institutions: Mutual Funds, Hedge Funds, and Finance Companies

11.2

Learning Objective
Distinguish between mutual funds and hedge funds and describe their roles in the financial system.

Investment institution
A financial firm, such as a mutual fund or a hedge fund, that raises funds to invest in loans and securities.

Mutual fund A financial intermediary that raises funds by selling shares to individual savers and invests the funds in a portfolio of stocks, bonds, mortgages, and money market securities.

Investment banks are not the only important nonbank financial firms. **Investment institutions** are financial firms that raise funds to invest in loans and securities. The most important investment institutions are mutual funds, hedge funds, and finance companies. Mutual funds and hedge funds, in particular, have come to play an increasingly important role in the financial system.

Mutual Funds

Mutual funds are financial intermediaries that allow savers to purchase shares in a portfolio of financial assets, including stocks, bonds, mortgages, and money market securities. Mutual funds offer savers the advantage of reducing transactions costs. Rather than buying many stocks, bonds, or other financial assets individually—each with its own transactions costs—a saver can buy a proportional share of these assets by buying into the fund with one purchase. Mutual funds provide risk-sharing benefits by offering a diversified portfolio of assets and liquidity benefits because savers can easily sell the shares. Moreover, the company managing the fund—for example, Fidelity or Vanguard—specializes in gathering information about different investments.

The mutual fund industry in the United States dates back to the organization of the Massachusetts Investors Trust (managed by Massachusetts Financial Services, Inc.) in March 1924. The fund's marketing stressed the usefulness of mutual funds for achieving a diversified portfolio for retirement saving. Later in 1924, the State Street Investment Corporation was organized. In 1925, Putnam Management Company introduced the Incorporated Investment Fund. These three investment managers are still major players in the mutual fund industry.

Types of Mutual Funds Mutual funds operate as either closed-end or open-end funds. In *closed-end mutual funds*, the mutual fund company issues a fixed number of nonredeemable shares, which investors may then trade in over-the-counter markets, just as stocks are traded. The price of a share fluctuates with the market value of the assets—often called the net asset value (NAV)—in the fund. Due to differences in the quality of fund management or the liquidity of the shares, fund shares may sell at a discount or a premium relative to the market value of the underlying assets in the fund. More common are *open-end mutual funds*, which issue shares that investors can redeem each day after the markets close for a price tied to the NAV.

In the past 15 years, *exchange-traded funds* (*ETFs*) have become popular. ETFs are similar to closed-end mutual funds in that they trade continually throughout the day, as stocks do. However, ETFs differ from closed-end funds in that market prices track the prices of the assets in the fund very closely. Unlike closed-end funds, ETFs are not actively managed, which means they hold a fixed portfolio of assets that managers do not change. (However, some actively managed ETFs are starting to appear.) Large institutional investors who purchase above a certain number of shares of an ETF—called a *creation unit aggregation*—have the right to redeem those shares for the assets in the fund. For instance, the Vanguard Large-Cap ETF contains 751 stocks. If the price of the underlying stocks were greater than the price of the ETF, institutional investors could make arbitrage profits by redeeming the ETF for the underlying stocks. Similarly, no institutional investor would buy an ETF if its price were greater than the prices of the underlying assets. Because arbitrage keeps the prices of ETFs very close to the prices of the underlying assets, small investors can use them as an inexpensive way of buying a diversified portfolio of assets.

Many mutual funds are called *no-load funds* because they do not charge buyers a commission, or "load." Mutual fund companies earn income on no-load funds by charging a management fee—typically about 0.5% of the value of the fund's assets—for running the fund. The alternative, called *load funds*, charge buyers a commission to both buy and sell shares.

Funds that invest in stocks or bonds are the largest category of mutual funds. Large mutual fund companies, such as Fidelity, Vanguard, and T. Rowe Price, offer many stock and bond funds. Some funds hold a wide range of stocks or bonds, others specialize in securities issued by a particular industry or sector, and still others invest as an *index fund* in a fixed-market basket of securities, such as the stocks in the S&P 500 stock index. Large mutual fund companies also offer funds that specialize in the stocks and bonds of foreign firms, and these provide a convenient way for small investors to participate in foreign financial markets.

Money market mutual fund A mutual fund that invests exclusively in short-term assets, such as Treasury bills, negotiable certificates of deposit, and commercial paper.

Money Market Mutual Funds The greatest growth in mutual funds has been in **money market mutual funds**, which hold high-quality, short-term assets, such as Treasury bills, negotiable certificates of deposit, and commercial paper. Most money market mutual funds allow savers to write checks above a specified amount, say $500, against their accounts. Money market mutual funds have become very popular with small savers as an alternative to commercial bank checking and savings accounts, which typically pay lower rates of interest.

Starting in the 1980s, money market mutual funds began successfully competing with commercial banks for the business of providing short-term credit to large firms.

Rather than taking out loans from banks, firms sold commercial paper to the funds. The interest rates the firms paid on the paper were lower than banks charged on loans but higher than the interest rate money market mutual funds would receive from investing in Treasury bills. The funds were taking on more credit risk by buying commercial paper rather than Treasury bills, but the risk was minimized because the maturities were short—generally, less than 90 days—and the commercial paper received high ratings from the rating agencies. By the 2000s, many financial corporations, including investment banks, also began to rely on selling commercial paper to finance their need for short-term credit. As we have seen, some investment banks took on the risk of relying on commercial paper to finance long-term investments.

The financial crisis of 2007–2009 revealed that market participants had underestimated two sources of risk arising from the increased use of commercial paper. First, firms using commercial paper to fund their operations faced the risk that they might have difficulty selling new commercial paper when their existing commercial paper matured. This funding risk could leave firms scrambling to find alternative sources of credit. Second, money market mutual funds and other buyers of commercial paper faced the possibility that the modestly higher interest rates they were receiving compared with Treasury bills did not sufficiently compensate them for the credit risk they were taking on.

Because the underlying assets in a money market mutual fund are both short term and, presumably, of high quality, the funds keep their net asset values (NAVs) stable at $1 per share. Small day-to-day price declines that would otherwise drive the NAV of a fund's shares below $1 are absorbed by the fund because the fund's managers know that they will receive the face value of their investments in a brief period of time when the investments mature. So, unlike with other types of mutual funds, buyers do not have to worry about a loss of principal—or so most investors thought until the financial crisis.

To the shock of most investors, Reserve Fund announced in September 2008 that its Primary Fund, a well known money market mutual fund, had lost so much money when Lehman Brothers declared bankruptcy and defaulted on its commercial paper that Reserve would have to "break the buck." Breaking the buck meant that Reserve would allow the NAV of the fund to fall to $0.97, which meant a 3% loss of principal for investors in the fund. In addition, Reserve announced that it would delay allowing investors to redeem their shares or write checks against them. The fact that investors in a well-known fund had suffered a loss of principal and had been unable to redeem their shares caused large withdrawals from other money market mutual funds. These withdrawals led the U.S. Treasury to announce that it would guarantee the holdings of money market mutual funds against losses, thereby ensuring that other funds would not be forced to break the buck.

Although the Treasury's guarantee slowed withdrawals from money market mutual funds, the funds cut back significantly on their purchases of commercial paper. Because the funds made up such a large fraction of the market for commercial paper and because many firms had become heavily dependent on sales of commercial paper to finance their operations, the adverse consequences for the financial system were severe. In October 2008, the Federal Reserve stepped in to stabilize the market by directly purchasing commercial paper for the first time since the Great Depression of the 1930s. The Fed's actions helped restore the flow of funds to firms that were dependent on commercial paper.

Hedge Funds

Hedge fund A financial firm organized as a partnership of wealthy investors that make relatively high-risk, speculative investments.

Hedge funds are similar to mutual funds in that they use money collected from savers to make investments. There are several differences between mutual funds and hedge funds, however. Hedge funds are typically organized as partnerships of 99 investors or fewer, all of whom are either wealthy individuals or institutional investors, such as pension funds. Because hedge funds consist of a relatively small number of wealthy investors, they are largely unregulated. Being unregulated allows hedge funds to make risky investments that mutual funds would be unable to make.

Hedge funds frequently *short* securities whose prices they think may decline, meaning that they borrow the securities from a dealer and sell them in the market, planning to buy them back after their prices decline. A typical strategy of early hedge funds was to pair a short position in a security with a long position by, for instance, buying a futures contract on the security, so that the fund would stand to gain from either an increase or a decrease in the price of the security. Because this type of strategy resembles conventional hedging strategies (see Chapter 7), these early funds acquired the name "hedge funds." Modern hedge funds, though, typically make investments that involve speculating, rather than hedging, so their name is no longer an accurate description of their strategies. Although reliable statistics on hedge funds are difficult to obtain, in 2012 there were as many as 10,000 operating in the United States, managing more than $2 trillion in assets.

Hedge funds have been controversial for several reasons:

1. While mutual fund managers typically charge the fund a fee for managing it, hedge fund managers also receive a share of any profits the fund earns. A typical hedge fund charges investors a fee of 2% of the value of the fund's assets plus 20% of any profits the fund earns (these fees are sometimes called "carried interest," on which managers pay taxes at the capital gains tax rate rather than the ordinary income tax rate).

2. Investments in hedge funds are typically illiquid, with investors often not being allowed to withdraw their funds for one to three years. And even then, typically investors are given only a narrow window of time during which they can redeem their investment.

3. Several hedge funds have experienced substantial losses that led to potential risk to the financial system. Most notably, in 1998 the hedge fund Long-Term Capital Management (LTCM), whose founders included Myron Scholes and Robert Merton, both winners of the Nobel Prize in Economics, made speculative investments that would return a profit if interest rates on high-risk debt fell relative to interest rates on low-risk debt. Unfortunately for LTCM, rather than narrowing, the spread between high-risk and low-risk debt widened, and LTCM was driven to the edge of bankruptcy. Although LTCM had used only $4 billion in equity to make its investments,

through borrowing and using derivative contracts, the total value of its holdings was more than $1.1 trillion. The Federal Reserve feared that if LTCM declared bankruptcy and defaulted on its loans and derivative contracts, many of the hedge fund's counterparties would suffer losses, and these losses would undermine the stability of the financial system. So in September 1998, the Federal Reserve Bank of New York organized a bailout in which 16 financial firms agreed to invest in LTCM to stabilize the firm so that its investments could be sold off—or "unwound"—in a way that would not destabilize financial markets. Some economists believe that the Fed's actions to support LTCM led other investment managers to take on more risk because they believed the Fed would also intervene to save their firms from failure. Other economists, though, are skeptical that the Fed's actions in the LTCM bailout had a significant effect on the actions of other financial firms.

4. Finally, hedge funds have been criticized for their heavy use of short selling. Short selling can cause security prices to fall by increasing the volume of securities being sold. During the financial crisis, the leaders of the large investment banks claimed that short selling by hedge funds had driven the prices of their stocks to artificially low levels, thereby contributing to their financial problems. In 2010, the German government became concerned that speculation against bonds issued by some European governments and against the stocks of some German financial firms was destabilizing financial markets in Europe. In May, the German government banned "naked" short sales, which involve selling a security short without first borrowing the security. The German government also pushed for the European parliament to pass a bill that would regulate hedge funds.

Many economists, however, believe that hedge funds play an important role in the financial system. Because hedge funds are able to mobilize large amounts of money and leverage the money when buying securities, they are able to quickly force price changes that can correct market inefficiencies.

| Making the Connection | In Your Interest |

Would You Invest in a Hedge Fund if You Could?

Many people are disappointed by what they see as the inadequate returns they are receiving on their investments in mutual funds. For these people, do hedge funds represent the promised land of investing? Potential hedge fund investors face two problems. To begin with, hedge funds are not available to the average investor. To buy into a hedge fund, you must be an "accredited investor," as defined by the Securities and Exchange Commission (SEC). In the fall of 2012, to be an accredited investor, you needed net worth of $1 million or more and income of $200,000 or more in the two years prior to making the investment, as well as a reasonable expectation of having the same income in the year of the investment. Those requirements rule out most investors, but if you were an accredited investor, would buying into a hedge fund be likely to earn you a higher return than if you purchased shares in a mutual fund? The Vanguard 500 Index Fund, which invests in the stocks included in the S&P 500, for example, is within the reach of most investors because it has a minimum investment of only $3,000 and has no income requirement for investors.

Do hedge funds provide higher returns than the Vanguard 500 Index Fund and similar mutual funds? The answer to this question is not perfectly clear because, unlike mutual funds, most hedge funds do not have to provide detailed reports to the SEC on the returns their investors earn. While every year there are some funds that earn very high returns, which are widely publicized in the financial press, estimates of hedge fund returns indicate that in some recent years they have on average not done well. For example, one estimate of the returns earned by 2,000 large hedge funds in 2011 indicates that these funds had an average rate of return of −5%, while the S&P 500 gained 2% that year. Even funds that have huge returns for a few years often suffer heavy losses in other years. For example, the hedge funds managed by John Paulson invested heavily in securities that would increase in value if housing prices declined. When housing prices did decline in 2007 and 2008, the funds earned a profit of $15 billion. Paulson's fees were more than $4 billion in 2007 alone—the largest return ever earned by an individual in a single year in U.S. financial markets. If you were an accredited investor, then of course you would want to invest now in Paulson's funds, right? In fact, in 2011, Paulson invested in securities that lost value when the U.S. recovery turned out to be slower than he had forecast. As a result, his largest fund suffered a 35% loss, and another of his funds lost more than 50%, leading a number of large investors to redeem their shares. One reason that hedge funds often incur large losses as well as large gains is that they tend to be much more heavily leveraged than are mutual funds.

In addition to earning erratic returns, hedge funds have several other drawbacks. As we have already noted, the fees hedge fund managers charge are much higher than the fees mutual fund managers charge. For example, Vanguard charges 0.17% of the value of the 500 Index Fund as a management fee, while hedge fund managers such as John Paulson typically charge a fee of 2% of the value of the fund's assets plus 20% of any profits the fund earns. With such high management fees, a hedge fund has to make very profitable investments for investors to receive an above-average return. Unlike an investment in a mutual fund, an investment in a hedge fund is typically illiquid because investors can withdraw their funds only at specific times. Hedge funds also typically invest in assets that are more illiquid than the assets that mutual funds invest in. Because these illiquid assets may not frequently be bought and sold, it can be difficult for investors to determine their market prices and, therefore, the true value of the funds' investments.

The Dodd-Frank Act of 2010 required large hedge funds to register with the SEC for the first time, but hedge funds are not required to make detailed disclosures of their asset holdings, as mutual funds are. Hedge fund managers argue that full disclosure would allow other managers to copy their investment strategies. Lack of full disclosure makes it difficult for investors to evaluate hedge funds as easily as they can mutual funds. In extreme cases, the lack of disclosure can help conceal fraud. In 2008, the funds Bernard Madoff had been running for decades turned out to have been using funds from new investors to pay off previous investors rather than using them to buy securities. Investors lost billions of dollars in the fraud, and Madoff was sentenced to more than 150 years in prison.

The table below summarizes the benefits and drawbacks of hedge funds relative to mutual funds.

Mutual funds		Hedge funds	
Benefits	Drawbacks	Benefits	Drawbacks
1. Low management fees	1. Not allowed to follow some investment strategies	1. Allowed to use sophisticated investment strategies	1. High management fees
2. Full disclosure of holdings	2. Possibly lower return	2. Possibly higher return	2. Limited disclosure of holdings
3. Shares are liquid			3. Investment in fund may be illiquid
4. Lower risk			4. Higher risk

The table shows that the key advantage of hedge funds is that they can use sophisticated investment strategies to earn high returns. An important idea in financial markets, though, is the trade-off between risk and return. Even if investors in hedge funds receive an above-average return on their investment—which is by no means clear—they take on substantially more risk than investors in diversified mutual funds. So, even if you were qualified to invest in a hedge fund, you would want to closely consider the fund's track record, its fees, and its investment strategy before doing so.

Sources: Securities and Exchange Commission, *Investor Bulletin: Hedge Funds*, October 2012; Julie Creswell and Azam Ahmed, "Large Hedge Funds Fared Well in 2011," *New York Times*, March 29, 2012; and David Weidner, "For Investors, 'Average' Is the New 'Above Average.'" *Wall Street Journal*, August 15, 2012.

See related problem 2.9 at the end of the chapter.

Finance Companies

Finance companies are financial intermediaries that raise money through sales of commercial paper and other securities and use the funds to make small loans to households and firms. Some investment banks also provide funds to finance companies through short-term loans or revolving lines of credit. Before making loans, finance companies gather information about borrowers' default risks. Because finance companies do not accept deposits as commercial banks do, however, federal and state governments generally have seen little need for regulation beyond information disclosure to potential borrowers and fraud prevention. The lower degree of regulation allows finance companies to provide loans tailored to match the needs of borrowers more closely than do the standard loans that other, more regulated institutions can provide.

The three main types of finance companies are consumer finance, business finance, and sales finance companies.

Consumer finance companies make loans to enable consumers to buy cars, furniture, and appliances; to finance home improvements; and to refinance household debts. Finance company customers have higher default risk than do good-quality bank customers and so may be charged higher interest rates.

Finance company
A nonbank financial intermediary that raises money through sales of commercial paper and other securities and uses the funds to make small loans to households and firms.

Business finance companies engage in factoring—that is, purchasing at a discount accounts receivables of small firms. Accounts receivables represent money that a firm is owed for goods or services sold on credit. For example, CIT, which is a business finance company headquartered in New York City, might buy $100,000 of short-term accounts receivable from Axle Tire Company for $90,000. CIT is effectively lending Axle $90,000 and earning a $10,000 return when CIT collects the accounts receivable. Axle Tire is willing to sell its receivables to CIT because it needs the cash to pay for inventory and labor costs, and it might have a cash flow problem if it waited for all its customers to pay their bills. Another activity of business finance companies is to purchase expensive equipment, such as airplanes or large bulldozers, and then lease the equipment to firms over a fixed length of time.

Sales finance companies are affiliated with companies that manufacture or sell big-ticket goods. For example, department stores such as Macy's or JCPenney issue credit cards that consumers can use to finance purchases at those stores. This convenient access to credit is part of the selling effort of the store.

Many economists believe that finance companies fill an important niche in the financial system because they have an advantage over commercial banks in monitoring the value of collateral, making them logical players in lending for consumer durables, inventories, and business equipment. Other economists, though, note that finance companies take on more risk than do commercial banks and rely on short-term financing that may not be rolled over by lenders. These characteristics may make finance companies vulnerable to failure during a severe recession or financial crisis.

Contractual Savings Institutions: Pension Funds and Insurance Companies

11.3

Learning Objective

Explain the roles that pension funds and insurance companies play in the financial system.

Contractual saving institution A financial intermediary such as a pension fund or an insurance company that receives payments from individuals as a result of a contract and uses the funds to make investments.

Pension fund A financial intermediary that invests contributions of workers and firms in stocks, bonds, and mortgages to provide for pension benefit payments during workers' retirements.

Pension funds and insurance companies may not seem much like commercial banks, but they are also financial intermediaries that accept payments from individuals and use the payments to make investments. Pension funds and insurance companies are called **contractual saving institutions** because the payments individuals make to them are the result of a contract, either an insurance policy or a pension fund agreement.

Pension Funds

For many people, saving for retirement is their most important form of saving. People can accumulate retirement savings in two ways: through pension funds sponsored by employers or through personal savings accounts. Because retirements are predictable, **pension funds** can invest the contributions of workers and firms in long-term assets, such as stocks, bonds, and mortgages, to provide for pension benefit payments during workers' retirements. Representing more than $9 trillion in assets in the United States in 2012, private and state and local government pension funds are the largest institutional participants in capital markets. Figure 11.2 shows the investments of private and public pension funds during the second quarter of 2012. With about 20% of all U.S. financial assets under their control, pension funds hold about 22% of the nation's publicly traded equities and about 5% of the value of corporate bonds.

When you work for a firm that has a pension fund, you receive pension benefits only if you are vested. *Vesting* is the number of years you must work in order to receive

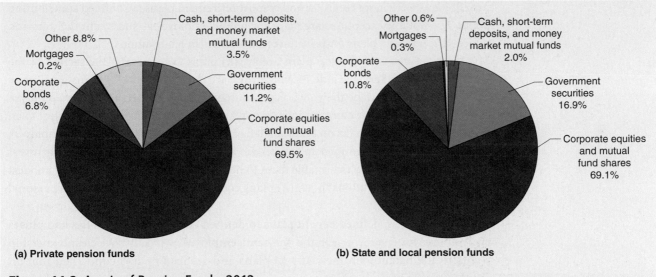

(a) Private pension funds

(b) State and local pension funds

Figure 11.2 Assets of Pension Funds, 2012

Both private and state and local pension funds concentrate their investments in stocks, bonds, and other capital market securities.

Source: Board of Governors of the Federal Reserve System, *Flow of Funds Accounts of the United States*, September 20, 2012.

benefits after retirement. The vesting period required varies across pension plans. Employees may prefer to save through pension plans provided by employers rather than through savings accounts for three reasons. First, pension funds may be able to manage a financial portfolio more efficiently, with lower transactions costs, than employees can. Second, pension funds may be able to provide benefits such as life annuities, which are costly for individual savers to obtain on their own. Third, the special tax treatment of pensions can make pension benefits more valuable to employees than cash wages.[3]

A key distinction among pension plans is whether they have defined contributions or defined benefits. In a *defined benefit plan*, the firm promises employees a particular dollar benefit payment, based on each employee's earnings and years of service. The benefit payments may or may not be indexed to increase with inflation. If the funds in the pension plan exceed the amount promised, the excess remains with the firm running the plan. If the funds in the pension plan are insufficient to pay the promised benefit, the plan is *underfunded*, and the issuing firm is liable for the difference.

In a *defined contribution plan*, the firm places contributions from employees into investments, such as mutual funds, chosen by the employees. The employees own the value of the funds in the plan. If an employee's investments are profitable, the employee's income during retirement will be high; if the employee's investments are not profitable, the employee's income during retirement will be low. Although at one time defined

---

[3]Your contribution to a pension fund can be excluded from your current income for tax purposes, and your employer's matching contribution is tax deductible for your employer. In addition, you can't be taxed on the investment earnings of a pension fund. Your taxation is deferred until you receive retirement benefits from your pension. You also have the option of transferring pension benefit payments into an individual retirement account (IRA) or another favorable distribution plan, which can reduce the tax you would otherwise owe on a lump-sum payment from your pension plan.

benefit plans were more common, today most retirement plans are defined contribution plans. The notable exceptions are plans for public employees—such as firefighters and police officers—and plans for private-sector workers in labor unions.

Most defined contribution plans are 401(k) plans. Named after the section of the Internal Revenue Service Code in which they are described, 401(k) plans give many employees a chance to be their own pension managers. In a 401(k) plan, an employee can make tax-deductible contributions through regular payroll deductions, subject to an annual limit, and pay no tax on accumulated earnings until retirement. Some employers match employee contributions up to a certain amount. Many 401(k) participants invest through mutual funds, which enable them to hold a large collection of assets at a modest cost. By 2012, contributions to 401(k) plans equaled more than one-third of personal saving.

The shift from defined benefit plans to defined contribution plans has had pluses and minuses for employees. On the one hand, employees typically have clear ownership rights to the balances in their 401(k) plans and so need be less concerned that an employer's financial problems might undermine the solvency of a defined benefit plan. Employees also typically have an opportunity to choose from a range of mutual funds in which to invest their 401(k) contributions. On the other hand, with a defined benefit plan, the employer bears the risk that bad investments may require the firm to divert some current revenues to make promised pension payments. With a defined contribution plan, the employees bear the risk of poor investment returns.

In response to difficulties firms encountered in administering pension plans, Congress passed the Employee Retirement Income Security Act (ERISA) in 1974. This landmark legislation set national standards for pension fund vesting and funding, restricted plans' ownership of certain types of risky investments, and enacted standards for information reporting and disclosure. The act authorized creation of the Pension Benefit Guaranty Corporation (PBGC, or "Penny Benny") to insure pension benefits up to a dollar limit if a firm cannot meet its unfunded obligations under a defined benefit plan because of bankruptcy or other reasons. In 2012, the limit was $55,841 per beneficiary per year. The PBGC charges firms a premium on pension liabilities and has an implicit line of credit from the U.S. Treasury. The current underfunding of defined benefit private pension funds greatly exceeds the reserves of the PBGC. This fact has led some economists to fear that a pension insurance crisis may be on the horizon.

Insurance Companies

Insurance company
A financial intermediary that specializes in writing contracts to protect policyholders from the risk of financial loss associated with particular events.

Insurance companies are financial intermediaries that specialize in writing contracts to protect their policyholders from the risk of financial loss associated with particular events—such as automobile accidents or house fires. Insurers obtain funds by charging *premiums* to policyholders and use these funds to make investments. For example, individuals may pay annual premiums of $1,000 each to obtain life insurance policies from an insurance company, and the company will use these funds to make a loan to a hotel chain that is remodeling or expanding. Policyholders pay the premiums in exchange for the insurance company assuming the risk that if the insured event occurs, the company will pay the policyholder. Insurance companies invest policyholders' premiums in stocks, bonds, mortgages, and direct loans to firms, known as *private placements*.

The insurance industry has two segments: *Life insurance companies* sell policies to protect households against a loss of earnings from the disability, retirement, or death of the insured person. *Property and casualty companies* sell policies to protect households and firms from the risks of illness, theft, fire, accidents, or natural disasters. Insurance companies typically do not make a profit on the insurance policies themselves because they pay out more in claims than they receive in premiums. Instead, their profits come from investing the premiums. Figure 11.3 shows that the asset portfolios of property and casualty insurance companies differ from those of life insurance companies. In the second quarter of 2012, life insurance companies held about $5.5 trillion in assets, while property and casualty insurance companies held about $1.4 trillion in assets. The funds invested by life insurance companies are exempt from taxation, but property and casualty insurance companies do not receive this exemption. This tax difference is reflected in their asset portfolios: Property and casualty insurance companies invest more heavily in municipal bonds because the interest received is not taxable, while life insurance companies invest more heavily in corporate bonds, which pay higher interest rates.

The profitability of insurance companies depends in large part on their ability to reduce risks involved in providing insurance. The key risks to the profitability of insurers arise from adverse selection and moral hazard. Insurance companies have several ways of reducing the risks in providing insurance, which we discuss in the following sections.

Risk Pooling Insurance companies can reliably predict when and how much they will pay out to policyholders by using the *law of large numbers*. This statistical concept states that although the death, illness, or injury risks of an individual cannot be predicted, the average occurrences of any such event for large numbers of people generally can be predicted. By issuing a sufficient number of policies, insurance companies take advantage of risk pooling and diversification to estimate the size of reserves needed to pay potential claims. Statisticians known as *actuaries* compile probability tables to help predict the risk of an event occurring in the population.

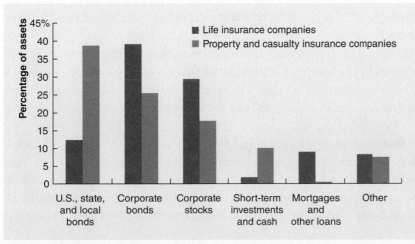

Figure 11.3

Financial Assets of U.S. Insurance Companies

Life insurance companies have larger asset portfolios than do property and casualty insurance companies. Property and casualty insurance companies hold more municipal bonds because the interest on them is tax exempt, while life insurance companies hold more corporate bonds because they pay higher interest rates.

Source: Board of Governors of the Federal Reserve System, *Flow of Funds Accounts of the United States*, September 20, 2012.

Reducing Adverse Selection Through Screening and Risk-Based Premiums Insurance companies suffer from adverse selections problems. The people most eager to purchase insurance are those with the highest probability of requiring an insurance payout. Severely ill people may want to buy large life insurance policies, and people in neighborhoods plagued by arson will want large fire insurance policies. To reduce adverse selection problems, insurance company managers gather information to screen out poor insurance risks. If you apply for an individual health insurance policy, you have to disclose information about your health history to the insurance company. Similarly, if you try to buy automobile insurance, you have to supply information about your driving record, including speeding tickets and accidents.

Insurance companies also reduce adverse selection by charging *risk-based premiums*, which are premiums based on the probability that an individual will file a claim. For example, insurance companies charge higher premiums on automobile insurance policies for drivers who have had multiple accidents and speeding tickets than for drivers who have clean driving records. Similarly, premiums of life insurance policies are higher for older people than for younger people.

Reducing Moral Hazard With Deductibles, Coinsurance, and Restrictive Covenants
Moral hazard is also a problem for insurance companies because policyholders may change their behavior once they have insurance. For example, after a firm has bought a fire insurance policy for a warehouse, the firm has less incentive to spend money fixing the sprinkler system in the warehouse. One way for insurance companies to reduce the likelihood that an insured event takes place is to make sure that some of the policyholder's money is at risk. Insurance companies do this by requiring a *deductible*, which is a specified amount of a claim that an insurance company does not pay. For example, a $500 deductible on your automobile insurance means that if you have an accident that results in $2,000 in damages to your car, the insurance company will pay you only $1,500. To give policyholders a further incentive to hold down costs, insurance companies may offer *coinsurance* as an option in exchange for charging a lower premium. This option requires policyholders to pay a certain percentage of the costs of a claim after the deductible has been satisfied. For example, if you have a health insurance policy with a $200 deductible and a 20% coinsurance, or *copayment*, requirement, then on a $1,000 claim, you would pay $360 (= $200 + (0.20 × $800)), and the insurance company would pay the other $640 on your behalf.

To cope with moral hazard, insurers also sometimes use *restrictive covenants*, which limit risky activities by the insured if a subsequent claim is to be paid. For example, a fire insurance company may refuse to pay a firm's claim if the firm failed to install and maintain smoke alarms, fire extinguishers, or a sprinkler system in accordance with its contract.

The tools that insurance companies use to reduce adverse selection and moral hazard problems are intended to align the interests of policyholders with the interests of the insurance companies. To the extent that the companies succeed, the cost of providing insurance is reduced. Competition among insurance companies results in these cost savings being passed along to policyholders, in the form of lower insurance premiums.

Risk, Regulation, and the Shadow Banking System

We have seen that in the 15 years before the financial crisis of 2007–2009, nonbank financial institutions, such as investment banks, hedge funds, and money market mutual funds, had become an increasingly important means for channeling money from lenders to borrowers. These nonbank financial institutions have been labeled the "shadow banking system"—matching savers and borrowers, but outside the commercial banking system, and, in principle, lowering costs to borrowers and raising returns to savers. On the eve of the financial crisis, the size of the shadow banking system was greater than the size of the commercial banking system.[4] What importance, if any, did this change in funding channels have for the financial system and the economy? Did the growth of the shadow banking system play a role in the financial crisis?

11.4

Learning Objective

Explain the connection between the shadow banking system and systemic risk.

Systemic Risk and the Shadow Banking System

In a market system, firms are generally free to operate as they please, subject to laws concerning fraud, racial and other discrimination, and so on. We have seen, though, that dating back to the early days of the country, fears of the financial power of banks had resulted in the government regulating banks in a number of ways, including restricting the number of bank branches and prohibiting interstate banking (see Chapter 10). Although some of these regulations had been removed by the 1990s, banks still remained more closely regulated than most other firms, including most financial firms.

During the 1930s, the sharp decline in stock prices and widespread bank failures led the federal government to enact new financial regulations. To help stabilize the banking system, Congress established the Federal Deposit Insurance Corporation (FDIC), which insures deposits in commercial banks. To help reduce information problems in financial markets, Congress established the Securities and Exchange Commission (SEC), which was given responsibility for regulating the stock and bond markets.

In the absence of deposit insurance, bank managers had an incentive to avoid risky investments that would alarm depositors and endanger the solvency of the bank. Depositors had an incentive to monitor how banks invested their deposits to avoid losses in the event that the bank failed. Although bank failures imposed losses on the owners of banks and on depositors, the possibility of losses always exists in a market system. Moreover, as Congress realized, the enactment of deposit insurance increased moral hazard by reducing the incentive bank managers had to avoid risky investments and by reducing the incentive depositors had to monitor the actions of bank managers. Why, then, did Congress establish the FDIC? The goal was not primarily to protect depositors from the risk of losing money if their banks failed. Instead, Congress was trying to stop bank panics. Congress intended to reduce the likelihood that the failure of an individual bank would lead depositors to withdraw their money from other banks, a process called *contagion*. Deposit insurance largely eliminated bank runs because depositors no longer had to fear the loss of funds in their checking and savings accounts in the

---

[4]Timothy Geithner, in the speech cited in the chapter opener, noted that in 2007 the value of the assets held by investment banks and hedge funds plus the value of asset-backed commercial paper plus repurchase agreements was greater than the value of loans, securities, and all other assets held by commercial banks.

Systemic risk Risk to the entire financial system rather than to individual firms or investors.

event that their bank failed. Essentially, then, in enacting deposit insurance, Congress was less concerned with the risk to individual depositors than with **systemic risk** to the entire financial system.

Deposit insurance stabilized the banking system, maintaining the flow of funds from depositors through banks to borrowers, particularly businesses dependent on bank loans. But there is no equivalent to deposit insurance in the shadow banking system. In the shadow banking system, short-term loans take such forms as repurchase agreements, purchases of commercial paper, and purchases of money market mutual fund shares rather than the form of bank deposits. During the financial crisis, the Treasury temporarily guaranteed owners of money market mutual fund shares against losses of principal for shares they already owned, but that program ended in September 2009. With that exception, the government does not reimburse investors and firms who make loans to shadow banks in the event that they suffer losses. So, while commercial bank runs are largely a thing of the past, runs on shadow banks decidedly are not. During the financial crisis, the shadow banking system was subject to the same type of systemic risk that the commercial banking system experienced during the years before Congress established the FDIC in 1934.

Regulation and the Shadow Banking System

Historically, the commercial banking system had been the primary source of credit to most firms and had been subject to periods of instability. So, the federal government has over the years regulated the types of assets commercial banks can hold and the extent of their leverage. Shadow banking firms, such as investment banks and hedge funds, have not been subject to these regulations. There have been two main rationales for exempting many nonbanks from restrictions on the assets they can hold and the degree of leverage they can have: First, policymakers did not consider these firms as being as important to the financial system as were commercial banks, and regulators did not believe that the failure of these firms would damage the financial system. Second, these firms deal primarily with other financial firms, institutional investors, or wealthy private investors rather than with unsophisticated private investors. Policymakers assumed that because investment banks and hedge funds were dealing with sophisticated investors, these investors could look after their own interests, without the need for federal regulations.

In 1934, Congress gave the SEC broad authority to regulate the stock and bond markets. With the growth of trading in futures contracts, Congress in 1974 established the Commodity Futures Trading Commission (CFTC) to regulate futures markets. Over time, though, financial innovation resulted in the development of complex financial securities that were not traded on exchanges and, therefore, not subject to regulation by the SEC and CFTC. By the time of the financial crisis, trillions of dollars' worth of securities such as credit default swaps were being traded in the shadow banking system, with little oversight from the SEC or CFTC. The financial crisis revealed that this trading involved substantial counterparty risk, particularly with respect to securities based on mortgages. When derivatives are traded on exchanges, the exchange serves as the counterparty, which reduces the default risk to buyers and sellers (see Chapter 7). In 2010, with passage of the Dodd-Frank Act, Congress enacted regulatory changes that have pushed more trading in derivatives onto exchanges.

Counterparty risk in the shadow banking system also increased over time, as some of these firms became highly leveraged. With high leverage, small losses would be magnified, increasing the probability of default.

The Fragility of the Shadow Banking System

We can summarize the vulnerability of the shadow banking system as follows: Many firms in the shadow banking system operate in a way similar to commercial banks in that they borrow short term—by issuing commercial paper or entering into repurchase agreements—and lend long term. However, for several reasons, they are more vulnerable than are commercial banks to incurring substantial losses and possible failure. First, unlike bank depositors, the investors providing investment banks and hedge funds with short-term loans have no federal insurance against loss of principal. This lack of federal insurance potentially makes investment banks and hedge funds as vulnerable to runs as commercial banks had been in the early 1930s. Second, because they are largely unregulated, shadow banks can invest in more risky assets and become more highly leveraged than commercial banks. Finally, shadow banks proved vulnerable in the financial crisis because during the early and mid-2000s, many had made investments that would rapidly lose value if housing prices in the United States were to decline. When housing prices began to decline, many shadow bank suffered heavy losses, and some were forced into bankruptcy. Given the increased importance of these firms in the financial system, the result was the worst financial crisis since the Great Depression.

Are Shadow Banks Still Vulnerable to Runs Today?

During and immediately following the financial crisis, some economists and policymakers called for extensive new regulations on shadow banks. In the end, the Dodd-Frank Act, which Congress passed in 2010, contained limited additional regulation of shadow banks. Some trading in derivatives was required to be carried out on exchanges, large hedge funds were required for the first time to register with the SEC, and firms selling mortgage-backed securities and similar assets were required to retain 5% of the credit risk. In addition, federal regulators were given the authority to take over large financial firms—not just large commercial banks—that appeared likely to fail and to require "systemically important financial firms" to hold additional capital.

Fundamentally, though, Dodd-Frank and other legislation left unchanged the basic problem the financial crisis revealed about shadow banks: Some shadow banks borrow short term to make (often highly leveraged) long-term investments. Because the lenders providing the short-term loans to shadow banks do not receive the same federal insurance as commercial bank deposits, shadow banks appear to be as vulnerable to runs now as they were at the time of the financial crisis. Some economists and policymakers advocate extending federal insurance to a wide range of short-term loans, thereby ending runs in the shadow banking system in the same way that the establishment of the FDIC ended runs in the commercial banking system. Other economists are skeptical of this proposal because they believe that insuring other types of short-term lending would greatly increase moral hazard problems, as lenders would have less incentive to monitor borrowers. In addition, the federal government would potentially be liable for enormous payments if during a financial crisis shadow banks defaulted on their short-term borrowing.

A more optimistic view held by some economists and policymakers is that there is an important distinction between runs on commercial banks and runs on shadow banks. Prior to the establishment of the FDIC, many people with commercial bank deposits had only limited ability to monitor the investments that bank managers were making with their deposits. Their deposits were also not secured by any specific collateral. In those circumstances, any bad news about a bank could set off a bank run and, through the mechanism of contagion, possibly a bank panic. The lenders to shadow banks, in contrast, are in many cases other financial firms, institutional investors, and wealthy investors. These lenders have much greater ability to monitor the quality of the investments shadow bank managers are making and typically require specific collateral for their loans, as when repurchase agreements are secured by Treasury securities. In this view, the shadow bank runs during the financial crisis that led to the failure of Lehman Brothers and the near failure of Bear Stearns and AIG were the result of a historically unusual event, namely the widespread use of financial securities based on a single type of financial asset: residential mortgages. In this view, the likelihood is low that financial firms, institutional investors, and wealthy investors will again so greatly misjudge the riskiness of a financial asset. Therefore, in this view, the original reason for exempting shadow banks from detailed regulation—that shadow banks deal primarily with sophisticated investors—still holds.

Answering the Key Question

Continued from page 313

At the beginning of this chapter, we asked:

"Does the shadow banking system pose a threat to the stability of the U.S. financial system?"

The shadow banking system clearly played a key role in the financial crisis of 2007–2009. Many shadow banks, particularly investment banks and hedge funds, were overly reliant on financing long-term investments with short-term borrowing, were highly leveraged, and held securities that would lose value if housing prices fell. When housing prices did fall, these firms suffered heavy losses, and some were forced into bankruptcy. Given the importance of shadow banking to the financial system, the result was a financial crisis.

Do shadow banks still pose a threat to the stability of the financial system? Because shadow banks can fill a role in the financial system more efficiently than can commercial banks, shadow banks continue to operate much as they did before the financial crisis. In particular, shadow banks continue to borrow short-term funds that, unlike commercial bank deposits, are not federally insured, and they use those funds for long-term investments. Therefore, shadow banks remain vulnerable to runs similar to those that occurred during the financial crisis.

Key Terms and Problems

Key Terms

Contractual saving institution, p. 334

Finance company, p. 333

Hedge fund, p. 330

Initial public offering (IPO), p. 315

Insurance company, p. 336

Investment banking, p. 314

Investment institution, p. 327

Money market mutual fund, p. 328

Mutual fund, p. 327

Pension fund, p. 334

Syndicate, p. 315

Systemic risk, p. 340

Underwriting, p. 315

11.1 Investment Banking
Explain how investment banks operate.

Review Questions

1.1 What are the key differences between investment banks and commercial banks?

1.2 During the 2000s, why did investment banks become more reliant on repo financing and also more highly leveraged? In your answer, be sure to define repo financing and leverage.

1.3 What became of the large, standalone investment banks during the financial crisis of 2007–2009?

Problems and Applications

1.4 An article in the *Economist* magazine says about investment banks: "By unlocking the capital markets and helping firms to manage risks, investment banks are important conduits of credit." How do investment banks "unlock capital markets"? How do investment banks help firms to manage risk? How do these activities make investment banks conduits of credit?

Source: "Pity the Investment Bankers," *Economist*, September 15, 2012.

1.5 A review of a biography of the British investment banker Siegmund Warburg states that Warburg believed:

> Investment banking should not be about gambling but about . . . financial intermediation built on client relationships, not speculative trading. . . . Warburg was always queasy about profits made from [investing] the firm's own capital, preferring income from advisory and underwriting fees.

a. What is underwriting? In what sense is an investment bank that engages in underwriting acting as a financial intermediary?

b. Is an investment bank that buys securities with its own capital acting as a financial intermediary? Briefly explain.

Source: "Taking the Long View," *Economist*, July 24, 2010.

1.6 In referring to the collapse of the Long-Term Capital Management hedge fund in 1998, an article in the *New York Times* noted that:

> Starting with just $5 billion in capital, the fund was able to get $125 billion in additional funds. Using that leverage, it took on trading positions with an estimated potential value of $1.25 trillion.

a. What is leverage? What information from this excerpt indicates that Long-Term Capital Management was highly leveraged?

b. What risks did Long-Term Capital Management's high leverage pose to the firm? What risks did it pose to the financial system?

Source: Anna Bernasek, "Hedge Funds' Heft Raises Increasing Concern About Their Risks," *New York Times*, July 5, 2005.

1.7 In 2005, before the financial crisis, Timothy Geithner, who was then president of the Federal Reserve Bank of New York, thought that leverage at hedge funds was rising, "probably because of heightened competitive pressure." Why might competitive pressure lead a hedge fund manager to take on more leverage? Would the same reasoning apply to the managers of an investment bank? Briefly explain.

Source: Anna Bernasek, "Hedge Funds' Heft Raises Increasing Concern About Their Risks," *New York Times*, July 5, 2005.

1.8 **[Related to** Solved Problem 11.1 **on page 319]** Suppose that you intend to buy a house for $200,000. Calculate your leverage ratio for this investment in each of the following situations:

a. You pay the entire $200,000 price in cash.

b. You make a 20% down payment.

c. You make a 10% down payment.

d. You make a 5% down payment.

Now assume that at the end of the year, the price of the house has risen to $220,000.

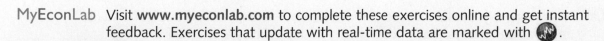

Calculate the return on your investment for each of the situations listed above. In your calculations, ignore interest you pay on the mortgage loan and the value of any housing services you receive from owning your home.

1.9 [Related to the Making the Connection **on page 322**] What incentives would the partners in an investment bank have to turn it into a public corporation? If becoming a public corporation increases the risk in investment banking, how do publicly traded investment banks succeed in selling stock to investors?

1.10 [Related to the Making the Connection **on page 326**] Many investment banks practice an "up or out" policy, with new hires being either fired or promoted within a few years. Many large law firms and accounting firms use a similar policy, as do colleges, with respect to their tenure-track faculty. Most firms, however, do not use this policy. In a typical firm, after a short probationary period, most employees continue to work for the firm indefinitely, with no set time before they are considered for promotion. What are the advantages and disadvantages to investment banks and other firms of using an "up or out" employment policy? Are there advantages to employees? If there are no advantages to employees, how are investment banks able to find people willing to work for them?

11.2 Investment Institutions: Mutual Funds, Hedge Funds, and Finance Companies
Distinguish between mutual funds and hedge funds and describe their roles in the financial system.

Review Questions

2.1 In what ways are investment institutions similar to commercial banks? In what ways are they different?

2.2 What are the key differences between mutual funds and hedge funds?

2.3 How are finance companies able to compete against commercial banks?

Problems and Applications

2.4 How are banks able to attract small savers if small savers can usually receive a higher interest rate from money market mutual funds than from bank savings accounts?

2.5 Financial journalist David Wessel has described what happened with the Reserve Primary Fund, a money market mutual fund, on September 16, 2008:

At 4:15 P.M., the fund issued a press release. The Lehman paper in its portfolio was worthless and the fund's shares were worth not $1, but only 97 cents: breaking the buck. The news triggered a run that spread through the $3.4 trillion [money market mutual fund] industry.

a. What is "Lehman paper"? Why was the Lehman paper in the fund's portfolio worthless?

b. What does "breaking the buck" mean? Why was it significant to the financial system?

c. What is a "run"? Why would one money market mutual fund having broken the buck cause a run on other money market mutual funds?

Source: David Wessel, *In Fed We Trust*, New York: Crown Business, 2009, p. 207.

2.6 When Chrysler Corporation was considering setting up its own auto finance company, it sent a memo to its dealers that contained the following: "Chrysler Group is in private discussions with multiple financial institutions, including Ally, to optimize the financial services offering available to our dealers and customers."

a. What is an auto finance company?

b. What advantages might automobile dealers gain from using a finance company, rather than a bank, to finance their purchases of autos from the manufacturer and their customers' purchases of autos from the dealers? What advantages might customers gain? What advantages would Chrysler gain from setting up its own auto finance company rather than relying on an independent company?

Source: Jeff Bennett and Andrew R. Johnson, "Chrysler Moves Closer to Setting Up Finance Unit," *Wall Street Journal*, April 25, 2012.

2.7 An article in the *Economist* magazine remarks that the average hedge fund is unlikely to earn more than the average mutual fund, and "since their fees are higher, the result will be disappointing returns for the average investor."

a. What is a hedge fund?

b. Are "average investors" able to invest in hedge funds? Briefly explain.

c. Why are the fees hedge funds charge higher than the fees mutual funds charge?

Source: "Mastered by the Universe" *Economist*, July 11, 2012.

2.8 In describing the work of hedge funds, financial journalist Sebastian Mallaby has observed:

[Research] showed that the unglamorous "value" stocks were underpriced relative to overhyped "growth" stocks. This meant that capital was being provided too expensively to

solid, workhorse firms and too cheaply to their flashier rivals. . . . It was the function of hedge funds to correct inefficiencies like this.

a. Explain what the first two sentences in this excerpt mean: What is the connection between the relative prices of these two types of firms and their cost of raising capital? Who is "providing" capital to these firms?

b. How can hedge funds correct this inefficiency?

Source: Sebastian Mallaby, *More Money Than God: Hedge Funds and the Making of a New Elite*, New York: The Penguin Press, 2010, pp. 8–9.

2.9 [Related to the Making the Connection on page 331] A New York Stock Exchange (NYSE) publication asks the question: "Do all investors fully understand the riskier characteristics of hedge funds as they pursue potentially greater returns?"

a. What does the NYSE mean by the "riskier characteristics of hedge funds"?

b. Do hedge funds provide investors with higher returns than alternative investments such as mutual funds? Should all investors who are eligible to invest in hedge funds do so? Briefly explain.

Source: New York Stock Exchange, "Hedge Fund Investing," http://www.nyse.com/pdfs/Hedge_Fund_Investing.pdf.

11.3 **Contractual Savings Institutions: Pension Funds and Insurance Companies**
Explain the roles that pension funds and insurance companies play in the financial system.

Review Questions

3.1 In what ways are contractual savings institutions similar to commercial banks? In what ways are they different?

3.2 What is the difference between a defined contribution pension plan and a defined benefit plan? What benefits do employees receive from saving for retirement using 401(k) plans?

3.3 In what ways are insurance companies financial intermediaries? What is the difference between a life insurance company and a property and casualty insurance company?

Problems and Applications

3.4 Suppose that as an employee of a large firm, you are given the choice between a defined benefit pension plan and a defined contribution pension plan. From your point of view, what are the advantages and disadvantages of each type of plan? From your employer's point of view, what are the advantages and disadvantages?

3.5 An article in the *New York Times* observes that 401(k) plans:

> have largely supplanted traditional pensions and become the central pillar of America's employer-sponsored retirement system, with 60 million workers participating in them.

a. What are "traditional pension plans," and how do they differ from 401(k) plans?

b. Briefly explain why 401(k) plans might be more desirable to employers and employees than traditional pension plans. Are there any reasons why 401(k) plans might be less desirable to either group?

Source: Steven Greenhouse, "Should the 401(k) Be Reformed or Replaced?" *New York Times*, September 11, 2012.

3.6 Why do pension funds have vesting periods? Do vesting periods have any advantages to employees relative to a system where new hires are eligible to participate in a pension plan right away?

3.7 Suppose that insurance companies in Ohio are reluctant to offer fire insurance to firms in low-income neighborhoods because of the prevalence of arson fires in those neighborhoods. Suppose that the Ohio state legislature passes a law stating that insurance companies must offer fire insurance to every business in the state and may not take into account the prevalence of arson fires when setting insurance premiums. What will be the likely effect on the market for fire insurance in Ohio?

3.8 Insurance companies never know the exact amounts of their future payouts. So, why do they hold large amounts of long-term, relatively illiquid assets, such as corporate bonds, that may be difficult to sell quickly if they need to make payments to policyholders?

3.9 Some private companies offer medical insurance policies that allow policyholders to make premium payments in exchange for the insurance company paying some or all of the policyholders' medical bills. An article in the *Economist* magazine observes that: "health insurance is an unusual product in that it guarantees a basket of services which is always improving and getting more expensive."

a. What basket of services does a medical insurance policy guarantee?

b. Why might the fact that medical services are always improving and getting more expensive create difficulties for companies offering medical insurance policies?

Source: "You Didn't Pay for It," *Economist*, October 15, 2012.

11.4 | **Risk, Regulation, and the Shadow Banking System**
Explain the connection between the shadow banking system and systemic risk.

Review Questions

4.1 In what ways does the shadow banking system differ from the commercial banking system?

4.2 Why have runs on commercial banks become rare, while several shadow banking firms experienced runs during the financial crisis?

Problems and Applications

4.3 During the financial crisis, the U.S. Treasury implemented the Guarantee Program for Money Market Funds, which insured investors against losses on their existing money market mutual fund shares. (The program expired in September 2009.) In explaining the program, a Treasury statement noted: "Maintaining confidence in the money market mutual fund industry was critical to protecting the integrity and stability of the global financial system." Why is the money market mutual fund industry so important? If money market mutual funds have problems, can't savers just deposit their money in banks?

Source: U.S. Department of the Treasury, "Treasury Announces Expiration of Guarantee Program for Money Market Funds," September 18, 2009.

4.4 In a speech in October 2012, Federal Reserve Governor Daniel Tarullo made the following observation: "Money market funds remain a major part of the shadow banking system and a key potential systemic risk even in the post-crisis financial environment." Tarullo went on to say that he did not believe that existing regulations "are sufficient to mitigate the run potential in money market funds."

a. What is "systemic risk"?

b. What is the "run potential" in money market mutual funds? How is this run potential related to systemic risk in the financial system?

Source: Daniel K. Tarullo, "Financial Stability Regulation," Distinguished Jurist Lecture, University of Pennsylvania Law School, Philadelphia, Pennsylvania, October 10, 2012.

4.5 In an account of the financial crisis, Roger Lowenstein described the problems affecting the Merrill Lynch investment bank: "too much leverage, too much relying on short-term [borrowing], and assets, especially real estate, of dubious value." Why might too much leverage be a problem for an investment bank? Why might relying too much on short-term borrowing be a problem?

Source: Roger Lowenstein, *The End of Wall Street*, New York: Penguin Press, 2010, p. 172.

4.6 Gary Gorton, a professor at Yale University, has compared repurchase agreements used by shadow banks to bank deposits in commercial banks. He notes: "If the depositors become concerned that their deposits are not safe, they can withdraw from the bank by not renewing their repo."

a. In what way is a repurchase agreement like a bank deposit?

b. What would be the consequences for a shadow bank if "depositors" failed to renew their repos?

Source: Gary Gorton, "Banking Panics: Déjà Vu All Over Again," *New York Times*, October 5, 2009.

4.7 In March 2008, the U.S. Treasury and the Federal Reserve arranged for the sale of the Bear Stearns investment bank to JPMorgan Chase in order to prevent Bear Stearns from having to declare bankruptcy. A columnist for the *New York Times* noted:

> It was an old-fashioned bank run that forced Bear Stearns to turn to the federal government for salvation. . . . The difference is that Bear Stearns is not a commercial bank, and is therefore not eligible for the protections those banks received 75 years ago when Franklin D. Roosevelt halted bank runs with government guarantees.

a. How can an investment bank be subject to a run?

b. What "government guarantees" did commercial banks receive 75 years ago?

c. How did these government guarantees halt commercial bank runs?

Source: Floyd Norris, "F.D.R.'s Safety Net Gets a Big Stretch," *New York Times*, March 15, 2008.

4.8 [Related to the Chapter Opener on page 313] In 2009, Congress and the president set up the Financial Crisis Inquiry Commission to investigate the causes of the financial crisis. At a hearing of the commission in 2010, Robert Rubin—who had served in top management at Goldman Sachs, had been secretary of the Treasury in the Clinton administration, and had served on the board of directors at Citigroup during the crisis—testified that "all of us in the [financial] industry failed to see the potential for this serious crisis." Why might the financial crisis have been difficult to foresee, even by people working in high-level positions in the financial system? Were there changes in the financial system that—at least with hindsight—might have indicated that by 2007 a financial crisis had become more likely? Briefly explain.

Source: Ezra Klein, "Wall Street Says Washington Doesn't Understand Finance. Well, Neither Does Wall Street," *Washington Post*, April 19, 2010.

Data Exercises

D11.1: [Money market mutual funds] Go to the Web site of the Federal Reserve Bank of St. Louis (FRED) (research.stlouisfed.org/fred2/) and download and graph the data series for Retail Money Funds (WRMFSL) and for Institutional Money Funds (WIMFNS) from the earliest week available until the most recent week available.

   a. Explain the difference between retail and institutional money market mutual funds.

   b. How have the trends in retail and institutional money market mutual funds differed?

D11.2: [Value of mutual fund shares and recessions] Go to the Web site of the Federal Reserve Bank of St. Louis (FRED) (research.stlouisfed.org/fred2/)

and download and graph the data series for the value of mutual fund shares owned by households (MFSABSHNO) from the first quarter of 1952 until the most recent quarter available. Go to the Web site of the National Bureau of Economic Research (nber.org) and find the dates for business cycle peaks and troughs (the period between a business cycle peak and trough is a recession).

   a. Describe how the value of mutual fund shares owned by households moves just before, during, and just after a recession. Is the pattern the same across recessions?

   b. What factors can cause the value of mutual fund shares owned by households to change?

CHAPTER 12

Financial Crises and Financial Regulation

Learning Objectives

After studying this chapter, you should be able to:

12.1 Explain what financial crises are and what causes them (pages 350–359)

12.2 Understand the financial crisis that occurred during the Great Depression (pages 360–365)

12.3 Understand what caused the financial crisis of 2007–2009 (pages 365–368)

12.4 Discuss the connection between financial crises and financial regulation (pages 368–379)

A Cloudy Crystal Ball on the Financial Crisis

We now know that problems in the U.S. housing market—particularly the widespread use of subprime mortgages—ultimately led to the financial crisis of 2007–2009 and to the worst recession since the Great Depression of the 1930s. But many policymakers, business leaders, and economists failed to see the crisis approaching. For instance, Federal Reserve Chairman Ben Bernanke made this comment during a speech at a banking conference in May 2007:

> Given the fundamental factors in place that should support the demand for housing, we believe the effect of the troubles in the sub-prime sector on the broader housing market will likely be limited, and we do not expect significant spillovers from the subprime market to the rest of the economy or to the financial system. The vast majority of mortgages,

including even subprime mortgages, continue to perform well.

As late as the fall of 2007, with employment declining and the start of the recession only a few months away, many economists doubted that even a mild recession would occur. The chief economist at Bank of America was quoted as saying, "The financial turmoil and extended problems in housing put the risks for the economy clearly to the downside, no question. But there are also factors that suggest a longer period of slower growth, but not recession." Similarly, an economist for Wachovia Bank argued, "None of the numbers we've seen on the economy point to recession. It points to moderate economic growth." And in November 2007, the chief economist of the National Association of Manufacturers was quoted as saying, "For the next year or so, the global economy is strong."

Continued on next page

Key Issue and Question

Issue: The financial crisis of 2007–2009 was the most severe since the Great Depression of the 1930s.

Question: Was the severity of the 2007–2009 recession due to the financial crisis?

Answered on page 380

The forecasts of many business executives also proved to be inaccurate. A Business Roundtable survey of 105 CEOs of large U.S. companies indicated that they were actually more optimistic about the U.S. economy at the end of 2007, with the recession about to begin, than they had been earlier in the year. Many more of the CEOs surveyed expected to increase hiring during 2008 than expected to decrease it.

The point is *not* that these people were poor forecasters. Recessions are generally difficult to predict, and very few people anticipated the severity of the 2007–2009 recession. Only those few people who had lived through the 1930s had experienced a financial crisis as severe as the one brought on by the collapse in the market for subprime mortgages. (There were *some* policymakers, economists, and CEOs who by 2007, or even earlier, believed that the U.S. economy was headed for recession. A few even predicted a severe recession.) As we discuss the financial crisis in this chapter, keep in mind that policymakers, managers of financial firms, investors, and households were struggling to deal with unprecedented events.

Sources: Ben S. Bernanke, "The Subprime Mortgage Market," speech at the Federal Reserve Bank of Chicago's 43rd Annual Conference on Bank Structure and Competition, Chicago, May 17, 2007, www.federalreserve.gov/newsevents/speech/bernanke20070517a.htm; David Leonhardt and Jeremy W. Peters, "Unexpected Loss of Jobs Raises Risk of Recession," *New York Times*, September 8, 2007; Associated Press, "Growth Slows in Services, but a Recession Is Doubted," *New York Times*, October 4, 2007; Peter S. Goodman, "Companies Bolster Sales Abroad to Offset Weakness at Home," *New York Times*, November 20, 2007; and Floyd Norris, "Pessimism Is Growing in Executive Suites," *New York Times*, December 6, 2007.

We have seen that the growth of the shadow banking system over the past 20 years has significantly changed the way funds flow from lenders to borrowers. In this chapter, we look at the origins and consequences of financial crises and then look specifically at how problems in the shadow banking system contributed to the financial crisis of 2007–2009.

12.1 The Origins of Financial Crises

Learning Objective

Explain what financial crises are and what causes them.

The key function of the financial system is to facilitate the flow of funds from lenders to borrowers. A **financial crisis** is a significant disruption in this flow. Economic activity depends on the ability of households to borrow to finance purchases and the ability of firms to borrow to finance their day-to-day activities as well as their long-term investments in new factories, machinery, and equipment. So, a financial crisis typically leads to an economic recession as households and firms cut back their spending in the face of difficulty in borrowing money. From before the Civil War through the 1930s, most of the financial crises in the United States involved the commercial banking system. We begin our discussion of financial crises with bank panics.

Financial crisis A significant disruption in the flow of funds from lenders to borrowers.

The Underlying Fragility of Commercial Banking

The basic activities of commercial banks are to accept short-term deposits, such as checking account deposits, and use the funds to make loans, including car loans, mortgages, and business loans, and buy long-term securities, such as municipal bonds. In other words, banks borrow short term from depositors and lend, often long term, to households, firms, and governments. As a result, banks have a maturity mismatch because the maturity of their liabilities—primarily deposits—is much shorter than the maturity of their assets—primarily loans and securities. Banks are relatively *illiquid* because depositors can demand their money back at any time, while banks may have difficulty selling the loans in which they have invested depositors' money. Banks, therefore, face *liquidity risk* because they can have difficulty meeting their depositors' demands to withdraw their money. If more depositors ask to withdraw their money than a bank has money on hand, the bank has to borrow money, usually from other banks. If banks are unable to borrow to meet deposit withdrawals, then they have to sell assets to raise the funds. If a bank has made loans and bought securities that have declined in value, the bank may be **insolvent**, which means that the value of its assets is less than the value of its liabilities, so its net worth, or capital, is negative. An insolvent bank may be unable to meets its obligations to pay off its depositors.

Insolvent The situation for a bank or another firm of having a negative net worth because the firm's assets have less value than its liabilities.

Bank Runs, Contagion, and Bank Panics

Liquidity risk is a particular problem for banks if the government does not provide insurance for deposits and if there is no central bank. Between 1836 and 1914, the United States had no central bank. Prior to 1933, the federal government had no system of deposit insurance. In those years, if depositors suspected that a bank had made bad loans or other investments, depositors had a strong incentive to rush to the bank to withdraw their money. Depositors knew that the bank would only have enough cash and other liquid assets available to pay off a fraction of the bank's deposits. Once the bank's liquid assets were exhausted, the bank would have to shut its doors, at least temporarily, until it could raise additional funds. A bank that was forced to raise cash by selling illiquid assets at sharply discounted prices might become insolvent and permanently close its doors. Depositors of a failed bank were likely to receive only some of their money back, and then usually only after a long delay. The process by which simultaneous withdrawals by a bank's depositors results in the bank closing is called a **bank run**.

As a depositor in a bank during this period, if you had any reason to suspect that the bank was having problems, you had a strong incentive to be one of the first in line to withdraw your money. Even if you were convinced that your bank was well managed and its loans and investments were sound, if you believed the bank's other depositors thought there was a problem, you still had an incentive to withdraw your money before the other depositors arrived and forced the bank to close. In other words, in the absence of deposit insurance, *the stability of a bank depends on the confidence of its depositors*. In such a situation, if bad news—or even false rumors—shakes that confidence, a bank will experience a run.

Bank run The process by which depositors who have lost confidence in a bank simultaneously withdraw enough funds to force the bank to close.

Moreover, without a system of government deposit insurance, bad news about one bank can snowball and affect other banks, in a process called **contagion**. Once one bank has experienced a run, depositors of other banks may become concerned that their banks might also have problems. These depositors have an incentive to withdraw their money from their banks to avoid losing it should their banks be forced to close. These other banks will be forced to sell loans and securities to raise money to pay off depositors. A key point is that if multiple banks have to sell the same assets—for example, mortgage-backed securities in the modern banking system—the prices of these assets are likely to decline. As asset prices fall, the net worth of banks is undermined and some banks may even be pushed to insolvency. If multiple banks experience runs, the result is a **bank panic**, which may force many, perhaps all, banks in the system to close. A bank panic feeds on a self-fulfilling perception: If depositors *believe* that their banks are in trouble, the banks *are* in trouble.

Contagion The process by which a run on one bank spreads to other banks resulting in a bank panic.

The underlying problem in contagion and bank panics is that banks build their loan portfolios on the basis of private information about borrowers, which they gather to determine which loans to make. Because this information is private, depositors can't review it to determine which banks are strong and which are weak. This situation is similar to adverse selection in financial markets, in which lenders cannot distinguish

Bank panic The situation in which many banks simultaneously experience runs.

good from bad loan applicants. Because of the private information that banks obtain when accumulating assets, depositors have little basis for assessing the quality of their banks' portfolios and distinguishing solvent from insolvent banks. So, bad news about one bank can raise fears about the financial health of others, resulting in a bank panic.

Government Intervention to Stop Bank Panics

Policymakers want to maintain the health of the banking industry because banks reduce information costs in the financial system. The failure of financially healthy banks due to liquidity problems hurts the ability of households and small and medium-sized firms to obtain loans, thereby reducing the efficiency with which the financial system matches savers and borrowers.

Governments have used two approaches to avoid bank panics: (1) A central bank can act as a lender of last resort, and (2) the government can insure deposits. In the United States, Congress reacted to bank panics by establishing the Federal Reserve System in 1913. Policymakers and economists argued that the banking industry needed a "banker's bank," or *lender of last resort*. By acting as a **lender of last resort**, the Fed would be an ultimate source of credit to which banks could turn for loans during a panic. The Fed would make loans to solvent banks, using the banks' good, but illiquid, loans as collateral. Policymakers expected the Fed to make loans only to solvent banks, allowing insolvent banks to fail.

As we will see, the Fed failed to stop the bank panics of the early 1930s, which led Congress to create the **Federal Deposit Insurance Corporation (FDIC)** in 1934. By reassuring depositors that they would receive their money back even if their bank failed, deposit insurance effectively ended the era of commercial bank panics in the United States.

Lender of last resort
A central bank that acts as the ultimate source of credit to the banking system, making loans to solvent banks against their good, but illiquid, loans.

Federal Deposit Insurance Corporation (FDIC) A federal government agency established by Congress in 1934 to insure deposits in commercial banks.

Solved Problem 12.1

Would Requiring Banks to Hold 100% Reserves Eliminate Bank Runs?

The Federal Reserve requires banks to hold reserves equal to 10% of their holdings of checkable deposits above a certain level. In the 1950s, Milton Friedman of the University of Chicago and winner of the Nobel Prize in Economics proposed that banks be required to hold 100% reserves. More recently, Laurence J. Kotlikoff of Boston University has advocated a similar plan. If required to hold 100% reserves, banks would make loans and buy securities with their capital rather than with deposits. Briefly discuss how this proposal would affect the likelihood of bank runs.

Source: Kotlikoff's account of 100% reserve banking is part of his general proposal for financial reform in Laurence J. Kotlikoff, *Jimmy Stewart Is Dead*, Hoboken, NJ: John Wiley & Sons, 2010.

Solving the Problem

Step 1 **Review the chapter material.** This problem is about what causes bank runs, so you may want to review the section "Bank Runs, Contagion, and Bank Panics," which begins on page 351.

Step 2 **Solve the problem by discussing what causes bank runs and whether requiring banks to hold 100% reserves would affect the likelihood of runs.** We have seen that bank runs are caused by depositors' knowledge that banks keep only a fraction of deposits on reserve and loan out or invest the remainder. In a system without a lender of last resort or government deposit insurance, banks can quickly exhaust their reserves in a run, so that only the first depositors in line will receive all their money back. If banks held 100% reserves, rather than, say, 10%, depositors would no longer have to fear that their money would not be available should they choose to withdraw it. Depositors would also not be at risk of losing money if banks made poor investments because the value of a bank's loans and securities would no longer be connected to the bank's ability to refund depositors' money.

We can conclude that whatever the other merits or drawbacks of a system of 100% reserve banking, such a system would not be subject to runs.

See related problem 1.7 at the end of the chapter.

Bank Panics and Recessions

As Table 12.1 shows, the United States was plagued by bank panics from the early nineteenth century through 1933, when federal deposit insurance was enacted. The National Bureau of Economic Research (NBER) provides the generally accepted dates

Table 12.1 U.S. Bank Panics

Date of the bank panic	Did the bank panic occur during a recession?
August 1857	Yes
December 1861	No
April 1864	No
September 1873	Yes
June 1884	Yes
November 1890	Yes
May 1893	Yes
October 1896	Yes
October 1907	Yes
October 1930	Yes
April 1931	Yes
September–October 1931	Yes
January–February 1933	Yes

Note: Recessions are dated according to the National Bureau of Economic Research's (NBER's) business cycle reference dates, which begin in 1854. The bank panic of September 1873 occurred the month before a recession began.

Sources: Carmen M. Reinhart and Kenneth S. Rogoff, *This Time Is Different: Eight Centuries of Financial Folly*, Princeton, NJ: Princeton University Press, 2009, Table A.4.1; Michael Bordo, Barry Eichengreen, Daniela Klingebiel, and Maria Soledad Martinez-Peria, "Is the Crisis Problem Growing More Severe?" *Economic Policy*, Vol. 32, Spring 2001, pp. 52–82, Web appendix; Michael Bordo and Joseph G. Haubrich, "Credit Crises, Money and Contractions: An Historical Review," *Journal of Monetary Economics*, Vol. 57, January 2010, pp. 1–18; and National Bureau of Economic Research.

for recessions in the United States. From the 1854 recession until 1933, every bank panic was associated with a recession, apart from the two panics that occurred in the 1860s, during the Civil War.

It isn't a coincidence that bank panics and recessions occurred together. A bank panic can lead to declines in production and employment, either causing a recession or making an existing recession worse. Bank failures can directly affect the ability of households and firms to spend by wiping out some of the wealth they hold as deposits. Shareholders of banks also suffer losses to their wealth when banks fail. In addition, households and firms that relied on failed banks for credit will no longer have access to the loans they need to fund some of their spending. Typically in a panic, even banks that remain solvent will reduce their lending as they attempt to accumulate reserves to meet deposit withdrawals. The result can be a *credit crunch*, as households and firms that previously qualified for bank loans no longer do. Finally, by destroying checking account deposits, bank failures can result in a decline in the money supply.

There can also be negative feedback between a bank panic and a recession. As we have seen, if a recession triggers a panic, the panic can make the recession worse. But as the recession worsens, with the profitability of firms declining and household incomes falling, more borrowers are likely to default on their loans, and the prices of securities held by banks are likely to fall, further undermining the confidence of depositors and leading to increased withdrawals. The threat of increased withdrawals and the decreasing number of creditworthy borrowers can lead banks to further curtail their loans, thereby reducing the ability of households and firms to spend, which deepens the recession. Figure 12.1 illustrates the negative feedback loop during a bank panic.

Figure 12.1

The Feedback Loop During a Bank Panic

Bank runs can cause good banks, as well as bad banks, to fail. Bank failures are costly because they reduce credit availability to households and firms. Once a panic starts, falling income, employment, and asset prices can cause more bank failures. This feedback loop can cause a panic to continue, unless the government intervenes.

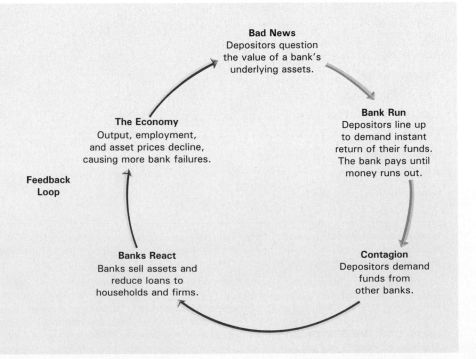

Bad News
Depositors question the value of a bank's underlying assets.

Bank Run
Depositors line up to demand instant return of their funds. The bank pays until money runs out.

Contagion
Depositors demand funds from other banks.

Banks React
Banks sell assets and reduce loans to households and firms.

The Economy
Output, employment, and asset prices decline, causing more bank failures.

Feedback Loop

Why Was the Severity of the 2007–2009 Recession So Difficult to Predict?

We saw in the chapter opener that policymakers, economists, and corporate CEOs were all surprised by the severity of the 2007–2009 recession in the United States. A key reason for the surprise was that the United States had not experienced a financial panic since the 1930s. Business cycle recessions can have a number of causes. The recession of 2001 was caused by a decline in investment spending after many firms had overspent on information technology during the "dot-com boom" of the late 1990s. Spikes in oil prices have also caused recessions. But recessions in the United States between 1933 and 2007, regardless of their cause, were not accompanied by bank panics. A series of bank panics occurred at the beginning of the Great Depression of the 1930s. The recession of 2007–2009 was also accompanied by a bank panic, but it was primarily in the "shadow banking system" rather than in the commercial banking system. Both the Great Depression and the recession of 2007–2009 were severe. Was their severity the result of the accompanying bank panics? More generally, do recessions accompanied by bank panics tend to be more severe than recessions that do not involve bank panics?

Carmen Reinhart and Kenneth Rogoff of Harvard University have gathered data on recessions and bank panics, or bank crises, in a number of countries in an attempt to answer this question. The table below shows the average change in key economic variables during the period following a bank crisis for the United States during the Great Depression and a variety of other countries in the post–World War II era, including Japan, Norway, Korea, and Sweden:

Economic variable	Average change	Average duration of change	Number of countries
Unemployment rate	+ 7 percentage points	4.8 years	14
Real GDP per capita	− 9.3%	1.9 years	14
Real stock prices	− 55.9%	3.4 years	22
Real house prices	− 35.5%	6 years	21
Real government debt	+ 86%	3 years	13

The table shows that for these countries, on average, the recessions following bank crises were quite severe. Unemployment rates increased by 7 percentage points—for example, from 5% to 12%—and continued increasing for nearly five years after a crisis had begun. Real GDP per capita also declined sharply. The average length of a recession following a bank crisis has been nearly two years. Adjusted for inflation, stock prices dropped by more than half, and housing prices dropped by more than one-third. Government debt soared by 86%. The increased public debt was partly the result of increased government spending, including spending to bail out failed financial institutions. But most of the increased debt was the result of government budget deficits resulting from sharp declines in tax revenues as incomes and profits fell as a result of the recession.

The table below shows some key indicators for the 2007–2009 U.S. recession compared with other U.S. recessions of the post–World War II period:

	Duration	Decline in real GDP	Peak unemployment rate
Average for postwar recessions	10.4 months	− 1.7%	7.6%
Recession of 2007–2009	18 months	− 4.1%	10.0%

Consistent with Reinhart and Rogoff's findings that recessions following bank panics tend to be unusually severe, the 2007–2009 recession was the worst in the United States since the Great Depression of the 1930s. The recession lasted nearly twice as long as the average of earlier postwar recessions, GDP declined by more than twice the average, and the peak unemployment rate was about one-third higher than the average.

Because most people did not see the financial crisis coming, they also failed to anticipate the severity of the 2007–2009 recession.

Note: In the second table, the duration of recessions is based on NBER business cycle dates, the decline in real GDP is measured as the simple percentage change from the quarter of the cyclical peak to the quarter of the cyclical trough, and the peak unemployment rate is the highest unemployment rate in any month following the cyclical peak.

Sources: The first table is adapted from data in Carmen M. Reinhart and Kenneth S. Rogoff, *This Time Is Different: Eight Centuries of Financial Folly*, Princeton, NJ: Princeton University Press, 2009, Figures 14.1–14.5; and the second table uses data from the U.S. Bureau of Labor Statistics, the U.S. Bureau of Economic Analysis, and the National Bureau of Economic Research.

See related problems 1.9 and 1.10 at the end of the chapter.

While the United States has experienced financial crises primarily as bank panics, other countries have experienced exchange-rate crises, sometimes called *currency crises*, and *sovereign debt crises*.

Exchange-Rate Crises

Exchange rates between currencies—for instance, the exchange rate between the U.S. dollar and the euro or between the Japanese yen and the Australian dollar—are determined by the interaction of demand and supply, as are other prices (see Chapter 8). In some cases, though, countries have attempted to keep the value of their currency fixed by *pegging* it against another currency. For instance, during the 1990s, a number of developing countries pegged the value of their currencies against the U.S. dollar. Having a fixed exchange rate can provide important advantages for a country that has extensive trade with another country. When the exchange rate is fixed, business planning becomes much easier. For example, if the value of the South Korean won increases relative to the U.S. dollar, Korean television manufacturers may have to raise the dollar prices of televisions they export to the United States, thereby reducing sales. If the exchange rate between the Korean won and the dollar is fixed, these manufacturers will have an easier job of planning.

In addition, if firms in a country want to borrow directly from foreign investors or indirectly from foreign banks, a fluctuating exchange rate will cause fluctuations in their debt payments. For example, a Thai firm might borrow U.S. dollars from a Japanese bank. If the Thai firm wants to build a new factory in Thailand with borrowed dollars, the firm has to exchange the dollars for an equivalent amount of Thai currency, the baht. When the factory opens and production begins, the Thai firm will be earning the additional baht it needs to exchange for dollars to make the interest payments on the loan. A problem arises if the value of the baht falls against the dollar because the Thai firm will now have to pay more baht to buy the dollars it needs. By pegging the value of the baht against the dollar, the Thai government reduces the risks to Thai firms from foreign-currency loans.

Pegging can lead to problems, particularly if the pegged exchange rate ends up substantially above the equilibrium rate that would prevail in the absence of the peg. Figure 12.2 illustrates the problem that several East Asian countries faced in the late 1990s, as they attempted to peg exchange rates against the dollar above their equilibrium levels. In the absence of pegging, the equilibrium exchange rate between the Korean won and the dollar would be E_1, and the equilibrium quantity of won traded per day would be Won_1. Because the Korean government pegs the value at a level, E_2, that is above the equilibrium level, there is an excess supply of won equal to $Won_3 - Won_2$. With more people wanting to trade won for dollars at that exchange rate than want to trade dollars for won, the Korean central bank, which would be responsible for maintaining the peg, must use its previously accumulated reserves of dollars to buy surplus won, or else the peg cannot be maintained.

Eventually the central bank will exhaust its holding of dollars. To maintain the peg as long as possible, Korea and other East Asian countries in similar situations took steps to raise domestic interest rates. Higher interest rates were intended to attract foreign investors to buy domestic bonds, thereby raising the demand for the domestic currency, and, potentially, preserving the peg. Unfortunately, higher domestic interest rates also discouraged domestic firms from engaging in real capital investment and domestic

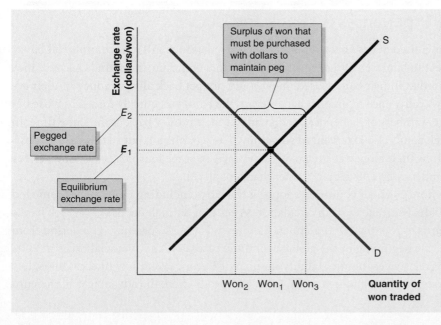

Figure 12.2

Pegging the Exchange Rate between the Won and the Dollar

The government of South Korea pegged the value of the won against the dollar. The pegged exchange rate, E_2, was above the equilibrium exchange rate, E_1. To maintain the peg, the Korean central bank had to use dollars to buy surplus won equal to $Won_3 - Won_2$.

households from borrowing to finance spending on houses and consumer durables. In the end, the East Asian currency crises of the late 1990s resulted in recessions in these countries, and the countries decided to abandon their currency pegs.

Sovereign Debt Crises

Sovereign debt refers to bonds issued by a government. A sovereign debt crisis occurs when a country has difficulty making interest or principal payments on its bonds or when investors expect a country to have this difficulty in the future. If a sovereign debt crisis leads to actual default, a government may for a period of time be unable to issue bonds, which means that it will have to rely exclusively on tax revenues to pay for government spending. Even if the government avoids default, it will probably have to pay much higher interest rates when it issues bonds. The resulting decreases in other government spending or increases in taxes can push the economy into recession.

Sovereign debt crises occur frequently and typically result from either of two circumstances:

1. Chronic government budget deficits that eventually result in the interest payments required on government bonds taking up an unsustainably large fraction of government spending
2. A severe recession that increases government spending and reduces tax revenues, resulting in soaring budget deficits.

Following the 2007–2009 recession, several European governments, most notably that of Greece, were pushed to the edge of debt crises, as investors began to doubt their ability to pay the interest on their bonds. These countries imposed sharp spending cuts and higher taxes to close their government budget deficits.

Making the Connection

Greece Experiences a "Bank Jog"

Before the United States enacted federal deposit insurance in 1934, commercial banks were subject to bank runs. In a bank run, depositors withdrew their funds because they were afraid that if their bank closed, they would not get back all the money in their accounts. Typically, once a run on a bank began, the bank was quickly forced to close because large numbers of its depositors demanded their money back at the same time. In 2012, Greek banks also experienced something like a bank run, but in this case, depositors withdrew their money at a relatively slow pace, so some journalists described Greek banks as undergoing a "bank jog" rather than a bank run.

After June 2002, all countries adopting the euro, including Greece, had removed their individual currencies from circulation. After that date, all deposits in Greek banks were in euros, rather than in drachmas, the previous Greek currency. The period from 2001 until the beginning of the global economic recession and financial crisis in 2007 was one of relative economic stability in most of Europe. With low interest rates, low inflation rates, and expanding employment and production, the advantages of the euro seemed obvious. The countries using the euro no longer had to deal with problems caused by fluctuating exchange rates. Having a common currency also makes it easier for consumers and firms to buy and sell across borders.

The recession and financial crisis resulted in falling real GDP and higher unemployment. The recession caused large increases in government spending and reductions in tax revenues as incomes and profits declined. Governments in a number of European countries, particularly Greece, Ireland, Spain, Portugal, and Italy, paid for the resulting budget deficits by selling bonds to investors. By the spring of 2010, many investors began to doubt the ability of some countries, particularly Greece, to make the interest payments on the bonds. If Greece defaulted, investors would be likely to stop buying bonds issued by several other European governments, and the continuation of the euro would be called into question.

The European Central Bank (ECB) helped Greece avoid a default by directly buying its bonds. The central bank extended similar help to Spain, Ireland, and Italy. The International Monetary Fund and the European Union put together aid packages meant to keep Greece and other countries from defaulting. In exchange for the aid, these countries were required to adopt an austerity policy of cutting government spending and raising taxes even though doing so resulted in significant protests from unions, students, and other groups.

In 2012, discontent over spending cuts and higher taxes, along with continuing high unemployment, led Greek voters to elect politicians who vowed to reverse the austerity policy. As a result, speculation increased that Greece would abandon the euro. Many Greeks were afraid that the government might decide to exchange their euro bank deposits for drachmas at a rate of one for one. If the drachma then depreciated—as was widely expected—bank depositors would suffer heavy losses. In response, beginning in May, Greek banks began to lose deposits. Depositors either held their withdrawals as cash or deposited them in foreign banks. Unlike with a normal bank run, however, Greek depositors believed that they had ample time to withdraw their money because the ECB was willing to provide euro currency to Greek banks to meet withdrawals and because it was unclear whether Greece actually would stop using the euro.

The Greek bank jog indicated a potential new source of instability in the global financial system: Not only might depositors in euro countries lose faith in banks because of actions by the banks—for instance, making bad loans—depositors could also become concerned that their country might leave the euro or that the ECB would not be willing to supply an unlimited amount of euros to local banks.

Sources: David Enrich, Sara Schaefer Muñoz, and Charles Forelle, "Europe Banks Fear Flight of Deposits," *Wall Street Journal*, May 20, 2012; Matthew O'Brien, "End of the Marathon: The Meaning of Greece's 'Bank Jog,'" *Atlantic*, May 17, 2012; and Damien McElroy, "Greeks Withdraw Savings in National 'Bank Jog,'" (UK) *Telegraph*, May 20, 2012.

See related problems 1.11 and 1.12 at the end of the chapter.

12.2

Learning Objective

Understand the financial crisis that occurred during the Great Depression.

The Financial Crisis of the Great Depression

The two most significant financial crises in the past 100 years in the United States were the ones that accompanied the Great Depression of the 1930s and the recession of 2007–2009. In this section and the next section, we look more closely at these crises.

The Start of the Great Depression

Panel (a) of Figure 12.3 shows movements for the years from 1929 to 1939 in real GDP; real investment spending by firms on factories, office buildings, and other physical capital and by households on residential construction; and real consumption spending by households on goods and services. The data are expressed as index numbers relative to their values in 1929. Real GDP declined by 27% between 1929 and 1933, while real consumption declined by 18% and real investment by an astonishing 81%. These declines were by far the largest of the twentieth century. Panel (b) shows the unemployment rate for the same years. The unemployment rate tripled from 1929 to 1930, was above 20% in 1932 and 1933, and was still above 10% in 1939, a decade after the Great Depression had begun.

Although many people think the Great Depression started with the famous stock market crash of October 1929, the NBER dates the Depression as starting two months earlier, in August 1929. Figure 12.4 shows movements in the S&P 500 Composite Stock Price Index from 1920 to 1939. By 1928, the Federal Reserve had become concerned

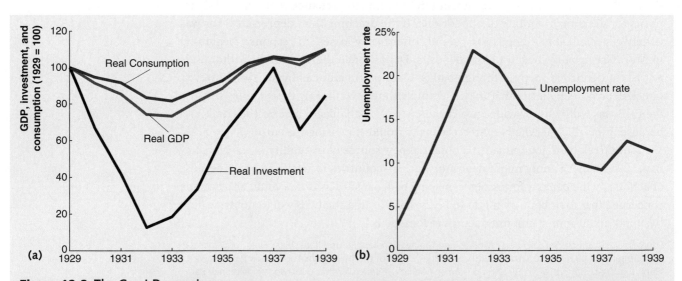

Figure 12.3 The Great Depression

In panel (a), the data are expressed as index numbers relative to their values in 1929. Real GDP declined by 27% between 1929 and 1933, while real consumption declined by 18% and real investment fell by an astonishing 81%. These declines were by far the largest of the twentieth century. Panel (b) shows that the unemployment rate tripled from 1929 to 1930, was above 20% in 1932 and 1933, and was still above 10% in 1939, a decade after the Great Depression had begun.

Sources: Panel (a): U.S. Bureau of Economic Analysis; panel (b): Economic historians have compiled varying estimates of unemployment in the 1930s, years during which the federal government did not collect data on unemployment. The estimates used in the panel are from David R. Weir, "A Century of U.S. Unemployment, 1890–1990," in Roger L. Ransom, Richard Sutch, and Susan B. Carter (eds.), *Research in Economic History*, Vol. 14, Westport, CT: JAI Press, 1992, Table D3, pp. 341–343.

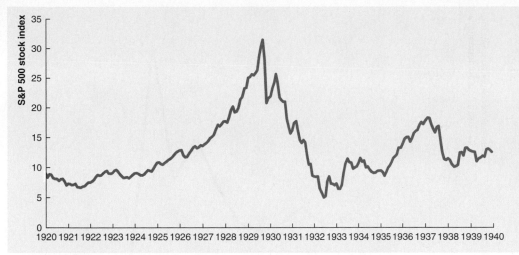

Figure 12.4

The S&P 500, 1920–1939

The Federal Reserve raised interest rates after it became concerned by the rapid increases in stock prices during 1928 and 1929. The decline in stock prices from 1929 to 1932 was the largest in U.S. history.

Source: Robert J. Shiller, *Irrational Exuberance*, Princeton, NJ: Princeton University Press, 2005, as updated at www.econ.yale.edu/~shiller/data.htm.

about the rapid increases in stock prices shown in the figure. As the Federal Reserve increased interest rates to reduce what it saw as a speculative bubble in stock prices, growth in the U.S. economy slowed during early 1929, and the economy eventually entered a recession.

Several factors increased the severity of the downturn during the period from the fall of 1929 to the fall of 1930. Between September 1929 and September 1930, stock prices plunged by more than 40%, thereby reducing household wealth, making it more difficult for firms to raise funds by issuing stock, and increasing the uncertainty of households and firms about their future incomes. This increase in uncertainty may account for the sharp fall in household spending on consumer durables, such as automobiles, and firm spending on factories, office buildings, and other physical capital. In addition, Congress passed the Smoot-Hawley Tariff Act in June 1930, which led to retaliatory increases in foreign tariffs, thereby reducing U.S. exports. Some economists also believe that the downturn was made worse by a decline in spending on new houses. This decline resulted from a slowdown in population growth caused in part by legislation Congress passed in the early 1920s restricting immigration.

The Bank Panics of the Early 1930s

If the downturn that began in August 1929 had ended in the fall of 1930, it would still have been one of the most severe on record. Far from ending, though, the downturn continued until March 1933. A slow recovery then took place until another recession began in May 1937 that lasted until June 1938. As a result, in 1939, a decade after the beginning of the Depression, many firms were still producing well below their capacity, and the unemployment rate remained high. The U.S. economy did not return to normal conditions until after the end of World War II in 1945.

Many economists believe that the series of bank panics that began in the fall of 1930 greatly contributed to the length and severity of the Depression. The bank panics came in several waves: the fall of 1930, the spring of 1931, the fall of 1931, and the spring of 1933. The large number of small, poorly diversified banks—particularly those that

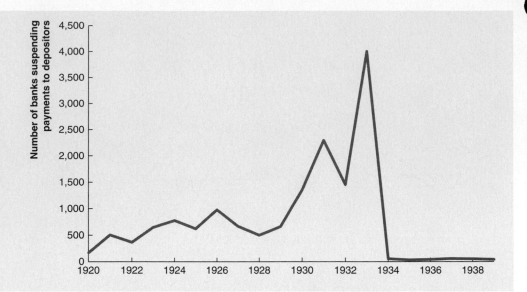

Figure 12.5

Bank Suspensions, 1920–1939

Bank suspensions, during which banks are closed to the public either temporarily or permanently, soared during the bank panics of the early 1930s before falling to low levels following the establishment of the FDIC in 1934.

Source: Board of Governors of the Federal Reserve System, *Banking and Monetary Statistics of the United States, 1914–1941*, Washington, DC: U.S. Government Printing Office, November 1943.

held agricultural loans as commodity prices fell—helped fuel the crises. A bank suspension occurs when a bank is closed to the public either temporarily or permanently. Figure 12.5 shows the number of bank suspensions for the years from 1920 to 1939. The panic of 1933 was the most severe, with several states declaring "bank holidays" in which all banks in the state were closed. Finally, shortly after taking office in March 1933, President Franklin Roosevelt declared a national bank holiday, and nearly every bank in the country closed. Of the 24,500 commercial banks operating in the United States in June 1929, only 15,400 were still operating in June 1934. The figure shows that with the establishment of the FDIC in 1934, bank suspensions fell to low levels.

We have already discussed how bank panics can deepen a recession. In addition, during the Depression, the bank panics fueled a **debt-deflation process** first described at the time by Irving Fisher of Yale University. Fisher argued that as banks were forced to sell assets, the prices of those assets would decline, causing other banks and investors holding the assets to suffer declines in net worth, leading to additional bank failures and to investors going bankrupt. These failures and bankruptcies would lead to further asset sales and further declines in asset prices. In addition, as the economic downturn worsened, the price level would fall—as it did in the early 1930s—with two negative effects: Real interest rates would rise, and the real value of debts would increase. The consumer price index declined by about 25% between 1929 and 1933, which means that fixed payments on loans and bonds had to be made with dollars of greater purchasing power, increasing the burden on borrowers and raising the likelihood of defaults. This process of falling asset prices, falling prices of goods and services, and increasing bankruptcies and defaults can increase the severity of an economic downturn.

Debt-deflation process
The process first identified by Irving Fisher in which a cycle of falling asset prices and falling prices of goods and services can increase the severity of an economic downturn.

The Failure of Federal Reserve Policy During the Great Depression

Some bank failures during the early 1930s resulted from the severity of the Depression, as banks suffered losses on their loans and security investments, became insolvent, and failed. But some bank failures resulted from the instability of the system as banks that were illiquid but not insolvent suffered runs and were forced to close. Ironically, the Federal Reserve, which Congress established in 1913 to end bank panics, presided over the worst panics in U.S. history.

Why did the Fed not intervene to stabilize the banking system? Economists have discussed four possible explanations:

1. *No one was in charge.* Today, the chairman of the Federal Reserve is clearly in charge. He is chairman of both the Board of Governors and the Federal Open Market Committee, which determines the Fed's most important policies. The current structure of the Federal Reserve System was not put in place until 1935, however, and in the early 1930s, power within the Federal Reserve System was much more divided. The secretary of the Treasury and the comptroller of the currency, both of whom report directly to the president of the United States, served on the Federal Reserve Board, which was the predecessor to the Board of Governors. The secretary of the Treasury served as the board's chairman. So, the Fed had less independence from the executive branch of the government than it does today. In addition, the heads of the 12 Federal Reserve District Banks operated much more independently than they do today, with the head of the Federal Reserve Bank of New York having nearly as much influence within the system as the head of the Federal Reserve Board. At the time of the bank panics, George Harrison, the head of the Federal Reserve Bank of New York, served as chairman of the Open Market Policy Conference, the predecessor of the current Federal Open Market Committee. Harrison frequently acted independently of Roy Young and Eugene Meyer, who served as heads of the Federal Reserve Board during those years. Important decisions required forming a consensus among these different groups. During the early 1930s, a consensus proved hard to come by, and taking decisive policy actions was difficult.

2. *The Fed was reluctant to rescue insolvent banks.* The Federal Reserve was established to serve as a lender of last resort to solvent banks that were experiencing temporary liquidity problems because of bank runs. Many of the banks that failed during the bank panics of the early 1930s were insolvent if their assets were valued at market prices, and many Fed officials believed that taking actions to save them might encourage risky behavior by bank managers. In other words, the Fed was afraid of the problem that economists now call moral hazard.

3. *The Fed failed to understand the difference between nominal and real interest rates.* The Fed closely monitored nominal interest rates, particularly rates on short-term loans, which fell to very low levels during the early 1930s. Many Fed officials believed that these low interest rates indicated that there was no shortage of available loans to borrowers. Economists, though, believe that the real interest rate is a better indicator than the nominal interest rate of conditions in the loan market. During the early 1930s, the U.S. economy experienced *deflation*, with the price level falling at an annual average rate of 6.6% between 1930 and 1933. So, measured in real terms, interest rates were much higher in the early 1930s than policymakers at the Fed believed them to be.

4. *The Fed wanted to "purge speculative excess."* Many members of the Fed believed that the Depression was the result of financial speculation during the late 1920s, particularly the bubble in stock prices that occurred in 1928 and 1929. They argued that

only after the results of the excesses had been "purged" would a lasting recovery be possible. Some economists believe that the Fed followed the "liquidationist" policy said to be promoted by Secretary of the Treasury Andrew Mellon. According to this policy, allowing the price level to fall and weak banks and weak firms to fail was necessary before a recovery could begin.

Making the Connection

Did the Failure of the Bank of United States Cause the Great Depression?

In the early 1960s, Milton Friedman of the University of Chicago and Anna Schwartz of the National Bureau of Economic Research published an influential discussion of the importance of bank panics in their book *A Monetary History of the United States, 1867–1960*. In that book and later writings, Friedman and Schwartz singled out the failure in December 1930 of the Bank of United States, a large private bank located in New York City, as being particularly important:

> [The bank's] failure on Dec. 11, 1930, marked a basic change in character of the contraction that had started in August 1929, from a severe recession, with no sign of any financial crisis, to a catastrophe that reached its climax in the banking holiday of March 1933, when all banks were closed for a week. . . .

The Bank of United States ran into trouble in part because an unusually high percentage of its loans were in real estate, which by the fall of 1930 was suffering from falling prices and mortgage defaults. In addition, its owners had been using the bank's funds to support the price of the bank's stock, an illegal activity for which two of the owners later went to jail. In the weeks leading up to the bank's closure, the Federal Reserve Bank of New York attempted to arrange for the bank to merge with two other New York City banks. When plans for the merger fell through, the bank was closed, becoming the largest bank to have failed in the United States up to that time.

The failure of the Bank of United States caused much discussion at the time, and economists continue to debate this episode today. The bank appears to have been insolvent at the time it closed, which is probably why the plan to save it by merging it with other banks failed. There is some evidence, though, that George Harrison, who headed the Federal Reserve Bank of New York, did not support the merger plan, which may have played a role in its rejection by the other banks. Economists continue to disagree as to whether the Federal Reserve should have moved more forcefully to keep the bank from closing.

Many economists are skeptical of Friedman and Schwartz's emphasis on the importance of the bank's failure. Immediately after the bank failed, other New York City banks did not suffer severe liquidity problems, and none failed. Several months passed before the next bank panic, and many of the banks involved in that panic were smaller banks outside New York City. In addition, whether that panic had any connection to the failure of the Bank of United States is unclear. Following the failure of the Bank of United States, interest rates on low-rated corporate bonds began to rise relative to interest rates on high-rated corporate bonds, which might indicate that investors interpreted the bank's failure as bad news about the future state of the economy. But, once again, it is unclear whether this movement in interest rates was the result of the bank's failure.

The details of the failure of the Bank of United States are less important than the later impact of this episode on policymakers. Particularly after publication of Friedman and Schwartz's book, many economists, both inside and outside the Fed, became convinced that allowing the bank to fail had been a significant policy mistake. Some economists even argue that this episode was important in leading the Fed to develop the "too-big-to-fail" doctrine, which holds that no large financial institution can be allowed to fail because its failure may destabilize the financial system. This doctrine was subject to intensive debate during the 2007–2009 financial crisis and its aftermath.

Although the Bank of United States failed more than 80 years ago, the consequences of its failure continue to influence current policy.

Sources: Milton Friedman and Anna Schwartz, *A Monetary History of the United States, 1867–1960*, Princeton, NJ: Princeton University Press, 1963, pp. 308–313; Friedman quote from Milton Friedman, "Anti-Semitism and the Great Depression," *Newsweek*, Vol. 84, November 16, 1974, p. 90; Allan H. Meltzer, *A History of the Federal Reserve: Volume 1: 1913–1951*, Chicago: University of Chicago Press, 2003, pp. 323–326; Elmus Wicker, *The Banking Panics of the Great Depression*, Cambridge, UK: Cambridge University Press, 1996; and Arthur J. Rolnick, "Interview with Ben S. Bernanke," Federal Reserve Bank of Minneapolis, *The Region*, June 2004.

See related problem 2.9 at the end of the chapter.

The Financial Crisis of 2007–2009

12.3

Learning Objective
Understand what caused the financial crisis of 2007–2009.

Several factors contributed to the severity of the recession of 2007–2009, including an increase in oil prices from $34 per barrel in 2004 to $147 per barrel in 2008. The most important cause, though, was clearly the bursting of the housing market bubble.

The Housing Bubble Bursts

New home sales rose by 60% between January 2000 and July 2005, by which time many economists believed that a *bubble* had formed in the housing market. Recall that in a bubble, the price of an asset is greater than its fundamental value. We have seen that the fundamental value of a share of stock equals the present value of the dividends investors expect to receive from owning the stock. Similarly, the fundamental value of a house equals the present value of the housing services the homeowner expects to receive. We would anticipate, then, that housing prices and rents would increase at roughly the same rate.[1] Accordingly, if prices of single-family homes rise significantly relative to rental rates for single-family homes, it is more likely that the housing market is experiencing a bubble. As Figure 12.6 shows, housing prices and housing rents generally increase at about the same rate, but between January 2000 and May 2006, housing prices more than doubled, while rents increased by less than 25%. This divergence between housing prices and rents is evidence of a bubble.

---

[1]It is possible that housing prices might rise while current rents remain unchanged if homebuyers are anticipating an increase in *future* rents. But there was not much indication during 2000–2005 that homebuyers or economists were expecting sharp increases in rents in the future.

Figure 12.6

Housing Prices and Housing Rents, 1987-2012

Typically, housing prices increase at about the same rate as housing rents. But during the housing bubble, housing prices increased far more than did rents.

Source: Federal Reserve Bank of St. Louis and S&P/Case-Shiller, standardandpoors.com.

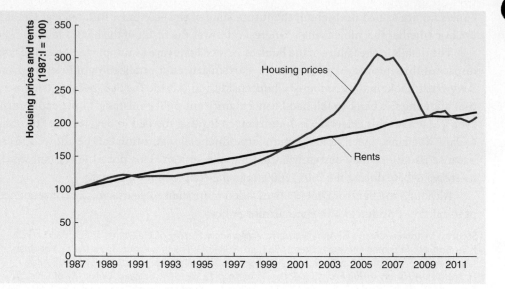

As prices of new and existing homes began to decline during 2006, some homebuyers had trouble making the payments on their mortgage loans. When lenders foreclosed on defaulted mortgages, the lenders sold the homes, causing housing prices to decline further. Mortgage lenders that had concentrated on making subprime loans suffered heavy losses, and some went out of business. Most banks and other lenders tightened their requirements for borrowers. This *credit crunch* made it more difficult for potential homebuyers to obtain mortgages, which further depressed the housing market. The decline in the housing market not only resulted in lower spending on residential construction but also affected markets for furniture, appliances, and home improvements, as homeowners found it more difficult to borrow against the declining value of their homes.

Bank Runs at Bear Stearns and Lehman Brothers

By early 2007, it had become clear that investors, including banks and other financial firms, that owned mortgage-backed securities made up of subprime mortgages would suffer significant losses. Many economists and policymakers, though, agreed with the opinion of Fed Chairman Ben Bernanke quoted in the chapter opener that rising defaults on subprime mortgages would not cause problems for the wider economy. The first strong indication that a financial crisis might be approaching came in August 2007, when the French bank BNP Paribas announced that it would not allow investors in three of its investment funds to redeem their shares. The funds had held large amounts of mortgage-backed securities and because trading in these securities had dried up, it had become difficult to determine the securities' market prices and, therefore, the value of the funds' shares.

In the fall of 2007 and the spring of 2008, credit conditions worsened. Many lenders became reluctant to lend to financial firms for more than very short terms and often insisted on government bonds as collateral. Some investment banks had funded long-term investments with short-term borrowing from banks and other financial firms (see Chapter 11). These investment banks were in a situation similar to that of commercial banks before the establishment of federal deposit insurance. In particular, the investment banks were subject to runs if lenders declined to renew the banks' short-term loans, which is what happened to Bear Stearns in March 2008. Lenders became concerned that Bear's investments in mortgage-backed securities had declined in value so much that the investment bank was insolvent. With aid from the Federal Reserve, Bear was saved from bankruptcy only by being acquired by the bank JPMorgan Chase at a price of $10 per share; one year earlier, Bear's shares had sold for $170.

By August 2008, the crisis was deepening, as nearly 25% of subprime mortgages were at least 30 days past due. On September 15, the Lehman Brothers investment bank filed for bankruptcy protection after the Treasury and Federal Reserve declined to commit the funds necessary to entice a private buyer to purchase the firm. At the same time, the Merrill Lynch investment bank agreed to sell itself to Bank of America. The failure of Lehman Brothers marked a turning point in the crisis. On September 16, Reserve Primary Fund, a large money market mutual fund, announced that because it had suffered heavy losses on its holdings of Lehman Brothers commercial paper, it would "break the buck" by allowing the price of shares in the fund to fall from $1.00 to $0.97 (see Chapter 11). This announcement led to a run on money market mutual funds, as investors cashed in their shares. Many parts of the financial system became frozen as trading in securitized loans largely stopped, and large firms as well as small ones had difficulty arranging for even short-term loans.

The Federal Government's Extraordinary Response to the Financial Crisis

Prior to the financial crisis, the federal government's policymaking and regulatory structure had been focused on the commercial banking system and the stock market. This focus left the government poorly equipped to deal with a crisis centered on the shadow banking system of investment banks, money market mutual funds, insurance companies, and hedge funds. In addition, as we have seen, most policymakers did not realize until well into 2007 that the subprime crisis might evolve into a full-blown financial crisis.

Nevertheless, the Federal Reserve, the Treasury, Congress, and President George W. Bush responded vigorously once the crisis had begun. On September 18, 2007, the Fed began aggressively driving down short-term interest rates by cutting its target for the federal funds rate, the interest rate that commercial banks charge each other for short-term loans. By December 2008, the federal funds rate was close to zero, its lowest rate in history. In September 2008, the federal government effectively nationalized Fannie Mae and Freddie Mac, the government-sponsored enterprises responsible for securitizing a majority of mortgage loans, by having the Treasury pledge to provide up to $100 billion to each firm in exchange for 80% ownership of the firms. The Treasury gave management control of the firms to the Federal Finance Housing Agency. That same month, the Treasury moved to stop the runs on money market mutual funds by announcing a $50 billion plan to insure shares in these funds. In October, the Fed announced that for the first time since the Great Depression, it would lend directly to corporations through the *Commercial Paper Funding Facility* by purchasing three-month commercial paper issued by nonfinancial corporations.

In September 2008, the Federal Reserve and the Treasury also unveiled a plan for Congress to authorize $700 billion to be used to purchase mortgages and mortgage-backed securities from financial firms and other investors. The objective of the *Troubled*

Asset Relief Program (TARP), which Congress passed in early October 2008, was to restore a market in these securities to provide relief to financial institutions that had trillions of dollars of these assets on their balance sheets. Ultimately, devising a program for purchasing mortgages and mortgage-backed securities proved difficult, and most of the TARP funds were used to make direct preferred stock purchases in banks to increase their capital and to provide funds to automobile firms that were in danger of failing.

These policy initiatives represented one of the most extensive government interventions in the financial system in U.S. history. Whether these initiatives may have unintended negative consequences in the long run remains to be seen. But most economists and policymakers believe that they served the purpose of stabilizing the financial system during the fall of 2008 and the spring of 2009. Also helping to stabilize the system was a *stress test* administered by the Treasury to 19 large financial firms during early 2009. The test was intended to gauge how well these firms would fare if the recession deepened. Many investors were reassured when the tests indicated that the firms would need to raise less than $100 billion in new capital to have the resources to deal with a severe economic downturn.

After the crisis had passed, Congress turned to the task of examining whether regulations governing the financial system needed to be overhauled. In July 2010, Congress passed, and President Barack Obama signed, the Wall Street Reform and Consumer Protection Act, which we will discuss in the next section.

Financial Crises and Financial Regulation

12.4

Learning Objective

Discuss the connection between financial crises and financial regulation.

The federal government's response to the 2007–2009 financial crisis highlights that new government financial regulations typically occur in response to a crisis. As we look at different types of regulations that the government has enacted over the years, we will see that there is a regular pattern:

1. A crisis in the financial system occurs
2. The government responds to the crisis by adopting new regulations
3. Financial firms respond to the new regulations
4. Government regulators adapt policies as financial firms try to evade regulations

The first stage in the regulatory pattern is a *crisis* in the financial system. For example, if savers lose confidence in banks, they will withdraw their funds, and a bank panic will result. In a panic, banks are unable to fulfill their role as financial intermediaries and many households and firms lose access to loans.

The second stage occurs when the government steps in to end the crisis through *regulation*. The government generally intervenes when it perceives instability in financial institutions and when political pressures make intervention advisable. For example, government regulation in the United States and other countries has responded to bank panics by enacting deposit insurance.

The third stage is the *response by the financial system*. A major new regulation—deposit insurance, for example—leads to changes and innovation in the activities of financial institutions. For example, banks may take on more risk once deposit insurance reduces the extent to which depositors monitor bank investments. As with manufacturing companies or other nonfinancial businesses, innovation (the development of new products or lines of business to serve consumers) gives one company an edge over its competitors. The motivation for financial innovation is the same as in other businesses: profit.

The fourth stage is the *regulatory response*. Regulators observe the effect of regulation on how financial institutions do business. In particular, when financial innovations circumvent regulatory restrictions, regulators must adapt their policies or seek new authority as a regulatory response. For example, when Congress adopted a regulation to keep banks from paying interest on checking accounts, banks eventually circumvented the ban by developing accounts similar to checking accounts, called NOW accounts, that paid interest. Congress then had to adapt regulations to either ban NOW accounts or to allow them. In this case, Congress decided to allow the accounts.

Lender of Last Resort

We have already seen that Congress created the Federal Reserve System in 1913 as the lender of last resort to provide liquidity to banks during bank panics. We have also seen, though, that the Fed failed its first crucial test when it stood by while the banking system collapsed in the early 1930s. Congress responded to this failure by establishing the FDIC in 1934 and by reorganizing the Fed to make the Federal Open Market Committee (FOMC) the Fed's main policy body. The chairman of the Board of Governors, rather than the president of the Federal Reserve Bank of New York, was made the chairman of the FOMC. This last change helped to centralize decision making at the Fed by ensuring that the Board of Governors, based in Washington, DC, rather than the 12 Federal Reserve District Bank presidents, would be the dominant force in the system.

Success in the Postwar Years and the Development of the "Too-Big-to-Fail" Policy

Despite its shaky start as a lender of last resort during the Great Depression, the Fed has performed this role well during most of the post–World War II period. For example, when the Penn Central Railroad, once one of the largest corporations in the United States, filed for bankruptcy in 1970, it defaulted on $200 million of commercial paper. Investors started to doubt the quality of commercial paper issued by other large corporations and became cautious about investing in that market. The Fed helped to avoid a crisis by providing commercial banks with loans that allowed the banks to lend to firms that would ordinarily have borrowed in the commercial paper market.

In a similar episode in 1974, the Franklin National Bank began to experience a run by depositors who held negotiable certificates of deposit (CDs). Because these CDs were worth more than $40,000, they were beyond what was then the limit for federal deposit insurance, and investors feared that they would suffer heavy losses if the bank failed. Other banks feared that they would also be subject to runs by depositors holding negotiable CDs. Because negotiable CDs were a significant source of funds to banks, banks would have had to cut back on their own loans, reducing the credit available to households and firms. The Fed avoided this result by making short-term loans of more than $1.5 billion to Franklin National until the Fed was able to find another bank willing to merge with Franklin National. The Fed's prompt action avoided what could have been a significant blow to the financial system.

The stock market crash of October 19, 1987, raised fears of a repetition of the events that followed the 1929 crash. In particular, many securities firms had suffered heavy losses because of the fall in stock prices. The failure of those firms would have disrupted trading on the New York Stock Exchange. Before the stock market opened for trading the following day, Federal Reserve Chairman Alan Greenspan announced to the news media the Fed's readiness to provide liquidity to support the economic and financial systems. At the same time, the Fed, acting as lender of last resort, encouraged banks to lend to securities firms and extended loans to banks. These actions reassured both banks and investors and preserved the smooth functioning of financial markets.

In these and other similar actions, the Fed had successfully used its role as lender of last resort to stabilize the financial system, thereby avoiding the errors of the 1930s when the Fed's unwillingness to save insolvent banks led it to stand by while the financial system collapsed. But was it possible that the Fed was starting to err in the opposite direction? In principle, central banks should provide short-term loans to banks that are illiquid but not insolvent. By lending to banks that are insolvent, the central bank runs the risk that bank managers will take on too much risk, knowing that if their investments fail and they become insolvent, the central bank will save them. In other words, by lending to insolvent banks, the Fed increases the level of moral hazard in the system. It became clear by the early 1980s that the largest banks were considered **"too big to fail"** by the Fed and the FDIC. In 1984, the comptroller of the currency, who regulates national banks, provided Congress with a list of banks that were considered too big to fail. A failure by any of these banks was thought to pose *systemic risk* to the financial system.

Too-big-to-fail policy
A policy under which the federal government does not allow large financial firms to fail, for fear of damaging the financial system.

Because the Fed and the FDIC would not allow these large banks to fail, depositors in them effectively had unlimited deposit insurance. Large depositors, including holders of negotiable CDs, would not lose any money if these banks failed, even though their deposits were above what was then the federal deposit limit of $100,000. So, these depositors had much less incentive to monitor the behavior of bank managers and to withdraw their deposits or demand higher interest rates if the managers made reckless investments.

Moreover, the too-big-to-fail policy was criticized for being unfair because it treated small and large banks differently. When the FDIC closed the African-American-owned Harlem's Freedom National Bank in 1990, its large depositors—including such charitable organizations as the United Negro College Fund and the Urban League—received only about 50 cents per dollar of uninsured deposits. Only a few months later, in January 1991, the much larger Bank of New England failed, as a result of a collapse of its real estate portfolio. Its large depositors were fully protected by the FDIC, costing taxpayers about $2.3 billion.

Concern with the unfairness and increased moral hazard resulting from the too-big-to-fail policy was one reason that Congress passed the Federal Deposit Insurance Corporation Improvement Act of 1991 (FDICIA). The act required the FDIC to deal with failed banks using the method that would be least costly to the taxpayer, which typically means closing the bank, reimbursing the bank's insured depositors, and using whatever funds can be raised from selling the bank's assets to reimburse uninsured depositors. Because the value of a failed bank's assets is almost always less than the value of its liabilities, uninsured depositors suffer losses. The act did contain an exception, however, for cases in which a bank's failure would cause "serious adverse effects on economic conditions or financial stability." To invoke this exception, two-thirds of the directors of the FDIC, two-thirds of the members of the Fed's Board of Governors, and the secretary of the Treasury would have to approve. During the financial crisis of 2007–2009, this exception proved to be important.

The Financial Crisis and A Broader Fed Role As Lender of Last Resort Because investment banks, rather than commercial banks, were most directly affected at the beginning of the financial crisis, policymakers faced unexpected challenges. Unlike commercial banks, investment banks were not eligible to borrow directly from the Fed. While deposits in commercial banks are covered by insurance through the FDIC, loans to investment banks are not. We have already seen that the Fed dealt with these problems by lending to large investment banks and by buying commercial paper to ensure that corporations would be able to meet their short-term credit needs. In addition, the Treasury provided temporary insurance to investors owning money market mutual fund shares.

Perhaps the most controversial of the Fed's actions was the decision in March 2008 to participate with the Treasury to keep Bear Stearns from failing by arranging for the investment bank to be purchased by JPMorgan Chase. As part of the arrangement, the Fed agreed to cover up to $29 billion in losses that JPMorgan Chase might suffer on Bear's holdings of mortgage-backed securities. Some economists and policymakers criticized this action, saying that it increased moral hazard in the financial system. This criticism may have played a role in the Fed's decision not to attempt to save Lehman Brothers from bankruptcy in September 2008. A few days later, though, the Fed made a large loan to the American International Group (AIG) insurance company in exchange for 80% ownership of the firm. In fact, with the exception of Lehman Brothers, the Fed, FDIC, and Treasury combined to take actions that resulted in no large financial firms failing. The too-big-to-fail policy appeared to be back.

The 2010 Financial Overhaul: The End of the Too-Big-to-Fail Policy? Although the actions of the Fed, FDIC, and Treasury received praise from some economists and policymakers for helping restore stability to the financial system, many members of Congress criticized what was called the "Wall Street bailout" that they believed resulted from TARP and the actions taken to keep large financial firms from failing. Accordingly, Congress passed the Wall Street Reform and Consumer Protection Act, or Dodd-Frank Act, in July 2010, which included provisions intended to end the too-big-to-fail policy. The act allows the Fed, FDIC, and Treasury to seize and "wind down" large financial firms, which means that the firms' assets are to be sold off in a way that will not destabilize financial markets. Previously, only the FDIC had this power, and it could use it only in closing commercial banks. The intent was to give policymakers a third option besides allowing a large firm to go bankrupt or taking action to save it. Sheila Bair, who was then chair of the FDIC, predicted that the act would lead investors to shift funds toward smaller firms, where the information costs of determining the riskiness of investments would be lower. Larger firms would have to provide investors with higher expected returns to compensate them for the ending of the too-big-to-fail policy. As of 2012, the largest U.S. banks had maintained their importance in the financial system. In 2012, the five largest bank

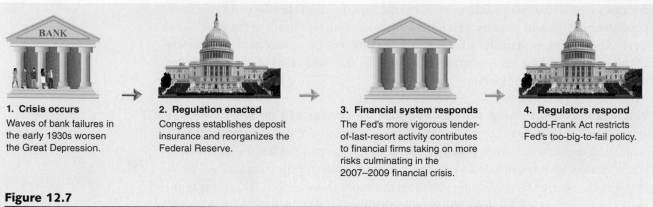

1. Crisis occurs
Waves of bank failures in the early 1930s worsen the Great Depression.

2. Regulation enacted
Congress establishes deposit insurance and reorganizes the Federal Reserve.

3. Financial system responds
The Fed's more vigorous lender-of-last-resort activity contributes to financial firms taking on more risks culminating in the 2007–2009 financial crisis.

4. Regulators respond
Dodd-Frank Act restricts Fed's too-big-to-fail policy.

Figure 12.7

Lender of Last Resort: Crisis, Regulation, Financial System Response, and Regulatory Response

holding companies owned more than one-half of all bank assets, compared with about one-quarter of all assets 10 years earlier. Whether the Dodd-Frank Act has actually put an end to the too-big-to-fail policy remains to be seen, as the new law left important details for regulators to implement.

Figure 12.7 summarizes the Fed's role of lender of last resort in the context of financial crisis, regulation, financial system response, and regulatory response.

Making the Connection

The Consumer Financial Protection Bureau: The New Sheriff of Financial Town

In July 2010, Congress passed the Wall Street Reform and Consumer Protection Act, or Dodd-Frank Act. One of the act's provisions was the creation of the Consumer Financial Protection Bureau (CFPB), in response to complaints about deceptive practices by banks, credit card companies, and mortgage brokers before and during the financial crisis. Many policymakers believed that thousands of Americans had lost their homes because they had taken out mortgage loans that they had either not understood or could not afford.

The CFPB was charged with consolidating responsibilities that had resided with several other federal agencies, and in July 2011, it took over enforcement of 18 existing consumer laws. Since then, the CFPB has used a range of powers to restrict what it considers problem lending, misleading marketing, and secret deals among companies that raise the costs of loans to consumers. The CFPB has a powerful enforcement tool: the threat of civil charges against violators of laws involving money transfers, foreclosures, and many other financial products and services.

The CFPB is part of, and funded by, the Federal Reserve System, but it is responsible for hiring its own personnel and setting its own rules. Although supporters welcomed the new bureau as an advocate for consumers, critics worried about the costs and complexity of additional regulation. Critics also saw the bureau's unusual level of independence as exempting it from the typical checks on the activities of government agencies. In its first year of existence, the CFPB carried out investigations of credit card companies, for-profit colleges, and mortgage lenders, as well as dozens of other firms. One of its most significant actions was an agreement it reached with Capital One Financial to refund $150 million in fees to over 2.5 million customers who, it was charged, purchased credit card protection and other services as a result of misleading marketing.

Critics questioned whether the gains for consumers from the bureau's activities were worth the costs. One rule issued by the CFPB for mortgage simplification was over 1,000 pages long; the entire Federal Reserve Act is only 32 pages long. Small banks, in particular, have complained that following complex rules makes it more costly to offer their services, and these costs are then passed through to consumers. Other costs include legal bills for firms subject to CFPB investigations. Jonathan Pompa, an attorney whose firm represents companies that have been investigated, claimed that the CFPB aggressively examines firms that offer financial products that it believes might harm consumers. As Pompa explains: "They're not messing around. . . . A year ago, we said there was a new sheriff in town. It's not just a sheriff—it's an army."

The CFPB also came under criticism for establishing a Web site devoted to consumer complaints about credit card companies. The American Bankers Association argued that because the Web site provides publicity for allegations that have not yet been verified, the action "raises serious questions about the balanced review we expect from our government agencies."

Supporters of the CFPB argue, though, that the financial crisis revealed that more regulation of consumer lending and related financial services was necessary and that effective regulation could make another financial crisis less likely. Supporters argue that criticism of the bureau comes mainly from financial firms that would rather not comply with new regulations.

Economists and policymakers continue to debate whether the CFPB is supplying needed regulation of financial firms or whether it is unnecessarily increasing the costs and reducing the efficiency of the services those firms provide.

Sources: Mary Kissel, "Ripoffreport.gov," *Wall Street Journal*, June 25, 2012; "Too Big Not to Fail," *Economist*, February 18, 2012; "Consumer Financial Protection Bureau's Impact Has Come as a Surprise," Associated Press, September 16, 2012; Jenna Greene, "One Year In, Consumer Financial Agency Has Had 'Extraordinary' Impact," BLT: The Blog of LegalTimes, July 20, 2012; and "Bureau of Consumer Financial Protection (C.F.P.B.)," *New York Times*, August 10, 2012.

See related problem 4.7 at the end of the chapter.

Reducing Bank Instability

The banking crisis of the Great Depression led not only to a reorganization of the Federal Reserve and the establishment of the FDIC but also to Congress's enactment of new regulations aimed at directly increasing the stability of the commercial banking system. One way that Congress attempted to reach this goal was by reducing competition among banks. Congress's intention was to reduce both the likelihood of bank runs and the extent of moral hazard in banks' behavior. One argument for limiting competition is that it increases a bank's value, thereby reducing bankers' willingness to make excessively risky investments.

In the long run, however, anticompetitive regulations do not promote bank stability because they create incentives for unregulated financial institutions and markets to compete with banks by offering close substitutes for bank deposits and loans. A dramatic example of how anticompetitive regulation actually led to competition occurred in the fight over limits on the interest rates that banks could pay on deposits. The battle began with the Banking Act of 1933, which authorized Regulation Q. *Regulation Q*, which was administered by the Fed, placed ceilings on the interest rates bank could pay on time and savings deposits and prohibited banks from paying interest on demand deposits, which were then the only form of checkable deposits. Regulation Q was intended to maintain banks' profitability by limiting competition for funds among banks and by guaranteeing a reasonable spread between interest rates banks received on loans and interest rates they paid on deposits. In practice, the regulation forced banks to innovate in order to survive.

In setting a ceiling on interest rates that banks could pay depositors, Congress intended to give banks a competitive advantage in the market for loans. Because they paid relatively little for deposits, banks could charge lower interest rates on loans and were the leading lenders to households and firms. But whenever market interest rates rose above the Regulation Q interest rate ceilings, savers had an incentive to withdraw money from bank deposits, thereby starving banks of the funds they needed to make loans. For instance, in the late 1960s, as rising inflation rates drove interest rates above the Regulation Q ceilings, large corporations and wealthy households, in particular, substituted short-term investments in Treasury bills, commercial paper, and repurchase agreements for short-term deposits in banks. The introduction of money market mutual funds in 1971 gave savers an additional alternative to bank deposits.

As we have seen, the development of money market mutual funds also provided *borrowers* with a new source of funds. Large, well-established firms could raise short-term funds in the commercial paper market. Firms sold a substantial portion of their commercial paper to money market mutual funds. Banks suffered from losing their commercial loan business to the commercial paper market because, as our analysis of adverse selection predicts, only high-quality borrowers can successfully sell commercial paper, leaving banks with lower-quality borrowers. The exit of savers and borrowers from banks to financial markets is known as **disintermediation**, and it costs banks lost revenue because it means they do not have savers' funds to loan.

Disintermediation
The exit of savers and borrowers from banks to financial markets.

To circumvent Regulation Q, banks developed four new financial instruments for savers:

1. Negotiable certificates of deposit (CDs)
2. Negotiable order of withdrawal (NOW) accounts
3. Automatic trasfer system (ATS) accounts
4. Money market deposit (MMDA) accounts

Citibank introduced *negotiable certificates of deposit* (or *negotiable CDs*) in 1961 as time deposits with a fixed maturity of, say, six months. These CDs had two important features: Because they had values of at least $100,000, they were not subject to Regulation Q interest rate ceilings. Because they could be bought and sold, negotiable CDs provided competition to commercial paper.

In addition, banks attempted to get around the prohibition of paying interest on demand deposits by developing *negotiable order of withdrawal (NOW) accounts* on which they paid interest. A depositor with a NOW account received "negotiable orders of withdrawal" that he or she could sign over when transferring funds to someone else. Although these negotiable orders of withdrawal were not called checks, they looked like checks and were treated like checks, so NOW accounts were effectively interest-paying checking accounts.

Banks also developed *automatic transfer system (ATS) accounts* as a means of helping large depositors avoid interest-rate ceilings. ATS accounts effectively pay interest on checking accounts by "sweeping" a customer's checking account balance at the end of the day into an interest-paying overnight repurchase agreement.

Finally, in response to the breakdown of interest-rate regulation in banking, Congress enacted two pieces of legislation: the Depository Institutions Deregulation and Monetary Control Act of 1980 (DIDMCA) and the Garn-St. Germain Act of 1982. With the passage of DIDMCA, Congress eased the anticompetitive burden on banks by phasing out Regulation Q—which disappeared entirely in 1986—and by formally allowing NOW and ATS accounts. In addition, the act eliminated interest-rate ceilings on mortgage loans and commercial loans. Congress passed the Garn-St. Germain Act to help reverse disintermediation by giving banks a more potent weapon against money market mutual funds. The act permitted banks to offer *money market deposit accounts (MMDAs)*, which would be covered by FDIC insurance, but banks were not required to hold reserves against them. Depositors were allowed to write only six checks per month. The costs of MMDAs to banks were low because the banks were not required to hold reserves against them or process many checks, so the banks could afford to pay higher interest rates on them than on NOW accounts. The combination of market interest rates and the safety and familiarity of banks made the new accounts instantly successful with depositors.

Figure 12.8 summarizes the process of financial crisis, regulation, financial system response, and regulatory response as it applies to interest-rate ceilings.

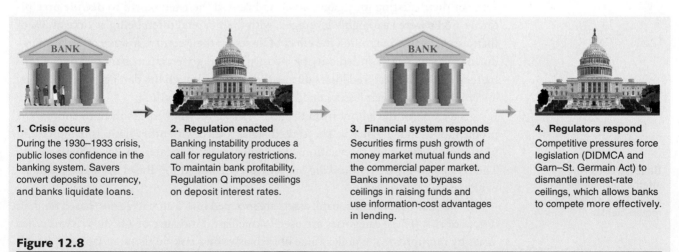

1. Crisis occurs
During the 1930–1933 crisis, public loses confidence in the banking system. Savers convert deposits to currency, and banks liquidate loans.

2. Regulation enacted
Banking instability produces a call for regulatory restrictions. To maintain bank profitability, Regulation Q imposes ceilings on deposit interest rates.

3. Financial system responds
Securities firms push growth of money market mutual funds and the commercial paper market. Banks innovate to bypass ceilings in raising funds and use information-cost advantages in lending.

4. Regulators respond
Competitive pressures force legislation (DIDMCA and Garn–St. Germain Act) to dismantle interest-rate ceilings, which allows banks to compete more effectively.

Figure 12.8

Interest-Rate Ceilings: Crisis, Regulation, Financial System Response, and Regulatory Response

Capital Requirements

One way the federal government attempts to promote stability in the banking system is by sending examiners from the FDIC, the Fed, and the Office of the Comptroller of the Currency to banks to check whether they are following regulations. (The Office of the Comptroller of the Currency confines its examinations primarily to large national banks.) After an examination, a bank receives a grade in the form of a *CAMELS* rating, based on the following:

Capital adequacy
Asset quality
Management
Earnings
Liquidity
Sensitivity to market risk

A poor CAMELS rating can lead to a cease-and-desist order being issued to a bank to change its behavior. Such a system mimics the way private markets approach moral hazard by inserting restrictive covenants in financial contracts.

Of the CAMELS categories, along with asset quality, capital adequacy has typically received the most attention. Moral hazard occurs when banks use their equity capital in risky investments in an attempt to increase their return on equity. Regulating the minimum amount of capital that banks are required to hold reduces the potential for moral hazard and the cost to the FDIC of bank failures. Regulators increased their focus on capital requirements following the *savings-and-loan (S&L) crisis* of the 1980s. To promote mortgage lending, federal regulation created S&Ls in the 1930s. S&Ls held long-term, fixed-rate mortgages and financed them with short-term time deposits. Although this structure guaranteed that S&Ls would suffer from a severe maturity mismatch, as long as interest rates were stable and regulation limited the interest rates that S&Ls and banks could pay on deposits, little went wrong. Beginning in 1979, however, sharply rising market interest rates increased the cost of funds for S&Ls, decreased the present value of their existing mortgage assets, and caused their net worth to decline precipitously. S&Ls were also highly leveraged, with their capital often being as little as 3% of their assets, which magnified the effect of losses on their equity. A wave of S&L failures during the 1980s was ended only by a costly federal government bailout. Many commercial banks also suffered losses during the 1980s, although the damage was limited by lower leverage and their lesser concentration in mortgage lending.

As a result of the fallout from the S&L crisis, policymakers resolved to address the problem of capital adequacy. The United States joined with other nations in a program begun by the Bank for International Settlements (BIS), located in Basel, Switzerland. The *Basel Committee on Banking Supervision* developed the **Basel accord** to regulate bank capital requirements.

Under the Basel accord, bank assets are grouped into four categories, based on their degree of risk. These categories are used to calculate a measure of a bank's *risk-adjusted assets* by multiplying the dollar value of each asset by a risk-adjustment factor. A bank's capital adequacy is then calculated using two measures of the bank's capital relative to its risk-adjusted assets. *Tier 1 capital* consists mostly of what we have been calling bank

Basel accord An international agreement about bank capital requirements.

capital: shareholders' equity. *Tier 2 capital* equals the bank's loan loss reserves, its subordinated debt, and several other bank balance sheet items. Banks set aside part of their capital as a *loan loss reserve* to anticipate future loan losses. Using a loan loss reserve enables a bank to avoid large swings in its reported profits. When banks sell bonds, some of the bonds are *senior debt*, while others are *subordinated* debt, or *junior* debt. If the bank were to fail, the investors owning senior debt would be paid before the investors owning junior debt. Because the investors owning junior debt have a greater incentive to monitor the behavior of bank managers, junior debt was included in Tier 2 capital under the Basel accord.

Bank regulators determine a bank's capital adequacy by calculating two ratios: the bank's Tier 1 capital relative to its risk-adjusted assets and the bank's total capital (Tier 1 plus Tier 2) relative to its risk-adjusted assets. On the basis of these two *capital ratios*, also called *leverage ratios*, banks are assigned to five risk categories, as shown in Table 12.2. Note that the higher a bank's capital ratio, the lower its leverage and the better able it is to weather short-term losses.

Banks in Category 1 have no restrictions on their activities beyond those specified in general banking regulations. Banks in Category 2 must abide by certain restrictions on their activities but are not required to take any actions. Banks in Categories 3, 4, and 5 must take steps to raise their capital ratios. Ordinarily, the FDIC enters a formal agreement with a bank in Categories 3, 4, and 5, specifying the actions that must be taken and deadlines for completing the actions. A bank in Category 5 must convince the FDIC that it has a plan to immediately increase its capital, or it will be closed. Note that a bank in Category 5 might be solvent—its capital may be positive, so the value of its assets may be greater than the value of its liabilities—but it will still be closed by the FDIC if it cannot raise additional capital immediately.

Implementation of these capital requirements meant that banks with low capital ratios were forced to close or to raise additional capital, thereby increasing the stability of the commercial banking system. But the requirements also led to a response by large commercial banks involving financial innovations that allowed these banks to push some assets off their balance sheets. Because holding relatively risky assets, such as mortgage-backed securities, required banks to hold additional capital, some large banks, such as Citigroup, formed *special investment vehicles* (*SIVs*) to hold these assets. SIVs had separate management and separate capital from the banks that sponsored them. But in buying and selling securities, the SIVs benefited from their association with the sponsoring banks. By the time of the financial crisis, there were about 30 SIVs,

Table 12.2 Measuring Banks' Capital Adequacy

Category	Description	Tier 1 capital ratio	Total capital ratio
1	Well capitalized	6% or greater	10% or greater
2	Adequately capitalized	4% or greater	8% or greater
3	Undercapitalized	Less than 4%	Less than 8%
4	Significantly undercapitalized	Less than 3%	Less than 6%
5	Critically undercapitalized	Less than 2%	—

Source: Federal Deposit Insurance Corporation.

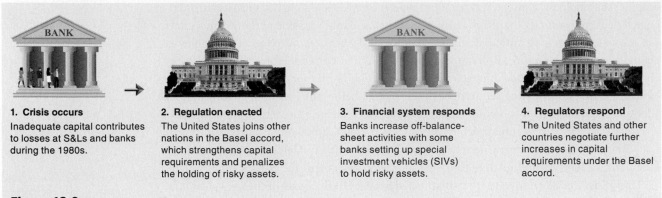

1. Crisis occurs

Inadequate capital contributes to losses at S&Ls and banks during the 1980s.

2. Regulation enacted

The United States joins other nations in the Basel accord, which strengthens capital requirements and penalizes the holding of risky assets.

3. Financial system responds

Banks increase off-balance-sheet activities with some banks setting up special investment vehicles (SIVs) to hold risky assets.

4. Regulators respond

The United States and other countries negotiate further increases in capital requirements under the Basel accord.

Figure 12.9

Capital Requirements: Crisis, Regulation, Financial System Response, and Regulatory Response

holding about $320 billion in assets. As the assets held by the SIVs lost value, a sponsoring bank was faced with the hard choice of allowing the SIV to fail or bringing it back on the bank's balance sheet. In the end, most banks chose the second course, increasing the damage to their balance sheets during the financial crisis but preserving their relationships with customers who had invested in commercial paper and other debt issued by the SIVs.

In September 2010, a new agreement was reached under the Basel accord that requires banks to increase their capital ratios. Banks were given more than eight years to comply with the new rules, and most large banks would have to raise little additional capital. Although, in the short run, the new agreement seemed unlikely to have much effect on the international banking system, regulators believed that, in the long run, it would reduce the need for government aid to banks in a future crisis. Figure 12.9 summarizes the process of financial crisis, regulation, financial system response, and regulatory response as it applies to capital requirements.

The 2007–2009 Financial Crisis and the Pattern of Crisis and Response

The events during and after the 2007–2009 financial crisis fit the pattern of crisis and response that we have seen several times in this chapter. Clearly, the housing collapse brought on a crisis greater than any the U.S. financial system had experienced since the Great Depression of the 1930s. The collapse of housing prices reduced the net worth of households, causing them to cut back on spending to pay down debt. Households that attempted to borrow, including borrowing to refinance mortgages, found it difficult to obtain credit because their net worth had declined and because lenders had tightened lending standards. Many smaller firms were in a similar position, as commercial real estate prices declined sharply, reducing the value of the buildings many firms rely on as collateral when borrowing.

Falling prices of mortgage-backed securities and other housing-related assets led to losses at banks and other intermediaries. The initial regulatory response by the Treasury and the Federal Reserve was to stabilize the financial system through bailouts of firms such as AIG, capital injections to commercial banks through TARP, and aggressive lending by the Federal Reserve.

Banks responded to the crisis and the regulatory pressure to rebuild their capital and reduce the nonperforming loans on their balance sheets by reducing lending and accumulating reserves in an attempt to *deleverage*. In addition, banks became more risk averse as they reassessed their lending rules. Many small businesses found themselves cut off from credit, even at banks with which they had had long-term relationships.

As the crisis passed, Congress attempted to overhaul regulation of the financial system with the passage in July 2010 of the Wall Street Reform and Consumer Protection Act, referred to as the Dodd-Frank Act. Here are some of the key provisions of the act:

- Created the Consumer Financial Protection Bureau, housed in the Federal Reserve, to write rules intended to protect consumers in their borrowing and investing activities.
- Established the Financial Stability Oversight Council, which includes representatives from all the major federal financial regulatory bodies, including the SEC and the Fed. The council is intended to identify and act on systemic risks to the financial system.
- Ended the too-big-to-fail policy for large financial firms, as discussed earlier in this chapter.
- Made several changes to the Fed's operations.
- Required certain derivatives to be traded on exchanges rather than over the counter.
- Implemented the *Volcker Rule*, which bans most proprietary trading at commercial banks.
- Required hedge funds and private equity firms to register with the SEC.
- Required that firms selling mortgage-backed securities and similar assets retain at least 5% of the credit risk.

The effects of the Dodd-Frank Act on the financial system remain to be seen. But if history is a guide, we can be certain that financial firms will respond with innovations intended to reduce the effect of the new rules on their activities.

Figure 12.10 summarizes the process of financial crisis, regulation, financial system response, and regulatory response as it applies to the financial crisis of 2007–2009.

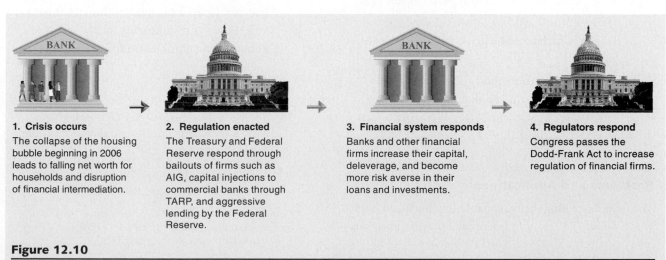

1. Crisis occurs
The collapse of the housing bubble beginning in 2006 leads to falling net worth for households and disruption of financial intermediation.

2. Regulation enacted
The Treasury and Federal Reserve respond through bailouts of firms such as AIG, capital injections to commercial banks through TARP, and aggressive lending by the Federal Reserve.

3. Financial system responds
Banks and other financial firms increase their capital, deleverage, and become more risk averse in their loans and investments.

4. Regulators respond
Congress passes the Dodd-Frank Act to increase regulation of financial firms.

Figure 12.10

The Financial Crisis of 2007–2009: Crisis, Regulation, Financial System Response, and Regulatory Response

Answering the Key Question

Continued from page 349

At the beginning of this chapter, we asked:

"Was the severity of the 2007–2009 recession due to the financial crisis?"

We have seen that the recession of 2007–2009 was the most severe since the Great Depression of the 1930s. It was also the first recession since the 1930s to be accompanied by a financial crisis. We discussed research by Carmen Reinhart and Kenneth Rogoff that shows that recessions have typically been longer and deeper when they involve financial crises than when they don't. We noted that because financial crises disrupt the flow of funds from savers to households and firms, they cause substantial reductions in spending, which is the key reason they make recessions worse. So, it is likely that the severity of the 2007–2009 financial crisis explains the severity of the recession. Not all economists accept this conclusion. Some economists believe that policy errors by the Federal Reserve and policy uncertainty during and after the recession explain the severity of the recession and the weakness of the recovery.

Key Terms and Problems

Key Terms

Bank panic, p. 351

Bank run, p. 351

Basel accord, p. 376

Contagion, p. 351

Debt-deflation process, p. 362

Disintermediation, p. 374

Federal Deposit Insurance
    Corporation (FDIC), p. 352

Financial crisis, p. 350

Insolvent, p. 351

Lender of last resort, p. 352

Too-big-to-fail policy, p. 370

12.1 The Origins of Financial Crises
Explain what financial crises are and what causes them.

Review Questions

1.1   Why does a financial crisis typically result in a recession?

1.2   Does a bank have to be insolvent to experience a run?

1.3   What are the two methods that governments typically use to avoid bank panics?

1.4   How do currency crises occur? Why have some European countries been suffering from a sovereign debt crisis?

Problems and Applications

1.5   In describing the bank panic that occurred in the fall of 1930, Milton Friedman and Anna Schwartz wrote:

A contagion of fear spread among depositors, starting from the agricultural areas, which had experienced the heaviest impact of bank failures in the twenties. But such contagion knows no geographical limits.

a. What do the authors mean by a "contagion of fear"?

b. What did bank depositors have to fear in the early 1930s? Do depositors today face similar fears? Briefly explain.

c. What do the authors mean that "such contagion knows no geographical limits"?

Source: Milton Friedman and Anna Schwartz, *A Monetary History of the United States, 1867–1960*, Princeton, NJ: Princeton University Press, 1963, p. 308.

1.6 An article in the *Economist* on the Dodd-Frank Act noted the following about a provision of the act that would require that trading in some derivatives be moved from over the counter to exchanges:

> The bill would further reduce the risk of contagion by moving derivatives trading onto clearing-houses, which would make it easier to determine firms' exposure to counterparties and would guarantee payment in the event of a default.

a. What does "exposure to counterparties" mean?

b. If it becomes easier to determine the exposure of a bank or another financial firm to counterparties, why might that reduce the risk of contagion?

Source: "In Praise of Doddery," *Economist*, March 18, 2010.

1.7 **[Related to** Solved Problem 12.1 **on page 352]** Economist Laurence Kotlikoff of Boston University has proposed that the banking system be reformed so that all banks become "limited purpose banks." As he explains:

> [Banks] would simply function as middlemen. They would never own financial assets or borrow to invest in anything. . . . [Limited purpose banking] effectively provides for 100 percent reserve requirements on checking accounts. This eliminates any need for FDIC insurance and any possibility of traditional bank runs.

Why would 100% reserve requirements on checking accounts eliminate the need for FDIC insurance? Would depositors need to fear losing money if their bank failed?

Source: Laurence J. Kotlikoff, *Jimmy Stewart Is Dead*, Hoboken, NJ: John Wiley & Sons, 2010, pp. 123–124, 132.

1.8 In 2012, the euro-zone countries began the process of increasing the integration of their banking systems by giving the European Central Bank the authority to supervise banks in all member countries. There was less progress on a proposal to have a single deposit insurance program for all countries. An article in the *Wall Street Journal* called a common deposit insurance program "a difficult political issue." Why might the countries in the euro zone consider it necessary to have a common deposit insurance system? Why might these countries have difficulty implementing a common system?

Source: Richard Barley, "Europe Inches Forward," *Wall Street Journal*, October 19, 2012.

1.9 **[Related to the** Making the Connection **on page 355]** In their book *This Time Is Different*, Carmen Reinhart and Kenneth Rogoff conclude: "An examination of the aftermath of severe postwar financial crises shows that they have had a deep and lasting effect on asset prices, output, and employment." Why should a recession accompanied by a financial crisis be more severe than a recession not accompanied by a financial crisis?

Source: Carmen M. Reinhart and Kenneth S. Rogoff, *This Time Is Different: Eight Centuries of Financial Folly*, Princeton, NJ: Princeton University Press, 2009, p. 248.

1.10 **[Related to the** Making the Connection **on page 355]** Carmen Reinhart and Kenneth Rogoff have argued that the 2007–2009 financial crisis explains not just the severity of the accompanying recession but also the slowness of the subsequent recovery. Michael Bordo of Rutgers University has argued that Reinhart and Rogoff's argument is incorrect. Instead, he argues that the slow recovery was due to "the unprecedented housing bust" and "uncertainty over changes in fiscal and regulatory policy." If you were attempting to evaluate the relative merits of Reinhart and Rogoff's and Bordo's arguments, what type of evidence would you look at? Is it likely that you could definitively identify the causes of the slow recovery? Briefly explain.

Source: Michael Bordo, "Financial Recessions Don't Lead to Weak Recoveries," *Wall Street Journal*, September 27, 2012.

1.11 **[Related to the** Making the Connection **on page 358]** In 2012, some economists and policymakers continued to worry about the state of the European financial system. An article in the *Economist* magazine commented on the actions of the European Central Bank (ECB): "The ECB's role has steadily evolved and has in the process reduced the risk of an implosion of the banking system and contagion across sovereign debt markets."

a. Why might any banking system face "implosion"? What steps can a central bank take to keep a banking system from imploding?

b. What does the article mean by the risk of "contagion across sovereign debt markets"? What steps did the ECB take to reduce the risk of contagion?

Source: "Getting Worse More Slowly Isn't Good Enough," *Economist*, October 1, 2012.

1.12 **[Related to the** Making the Connection **on page 358]** In 2012, as speculation increased that Greece might stop using the euro as its currency, the *Wall Street Journal* published an article that included this observation: "The Continent's financial system remains vulnerable to the prospect that stampedes of customers could yank their deposits from [banks] perceived as shaky." Were bank depositors afraid that banks were likely to fail? If not, what were they afraid of? Would depositors in U.S. banks be likely to have similar fears about U.S. banks? Briefly explain.

Source: David Enrich, Sara Schaefer Muñoz, and Charles Forelle, "Europe Banks Fear Flight of Deposits," *Wall Street Journal*, May 20, 2012.

12.2 The Financial Crisis of the Great Depression

Understand the financial crisis that occurred during the Great Depression.

Review Questions

2.1 What role did the bank panics of the early 1930s play in explaining the severity of the Great Depression?

2.2 How did the debt-deflation process contribute to the severity of the Great Depression?

2.3 Briefly summarize the explanations for the failure of the Federal Reserve to intervene to stabilize the banking system in the early 1930s.

Problems and Applications

2.4 In June 1930, a delegation of businessmen appeared at the White House to urge President Herbert Hoover to propose an economic stimulus package. Hoover told them: "Gentlemen, you have come sixty days too late. The depression is over." When did the Great Depression begin? Why might Hoover have reasonably expected that it to be over by June 1930? Why did the Depression continue much longer?

Source: Arthur M. Schlesigner, Jr., *The Crisis of the Old Order*, Boston: Houghton-Mifflin, 1957, p. 331.

2.5 In academic research published before he entered government, Fed Chairman Ben Bernanke wrote:

[In] a system without deposit insurance, depositor runs and withdrawals deprive banks of funds for lending; to the extent that bank lending is specialized or information sensitive, these loans are not easily replaced by nonbank forms of credit.

a. What does it mean to say that bank lending is "information sensitive"?

b. What are "nonbank forms of credit"? Why would bank lending being "information sensitive" make it difficult to replace with nonbank forms of credit?

c. Does Bernanke's observation help to explain the role bank panics played in the severity of the Great Depression?

Source: Ben S. Bernanke, *Essays on the Great Depression*, Princeton, NJ: Princeton University Press, 2000, p. 26.

2.6 In his memoirs, Herbert Hoover described the reaction of his Treasury Secretary to the Great Depression:

> First was the "leave it alone liquidationists" headed by Secretary of the Treasury Mellon, who felt that government must keep its hands off and let the slump liquidate itself. Mr. Mellon had only one formula: "Liquidate labor, liquidate stocks, liquidate the farmers, liquidate real estate."

a. What does "liquidate" mean in this context?

b. Can these views help to explain the Fed's actions during the early years of the Great Depression? Briefly explain.

Source: Herbert Hoover, *The Memoirs of Herbert Hoover: Volume 3: The Great Depression, 1929–1941*, New York: Macmillan, 1952, p. 30.

2.7 In 2010, an article in the *Wall Street Journal* observed:

> In the bond market . . . investors have been flocking to all manner of [bonds] . . . from Treasuries to "junk" bonds. The attraction: steady interest payments which would become increasingly valuable if deflation were to take hold.

a. Why would the interest payments on bonds become more "valuable" if deflation were to occur?

b. If deflation occurred, would the nominal interest rates on these bonds be higher or lower than the real interest rates? Briefly explain.

Source: Jane J. Kim and Eleanor Laise, "How to Beat Deflation," *Wall Street Journal*, August 7–8, 2010.

2.8 In his history of the Federal Reserve, Allan Meltzer of Carnegie Mellon University describes the views of Federal Reserve officials in the fall of 1930:

> Most of the policymakers regarded the substantial decline in short-term market interest rates . . . as the main . . . indicators of the current position of the monetary system. . . . [Policy] was "easy" and had never been easier in the experience of the policymakers of the Federal Reserve System.

a. What does it mean to say that Fed policy is "easy"?

b. In the context of the early 1930s, were low nominal interest rates a good indicator that policy was easy? Why might Fed officials have believed that they were?

Source: Allan H. Meltzer, *A History of the Federal Reserve: Volume 1: 1913–1951*, Chicago: University of Chicago Press, 2003, p. 315.

2.9 [**Related to the** Making the Connection **on page 364**] Arthur Rolnick of the Federal Reserve Bank of Minneapolis has argued that in their account of the failure of the Bank of United States:

> Friedman and Schwartz provide the rationale for the policy that today is known as "too big to fail"—that there are some institutions that are so big that we can't afford to let them fail because of the systemic impact on the rest of the economy. . . . They suggest that if the Fed had rescued this bank, the Great Depression might only have been a short, albeit severe, recession.

a. What was the Bank of United States? When did it fail? Why did it fail?

b. Why might the Fed's failure to save the Bank of United States provide a rationale for the policy of "too big to fail"?

c. Are there counterarguments to Rolnick's view?

Source: Arthur J. Rolnick, "Interview with Ben S. Bernanke," Federal Reserve Bank of Minneapolis, *The Region*, June 2004.

12.3 The Financial Crisis of 2007–2009

Understand what caused the financial crisis of 2007–2009.

Review Questions

3.1 What does it mean to say that there is a bubble in the housing market? Briefly describe the effect that the bursting of the housing bubble had on the U.S. economy.

3.2 How can an investment bank experience a "run"? Briefly describe the effect the runs on Bear Stearns and Lehman Brothers had on the U.S. economy.

3.3 Briefly discuss the policy actions the Federal Reserve and the Treasury took during the financial crisis.

Problems and Applications

3.4 An article in the *New York Times* quoted former Fed Chairman Alan Greenspan as arguing in 2010:

> The global house price bubble was a consequence of lower interest rates, but it was long-term interest rates that galvanized home asset prices, not the overnight rates of central banks, as has become the seemingly conventional wisdom.

a. What is a "house price bubble"?

b. Why would long-term interest rates have a closer connection than overnight interest rates to house prices?

c. Why would it matter to Greenspan whether low long-term interest rates were more responsible than low short-term interest rates for the housing bubble?

Source: Sewell Chan, "Greenspan Concedes That the Fed Failed to Gauge the Bubble," *New York Times*, March 18, 2010.

3.5 An article in the *New York Times* published just after the Fed helped to save Bear Stearns from bankruptcy noted:

> If Bear Stearns failed, for example, it would result in a wholesale dumping of mortgage securities and other assets onto a market that is frozen and where buyers are in hiding. This fire sale would force surviving institutions carrying the same types of securities on their books to mark down their positions.

a. Why did Bear Stearns almost fail?

b. How did the Federal Reserve rescue Bear Stearns?

c. What is the debt-deflation process? Does this process provide any insight into why the Federal Reserve rescued Bear Stearns?

Source: Gretchen Morgenson, "Rescue Me: A Fed Bailout Crosses a Line," *New York Times*, March 16, 2008.

3.6 Financial journalist Joe Nocera observed about the decision of the Federal Reserve and the Treasury not to help save Lehman Brothers:

> Ever since that weekend, most people, including me, have viewed the decision by Henry Paulson Jr., the Treasury secretary at the time, and Ben Bernanke, the Federal Reserve chairman, to allow Lehman to go bust as the single biggest mistake of the crisis.

Why did the Treasury and the Federal Reserve allow Lehman Brothers to fail? Why do some consider the decision to be the biggest mistake of the crisis?

Source: Joe Nocera, "Lehman Had to Die So Global Finance Could Live," *New York Times*, September 11, 2009.

3.7 [Related to the Chapter Opener on page 349] Looking back at the financial crisis several years later, former Fed Chair Alan Greenspan argued:

> At least partly responsible [for the severity of the financial collapse] may have been the failure of risk managers to fully understand the impact of the emergence of shadow banking that increased financial innovation, but as a consequence, also increased the level of risk. The added risk had not been compensated by higher capital.

a. How did the emergence of shadow banking increase the risk to the financial system?

b. What does Greenspan mean that "the added risk had not been compensated by higher capital"? By holding more capital, what problems could shadow banks have potentially avoided?

Source: Alan Greenspan, "The Crisis," *Brookings Papers on Economic Activity*, Spring 2010, p. 219.

12.4 **Financial Crises and Financial Regulation**
Discuss the connection between financial crises and financial regulation.

Review Questions

4.1 How is being a lender of last resort connected to the too-big-to-fail policy?

4.2 What innovations did banks develop to get around ceilings on deposit interest rates?

4.3 Why might deposit insurance encourage banks to take on too much risk? Is deposit insurance, therefore, a bad idea? Briefly explain.

Problems and Applications

4.4 A column in the *Wall Street Journal* by the governor of the central bank of Sweden discussing the Basel accord makes the following observation: "One clear lesson from the [financial] crisis is that regulatory capital requirements for the banking system were too low. In other words, leverage was too high."

a. What are "regulatory capital requirements"?

b. Why would regulatory capital requirements being too low result in leverage being too high?

c. What does leverage being too high have to do with the financial crisis?

Source: Stefan Ingves, "Basel III Is Simpler and Stronger" *Wall Street Journal*, October 14, 2012.

4.5 The financial writer Sebastian Mallaby made the following observation about hedge funds:

Leverage also made hedge funds vulnerable to shocks: If their trades moved against them, they would burn through thin cushions of capital at lightning speed, obliging them to dump positions fast—*destabilizing* prices.

a. What does a hedge fund's trades "moving against it" mean?

b. Why would a fund's trades moving against it cause it to burn through its capital?

c. What is the connection between a fund's being highly leveraged and its having a "thin cushion of capital"?

d. What does a fund's "dumping its positions" mean?

e. Why might a fund's dumping its positions cause prices to be destabilized? Prices of what?

Source: Sebastian Mallaby, *More Money Than God*, New York: Penguin Press, 2010, p. 10.

4.6 In a paper looking back at the financial crisis, former Fed Chairman Alan Greenspan wrote:

Some bubbles burst without severe economic consequences, the dotcom boom and the rapid run-up of stock prices in the spring of 1987, for example. Others burst with severe deflationary consequences. That class of bubbles . . . appears to be a function of the degree of debt leverage in the financial sector, particularly when the maturity of debt is less than the maturity of the assets it funds.

a. What does Greenspan mean by "debt leverage"?

b. Why would it matter if "the maturity of the debt is less than the maturity of the assets it funds"?

c. Does Greenspan's analysis provide insight into why the Fed during his tenure may have been reluctant to take action against asset bubbles?

Source: Alan Greenspan, "The Crisis," *Brookings Papers on Economic Activity*, Spring 2010, pp. 210–11.

4.7 [Related to the Making the Connection on page 372] An article in the *Economist* explained that, although many bankers do not support the regulations imposed by the Consumer Financial Protection Bureau (CFPB), they are reluctant to criticize the CFPB publicly: "This is in part due to the risk that, given the industry's low public esteem, complaining would be inflammatory and counterproductive, perhaps also bringing with it regulatory retribution. A few also see the possibility of gaining an edge." Briefly explain why costly regulations imposed by the CFPB could result in an advantage for some financial firms over their rivals.

Source: "Too Big Not to Fail," *Economist*, February 18, 2012.

4.8 Shortly after the Federal Reserve arranged for JPMorgan Chase to purchase Bear Stearns in March 2008, the *Wall Street Journal* recounted the events that led to the extraordinarily low price that JPMorgan paid for Bear Stearns:

"The bank was mulling a price of $4 or $5 a share. 'That sounds high to me,' Mr. Paulson said. 'I think this should be done at a low price.'"

a. Why did Treasury Secretary Paulson want Bear Stearns to sell for such a low price?

b. Why was the Fed's decision to orchestrate the purchase of Bear Stearns so controversial?

Source: Kate Kelly, "Bear Stearns Neared Collapse Twice in Frenzied Last Days," *Wall Street Journal*, May 29, 2008.

Data Exercises

D12.1: [Unemployment and the recession of 2007–2009]

 Go to the Web site of the Federal Reserve Bank of St. Louis (FRED) (research.stlouisfed.org/fred2/) and download and graph the data series for the unemployment rate (UNRATE) from January 1948 until the most recent month available. Go to the Web site of the National Bureau of Economic Research (nber.org) and find the dates for business cycle peaks and troughs. (The period between a business cycle peak and trough is a recession.) Describe how the unemployment rate moves just before, during, and just after a recession. How does the pattern for the 2007–2009 recession compare to the patterns for other recessions?

D12.2: [Credit markets and the recession of 2007–2009]

 Go to the Web site of the Federal Reserve Bank of St. Louis (FRED) (research.stlouisfed.org/fred2/) and download and graph the data series for the interest rate on Baa-rated corporate bonds (DBAA) from January 1986 until the most recent data available. Go to the Web site of the National Bureau of Economic Research (nber.org) and find the dates for business cycle peaks and troughs. (The period between a business cycle peak and trough is a recession.)

a. Describe how the interest rate on these bonds typically moves just before, during, and just after a recession.

b. How does the pattern for the 2007–2009 recession compare to the patterns for other recessions?

c. If you had to date the financial crisis just on the basis of movements in the interest rates on these bonds, in which month would you say the financial crisis began, and in which month would you say the financial crisis ended? Briefly explain your choices.

CHAPTER 13

The Federal Reserve and Central Banking

Learning Objectives

After studying this chapter, you should be able to:

13.1 Explain why the Federal Reserve System is structured the way it is (pages 388–399)

13.2 Explain the key issues involved in the Fed's operations (pages 399–406)

13.3 Discuss the issues involved with central bank independence outside the United States (pages 406–409)

Has the Fed Become Too Powerful?

In July 2012, the U.S. House of Representatives voted overwhelmingly to authorize the Government Accountability Office (GAO) to audit the monetary policy actions of the Federal Reserve. Many economists and some policymakers, including Fed Chairman Ben Bernanke, saw the vote as an attempt to reduce the independence of the Fed. Bernanke argued that passage of the bill would be a "nightmare scenario" for the Fed because it would increase political influence on Fed decision making. In late 2012, it appeared doubtful that the Senate would pass the bill, so it was unlikely to become law.

But the bill was only one of several indications in recent years that many members of Congress were in favor of reducing the Fed's independence. We have

seen that the Federal Reserve Act of 1913, which established the Federal Reserve System, had intended to make the Fed financially independent from the rest of the federal government, and, to an extent, politically independent as well. We have also seen that from the beginning, critics have questioned whether the Fed should be independent. Accountants typically perform audits of a firm's financial statements to verify that the statements are accurate. Since 1978, the Office of Inspector General (OIG) has been charged by Congress with hiring an outside firm to audit the Federal Reserve's financial statements. In 2010, Congress went beyond these routine audits in a provision of the Wall Street Reform and Consumer Protection Act, or Dodd-Frank Act. The provision required the GAO to audit the

Continued on next page

Key Issue and Question

Issue: Following the financial crisis, Congress debated whether to reduce the independence of the Federal Reserve.

Question: Should Congress and the president be given greater authority over the Federal Reserve?

Answered on page 409

Fed's emergency lending programs that had begun in December 2007 to deal with the financial crisis.

Over the years, some members of Congress have criticized the Fed's expenditures on relatively small projects, such as Reserve Bank buildings. But ordering an audit of a Fed program was highly unusual. The bill that passed the House in 2012 would have gone much further, however, by requiring the GAO to audit all of the Fed's monetary policy actions. These steps by Congress indicate that as the Fed's role in the financial system expanded during and after the financial crisis, the Fed has come under closer scrutiny.

Many critics see the Fed as having assumed far too important a role in the economy. One indication of the Fed's importance is the way the financial markets react to speeches and testimony by the Fed's chairman. For example, in 2010, many investors were worried that the United States might soon experience a "double-dip recession." Although the recession that began in 2007 had ended in mid-2009, some economists were forecasting that the U.S. economy would fall back into recession in late 2010. So, many investors hoped that when Fed Chairman Ben Bernanke testified before Congress in July 2010, he would announce new policies that would help to expand the economy. When Bernanke's testimony did not include such policies, the Dow Jones Industrial Average immediately plunged by more than 160 points. It is little wonder that many people consider the chairman of the Federal Reserve second only to the president of the United States in his ability to affect the economy and the financial system.

But should the unelected head of the central bank have so much power? Economists and policymakers have debated this question for decades.

Sources: Kristina Peterson and Siobhan Hughes, "House Passes Ron Paul's 'Audit the Fed' Bill," *Wall Street Journal*, July 25, 2012; and Annalyn Censky, "Audit the Fed? Bernanke Fights Back Against Ron Paul," money.cnn.com, July 18, 2012.

In this chapter, we discuss the Fed's organization and structure and its role as an economic policymaking body. We also describe the political arena in which the Fed operates and the debate over the independence of the central bank that has become more intense in Congress in recent years. We then examine the organization and independence of central banks outside the United States, including the European Central Bank.

13.1

Learning Objective

Explain why the Federal Reserve System is structured the way it is.

The Structure of the Federal Reserve System

Few countries have as complex a structure for their central bank as the United States has in its Federal Reserve System. The Fed's organization was shaped by the same political struggle that gave the United States a fragmented banking system: advocates of strong financial institutions versus those who feared such strong institutions would abuse their economic power. We hear echoes of those earlier political struggles in the fight over recent Congressional legislation aimed at reducing the Fed's independence. To understand why the Fed is organized as it is, we need to look back in history at the nation's earlier attempts to create a central bank.

Creation of the Federal Reserve System

Not long after the United States won its independence, Treasury Secretary Alexander Hamilton organized the Bank of the United States, which was meant to function as a central bank but had both government and private shareholders. The Bank attempted to stabilize the financial system by taking steps to ensure that local banks did not extend too many loans relative to their capital. And the Bank rapidly accumulated enemies.

Local banks resented the Bank's supervision of their operations. Many advocates of a limited federal government distrusted the Bank's power. Farmers and owners of small businesses, particularly in the West and South, resented the Bank's interfering with their ability to obtain loans from their local banks.

Congress granted the Bank a 20-year charter in 1791, making it the only federally chartered bank. All other banks at the time had their charters from state governments. There was not enough Congressional support to renew the charter, so the Bank ceased operations in 1811. Partly because of the federal government's problems in financing the War of 1812, political opinion in Congress shifted back toward the need for a central bank. In 1816, Congress established the Second Bank of the United States, also under a 20-year charter. The Second Bank encountered many of the same controversies as the First Bank. As the time approached for renewal of the Second Bank's charter, an epic political battle broke out between the populist President Andrew Jackson and Nicholas Biddle, the president of the Second Bank. Although in 1832, Congress passed a bill to recharter the Bank, Jackson vetoed the bill, and the Bank's charter expired in 1836. (The Bank survived for a time as a state-chartered bank in Pennsylvania.)

The disappearance of the Second Bank of the United States left the nation without a central bank and, therefore, without an official lender of last resort for banks. Private institutions, such as the New York Clearing House, attempted to fill the void, but severe nationwide financial panics in 1873, 1884, 1893, and 1907—and accompanying economic downturns—raised fears in Congress that the U.S. financial system was unstable. After a panic and economic recession in 1907, Congress considered options for government intervention. Many officials worried that bankers such as New York financier J. P. Morgan, who in the past had helped organize loans to banks suffering temporary liquidity problems, would be unable to manage future crises. Congress appointed the National Monetary Commission to study the possibility of establishing a central bank. Congress modified the commission's recommendations, but with the support of President Woodrow Wilson, the Federal Reserve Act became law in 1913.

The Federal Reserve Act established the **Federal Reserve System** as the central bank of the United States. Many in Congress believed that a unified central bank based in Washington, DC, would concentrate too much economic power in the hands of the officials running the bank. So, the act divided economic power within the Federal Reserve System in three ways: among bankers and business interests, among states and regions, and between government and the private sector. The act and subsequent legislation created four groups within the system, each empowered, in theory, to perform separate duties: the Federal Reserve Banks, private commercial member banks, the Board of Governors, and the Federal Open Market Committee (FOMC). All national banks—commercial banks with charters from the federal government—were required to join the system. State banks—commercial banks with charters from state governments—were given the option to join. The original intent of the Federal Reserve Act was to give the central bank control over the amount of currency outstanding and the volume of loans—known as *discount loans*—to member banks under the lender-of-last-resort function. In 1913, the president and Congress didn't envision the Fed as a centralized authority with broad control over most aspects of money and the banking system. As we will see in the rest of this section, over time, the Fed has expanded its role in the financial system.

Federal Reserve System
The central bank of the United States.

Federal Reserve Banks

As part of its plan to divide authority within the Federal Reserve System, Congress declined to establish a single central bank with branches, which had been the structure of both the First and Second Banks of the United States. Instead, the Federal Reserve Act divided the United States into 12 Federal Reserve districts, each of which has a **Federal Reserve Bank** in one city (and, in most cases, additional branches in other cities in the district). Congress intended that the primary function of the Reserve Banks would be to make discount loans to member banks in its region. These loans were to provide liquidity to banks, thereby fulfilling in a decentralized way the system's role as a lender of last resort and putting an end to bank panics—or so Congress hoped!

Figure 13.1 shows the Federal Reserve districts and locations of the Federal Reserve Banks. The map may appear strange at first glance. Some states are split by district boundaries, and economically dissimilar states are grouped in the same district. Most Federal Reserve districts contain a mixture of urban and rural areas, as well as manufacturing, agriculture, and service business interests. This arrangement was intentional, to prevent any one interest group or any one state from obtaining preferential treatment from the district Federal Reserve Bank.

Federal Reserve Bank
A district bank of the Federal Reserve System that, among other activities, conducts discount lending.

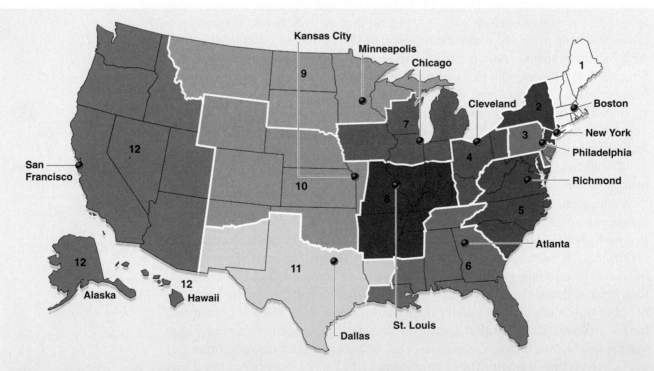

Figure 13.1 Federal Reserve Districts

The division of the United States into 12 Federal Reserve districts was designed so that each district contains a mixture of urban and rural areas and manufacturing, agricultural, and service industries.

Note that Hawaii and Alaska are included in the Twelfth Federal Reserve District.

Source: Federal Reserve Bulletin.

Making the Connection

St. Louis *and* Kansas City? What Explains the Locations of the District Banks?

The current Fed is not exactly what Congress had in mind when it passed the Federal Reserve Act. In particular, the Reserve Banks were intended to have much more independence than they have today. So, where the banks would be located was a significant issue during the Congressional debates over the act. The act allowed for 8 to 12 districts but did not specify their boundaries or indicate in which cities Federal Reserve Banks would be located. That decision was given to a Reserve Bank Organizing Committee, consisting of the secretary of the Treasury, the secretary of Agriculture, and the comptroller of the currency. The district boundaries and Federal Reserve Bank cities that the committee announced in April 1914 have remained unchanged to the present.

The committee's choices were controversial because the three committee members were all appointees of Democratic President Woodrow Wilson. Some critics argued that Democratic Party politics dictated which cities the committee chose. For instance, the only state with two banks is Missouri, with Kansas City serving as the Federal Reserve Bank for the tenth district and St. Louis serving as the bank for the eighth district. Critics pointed out that the Democratic Speaker of the House was from Missouri. Similarly, Richmond, Virginia, the home of Democratic Senator Carter Glass, one of the sponsors of the Federal Reserve Act, was awarded a bank. Attempts were made to convince officials of the Federal Reserve System to overturn the committee's decisions, until finally in 1916, the U.S. attorney general ruled that the district boundaries and locations of the Federal Reserve Banks could be changed only if Congress amended the Federal Reserve Act.

Although the view that the locations of the Federal Reserve Banks represent early twentieth century politics is widespread among economists, recent research has questioned this idea. Michael McAvoy, of the State University of New York, Oneonta, reexamined the choices of the Reserve Bank Organizing Committee to see whether political or economic factors were more important. He found that there was agreement among most groups at the time on locating Federal Reserve Banks in six of the cities: Boston, Chicago, New York, Philadelphia, St. Louis, and San Francisco. McAvoy estimated a statistical model to see whether political variables—such as whether the city was represented by a Democrat in Congress—or economic variables—such as the city's population, the growth in bank capital, and the preferences of bankers surveyed by the committee—were able to predict the cities chosen. McAvoy's conclusion was that economic variables could correctly predict the cities chosen, while political factors could not.

So, while it may seem odd today for Missouri to have two Federal Reserve Banks, it appears to have made economic sense in 1914.

Sources: Michael R. McAvoy, "How Were the Federal Reserve Bank Locations Selected?" *Explorations in Economic History*, Vol. 43, No. 3, July 2006; and Allan H. Meltzer, *A History of the Federal Reserve, Volume I: 1913–1951*, Chicago: University of Chicago Press, 2003, pp. 73–75.

See related problem 1.9 at the end of the chapter.

Who owns the Federal Reserve Banks? When banks join the Federal Reserve System, they are required to buy stock in their District Bank. Member banks receive fixed dividends of 6% on the shares of stock they own in the District Bank. So, in principle, the private commercial banks in each district that are members of the Federal Reserve System own the District Bank. In fact, each Federal Reserve Bank is a private–government joint venture because the member banks enjoy few of the rights and privileges that shareholders ordinarily exercise. For example, member banks do not have a legal claim on the profits of the District Banks, as shareholders of private corporations do.

A guiding principle of the 1913 Federal Reserve Act was that one constituency (for example, finance, industry, commerce, or agriculture) would not be able to exploit the central bank's economic power at the expense of another constituency. Therefore, Congress restricted the composition of the boards of directors of the Federal Reserve Banks. The directors represent the interests of three groups: banks, businesses, and the general public. Member banks elect three bankers (Class A directors) and three leaders in industry, commerce, and agriculture (Class B directors). The Fed's Board of Governors appoints three public interest directors (Class C directors). For much of the Federal Reserve System's history, the nine directors of a Federal Reserve Bank have elected the president of that bank, subject to approval by the Board of Governors. Under the Dodd-Frank Act, the Class A directors no longer participate in the election of bank presidents.

The 12 Federal Reserve Banks carry out duties related to the Fed's roles in the payments system, control of the money supply, and financial regulation. Specifically, the Federal Reserve Banks:

- Manage check clearing in the payments system
- Manage currency in circulation by issuing new Federal Reserve notes and withdrawing damaged notes from circulation
- Conduct discount lending by making and administering discount loans to banks within the district
- Perform supervisory and regulatory functions such as examining state member banks and evaluating merger applications
- Provide services to businesses and the general public by collecting and making available data on district business activities and by publishing articles on monetary and banking topics written by professional economists employed by the banks
- Serve on the Federal Open Market Committee, the Federal Reserve System's chief monetary policy body

The Federal Reserve Banks engage in monetary policy both directly (by making discount loans) and indirectly (through membership on Federal Reserve committees). In theory, Federal Reserve Banks establish the discount rate that banks pay on discount loans and determine the amounts that individual (member and nonmember) banks are allowed to borrow. In practice, however, in recent decades, the discount rate has been set by the Board of Governors in Washington, DC, and it is the same in all 12 districts. The Federal Reserve Banks also influence policy through their representatives on the Federal Open Market Committee and on the Federal Advisory Council, a consultative body composed of district bankers.

Member Banks

Although the Federal Reserve Act required all national banks to become member banks of the Federal Reserve System, state banks were given the option to join, and many chose not to. Currently, only about 16% of state banks are members. About 38% of all banks in the United States now belong to the Federal Reserve System, although these member banks hold a substantial majority of all bank deposits.

Historically, state banks often chose not to join the Federal Reserve System because they saw membership as costly. In particular, state banks that did not join the system could avoid the Fed's reserve requirements. Because the Fed did not pay interest on required reserves, banks saw the reserve requirement as effectively being a tax because the banks were losing the interest they could have earned by lending the funds. In other words, being a member of the Fed imposed a significant opportunity cost on banks, in the form of lost interest earnings. As nominal interest rates rose during the 1960s and 1970s, the opportunity cost of Fed membership increased, and fewer state banks elected to become or remain members.

During the 1970s, the Fed argued that the so-called reserve tax on member banks placed these banks at a competitive disadvantage relative to nonmember banks. The Fed claimed that declining bank membership eroded its ability to control the money supply and urged Congress to compel all commercial banks to join the Federal Reserve System. Although Congress did not legislate such a requirement, the Depository Institutions Deregulation and Monetary Control Act (DIDMCA) of 1980 required that all banks maintain reserve deposits with the Fed on the same terms. This legislation gave member and nonmember banks equivalent access to discount loans and to payment system (check-clearing) services. DIDMCA effectively blurred the distinction between member and nonmember banks and halted the decline in Fed membership. In October 2008, the Fed began paying banks an interest rate of 0.25% on reserves, which lowered the opportunity cost to banks of holding reserves.

Solved Problem 13.1

How Costly Are Reserve Requirements to Banks?

Suppose that Wells Fargo pays a 1% annual interest rate on checking account balances, while having to meet a reserve requirement of 10%. Assume that the Fed pays Wells Fargo an interest rate of 0.25% on its holdings of reserves and that Wells Fargo can earn 5% on its loans and other investments.

a. How do reserve requirements affect the amount that Wells Fargo can earn on $1,000 in checking account deposits? Ignore any costs Wells Fargo incurs on the deposits other than the interest it pays to depositors.

b. Is the opportunity cost to banks of reserve requirements likely to be higher during a recession or during an economic expansion? Briefly explain.

Solving the Problem

Step 1 **Review the chapter material.** This problem is about the effect of reserve requirements on banks, so you may want to review the section "Member Banks" on this page.

Step 2 **Answer part (a) by calculating the effective cost of funds to Wells Fargo.**
With a 10% reserve requirement, Wells Fargo must hold $100 of a $1,000 checking account deposit as reserves with the Fed, on which it receives an interest rate of 0.25%. The bank can invest the remaining $900. So, it will earn ($900 × 0.05) + ($100 × 0.0025) = $45.00 + $0.25 = $45.25. If the bank did not need to hold reserves against the deposit, it would earn $1,000 × 0.05 = $50. So, the reserve requirement is reducing Well Fargo's return by $4.75, or $4.75/$1,000 = 0.475%.

Step 3 **Answer part (b) by explaining how the reserve tax varies over the business cycle.** The higher the interest rate banks can earn on their loans and other investments, the higher the opportunity cost of having to hold reserves at the Fed that are earning a low interest rate. Interest rates tend to fall during economic recessions and rise during economic expansions (see Chapter 4). So, the opportunity cost to banks of reserve requirements is likely to be higher during economic expansions than during economic recessions.

See related problem 1.10 at the end of the chapter.

Board of Governors

Board of Governors
The governing board of the Federal Reserve System, consisting of seven members appointed by the president of the United States.

The **Board of Governors**, which is headquartered in Washington, DC, has ultimate authority over the Federal Reserve System. Its seven members are appointed by the president of the United States and confirmed by the U.S. Senate. To provide for central bank independence, the terms of board members are set so that governors serve nonrenewable terms of 14 years, which are staggered so that one term expires every other January 31. As a result, it is unlikely that one U.S. president will be able to appoint a full Board of Governors. On average, presidents appoint a new member every other year. It is possible for one person to serve longer than 14 years: If the person begins by serving out the remainder of the unexpired term of a governor who has retired, he or she may be reappointed to a full term. By this method, Alan Greenspan served from 1987 to 2006. No Federal Reserve District can be represented by more than one member on the Board of Governors.

The president chooses one member of the Board of Governors to serve as chairman. Chairmen serve four-year terms and may be reappointed. For instance, Ben Bernanke was appointed chair in January 2006 by President George W. Bush and reappointed in January 2010 by President Barack Obama.

Currently, many board members are professional economists from business, government, and academia. Chairmen of the Board of Governors since World War II have come from various backgrounds, including Wall Street (William McChesney Martin), academia (Arthur Burns and Ben Bernanke), business (G. William Miller), public service (Paul Volcker), and economic forecasting (Alan Greenspan).

The Board of Governors administers monetary policy to influence the nation's money supply and interest rates through open market operations, reserve requirements, and discount lending. Since 1935, the board has had the authority to determine reserve requirements within limits set by Congress. The board also effectively sets the discount rate charged on loans to banks. It holds 7 of the 12 seats on the Federal Open Market Committee and therefore influences the setting of guidelines for open market operations. In addition to its formal responsibilities, the board informally influences national and international economic policy decisions. The chairman of the Board of Governors advises the president and testifies before Congress on economic matters, such as economic growth, inflation, and unemployment.

The Board of Governors is responsible for some financial regulation. It sets margin requirements, or the proportion of the purchase price of securities that an investor must pay in cash rather than buy on credit. In addition, it determines permissible activities for bank holding companies and approves bank mergers. The chairman of the Board of Governors also serves on the Financial Stability Oversight Council (FSOC), which the Dodd-Frank Act established in 2010 to regulate the financial system. Finally, the Board of Governors exercises administrative controls over individual Federal Reserve Banks, reviewing their budgets and setting the salaries of their presidents and officers.

The Federal Open Market Committee

The 12-member **Federal Open Market Committee (FOMC)** directs the Fed's open market operations. Members of the FOMC are the chairman of the Board of Governors, the other Fed governors, and 5 of the 12 presidents of Federal Reserve Banks. The president of the Federal Reserve Bank of New York is always a member, with the other 11 Federal Reserve Bank presidents serving one-year terms on a rotating basis. All 12 Federal Reserve Bank presidents attend meetings and participate in discussions. The chairman of the Board of Governors serves as chairman of the FOMC. The committee meets in Washington, DC, eight times each year.

In recent decades, the FOMC has been at the center of Fed policymaking. Until the financial crisis of 2007–2009, the Fed's most important policy tool was setting the target for the federal funds rate, which is the interest rate that banks charge each other on short-term loans (see Chapter 15). During the financial crisis, Fed Chairman Ben Bernanke needed to make decisions rapidly and to use new policy tools. As a result, the focus of monetary policy moved away from the FOMC. As more normal conditions have been returning to the economy and the financial system, the FOMC is resuming its traditional importance.

Prior to each meeting, FOMC members access data from three books: The "Green Book," prepared by board staff, contains a national economic forecast for the next two years; the "Blue Book," also prepared by board staff, contains projections for monetary aggregates and other information useful in providing context for alternative monetary policies; and the "Beige Book," prepared by the Federal Reserve Banks, contains summaries of economic conditions in each district. At the end of each meeting, after all members of the Board of Governors and all Reserve Bank presidents have been heard from, Chairman Bernanke summarizes the discussion. The FOMC then takes a formal vote that sets a target for the federal funds rate. The committee summarizes its views in a public statement of the balance or risks between higher inflation and a weaker economy. Typically, the board's staff has prepared three statements with slightly different language for the members to choose from. In times of uncertainty over the Fed's future policy, the precise wording of the statement can be very important.

Federal Open Market Committee (FOMC)
The 12-member Federal Reserve committee that directs open market operations.

To reach its target for the federal funds rate, the Fed needs to adjust the level of reserves in the banking system by buying and selling Treasury securities. The FOMC doesn't itself buy or sell securities for the Fed's account. Instead, at the end of each meeting, it issues a directive to the Fed's trading desk at the Federal Reserve Bank of New York. There, the manager for domestic open market operations carries out the directive by buying and selling Treasury securities with *primary dealers*, which are private financial firms that deal in these securities.

Making the Connection

On the Board of Governors, Four Can Be a Crowd

Because the Fed's most important monetary policy tool is setting the target for the federal funds rate, by the 1980s, the key monetary policy debates within the Fed took place during meetings of the FOMC. Economists and Wall Street analysts closely watched the outcome of each meeting for clues about the direction of Fed policy. During the financial crisis of 2007–2009, however, it became clear that the Fed could not confine its actions to changes in the target for the federal funds rate. As in other recessions, the FOMC moved quickly to cut the target beginning in September 2007. But by December 2008, the target had effectively been cut to zero, yet the economy continued to contract, and the financial system was in crisis.

Fed Chairman Ben Bernanke responded by taking a series of policy actions, some of which were unprecedented (see Chapter 12). Because events were moving swiftly, waiting for the next FOMC meeting to discuss potential policy moves was not feasible. In addition, because FOMC meetings were attended by all the members of the Board of Governors and the 12 Reserve Bank presidents, its size was a barrier to quick decision making. The alternative of relying on the Board of Governors was also problematic. In 1976, Congress passed the Government in the Sunshine Act, which requires most federal government agencies to give public notice before a meeting. If four or more members of the Board of Governors meet to consider a policy action, it is considered an official meeting under the act and cannot be held without prior public notice. Given that Bernanke needed to make decisions rapidly as events unfolded hour by hour, the requirement of prior public notice made it infeasible for him to meet with more than two other members of the Board of Governors.

As a result, Bernanke relied on an informal group of advisers consisting of Board of Governors members Donald Kohn and Kevin Warsh and New York District Bank president Timothy Geithner. Geithner was a member of the FOMC but not of the Board of Governors, so his presence at meetings did not trigger the Sunshine Act requirement. The "four musketeers," as they came to be called, were the key policymaking body at the Fed for the duration of the crisis. The unintended consequence of the Sunshine Act requirements was to drastically limit the input of the other members of the Board of Governors into monetary policymaking.

Source: David Wessel, *In Fed We Trust: Ben Bernanke's War on the Great Panic*, New York: Crown Business, 2009.

See related problem 1.11 at the end of the chapter.

Power and Authority Within the Fed

Congress designed the Federal Reserve System to have checks and balances to ensure that no one group could control it. There was therefore little central (or national) control of the system during its first years. The Governors Conference, consisting of the heads of the 12 Federal Reserve Banks, vied with the Federal Reserve Board in Washington for control of the system.[1] After the severe banking crisis of the early 1930s, many analysts concluded that the decentralized Reserve Bank system could not adequately respond to national economic and financial disturbances. The Banking Acts of 1933 and 1935 gave the Board of Governors authority to set reserve requirements and the FOMC the authority to direct open market operations. The Banking Act of 1935 also centralized the Board of Governors' control of the system, giving it a majority (7 of 12) of votes on the FOMC. In addition, the secretary of the Treasury and the comptroller of the currency were removed from the Board of Governors, thereby increasing the Fed's independence.

The Board of Governors and the FOMC exert most of the Fed's *formal* influence on monetary policy. However, many Fed watchers believe that the *informal* authority of the chairman, the board's staff economists, and the members of the FOMC predominates. In other words, the informal power structure within the Fed is more concentrated than the formal power structure. Because the Federal Reserve Bank of New York always occupies a seat on the FOMC, the president of that bank can be quite influential. Figure 13.2 shows the organizational and power-sharing arrangements within the Fed. Ultimately, the Fed chairman wields the most power in the system. Some board members and District Bank presidents on the FOMC may challenge the chairman's agenda, but the chairman's influence still prevails.

Member banks, which are the nominal owners of Federal Reserve Banks, have little actual influence within the system. The distinction between *ownership* and *control* within the Federal Reserve System is clear: Member banks own shares of stock in the Federal Reserve Banks, but this ownership confers few of the rights that are typically granted to shareholders of private corporations. Member banks receive a fixed 6% annual dividend, regardless of the Fed's earnings, and so do not have the residual claim to a firm's profits that shareholders in a private corporation enjoy. Moreover, member banks have virtually no control over how their investment in the system is used because the Board of Governors in Washington, DC, formulates policy. Although member banks elect the six Class A and Class B directors, these are not contested elections. Officials at the Federal Reserve Bank or the Board of Governors typically suggest the one candidate for each position.

Changes to the Fed Under the Dodd-Frank Act

The severity of the financial crisis and some of the unprecedented policy actions the Fed took during that time led many economists and policymakers to reconsider the role of the Fed in the financial system. During the long debate over financial reform, members of Congress offered many proposals to alter the Fed's structure or its responsibilities.

---

[1]At the time, the heads of the Reserve Banks were called governors. The Governors Conference controlled open market operations in the early years of the Fed. Open market operations came under the control of the Open Market Investment Committee during the 1920s. The Open Market Investment Committee was then replaced by the Federal Open Market Committee in 1933.

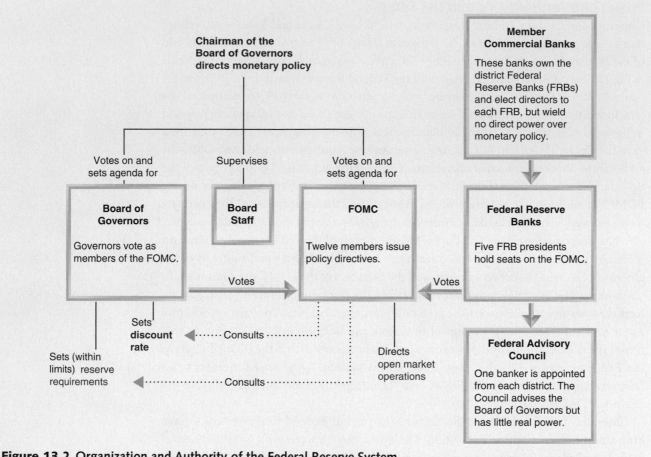

Figure 13.2 Organization and Authority of the Federal Reserve System

The Federal Reserve Act of 1913 established the Federal Reserve System and incorporated a series of checks and balances into the system. However, informal power within the Fed is more concentrated in the hands of the chairman of the Board of Governors than the formal structure suggests.

Wall Street Reform and Consumer Protection Act (Dodd-Frank Act)
Legislation passed during 2010 that was intended to reform regulation of the financial system.

When the **Wall Street Reform and Consumer Protection Act**, also known as the **Dodd-Frank Act**, finally passed in July 2010, however, its changes to the Fed were relatively minor. The following are the main provisions of the bill that affect the Fed:

- The Fed was made a member of the new Financial Stability Oversight Council (FSOC), along with members of nine other regulatory agencies, including the SEC and the FDIC. Although how the council will operate in practice remains to be seen, Congress intends for the FSOC to increase capital requirements at financial firms and provide a mechanism for closing insolvent firms in a way that does not result in financial instability. The objective is to avoid situations, such as the failure of Lehman Brothers in 2008, in which the insolvency of one large financial firm threatens the stability of the system.
- One member of the Board of Governors is now designated the vice chairman for supervision, with particular responsibility for coordinating the Fed's regulatory actions.
- As we saw at the beginning of the chapter, the Government Accountability Office (GAO) was ordered to perform an audit of the emergency lending programs the Fed had carried out during the financial crisis.

- As already mentioned, the Class A directors of the Federal Reserve Banks will no longer participate in elections of the bank presidents.
- To increase the transparency of its operations, the Fed was ordered to disclose the names of financial institutions to which it makes loans and with which it buys and sells securities.
- The new Consumer Financial Protection Bureau was established at the Fed. Although the bureau is physically located at the Fed and its budget comes from Fed revenues, Fed officials have no managerial oversight of it. The bureau's director is appointed by the president, subject to confirmation by the Senate, and functions independently of other Fed officials. The purpose of the bureau is to write rules concerning consumer protection that will apply to all financial firms. Some of the responsibility that the Fed had for regulating consumer lending has been transferred to the bureau.

How the Fed Operates

The government created the Fed to oversee aspects of the banking system and to manage the money supply. Lacking a constitutional mandate, the Fed operates in a political arena, and it is subject to pressure from members of Congress and the White House. In this section, we describe how the Fed operates in the political environment, and we discuss the debate over the independence of the central bank.

Handling External Pressure

Congress intended the Federal Reserve System to operate largely independently of external pressures from the president, Congress, the banking industry, and business groups. Members of the Board of Governors are appointed for long, nonrenewable terms of office, reducing any one president's influence on the board's composition and reducing the temptation for governors to take actions merely to please the president and Congress.

The Fed's financial independence allows it to resist external pressure. Generally, federal agencies must ask Congress for the funds they need to operate. Congress scrutinizes these budgetary requests and can reduce the amounts requested by agencies that have fallen out of favor with key members of the House or Senate. Not only is the Fed exempt from this process, but it is also a profitable organization that actually contributes funds to the Treasury rather than receiving funds from it. Most of the Fed's earnings come from interest on the securities it holds, with smaller amounts coming from interest on discount loans and fees that are received from financial institutions for check-clearing and other services. In 2011, the Fed's net income was $77 billion—substantial profits when compared with even the largest U.S. corporations. For instance, ExxonMobil earned $70 billion in profits in 2011, while Apple earned $36 billion, and Microsoft earned $31 billion. Unlike with these corporations, however, any income the Fed earns in excess of its expenses is transferred to the U.S. Treasury.

Despite the attempt to give the Fed independence, it isn't completely insulated from external pressure. First, the president can exercise control over the membership of the Board of Governors. Often, governors do not serve their full 14-year terms because they can earn higher incomes in private business. Therefore, a president who serves two terms in office may be able to appoint several governors. In addition, the president may

13.2

Learning Objective

Explain the key issues involved in the Fed's operations.

appoint a new chairman every four years. A chairman who is not reappointed may serve the remainder of his or her term as a governor but traditionally resigns, thereby giving the president another vacancy to fill.

Second, although the Fed's significant net income exempts it from requesting money from Congress, the Fed remains a creation of Congress. The U.S. Constitution does not specifically mandate a central bank, so Congress can amend the Fed's charter and powers—or even abolish it entirely. Members of Congress are usually not shy about reminding the Fed of this fact. In the middle and late 1970s, Congress forced the Fed to explain its goals and procedures. The Humphrey-Hawkins Act (officially the Full Employment and Balanced Growth Act of 1978) requires the Fed to explain how its procedures are consistent with the president's economic objectives. Most recently, the Dodd-Frank Act changed some aspects of the Fed's organization and procedures. In 2012, a bill was proposed to have the GAO audit the Fed's monetary policy actions, but the Senate is not expected to pass the bill into law. So, in practice, Congress has reduced some aspects of the Fed's independence, but it has not yet limited the Fed's ability to conduct an independent monetary policy.

The Fed has independence from Congress, but the Fed chairman testifies before Congress on the state of the economy and the goals of monetary policy. Under the leadership of Ben Bernanke, the Fed has become more communicative and transparent with the general public. Economists debate the benefits of Bernanke's approach.

Making the Connection

Fedspeak vs. Transparency

Alan Greenspan, who served as chairman of the Federal Reserve Board from 1987–2006, earned a reputation for what financial reporters called "Fedspeak." In his statements to Congress and the general public, Greenspan often used ambiguous and vague language that was difficult for people to understand. One reason for Greenspan's cautious statements was a concern that securities traders were listening for hints that the Fed would take actions to affect interest rates and stock prices—and the traders' profits.

When Ben Bernanke became chairman, he made a commitment to avoid Fedspeak. The television program *60 Minutes* interviewed Bernanke in April 2011, and he became the first Fed chairman to hold a news conference following a meeting of the Federal Open Market Committee. In an October 2012 speech, Bernanke explained that: "One of my principal objectives as Chairman has been to make monetary policy . . . as transparent as possible . . . the Federal Open Market Committee explains the reasons for its policy decisions . . . after each regularly scheduled meeting . . ." Perhaps reacting to the Fed's example, Mario Draghi, president of the European Central Bank (ECB), announced his own commitment to transparency by endorsing a proposal to publish the minutes of the ECB's monetary policy meetings.

Economists have generally welcomed the Fed's moves toward greater transparency. Knowing the central bank's policy intentions can help households and firms make better saving, investment, and spending decisions. However, some critics argue that the Fed's push for transparency may go too far and the Fed's decision-makers would have more leeway to respond to changes in the economy if they did not commit to particular courses of action. The Fed may have to come to agree to some extent with these critics. For example, in September 2012, the Fed announced that it would pursue an expansionary monetary policy until the labor market improved "substantially." But it did not set a time limit on how long the policy might continue or state an explicit goal for the increase in employment that would represent "substantial" improvement in the labor market. A columnist in the *Wall Street Journal* applauded the Fed's approach, arguing that: "While Bernanke welcomes making the Fed more open, less transparency isn't necessarily a bad development."

Still some critics continued to argue that the Fed was providing more information than investors, firms, or households could interpret. One critic argued in regard to a particular Fed policy that: "The Fed's action would have a better chance of producing the sustained positive market reaction the Fed apparently is after, if the Fed had simply taken the action and shut-up."

In the end, though, when faced with sustained political criticism of many of its actions, the Fed may have little choice but to be more transparent than in the days of Alan Greenspan and Fedspeak.

Sources: Ben S. Bernanke, "Five Questions about the Federal Reserve and Monetary Policy," Address before the Economic Club of Indiana, Indianapolis, Indiana, October 1, 2012; Christopher Lawton, "ECB to Publish Minutes From Its Monetary Policy Meetings?" *Wall Street Journal*, September 20, 2012; Gary Crosse and Jan Paschal, "Timeline: Federal Reserve's Transparency Steps," Reuters, January 25, 2012; Kathleen Madigan, "In Future, QE Could Stand for 'Quit Explaining'," *Wall Street Journal*, September 17, 2012; and Sy Harding, "Enough with the Fed's Transparency Already," *Forbes*, September 14, 2012.

See related problem 2.10 at the end of the chapter.

Examples of Conflict between the Fed and the Treasury

Elected officials lack formal control of monetary policy, which has occasionally resulted in conflicts between the Fed and the president, who is often represented by the secretary of the Treasury. During World War II, the Roosevelt administration increased its control over the Fed. To help finance wartime budget deficits, the Fed agreed to hold interest rates on Treasury securities at low levels: 0.375% on Treasury bills and 2.5% on Treasury bonds. The Fed could keep interest rates at these low levels only by buying any bonds that were not purchased by private investors, thereby predetermining (pegging) the rates. When the war ended in 1945, the Treasury wanted to continue this policy, but the Fed didn't agree. The Fed's concern was inflation: Larger purchases of Treasury securities by the Fed could increase the growth rate of the money supply and the rate of inflation. As the war ended, the government lifted the price controls that had restrained inflation.

Fed Chairman Marriner Eccles strongly objected to the policy of fixing interest rates. His opposition to the desires of the Truman administration cost him the Fed chairmanship in 1948, although he continued to fight for Fed independence during the remainder of his term as a governor. On March 4, 1951, the federal government formally abandoned the wartime policy of fixing the interest rates on Treasury securities with the *Treasury–Federal Reserve Accord*. This agreement was important in reestablishing the Fed's ability to operate independently of the Treasury.

Conflicts between the Treasury and the Fed didn't end with that agreement, however. For example, President Ronald Reagan and Federal Reserve Chairman Paul Volcker argued over who was at fault for the severe economic recession of the early 1980s. Reagan blamed the Fed for soaring interest rates. Volcker held that the Fed could not take action to bring down interest rates until the budget deficit—which results from policy actions of the president and Congress—was reduced. Similar conflicts occurred during the administrations of George H. W. Bush and Bill Clinton, with the Treasury frequently pushing for lower short-term interest rates than the Fed considered advisable.

During the financial crisis of 2007–2009, the Fed worked closely with the Treasury. They worked so closely, in fact, that some economists and policymakers worried that the Fed might be sacrificing some of its independence. The frequent consultations between Fed Chairman Ben Bernanke and then Treasury Secretary Henry Paulson during the height of the crisis in the fall of 2008 were a break with the tradition of Fed chairmen formulating policy independently of the administration. If such close collaboration were to continue, it would raise the question of whether the Fed would be able to pursue policies independent of those of the administration in power. A proposal in early 2010 that the president of the United States appoint the presidents of the District Banks raised further concerns about Fed independence. In the end, though, the provisions of the Dodd-Frank Act did little to undermine Fed independence.

Factors That Motivate the Fed

We have shown that the Fed has legal authority for monetary policy. We now examine two views of what motivates the Fed in using its authority: the public interest view and the principal–agent view.

Public interest view
A theory of central bank decision making that holds that officials act in the best interest of the public.

The Public Interest View The usual starting point for explaining the motivation of business managers is that they act in the interest of the constituency they serve: their shareholders. The **public interest view** of Fed motivation holds that the Fed, too, acts in the interest of its primary constituency (the general public) and that it seeks to achieve economic goals that are in the public interest. Examples of such goals are price stability, high employment, and economic growth.

Does the evidence support the public interest view of the Fed? Some economists argue that it doesn't with regard to price stability. The record of persistent inflation since World War II, particularly the high rates of inflation during the late 1970s and early 1980s, undercuts the claim that the Fed has emphasized price stability. Other economists argue that the Fed's record on price stability is relatively good and that the high inflation rates of the 1970s were primarily due to soaring oil prices that took the Fed by surprise. There are similar debates over the Fed's contributions to the stability of other economic indicators.

The Principal–Agent View Many economists view organizations as having conflicting goals. Although they are created to serve the public and perform a public service, government organizations also have internal goals that might not match their stated mission. In effect, public organizations face the principal–agent problem just as private corporations do.

Recall that when managers (agents) have little stake in their businesses, their incentives to maximize the value of shareholders' (principals') claims may be weak.

In such situations, the agents don't always act in the interest of the principals. Gordon Tullock and Nobel Laureate James Buchanan of George Mason University formulated a **principal–agent view** of motivation in bureaucratic organizations such as the Fed. This view contends that the objective of bureaucrats is to maximize their personal well-being—power, influence, and prestige—rather than the well-being of the general public. So, the principal–agent view of Fed motivation predicts that the Fed acts to increase its power, influence, and prestige as an organization, subject to constraints placed on it by principals such as the president and Congress.

If the principal–agent view accurately explains the Fed's motivation, we would expect the Fed to fight to maintain its autonomy—which it does. The Fed has frequently resisted Congressional attempts to control its budget. In fact, the Fed has been very successful at mobilizing constituents (such as bankers and business executives) in its own defense. Although early drafts of the Dodd-Frank Act included provisions that would have reduced the Fed's independence and its regulatory power, the Fed successfully lobbied Congress to strip most of these provisions from the final version of the act. Supporters of the public interest view, though, argue that the Fed guards its autonomy so as to better serve the public interest.

Proponents of the principal–agent view also think that the Fed would avoid conflicts with groups that could limit its power, influence, and prestige. For example, the Fed could manage monetary policy to assist the reelection efforts of presidential incumbents who are unlikely to limit its power. The result would be a **political business cycle**, in which the Fed would try to lower interest rates to stimulate economic activity before an election to earn favor with the incumbent party running for reelection. After the election, the economy would face the consequences when the Fed contracted economic activity to reduce the inflationary pressure caused by its earlier expansion—but, by then, the president who was sympathetic to the Fed would have been reelected. The facts for the United States don't generally support the political business cycle theory, however. For example, an expansion of money supply growth preceded President Richard Nixon's reelection in 1972, but a contraction of money supply growth preceded President Jimmy Carter's and President George H. W. Bush's unsuccessful bids for reelection in 1980 and 1992, respectively.

Nevertheless, the president's desires may subtly influence Fed policy. One study of the influence of politics on changes in monetary policy from 1979 through 1984 measured the number of times members of the administration were quoted about desired changes in monetary policy in articles appearing in the *Wall Street Journal*. The author found a close correlation between changes in monetary policy and the number of these signals from the administration that they desired a policy change.[2]

One criticism of the principal–agent view addresses the need to separate the Fed's intentions from external pressure: The Fed itself might want to act in one way, whereas Congress and the president might try to get the Fed to pursue other goals. The principal–agent view also fails to explain why Congress allows the Fed to be relatively independent through self-financing. Some economists suggest that the Fed may provide

Principal–agent view A theory of central bank decision making that holds that officials maximize their personal well-being rather than that of the general public.

Political business cycle The theory that policymakers will urge the Fed to lower interest rates to stimulate the economy prior to an election.

---

[2]Thomas Havrilesky, "Monetary Policy Signaling from the Administration to the Federal Reserve," *Journal of Money, Credit, and Banking*, Vol. 20, No. 1, February 1988, pp. 83–101.

Congress with long-run benefits through self-financing. If self-financing gives the Fed an incentive to conduct more open market purchases, thereby expanding the money supply, the Treasury will collect more tax revenue that Congress can spend.

Fed Independence

Usually, the political issue of Fed independence arises not because of disagreement over monetary policy or even over the role of the Fed in managing monetary policy but because of the public's negative reaction to Fed policy. An example is the bill mentioned in the chapter opener that the House passed in 2012, which would have directed the GAO to audit the Fed's monetary policy actions. This bill resulted in part from the public reaction to the Fed's inability to increase the speed of the economy's recovery from the 2007–2009 recession. We now analyze the arguments for and against Fed independence.

Arguments for Fed Independence The main argument for Fed independence is that monetary policy—which affects inflation, interest rates, exchange rates, and economic growth—is too important and technical to be determined by politicians. Because of the frequency of elections, politicians may be shortsighted, concerned with short-term benefits without regard for potential long-term costs. The short-term desire of politicians to be reelected may clash with the country's long-term interest in low inflation. Therefore, the Fed cannot assume that the objectives of politicians reflect public sentiment. The public may well prefer that the experts at the Fed, rather than politicians, make monetary policy decisions.

Another argument for Fed independence is that complete control of the Fed by elected officials increases the likelihood of political business cycle fluctuations in the money supply and interest rates. For example, those officials might pressure the Fed to assist the Treasury's borrowing efforts by buying government bonds, which would increase the money supply, lower interest rates, and fuel inflation.

Arguments Against Fed Independence The importance of monetary policy for the economy is also the main argument against central bank independence. Supporters of this argument claim that in a democracy, elected officials should make public policy. Because the public can hold elected officials responsible for perceived monetary policy problems, some analysts advocate giving the president and Congress more control over monetary policy. The counterargument to the view that monetary policy is too technical for elected officials is that national security and foreign policy also require sophisticated analysis and a long time horizon, and these functions are entrusted to elected officials. In addition, critics of Fed independence argue that placing the central bank under the control of elected officials could confer benefits by coordinating and integrating monetary policy with government taxing and spending policies.

Those who argue for greater Congressional control make the case that the Fed has not always used its independence well. For example, some critics note that the Fed failed to assist the banking system during the economic contraction of the early 1930s. Another example that many critics cite is that Fed policies were too inflationary in the 1960s and 1970s. Finally, some analysts believe that the Fed ignored the housing market bubble in the early 2000s and then moved too slowly to contain the effects on the financial system when the bubble finally burst in 2006.

Concluding Remarks Economists and policymakers don't universally agree on the merits of Fed independence. Under the present system, however, the Fed's independence is not absolute, and so it sometimes satisfies one group of critics or the other. In practice, debates focus on proposals to limit Fed independence in some respects, not to eliminate its formal independence. The extended debate over the Dodd-Frank Act gave critics of Fed independence the opportunity to have a number of proposals considered. In the end, though, there was support among a majority of Congress for only relatively minor changes to the law.

Making the Connection

End the Fed?

The U.S. Constitution does not explicitly give the federal government the authority to establish a central bank. This fact entered into the debate over the First and Second Banks of the United States in the early nineteenth century. Some of the opponents of those banks saw them as a means of exerting federal power over the states in a way that was not authorized in the Constitution. Many slaveholders in the South opposed the Second Bank of the United States partly because they feared that if the federal government claimed to have the power to establish a central bank, it might also claim to have the power to abolish slavery.

During the debate over the Federal Reserve Act in 1913, the issue of whether a central bank was constitutional was raised again. The standard argument in favor of the constitutionality of the Federal Reserve is that Article 1, Section 8 of the U.S. Constitution states that Congress has the power "To coin money [and] regulate the value thereof. . . ." Congress delegated this power to the Federal Reserve in the Federal Reserve Act. The federal courts have upheld the constitutionality of the Federal Reserve Act, notably in the 1929 case *Raichle v. Federal Reserve Bank of New York*.

Modern arguments against the Fed have been mostly based not on its supposed unconstitutionality but on the issue of whether having an independent central bank is the best means of carrying out monetary policy. During 2012, Congressman Ron Paul ran for the Republican nomination for president and argued forcefully that the Federal Reserve should be abolished. His book *End the Fed* had been a bestseller. Among the benefits he saw from abolishing the Fed were "stopping the business cycle, ending inflation, building prosperity for all Americans, and putting an end to the corrupt collaboration between government and banks. . . ." In addition to abolishing the Fed, Congressman Paul advocated a return to the gold standard and a move to 100% reserve banking, which would eliminate the need for deposit insurance because banks could make loans and other investments only by using their capital.

In the debate in Congress over the Dodd-Frank Act, calls to abolish the Fed did not gain much support. But several proposals to significantly restructure the Fed or reduce its independence were included in early versions of the bill. For example, drafts of the bill contained provisions that would have stripped the Fed of most of its supervisory authority over banks and that would have made the Reserve Bank presidents presidential appointees. These provisions did not survive in the final version of the Dodd-Frank Act that became law in July 2010.

Even after passage of the Dodd-Frank Act, some economists and members of Congress remained unhappy with both the unusual policy measures the Fed had adopted during and after the financial crisis and the possibility that Fed actions had contributed to the slow recovery from the recession. As we saw in the chapter opener, Congressman Paul's proposal to have the GAO audit the Fed's monetary policy actions passed overwhelmingly in the House. The Fed's defenders argued that far from contributing to the slow recovery from the recession, the Fed's policy actions had kept the economy from spiraling down into depression and had aided what would otherwise have been an even slower recovery. The Fed's defenders also argued that in the long run, reducing the Fed's independence would reduce the effectiveness of monetary policy.

Given the Fed's power and the fact that its officials are unelected, its role is likely to remain a subject of debate among economists and policymakers.

Sources: Kristina Peterson and Siobhan Hughes, "House Passes Ron Paul's 'Audit the Fed' Bill," *Wall Street Journal*, July 25, 2012; Ron Paul, *End the Fed*, New York: Grand Central Publishing, 2009; and Stephen Labaton, "Senate Plan Would Expand Regulation of Risky Lending," *New York Times*, November 10, 2009.

See related problem 2.11 at the end of the chapter.

13.3

Learning Objective

Discuss the issues involved with central bank independence outside the United States.

Central Bank Independence Outside the United States

The degree of central bank independence varies greatly from country to country. When we compare the structure of the Fed with that of central banks in Canada, Europe, and Japan, some patterns emerge. First, in countries in which central bank board members serve fixed terms of office, none is as long as the 14-year term for Federal Reserve governors, implying nominally greater independence in the United States. Second, in those other countries, the head of the central bank has a longer term of office than the four-year term of office of the chairman of the Board of Governors in the United States, implying somewhat greater political control in the United States. So, whether the Fed's structure makes it more or less independent of political control than are other central banks is unclear.

An independent central bank is free to pursue its goals without direct interference from other government officials and legislators. Most economists believe that an independent central bank can more freely focus on keeping inflation low. The European Central Bank is, in principle, extremely independent, whereas the Bank of Japan and the Bank of England traditionally have been less independent, though by the late 1990s, both had become more independent and more focused on price stability.

The Bank of England, founded in 1694 and one of the world's oldest central banks, obtained the power to set interest rates independently of the government in 1997. The government can overrule the Bank of England in "extreme circumstances," but to date it has not done so. The chancellor of the exchequer does, however, set the Bank of England's inflation target. Interest rate determination falls to the Monetary Policy Committee, whose members are the Bank of England's governor, two deputy governors, two members appointed by the governor (after consulting with the chancellor of the exchequer), and four external economic experts named by the chancellor.

The Bank of Japan's Policy Board members include the governor, two deputy governors, and six outside members named by the cabinet and confirmed by the Diet, which is Japan's national legislature. While the government may send representatives to meetings of the policy board, it lacks a vote. The Ministry of Finance does, however, retain control over parts of the Bank of Japan's budget that are unrelated to monetary policy. The Bank of Japan Law, in force since April 1998, gives the Policy Board more autonomy to pursue price stability.

The Bank of Canada has an inflation target as a goal for monetary policy, but that target is set jointly by the Bank of Canada and the government. While since 1967 the government has had the final responsibility for monetary policy, the Bank of Canada has generally controlled monetary policy. The finance minister can direct the bank's action, but such direction must be written and public, and none has been issued up to this time.

The push for increasing the independence of central banks to pursue a goal of low inflation has increased in recent years. Indeed, in most of the industrialized world, central bank independence from the political process is gaining ground as the way to organize monetary authorities. In practice, the degree of actual independence in the conduct of monetary policy varies across countries. What conclusions should we draw from differences in central bank structure? Many analysts believe that an independent central bank improves the economy's performance by lowering inflation without raising output or employment fluctuations. A study by Alberto Alesina and Lawrence Summers found that the countries with the most independent central banks had the lowest average rates of inflation during the 1970s and 1980s (see Chapter 2). The countries with much less independent central banks had significantly higher rates of inflation.

What constitutes meaningful central bank independence? Economists emphasize that declarations by a government that the country's central bank is independent are insufficient. The central bank must be able to conduct policy without direct interference from the government. The central bank also must be able to set goals for which it can be held accountable. The leading example of such a goal is a target for inflation. Central banks in Canada, Finland, New Zealand, Sweden, and the United Kingdom have official inflation targets, as does the European Central Bank. After years of debate, the U.S. Fed followed these other central banks by adopting an inflation target of 2%.

The European Central Bank

As part of the move toward economic integration in Europe, the European Central Bank (ECB) is charged with conducting monetary policy for the 17 countries that participate in the European Monetary Union, or Eurosystem, and use the euro as their common currency. Representatives of many European nations signed an important agreement in Maastricht, the Netherlands, in December 1991. This agreement detailed a gradual approach to monetary union to be completed between 1994 and 1999. Although the monetary union did not become effective until January 1, 1999, groundwork for the ECB had been laid in advance.

The ECB's organization is in some respects similar to that of the U.S. Fed. The ECB's executive board, chaired in 2012 by Mario Draghi, who serves as president of the ECB, has six members who work exclusively for the bank. Board members (a vice president and four others) are appointed by the heads of state and government, based on the recommendation of the Council of Ministers of Economics and Finance, after consulting the European Parliament and the Governing Council of the ECB. Executive board members serve nonrenewable eight-year terms. Also participating in the governance of the ECB are the governors of each of the member national central banks, each of whom serves a term of at least five years. The long terms of office are designed to increase the political independence of the ECB.

In principle, the ECB has a high degree of overall independence, with a clear mandate to emphasize price stability, and it is free from interference by the European Union or national governments in the conduct of policy. Moreover, the ECB's charter can be changed only by changing the Maastricht Treaty, which would require the agreement of all the countries that signed the original treaty. Whether legal independence is enough to guarantee actual independence is another matter, however. Based on the historical experience of the Federal Reserve, there may be cause for concern about the ECB. The decentralized central banking system envisioned in the original Federal Reserve Act of 1913 led to power struggles within the system and offered no mechanism to achieve consensus during the financial crisis of the early 1930s. National central banks have considerable power in the ECB. The governors of the European System of Central Banks (ESCB) hold a majority of votes in the ECB's governing council. And national central banks collectively have a much larger staff than the ECB.

Where might conflict arise? While the law establishing the ECB emphasizes price stability, countries have argued over the merits of expansionary or contractionary monetary policy. This conflict became particularly evident during the financial crisis of 2007–2009, when countries such as Greece, Spain, and Ireland suffered severe declines in production and employment and urged that the ECB follow a more expansionary policy. Countries such as Germany that had fared better during the financial crisis were reluctant to see the ECB abandon its inflation target.

The European Central Bank and the Sovereign Debt Crisis

The European Central Bank has a complicated mission. Unlike the Fed, the Bank of England, or the Bank of Japan, which each conduct monetary policy for a single country, the ECB is responsible for the monetary policy of the 17 sovereign countries that use the euro as their currency. The 2007–2009 financial crisis and the recession that accompanied it affected these 17 countries to differing extents. Even before euro coins and paper currency were introduced in 2002, some economists voiced doubts that a single currency controlled by one central bank could work, given the differences among the economies of the countries participating. Typically, during a recession, a country's central bank can pursue an expansionary policy that is as aggressive as might be needed. But during the 2007–2009 recession, the 17 countries that are part of the European Monetary Union had to rely on the ECB and were not able to pursue independent policies.

The recession hit some countries much harder than others. For example, the unemployment rate in Germany had fallen below pre-recession levels by 2010 and had dropped below 6% in 2012. In contrast, the unemployment rates in Ireland and Portugal were at 15% in late 2012, and the unemployment rates in Spain and Greece were above 20%. The countries in which unemployment was high would have preferred the ECB to follow a more expansionary policy than did Germany, where officials continued to stress the importance of the ECB's goal of price stability.

The countries where the recession had been particularly severe also suffered from large government budget deficits as tax revenues declined and government spending increased. To finance the deficits, these governments had to issue bonds, or *sovereign debt*. By the spring of 2010, Greece had issued so many bonds that private investors began to doubt that Greece could afford to continue making the interest payments on this debt. Doubts also arose about debt issued by Ireland, Spain, and Portugal. The resulting *sovereign debt crisis* posed a dilemma for the ECB: It could intervene to buy some of the debt, but doing so might further increase the amount of liquidity in the European financial system, raising expectations of higher future inflation. In addition, buying debt might be seen as approving the poor budgetary policies of some of these governments, thereby increasing moral hazard.

Despite objections, then ECB President Jean-Claude Trichet began buying sovereign debt in May 2010. Trichet argued that the intervention was necessary to ensure that the affected governments would still be able to raise funds by selling bonds and to protect the solvency of European banks that had purchased large amounts of these government bonds. The action resulted in considerable controversy, however, and Axel Weber, the president of the German central bank and a member of the ECB's governing council, took the rare step of criticizing it publicly. Trichet's successor, Mario Draghi, expanded the buying program through 2012 in an attempt to contain the sovereign debt crisis and ensure the stability of the European banking system. In October 2012, Draghi took the unusual step of directly addressing members of Germany's parliament in an attempt to ensure that Germany remained behind the ECB's policies. In addition, the governments of the euro-zone countries agreed in 2012 to give the ECB authority to oversee the banking systems of all member countries, although the governments were unable to agree on instituting a unified system of deposit insurance.

Although in late 2012 the sovereign debt crisis appeared to be contained, whether the European experiment of a single currency and a single central bank would ultimately be successful remained in question.

Answering the Key Question

Continued from page 387

At the beginning of this chapter, we asked:

"Should Congress and the president be given greater authority over the Federal Reserve?"

As we have seen in this chapter, almost since the founding of the Fed, economists and policymakers have debated how independent the Fed should be from the rest of the government. In 1913, the Federal Reserve Act placed the secretary of the Treasury and the comptroller of the currency—both presidential appointees—on the Federal Reserve Board, making the secretary of the Treasury the board's chairman. In 1935, Congress removed these officials from the board to increase the Fed's independence. During the debate over financial reform in 2010, Congress seriously considered allowing the president to appoint the presidents of the 12 Federal Reserve Banks, although this proposal was dropped from the final version of the Dodd-Frank Act. In 2012, legislation to direct the GAO to audit the Fed's monetary policy actions passed the House of Representatives, although it appeared unlikely to become law. Given its importance in the financial system, economists and policymakers will continue to debate the merits of the Fed's independence.

Key Terms and Problems

Key Terms

Board of Governors, p. 394

Federal Open Market Committee
(FOMC), p. 395

Federal Reserve Bank, p. 390

Federal Reserve System, p. 389

Political business cycle, p. 403

Principal–agent view, p. 403

Public interest view, p. 402

Wall Street Reform and Consumer
Protection Act (Dodd-Frank
Act), p. 398

13.1 The Structure of the Federal Reserve System
Explain why the Federal Reserve System is structured the way it is.

Review Questions

1.1 What happened to the First and Second Banks of the United States?

1.2 Why was the Federal Reserve System split into 12 districts?

1.3 Which body is more important within the Federal Reserve System, the Board of Governors or the Federal Open Market Committee? Briefly explain.

1.4 What changes did the Dodd-Frank Act make to the Fed?

Problems and Applications

1.5 Why did Congress pass the Federal Reserve Act in 1913, when the United States had functioned without a central bank since 1836?

1.6 Why did Congress want the member banks to own the Federal Reserve Banks? Does the current relationship between the member banks and the Federal Reserve Banks indicate that Congress achieved its goal?

1.7 According to economist Allan Meltzer of Carnegie Mellon University, who has written about the history of the Federal Reserve:

> Tension between the [Federal Reserve] Board and the reserve banks began before the System opened for business. . . . [Paul] Warburg described the problem. Dominance by the Board would allow political considerations to dominate decisions about interest rates. Dominance by the reserve banks "would . . . reduce the Board to a position of impotence."

Paul Warburg was one of President Wilson's initial appointments when the Federal Reserve Board began operations in 1914.

a. Why did Congress set up a system that had this tension between the Federal Reserve Banks and the Federal Reserve Board?

b. Has the tension been resolved in the modern Fed? If so, how?

Source: Allan H. Meltzer, *A History of the Federal Reserve, Volume I: 1913–1951*, Chicago: University of Chicago Press, 2003, p. 75.

1.8 David Wheelock of the Federal Reserve Bank of St. Louis describes the following episode at the beginning of the Great Depression:

> Following the stock market crash [of October 1929], the Federal Reserve Bank of New York used open market purchases [of Treasury securities] and liberal discount window lending [to commercial banks] to inject reserves into the banking system. . . . The Federal Reserve Board reluctantly approved the New York Fed's actions ex post, but many members expressed displeasure that the New York Fed had acted independently.

a. What are the arguments for and against a Federal Reserve Bank operating independently?

---

b. In the modern Fed, would it be possible for a Federal Reserve Bank to act as the New York Fed did in 1929?

Source: David C. Wheelock, "Lessons Learned? Comparing the Federal Reserve's Responses to the Crises of 1929–1933 and 2007–2009," Federal Reserve Bank of St. Louis *Review*, Vol. 92, No. 2, March/April 2010, pp. 97–98.

1.9 [Related to the Making the Connection on page 391] Suppose Congress were to amend the Federal Reserve Act and set up a new commission to reexamine the Federal Reserve district boundaries. What considerations should the commission use in drawing the boundaries? Would the boundaries likely be much different than the original boundaries? Does it matter as much today as it did in 1914 where the district boundaries lie?

1.10 [Related to Solved Problem 13.1 on page 393] Suppose that Bank of America pays a 2% annual interest rate on checking account balances while having to meet a reserve requirement of 10%. Assume that the Fed pays Bank of America an interest rate of 0.25% on its holdings of reserves and that Bank of America can earn 7% on its loans and other investments.

a. How do reserve requirements affect the amount that Bank of America can earn on $1,000 in checking account deposits? Ignore any costs Bank of America incurs on the deposits other than the interest it pays to depositors.

b. Is the opportunity cost to banks of reserve requirements likely to be higher during a period of high inflation or during a period of low inflation? Briefly explain.

1.11 [Related to the Making the Connection on page 396] What is the purpose of the Government in the Sunshine Act? In your opinion, was Fed Chairman Bernanke justified in evading the requirements of this act during the financial crisis of 2007–2009?

13.2 **How the Fed Operates**
Explain the key issues involved in the Fed's operations.

Review Questions

2.1 In what ways is the Fed subject to external pressure?

2.2 What are the major differences between the public interest view of the Fed's motivation and the principal–agent view? How are these views connected to the theory of the political business cycle?

2.3 Briefly discuss the main arguments for and against the Fed's independence.

Problems and Applications

2.4 In the first volume of his history of the Federal Reserve System, Allan Meltzer titled one of his chapters "Under Treasury Control, 1942–1951." Why would Meltzer have considered the Fed to have been under Treasury control during those years?

Source: Allan H. Meltzer, *A History of the Federal Reserve, Volume I: 1913–1951*, Chicago: University of Chicago Press, 2003, Ch. 7.

2.5 [Related to the Chapter Opener on page 387] At a hearing before a committee of the House of Representatives, Fed Chair Ben Bernanke was asked about the legislation that would direct the GAO to audit the Fed's monetary policy actions. He replied:

The term "audit the Fed" is deceptive. The public thinks that auditing means checking the books, looking at the financial statements, making sure that you're not doing special deals, and that kind of thing. All of those things are (already) completely open....

The nightmare scenario I have is one in which some future Fed chairman would decide to raise the federal funds rate by 25 basis points, and somebody in this room would say, "I don't like that decision. I want the GAO to go in and get all the records, get all the transcripts, get all the preparatory materials and give us an independent opinion on whether or not that was the right decision."

Why would the situation Bernanke is describing be a "nightmare scenario"? Wouldn't it be good to have the GAO give an independent opinion on whether a particular monetary policy action was the right decision?

Source: Board of Governors of the Federal Reserve System, "Testimony of Chairman Ben S. Bernanke before the House Financial Services Committee, July 18, 2012."

2.6 Evaluate the following statement: "Because the Fed does not have to ask Congress for money to fund its operations, the principal–agent view of the Fed's motivation cannot be correct."

2.7 [Related to the Making the Connection on page 391] Is Michael McAvoy's explanation of how the Federal Reserve Bank cities were selected more consistent with a public interest view of how the decision was made or a principal-agent view? Briefly explain.

2.8 Are the high rates of inflation that the United States experienced during the 1970s consistent with the public interest view of the Fed's motivation?

2.9 In late 2009, during the debate over the Dodd-Frank Act, a newspaper article noted:

> Last summer, the central bank hired an experienced Democratic hand and former lobbyist, Linda Robertson, to help deal with members of Congress. . . . Mindful that

Democrats now control the White House and Congress, Mr. Bernanke put up virtually no opposition to President Obama's proposal for a new consumer agency that would take over the Fed's authority over consumer lending issues.

Do the points raised in the article shed light on the Fed's motivations? Briefly explain.

Source: Edmund L. Andrews, "Under Attack, Fed Chief Studies Politics," *New York Times*, November 10, 2009.

2.10 [Related to the Making the Connection on page 400] In a speech, Fed Chairman Ben Bernanke argued that: "Democratic principles demand that, as an agent of the government, a central bank must be accountable in the pursuit of its mandated goals, responsive to the public and its elected representatives, and transparent in its policies." Do you agree that democratic principles require that central banks be transparent in their policies? Briefly explain.

Source: Ben S. Bernanke, "Central Bank Independence, Transparency, and Accountability," Speech delivered at the Institute for Monetary and Economic Studies International Conference, Bank of Japan, Tokyo, Japan, May 25, 2010.

2.11 [Related to the Making the Connection on page 405] Suppose that the U.S. Constitution were amended to include the following: "Congress shall establish a central bank that will be responsible for conducting the monetary policy of the United States." What effect would such an amendment be likely to have on the Fed?

13.3 **Central Bank Independence Outside the United States**
Discuss the issues involved with central bank independence outside the United States.

Review Questions

3.1 Compare the length of terms of office for central bank heads and members of central bank governing boards between the U.S. Federal Reserve and foreign central banks.

3.2 What is the main problem with having a central bank that is not independent of the rest of the government?

3.3 How is the European Central Bank organized? What special problems does it confront? What difficulties did it encounter during the financial crisis of 2007–2009 and the subsequent sovereign debt crisis?

Problems and Applications

3.4 Is it easier for a central bank to be independent in a high-income country or in a low-income country? What implications does your answer have for what the average inflation rate is likely to be in high-income countries as opposed to low-income countries?

3.5 In October 2012, a newspaper article describing a meeting between ECB President Mario Draghi and members of the German parliament quoted Draghi as saying that in deciding to buy sovereign debt, the ECB was attempting to reduce "unfounded fears about the future of the euro area . . . and the only way to do so was to establish a fully credible backstop against disaster scenarios."

   a. Why did some people have fears about the future of the euro?

   b. What "disaster scenarios" was the ECB worried about? How would buying sovereign debt provide a "backstop" against these scenarios?

   c. The German central bank, the Bundesbank, criticized the plan, calling it "tantamount to financing governments by printing bank notes." Briefly explain what the Bundesbank meant by this statement. What is a potential problem with financing governments by printing currency?

   Source: Brian Blackstone and William Boston, "Draghi Defends Bond Buying Program," *Wall Street Journal*, October 24, 2012.

3.6 A newspaper article in 2012 referred to "growing expectations the Bank of Japan, pressed by the government, will take a large-scale easing step next week." It also noted that: "Japan's finance minister Koriki Jojima denied the report, although he indicated his desire to see further easing."

   a. What does the article mean by "further easing"?

   b. Why might the finance minister not want it to appear that the Japanese government was dictating policy to the Bank of Japan?

   Source: Nicole Hong, "Dollar Gives Up Gains as BOJ Easing Expectations Dim," *Wall Street Journal*, October 23, 2012.

3.7 Adam Posen, then a member of the Bank of England's Monetary Policy Committee, was quoted as arguing in a speech that:

   > Central banks' purchases of government debt . . . far from undermining their independence . . . should enhance their credibility. . . . Mr. Posen said, . . . "What matters for our independence is our ability to say no and to mean it, and to be responsible about when we choose to say yes."

   a. Why might purchasing government debt be seen as undermining a central bank's independence?

   b. Why might a central bank sometimes want to say "no" to calls for it to purchase government debt? Why might it sometimes want to say "yes"?

   Source: Natasha Brereton, "BOE's Posen Defends ECB's Actions," *Wall Street Journal*, June 15, 2010.

Data Exercises

D13.1: [**The ECB and differences among European economies**] Go to the Web site of the Federal Reserve Bank of St. Louis (FRED) (research.stlouisfed.org/fred2/) and download and graph the growth rate for real GDP in Greece (GRCGDPRQPSMEI) from the first quarter of 2000 to the most recent quarter available. On the same graph download the growth rate for real GDP in Germany (DEURGDPR) for the same period. Note that to add the data for Germany to the graph for Greece, you will first need to click on "Edit Graph," the click on "Add Data Series." When you find the data series for real GDP for Germany, you will need to change the units to "Percentage Change from Year Ago." Briefly compare movements in the two series. What challenges do these movements in real GDP pose for the European Central Bank (ECB)?

D13.2: **[The ECB and the sovereign debt crisis]** Go to sdw.ecb.europa.eu and select "Government Debt (as a % of GDP)." What is the current euro-zone debt/GDP ratio? What is the deficit/GDP ratio? What challenges do the deficit and debt data pose for the European Central Bank (ECB)?

CHAPTER 14

The Federal Reserve's Balance Sheet and the Money Supply Process

Learning Objectives

After studying this chapter, you should be able to:

14.1 Explain the relationship between the Fed's balance sheet and the monetary base (pages 416–424)

14.2 Derive the equation for the simple deposit multiplier and understand what it means (pages 424–429)

14.3 Explain how the behavior of banks and the nonbank public affect the money multiplier (pages 429–439)

14A Appendix: Describe the money supply process for M2 (page 446)

High Times for "Gold Bugs"

At one time, gold was the basis for the money supply in the United States and other high-income countries, but that is no longer the case. The United States went off the gold standard in 1933 and stopped minting gold coins as currency. The U.S. Mint still produces gold coins that commemorate famous people and historical events. Coin collectors buy most of these coins. Some people are interested in gold coins as an investment, so the Mint also produces American Eagle Bullion coins. Beginning in 2008, as the financial crisis was at its worst, those coins were very hot. Sales of the 1-ounce American Eagle gold coin soared to more than 10 times the pre-crisis levels and remained there for several years. BullionVault, a Web-based company that allows investors to buy title to gold bars stored in underground vaults in New York, London, and Zurich, reported very strong sales. Although some investors like to have direct ownership of gold, other investors prefer to bet on gold indirectly by buying gold exchange-traded funds (ETFs). Gold ETFs can be bought and sold on financial markets and are designed to track the price of gold. Investments in gold seemed to be paying off when the price per ounce soared to a record high of $1,780 in September 2011.

While some individual investors, known as "gold bugs," have always wanted to hold gold, the surge in demand for gold beginning in 2008 surprised many economists. In 2009, for the first time, sales of gold for investment were greater than sales of gold for use in jewelry. It wasn't just individual investors who were driving up the price of gold. Billionaire hedge fund managers

Continued on next page

Key Issue and Question

Issue: Years after the end of the financial crisis, banks continued to hold record levels of reserves.

Question: Why did bank reserves increase rapidly during and after the financial crisis of 2007–2009, and should policymakers be concerned about the increase?

Answered on page 440

George Soros and John Paulson invested in gold bullion and shares of stock in gold mining companies. Soros is famous for having made more than $1 billion by betting against the value of the British pound in 1992. So, his purchases of gold attracted the interest of many investors. Paulson, who had made billions during 2007 and 2008 by betting on a fall in housing prices, made an additional $5 billion in profits in 2010 from an increase in gold prices. Thomas Kaplan, manager of the Tigris Financial Group, invested more than $2 billion in gold mining companies and purchases of land in 17 countries that geologists considered were likely to have gold deposits.

Why the great interest in gold as an investment? The motives of investors differed, but many were concerned about a consequence of government actions during the financial crisis: In many countries, including the United States, the money supply had increased rapidly. Moreover, banks were sitting on record amounts of reserves. Inflation remained low through 2012, but some investors predicted soaring inflation in the years to come and saw holding gold as the best way to hedge that risk.

How significant the risk of rising inflation was and historically how good a hedge against inflation gold has been are two of the questions we will explore in this chapter.

Sources: Michael Howard Saul, "$100 Million Gift to Benefit Central Park," *Wall Street Journal*, October 23, 2012; Tatyana Shumsky and Liam Pleven, "Some Gold Bulls See Bright Future," *Wall Street Journal*, August 22, 2012; Nelson Schwartz, "Uncertainty Restores Glitter to an Old Refuge, Gold," *New York Times*, June 12, 2010; "Store of Value," *Economist*, July 8, 2010; and U.S. Mint, *American Eagle Bullion Sales Totals, 1986–2012*, October 2012.

Economists, policymakers, and investors are interested in the money supply because it can affect interest rates, exchange rates, the inflation rate, and the economy's output of goods and services. As a result, the central bank—whether it is the European Central Bank, the Fed in the United States, the Bank of Japan, or the Bank of England—attempts to manage the money supply. To understand how a central bank manages the money supply, we need to analyze the factors that determine the money supply and how a central bank can increase or decrease the amount of money in circulation. In this chapter, we construct a model that explains the size of the money supply and explains why the money supply fluctuates. How a country's money supply is created is called the *money supply process*. We devote this chapter to understanding the money supply process in the United States. In the course of our discussion, we will see why bank reserves in the United States soared during and after the 2007–2009 financial crisis.

14.1

Learning Objective

Explain the relationship between the Fed's balance sheet and the monetary base.

The Federal Reserve's Balance Sheet and the Monetary Base

We begin our investigation of the money supply process by first describing the monetary base and then determining how the monetary base is linked to the money supply. Our model of how the money supply is determined includes the behavior of three actors:

1. The *Federal Reserve*, which is responsible for controlling the money supply and regulating the banking system.
2. The *banking system*, which creates the checking accounts that are the most important component of the M1 measure of the money supply.
3. The *nonbank public*, which refers to all households and firms other than banks. The nonbank public decides the form in which they wish to hold money—for instance, as currency or as checking account balances.

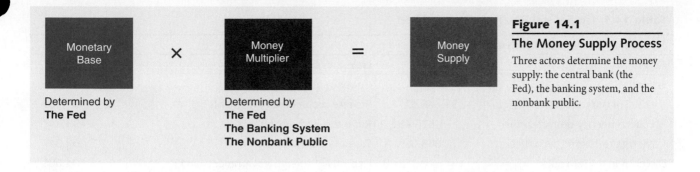

Figure 14.1

The Money Supply Process

Three actors determine the money supply: the central bank (the Fed), the banking system, and the nonbank public.

Figure 14.1 represents the money supply process and shows which actors in the economy influence each variable in the process. In a nutshell, this figure shows the components of the model and is the backbone of our analysis in this chapter. The process starts with the **monetary base**, which is also called **high-powered money**. The monetary base equals the amount of currency in circulation plus the reserves of the banking system:[1]

Monetary base (or high-powered money) The sum of bank reserves and currency in circulation.

$$\text{Monetary base} = \text{Currency in circulation} + \text{Reserves of banks.}$$

As we will see, the Fed has good control of the monetary base. The money multiplier links the monetary base to the money supply. As long as the value of the money multiplier is stable, the Fed can control the money supply by controlling the monetary base.

Our model of the money supply process applies to the monetary aggregate, M1, which is the Fed's narrow measure of money. The chapter appendix describes the money supply process for the broader measure of the money supply, M2.

The Federal Reserve's Balance Sheet

There is a close connection between the monetary base and the Fed's balance sheet, which lists the Fed's assets and liabilities. In Table 14.1, we show both the full Fed balance sheet and a simplified version that includes only the four entries that are most relevant to the Fed's actions in increasing and decreasing the monetary base. In most years, the Fed's most important assets are its holdings of U.S. Treasury securities—Treasury bills, notes, and bonds—and the discount loans it has made to banks. The financial crisis of 2007–2009 and the slow economic recovery that followed led the Fed to greatly expand its purchases of Treasury securities as it tried to reduce interest rates and spur spending by households and firms. In addition, the Fed purchased mortgage-backed securities guaranteed by Fannie Mae and Freddie Mac in an attempt to help revive the very weak housing market. The Fed participated in actions to save the investment bank Bear Stearns and the insurance company AIG from bankruptcy, and securities related to those actions remained on the Fed's books in 2012, although to a much smaller extent than in earlier years. The Fed has participated in liquidity swaps with foreign central banks and has accumulated substantial assets related to those swaps.

---

[1]Note that the "reserves" component of the monetary base is technically called "reserve balances" and includes deposits at the Fed by some nonbank depository institutions, such as savings and loans.

Table 14.1 The Federal Reserve's Balance Sheet

(a) Federal Reserve balance sheet, October 2012

Assets		Liabilities and Capital	
Securities		Currency in circulation	$1,092,845
U.S. Treasury securities	$1,646,524	Reverse repurchase agreements	91,709
Federal agency debt securities	82,746	Reserve balances of banks	1,433,241
Mortgage-backed securities	868,069	Treasury deposits	52,847
Discount loans to banks	1,312	Deposits of foreign governments and international organizations, and other deposits	104,601
Gold	16,237	Deferred availability cash items	780
AIG and Bear Stearns–related holdings	2,498	Other liabilities	11,842
Items in the process of collection	203	Total liabilities	$2,787,866
Buildings	2,350		
Coins	2,167	Capital	$54,750
Central bank liquidity swaps	12,177		
Other assets	208,332		
Total assets	$2,842,615	Total liabilities and capital	$2,842,615

(b) Simplified Federal Reserve balance sheet

Assets	Liabilities
U.S. Government securities	Currency in circulation
Discount loans to banks	Reserves of banks

Note: Values for panel (a) are in millions of dollars. Components may not sum to totals because of rounding.

Source for panel (a): *Federal Reserve Statistical Release H.4.1, Factors Affecting Reserve Balances of Depository Institutions and Condition Statement of Federal Reserve Banks*, October 25, 2012.

When economists, policymakers, or journalists refer to the "size of the Fed's balance sheet," they are typically referring to the value of the Fed's assets. In this sense, in October 2012, the size of the Fed's balance sheet was $2.8 trillion, more than three times as large as it was in December 2007, at the beginning of the 2007–2009 recession and financial crisis.

Panel (a) of Table 14.1 also shows that the Fed's main liabilities are currency in circulation and reserve balances of banks—or, simply, *reserves*. In its role as the government's bank, the Fed also holds deposits for the U.S. Treasury and for foreign governments and international agencies. As part of its open market operations, the Fed incurs a liability in the form of reverse repurchase agreements. Finally, the asset "Items in the process of collection" and the liability "Deferred availability cash items" relate to the Fed's role in check clearing.

Panel (b) of Table 14.1 strips out the detail from the Fed's balance sheet to focus on the two assets and two liabilities that are most directly involved in the Fed's actions to increase or decrease the monetary base.

The Monetary Base

Notice that the sum of currency in circulation and bank reserves, the Fed's two liabilities shown in panel (b) of Table 14.1, equals the monetary base. We are treating currency in circulation as the amount of paper currency printed by the Fed, or *Federal Reserve Notes*, that is circulating in the economy.[2] **Currency in circulation** includes currency held by banks, which is called **vault cash**. Currency held by the nonbank public (households and firms) is called **currency in M1**. It equals currency in circulation minus vault cash:

$$\text{Currency in M1} = \text{Currency in circulation} - \text{Vault cash.}$$

Reserve balances of banks on the Fed's balance sheet equal deposits by commercial banks with the Fed. But by law, vault cash is also included in **bank reserves**. If we subtract vault cash from currency in circulation and add it to bank deposits with the Fed, we have a more exact definition of the monetary base:

$$\text{Monetary base} = \text{Currency in M1} + \text{Total reserves of banks,}$$

where the last term is the sum of vault cash and bank deposits with the Fed. Hereafter, for simplicity, we will refer to the monetary base as being equal to currency plus reserves.

Reserve deposits are assets for banks, but they are liabilities for the Fed because banks can request that the Fed repay the deposits on demand with Federal Reserve Notes. The situation is analogous to your checking account's being an asset to you but a liability to the bank where you have your account.

Total reserves are made up of the amounts that the Fed requires banks to hold, called **required reserves**, and the extra amounts that banks elect to hold, called **excess reserves**:

$$\text{Reserves} = \text{Required reserves} + \text{Excess reserves.}$$

The Fed specifies a percentage of checkable deposits that banks must hold as reserves, which is called the **required reserve ratio**. For example, if the required reserve ratio is 10%, a bank must set aside 10% of its checkable deposits as reserve deposits with the Fed or as vault cash. In October 2008, the Fed for the first time began paying interest to banks on their reserve accounts, although the interest rate is quite modest (0.25% in 2012). Historically, banks have not held much in excess reserves. During and after the financial crisis of 2007–2009, however, banks greatly increased their holdings of excess reserves. The key reason seems to be that although the interest rate the Fed paid on reserves was low, the investment was risk free, and the interest rate was competitive with the returns on other safe short-term investments the banks could make. In addition, given the historically high level of uncertainty in the financial system, many banks wanted to increase their liquidity.

How the Fed Changes the Monetary Base

The Fed increases or decreases the monetary base by changing the levels of its assets—that is, the Fed changes the monetary base by buying and selling Treasury securities or by making discount loans to banks.

Currency in circulation Paper money circulating outside of the Fed.

Vault cash Currency held by banks.

Currency in M1 Currency held by the nonbank public.

Bank reserves Bank deposits with the Fed plus vault cash.

Required reserves Reserves that the Fed requires banks to hold.

Excess reserves Reserves that banks hold over and above those the Fed requires them to hold.

Required reserve ratio The percentage of checkable deposits that the Fed specifies that banks must hold as reserves.

---

[2]Technically, the monetary base also includes U.S. Treasury currency outstanding, which is primarily coins. Because the value of coins in circulation is small compared to the Fed's currency outstanding or to bank reserves, we will ignore it. The reserve balances shown on the Fed's balance sheet include deposits at the Fed by all depository institutions, whether or not they are commercial banks. For convenience, we assume that all of these depository institutions are commercial banks.

Open market operations
The Federal Reserve's purchases and sales of securities, usually U.S. Treasury securities, in financial markets.

Open market purchase
The Federal Reserve's purchase of securities, usually U.S. Treasury securities.

Open Market Operations The most direct method the Fed uses to change the monetary base is **open market operations**, which involve buying or selling securities, generally U.S. Treasury securities. Open market operations are carried out by the Fed's trading desk, located at the Federal Reserve Bank of New York. Fed employees on the trading desk buy and sell securities electronically with *primary dealers*. In 2012, there were 21 primary dealers, who are commercial banks, investment banks, and securities dealers. Those dealers that are not commercial banks keep their accounts with commercial banks, so we can think of open market operations as being carried out between the Fed and the banking system. In an **open market purchase**, which raises the monetary base, the Fed buys Treasury securities. Suppose the Fed buys $1 million worth of Treasury bills from Bank of America. Bank of America will electronically transfer ownership of the bills to the Fed, and the Fed will pay for them by depositing $1 million in Bank of America's reserve account at the Fed.

We can illustrate the effect of the Fed's open market purchase by using a *T-account*, which is a stripped-down version of a balance sheet. We will use T-accounts to show only how a transaction *changes* a balance sheet. Although in our example, the Fed purchased securities from only one bank, in practice, the Fed typically buys securities from multiple banks at the same time. So, we use a T-account for the whole banking system to show the results of the Fed's open market purchase: The banking system's balance sheet shows a decrease in security holdings of $1 million and an increase in reserves of the same amount (note that the banking system's balance sheet simply adds together the assets and liabilities of all the commercial banks in the United States):

BANKING SYSTEM

Assets		Liabilities
Securities	−$1 million	
Reserves	+$1 million	

We can use another T-account to show the changes in the Fed's balance sheet. The Fed's holdings of securities (an asset) increase by $1 million, and bank reserve deposits (a liability) also increase by $1 million:

FEDERAL RESERVE

Assets		Liabilities	
Securities	+$1 million	Reserves	+$1 million

The Fed's open market purchase from Bank of America increases reserves by $1 million and, therefore, the monetary base increases by $1 million. A key point is that *the monetary base increases by the dollar amount of an open market purchase.*

Open market sale The Fed's sale of securities, usually Treasury securities.

Similarly, the Fed can reduce the monetary base through an **open market sale** of Treasury securities. For example, suppose the Fed sells $1 million of Treasury securities to Barclays Bank. The Fed transfers the securities to Barclays, and Barclays pays with funds in its reserve account. As a result, the banking system's holdings of securities will increase by $1 million, and its reserves will fall by $1 million, as shown in the following T-account:

BANKING SYSTEM

Assets		Liabilities
Securities	+$1 million	
Reserves	−$1 million	

The Fed's holdings of securities will decrease by $1 million, as will bank reserves:

FEDERAL RESERVE

Assets		Liabilities	
Securities	−$1 million	Reserves	−$1 million

Because reserves have fallen by $1 million, so has the monetary base. We can conclude that *the monetary base decreases by the dollar amount of an open market sale.*

As we will see, a key role the nonbank public plays in the money supply process is deciding how much currency it wishes to hold relative to checkable deposits. However, the public's preference for currency relative to checkable deposits does not affect the monetary base. To see why, consider what happens if households and firms decide to withdraw $1 million from their checking accounts. The following T-account shows the change in the balance sheet of the nonbank public (note that the nonbank public's balance sheet simply adds together the assets and liabilities of all of the households and firms in the United States):

NONBANK PUBLIC

Assets		Liabilities
Checkable deposits	−$1 million	
Currency	+$1 million	

As the banking system withdraws $1 million from its reserves at the Fed to provide the currency to households and firms, the banking system's balance sheet will change as follows:

BANKING SYSTEM

Assets		Liabilities	
Reserves	−$1 million	Checkable deposits	−$1 million

The Fed's balance sheet will also change as currency in circulation increases, while bank reserves fall:

FEDERAL RESERVE

Assets	Liabilities	
	Currency in circulation	+$1 million
	Reserves	−$1 million

Notice that although one component of the monetary base (reserves) has fallen by $1 million, the other component (currency in circulation) has risen by $1 million. So, the monetary base is unaffected. This result is important because it means that the Fed can increase and decrease the monetary base through open market operations without the changes being affected by how much currency the nonbank public wishes to hold relative to checkable deposits.

Discount Loans Although the Fed typically uses open market operations in managing the monetary base, it can also increase or decrease reserves by making **discount loans** to commercial banks. This change in bank reserves changes the monetary base.

Discount loan A loan made by the Federal Reserve, typically to a commercial bank.

Suppose that banks increase their discount loans from the Fed by $1 million. The Fed provides the funds to the banks by increasing their reserve accounts. For the Fed, assets rise by $1 million from the additional discount loans, and liabilities rise by $1 million from the additional bank reserves. So, the increase in discount loans affects both sides of the Fed's balance sheet:

FEDERAL RESERVE

Assets		Liabilities	
Discount loans	+$1 million	Reserves	+$1 million

Both sides of the banking system's balance sheet are also affected. Banks increase their assets by $1 million in the form of reserves and increase their liabilities by $1 million in the form of discount loans payable to the Fed:

BANKING SYSTEM

Assets		Liabilities	
Reserves	+$1 million	Discount loans	+$1 million

As a result of the Fed's making $1 million of discount loans, bank reserves and the monetary base increase by $1 million.

If banks repay $1 million in discount loans to the Fed, reducing the total amount of discount loans, then the preceding transactions are reversed. Discount loans fall by $1 million, as do reserves and the monetary base:

FEDERAL RESERVE

Assets		Liabilities	
Discount loans	−$1 million	Reserves	−$1 million

BANKING SYSTEM

Assets		Liabilities	
Reserves	−$1 million	Discount loans	−$1 million

Comparing Open Market Operations and Discount Loans

Although open market operations and discount loans both change the monetary base, the Fed has greater control over open market operations than over discount loans. The Fed completely controls the volume of open market operations because it initiates purchases or sales of securities by having the trading desk at the New York Fed place orders with the primary dealers. The Fed is willing to buy and sell securities at whatever price is needed to carry out its open market operations successfully.

The Fed's control over discount lending is much less complete than its control over open market operations because banks decide whether to borrow from the Fed. The Fed has some control over discount loans because it sets the **discount rate**, which is the interest rate the Fed charges on discount loans. In fact, the discount rate differs from most interest rates because it is set by the Fed, whereas most interest rates are determined by demand and supply in financial markets.

Discount rate The interest rate the Federal Reserve charges on discount loans.

As a result of the difference between the Fed's control over open market operations and its control over discount loans, economists think of the monetary base as having two components: the nonborrowed monetary base, B_{non}, and borrowed reserves, BR, which is another name for discount loans. We can express the monetary base, B, as

$$B = B_{non} + BR.$$

Although decisions by both the Fed and banks determine the volume of discount loans, the Fed has control over the nonborrowed monetary base.

Making the Connection

Explaining the Explosion in the Monetary Base

As the graph below shows, the monetary base increased sharply in the fall of 2008, doubling between September and the end of December. The base remained at high levels through the fall of 2012. The graph also shows that reserves, which had made up only about 5% of the monetary base before the financial crisis began, made up more than 50% by the spring of 2009. In fact, more than 80% of the increase in the monetary base occurred because of an increase in the bank reserves component rather than in the currency in circulation component.

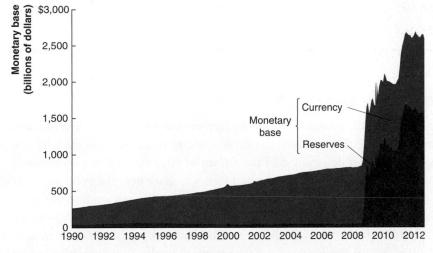

MyEconLab Real-time data

Source: Federal Reserve Bank of St. Louis.

We have seen that the Fed has the ability through open market purchases of Treasury securities to increase bank reserves and, thereby, the monetary base. Typically, then, a large increase in the monetary base means that the Fed has made large purchases of Treasury bills and other Treasury securities. In this case, though, the Fed's holdings of Treasury securities actually *fell* while the base was exploding. The Fed held $779 billion in Treasury securities of all types in January 2007 but only $475 billion in January 2009.

The Fed's holdings of Treasury bills plunged from $277 billion in January 2007 to only $18 billion in January 2009.

So the increase in the monetary base was not a result of typical open market purchases. Instead, it reflected the Fed's innovative policy measures. As the Fed began to purchase mortgage-backed securities, commercial paper, and assets connected with the investment bank Bear Stearns and the insurance company AIG, the asset side of its balance sheet expanded, and so did the monetary base. There is an important point connected with this episode for understanding the mechanics of increases in the monetary base: *Whenever the Fed purchases assets of any kind, the monetary base increases.* It doesn't matter if the assets are Treasury bills, mortgage-backed securities, or computer systems. For instance, if the Federal Reserve Bank of Dallas buys a computer system from a local information technology company for $10 million, it will pay for the computers with a check. When the company deposits the check into the company's bank, the bank will send the check to the Fed, which will increase the bank's reserves by $10 million. The result is an increase in the monetary base of $10 million. If the computer company decided to cash the check, the result would be the same: Currency in circulation would rise by $10 million, while the reserves of the computer company's bank would be unchanged, so the monetary base would still rise by $10 million.

When in the fall of 2008, the Fed began to purchase hundreds of billions of dollars' worth of mortgage-backed securities and other financial assets, it was inevitable that the monetary base would increase.

Source: William T. Galvin, "More Money: Understanding Recent Changes in the Monetary Base," *Federal Reserve Bank of St. Louis Review*, Vol. 91, No. 2, March/April 2009, pp. 49–59.

See related problem 1.7 at the end of the chapter.

14.2

Learning Objective

Derive the equation for the simple deposit multiplier and understand what it means.

The Simple Deposit Multiplier

We now turn to the money multiplier to further understand the factors that determine the money supply. Our analysis has three steps, to reflect the fact that the size of the money multiplier is determined by the actions of three actors in the economy: the Fed, the nonbank public, and banks. The first step, which we describe in this section, shows how the money supply can be increased or decreased through a process called *multiple deposit expansion*. In this part of the analysis, we determine the *simple deposit multiplier*. The second step shows how the actions of the nonbank public affect the money multiplier, and the third step incorporates the actions of banks. We cover these last two steps in Section 14.3.

Multiple Deposit Expansion

What happens to the money supply when the Fed increases bank reserves through an open market purchase? To answer this question, we first analyze the changes that occur at a single bank and then look at the changes for the whole banking system.

How a Single Bank Responds to an Increase In Reserves Suppose that the Fed purchases $100,000 in Treasury bills (or T-bills) from Bank of America, increasing Bank of

America's reserves by $100,000. We can use a T-account to show how Bank of America's balance sheet changes to reflect these transactions:

BANK OF AMERICA

Assets		Liabilities
Securities	−$100,000	
Reserves	+$100,000	

The Fed's purchase of T-bills from Bank of America increases the bank's excess reserves but not its required reserves. The reason is that required reserves are determined as a percentage of the bank's checkable deposits. Because this transaction has no effect on Bank of America's checkable deposits, it doesn't change the amount of reserves that the bank is required to hold. Bank of America earns only a low interest rate from the Fed on the additional reserves obtained from the T-bill sale and therefore has an incentive to loan out or invest these funds.

Suppose that Bank of America loans $100,000 to Rosie's Bakery to enable it to buy two new ovens. We will assume that Bank of America extends the loan by creating a checking account for Rosie's and depositing the $100,000 principal of the loan in it. Both the asset and liability sides of Bank of America's balance sheet increase by $100,000:

BANK OF AMERICA

Assets		Liabilities	
Securities	−$100,000	Checkable deposits	+$100,000
Reserves	+$100,000		
Loans	+$100,000		

Recall that the money supply—using the M1 definition—equals currency plus checkable deposits. By lending money to Rosie's, Bank of America creates checkable deposits and, therefore, increases the money supply. Suppose that Rosie's then spends the loan proceeds by writing a check for $100,000 to buy the ovens from Bob's Bakery Equipment. Bob's deposits the check in its account with PNC Bank. Once the check has cleared and PNC Bank has collected the funds from Bank of America, Bank of America will have lost $100,000 of reserves and checkable deposits:

BANK OF AMERICA

Assets		Liabilities	
Securities	−$100,000	Checkable deposits	$0
Loans	+$100,000		
Reserves	$0		

Bank of America is now satisfied because it has exchanged some of its low-interest Treasury bill holdings for a higher-interest loan. But the impact of the open market purchase on the banking system is not finished.

How the Banking System Responds to an Increase in Reserves We can trace the further effect of the open market operation by considering the situation of PNC Bank after it has received the check for $100,000 from Bob's Bakery Equipment. After PNC has cleared the check and collected the funds from Bank of America, PNC's balance sheet changes as follows:

PNC BANK

Assets		Liabilities	
Reserves	+$100,000	Checkable deposits	+$100,000

PNC's deposits and reserves have both increased by $100,000. For simplicity, let's assume that when it received Bob's deposit, PNC had no excess reserves. If the required reserve ratio is 10%, PNC must hold $10,000 (= 0.10 × $100,000) against its increase of $100,000 in checkable deposits. The other $90,000 of the reserves it has gained are excess reserves. PNC knows that it will lose reserves equal to the amount of any loan it grants because the amount of the loan will be spent and the funds will be deposited in another bank. So, *PNC can only safely lend out an amount equal to its excess reserves.* Suppose that PNC makes a $90,000 loan to Jerome's Printing to purchase new office equipment. Initially, PNC's assets (loans) and liabilities (checkable deposits) rise by $90,000. But this is temporary because Jerome's will spend the loan proceeds by writing a $90,000 check to buy equipment from Computer Universe, which has an account at SunTrust Bank. When SunTrust clears the $90,000 check against PNC, PNC's balance sheet changes as follows:

PNC BANK

Assets		Liabilities	
Reserves	+$10,000	Checkable deposits	+$100,000
Loans	+$90,000		

These are the changes in SunTrust's balance sheet:

SUNTRUST BANK

Assets		Liabilities	
Reserves	+$90,000	Checkable deposits	+$90,000

To this point, checkable deposits in the banking system have risen by $190,000 as a result of the Fed's $100,000 open market purchase.

SunTrust faces the same decisions that Bank of America and PNC faced. SunTrust wants to use the increase in reserves to expand its loans, but it can safely lend only the increase in excess reserves. With a required reserve ratio of 10%, SunTrust must add $90,000 × 0.10 = $9,000 to its required reserves and can lend only $81,000. Suppose that SunTrust lends the $81,000 to Howard's Barber Shop to use for remodeling. Initially, SunTrust's assets (loans) and liabilities (checkable deposits) rise by $81,000. But when Howard's spends the loan proceeds and a check for $81,000 clears against it, the changes in SunTrust's balance sheet will be as follows:

SUNTRUST BANK

Assets		Liabilities	
Reserves	+$9,000	Checkable deposits	+$90,000
Loans	+$81,000		

If the proceeds of the loan to Howard's Barber Shop are deposited in another bank, checkable deposits in the banking system will rise by another $81,000. To this point, the $100,000 increase in reserves supplied by the Fed has increased the level of checkable deposits by $100,000 + $90,000 + $81,000 = $271,000. This process is called **multiple deposit creation**. The money supply is growing with each loan. The initial increase in bank reserves and in the monetary base is resulting in a multiple change in the money supply.

The process still isn't complete. The recipient of the $81,000 check from Howard's Barber Shop will deposit it, and checkable deposits at some other bank will expand. The process continues to ripple through the banking system and the economy. We illustrate the results in Table 14.2. Note from the table that new checkable deposits continue to be created each time checks are deposited and banks make new loans, but the size of the increase gets smaller each time because banks must hold part of the money at each step as required reserves.

Multiple deposit creation Part of the money supply process in which an increase in bank reserves results in rounds of bank loans and creation of checkable deposits and an increase in the money supply that is a multiple of the initial increase in reserves.

Calculating the Simple Deposit Multiplier

Table 14.2 shows that the Fed's open market purchase of $100,000 increases the reserves of the banking system by $100,000 and, ultimately, increases checkable deposits by $1,000,000. The ratio of the amount of deposits created by banks to the amount of new reserves created is called the **simple deposit multiplier**. In this case, the simple deposit multiplier equals $1,000,000/$100,000 = 10. Why 10? How do we know that the initial increase in bank reserves of $100,000 ultimately leads to an increase in deposits of $1,000,000?

Simple deposit multiplier The ratio of the amount of deposits created by banks to the amount of new reserves.

There are two ways to answer this question. First, each bank in this process is keeping reserves equal to 10% of its deposits because we are assuming that no bank holds excess reserves. For the banking system as a whole, the increase in reserves is $100,000—the amount of the Fed's open market purchase. Therefore, the system as a whole will end up with $1,000,000 in deposits because $100,000 is 10% of $1,000,000.

Table 14.2 Multiple Deposit Creation, Assuming a Fed Open Market Purchase of $100,000 and a Required Reserve Ratio of 10%

Bank	Increase in deposits	Increase in loans	Increase in reserves
PNC Bank	$ 100,000	$ 90,000	$ 10,000
SunTrust Bank	90,000	81,000	9,000
Third Bank	81,000	72,900	8,100
Fourth Bank	72,900	65,610	7,290
Fifth Bank	65,610	59,049	6,561
.	.	.	.
.	.	.	.
.	.	.	.
Total increase	$1,000,000	$900,000	$100,000

A second way to answer the question is by deriving an expression for the simple deposit multiplier. From Table 14.2, we can write an expression for the total increase in deposits:

$$\Delta D = \$100,000 + [0.9 \times \$100,000] + [(0.9 \times 0.9) \times \$100,000] + [(0.9 \times 0.9 \times 0.9) \times \$100,000] + \ldots$$

Or, simplifying:

$$\Delta D = \$100,000 \times [1 + 0.9 + 0.9^2 + 0.9^3 + \ldots].$$

The rules of algebra tell us that an infinite series like the one in the expression sums to:

$$\frac{1}{1 - 0.9} = \frac{1}{0.1} = 10.$$

So, $\Delta D = \$100,000 \times 10 = \$1,000,000$. Note that 10 is 1 divided by the required reserve ratio, rr_D, which in this case is 10%, or 0.10. This gives us another way of expressing the simple deposit multiplier:

$$\text{Simple deposit multiplier} = \frac{1}{rr_D}.$$

So, now we have an equation showing how a change in deposits, ΔD, is related to an initial change in reserves, ΔR:

$$\Delta D = \frac{\Delta R}{rr_D},$$

or, in our example,

$$\Delta D = \frac{\$100,000}{0.1} = \$1,000,000.$$

If a bank decides to invest all or some of its excess reserves in municipal bonds or other securities rather than make loans, the deposit expansion process will be the same as if the bank had made loans. Suppose that PNC decided to purchase $90,000 worth of municipal bonds from the Goldman Sachs investment bank instead of extending the $90,000 loan to Jerome's. PNC would write Goldman Sachs a check in the amount of $90,000, which Goldman Sachs would deposit in its bank. Goldman Sachs's bank would then have excess reserves, which it could lend or invest, and so on. The effect on multiple deposit creation is the same whether banks use excess reserves to make loans or buy securities.

At first you might think that individual banks are creating money. However, an individual bank can lend only an amount equal to its excess reserves. New deposits are created when borrowers spend the funds they borrow from banks and the funds are then deposited back into the banking system. Multiple deposit creation refers to the actions of the banking system as a whole, not to the action of an individual bank.

Finally, note that while the Fed can expand the volume of checkable deposits in the banking system by increasing reserves, it can also contract the volume of deposits by reducing reserves. The Fed reduces reserves by selling government securities in an *open market sale*. This action has a ripple effect that is similar to deposit expansion in the banking system, but in the opposite direction. The result of the open market sale is *multiple deposit contraction*. Suppose that the Fed sells $100,000 in Treasury securities to Bank of America, thereby reducing that bank's reserves by $100,000. With a simple deposit multiplier of 10, we know that a decline in reserves of $100,000 will eventually lead to a decline in checkable deposits of $1,000,000.

Banks, the Nonbank Public, and the Money Multiplier

14.3

Learning Objective
Explain how the behavior of banks and the nonbank public affect the money multiplier.

Understanding the simple deposit multiplier is an important step in understanding the money supply process, but it is not the complete story. In deriving the simple deposit multiplier, we made two key assumptions:

1. Banks hold no excess reserves.
2. The nonbank public does not increase its holdings of currency.

In other words, we assumed in the previous section that whenever banks have excess reserves, they lend them all out. We also assumed that if households or firms receive a check, they deposit the whole amount in a checking account, keeping none of the funds as cash. Neither of these assumptions is correct: Banks hold some excess reserves, and the nonbank public typically increases its holdings of currency when its checking account balances rise. In this section, we find out what happens to our story of the money supply process if we relax these assumptions.

The Effect of Increases in Currency Holdings and Increases in Excess Reserves

In our story of the money supply process in the previous section, once Bank of America had acquired $100,000 in excess reserves as a result of selling Treasury bills to the Fed, the bank loaned the entire amount to Rosie's Bakery. Rosie's then spent the loan proceeds by writing a check for $100,000 to Bob's Bakery Equipment, and Bob's deposited the entire $100,000 check in its account with PNC Bank. Once the check cleared, PNC Bank gained $100,000 in reserves. But suppose that instead of depositing the whole $100,000, Bob's had deposited $90,000 and taken $10,000 in cash? In that case, PNC would have a gain in reserves of $90,000, not $100,000, thereby reducing the amount PNC had available to lend.

Throughout the process of banks making loans and creating new checkable deposits, households and firms will hold some of the increased funds as currency rather than as deposits. Funds deposited in banks are subject to the multiple deposit creation process, while funds held as currency are not. We can conclude that *the more currency the nonbank public holds relative to checkable deposits, the smaller the multiple deposit creation process will be*.

Now suppose that when Bob's Bakery deposits the $100,000 in its account at PNC Bank, the bank decides that instead of holding $10,000 as required reserves and loaning out the other $90,000, it will hold the entire $100,000 as excess reserves. If PNC takes this action, the process of multiple deposit creation will come to an immediate stop because no more loans are made and no more deposits are created. Rather than resulting in a $1,000,000 increase in deposits, the Fed's $100,000 open market purchase will have resulted in only a $100,000 increase in deposits. The deposit multiplier will have declined from 10 to 1. We can conclude that *the more excess reserves banks hold relative to their checkable deposits, the smaller the multiple deposit creation process will be.*

Figure 14.1 on page 417 illustrates our ultimate goal in understanding the money supply process: to find a stable money multiplier that will link the monetary base to the money supply. We have seen that the Fed can control the size of the monetary base through open market operations. Provided that the money multiplier is stable, the Fed's control over the monetary base allows it to also control the money supply. The simple deposit multiplier is useful in understanding how reserve creation leads to increases in loans and deposits, which is the heart of the money supply process. But we need to elaborate on the simple deposit multiplier in three ways:

1. Rather than a link between reserves and deposits, we need a link between the monetary base and the money supply.
2. We need to include the effects on the money supply process of changes in the nonbank public's desire to hold currency relative to checkable deposits.
3. We need to include the effects of changes in banks' desire to hold excess reserves relative to deposits.

In the next section, we make these changes to the simple deposit multiplier story in order to build a complete account of the money supply process.

Deriving a Realistic Money Multiplier

We need to derive a money multiplier, m, that links the monetary base, B, to the money supply, M:

$$M = m \times B.$$

This equation tells us that the money multiplier is equal to the ratio of the money supply to the monetary base:

$$m = \frac{M}{B}.$$

Recall that the money supply is the sum of currency, C, and checkable deposits, D, while the monetary base is the sum of currency and bank reserves, R. Because we want to take into account banks' decisions about holding excess reserves, we can separate reserves into its components: required reserves, RR, and excess reserves, ER. So, we can expand the expression for the money multiplier to:

$$m = \frac{C + D}{C + RR + ER}.$$

Currency-to-deposit ratio (C/D) The nonbank public's holdings of currency, C, relative to their holdings of checkable deposits, D.

Keep in mind that we are interested in the nonbank public's desire to hold currency relative to checkable deposits and banks' desire to hold excess reserves relative to checkable deposits. To capture this behavior in our expression for the money multiplier, we want to include the **currency-to-deposit ratio (C/D)**, which measures the nonbank public's holdings of currency relative to their holdings of checkable deposits, and the excess reserves-to-deposit ratio (*ER/D*), which measure banks' holdings of excess reserves relative to their checkable deposits. To include these ratios in the expression for the money multiplier, we can rely on the basic rule of arithmetic that multiplying the numerator and denominator of a fraction by the same variable preserves the value of the fraction. So, we can introduce the deposit ratios into our expression for the money multiplier this way:

$$m = \left(\frac{C + D}{C + RR + ER}\right) \times \frac{(1/D)}{(1/D)} = \frac{(C/D) + 1}{(C/D) + (RR/D) + (ER/D)}.$$

Recall that the ratio of required reserves to checkable deposits is the required reserve ratio, rr_D. We can use this fact to arrive at our final expression for the money multiplier:

$$m = \frac{(C/D) + 1}{(C/D) + rr_D + (ER/D)}.$$

So, we can say that because:

$$\text{Money supply} = \text{Money multiplier} \times \text{Monetary base,}$$

then,

$$M = \left(\frac{(C/D) + 1}{(C/D) + rr_D + (ER/D)}\right) \times B.$$

For example, suppose that we have the following values:

$$C = \$500 \text{ billion}$$
$$D = \$1,000 \text{ billion}$$
$$rr_D = 0.1$$
$$ER = \$150 \text{ billion}$$

Then the currency-to-deposit ratio = $500 billion/$1,000 billion = 0.50, and the excess reserves-to-deposit ratio = $150 billion/$1,000 billion = 0.15. So, the value of the money multiplier is:

$$m = \frac{0.5 + 1}{0.5 + 0.1 + 0.15} = \frac{1.5}{0.75} = 2.$$

With a money multiplier of 2, every $1 billion increase in the monetary base will result in a $2 billion increase in the money supply.

There are several points to note about our expression linking the money supply to the monetary base:

1. The money supply will increase if either the monetary base or the money multiplier increases in value, and it will decrease if either the monetary base or the money multiplier decreases in value.
2. An increase in the currency-to-deposit ratio (*C/D*) causes the value of the money multiplier to decline and, if the monetary base is unchanged, the value of the money supply to decline. For instance, in the previous example, if (*C/D*) increases from 0.5 to 0.6, then the value of the multiplier falls from 1.5/0.75 = 2 to 1.6/0.85 = 1.88. This result makes economic sense: If households and firms increase their holdings of

currency relative to their holdings of checkable deposits, banks will have a relatively smaller amount of funds they can lend out, which reduces the multiple creation of deposits.

3. An increase in the required reserve ratio, rr_D, causes the value of the money multiplier to decline and, if the monetary base is unchanged, the value of the money supply to decline. The arithmetic of this result is straightforward: Because rr_D is in the denominator of the money multiplier expression, as the value of rr_D increases, the value of m declines. Economically, an increase in rr_D means that for any increase in reserves banks receive, a larger fraction must be held as required reserves and are, therefore, not available to be loaned out as part of the process of multiple deposit creation.

4. An increase in the excess reserves-to-deposit ratio (ER/D) causes the value of the money multiplier to decline and, if the monetary base is unchanged, the value of the money supply to decline. Once again, the arithmetic of this result is straightforward because (ER/D) is in the denominator of the money multiplier expression. Economically, an increase in (ER/D) means that banks are holding relatively more excess reserves, so they are not using these funds to make loans as part of the process of multiple deposit creation.

Solved Problem 14.3

Using the Expression for the Money Multiplier

Consider the following information:

$$\text{Bank reserves} = \$500 \text{ billion}$$
$$\text{Currency} = \$400 \text{ billion}$$

a. If banks are holding $80 billion in required reserves, and the required reserve ratio $= 0.1$, what is the value of checkable deposits?

b. Given this information, what is the value of the money supply (M1)? What is the value of the monetary base? What is the value of the money multiplier?

Solving the Problem

Step 1 **Review the chapter material.** This problem is about the money multiplier, so you may want to review the section "Deriving a Realistic Money Multiplier," which begins on page 430.

Step 2 **Answer part (a) by calculating the value of checkable deposits.** The value of required reserves is equal to the value of checkable deposits multiplied by the required reserve ratio:

$$RR = D \times rr_D$$
$$\$80 \text{ billion} = D \times 0.1$$
$$D = (\$80 \text{ billion}/0.1) = \$800 \text{ billion}$$

Step 3 **Answer part (b) by calculating the values of the money supply, the monetary base, and the money multiplier.** The M1 measure of the money supply equals the value of currency plus the value of checkable deposits:

$$M = C + D$$
$$= \$400 \text{ billion} + \$800 \text{ billion}$$
$$= \$1,200 \text{ billion}.$$

The monetary base is equal to the value of currency plus the value of bank reserves:

$$B = C + R$$
$$= \$400 \text{ billion} + \$500 \text{ billion}$$
$$= \$900 \text{ billion}.$$

We can calculate the money multiplier two ways. First, note that the money multiplier is equal to the ratio of the money supply to the monetary base:

$$m = \frac{M}{B} = \frac{\$1,200 \text{ billion}}{\$900 \text{ billion}} = 1.33.$$

Or, we can calculate the value of the money multiplier using the expression derived on page 430:

$$m = \frac{(C/D) + 1}{(C/D) + rr_D + (ER/D)}.$$

To use this expression, we need to calculate the value of excess reserves. Because we know that total reserves equal \$500 billion and required reserves equal \$80 billion, the value of excess reserves must equal \$420 billion. Inserting values into the expression for the money multiplier gives us:

$$m = \frac{(\$400 \text{ billion}/\$800 \text{ billion}) + 1}{(\$400 \text{ billion}/\$800 \text{ billion}) + 0.1 + (\$420 \text{ billion}/\$800 \text{ billion})}$$

$$= \frac{1.5}{1.125} = 1.33.$$

So, the two approaches to calculating the value of the money multiplier give us the same result.

See related problems 3.7 and 3.8 at the end of the chapter.

We saw earlier in the chapter that economists think of the monetary base as having two components—the nonborrowed monetary base, B_{non}, and borrowed reserves, BR, which is another name for discount loans: $B = B_{non} + BR$. Because the actions of both the Fed and banks determine the volume of discount loans, the Fed has greater control over the nonborrowed monetary base. We can recognize this fact by rewriting the relationship between the money supply and the monetary base:

$$M = \left(\frac{(C/D) + 1}{C/D + rr_D + (ER/D)} \right) \times (B_{non} + BR).$$

We now have a complete description of the money supply process:

1. The money supply equals the monetary base times the money multiplier.
2. The monetary base equals the nonborrowed base, determined primarily by the Fed through open market operations, and discount loans, determined jointly by the banks and the Fed.
3. The money multiplier depends on the required reserve ratio (determined by the Fed), the ratio of excess reserves-to-deposits (determined by banks), and the currency-to-deposit ratio (determined by the nonbank public: households and firms).

Table 14.3 summarizes the variables that determine the money supply. Note that decreases in the variables listed in the first column would have the opposite effect on the money supply to that given in the third column.

We stated earlier that the Fed controls the money supply. We now know that this statement is not quite correct. The Fed can set the value of the nonborrowed base at whatever level it chooses. But the behavior of the nonbank public influences the money supply through the currency-to-deposit ratio, and the behavior of banks influences the money supply through the volume of discount loans and the excess reserves-to-deposit ratio. In the next section, we can use this analysis to understand changes in the monetary base and in the money supply during the financial crisis of 2007–2009 and the following period.

Table 14.3 Variables in the Money Supply Process

An increase in the . . .	based on the actions of . . .	causes the money supply to . . .	because . . .
nonborrowed base, B_{non}	the Fed through open market operations	increase	the monetary base increases, and more reserves are available for deposit expansion.
required reserve ratio, rr_D	the Fed through changes in reserve requirements	decrease	fewer reserves can be lent out, and the value of the money multiplier falls.
currency-to-deposit ratio (C/D)	the nonbank public	decrease	the value of the money multiplier falls, reducing deposit expansion.
excess reserves-to-deposit ratio (ER/D)	banks	decrease	the value of the money multiplier falls, reducing deposit expansion.

The Money Supply, the Money Multiplier, and the Monetary Base During and After the 2007–2009 Financial Crisis

We have already seen that beginning in the fall of 2008, in response to the financial crisis, the Fed bought huge amounts of financial assets, including mortgage-backed securities. Panel (a) of Figure 14.2 shows that, as a result, the size of the monetary base soared. M1 also increased, but not by nearly as much. As panel (b) shows, the value of the money multiplier declined sharply during the same period. The value of the money multiplier had been trending down, declining from a value of about 3 at the beginning of 1990 to about 1.7 at the beginning of 2007. The value then declined by more than 50% during the financial crisis, dropping below 1 by late 2008. In fact, with the value of the monetary base having risen above the value of the money supply, the money multiplier had turned into a money *divider*!

Why did the monetary base increase so much more than M1? Figure 14.3 helps solve the mystery. The figure shows movements in the currency-to-deposit ratio (*C/D*) and the excess reserves-to-deposit ratio (*ER/D*). While the currency-to-deposit ratio had been gradually trending upward since 1990, it fell during the financial crisis because households and firms shifted funds into checkable deposits from money market mutual funds and other assets whose riskiness they believed had increased. Recall from our discussion of the effect of changes in (*C/D*) on the money multiplier that a decrease in (*C/D*), holding all else constant, will cause the value of the money multiplier to increase and the value of M1 to also increase for any given value of the monetary base. We know from panel (b) of Figure 14.2 that, in fact, the value of the money multiplier *decreased*. The reason is that the value of (*ER/D*) soared, increasing from almost zero in

MyEconLab Real-time data

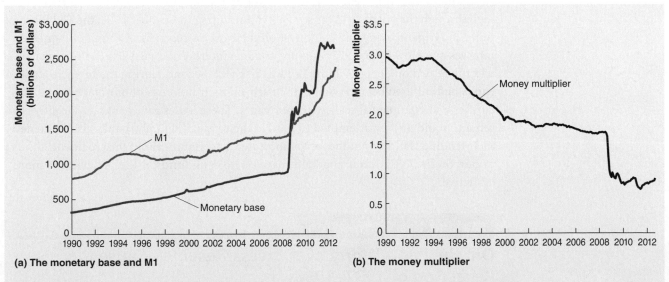

(a) The monetary base and M1

(b) The money multiplier

Figure 14.2 Movements in the Monetary Base, M1, and the Money Multiplier, 1990–2012

Panel (a) shows that beginning in the fall of 2008, the size of the monetary base soared. M1 also increased, but not nearly as much.

As panel (b) shows, the value of the money multiplier declined sharply during the same period.

Source: Federal Reserve Bank of St. Louis.

MyEconLab Real-time data

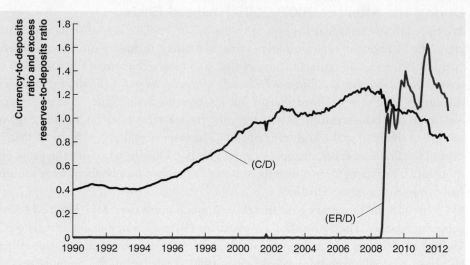

Figure 14.3

Movements in (C/D) and (ER/D)

The currency-to-deposit ratio (C/D) had been gradually trending upward since 1990, but it fell during the financial crisis of 2007–2009. At the same time, the excess reserves-to-deposits ratio (ER/D) soared, increasing from almost zero in September 2008—because banks were holding very few excess reserves— to about 1.3 in the fall of 2009. Banks began to hold more excess reserves than they had checkable deposits.

Source: Federal Reserve Bank of St. Louis.

September 2008—because banks were holding very few excess reserves—to about 1.3 in the fall of 2009. In other words, banks began to hold more excess reserves than they had checkable deposits.

Because the increase in (ER/D) was significantly larger than the decline in (C/D), the value of the money multiplier declined, and the increase in the monetary base resulted in a much smaller increase in M1 than would have occurred if the value of the money multiplier had remained what it was at the beginning of the financial crisis.

Banks' holdings of excess reserves shot up during the fall of 2008 and remained high through the fall of 2012 for several reasons. First, in October 2008, the Fed for the first time began paying banks interest on their excess reserves. Although the interest rate was quite low—only 0.25%—other nominal interest rates had also declined sharply and the return on deposits at the Fed was risk free. Second, during the financial crisis, banks had suffered heavy losses, particularly on their holdings of mortgage-backed securities and commercial real estate mortgages. These losses gave banks an incentive to remain liquid as they attempted to rebuild their capital. Finally, banks also tightened their lending standards in the face of increased uncertainty about the creditworthiness of borrowers. With fewer good alternatives, holding funds at the Fed became more attractive.

Making the Connection

Did the Fed's Worry over Excess Reserves Cause the Recession of 1937–1938?

If the Fed is worried about the level of excess reserves in the banking system, one solution is to turn the *excess* reserves into *required* reserves by increasing the required reserve ratio. This is what the Fed did in the mid-1930s, during the Great Depression.

As the graph below shows, following the end of the bank panics in early 1933, excess reserves in the banking system rose sharply.

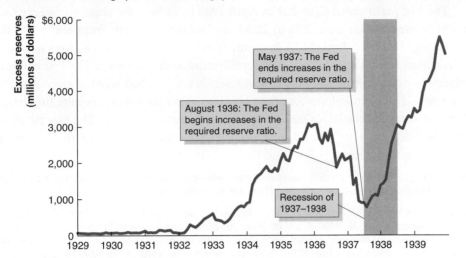

Source: Banking and Monetary Statistics of the United States.

Banks accumulated excess reserves during the mid-1930s for reasons similar to the reasons banks accumulated excess reserves after 2008. Although bank panics had ended following the establishment of the FDIC, many banks had suffered heavy losses and strongly desired to remain liquid. Nominal interest rates had also fallen to very low levels, which reduced the opportunity cost of holding reserves at the Fed. Finally, given the severity of the Depression, the creditworthiness of most borrowers had deteriorated. By late 1935, the unemployment rate remained very high, at more than 14%, and the inflation rate remained low, at less than 2%. Nevertheless, some members of the Fed's Board of Governors were worried about a rapid increase in stock prices, which, despite the depressed economy, they felt might be a speculative bubble similar to the one that had preceded the great stock market crash of October 1929. Some members were also afraid of an increase in the inflation rate. A memorandum by the Federal Reserve's staff referred to the "general fear which many people entertain that excess reserves of the present magnitude must sooner or later set in motion inflationary forces which, if not dealt with before they get strongly under way, may prove impossible to control. . . ."

The Board of Governors decided to reduce excess reserves in the banking system by raising the required reserve ratio on checkable deposits in four steps, from 10% to 20%, beginning in August 1936. The board also raised the required reserve ratio on time deposits from 3% to 6%. The graph above indicates that at first the Fed's actions succeeded in reducing excess reserves. But the Fed's policy ignored the reasons banks during this period were holding excess reserves. Following the increases in the required reserve ratio, the only way banks could restore their previous holdings of excess reserves was to make fewer loans and, thereby, hold fewer demand deposits. As bank loans contracted, so did the money supply. Households and firms, unable to obtain credit, cut back on their spending, and the economy fell into recession in 1937.

The unemployment rate, which was still far from the full employment levels of 1929, started increasing again.

The Fed partly reversed course in April 1938 by cutting the required reserve ratio on checkable deposits from 20% to 17.5% and on time deposits from 6% to 5%. But the damage had been done. Most economists believe that the Fed's actions in raising the required reserve ratio contributed significantly to the recession. The Fed had misjudged the desire of banks to hold excess reserves and, so, had failed to anticipate that banks would take action to restore their holdings of excess reserves despite the sharply higher reserve requirements. One Fed economist recently observed: "The experience [of the 1930s] demonstrates that raising reserve requirements is surely *not* the best way to eliminate excess reserves."

Note: In the 1930s, the Fed set different reserve requirements for banks, depending on their size and location. The reserve requirements discussed here are for reserve city banks.

Sources: David Wheelock, "How *Not* to Reduce Excess Reserves," *Federal Reserve Bank of St. Louis Economic Synopses*, No. 38, 2009; Board of Governors of the Federal Reserve System, *Banking and Monetary Statistics of the United States, 1914–1941*, Washington, DC, November 1943; the quote from the 1935 Fed memorandum is from Milton Friedman and Anna Schwartz, *A Monetary History of the United States, 1867–1960*, Princeton, NJ: Princeton University Press, 1963, p. 523.

See related problem 3.10 at the end of the chapter.

In 2012, banks' enormous holdings of excess reserves left investors, policymakers, and economists concerned about the implications for future inflation. As we have seen, in normal economic times—and in the absence of the Fed paying interest on bank reserves—banks typically lend out nearly all of their excess reserves. If banks were to suddenly begin lending the more than $1.4 trillion in excess reserves they held in November 2012, the result would be an explosion in the money supply and, potentially, a rapid increase in inflation. Fear of this potential for a much higher rate of inflation in the future drove some investors in 2012 to buy gold.

Making the Connection | In Your Interest

If You Are Worried About Inflation, Should You Invest in Gold?

Beginning in 2008, many investors bought gold because they were worried about the possibility that increases in bank reserves and the money supply might lead to much higher rates of inflation in the future. But how good an investment is gold? Gold clearly has some drawbacks as an investment: Unlike a bond, gold pays no interest; unlike a stock, gold pays no dividend. At a time when many investments—including most stocks and bonds—exist only in electronic form, gold is a real tangible asset that has to be stored and safeguarded. For instance, an individual investor who owns American Eagle coins issued by the U.S. Mint must find a place to store them—perhaps paying a fee to a bank for a safety deposit box—and may have to pay for insurance on them. An investor can avoid these costs by buying gold ETFs, although people who buy gold because they are afraid of a future collapse of the financial system prefer to hold physical gold.

Because gold pays no interest, it is difficult to determine its fundamental value as an investment. Ultimately, the minimum price of gold is set by its value as a metal that can be used in jewelry and that also has some limited industrial uses. Gold's value as an investment depends on how likely its price is to increase in the future because its rate of return is entirely in the form of capital gains. Many individual investors believe that gold is a good hedge against inflation because the price of gold can be relied on to rise if the general price level rises. But is this view correct? The blue line in the graph below shows the monthly price of gold from January 1975 through September 2012.

MyEconLab Real-time data

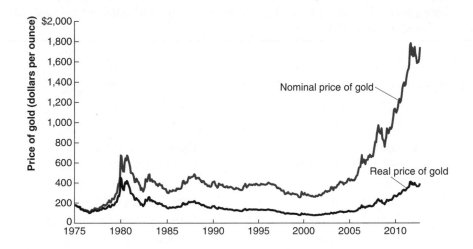

The graph shows that the price of gold soared during the high-inflation years of the late 1970s. Gold was selling for about $175 per ounce in January 1975 and increased to $670 in September 1980. Unfortunately for investors in gold, while the overall price level continued to rise during the years following 1980, the price of gold actually fell. In August 1999, gold was selling for only about $255 per ounce, or about 60% less than at its peak nearly 20 years earlier. Meanwhile, the price level, as measured by the consumer price index, had doubled. The red line on the graph shows the real price of gold, calculated by dividing the nominal price of gold by the consumer price index. The red line shows that even after the strong nominal price increases beginning in 2009, by the fall of 2012, the real price of gold was still below its September 1980 level. In other words, in the long run, gold has proven to be a poor hedge against inflation.

Although investors who were buying gold in 2012 may have been making a shrewd investment, the record of the past 30 years was not encouraging.

Note: The nominal price of gold is the "gold fixing price" in the London Bullion Market. The real price of gold is calculated by dividing by the consumer price index, using January 1975 = 100 as a base.

Source: Federal Reserve Bank of St. Louis.

See related problem 3.11 at the end of the chapter.

Answering the Key Question

Continued from page 415

At the beginning of this chapter, we asked:

"Why did bank reserves increase rapidly during and after the financial crisis of 2007–2009, and should policymakers be concerned about the increase?"

As we have seen, the rapid increase in bank reserves that began in the fall of 2008 was a result of the Fed purchasing assets. Whenever the Fed purchases an asset, the monetary base increases. Both the currency and bank reserves components of the base increased in 2008, but the increase in reserves was particularly large. Banks were content to hold large balances of excess reserves because the Fed was paying interest on them and because of the increased risk in alternative uses of the funds. Inflation remained very low through 2012, but some policymakers were concerned that, ultimately, if banks began to lend out their holdings of excess reserves, the inflation rate could increase in the future.

Key Terms and Problems

Key Terms

Bank reserves, p. 419

Currency-to-deposit ratio (*C/D*), p. 430

Currency in circulation, p. 419

Currency in M1, p. 419

Discount loan, p. 421

Discount rate, p. 422

Excess reserves, p. 419

Monetary base (or high-powered money), p. 417

Multiple deposit creation, p. 427

Open market operations, p. 420

Open market purchase, p. 420

Open market sale, p. 420

Required reserve ratio, p. 419

Required reserves, p. 419

Simple deposit multiplier, p. 427

Vault cash, p. 419

14.1 ## The Federal Reserve's Balance Sheet and the Monetary Base

Explain the relationship between the Fed's balance sheet and the monetary base.

Review Questions

1.1 How does the monetary base differ from the money supply?

1.2 What are the two most important assets and the two most important liabilities on the Fed's balance sheet? Because currency is valuable, why is it a liability to the Fed rather than an asset?

1.3 Use a T-account for Bank of America and a T-account for the Fed to show the result of the Fed buying $1 million in Treasury bills from Bank of America.

Problems and Applications

1.4 An article in the *Wall Street Journal* titled "Why the Fed's Balance Sheet Is Shrinking," observed

that: "As people pay back their mortgages . . . the Fed's holdings of mortgage backed securities shrink until it can use those funds to buy more."

a. What are mortgage-backed securities? Where do they appear on the Fed's balance sheet?

b. What does it mean to say that the Fed's balance sheet is "shrinking"? Why would people paying off their mortgages cause the Fed's balance sheet to shrink?

Source: Kristina Peterson and Eric Morath, "Why the Fed's Balance Sheet Is Shrinking," *Wall Street Journal*, November 2, 2012.

1.5 In August 2010, the Federal Reserve announced that as the mortgage-backed securities it owns matured, it would reinvest the funds by buying

U.S. Treasury securities. How would these actions affect the size of the Fed's balance sheet? Would the Fed be more likely to take this action if it saw future U.S. economic growth as strong or as weak? Briefly explain.

1.6 Use T-accounts to show the effect of the following on the balance sheets of the Fed and the banking system:

a. The Fed increases discount loans by $2 billion.

b. The Fed carries out a $2 billion open market sale.

1.7 [Related to the Making the Connection **on page 423**] In the fall of 2012, an article in the *New York*

Times speculated that the Federal Reserve "could announce a new round of asset purchases, expanding its balance sheet for the third time since 2008."

a. What are asset purchases?

b. How do asset purchases expand the Fed's balance sheet?

c. Why had the Fed expanded its balance sheet since 2008?

Source: Binyamin Appelbaum, "Economic Stimulus as the Election Nears? It's Been Done Before," *New York Times*, September 11, 2012.

14.2 The Simple Deposit Multiplier
Derive the equation for the simple deposit multiplier and understand what it means.

Review Questions

2.1 Suppose that PNC Bank sells $1 million in Treasury bills to the Fed and then makes a $1 million loan to David's Donut Emporium and Boat Repair. Use a T-account to show the results of these transactions on PNC's balance sheet.

2.2 Why does the Fed's purchase of Treasury bills lead to "multiple deposit expansion"?

2.3 If the required reserve ratio is 15%, what is the value of the simple deposit multiplier?

Problems and Applications

2.4 Suppose that Bank of America lends $100,000 to Jill's Jerseys. Using T-accounts, show how this transaction is recorded on the bank's balance sheet. If Jill's spends the money to buy materials from Zach's Zippers, which has its checking account at PNC Bank, show the effect on Bank of America's balance sheet. What is the total change in Bank of America's assets and liabilities?

2.5 Suppose that a bank with no excess reserves receives a deposit into a checking account of $10,000 in currency. If the required reserve ratio is 0.10, what is the maximum amount that the bank can lend out?

2.6 Suppose that JPMorgan Chase sells $100 million in Treasury bills to the Fed.

a. Use T-accounts to show the immediate effect of this sale on the balance sheets of JPMorgan Chase and the Fed.

b. Suppose that before selling the Treasury bills, JPMorgan Chase had no excess reserves. Suppose that the required reserve ratio is 20%. Suppose that JPMorgan Chase makes the maximum loan it can from the funds acquired by selling the Treasury bills. Use a T-account to show the initial impact of granting the loan on JPMorgan Chase's balance sheet. Also include on this T-account the transaction from part (a).

c. Now suppose that whoever took out the loan in part (b) writes a check for this amount and that the person receiving the check deposits it in Wells Fargo Bank. Show the effect of these transactions on the balance sheets of JPMorgan Chase and Wells Fargo after the check has cleared. (On the T-account for JPMorgan Chase, include the transactions from parts (a) and (b).)

d. If currency is $400 billion, total reserves of the banking system are $600 billion, and total checkable deposits are $2,100 billion, what is

MyEconLab Visit **www.myeconlab.com** to complete these exercises online and get instant feedback. Exercises that update with real-time data are marked with 🕸.

the maximum increase in the money supply that can result from the transaction in part (a) (that is, the maximum increase after all actions resulting from the transaction in part (a) have occurred)?

2.7 In the following bank balance sheet, amounts are in millions of dollars. The required reserve ratio is 3% on the first $30 million of checkable deposits and 12% on any checkable deposits over $30 million.

Assets		Liabilities	
Reserves	$18.9	Checkable deposits	$180.0
Loans	150.0	Net worth	20.0
Securities	31.1		
	$200.0		$200.0

a. Calculate the bank's excess reserves.

b. Suppose that the bank sells $5 million in securities to an investor. Show the bank's balance sheet after this transaction. Calculate what the banks excess reserves are now.

c. Suppose that the bank loans its excess reserves in part (b) to a local business. Show the bank's balance sheet after the loan has been made but before the business has spent the proceeds of the loan. Now what are the bank's excess reserves?

d. Suppose that the business spends the amount of the loan by writing a check. Revise the bank's balance sheet and calculate its excess reserves after the check has cleared.

2.8 In medieval times, goldsmiths would often offer to store gold in return for a fee. They provided anyone depositing gold with a warehouse receipt, which represented a legal claim on the goldsmith to exchange the receipt for the amount of gold written on it.

a. How are the medieval goldsmiths like modern banks, and how are they unlike modern banks?

b. Is multiple deposit creation possible in this system? Does your answer depend on whether the warehouse receipts can be bought and sold and redeemed by someone other than the person who deposited the gold?

2.9 A Fed publication refers to the multiple expansion of deposits as "the heart of banking theory."

a. Why is the process of the multiple expansion of deposits so important to understanding how the banking system operates?

b. The same publication refers to "the banking system's ability to multiply loans and deposits with the individual bank's inability to do so." How is the banking system able to multiply loans and deposits if an individual bank is unable to do so?

Source: Thomas M. Humphrey, "The Theory of Multiple Expansion of Deposits: What It Is and Whence It Came," *Federal Reserve Bank of Richmond Economic Review*, March/April 1987.

14.3 **Banks, the Nonbank Public, and the Money Multiplier**
Explain how the behavior of banks and the nonbank public affect the money multiplier.

Review Questions

3.1 What are the key differences between the simple deposit multiplier and the money multiplier?

3.2 Briefly explain whether under normal circumstances the money multiplier will increase or decrease following an increase in each of the following:

a. The currency-to-deposit ratio (C/D)

b. The excess reserves-to-deposit ratio (ER/D)

c. The required reserve ratio (rr_D)

3.3 Briefly explain what happened to the currency-to-deposit ratio (C/D) and the excess reserves-to-deposit ratio (ER/D) during the financial crisis of

2007–2009. What effect did these changes have on the size of the money multiplier?

Problems and Applications

3.4 Explain whether you agree with the following observation: "If the required reserve ratio were zero, the process of multiple deposit expansion would go on forever."

3.5 [**Related to the** Chapter Opener **on page 415**] According to an article in the *Wall Street Journal*: "The identity of who buys gold has changed radically. . . . Just five years ago, jewelry accounted for two-thirds of gold demand. Last year, it represented less than half." If the demand for gold to be used in jewelry has declined, who is buying gold? Does the change in who the most important demanders of gold are matter for long-term movements in the price of gold? Briefly explain.

Source: Liam Denning, "Central Bankers Rub Gold Bugs the Right Way," *Wall Street Journal*, February 17, 2012.

3.6 What will be the value of the money multiplier if banks hold no excess reserves, the currency-to-deposit ratio is 1, and the required reserve ratio for checkable deposits is 100%?

3.7 [**Related to** Solved Problem 14.3 **on page 432**] Consider the following data:

Currency	$ 100 billion
Bank reserves	200 billion
Checkable deposits	800 billion
Time deposits	1,200 billion
Excess reserves	40 billion

Calculate the values for the currency-to-deposit ratio, the ratio of total reserves to deposits, the monetary base, the money multiplier, and the M1 money supply.

3.8 [**Related to** Solved Problem 14.3 **on page 432**] Consider the following data:

Currency	$850 billion
Checkable deposits	700 billion
Bank reserves	700 billion

a. Calculate the values for the currency-to-deposit ratio, the ratio of total reserves to deposits, the monetary base, the money multiplier, and the M1 money supply.

b. Suppose that the ratio of total reserves to deposits changes from the value you calculated in part (a) to 2.0. (Assume that the currency-to-deposit ratio remains the same.) Now what is the value of the money multiplier?

3.9 Consider the following data (all values are in billions of dollars):

	June 1930	June 1931	June 1932
Currency	$3.681	$3.995	$4.959
Checkable deposits	21.612	19.888	15.490
Bank reserves	3.227	3.307	2.829

Calculate the values for each period for the currency-to-deposit ratio, the ratio of total reserves to deposits, the monetary base, the money multiplier, and the M1 money supply. Can you explain why the currency-to-deposit ratio and the ratio of total reserves to deposits moved as they did between 1930 and 1932?

3.10 [**Related to the** Making the Connection **on page 436**] Allan Meltzer of Carnegie Mellon University wrote the following about how the Federal Reserve Board's staff analyzed the likely effects of the large excess reserves banks were holding in the mid-1930s:

> [The] Board's staff . . . [assumed] that none of the excess reserves were held for reasons of safety based on experience. The result was a large overestimate of potential monetary and credit expansion and prospective inflation and an underestimate of the effect of higher reserve requirement ratios.

a. Why might banks in the mid-1930s have been holding reserves for "reasons of safety"?

b. What does Meltzer mean by "potential monetary and credit expansion"?

c. If banks were holding excess reserves for reasons of safety, why might the Fed's staff have been overestimating potential monetary and credit expansion?

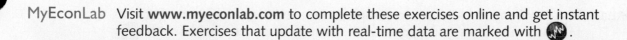

d. What was the effect on banks of the Fed's decision to increase the required reserve ratio? What insight does Meltzer give into why the Fed's staff underestimated the effect of the increase?

Source: Allan H. Meltzer, *A History of the Federal Reserve, Volume I: 1913–1951*, Chicago: University of Chicago 2003, p. 496.

3.11 [**Related to the** Making the Connection **on page 438**] An article in the *New York Times* noted that many people are increasing the types of investments in their retirement accounts

beyond just stocks and bonds to include gold: "This is nothing but speculation. And as is the case with most speculation, the average investor is not likely to make money."

a. Why might investing in gold be considered "nothing but speculation"?

b. What does it mean to say that the average investor "is not likely to make money" investing in gold? Do you agree? Briefly explain.

Source: Steven M. Davidoff, "The Risks of Tapping Your Retirement Fund for an Alternative Use," *New York Times*, October 30, 2012.

Data Exercises

D14.1: [**Calculating the money multiplier**] Go to the Web site of the Federal Reserve Bank of St. Louis (FRED) (research.stlouisfed.org/fred2/) and find the most recent values for the for the M1 Money Stock (M1SL) and the St. Louis Adjusted Monetary Base (AMBSL).

a. Using these data, calculate the value of the money multiplier.

b. Assuming the multiplier is equal to the value computed in part (a), if the monetary base increases by $400 million, by how much will the money supply increase?

D14.2: [**Calculating the money multiplier**] Go to the Web site of the Federal Reserve Bank of St. Louis (FRED) (research.stlouisfed.org/fred2/) and find the most recent values for the Currency Component of M1 (CURRNS), Total Checkable Deposits (TCDSL), and Excess Reserves of Depository Institutions (EXCRESNS).

a. Using these data, calculate the value of the currency-to-deposit ratio.

b. Using these data, calculate the value of the excess reserve-to-deposit ratio.

c. Using these data and assuming a required reserve ratio of 11%, calculate the value of the money multiplier.

D14.3: [**Analyzing changes in the money supply**] Go to the Web site of the Federal Reserve Bank of St. Louis (FRED) (research.stlouisfed.org/fred2/) and find the most recent value and the value from the same month one year earlier for Excess Reserves of Depository Institutions (EXCRESNS).

a. Using these data, calculate the percentage change in excess reserve balances between the two periods.

b. Based on your answer to part (a), briefly explain whether, holding all other factors that affect the money supply constant, the money supply should have increased, decreased, or remained the same during this period.

D14.4: [**The monetary base and recessions**] Go to the Web site of the Federal Reserve Bank of St. Louis (FRED) (research.stlouisfed.org/fred2/) and download the data series for the Board of Governors Monetary Base, Adjusted for Changes in Reserve Requirements (BOGAMBSL) from July 1959 until the most recent month available. In addition to the levels of the monetary base also find the compound annual rates of changes (choose "Edit Graph" and then under "Units" choose Compound

Annual Rate of Change). Graph both the levels and the rates of change of the monetary base. Go to the Web site of the National Bureau of Economic Research (nber.org) and find the dates for business cycle peaks and troughs. (The period between a business cycle peak and trough is a recession.)

a. What was the trend in the levels of the monetary base from 1959 through the most recent month available?

b. Describe how the levels of the monetary base change just before, during, and just after a recession. Is the pattern the same across recessions?

c. On the rate of change graph, which periods saw the most volatility in the monetary base?

Appendix

The Money Supply Process for M2

14.A

Learning Objective
Describe the money supply process for M2.

In the aftermath of financial innovation during the 1980s and 1990s, many analysts and policymakers became concerned that M1 no longer adequately represented assets functioning as a medium of exchange. As a result, they focused more attention on M2. As we saw in Chapter 2, M2 is a broader monetary aggregate than M1, including not only currency, C, and checkable deposits, D, but also nontransaction accounts. We can divide these nontransaction accounts into two components: N, which consists of savings accounts (including money market deposit accounts) and small time deposits, and MM, which consists of retail money market mutual funds. So we can represent M2 as:

$$M2 = C + D + N + MM.$$

The M2 measure of the money supply is less sensitive than M1 to shifts by households and firms—the nonbank public—from holding funds in one type of account to holding them in another type of account. Suppose that, for instance, the nonbank public wants to switch funds from checkable deposits to savings accounts. In that case, D would fall, but N would rise by the same amount, leaving M2 unchanged. However, M1, the sum of currency and checkable deposits, would fall.

We can express M2 as the product of an *M2 multiplier* and the monetary base:

$$M2 = (M2 \text{ multiplier}) \times \text{Monetary base.}$$

We can derive an expression for the M2 multiplier similar to the expression we derived for the M1 multiplier. The result is:

$$M2 \text{ multiplier} = \frac{1 + (C/D) + (N/D) + (MM/D)}{(C/D) + rr_D + (ER/D)}.$$

The M2 multiplier is significantly larger than the M1 multiplier because the terms (N/D) and (MM/D) are added to the numerator. With no reserve requirements for the accounts in N and MM, M2 money expansion from a change in the monetary base is greater than that for M1. The M2 multiplier has been more stable than the M1 multiplier since 1980.

Components of the M2 multiplier affect the size of the multiplier in a manner similar to that for M1. Increases in the required reserve ratio and the currency-to-deposit ratio reduce the extent of deposit expansion, thereby reducing the multiplier. However, an increase in the nonbank public's preference for nontransaction or money market–type accounts relative to checkable deposits increases the multiplier.

In recent years, many economists and policymakers have deemphasized the importance of changes in the money supply in forecasting future changes in other economic variables, such as real GDP. Nevertheless, some "Fed watchers" continue to study movements in the money supply. These Fed watchers predict the growth of M2 in much the same way as they do for M1. They forecast changes in the monetary base—particularly in the nonborrowed base—and changes in the components of the M2 multiplier.

CHAPTER 15

Monetary Policy

Learning Objectives

After studying this chapter, you should be able to:

15.1 Describe the goals of monetary policy (pages 448–451)

15.2 Understand how the Fed uses monetary policy tools to influence the federal funds rate (pages 451–459)

15.3 Trace how the importance of different monetary policy tools has changed over time (pages 459–467)

15.4 Explain the role of monetary targeting in monetary policy (pages 468–480)

Bernanke's Dilemma

In the fall of 2012, Federal Reserve Chairman Ben Bernanke was in a difficult position. During the financial crisis of 2007–2009, the Fed took extraordinary policy actions to keep the financial system from imploding. The crisis had deepened in the fall of 2008, following the bankruptcy of the Lehman Brothers investment bank. At that time, the Fed made huge asset purchases that greatly increased the size of its balance sheet, bank reserves, and the monetary base. The Fed's hope was that in two years, the economy would be in the middle of a strong recovery, and the Fed could begin what Bernanke called its "exit strategy." Although the Fed never described it in detail, the exit strategy was the process by which the Fed would shrink its balance sheet and return bank reserves and the monetary base to normal levels.

Unfortunately, as Bernanke testified before Congress in July 2012, more than three years after the end of the 2007–2009 recession, the economy was recovering much more slowly than the Fed had hoped. In the second quarter of 2012, real GDP had increased by only 1.3% at an annual rate. Although the economy grew at the faster rate of 2.0% in the third quarter, these growth rates were too slow to expand employment sufficiently to bring down the unemployment rate, which remained at nearly 8%. Would the economy grow more rapidly in the second half of the year? In a speech to a Fed conference in August 2012, Bernanke argued that unemployment was a "grave concern not only because of the enormous suffering and waste of human talent it entails, but also because persistently high levels

Continued on next page

Key Issue and Question

Issue: During the financial crisis, the Federal Reserve employed a series of new policy tools in an attempt to stabilize the financial system.

Question: Should price stability still be the most important policy goal of central banks?

Answered on page 480

of unemployment will wreak structural damage on our economy that could last for years." It was no surprise, then, that in September, the Fed announced a third round of *quantitative easing*, under which it would buy $40 billion in mortgage-backed securities each month and continue selling short-term Treasury securities and reinvesting the funds in long-term Treasury securities.

The focus on Bernanke and his colleagues at the Fed was not unusual. Although in early 2009, Congress and President Barack Obama had enacted a fiscal policy action that involved substantial increases in government spending and reductions in taxes, most macroeconomic policy consists of monetary policy

initiatives from the Fed. Fiscal policy involves changes in government spending and in taxes that require action by the president and the 535 members of Congress—a process that can be laborious and time-consuming. But monetary policy is concentrated in the hands of the Fed's Board of Governors and Federal Open Market Committee (FOMC). In practice, power over monetary policy is even more concentrated because both the Board of Governors and FOMC typically defer to the chairman's policy proposals. So, it was not surprising that economists, policymakers, and the general public all looked to Bernanke as the economy struggled through a slow recovery in 2012.

Source: Ben S. Bernanke, "Monetary Policy Since the Onset of the Crisis," Delivered at the Federal Reserve Bank of Kansas City Economic Symposium, Jackson Hole, Wyoming, August 31, 2012.

Although we can easily identify the goals of monetary policy, as Ben Bernanke acknowledged during 2012, it is not always so easy for the Fed to achieve those goals. The Fed has a limited number of monetary policy tools to use in attaining its goals. It uses these policy tools primarily to change the money supply and short-term interest rates. During and after the financial crisis, though, the Fed had to move beyond a focus on the money supply and short-term interest rates, as it attempted to reach its goals. In this chapter, we describe how the Fed conducts monetary policy and identify the difficulties that it encounters in designing effective monetary policies.

15.1

Learning Objective

Describe the goals of monetary policy.

The Goals of Monetary Policy

Most economists and policymakers agree that the overall aim of monetary policy is to advance the economic well-being of the population. Although there are many ways to assess economic well-being, it is typically determined by the quantity and quality of goods and services that individuals can enjoy. Economic well-being arises from efficient employment of labor and capital and steady growth in output. In addition, stable economic conditions—minimal fluctuations in production and employment, steady interest rates, and smoothly functioning financial markets—are qualities that enhance economic well-being. The Fed has set six *monetary policy goals* that are intended to promote a well-functioning economy:

1. Price stability
2. High employment
3. Economic growth
4. Stability of financial markets and institutions
5. Interest rate stability
6. Foreign-exchange market stability

The Fed and other central banks use monetary policy to achieve these goals.

Price Stability

Inflation, or persistently rising prices, erodes the value of money as a medium of exchange and as a unit of account. Especially since inflation rose dramatically and unexpectedly during the 1970s, policymakers in most high-income countries have set price stability as a policy goal. In a market economy, in which prices communicate information about costs and about demand for goods and services to households and firms, inflation makes prices less useful as signals for resource allocation. When the overall price level changes, families have trouble deciding how much to save for their children's education or for retirement, and firms facing uncertain future prices hesitate to enter into long-term contracts with suppliers or customers. Fluctuations in inflation can also arbitrarily redistribute income, as when lenders suffer losses when inflation is higher than expected.

Severe inflation inflicts even greater economic costs. Rates of inflation in the hundreds or thousands of percent per year—known as *hyperinflation*—can severely damage an economy's productive capacity. In extreme cases, money loses value so quickly that it no longer functions as a store of value or medium of exchange. People need a wheelbarrow full of cash to buy groceries. During the hyperinflation of the 1920s in Germany, production plummeted and unemployment soared. The resulting economic instability paved the way for Hitler's fascist regime to come to power 10 years later. The range of problems caused by inflation—from uncertainty to economic devastation—makes price stability a key monetary policy goal.

High Employment

High employment, or a low rate of unemployment, is another key monetary policy goal. Unemployed workers and underused factories and machines lower an economy's output. Unemployment causes financial distress and decreases self-esteem for workers who lack jobs. Congress and the president share responsibility with the Fed for the goal of high employment. Congress enacted the Employment Act of 1946 and the Full Employment and Balanced Growth Act of 1978 (the Humphrey-Hawkins Act) to promote high employment and price stability.

Although the Fed is committed to high employment, it does not seek a zero percent rate of unemployment. Even under the best economic conditions, some workers move into or out of the job market or are between jobs. Workers sometimes leave one job to pursue another and might be unemployed in the meantime. Individuals also leave the labor force to obtain more education and training or to raise a family, and reentry may take time. This type of *frictional unemployment* enables workers to search for positions that maximize their well-being. *Structural unemployment* refers to unemployment that is caused by changes in the structure of the economy, such as shifts in manufacturing techniques, increased use of computers, and increases in the production of services instead of goods. The tools of monetary policy are aimed at affecting economic conditions throughout the economy, so they are ineffective in reducing the levels of frictional and structural unemployment. Instead, the Fed attempts to reduce levels of *cyclical unemployment*, which is unemployment associated with business cycle recessions. Sometimes economists have difficulty distinguishing structural unemployment from cyclical unemployment. For example, in 2012, some economists argued that while the high level of unemployment had a large cyclical component, structural unemployment might also have risen as the decline in the residential construction industry was expected to persist for a number of years. How much an increase in structural unemployment was contributing to the high unemployment rate was unclear, however.

When all workers who want jobs have them (apart from the frictionally and structurally unemployed) and the demand and supply of labor are in equilibrium, economists say that unemployment is at its *natural rate* (sometimes called the *full-employment rate of unemployment*). Economists disagree on the exact value of the natural rate of unemployment, and there is good reason to believe that it varies over time in response to changes in the age and gender composition of the labor force and changes in government policies with respect to taxes, minimum wages, and unemployment insurance compensation. Currently, most economists estimate that the natural rate of unemployment is between 5% and 6%, which is well below the 7.7% unemployment rate the U.S. was experiencing in November 2012.

Economic Growth

Economic growth

Increases in the economy's output of goods and services over time; a goal of monetary policy.

Policymakers seek steady **economic growth**, or increases in the economy's output of goods and services over time. Economic growth provides the only source of sustained real increases in household incomes. Economic growth depends on high employment. With high employment, businesses are likely to grow by investing in new plant and equipment that raise profits, productivity, and workers' incomes. With high unemployment, businesses have unused productive capacity and are much less likely to invest in capital improvements. Policymakers attempt to encourage *stable* economic growth because a stable business environment allows firms and households to plan accurately and encourages the long-term investment that is needed to sustain growth.

Stability of Financial Markets and Institutions

When financial markets and institutions are not efficient in matching savers and borrowers, the economy loses resources. Firms with the potential to produce high-quality goods and services cannot obtain the financing they need to design, develop, and market these goods and services. Savers waste resources looking for satisfactory investments. The stability of financial markets and institutions makes possible the efficient matching of savers and borrowers.

Congress and the president created the Fed in response to the financial panics of the late 1800s and early 1900s. However, the Fed failed to stop the bank panics of the early 1930s that increased the severity of the Great Depression (see Chapter 12). During the post–World War II period, the Fed experienced greater success in averting potential panics in the commercial paper, stock, and commodity markets. The Fed's attention to financial stability was shown by its interventions following the stock market crash of 1987 and the terrorist attacks of September 11, 2001.

Although the Fed also responded vigorously to the financial crisis that began in 2007, it initially underestimated its severity and was unable to head off the deep recession of 2007–2009. The financial crisis led to renewed debate over whether the Fed should take action to forestall asset price bubbles such as those associated with the dot-com boom on the U.S. stock market in the late 1990s and the U.S. housing market in the mid 2000s. Fed policymakers and many economists have generally argued that asset bubbles are difficult to identify ahead of time and actions to deflate them may be counterproductive. But the severity of the 2007–2009 recession led some economists and policymakers to reassess this position. Financial stability has clearly become a more important Fed policy goal.

Interest Rate Stability

Like fluctuations in price levels, fluctuations in interest rates make planning and investment decisions difficult for households and firms. Increases and decreases in interest rates make it hard for firms to plan investments in plant and equipment and make households more hesitant about long-term investments in houses. Because people often blame the Fed for increases in interest rates, the Fed's goal of interest rate stability is motivated by political pressure as well as by a desire for a stable saving and investment environment. In addition, as we have seen, sharp interest rate fluctuations cause problems for banks and other financial firms. So, stabilizing interest rates can help to stabilize the financial system.

Foreign-Exchange Market Stability

In the global economy, foreign-exchange market stability, or limited fluctuations in the foreign-exchange value of the dollar, is an important monetary policy goal. A stable dollar simplifies planning for commercial and financial transactions. In addition, fluctuations in the dollar's value change the international competitiveness of U.S. industry: A rising dollar makes U.S. goods more expensive abroad and reduces exports, and a falling dollar makes foreign goods more expensive in the United States. In practice, the U.S. Treasury often originates changes in foreign-exchange policy, although the Fed implements these policy changes.

The Fed's Dual Mandate

How can the Fed pursue all these policy goals at once? As it turns out, these goals are really just two goals: price stability and maximum employment. If the Fed can attain these two goals, it will typically attain its other goals as well. Therefore, many economists and commentators refer to the Fed's *dual mandate* as price stability and high employment. An open question is whether the Fed's dual mandate is necessarily consistent with financial market stability, as we will discuss later in this chapter.

How can the Fed achieve these monetary policy goals? In the next section, we consider the monetary policy tools the Fed has available to reach its goals.

Monetary Policy Tools and the Federal Funds Rate

Until the financial crisis of 2007–2009, the Fed primarily relied on three monetary policy tools. During the financial crisis, the Fed announced several new policy tools. At the end of 2012, two of these new policy tools were still active. We first consider the Fed's three traditional policy tools:

1. **Open market operations** are the Fed's purchases and sales of securities in financial markets. Traditionally, the Fed concentrated on purchases and sales of Treasury bills, with the aim of influencing the level of bank reserves and short-term interest rates. During the financial crisis, the Fed began purchasing a wider variety of securities to affect long-term interest rates and to support the flow of credit in the financial system.

15.2

Learning Objective
Understand how the Fed uses monetary policy tools to influence the federal funds rate.

Open market operations
The Federal Reserve's purchases and sales of securities, usually U.S. Treasury securities, in financial markets.

Discount policy The policy tool of setting the discount rate and the terms of discount lending.

Discount window The means by which the Fed makes discount loans to banks, serving as the channel for meeting the liquidity needs of banks.

Reserve requirement The regulation requiring banks to hold a fraction of checkable deposits as vault cash or deposits with the Fed.

2. **Discount policy** includes setting the discount rate and the terms of discount lending. When Congress passed the Federal Reserve Act in 1913, it expected that discount policy would be the Fed's primary monetary policy tool. The **discount window** is the means by which the Fed makes discount loans to banks, and serves as the channel to meet banks' short-term liquidity needs.

3. **Reserve requirements** are the Fed's regulation requiring that banks hold a certain fraction of their checkable deposits as vault cash or deposits with the Fed.[1] We have seen that the required reserve ratio is a determinant of the money multiplier in the money supply process (see Chapter 14).

During the financial crisis, the Fed introduced two new policy tools connected with bank reserve accounts that were still active at the end of 2012.

1. *Interest on reserve balances.* In October 2008, the Fed introduced a new tool when it began for the first time to pay interest on banks' required reserve and excess reserve deposits.[2] Reserve requirements impose an implicit tax on banks because banks could otherwise receive interest on the funds by lending them out or by investing them. The Fed reduces the size of this tax by paying interest on reserve balances. The Fed also gains a greater ability to influence banks' reserve balances. By raising the interest rate it pays, the Fed can increase banks' holdings of reserves, potentially restraining banks' ability to extend loans and increase the money supply. By reducing the interest rate, the Fed can have the opposite effect.

2. *Term deposit facility.* In April 2010, the Fed announced that it would offer banks the opportunity to purchase term deposits, which are similar to the certificates of deposit that banks offer to households and firms. The Fed offers term deposits to banks in periodic auctions. The interest rates are determined by the auctions and have been slightly above the interest rate the Fed offers on reserve balances. For example, in November 2012, the interest rate on the Fed's auction of $3 billion in 28-day term deposits was 0.26%, which was higher than the interest rate of 0.25% the Fed was paying on reserve deposits. The term deposit facility gives the Fed another tool in managing bank reserve holdings, which were at the very high level of more than $1.5 trillion in late 2012. The more funds banks place in term deposits, the less they will have available to expand loans and the money supply.

The Federal Funds Market and the Fed's Target Federal Funds Rate

In the decades preceding the financial crisis of 2007–2009, the focus of Fed policy was setting a target for the **federal funds rate**, which is the interest rate that banks charge each other on very short-term loans. The target for the federal funds rate is set at meetings of the Federal Open Market Committee (FOMC), which take place eight times per year in Washington, DC. Although the Fed sets a target for the federal funds rate, the

Federal funds rate The interest rate that banks charge each other on very short-term loans; determined by the demand and supply for reserves in the federal funds market.

---

[1] Required reserves vary with the level of checkable deposits. As of December 2012, banks do not have to hold reserves on their first $12.4 million of checkable deposits. They must hold reserves of 3% on the next $67.1 million in checkable deposits and reserves of 10% on checkable deposits above $79.5 million.

[2] Technically, the Fed can set separate interest rates on required reserve balances and on excess reserve balances. In December 2012, the interest rate on both types of balances was the same: 0.25%.

actual rate is determined by the interaction of demand and supply for bank reserves in the *federal funds market.*

To analyze the determinants of the federal funds rate, we need to examine the banking system's demand for and the Fed's supply of reserves. We use a graph of the demand for and supply of reserves to see how the Fed uses its policy tools to influence the federal funds rate and the money supply.

Demand for Reserves Banks demand reserves both to meet their legal obligation to hold required reserves and because they may wish to hold excess reserves to meet their short-term liquidity needs. The demand curve for reserves, D, shown in Figure 15.1, includes banks' demand for both required reserves, RR, and excess reserves, ER. The demand curve is drawn assuming that factors other than the federal funds rate—such as other market interest rates or the required reserve ratio—that would affect banks' demand for reserves are held constant. As with other types of loans, we would expect that the higher the interest rate, the lower the quantity of loans demanded. As the federal funds rate, i_{ff}, increases, the opportunity cost to banks of holding excess reserves increases because the return they could earn from lending out those reserves goes up. So, as the federal funds rate increases, the quantity of reserves demanded will decline. The result is that banks' demand curve for reserves will be downward sloping.

Notice that in Figure 15.1, the demand curve for reserves becomes horizontal (or perfectly elastic) at the interest rate i_{rb}, which is the interest rate the Fed pays on banks' reserve balances. The interest rate that the Fed pays on reserves sets a floor for the federal funds rate. To see why, suppose that the Fed is paying banks 0.25% on their reserve balances, but the federal funds rate is only 0.10%. Banks could borrow funds in the federal funds market at 0.10%, deposit the money in their reserve balances at the Fed, and earn a risk-free 0.15%. Competition among banks to obtain the funds to carry out this

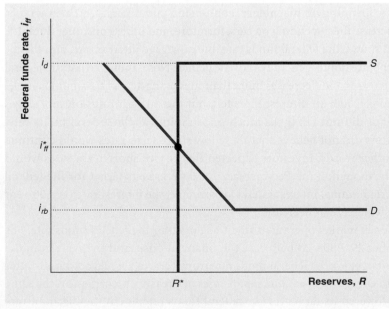

Figure 15.1

Equilibrium in the Federal Funds Market

Equilibrium in the federal funds market occurs at the intersection of the demand curve for reserves, D, and the supply curve for reserves, S. The Fed determines the level of reserves, R, the discount rate, i_d, and the interest rate on banks' reserve balances at the Fed, i_{rb}. Equilibrium reserves are R^*, and the equilibrium federal funds rate is i_{ff}^*.

risk-free arbitrage would force up the federal funds rate to 0.25%, which is the rate at which banks could no longer earn arbitrage profits.

Supply of Reserves Figure 15.1 also shows the supply curve for reserves, S. The Fed supplies borrowed reserves, in the form of discount loans, and nonborrowed reserves, through open market operations. The vertical portion of the supply curve reflects the assumption that the Fed can set reserves, R, at whatever level it needs to meet its objectives. So, the quantity of reserves does not depend on the federal funds rate, making this portion of the supply curve vertical. Note, though, that the supply curve becomes horizontal (or perfectly elastic) at i_d, which is the discount rate that the Fed sets. At a federal funds rate below the discount rate, borrowing from the Fed is zero because banks can borrow more cheaply from other banks. So, in this case, all bank reserves are nonborrowed reserves. The discount rate is a ceiling on the federal funds rate because banks would not pay a higher interest rate to borrow from other banks than the discount rate they can pay to borrow from the Fed. (For simplicity, we are assuming that banks face no restrictions on using the discount window.)

Equilibrium in the Federal Funds Market The equilibrium federal funds rate and level of reserves occur at the intersection of the demand and supply curves in Figure 15.1. Equilibrium reserves equal R^*, and the equilibrium federal funds rate equals i_{ff}^*.

Open Market Operations and the Fed's Target for the Federal Funds Rate

The centerpiece of Fed policymaking has been the meetings of the FOMC, at which the Fed announces a target for the federal funds rate. Although only banks and a few other financial institutions can borrow and lend at the federal funds rate, changes in this interest rate can have broad effects on the economy. For example, when the FOMC lowers the target for the federal funds rate, the lower cost of funds to banks typically leads to lower interest rates on bank loans to households and firms. Responding to the lower rates, firms increase their spending on machinery, equipment, and other investment goods, and households increase their spending on cars, furniture, and other consumer durables.

As Figure 15.2 shows, the federal funds rate, the mortgage interest rate, and the interest rates on corporate bonds generally move together. Note, though, that the federal funds rate often increases and decreases more than these long-term rates. For example, for several years after 2000, all interest rates fell, but the interest rates on mortgages and corporate bonds did not fall by as much or as rapidly as the federal funds rate. In this case, investors did not believe that these low short-term rates would continue for very long. In other words, investors expected that future short-term rates would increase. Generally, though, if the Fed increases or decreases its target for the federal funds rate, long-term nominal interest rates—for example, the interest rate on a 30-year mortgage—will also increase or decrease.

The Fed uses open market operations to hit its target for the federal funds rate. For example, on October 29, 2008, to help ease the financial crisis and the recession, the FOMC lowered its target for the federal funds rate from 1.5% to 1%. To accomplish this goal, the Fed had to engage in *open market purchases* of Treasury securities. At the same time that the Fed lowered its target for the federal funds rate, it cut the discount rate

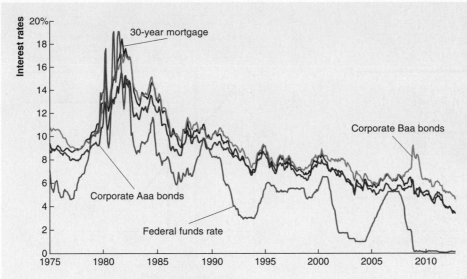

Figure 15.2

**The Federal Funds Rate
and the Interest Rates
on Corporate Bonds and
Mortgages**

The Fed controls the federal funds
rate. The long-term interest rates that
households pay to purchase a house
or that corporations pay to finance
investment generally rise and fall
with the federal funds rate.

Source: Board of Governors of the
Federal Reserve System.

from 1.75% to 1.25%. Panel (a) of Figure 15.3 illustrates the results of the Fed's actions.
If nothing else changes in the federal funds market, an open market purchase shifts the
reserve supply curve to the right, from S_1 to S_2, increasing bank reserves and decreasing
the federal funds rate. Because the discount rate was lowered, the horizontal portion of
the reserve supply curve also shifts down. The equilibrium level of bank reserves increases
from R_1^* to R_2^*, and the equilibrium federal funds rate declines from 1.5% to 1%.

To increase its target for the federal funds rate, the Fed engages in *open market sales*
of Treasury securities. For example, on June 29, 2006, the FOMC increased its target for
the federal funds rate from 5% to 5.25%. At the same time, the Fed raised the discount
rate from 6% to 6.25%. The Fed wanted to push up interest rates to slow the economy
in the face of the housing bubble and a rising inflation rate. Panel (b) of Figure 15.3
illustrates the result of an open market sale. The supply curve for reserves shifts to the
left, from S_1 to S_2, decreasing the equilibrium level of bank reserves from R_1^* to R_2^*, and
increasing the equilibrium federal funds rate from 5% to 5.25%. Because the discount
rate was increased, the horizontal portion of the reserve supply curve also shifts up.
(Note that because these events took place before the Fed began paying interest on
bank reserve deposits, we have omitted the horizontal segment of the demand curve for
reserves.)

In summary, an open market purchase of securities by the Fed decreases the federal
funds rate. An open market sale of securities increases the federal funds rate.

The Effect of Changes in the Discount Rate and in Reserve Requirements

The Fed adjusts the target for the federal funds rate almost exclusively through open
market operations, but we can briefly consider the effect on the market for reserves of
changes in the discount rate and changes in the required reserve ratio.

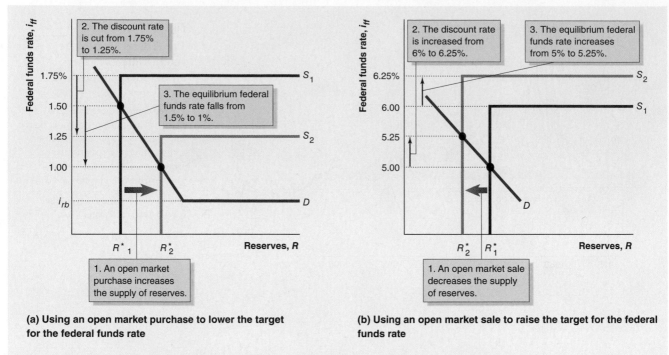

(a) Using an open market purchase to lower the target for the federal funds rate

(b) Using an open market sale to raise the target for the federal funds rate

Figure 15.3 Effects of Open Market Operations on the Federal Funds Market

In panel (a), an open market purchase of securities by the Fed increases reserves in the banking system, shifting the supply curve to the right from S_1 to S_2. The equilibrium level of reserves increases from R_1^* to R_2^*, while the equilibrium federal funds rate falls from 1.5% to 1%. The discount rate is also cut from 1.75% to 1.25%.

In panel (b), an open market sale of securities by the Fed reduces reserves, shifting the supply curve to the left from S_1 to S_2. The equilibrium level of reserves decreases from R_1^* to R_2^*, while the equilibrium federal funds rate rises from 5% to 5.25%. The discount rate is also increased from 6% to 6.25%.

Changes in the Discount Rate Since 2003, the Fed has kept the discount rate higher than the target for the federal funds rate. This makes the discount rate a *penalty rate*, which means that banks pay a penalty by borrowing from the Fed rather than from other banks in the federal funds market. Typically, the Fed has raised or lowered the discount rate at the same time that it raises or lowers the target for the federal funds rate.[3] As a result, changes in the discount rate have no independent effect on the federal funds rate. In the reserves market graph, the horizontal portion of the supply curve is always above the equilibrium federal funds rate.

Changes in the Required Reserve Ratio The Fed rarely changes the required reserve ratio. The last change took place in April 1992, when the required reserve ratio was reduced from 12% to 10%. It is possible, though, that the Fed might change the required reserve ratio in the future. Changing the required reserve ratio without also engaging in

---

[3]An exception to this rule came in February 2010, when the Fed increased the discount rate from 0.50% to 0.75% while leaving the target for the federal funds rate unchanged.

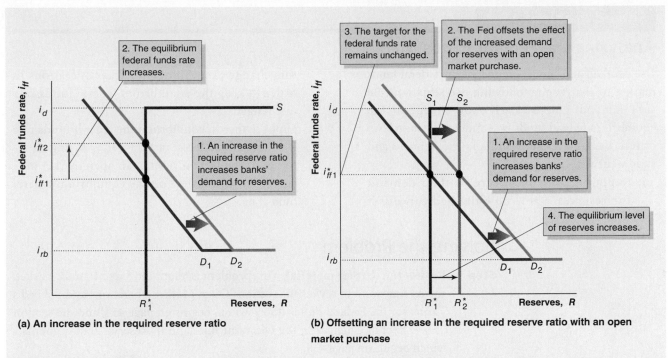

Figure 15.4 The Effect of a Change in the Required Reserve Ratio on the Federal Funds Market

In panel (a), the Fed increases the required reserve ratio, which shifts the demand curve for reserves from D_1 to D_2. The equilibrium federal funds rate rises from i_{ff1}^* to i_{ff2}^*. In panel (b), the Fed increases the required reserve ratio, which shifts the demand curve from D_1 to D_2. The Fed offsets the effects of the increase in the required reserve ratio with an open market purchase, shifting the supply curve from S_1 to S_2. The level of reserves increases from R_1^* to R_2^*, while the target federal funds rate remains unchanged, at i_{ff1}^*.

open market operations would cause a change in the equilibrium federal funds rate. We illustrate this result in panel (a) of Figure 15.4. If the other factors underlying the demand and supply curves for reserves are held constant, an increase in the required reserve ratio shifts the demand curve to the right, from D_1 to D_2, because banks have to hold more reserves. As a result, the equilibrium federal funds rate increases from i_{ff1}^* to i_{ff2}^* while the equilibrium level of reserves remains unchanged at R_1^*.

It is unlikely that the Fed would begin using changes in the required reserve ratio as a means of changing its target for the federal funds rate. It is more likely that if the Fed changes the required reserve ratio, it will carry out offsetting open market operations to keep the target for the federal funds rate unchanged. Panel (b) shows the situation where the Fed combines an increase in the required reserve ratio with an open market purchase so as to keep unchanged its target for the federal funds rate. As in panel (a), the increase in the required reserve ratio shifts the demand curve to the right, from D_1 to D_2, but in this case the open market purchase shifts the supply curve to the right, from S_1 to S_2, keeping the target for the federal funds rate unchanged, at i_{ff1}^*. The equilibrium level of reserves increases from R_1^* to R_2^*.

Solved Problem 15.2

Analyzing the Federal Funds Market

Use demand and supply graphs for the federal funds market to analyze the following two situations. Be sure that your graphs clearly show changes in the equilibrium federal funds rate and equilibrium level of reserves, and also any shifts in the demand and supply curves.

a. Suppose that banks decrease their demand for reserves. Show how the Fed can offset this change through open market operations in order to keep the equilibrium federal funds rate unchanged.

b. Suppose that in equilibrium the federal funds rate is equal to the interest rate the Fed is paying on reserves. If the Fed carries out an open market purchase, show the effect on the equilibrium federal funds rate.

Solving the Problem

Step 1 Review the chapter material. This problem is about the federal funds market, so you may want to review the section "Open Market Operations and the Fed's Target for the Federal Funds Rate," which begins on page 454, and the section "The Effect of Changes in the Discount Rate and in Reserve Requirements," which begins on page 455.

Step 2 Answer part (a) by drawing the appropriate graph. If banks decrease their demand for reserves, the demand curve will shift to the left. Unless the Fed offsets the effect of the shift, the equilibrium federal funds rate will decrease. To offset the decline in the demand for reserves, the Fed needs to carry out an open market sale, shifting the supply curve for reserves to the left. Your graph should show that after these two shifts the equilibrium federal funds rate is unchanged.

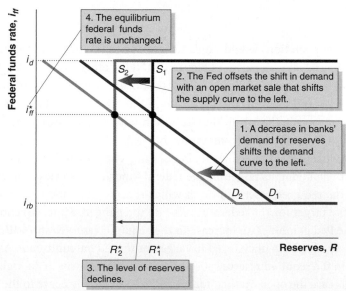

Step 3 Answer part (b) by drawing the appropriate graph. If the equilibrium federal funds rate is equal to the interest rate the Fed is paying banks on their reserve balances, the supply curve must be intersecting the demand curve on

the horizontal segment of the demand curve. An open market purchase will shift the supply curve to the right, which increases the equilibrium level of reserves, but because the supply curve is already in the horizontal segment of the demand curve, the equilibrium federal funds rate will not change.

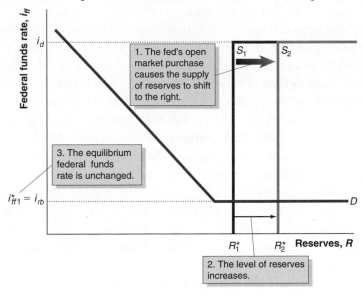

See related problems 2.7 and 2.8 at the end of the chapter.

More on the Fed's Monetary Policy Tools

Now that we have looked at how the Fed's monetary policy tools affect the federal funds rate, we can look more closely at each of the tools.

Open Market Operations

The original Federal Reserve Act didn't specifically mention open market operations because, at that time, neither policymakers nor financial market participants understood them well. The Fed began to use open market purchases as a policy tool during the 1920s, when it acquired World War I Liberty Bonds from banks, enabling banks to finance more business loans. Before 1935, district Federal Reserve Banks conducted limited open market operations in securities markets, but these transactions lacked central coordination and were not always used to achieve a monetary policy goal. The lack of coordinated intervention by the Fed during the banking crisis of the early 1930s led Congress in 1935 to establish the FOMC to guide open market operations.

When the Fed carries out an open market purchase of Treasury securities, the prices of these securities increase, thereby decreasing their yield. Because the purchase will increase the monetary base, the money supply will expand. An open market sale decreases the price of Treasury securities, thereby increasing their yield. The sale decreases the monetary base and the money supply. Because open market purchases reduce interest rates, they are considered an *expansionary policy*. Open market sales increase interest rates and are considered a *contractionary policy*.

15.3

Learning Objective

Trace how the importance of different monetary policy tools has changed over time.

Implementing Open Market Operations How does the Fed carry out open market operations? At the end of each meeting, the FOMC issues a statement that includes its target for the federal funds rate and its assessment of the economy, particularly with respect to its policy goals of price stability and economic growth. In addition, the FOMC issues a *policy directive* to the Federal Reserve System's account manager, who is a vice president of the Federal Reserve Bank of New York and who has the responsibility of implementing open market operations and hitting the FOMC's target for the federal funds rate. Open market operations are conducted each morning on the Open Market Trading Desk at the Federal Reserve Bank of New York. The trading desk is linked electronically through a system called the Trading Room Automated Processing System (TRAPS) to about 20 *primary dealers*, who are private securities firms that the Fed has selected to participate in open market operations. Each morning, the trading desk notifies the primary dealers of the size of the open market purchase or sale being conducted and asks them to submit offers to buy or sell Treasury securities. The dealers have just a few minutes to respond. Once the dealers' offers have been received, the Fed's account manager goes over the list, accepts the best offers, and then has the trading desk buy or sell the securities until the volume of reserves reaches the Fed's desired goal. These securities are either added to or subtracted from the portfolios of the various Federal Reserve banks according to their shares of total assets in the system.

How does the account manager know what to do? The manager interprets the FOMC's most recent policy directive, holds daily conferences with two members of the FOMC, and personally analyzes financial market conditions. Then the manager compares the level of reserves in the banking system with the level the trading desk staff estimates will be necessary to hit (or maintain) the target federal funds rate. If the level of reserves needs to be increased over the current level, the account manager orders the trading desk to purchase securities. If the level of reserves needs to be decreased, the account manager orders the trading desk to sell securities.

In conducting the Fed's open market operations, the trading desk makes both dynamic, or permanent, open market operations and defensive, or temporary, open market operations. *Dynamic open market operations* are intended to change monetary policy as directed by the FOMC. *Defensive open market operations* are intended to offset temporary fluctuations in the demand or supply for reserves, not to carry out changes in monetary policy. For example, when the U.S. Treasury purchases goods and services for the federal government, it does so by using funds in its account at the Fed. As the sellers of those goods and services deposit the funds in their banks, the supply of reserves in the banking system will increase. Similarly, if following a snowstorm transportation is delayed and there is a delay in check clearing, *Federal Reserve float* will increase. An increase in float temporarily increases the reserves of the banking system as banks that have had checks deposited see their reserves increase, while there is a delay in reducing the reserves of banks against which checks have been written. Dynamic open market operations are likely to be conducted as outright purchases and sales of Treasury securities—that is, by buying from or selling to primary dealers. Defensive open market operations are much more common than dynamic operations. Defensive open market purchases are conducted through repurchase agreements. With these agreements, the Fed buys securities from a primary dealer, and the dealer agrees to buy them back at a given price at a specified future date, usually within one week. In effect, the government securities serve as collateral for a short-term loan. For defensive open market sales, the trading desk often engages in *matched sale–purchase transactions* (sometimes called *reverse repos*), in which the Fed sells securities to primary dealers, and the dealers agree to sell them back to the Fed in the near future. Economic disturbances, such as natural disasters, also cause unexpected fluctuations in the demand for currency and bank reserves. The Fed's account manager must respond to these events and sell or buy securities to maintain the monetary policy indicated by the FOMC's guidelines.

Making the Connection

A Morning's Work at the Open Market Trading Desk

The following is an overview of activity at the Open Market Trading Desk at the Federal Reserve Bank of New York.

7:00 A.M. The account manager receives from the research staff an estimate of the supply of reserves for that day and for the remaining days of the current *maintenance period*. The maintenance period is the two-week period over which the Fed calculates banks' required reserve balances.

8:00 A.M.–9:00 A.M. The account manager begins informal discussions with market participants to assess conditions in the government securities market. From these discussions and from data supplied by the staff of the FOMC, the account manager estimates the demand for reserves and how the prices of government securities will change during the trading day. The account manager's staff compares forecasts on Treasury deposits and information on the timing of future Treasury sales of securities with the staff of the Office of Government Finance in the Treasury Department. These Treasury activities can affect the level of bank reserves and the monetary base.

9:10 A.M. After reviewing the information from the various staffs, the account manager studies the FOMC's directive. This directive identifies the level of the federal funds rate desired. The account manager must design *dynamic* open market operations to implement changes requested by the FOMC and *defensive* open market operations to offset temporary disturbances to reserves as predicted by the staff. The account manager places the daily conference call to at least two members of the FOMC to discuss trading strategy.

9:30 A.M. On approval of the trading strategy, the traders at the Federal Reserve Bank of New York notify the primary dealers in the government securities market of the Fed's desired transactions. If traders plan to make open market purchases, they request quotations for asked prices. If traders plan to make open market sales, they request quotations for bid prices. (Recall that the asked price is the price at which a dealer is willing to sell a security, and the bid price is the price at which a dealer is willing to buy a security.)

9:40 A.M. The primary dealers submit their propositions to the trading desk.

9:41 A.M. The trading desk selects the lowest prices offered when making purchases and accepts the highest prices when making sales and returns the results to dealers.

10:30 A.M. By this time, the transactions have been completed and the trading room at the Federal Reserve Bank of New York is less hectic. No long coffee breaks or three-martini lunches for the account manager and staff, though, because they are busy the rest of the day monitoring conditions in the federal funds market and the level of bank reserves to get ready for the next day of trading.

Source: Adapted from "A Morning at the Desk" from *Implementing Monetary Policy: The Federal Reserve in the 21st Century* by Christopher Burke, Federal Reserve Bank of New York, January 13, 2010.

See related problem 3.5 at the end of the chapter.

Open Market Operations Versus Other Policy Tools Open market operations have several benefits that other policy tools lack: control, flexibility, and speed of implementation. Because the Fed initiates open market purchases and sales, it completely controls their volume. Discount loans depend in part on the willingness of banks to request the loans and so are not as completely under the Fed's control.

Open market operations are flexible because the Fed can make both large and small open market operations. Often, dynamic operations require large purchases or sales, whereas defensive operations call for small purchases or sales. Other policy tools lack such flexibility. Reversing open market operations is simple for the Fed. For example, if the Fed decides that its open market sales have made reserves grow too slowly, it can quickly authorize open market purchases. Discount loans and reserve requirement changes are more difficult to reverse quickly. This is a key reason that the Fed has left reserve requirements unchanged since 1992.

The Fed can implement its open market operations rapidly, with no administrative delays. All that is required is for the trading desk to place buy or sell orders with the primary dealers. Changing the discount rate or reserve requirements requires lengthier deliberation.

Making the Connection

Why Can't the Fed Always Hit Its Federal Funds Target?

Although media reports routinely refer to the Fed as setting the federal funds rate, we know that, in fact, the Fed can only set a *target* for the federal funds rate. The actual federal funds rate is determined by the demand and supply for reserves in the federal funds market. Because the Fed cannot control the demand for reserves, it cannot ensure that the actual federal funds rate is equal to its target rate. It is the job of the trading desk at the New York Fed to use open market operations to try to keep the actual federal funds rate as close as possible to the target rate. The following graph shows weekly values for the target and actual federal fund rates from January 1998 through October 2012.

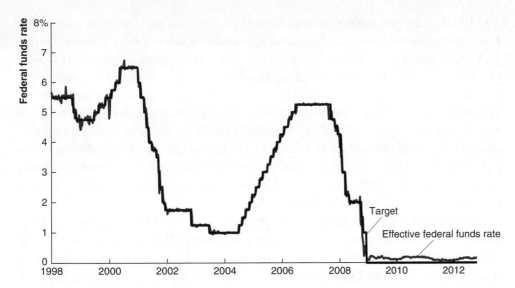

Overall, the trading desk has done a good job of keeping the actual rate close to the target rate. The figure shows the target rate as 0% beginning in December 2008. In fact, at that time, the FOMC announced that the target would be a range of 0% to 0.25%, and the actual federal funds rate remained in that range every week through October 2012. But in most of those weeks, the actual federal funds rate was *below* 0.25%, even though 0.25% was the interest rate that banks received from the Fed on their reserve deposits. Why would banks apparently be willing to lend in the federal funds market when they could receive a higher interest rate by leaving the money on deposit at the Fed? The answer is that some financial institutions that can borrow and lend in the federal funds market are not eligible to receive interest on deposits with the Fed. In particular, Fannie Mae and Freddie Mac, the government-sponsored enterprises that are major buyers of residential mortgages, supply sufficient funds in the reserves market to frequently drive the equilibrium federal funds market below the interest rate on reserve deposits.

By and large, though, the trading desk has the tools to keep the federal funds rate close to the target set by the FOMC.

Source: Federal Reserve Bank of St. Louis.

See related problem 3.10 at the end of the chapter.

"Quantitative Easing": Fed Bond Purchases During and After the Financial Crisis

In recent decades, Fed open market operations have concentrated on buying and selling short-term Treasury securities, with the intention of affecting the market for bank reserves and the equilibrium federal funds rate. But by December 2008, the Fed had driven the target for the federal funds rate nearly to zero, while the financial crisis and the economic recession had deepened. These continuing problems led the Fed to take the unusual step of buying more than $1.7 trillion in mortgage-backed securities and longer-term Treasury securities during 2009 and early 2010. This policy of a central bank attempting to stimulate the economy by buying long-term securities is called **quantitative easing**. The Fed's objective was to reduce the interest rates on mortgages and on 10-year Treasury notes.

Quantitative easing A central bank policy that attempts to stimulate the economy by buying long-term securities.

The interest rate on the 10-year Treasury note plays an important role in the financial system because it is a benchmark default-free interest rate. A lower interest rate on 10-year Treasury notes can help to lower interest rates on corporate bonds, thereby increasing investment spending. In addition, many adjustable rate mortgages have their interest rates determined by the interest rate on 10-year Treasury notes. When the interest rate on the 10-year Treasury note falls, the interest rates on these mortgages automatically fall. In November 2010, the Fed announced a second round of quantitative easing (dubbed QE2). With QE2, the Fed bought an additional $600 billion in long-term Treasury securities through June 2011. Because these bond purchases would greatly expand the monetary base, some economists and policymakers worried that they would eventually lead to higher inflation.

In September 2011, with economic recovery still proceeding more slowly than expected, the Fed announced that it would purchase $400 billion of long-term securities while also selling $400 billion of short-term securities. The financial press referred to this policy as *Operation Twist*. The policy's name reflects its goal of twisting the yield curve by increasing short-term interest rates and lowering long-term interest rates. Because Operation Twist attempted to directly reduce long-term interest rates through bond purchases, it was similar in its effects to quantitative easing. By selling $400 billion of short-term bonds at the same time that it bought $400 billion of long-term securities, the Fed did not increase the monetary base or the threat of future inflation.

In September 2012, the Fed announced a third round of quantitative easing (QE3), focused on purchases of mortgage-backed securities. The Fed pledged to continue QE3 until growth in real GDP and employment returned to more normal levels. Economists remain divided over whether the rounds of quantitative easing had significantly expanded the growth of employment and output in the U.S. economy.

Figure 15.5 shows how the Fed's policies during the financial crisis of 2007–2009 and the following years affected the *Fed's balance sheet*. The turmoil following the collapse of Lehman Brothers on September 15, 2008, led to a dramatic change in Fed policy. The Fed's assets exploded from $927 billion before the Lehman Brothers bankruptcy to $2.2 trillion on November 12, 2008. The increase came primarily from new loans to financial institutions and attempts to increase the liquidity of key markets such as commercial paper. Access to the commercial paper market is critical to the day-to-day operations of many large firms.

Discount Policy

Except for a brief period during 1966, before 1980, the Fed made discount loans only to banks that were members of the Federal Reserve System. Banks perceived the ability to borrow from the Fed through the discount window as an advantage of membership that partially offset the cost of the Fed's reserve requirements. Since 1980, all depository institutions have had access to the discount window. Each Federal Reserve Bank maintains its own discount window, although all Reserve Banks charge the same discount rate.

Categories of Discount Loans The Fed's discount loans to banks fall into three categories: (1) primary credit, (2) secondary credit, and (3) seasonal credit.

Primary credit is available to healthy banks that have adequate capital and supervisory ratings. Banks may use primary credit for any purpose and do not have to seek funds from other sources before requesting a discount window loan from the

Primary credit Discount loans available to healthy banks experiencing temporary liquidity problems.

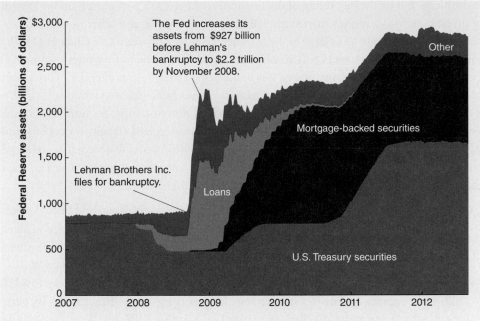

Figure 15.5

Federal Reserve Assets, 2007–2012

After the collapse of Lehman Brothers, the Fed dramatically increased the assets it owned from $927 billion to $2.2 trillion. Some of the increase came from loans to financial institutions and the rest came from purchases of assets such as commercial paper and mortgage-backed securities.

Source: Board of Governors of the Federal Reserve System.

primary credit facility, or *standing lending facility*. The loans are usually very short term—often overnight—but they can be for as long as several weeks. The primary credit interest rate is set above the federal funds rate and so is only a backup source of funds, because healthy banks will choose to borrow at a lower interest rate in the federal funds market or from other sources. The main purpose of primary credit is to make funds available to banks to deal with temporary liquidity problems. In that sense, primary credit represents the Fed's actions in its role as a lender of last resort. When economists and policymakers refer to the discount rate, they are referring to the interest rate on primary credit.

Secondary credit is intended for banks that are not eligible for primary credit because they have inadequate capital or low supervisory ratings. This type of credit is often used for banks that are suffering from severe liquidity problems, including those that may soon be closed. The Fed carefully monitors how banks are using the funds they obtain from these loans. The secondary credit interest rate is set above the primary credit rate, usually by 0.50 percentage point.

Seasonal credit consists of temporary, short-term loans to satisfy seasonal requirements of smaller banks in geographic areas where agriculture or tourism is important. For example, by using these loans, a bank in a ski resort area in Vermont won't have to maintain excess cash or sell loans and investments to meet the borrowing needs of local firms during the winter months. The seasonal credit interest rate is tied to the average of rates on certificates of deposit and the federal funds rate. Because of improvements in credit markets that allow even small banks access to market loans, many economists question whether a seasonal credit facility is still needed.

Discount Lending During the Financial Crisis of 2007–2009 From its founding in 1913 until 1980, with a few brief exceptions, the Fed made loans only to members of the Federal Reserve System. In 1980, Congress authorized the Fed to make loans to all depository

Secondary credit
Discount loans to banks that are not eligible for primary credit.

Seasonal credit Discount loans to smaller banks in areas where agriculture or tourism is important.

institutions. But by the beginning of the financial crisis in 2007, a shadow banking system of investment banks, money market mutual funds, hedge funds, and other nonbank financial firms had grown to be as large as the commercial banking system (see Chapter 11). The initial stages of the financial crisis involved these shadow banks rather than commercial banks. When the crisis began, the Fed was handicapped in its role as a lender of last resort because it had no recent tradition of lending to any firms but commercial banks.

The Fed did, however, have the authority to lend more broadly. Section 13(3) of the Federal Reserve Act authorizes the Fed in "unusual and exigent circumstances" to lend to any "individual, partnership, or corporation" that could provide acceptable collateral and could demonstrate an inability to borrow from commercial banks. The Fed used this authority to set up several temporary *lending facilities*:

- *Primary Dealer Credit Facility.* Under this facility, primary dealers could borrow overnight using mortgage-backed securities as collateral. This facility was intended to allow the investment banks and large securities firms that are primary dealers to obtain emergency loans. The facility was established in March 2008 and closed in February 2010.
- *Term Securities Lending Facility.* Under this facility, the Fed would loan up to $200 billion of Treasury securities in exchange for mortgage-backed securities. By early 2008, selling mortgage-backed securities had become difficult. This facility was intended to allow financial firms to borrow against those illiquid assets. It was established in March 2008 and closed in February 2010.
- *Commercial Paper Funding Facility.* Under this facility, the Fed purchased three-month commercial paper issued by nonfinancial corporations. When Lehman Brothers defaulted on its commercial paper in October 2008, many money market mutual funds suffered significant losses. As investors began redeeming their shares in these funds, the funds stopped buying commercial paper. Many corporations had come to rely on selling commercial paper to meet their short-term financing needs, including funding their inventories and their payrolls. By buying commercial paper directly from these corporations, the Fed allowed them to continue normal operations. This facility was established in October 2008 and closed in February 2010.
- *Term Asset-Backed Securities Loan Facility (TALF).* Under this facility, the Federal Reserve Bank of New York extended three-year or five-year loans to help investors fund the purchase of asset-backed securities. Asset-backed securities are securitized consumer and business loans, apart from mortgages. For instance, some asset-backed securities consist of consumer automobile loans that have been bundled together as a security to be resold to investors. Following the financial crisis, the market for asset-backed securities largely dried up. This facility was announced in November 2007, and the last loans were made in June 2010.

In addition to these lending facilities, the Fed set up a new way for banks to receive discount loans under the *Term Auction Facility*. In this facility, the Fed for the first time began auctioning discount loans at an interest rate determined by banks' demand for the funds. All banks eligible to borrow under the regular primary credit program could participate in the auctions. Depository institutions could pledge mortgage-backed securities, including those that were not otherwise marketable, as collateral for the loans. The length of the loans was 28 days or 84 days. Typically, the interest rate from these auctions was below the official discount rate. The length of the loans, the low interest rate, and the

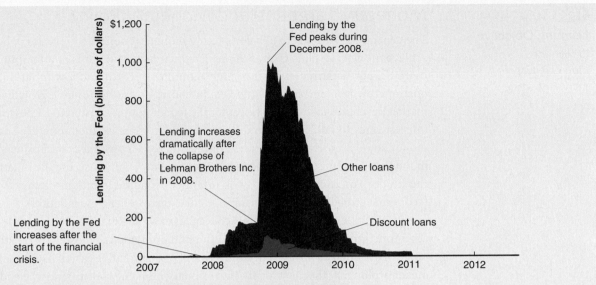

Figure 15.6 Lending by the Federal Reserve during the Financial Crisis

During the financial crisis, lending by the Federal Reserve increased from just a few hundred million dollars to $993.5 billion during December 2008. Since that time, lending by the Fed has steadily decreased.

Source: Board of Governors of the Federal Reserve System.

broader acceptability of collateral made these loans attractive to many banks during the crisis. The facility was established in December 2007 and closed in March 2010.

By mid-2010, with the financial system having recovered from the worst of the crisis, the Fed had ended these innovative discount programs.

Figure 15.6 shows that there was an explosion in all types of lending by the Fed during the financial crisis. Borrowing from the Fed amounted to just $2.1 billion as late as December 5, 2007. However, as the financial crisis worsened during the first months of 2008, financial institutions borrowed more and more from the Fed. After the collapse of Bear Stearns on March 19, 2008, total borrowing from the Fed had increased to $108.9 billion. On September 17, 2008, just days after Lehman Brothers filed for bankruptcy, total borrowing had reached $271.3 billion, skyrocketing from there to $993.5 billion on December 10, 2008, during the worst part of the financial crisis. Since that time, borrowing from the Fed has decreased steadily; it had fallen to $1.5 billion by the end of 2012.

Interest on Reserve Balances

Banks had long complained that the Fed's failure to pay interest on the banks' reserve deposits amounted to a tax. To respond to banks' complaints and to give the Fed greater control over movements in bank reserves, Congress authorized the Fed to begin paying interest on bank reserve deposits beginning in October 2011. In October 2008, during the financial crisis, Congress allowed the Fed to begin paying interest immediately, which it did. Paying interest on reserve balances gives the Fed another monetary policy tool. By increasing the interest rate, the Fed can increase the level of reserves banks are willing to hold, thereby restraining bank lending and increases in the money supply. Lowering the interest rate would have the opposite effect.

15.4

Learning Objective

Explain the role of monetary targeting in monetary policy.

Monetary Targeting and Monetary Policy

The central bank's objective in conducting monetary policy is to use its policy tools to achieve monetary policy goals. But the Fed often faces trade-offs in attempting to reach its goals, particularly the goals of high economic growth and low inflation. To demonstrate the problem, suppose the Fed, intending to spur economic growth, uses open market purchases to lower the target for the federal funds rate and to cause other market interest rates to fall. Open market purchases also increase the monetary base and the money supply. Lower interest rates typically increase consumer and business spending in the short run. But a larger money supply can potentially increase the inflation rate in the longer run. So, a policy that is intended to achieve one monetary policy goal (economic growth) may have an adverse effect on another (low inflation).

In 2012, Ben Bernanke and his colleagues at the Fed faced just this trade-off. With economic growth having slowed and the unemployment rate seemingly stuck in the range of 8%, the Fed engaged in a third round of quantitative easing. Doing so, however, meant prolonging the most highly expansionary monetary policy since the end of World War II. Some economists and policymakers worried that the result could be higher rates of inflation in the future.

The Fed faces another problem in reaching its monetary policy goals. Although it hopes to encourage economic growth and price stability, it has no direct control over real output or the price level. Interactions among households and firms determine real output and the price level. The Fed can influence the price level or output only by using its monetary policy tools—open market operations, discount policy, reserve requirements, and interest on bank reserves. But these tools don't permit the Fed to achieve its monetary policy goals directly.

The Fed also faces timing difficulties in using its monetary policy tools. The first obstacle preventing the Fed from acting quickly is the *information lag*. This lag is the Fed's inability to observe instantaneously changes in GDP, inflation, or other economic variables. If the Fed lacks timely information, it may set a policy that doesn't match actual economic conditions, and its actions can actually worsen the problems it is trying to correct. For example, some economists argue that an information lag resulted in the Fed reducing the target for the federal funds rate too slowly during 2006 and 2007 following the collapse of the housing bubble. A second timing problem is the *impact lag*. This lag is the time that is required for monetary policy changes to affect output, employment, or inflation. Changes in interest rates and the money supply affect the economy over time, not immediately. Because of this lag, the Fed's actions may affect the economy at the wrong time, and the Fed might not be able to recognize its mistakes soon enough to correct them. In 2012, some economists and policymakers argued that the Fed was neglecting to take into account the impact lag in keeping the target of the federal funds rate near zero for such an extended period.

One possible solution to the problems caused by the information lag and impact lag is for the Fed to use targets to meet its goals. Targets partially solve the Fed's inability to directly control the variables that determine economic performance, and they reduce the timing lags in observing and reacting to economic fluctuations. Unfortunately, targets also have problems, and some traditional targeting approaches have fallen out of favor at the Fed during the past 20 years. In the remainder of this section, we describe targets, their benefits and drawbacks, and their use in setting monetary policy.

Using Targets to Meet Goals

Targets are variables that the Fed can influence directly and that help achieve monetary policy goals. Traditionally, the Fed has relied on two types of targets: *policy instruments*—sometimes called *operating targets*—and *intermediate targets*. Although using policy instruments and intermediate targets is no longer the favored approach at the Fed, reviewing how they work can provide some insight into the difficulties the Fed faces in executing monetary policy.

Intermediate Targets Intermediate targets are typically either monetary aggregates, such as M1 or M2, or interest rates. The Fed can use as an intermediate target either a short-term interest rate, such as the interest rate on Treasury bills, or a long-term interest rate, such as the interest rate on corporate bonds or residential mortgages. The Fed typically chose an intermediate target that it believed would directly help it to achieve its goals. The idea was that by using an intermediate target—say, a monetary aggregate such as M2—the Fed had a better chance of reaching a goal, such as price stability or full employment, that is not directly under its control, than it would if it had focused solely on the goal. Using an intermediate target could also provide feedback on whether its policy actions were consistent with achieving the goal. For instance, from statistical studies, the Fed might have estimated that increasing M2 at a steady rate of 3% per year was consistent with its goal of price stability. If M2 was actually growing by 6%, the Fed would know immediately that it was on a course to miss its long-run goal of price stability. The Fed could then use its monetary policy tools (most likely open market operations) to slow M2 growth to the target rate of 3%. Hitting the M2 intermediate target had no value in and of itself. It would simply help the Fed to achieve its stated goals.

Policy Instruments, or Operating Targets The Fed controls intermediate target variables, such as the mortgage interest rate or M2, only indirectly because private-sector decisions also influence these variables. The Fed would therefore need a target that was a better link between its policy tool and intermediate targets. Policy instruments, or operating targets, are variables that the Fed controls directly with its monetary policy tools and that are closely related to intermediate targets. Examples of policy instruments include the federal funds rate and nonborrowed reserves. As we have seen, in recent decades, the federal funds rate is the Fed's most commonly used policy instrument because the market for bank reserves, which the Fed influences heavily, determines the federal funds rate. Most central banks in high-income countries use interest rates as policy instruments.

Figure 15.7 shows the Fed's traditional approach of using policy instruments and intermediate targets to reach its goals. Figure 15.7 also helps explain why we have used past tense in much of our discussion of targeting. Although the Fed selects goals, it ultimately controls only policy tools. For the targeting approach we have just outlined to be effective, the links between policy tools and policy instruments, between policy instruments and intermediate targets, and between intermediate targets and policy goals must be reliable. Over time, however, some of these links have broken down. For example, prior to 1980, there was a fairly consistent link between increases in the rate of growth of M1 and M2 and, after a lag of roughly two years, an increase in the inflation rate. This link made some economists argue that the Fed should concentrate on a monetary aggregate as its intermediate target. Unfortunately, the link between changes

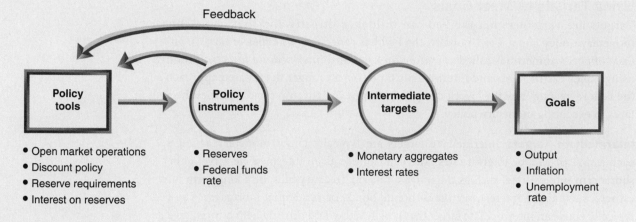

Figure 15.7 Achieving Monetary Policy Goals

The Federal Reserve establishes goals for such economic variables as the rate of inflation and the rate of unemployment. The Fed directly controls only its policy tools. It can use targets—intermediate targets and policy instruments—which are variables that the Fed can influence, to help achieve monetary policy goals. In recent years, the Fed has deemphasized the use of targeting procedures of this type.

in the money supply and changes in inflation has been erratic since 1980. The growth of the money supply has varied widely, while the inflation rate has varied much less. In general, in recent years, many economists and policymakers no longer believe that a stable relationship exists between the alternative intermediate targets and the Fed's policy goals.

Some discussion has continued, however, over whether the Fed should choose a reserve aggregate or the federal funds rate as its policy instrument. We analyze this discussion in the next section.

Making the Connection

What Happened to the Link Between Money and Prices?

In the United States, decades when the money supply has grown more rapidly have been decades when the inflation rate has been relatively high. But an economic relationship that holds over decades is not always useful for policymakers attempting to steer the economy in the short run. Prior to 1980, there was significant evidence that the link between money and prices held up in the short run of a year or two. In fact, many economists were convinced that the acceleration in inflation during the late 1960s and 1970s was due to the Fed's having allowed the growth rate of the money supply to sharply increase during those years.

The economists who argued this point most forcefully are known as *monetarists*. The most prominent monetarist was Nobel laureate Milton Friedman of the University of Chicago. The monetarists appeared to have gained favor in July 1979, when President Jimmy Carter appointed Paul Volcker as chairman of the Board of Governors of the Federal Reserve System. Volcker was committed to reducing inflation and chose monetary aggregates as intermediate targets. Under Volcker, the Fed shifted its policy to emphasize nonborrowed reserves as a policy instrument, or operating target. This episode is sometimes referred to as "The Great Monetarist Experiment." At first, the Fed's policy seemed successful, as it reduced the rate of growth of the money supply and, with a lag, the inflation rate fell. A severe recession began in July 1981, however, and by the end of the year, the rate of the growth of the money supply was increasing. From the third quarter of 1981 to the third quarter of 1983, M1 grew at an annual rate of more than 9%. Friedman predicted that with a lag, the result of this high rate of money growth would be a much higher inflation rate.

To support his argument, in an article in the *American Economic Review*, Friedman presented some of the data in the table below. Focus first on the unshaded entries in the table. Friedman argued that there was a close connection between the rate of growth of M1 over a two-year period and the inflation rate two years later. The unshaded entries in the table show that this relationship holds for the period from 1973 through 1981. Note in particular that a decline in the growth of the money supply from 8.6% during 1977–1979 to 6.1% during 1979–1981—the result of Volcker's policies—was associated with a decline in the inflation from 9.4% to 4.8%. So, Friedman seemed justified in predicting that because the Fed had allowed the growth of the money supply to increase to 9.2% during the 1981–1983 period, the inflation rate was likely to increase significantly. In fact, though, the values in the shaded areas of the table show that despite the increase in the money supply, the inflation rate *decreased rather than increased*. Moreover, money growth remained high during the following two years, while the inflation rate decreased even further. In the years that followed, the link between the growth in M1 or M2 and the inflation rate was no stronger.

Period for money growth	Growth in M1	Inflation rate two years later	Period for inflation
Third quarter of 1973 to third quarter of 1975	5.2%	6.3%	Third quarter of 1975 to third quarter of 1977
Third quarter of 1975 to third quarter of 1977	6.4	8.3	Third quarter of 1977 to third quarter of 1979
Third quarter of 1977 to third quarter of 1979	8.6	9.4	Third quarter of 1979 to third quarter of 1981
Third quarter of 1979 to third quarter of 1981	6.1	4.8	Third quarter of 1981 to third quarter of 1983
Third quarter of 1981 to third quarter of 1983	9.2	3.3	Third quarter of 1983 to third quarter of 1985
Third quarter of 1983 to third quarter of 1985	8.1	2.8	Third quarter of 1985 to third quarter of 1987

Why did the short-run link between the growth of the money supply and inflation break down after 1980? Most economists believe that the breakdown occurred because the nature of M1 and M2 changed after 1980. Before 1980, banks were not allowed to pay interest on checkable deposits. In 1980, Congress authorized negotiable order of withdrawal (NOW) accounts, on which banks can pay interest, so M1 changed from representing a pure medium of exchange to also representing a store of value. In addition, financial innovations at banks increased the amount of checkable deposits households and firms were willing to hold without spending them. *Automated transfer of saving* accounts move checkable deposit balances into higher-interest CDs each night and then back into checkable deposits in the morning. *Sweep accounts* are aimed at businesses and move their checkable deposits balances into money market deposit accounts at the end of each week and then move the funds back into checkable deposits at the beginning of the following week. (Recall that regulations bar firms from holding interest-earning checking [NOW] accounts.) As a result of these changes, a rapid increase in M1 need not translate directly into spending increases that would lead to higher inflation.

Because of the breakdown in the relationship between the growth of the money supply and inflation, since 1993, the Fed no longer announces targets for M1 and M2. Although at one time, investors closely followed the Fed's weekly announcements of data on M1 and M2, looking for clues about future inflation rates, today these announcements have little impact on financial markets.

Source: The table is adapted from Table 2 in Benjamin M. Friedman, "Lessons on Monetary Policy in the 1980s," *Journal of Economic Perspectives*, Vol. 2, No. 3, Summer 1988, p. 62. The original article by Milton Friedman is "Lessons from the 1979–1982 Monetary Policy Experiment," *American Economic Review*, Vol. 74, No. 2, May 1984, pp. 397–401.

See related problems 4.8 and 4.9 at the end of the chapter.

The Choice Between Targeting Reserves and Targeting the Federal Funds Rate

Traditionally, the Fed has used three criteria when evaluating variables that might be used as policy instruments. The Fed's main policy instruments have been *reserve aggregates*, such as total reserves or nonborrowed reserves, and the federal funds rate. We can briefly assess how well these instruments meet the Fed's three criteria:

1. *Measurable.* The variable must be measurable in a short time frame to overcome information lags. The Fed exercises significant control over both reserve aggregates and the federal funds rate and can accurately measure them hour by hour if it needs to.
2. *Controllable.* Although the Fed lacks complete control over the level of reserve aggregates and the federal funds rate because both depend on banks' demands for reserves, the trading desk at the Federal Reserve Bank of New York can use open market operations to keep both variables close to whatever target the Fed selects.
3. *Predictable.* The Fed needs a policy instrument that has a predictable effect on its policy goals. The effect of a change in either reserves or the federal funds rate on goals such as economic growth or price stability is complex. This complexity is one reason the Fed at one time relied on intermediate targets. Because it is not clear whether reserves or the federal funds rate best meets this last criterion, economists continue to discuss which policy instrument is best.

A key point to understand is that the Fed can choose a reserve aggregate for its policy instrument, or it can choose the federal funds rate, but it cannot choose both. To see why, look at Figure 15.8, which again shows the demand and supply for reserves in the federal funds market. In panel (a), we assume that the Fed has decided to use the level of reserves as its policy instrument by keeping reserves constant at R^*. With demand for reserves at D_1, the equilibrium federal funds rate is i_{ff1}^*. If households and firms decide to hold more checkable deposits or if banks decide to hold more excess reserves, the demand for reserves will shift to the right, from D_1 to D_2. The result will be

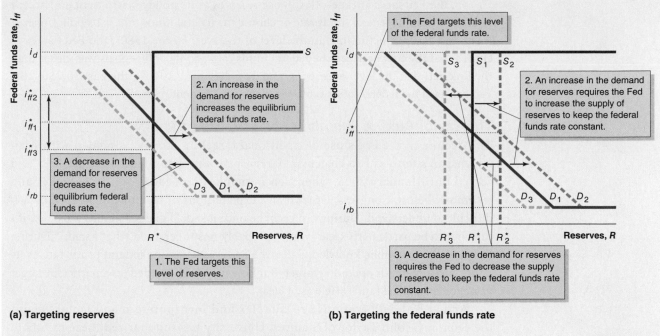

(a) Targeting reserves

(b) Targeting the federal funds rate

Figure 15.8 Choosing Between Policy Instruments

In panel (a), the Fed chooses the level of reserves as its policy instrument by keeping reserves constant, at R^*. With demand for reserves at D_1, the equilibrium federal funds rate is i_{ff1}^*. If the demand for reserves shifts to the right from D_1 to D_2, the equilibrium federal funds rate increases from i_{ff1}^* to i_{ff2}^*. Similarly, if the demand for reserves shifts to the left, from D_1 to D_3, the equilibrium federal funds rate decreases from i_{ff1}^* to i_{ff3}^*.

In panel (b), the Fed chooses the federal funds rate as its policy instrument by keeping the rate constant, at i_{ff}^*. If the demand for reserves increases from D_1 to D_2, the Fed will have to increase the supply of reserves from S_1 to S_2 in order to maintain its target for the federal funds rate at i_{ff}^*. If the demand for reserves decreases from D_1 to D_3, the Fed will have to decrease the supply of reserves from S_1 to S_3 to maintain its target for the federal funds rate.

an increase in the equilibrium federal funds rate from i_{ff1}^* to i_{ff2}^*. Similarly, if households and firms decide to hold fewer checkable deposits or banks decide to hold fewer excess reserves, the demand for reserves will shift to the left, from D_1 to D_3. The result will be a decrease in the equilibrium federal funds rate from i_{ff1}^* to i_{ff3}^*. We can conclude that *using reserves as the Fed's policy instrument will cause the federal funds rate to fluctuate in response to changes in the demand for reserves.*

In panel (b) of Figure 15.8, we assume that the Fed has decided to use the federal funds rate as its policy instrument by keeping the rate constant at i_{ff}^*. With demand for reserves at D_1, the equilibrium level of reserves is R_1^*. If the demand for reserves increases from D_1 to D_2, the Fed will have to increase the supply of reserves from S_1 to S_2 in order to maintain its target for the federal funds rate at i_{ff}^*. Shifting the supply curve from S_1 to S_2 causes the equilibrium level of reserves to increase from R_1^* to R_2^*. Similarly, if the demand for reserves decreases from D_1 to D_3, the Fed will have to decrease the supply of reserves from S_1 to S_3 to maintain its target for the federal funds rate. The result will be a decrease in the equilibrium level of reserves from R_1^* to R_3^*. We can conclude that *using the federal funds rate as the Fed's policy instrument will cause the level of reserves to fluctuate in response to changes in the demand for reserves.*

So, the Fed faces a trade-off: Choose reserves as its policy instrument and accept fluctuations in the federal funds rate or choose the federal funds rate as its policy instrument and accept fluctuations in the level of reserves. By the 1980s, the Fed had concluded that the link between the federal funds rate and its policy goals was closer than the link between the level of reserves and its policy goals. So, for the past 30 years, the Fed has used the federal funds rate as its policy instrument.

The Taylor Rule: A Summary Measure of Fed Policy

The decline in the Fed's use of traditional targeting largely coincided with Alan Greenspan's term as Fed chairman. Greenspan was appointed in August 1987 and served until January 2006, when Ben Bernanke succeeded him. In speeches and testimony before Congress, Greenspan's explanations of his policies were famously difficult to understand. During a speech, he once joked: "I guess I should warn you if I turn out to be particularly clear, you've probably misunderstood what I said."[4] During this time, it was public knowledge that the Fed was using the federal funds rate as its policy instrument, or operating target. But how the FOMC settled on a particular target value for the federal funds rate wasn't clear.

Taylor rule A monetary policy guideline developed by economist John Taylor for determining the target for the federal funds rate.

Actual Fed deliberations are complex and incorporate many factors about the economy. John Taylor of Stanford University has summarized these factors in the **Taylor rule** for federal funds rate targeting.[5] The Taylor rule begins with an estimate of the value of the real federal funds rate, which is the federal funds rate—adjusted for inflation—that would be consistent with real GDP being equal to potential real GDP in the long run. With real GDP equal to potential real GDP, cyclical unemployment should be zero, and the Fed will have attained its policy goal of high employment. According to the Taylor rule, the Fed should set its current federal funds rate target equal to the sum of the current inflation rate, the equilibrium real federal funds rate, and two additional terms. The first of these terms is the *inflation gap*—the difference between current inflation and a target rate; the second term is the *output gap*—the percentage difference of real GDP from potential real GDP. The inflation gap and the output gap are each given "weights" that reflect their influence on the federal funds rate target. With weights of one half for both gaps, we have the following Taylor rule:

$$\text{Federal funds rate target} = \text{Current inflation rate} + \text{Equilibrium real federal funds rate} + (1/2 \times \text{Inflation gap}) + (1/2 \times \text{Output gap}).$$

So when the inflation rate is above the Fed's target rate, the FOMC will raise the target for the federal funds rate. Similarly, when the output gap is negative—that is, when real GDP is less than potential GDP—the FOMC will lower the target for the federal funds rate. In calibrating this rule, Taylor assumed that the equilibrium real federal funds rate is 2% and the target rate of inflation is 2%. Figure 15.9 shows the level of the federal funds rate that would have occurred if the Fed had strictly followed the

---

[4]Floyd Norris, "What if the Fed Chief Speaks Plainly?" *New York Times*, October 28, 2005.

[5]Taylor's original discussion of the rule appeared in John B. Taylor, "Discretion Versus Policy Rules in Practice," *Carnegie-Rochester Conference Series on Public Policy*, Vol. 39, 1993, pp. 195–214.

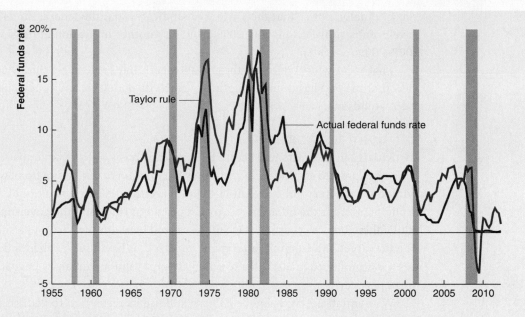

Figure 15.9 The Taylor Rule

The blue line shows the level of the federal funds rate that would have occurred if the Fed had strictly followed the Taylor rule, and the red line shows the actual federal funds rate. The figure shows that the Taylor rule does a reasonable job of explaining Federal Reserve policy during some periods, but it also shows the periods in which the target federal funds rate diverges from the rate predicted by the Taylor rule. The shaded areas represent periods of recession.

Sources: Federal Reserve Bank of St. Louis; and Congressional Budget Office. We thank our colleague Matthew Rafferty of Quinnipiac University for providing the data on the rate predicted by the Taylor rule.

Taylor rule and the actual federal funds rate. The figure indicates that because the two lines are close together during most years, the Taylor rule does a reasonable job of explaining Federal Reserve policy. There are some periods when the lines diverge significantly. During the late 1960s and early to mid-1970s, the federal funds rate predicted from the Taylor rule is consistently above the target federal funds rate. This gap is consistent with the view of most economists that in the face of a worsening inflation rate during those years, the FOMC should have raised the target for the federal funds rate more than it did.

Figure 15.9 also indicates that the FOMC lowered the federal funds rate following the severe 1981–1982 recession more slowly than is consistent with the Taylor rule. Finally, the figure indicates that the FOMC kept the federal funds rate at levels well below those indicated by the Taylor rule during the recovery from the 2001 recession. Some economists and policymakers have argued that by keeping the federal funds at a very low level for an extended period, the Fed helped provide fuel for the housing boom. The argument is that a low federal funds rate contributed to low mortgage interest rates, thereby increasing the demand for housing. At the time, Fed Chairman Alan Greenspan argued that low interest rates were needed to guard against the possibility that the economy might lapse into a period of deflation. Current Fed Chairman Ben Bernanke has argued that a global saving glut, rather than Fed policy, was the main reason long-term interest rates were low in the United States during the early

2000s. Finally, notice that the Taylor rule indicates that the federal funds rate should have been *negative* throughout 2009, which is another indication of the severity of the 2007–2009 recession.

That the Taylor rule tracks the actual federal funds rate fairly closely confirms the view that the Fed has been attempting to reach its policy goals through changes in the federal funds rate.

Inflation Targeting

Particularly in the years just before the financial crisis, many economists and central bankers expressed significant interest in using *inflation targeting* as a framework for carrying out monetary policy. With inflation targeting, a central bank publically sets an explicit target for the inflation rate over a period of time, and the government and the public then judge the performance of the central bank on the basis of its success in hitting the target. For example, after many years of not having an explicit inflation target, the Fed announced in 2012 that it would attempt to maintain an average inflation rate of 2% per year.

With inflation targeting, the Fed can still use its discretion to address special situations rather than following an inflexible rule. Nevertheless, an inflation target allows monetary policy to focus on inflation and inflation forecasts, except during times of severe recession. Arguments in favor of the Fed using an explicit inflation target focus on four points. First, announcing explicit targets for inflation would draw the public's attention to what the Fed can actually achieve in practice. Most economists believe that over the long run, monetary policy has a greater effect on inflation than on the growth of real output. Second, the establishment of transparent inflation targets for the United States would provide an anchor for inflationary expectations. If households, firms, and participants in financial markets believe that the Fed will hit an annual inflation target of 2%, then they will expect that if inflation were temporarily lower or higher, it will eventually return to the target rate. Third, announced inflation targets help institutionalize effective U.S. monetary policy. Finally, inflation targets promote accountability for the Fed by providing a yardstick against which its performance can be measured.

Some economists and policymakers were critical of the Fed's decision to adopt an explicit inflation target, however. Opponents of inflation targets also make four points. First, rigid numerical targets for inflation diminish the flexibility of monetary policy to address other policy goals. Second, because monetary policy affects inflation with a lag, inflation targeting requires that the Fed depend on forecasts of future inflation, uncertainty about which can create problems for the conduct of policy. Third, holding the Fed accountable only for a goal of low inflation may make it more difficult for elected officials to monitor the Fed's support for good economic policy overall. Finally, uncertainty about future levels of output and employment can impede economic decision making in the presence of an inflation target. That is, inflation targets may increase uncertainty over whether the Fed will take prompt action to return the economy to full employment following a recession.

The jury is still out on the question of whether inflation targets improve economic policy. Many economists and central bankers have suggested that gains from transparency and accountability can be achieved without explicit inflation targets and that the credibility of monetary policy is better established through experience. And an inflation target requires improved communication with the public. While an inflation target has the potential for increasing the understanding of policy objectives, the standard for communication becomes more exacting than it would in a world without explicit objectives.

International Comparisons of Monetary Policy

Although there are institutional differences in how central banks conduct monetary policy, there are two important similarities in recent practices. First, most central banks in high-income countries have increasingly used short-term interest rates—similar to the federal funds rate in the United States—as the policy instrument, or operating target, through which goals are pursued. Second, many central banks are focusing more on ultimate goals such as low inflation than on particular intermediate targets. In this section, we discuss these practices and the institutional settings for the conduct of monetary policy in Canada, Germany, Japan, the United Kingdom, and the European Union.

The Bank of Canada The Bank of Canada, like the U.S. Fed, became increasingly concerned about inflation during the 1970s. In 1975, the Bank of Canada announced a policy of gradually reducing the growth rate of M1. By the late 1970s, policy shifted toward an exchange rate target. By late 1982, M1 targets were no longer used. In 1988, John Crow, then governor of the Bank of Canada, announced the bank's commitment to price stability by announcing a series of declining inflation targets. To meet the inflation targets, the Bank of Canada sets explicit operational target bands for the overnight rate (analogous to the federal funds rate). While Fed policy has been concerned primarily with the inflation gap and the output gap, the Bank of Canada has also made the exchange value of the Canadian dollar a focus of policy. This focus on exchange rates—particularly between the Canadian dollar and the U.S. dollar—reflects the large role that exports have traditionally played in the Canadian economy.

During 2007–2009, the Bank of Canada received praise for helping the Canadian financial system weather the financial crisis with much less instability than occurred in the United States. The Canadian banking system, in particular, avoided the heavy losses from investments in mortgage-backed securities and commercial real estate suffered by many banks in the United States. In 2010, the Bank of Canada was the first central bank in an industrial country to raise its target for the overnight bank lending rate. This was another indication of the relatively strong performance of the Canadian economy during the global downturn.

The German Central Bank The German central bank, the Bundesbank, began experimenting with monetary targets in the late 1970s to combat inflation. The aggregate that it selected, *central bank money*, or M3, is defined as a weighted sum of currency, checkable deposits, and time and savings deposits. The Bundesbank believed that movements in central bank money had a predictable effect on nominal GDP and that this monetary aggregate was significantly controllable by using monetary policy tools. The Bundesbank set gradually lower target ranges for M3 growth each year during the late 1970s and through the 1980s. For the first half of the 1980s, the central bank successfully achieved its targets. But departures from its targets became more common from 1986 through 1988, as officials wanted to decrease the value of the (then) West German mark relative to the U.S. dollar. To do so, the Bundesbank increased money growth faster than its announced targets.

The reunification of Germany in 1991 posed problems for the Bundesbank's commitment to its announced targets. Two pressures were particularly significant. First, the exchange of West German currency for less valuable East German currency brought inflationary pressures. Second, political objectives for economic growth after reunification raised fears of a weakening resolve to keep inflation low. These pressures on the Bundesbank's operating procedures yielded a more flexible approach, similar to what the Fed uses.

Germany, which has had an informal inflation target since 1975, had an inflation goal of 2% per year prior to the inauguration of the European Central Bank in 1999. The Bundesbank believed that adherence to M3 targeting would keep inflation in check. The central bank used changes in the *lombard rate* (a short-term repurchase agreement rate) to achieve its M3 target.

The apparent German success in the conduct of monetary policy may be traceable to factors beyond monetary targeting. Many analysts note that the Bundesbank permitted substantial deviation from monetary targets for significant periods of time. The success of German monetary policy may lie more in the clear communication of the central bank's focus on controlling inflation than in a strict emphasis on monetary targeting, a lesson for the current debate over inflation targeting. Since Germany, along with 11 other European countries, began using the euro in 2002, the European Central Bank rather than the Bundesbank has been responsible for German monetary policy.

The Bank of Japan In the aftermath of the first OPEC oil shock in 1973, Japan experienced an inflation rate in excess of 20%. This high inflation rate led the Bank of Japan to adopt explicit money growth targets. In particular, beginning in 1978, the Bank of Japan announced targets for an aggregate corresponding to M2. Following the 1979 oil price shock, the central bank reduced money growth. The gradual decline in money growth over the period from 1978 through 1987 was associated with a faster decline in inflation than what the United States experienced. The consistency with which the Bank of Japan fulfilled its promises bolstered the public's belief in the bank's commitment to lower money growth and lower inflation. During this period, the Bank of Japan used a short-term interest rate in the Japanese interbank market—similar to the U.S. federal funds market—as its operating target.

As also happened in the United States, Japanese banks and financial markets experienced a wave of deregulation and financial innovation during the 1980s. As a consequence, the Bank of Japan began to rely less on the M2 aggregate in the conduct of monetary policy. From 1987 to 1989, the bank's concern over the foreign-exchange value of the yen—which had risen significantly against the U.S. dollar—dominated monetary policy. The rapid rate of money growth during this period led to a boom in Japanese asset prices, particularly in land and stocks. In an attempt to reduce speculation in asset markets during the boom, the Bank of Japan adopted a contractionary monetary policy, which led to a decline in asset prices and ultimately to a drop in Japanese economic growth. Despite the success of the Bank of Japan's fight against inflation during the 1978–1987 period, it has not adopted formal inflation targets, although the Bank emphasizes price stability as an objective. As an operating policy instrument, the central bank uses short-term interest rates and its discount rate.

Many financial market commentators viewed the continuing deflationary Japanese monetary policy in the late 1990s and 2000s as a significant factor in the weakness of Japanese economic performance during most of that period. A more expansionary monetary policy began to stimulate both economic growth and inflation in the mid-2000s. In 2006, the Bank of Japan began to scale back its expansionary policy. It also adopted a new policy framework focusing on the expected inflation rate one or two years ahead as opposed to the current inflation rate. The financial crisis that began in 2007 led the Bank of Japan to return to an expansionary policy. Since 2010, the Bank of Japan has intervened several times to reverse the soaring value of the yen against the U.S. dollar. The high value of the yen hampered Japanese exports and impeded Japan's economic recovery. In the years following the financial crisis, the Bank of Japan engaged in an ongoing struggle with the government of Japan, as the government attempted to pressure the Bank of Japan to be more aggressive in bringing down the exchange value of the yen, while the Bank of Japan fought to retain its independence in making monetary policy decisions.

The Bank of England In the United Kingdom, the Bank of England announced money supply targets in late 1973 in response to inflationary pressures. As was the case in the United States, money targets—in this case a broad aggregate, M3—were not pursued aggressively. In response to accelerating inflation in the late 1970s, the government of Prime Minister Margaret Thatcher formally introduced in 1980 a strategy for gradual deceleration of M3 growth. Just as achieving the M1 targets in the United States was made more complicated by financial innovation, the Bank of England had difficulty achieving M3 targets. Beginning in 1983, the bank shifted its emphasis toward targeting growth in the monetary base (again with an eye toward a gradual reduction in the rate of growth of the money supply). In 1992, the United Kingdom adopted inflation targets. Consistent with those targets, short-term interest rates have been the primary instrument of monetary policy. Since early 1984, interest-rate decisions have been made at monthly meetings between the governor of the Bank of England and the chancellor of the exchequer. When interest rates are changed, a detailed explanation is offered to emphasize that decisions reflect monetary policy's emphasis on inflation goals.

During the financial crisis, the Bank of England took several dramatic policy actions. The bank began cutting its *base rate*, the interest rate it charges banks for overnight loans—the equivalent of the Fed's discount rate—in the fall of 2007. By January 2009, the bank had cut the rate to 1.5%, the lowest it had been since the bank's founding in 1694. By March 2009, the bank had lowered the base rate to 0.5%, where it remained in the fall of 2012. Beginning in October 2008, the bank also rapidly lowered the interest rate it paid banks on reserves; by March 2009, the rate had declined from 5% to 0.5%. The bank also engaged in quantitative easing by buying long-term British government bonds. In late 2012, the Bank of England faced a challenge: Although the British economy had slipped into a so-called double-dip recession, with real GDP declining from late 2011 through mid-2012, inflation was above the government's target rate of 2%. Mervyn King, the governor of the Bank of England, argued that the bank should maintain its expansionary monetary policy and that the increase in inflation was due to temporary factors, such as higher oil and food prices.

The European System of Central Banks The European System of Central Banks (ESCB), consisting of the European Central Bank (ECB) and the national central banks of all member states of the European Union, commenced operation in January 1999, following the signing of the Maastricht Treaty. Modeled on the law governing the German Bundesbank, the primary objective of the ESCB is to maintain price stability. As a secondary objective, the ESCB must also support the general economic policies of the European Union. The ECB attaches a significant role to monetary aggregates—in particular, the growth rate of the M3 aggregate. In addition, however, the ECB has emphasized a goal of price stability, defined as an inflation range of 0% to 2%. In practice, the ECB's strategy has not always been clear, as it has not committed to either a monetary-targeting approach or an inflation-targeting approach.

During the financial crisis and its aftermath, the ECB struggled to forge a monetary policy appropriate to the very different needs of the member countries. In 2012, while some countries, notably Germany, had made a strong recovery from the recession, others, such as Greece, Ireland, Portugal, and Spain, struggled with high unemployment rates. In addition, the ECB felt obliged to intervene to buy Greek and Spanish government bonds when it appeared possible that those governments might default. This *sovereign debt crisis* put further strains on the ECB. In response to the debt crisis, euro-zone governments for the first time gave the ECB additional authority to regulate the banking systems of member countries.

Answering the Key Question

Continued from page 447

At the beginning of this chapter, we asked:

"Should price stability still be the most important policy goal of central banks?"

As we have seen in this chapter, economists debate whether central banks should have an explicit target for the inflation rate. Doing so would make price stability the most important goal of central banks. Although price stability in and of itself can increase economic well-being, most economists and policymakers see price stability as having broader benefits. In particular, few economies have managed to sustain high rates of economic growth and high rates of employment in the long run without also experiencing price stability. Whatever the merits of making price stability the focus of monetary policy, the severity of the financial crisis and recession led the Fed to put greater emphasis on its goals of high employment and economic growth.

Key Terms and Problems

Key Terms

Discount policy, p. 452

Discount window, p. 452

Economic growth, p. 450

Federal funds rate, p. 452

Open market operations, p. 451

Primary credit, p. 464

Quantitative easing, p. 463

Reserve requirement, p. 452

Seasonal credit, p. 465

Secondary credit, p. 465

Taylor rule, p. 474

15.1 The Goals of Monetary Policy
Describe the goals of monetary policy.

Review Questions

1.1 What is the purpose of monetary policy? What is meant by economic well-being? Why is the Fed said to have a "dual mandate"?

1.2 Which type of unemployment—frictional, structural, or cyclical—does the Federal Reserve seek to reduce? Why doesn't the Fed seek to reduce the unemployment rate to zero?

1.3 Why do fluctuations in interest rates make investment decisions by households and firms more difficult?

1.4 If you owned a firm that did business internationally, why would excess fluctuations in the foreign exchange value of the dollar make planning for business and financial transactions more difficult?

Problems and Applications

1.5 Given that *inflation* erodes the value of money, should the Federal Reserve pursue a goal of *deflation*? Would deflation create some of the same problems as inflation in terms of the information communicated by price changes and the arbitrary redistribution of income? Briefly explain.

1.6 A columnist in the *Wall Street Journal* has argued in favor of changing the Fed's dual mandate to a single mandate of price stability: "When an economy gets weak enough, extraordinary easing measures can be justified as the necessary battle against potentially highly damaging deflation rather than to reduce unemployment."

a. What does the author mean by "extraordinary easing measures"?

b. How would these measures end deflation? Why would deflation be "potentially highly damaging"?

c. Briefly explain whether you agree with the author's argument that the Fed's dual mandate should be replaced with a single mandate of price stability.

Source: Neal Lipschutz, "Should Fed Chairman Have a Single Term, Single Mandate?" *Wall Street Journal*, September 27, 2012.

1.7 The natural rate of unemployment varies over time, with changes in demographics, the structure of the economy, and government policies. For its goal of high employment, why would it be crucial for the Federal Reserve to be aware of variations in the natural rate of unemployment?

1.8 Achieving the goal of price stability with low and steady inflation allows the Fed to achieve other goals, such as stable interest rates and stable foreign exchange rates. If the Fed fails to achieve low and steady inflation, why will it be hard to achieve stable interest rates?

1.9 If the exchange rate between the Japanese yen and the dollar changes from ¥85 = $1 to ¥95 = $1, will this change make U.S. industries more or less competitive relative to Japanese industries? Briefly explain.

MyEconLab Visit **www.myeconlab.com** to complete these exercises online and get instant feedback. Exercises that update with real-time data are marked with .

15.2 Monetary Policy Tools and the Federal Funds Rate

Understand how the Fed uses monetary policy tools to influence the federal funds rate.

Review Questions

2.1 Which of the Fed's three traditional monetary policy tools is the most important?

2.2 How does the federal funds rate differ from the discount rate? Which rate is typically higher?

2.3 Why does an increase in the federal funds rate decrease the quantity of reserves demanded? At what interest rate does the demand curve for reserves become perfectly elastic?

2.4 Briefly explain what determines the supply curve for reserves. Why does the supply curve have a horizontal segment?

Problems and Applications

2.5 Use graphs of the federal funds market to illustrate the effect on the demand for reserves or the supply of reserves of each of the following Fed policy actions (be sure to explain what is happening in your graphs):

 a. A decrease in the required reserve ratio

 b. A decrease in the discount rate

 c. A decrease in the interest rate paid on reserves

 d. An open market sale of government securities

2.6 Suppose that the FOMC decides to lower its target for the federal funds rate. How can it use open market operations to accomplish this goal? How can the FOMC use open market operations to raise its target for the federal funds rate? Use a graph of the federal funds market to illustrate your answers.

2.7 [Related to Solved Problem 15.2 on page 458] Use graphs of the federal funds market to analyze each of the following three situations. Be sure that your graphs clearly show changes in the equilibrium federal funds rate, changes in the equilibrium level of reserves, and any shifts in the demand and supply curves.

 a. Suppose that the Fed decides to increase its target for the federal funds rate from 2% to 2.25% while also increasing the discount rate from 2.5% to 2.75%. Show how the Fed can use open market operations to bring about a higher equilibrium federal funds rate.

 b. Suppose that banks increase their demand for reserves. Show how the Fed can offset this change through open market operations in order to keep the equilibrium federal funds rate unchanged.

 c. Suppose that the Fed decides to decrease the required reserve ratio but does not want the increase to affect its target for the federal funds rate. Show how the Fed can use open market operations to accomplish this policy.

2.8 [Related to Solved Problem 15.2 on page 458] Suppose that in equilibrium, the federal funds rate is equal to the interest rate the Fed is paying on reserves. Use a graph of the federal funds market to analyze the effect of an open market sale of Treasury securities on the equilibrium federal funds rate.

2.9 The December 13, 2005, press release of the Federal Open Market Committee (FOMC) stated that the FOMC "decided today to raise its target for the federal funds rate by 25 basis points to 4¼ percent." The press release also stated that "In a related action, the Board of Governors unanimously approved a 25-basis point increase in the discount rate to 5¼ percent."

 a. Using a graph of the federal funds market, show the equilibrium federal funds rate and the discount rate before the policy action of December 13, 2005, when the federal funds rate was 4% and the discount rate 5%.

 b. Use your graph to explain how the Fed would raise the federal funds rate by 25 basis points (¼%). Show in your graph the 25-basis-point increase in the discount rate. What policy action would the Fed use to bring about this increase in the target federal funds rate?

Source: Board of Governors of the Federal Reserve System, "Press Release," December 13, 2005, www.federalreserve. gov/boarddocs/press/monetary/2005/20051213/.

2.10 The January 22, 2008, press release of the FOMC states that the FOMC "decided to lower its target for the federal funds rate by 75 basis points to 3½ percent." The press release goes on to say that "In a related action the Board of Governors approved a 75-basis point decrease in the discount rate to 4 percent."

a. Use a graph of the federal funds market to show the equilibrium federal funds rate and the discount rate before the policy action of January 22, 2008, when the federal funds rate was 4¼% and the discount rate 4¾%.

b. Use your graph to show how the Fed would lower the federal funds rate by 75 basis points (¾%). Show in your graph the 75-basis point decrease in the discount rate. What policy action would the Fed use to lower the federal funds rate by 75 basis points?

Source: Board of Governors of the Federal Reserve System, "Press Release," January 22, 2008, www.federalreserve.gov/ newsevents/press/monetary/20080122b.htm.

15.3 More on the Fed's Monetary Policy Tools
Trace how the importance of different monetary policy tools has changed over time.

Review Questions

3.1 How does an open market sale of Treasury securities by the Fed affect the price of Treasury securities, the interest rate on Treasury securities, the monetary base, and the money supply?

3.2 What advantages do open market operations have over other policy tools?

3.3 Why did the Fed begin using quantitative easing?

3.4 Before 1980, which banks could receive discount loans? After 1980, which banks could receive discount loans? During the financial crisis of 2007–2009, how did the Fed's discount lending expand?

Problems and Applications

3.5 [Related to the Making the Connection on page 461] To hit the target federal funds rate given in the FOMC's policy directive, does the account manager adjust the demand for reserves, the supply of reserves, or both? What monetary policy tool does the account manager use to hit the target federal funds rate? On most days, does the trading desk at the Federal Reserve Bank of New York carry out dynamic open market operations or defensive open market operations?

3.6 An article in the *Economist* magazine observed that when the Fed's "policy rate is effectively zero and long-term rates are close to all-time record lows. . . . [doesn't] additional easing amount to little more than pushing on a string?"

a. What is the Fed's "policy rate"?

b. What does the author mean by "additional easing"?

c. Why does the article describe additional easing as "pushing on a string"?

d. With short-term interest rates at or near zero and long-term interest rates at historic lows, do you think that additional quantitative easing by the Fed would amount to little more than pushing on a string? Briefly explain.

Source: "Is the Fed Pushing on a String?" *Economist*, July 3, 2012.

3.7 [Related to the Chapter Opener on page 447] In a letter to a member of Congress, Fed Chairman Ben Bernanke made the following statement:

> The monetary accommodation provided by the Federal Reserve has substantially helped the U.S. economy by easing financial conditions. . . . The easing in financial conditions has promoted economic activity through a variety of channels, including reducing the cost of capital, boosting the aggregate wealth of U.S. households, and improving the competitiveness of U.S. businesses in the global marketplace.

a. What does Bernanke mean by "monetary accommodation"?

b. What does Bernanke mean by "easing financial conditions"?

c. Briefly explain how easing financial conditions promoted economic activity through each of the three "channels" that Bernanke mentions.

Source: Letter from Ben S. Bernanke to Representative Darrell E. Issa, August 22, 2012.

3.8 The Fed continued to pursue unusual policy measures for several years after the end of the financial crisis of 2007–2009. Chairman Bernanke and other members of the FOMC continued to discuss an "exit strategy" to shrink its balance sheet and return bank reserves and the monetary base to more normal levels. How could the Federal Reserve use the interest rate it pays on bank reserves to restrain banks from lending large amounts of excess reserves and increasing the money supply excessively? In addition, how could the term deposit facility, the Fed's other new policy tool, restrain banks from lending large amounts of excess reserves all at once?

3.9 The following statement appeared in a feature in the *New York Times* that provides an overview of the Federal Reserve System: "The federal funds rate is set by the Fed's Open Market Committee, composed of the chairman, the six other governors, and five of the 12 regional bank presidents, on a rotating basis." Do you agree that the federal funds rate is set by the FOMC? Briefly explain.

Source: "Federal Reserve System," *New York Times*, October 17, 2012.

3.10 [Related to the Making the Connection on page 462] In addition to commercial banks, other financial institutions, such as Fannie Mae, Freddie Mac, and the Federal Home Loan Banks borrow and lend in the federal funds market. (The 12 Federal Home Loan Banks were created by Congress to raise funds in financial markets and make loans to local financial institutions to enable them to make mortgage and other loans.) Unlike commercial banks, these other financial institutions that can borrow and lend in the federal funds market are not eligible to receive interest on deposits with the Federal Reserve.

a. An article by two Federal Reserve economists notes that "the Federal Home Loan Banks use the federal funds market to warehouse liquidity to meet unexpected borrowing demands from members. . . ." What are the implications of this observation for the possibility that the equilibrium federal funds rate might drop below the interest rate the Fed pays on reserve deposits?

b. If only banks could borrow and lend in the federal funds market, explain why the actual federal funds rate could not drop below the interest rate the Fed pays on reserve deposits.

Source: Morten L. Bech and Elizabeth Klee, "The Mechanics of a Graceful Exit: Interest on Reserves and Segmentation in the Federal Funds Market," *Journal of Monetary Economics*, Vol. 58, No. 5, July 2011, pp. 415–31.

3.11 During the financial crisis of 2007–2009, the Fed set up the following temporary lending facilities: the Primary Dealer Credit Facility, the Term Securities Lending Facility, the Commercial Paper Funding Facility, and the Term Asset-Backed Securities Loan Facility. Review the discussion of each lending facility in the text. Indicate which type of institutions each lending facility was designed to help and which type of financial assets were involved with each lending facility.

15.4 Monetary Targeting and Monetary Policy
Explain the role of monetary targeting in monetary policy.

Review Questions

4.1 What trade-offs does the Fed face, particularly in the short run, in attempting to reach its goals?

4.2 What two timing difficulties does the Fed face in using its monetary policy tools?

4.3 Place the following in sequence, from what the Fed has the most influence on to what the Fed has the least influence on: policy goals, policy tools, policy instruments, intermediate targets.

4.4 How can the Taylor rule be used as a guide to evaluating Federal Reserve monetary policy over time?

4.5 Briefly describe the role of targeting in the monetary policies of the Bank of Canada, the Bank of England, the Bank of Japan, and the European Central Bank.

Problems and Applications

4.6 State whether each of the following variables is most likely to be a goal, an intermediate target, an operating target, or a monetary policy tool:

a. M2

b. Monetary base

c. Unemployment rate

d. Open market purchases

e. Federal funds rate

f. Nonborrowed reserves

g. M1

h. Real GDP

i. Discount rate

j. Inflation rate

4.7 If the Fed uses the federal funds rate as a policy instrument, will increases in the demand for reserves lead to an increase or a decrease in the level of reserves? If the Fed uses the level of reserves as a policy instrument, will increases in the demand for reserves lead to an increase or a decrease in the federal funds rate? Support your answers with a graph of the demand and supply of reserves.

4.8 [Related to the Making the Connection on page 470] What legislative changes and financial innovations occurred after 1979 that affected M1? How did these changes affect the short-run link between money and inflation?

4.9 [Related to the Making the Connection on page 470] Writing in the *Wall Street Journal* in 2012, a hedge fund manager observes: "With inflationary expectations not yet unsettled by the Federal Reserve's $2 trillion balance-sheet expansion, Mr. Bernanke has committed the Fed to an open-ended round of quantitative easing. . . ."

a. Why might "inflationary expectations" have been unsettled by the increase in the Fed's balance sheet? Why weren't inflationary expectations unsettled by the increase?

b. What does the author mean by Bernanke's "open-ended round of quantitative easing"? Would the Fed have been likely to engage in a third round of quantitative easing in 2012 if inflationary expectations had become unsettled? Briefly explain.

Source: Sean Fieler, "Easy Money Is Punishing the Middle Class," *Wall Street Journal*, September 26, 2012.

4.10 In a column in the *Wall Street Journal*, two economists at the Council on Foreign Relations argue: "Simply put, the Fed must choose between managing the level of reserves and managing rates. It cannot do both." Do you agree? Briefly explain.

Source: Benn Steil and Paul Swartz, "Bye-Bye to the Fed-Funds Rate," *Wall Street Journal*, August 19, 2010.

4.11 Using the Taylor rule, calculate the target for the federal funds rate for October 2012, using the following information: equilibrium real federal funds rate of 2%, target inflation rate of 2%, current inflation rate of 1.2%, and an output gap of 5.9%. In your calculations, the inflation gap is negative if the current inflation rate is below the target inflation rate. How does the targeted federal funds rate calculated using the Taylor rule compare to the actual federal funds rate of 0% to 0.25%?

4.12 John Taylor has argued that: "Considerable empirical work supports the view that interest rates were too low for too long in 2003-2005 and

were a major factor in the housing boom and bust that resulted."

a. What evidence is there that interest rates were too low in 2003–2005?

b. How might interest rates that were too low in 2003–2005 have contributed to the housing boom and bust?

Source: John Taylor, *First Principles: Five Keys to Restoring America's Prosperity*, New York: W.W. Norton & Company, 2012, p. 133.

Data Exercises

D15.1: **[Following news of FOMC meetings]** Go to www.federalreserve.gov, the Web site for the Federal Reserve Board of Governors, and read the most recent Federal Open Market Committee (FOMC) press release. At the Web site, select "Monetary Policy" at the top of the screen and then select "Federal Open Market Committee" on the far left of the screen. Select "Meeting Calendars, Statement, and Minutes." Finally, scroll down and select Statement for the date of the most recent FOMC meeting. Answer the following questions on the basis of the FOMC press release:

a. Did the FOMC change the target for the federal funds rate? If so, what was the change?

b. On balance, in its statement does the FOMC appear to be more concerned about slow economic growth or high inflation?

c. Did the FOMC change the interest rate paid on bank reserves?

d. Did the Fed announce any other monetary policy actions?

D15.2: **[Movements in the federal funds rate relative to the target]** Go to the Web site of the Federal Reserve Bank of St. Louis (FRED) (research.stlouisfed.org/fred2) and download and graph the data series for the effective federal funds rate

(DFF), the upper limit of the target range for the federal funds rate (DFEDTARU), and the lower limit for the target range (DFEDTARL). Plot values for all three data series from December 16, 2008 to the most recent day available on the same graph. Over this period, has the Fed been able to keep the effective federal funds rate within the target range? Briefly explain.

D15.3: Go to the Web site of the Bank of England, www.bankofengland.co.uk. The interactive database for the Bank of England has a section titled *Monetary financial institutions' balance sheets, income and expenditure*. That section has data on the Bank of England's balance sheet. What happened to the bank's balance sheet after 2007? How do these changes compare to the changes in the Fed's balance sheet during the same period?

D15.4: **[Movements in discount loans]** Go to the Web site of the Federal Reserve Bank of St. Louis (FRED) (research.stlouisfed.org/fred2) and download and graph the data series for discount loans (DISCBORR) from January 2000 until the most recent month available. Based only on these data, briefly explain when the financial crisis appears to have begun and when it ended.

MyEconLab Visit **www.myeconlab.com** to complete these exercises online and get instant feedback. Exercises that update with real-time data are marked with (W).

CHAPTER 16

The International Financial System and Monetary Policy

Learning Objectives

After studying this chapter, you should be able to:

16.1 Analyze how the Fed's interventions in foreign exchange markets affect the U.S. monetary base (pages 488–490)

16.2 Analyze how the Fed's interventions in foreign exchange markets affect the exchange rate (pages 490–494)

16.3 Understand how the balance of payments is calculated (pages 494–497)

16.4 Discuss the evolution of exchange rate regimes (pages 497–513)

Can the Euro Survive?

From the start, the euro was a gamble. The decision in 2002 by 12 sovereign countries to commit to using the same currency was an unprecedented experiment. Although there have been examples of smaller countries abandoning their own currencies to use the currency of a larger country, never before had economies as large as those of Germany, France, and Italy agreed to use a common currency. Of the four largest economies in Europe, only the United Kingdom declined to enter the "euro zone" and continued using its own currency. By 2012, 17 countries had adopted the euro. As we have seen, countries expect that their central banks will undertake monetary policy actions to reach key policy goals, such as price stability and full employment. But to undertake monetary policy, a country needs to control

its money supply. With the French franc, German deutsche mark, Italian lira, and other currencies no longer in existence, these countries have surrendered control of monetary policy to the European Central Bank (ECB). The ECB, not the central banks of the member countries, determines such key monetary policy variables as the overnight bank lending rate and the size of the monetary base.

During its first five years, the euro gamble seemed to be paying off. Businesses and households were benefitting from the cost savings of buying and selling goods and services across national borders without having to exchange currencies or worry about swings in the values of the currencies. With steady growth in output and employment, few people in euro countries complained about the ECB's conduct of monetary

Continued on next page

Key Issue and Question

Issue: The financial crisis led to controversy over the European Central Bank's monetary policy.

Question: Should European countries abandon using a common currency?

Answered on page 514

policy. But then the financial crisis of 2007–2009 hit. Although the crisis caused all countries in the euro zone to experience declines in output and employment, Greece, Spain, Portugal, and Ireland were hit particularly hard. Before the euro, the central banks of those countries would have responded to the recession by allowing their currencies to depreciate, thereby boosting exports and reducing imports. Each country also could have expanded its monetary base. But these options for fighting recession were no longer available. Compounding the problem was the fact that falling government revenues and increasing government spending were leading to large government budget deficits that could be met only by selling bonds—sovereign debt.

Investors became concerned that so much debt was being sold that the governments of Greece, Spain, and Italy in particular might default on their interest or principal payments. In 2012, the ECB took the unusual step of buying the debt of Spain and Italy. In addition, the governments of euro-zone countries agreed to give the ECB expanded powers to oversee banks in all member countries. These actions increased the likelihood that the system would hold together, although some economists and policymakers continued to argue that the euro was not sustainable in the long run.

Whatever the outcome, the saga of the euro illustrates the lengths to which countries are willing to go to achieve stability in exchange rates and the difficulties those countries can encounter.

Source: Brian Blackstone, "Europe Readies Bond Buying," *Wall Street Journal*, October 4, 2012; and James Kanter and Stephen Castle, "Leaders Say They Expect Agreement on Aid for Spanish Banks This Year," *New York Times*, October 18, 2012.

We have already described how the foreign exchange market operates (see Chapter 8). In this chapter, we focus on how the Fed and other central banks intervene in foreign exchange markets. We also describe different exchange rate systems, such as the euro, and how these systems affect domestic monetary policy. We begin by looking at how the actions the Fed takes in foreign exchange markets can affect the monetary base in the United States.

16.1

Learning Objective

Analyze how the Fed's interventions in foreign exchange markets affect the U.S. monetary base.

Foreign Exchange Intervention and the Monetary Base

In our analysis of the money supply process, we described the actions of three participants: the central bank, the banking system, and the nonbank public. However, because international financial markets are linked, foreign central banks, foreign banks, and foreign savers and borrowers can also affect the money supply in the United States. In particular, international financial transactions affect the money supply when central banks or governments try to influence the foreign exchange values of their currencies. As a result, such intervention may cause a conflict between the monetary policy goal of foreign exchange market stability and the policy goals of domestic price stability and economic growth.

The Federal Reserve and other central banks occasionally participate in international markets to affect the foreign exchange value of their nation's currency. A **foreign exchange market intervention** is a deliberate action by a central bank to influence the exchange rate. Foreign exchange market interventions alter a central bank's holdings of **international reserves**, which are assets that are denominated in a foreign currency and used in international transactions.

If the Fed wants the foreign exchange value of the dollar to rise, it can increase the demand for dollars by selling foreign assets and buying dollars in international currency markets. If the Fed wants the foreign exchange value of the dollar to fall, it can increase

Foreign exchange market intervention
A deliberate action by a central bank to influence the exchange rate.

International reserves
Central bank assets that are denominated in a foreign currency and used in international transactions.

the supply of dollars by selling dollars and buying foreign assets. Such transactions affect not only the value of the dollar but also the domestic monetary base. We can show how the monetary base is affected by using T-accounts to trace the effect of a foreign exchange market intervention on the Fed's balance sheet.

Suppose that in an effort to reduce the foreign exchange value of the dollar, the Fed buys foreign assets—such as short-term securities issued by foreign governments—worth a dollar value of $1 billion. This transaction increases the Fed's international reserves by $1 billion, so the entry for foreign assets on the Fed's balance sheet rises by $1 billion. If the Fed pays for the foreign assets by writing a check for $1 billion, it adds $1 billion to banks' reserve deposits at the Fed, which are a Fed liability. We can summarize the effect of this transaction on the Fed's balance sheet as follows:

FEDERAL RESERVE

Assets		Liabilities	
Foreign assets (international reserves)	+ $1 billion	Bank reserves at the Fed	+ $1 billion

Alternatively, the Fed could pay for the foreign assets with $1 billion of currency. Because currency in circulation also is a liability for the Fed, its liabilities still rise by $1 billion:

FEDERAL RESERVE

Assets		Liabilities	
Foreign assets (international reserves)	+ $1 billion	Currency in circulation	+ $1 billion

Because the monetary base equals the sum of currency and bank reserves, either transaction causes the monetary base to rise by the amount of the foreign assets (international reserves) purchased. *In other words, a purchase of foreign assets by a central bank has the same effect on the monetary base as an open market purchase of government bonds.* When a central bank buys foreign assets, its international reserves and the monetary base increase by the amount of foreign assets purchased.

Similarly, if the Fed in an effort to increase the foreign exchange value of the dollar sells foreign assets, the monetary base will decline, while the value of the dollar will rise. For instance, if the Fed sells $1 billion of short-term securities issued by foreign governments, the Fed's holdings of foreign assets will fall by $1 billion. At the same time, if the purchasers of the foreign assets sold by the Fed pay with checks drawn on U.S. banks, bank reserves at the Fed fall by $1 billion. The transaction affects the Fed's balance sheet as follows:

FEDERAL RESERVE

Assets		Liabilities	
Foreign assets (international reserves)	− $1 billion	Bank reserves at the Fed	− $1 billion

If the Fed instead purchased U.S. dollars with the proceeds of its sale of foreign assets, currency in circulation (another Fed liability) would fall by the value of the foreign assets sold. Because the monetary base is the sum of currency and reserves, it falls by the amount of foreign assets (international reserves) sold. Therefore, domestic bank reserves at the Fed or currency decline. *In other words, a sale of foreign assets by a central bank has the same effect on the monetary base as an open market sale of government bonds.* Purchases of domestic currency by a central bank financed by sales of foreign assets reduce international reserves and the monetary base by the amount of foreign assets sold.

When a central bank allows the monetary base to respond to the sale or purchase of domestic currency in the foreign exchange market, the transaction is called an **unsterilized foreign exchange intervention**. Alternatively, the central bank could use domestic open market operations to offset the change in the monetary base caused by a foreign exchange intervention. For example, consider a Fed sale of $1 billion of foreign assets. In the absence of any offsetting interventions, the monetary base falls by $1 billion. At the same time, however, the Fed could conduct an open market purchase of $1 billion of Treasury bills to eliminate the decrease in the monetary base arising from the foreign exchange intervention. The following T-account illustrates these transactions:

Unsterilized foreign exchange intervention
A foreign exchange market intervention in which the central bank does not offset the effect of the intervention on the monetary base.

Sterilized foreign exchange intervention
A foreign exchange market intervention in which the central bank offsets the effect of the intervention on the monetary base.

FEDERAL RESERVE

Assets		Liabilities	
Foreign assets (international reserves)	− $1 billion	Monetary base (currency plus reserves)	+ $0 billion
Treasury bills	+ $1 billion		

When a foreign exchange intervention is accompanied by offsetting domestic open market operations that leave the monetary base unchanged, it is called a **sterilized foreign exchange intervention**.

16.2

Learning Objective

Analyze how the Fed's interventions in foreign exchange markets affect the exchange rate.

Foreign Exchange Interventions and the Exchange Rate

Foreign exchange interventions can affect the domestic money supply, with potentially negative effects on the domestic economy. But central banks still occasionally intervene in foreign exchange markets because they seek to minimize fluctuations in exchange rates. A depreciating domestic currency raises the cost of foreign goods and may lead to inflation. As we saw in the previous section, central banks can attempt to limit depreciation by buying assets denominated in the domestic currency and selling foreign currency-denominated assets. An appreciating domestic currency can make a country's goods less competitive in world markets. Central banks attempt to limit appreciation by selling assets denominated in the domestic currency. In this section, we examine the effects of unsterilized and sterilized foreign exchange market interventions on the exchange rate.

Unsterilized Intervention

The exchange rate is determined by the demand and supply for dollars in the foreign exchange market (see Chapter 8). We can use demand and supply analysis to show the effects of central bank foreign exchange interventions on the exchange rate.

Assume that the Fed attempts to increase the exchange value of the dollar versus the Japanese yen through an unsterilized intervention. The Fed sells short-term Japanese government securities, which decreases the monetary base in the United States. The Fed has decreased the supply of dollars to the foreign exchange market, but a decrease in the monetary base will also raise U.S. interest rates (see Chapter 15). As U.S. interest rates rise relative to Japanese interest rates, foreign investors will demand more U.S. dollars in order to buy U.S. financial assets, and U.S. investors will want to buy fewer Japanese financial assets, so their supply of U.S. dollars in exchange for Japanese yen will fall. Panel (a) of Figure 16.1 shows the results of the demand curve for dollars in exchange for yen shifting to the right, from D_1 to D_2, and the supply curve shifting to the left, from S_1 to S_2. The equilibrium exchange rate increases from E_1 to E_2, indicating that the Fed has successfully increased the exchange value of the dollar. So, if nothing else changes, an unsterilized intervention in which the central bank sells foreign assets in exchange for domestic currency leads to a decrease in international reserves and in the monetary base and an appreciation of the domestic currency.

To lower the exchange rate with an unsterilized foreign exchange intervention, the Fed would buy short-term Japanese government securities, which increases the monetary base in the United States. As the monetary base increases, U.S. interest rates fall, causing the demand curve for dollars in exchange for yen to shift to the left and the supply curve of dollars to shift to the right. As panel (b) of Figure 16.1 shows, the result is a decrease in the equilibrium exchange rate. So, if nothing else changes, an unsterilized intervention in which the central bank buys foreign assets with domestic currency leads to an increase in international reserves and the monetary base and depreciation of the domestic currency.

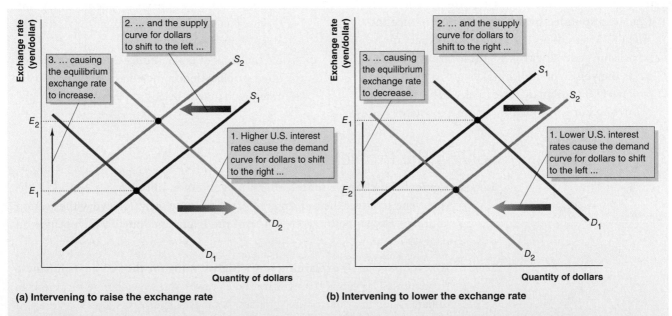

(a) Intervening to raise the exchange rate

(b) Intervening to lower the exchange rate

Figure 16.1 The Effect on the Exchange Rate of an Unsterilized Foreign Exchange Market Intervention

In panel (a), the Fed intervenes by selling short-term Japanese government securities. This action decreases the monetary base in the United States and raises U.S. interest rates. As a result, the demand for dollars in exchange for yen shifts to the right, from D_1 to D_2, and the supply of dollars shifts to the left, from S_1 to S_2. The equilibrium exchange rate increases from E_1 to E_2.

In panel (b), the Fed intervenes by buying short-term Japanese government securities. This action increases the monetary base in the United States and lowers U.S. interest rates. As a result, the demand for dollars in exchange for yen shifts to the left, from D_1 to D_2, and the supply of dollars shifts to the right, from S_1 to S_2. The equilibrium exchange rate decreases from E_1 to E_2. These two examples are both unsterilized interventions.

Sterilized Intervention

As we have seen, with a sterilized foreign exchange intervention, the central bank uses open market operations to offset the effects of the intervention on the monetary base. Because the monetary base is unaffected, domestic interest rates will not change. So, if the Fed sells short-term Japanese government securities but sterilizes the intervention by buying Treasury bills at the same time, U.S. interest rates will be unaffected. Therefore, the demand curve and supply curve for dollars in exchange for yen will also be unaffected, and the exchange rate will not change. We can conclude that a sterilized intervention does not affect the exchange rate. To be effective, central bank interventions that are intended to change the exchange rate need to be unsterilized.

Solved Problem 16.2

The Bank of Japan Counters the Rising Yen

In late 2012, the exchange rate between the yen and the U.S. dollar dropped below ¥78 = $1. An article in the *Wall Street Journal* noted that: "Weak economic data puts pressure on Japanese officials to fight the strong currency, which hurts exporters." The Bank of Japan responded by taking action to reduce the value of the yen. Another article noted that "monetary easing generally weakens the local currency."

a. Is the yen stronger if it takes more yen to buy one U.S. dollar or fewer yen? Why would a strong currency hurt Japanese exporters?

b. What is monetary easing? Would the Bank of Japan need to widen the gap between interest rates in Japan and the United States in order to reduce the value of the yen versus the dollar? In which direction would the gap have to widen? Use a graph of the market for yen in exchange for dollars to illustrate your answer.

c. Could the Bank of Japan reduce the value of the yen by buying dollar-denominated assets, leaving interest rates unchanged? Briefly explain.

Solving the Problem

Step 1 **Review the chapter material.** This problem is about how central banks intervene to affect the exchange rate, so you may want to review the section "Foreign Exchange Interventions and the Exchange Rate," which begins on page 490.

Step 2 **Answer part (a) by explaining why a higher value for the yen hurts Japanese exporters.** The yen is stronger if it takes fewer yen to exchange for one U.S. dollar. When the value of the yen rises, Japanese exporters, such as Toyota and Sony, face a difficult choice: raise the dollar prices of their products and suffer declining sales or keep the dollar prices unchanged and face declining profits. For example, suppose that Sony receives $200 from Best Buy and other U.S. retailers for each PlayStation 3 sold. If the exchange rate is ¥100 = $1, Sony receives ¥20,000 yen. But if the exchange rate is ¥80 = $1, Sony receives only ¥16,000—the difference between a comfortable profit and a loss.

Step 3 **Answer part (b) by explaining why the Bank of Japan would need to reduce interest rates in Japan relative to interest rates in the United States in order to reduce the exchange value of the yen. Draw a graph to illustrate your answer.** Monetary easing is another term for an expansionary monetary policy. Interest rates typically fall as a result of an expansionary monetary policy. If the Bank of Japan can reduce interest rates in Japan relative to interest rates in the United States, financial investments in Japan will become less desirable relative to financial investments in the United States. The graph below shows that lower Japanese interest rates will reduce the demand for yen in exchange for dollars from D_1 to D_2, and increase the supply of yen in exchange for dollars from S_1 to S_2. As a result, the equilibrium exchange rate will decline from E_1 to E_2. Notice that because you are drawing a graph from the perspective of the Bank of Japan, the vertical axis should be labeled "dollars/yen" rather than "yen/dollar."

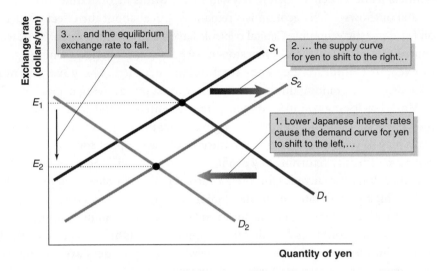

Step 4 **Answer part (c) by explaining that if the Bank of Japan carries out a sterilized intervention, the exchange rate will not change.** If the Bank of Japan were to intervene by purchasing U.S. dollar-denominated assets, such as Treasury bills, the effect on the Japanese monetary base would be the same as that of an open market purchase: The Japanese monetary base would rise, and Japanese interest rates would fall. This action would be an unsterilized intervention and would lower the exchange value of the yen. But if the Bank of Japan kept interest rates constant by engaging in an open market sale of Japanese government bonds at the same time that it purchased U.S. Treasury bills, this sterilized intervention would not reduce the exchange value of the yen.

Source: Nicole Hong, "Yen Rebounds on Dollar after BOJ Moves," *Wall Street Journal*, September 19, 2012; and Brian Baskin, "FX Global Call," *Wall Street Journal*, November 12, 2012.

See related problem 2.6 at the end of the chapter.

Capital Controls

Mexico suffered a *currency crisis* during 1994–1995, and several East Asian countries suffered currency crises during 1997–1998. During these crises, the countries involved suffered sharp declines in the exchange value of their currencies, which led to disruptions of their economies. These crises were fueled in part by sharp inflows and outflows of financial investments, or *capital inflows* and *capital outflows*, leading some economists and policymakers to advocate restrictions on capital mobility in emerging market countries. These restrictions, called **capital controls**, are government-imposed restrictions on foreign investors buying domestic assets or on domestic investors buying foreign assets. Capital controls also limit domestic investors' ability to diversify their portfolios internationally, leading those investors to require a higher expected return on domestic assets than on foreign assets.

Although capital outflows were an element of the currency crises—leading some political leaders such as then Malaysian Prime Minister Mahathir Mohamad to limit capital outflows—most economists remain skeptical about the effect of such controls on the domestic economy. Capital controls have significant problems. First, with capital controls, domestic firms and investors must receive permission from the government to exchange domestic currency for foreign currency. The government officials responsible for granting this permission may insist on receiving bribes before granting it. Most developing countries that have implemented capital controls have found that they result in a significant amount of government corruption. Second, multinational firms may be reluctant to invest in countries that have capital controls because the firms will have difficulty returning any profits they earn to their home countries if they can't exchange domestic currency for foreign currency. This problem is significant because to achieve high growth rates, many developing countries are dependent on the willingness of multinational firms to build factories and other facilities in their countries. Finally, in practice, many countries find that their capital controls are evaded by individuals and firms who resort to a black market where currency traders are willing to illegally exchange domestic currency for foreign currency.

Restrictions on capital inflows receive more support from some economists than do restrictions on capital outflows, in part because such inflows often lead to domestic lending booms and increased risk taking by domestic banks. Other economists point out that this problem could be made less severe by improving bank regulation and supervision in emerging-market countries. In this way, capital inflows could still serve as important financial mechanisms for channeling foreign investment to countries with promising investment opportunities.

Capital controls
Government-imposed restrictions on foreign investors buying domestic assets or on domestic investors buying foreign assets.

16.3

Learning Objective
Understand how the balance of payments is calculated.

The Balance of Payments

In describing the Fed's foreign exchange market interventions, we simply noted the increase or decrease in international reserves on the Fed's balance sheet, without discussing why the Fed holds international reserves or what factors account for the size of its reserve holdings. Transactions in international reserves are one of several capital flows between the United States and other countries. To understand how the Fed accumulates international reserves and how much it has available for foreign exchange market interventions, we must look at the broader flow of funds between the United States and foreign countries. We can use the balance of payments account to understand international capital flows. The **balance-of-payments account** measures all flows of private and government funds between a domestic economy (in this case, the United States) and all foreign countries.

The balance of payments for the United States is a bookkeeping procedure similar to ones that households or firms might use to record receipts and payments. In the balance of payments, inflows of funds from foreigners to the United States are receipts, which are recorded as positive numbers. Receipts include inflows of funds for purchases of U.S.-produced goods and services (U.S. exports), for acquisition of U.S. assets (capital inflows), and as gifts to U.S. citizens (unilateral transfers).

Outflows of funds from the United States to foreigners are payments, which are recorded with a minus sign. Payments include:

1. Purchases of foreign goods and services (imports)
2. Money spent on purchases of foreign assets by U.S. households and businesses (capital outflows)
3. Gifts to foreigners, including foreign aid (unilateral transfers)

The principal components of the balance-of-payments account summarize transactions for purchases and sales of goods and services (the *current account balance*, which includes the *trade balance*) and flows of funds for international lending or borrowing (the *financial account balance*, which includes *official settlements*).

Each international transaction represents an exchange of goods, services, or assets among households, firms, or governments. Therefore, the two sides of the exchange must always balance. In other words, the payments and receipts of the balance-of-payments account must equal zero, or:

$$\text{Current account balance } + \text{ Financial account balance} = 0.$$

The Current Account

The current account summarizes transactions between a country and its foreign trading partners for purchases and sales of currently produced goods and services. If the United States has a current account surplus (a positive number), U.S. citizens are selling more goods and services to foreigners than they are buying imports from foreigners. Therefore, U.S. citizens have funds to lend to foreigners. Typically, the U.S. current account has a negative balance, or is in deficit. In 2011, the United States had a current account deficit of $473.6 billion. When the United States has a current account deficit, it must borrow the difference to pay for goods and services purchased abroad. In general, a current account surplus or deficit must be balanced by international lending or borrowing or by changes in official reserve transactions. Policymakers have been concerned that the large U.S. current account deficits in the 1980s, 1990s, and 2000s have caused the United States to rely heavily on savings from abroad—international borrowing—to finance domestic consumption, investment, and the federal budget deficit. By the mid-2000s, U.S. policymakers and economists became particularly concerned about the country's growing reliance on funds from foreign central banks as opposed to private investors.

One reason for the U.S. current account deficits in the 2000s may have been a global "saving glut." The saving glut was partly the result of high rates of saving in countries such as Japan, which had aging populations that increased their saving as they prepared for retirement. In addition, the level of global saving increased because beginning in the late 1990s, developing countries such as China, Korea, and other Asian countries, as well as some countries in Eastern Europe, increased their saving as their incomes began to rise. With high saving rates and relatively limited opportunities for investment, funds from these countries flowed into the United States, bidding up the value of the dollar. The high value of the dollar reduced U.S. exports and increased imports, contributing to the current account deficit.

The Financial Account

The financial account measures trade in existing financial or real assets among countries. When someone in a country sells an asset (a skyscraper, a bond, or shares of stock, for example) to a foreign investor, the transaction is recorded in the balance-of-payments accounts as a capital inflow because funds flow into the country to buy the asset. When someone in a country buys an asset abroad, the transaction is recorded in the balance-of-payments accounts as a capital outflow because funds flow from the country to buy the asset. For example, when a wealthy Chinese entrepreneur buys a penthouse apartment in New York's Trump Tower, the transaction is recorded as a capital outflow for China and as a capital inflow for the United States.

The financial account balance is the amount of capital inflows minus capital outflows—plus the net value of *capital account* transactions, which consist mainly of debt forgiveness and transfers of financial assets by migrants when they enter the United States.[1] The financial account balance is in surplus if the citizens of the country sell more assets to foreigners than they buy from foreigners. The financial account balance is in deficit if the citizens of the country buy more assets from foreigners than they sell to foreigners. In 2011, the United States had capital inflows of $790.5 billion and capital outflows of $396.4 billion (plus net capital account transactions of −$1.1 billion) for a net financial account balance of $394.1 billion. This financial account balance represents an increase in U.S. assets held by foreigners.

Official Settlements

Not all capital flows among countries represent transactions by households and firms. Changes in asset holdings by governments and central banks supplement private capital flows. *Official reserve assets* are assets that central banks hold and that they use in making

---

[1]The capital account is a third, less important, part of the balance of payments. The capital account records relatively minor transactions, such as debt forgiveness, migrants' transfers—which consist of goods and financial assets people take with them when they leave or enter a country—and sales and purchases of nonproduced, nonfinancial assets. A nonproduced, nonfinancial asset is a copyright, patent, trademark, or right to natural resources. The definitions of the financial account and the capital account are often misunderstood because the capital account prior to 1999 recorded all the transactions included now in both the financial account and the capital account. In other words, capital account transactions went from being a very important part of the balance of payments to being a relatively unimportant part. Because the balance on what is now called the capital account is so small, for simplicity we merge it with the financial account here.

international payments to settle the balance of payments and to conduct international monetary policy. Historically, gold was the leading official reserve asset. Official reserves now are primarily government securities of the United States and other high-income countries, foreign bank deposits, and assets called Special Drawing Rights created by the International Monetary Fund (an international agency that we discuss later in this chapter). Official settlements equal the net increase (domestic holdings minus foreign holdings) in a country's official reserve assets.

The official settlements balance is sometimes called the *balance-of-payments surplus or deficit*. This terminology may be somewhat confusing. Earlier we saw that the balance of payments equals the sum of the current account and the financial account and is, therefore, always zero. An alternative way of thinking of the balance of payments is to exclude the official settlements balance from the financial account. This exclusion makes it possible for a country to have a balance of payments surplus or deficit. From this perspective, in 2011, the United States had a significant balance-of-payments deficit. When a country has a balance-of-payments surplus in this sense, it gains international reserves because its receipts exceed its payments. That is, foreign central banks provide the country's central bank with international reserves. When a country has a balance-of-payments deficit in this sense, it loses international reserves. Because U.S. dollars and dollar-denominated assets serve as the largest component of international reserves, a U.S. balance-of-payments deficit can be financed by a reduction in U.S. international reserves and an increase in dollar assets held by foreign central banks. Similarly, a combination of an increase in U.S. international reserves and a decrease in dollar assets held by foreign central banks can offset a U.S. balance-of-payments surplus.

The Relationship Among the Accounts

Recall that, in principle, the current account balance and financial account balance sum to zero. In reality, measurement problems keep this relationship from holding exactly. An adjustment for measurement errors, the statistical discrepancy, is reported in the financial account portion of the balance-of-payments accounts. In 2011, it equaled $80.6 billion (a capital inflow). Many analysts believe that large statistical discrepancies in countries' balance-of-payments accounts reflect hidden capital flows related to illegal activity, tax evasion, or capital flight because of political risk.

To summarize, international trade and financial transactions affect both the current account and the financial account in the balance of payments. To close out a country's international transactions from the balance of payments, its central bank and foreign central banks engage in official reserve transactions, which can affect the monetary base.

Exchange Rate Regimes and the International Financial System

The Fed and other central banks engage in foreign exchange market interventions to maintain the foreign exchange value of their nations' currencies. Political agreements influence the size and timing of each central bank's purchases and sales of international reserves. Specifically, countries may agree to participate in a particular

16.4

Learning Objective

Discuss the evolution of exchange rate regimes.

Exchange rate regime
A system for adjusting exchange rates and flows of goods and capital among countries.

exchange rate regime, or system for adjusting exchange rates and flows of goods and capital among countries. At times, countries have agreed to fix exchange rates among their national currencies, and these agreements have committed their central banks to act to maintain these exchange rates. At other times, countries have allowed exchange rates to fluctuate according to movements in demand and supply for different currencies, although central banks may still act to limit exchange-rate fluctuations. In this section, we analyze exchange rate regimes in terms of (1) how the agreement holds the system together, (2) how exchange rates adjust to maintain the agreement, and (3) how central banks act to maintain equilibrium in the international monetary and financial system. We also evaluate the successes and failures of each system.

Fixed Exchange Rates and the Gold Standard

Fixed exchange rate system A system in which exchange rates are set at levels determined and maintained by governments.

Gold standard A fixed exchange rate system under which currencies of participating countries are convertible into an agreed-upon amount of gold.

In the past, most exchange rate regimes were **fixed exchange rate systems**, in which exchange rates were set at levels that were determined and maintained by governments. Under a **gold standard**, currencies of participating countries are convertible into an agreed-upon amount of gold. The exchange rates between any two countries' currencies are fixed by their relative gold weights. The classical gold standard that prevailed from the late nineteenth century to the outbreak of World War I in 1914 illustrates the successes and failures of a fixed exchange rate system. Figure 16.2 shows the spread of the gold standard between 1870 and 1913.

Consider an example of how the gold standard operated: If $1 could be exchanged for 1/20 of an ounce of gold, while FF1 (1 French franc) could be exchanged for 1/80 of an ounce of gold, the exchange rate would be $1 = FF4, or $0.25 = FF1. Now let's consider an example of trade and capital flows between France and the United States to illustrate how this system of fixed exchange rates worked. Under a gold standard, a U.S. importer could buy goods from a French exporter by either (1) exchanging dollars for French francs in France and buying goods or (2) exchanging dollars for gold in the United States and shipping gold to France to buy francs and French goods.

Suppose that the demand for French goods rises relative to the demand for U.S. goods, leading to a rising demand for francs and a falling demand for dollars. The result is pressure for the exchange rate in francs per dollar to fall—say, from $1 = FF4 to $1 = FF3. In this situation, U.S. importers could make a profit from shipping gold to France to buy francs, as long as the governments of the United States and France continued to exchange currencies for gold at the agreed-upon rate.

Therefore, if Sally Sharp, a cloth importer in Philadelphia, wants to buy FF5,000 worth of cloth from Deluxe of Paris, she can use either of the two strategies described. First, if she tries to sell dollars for francs in the foreign exchange market, she will find that she must pay FF5,000 ÷ (3FF per $) = $1,666.67 for the cloth. Alternatively, she can exchange $1,250 for gold, ship the gold bars to France, and demand that the Bank of France exchange the gold for francs at the fixed exchange rate. At the official exchange rate of $1 = FF4, she will receive FF5,000 for her gold, which is enough to buy the cloth. The second strategy provides the cheaper solution for Sally. Her saving on this transaction, $416.67, makes it the better way to buy the cloth, as long as the cost of shipping the gold from Philadelphia to France does not exceed $416.67.

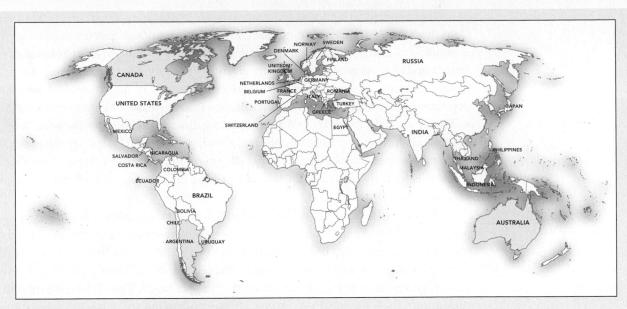

(a) Countries on the gold standard in 1870.

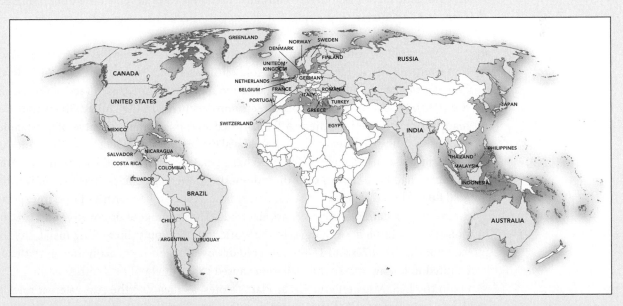

(b) Countries on the gold standard in 1913.

Figure 16.2 The Spread of the Gold Standard

In 1870, the only countries on the gold standard were those shaded in yellow: Great Britain, Canada, Australia, Portugal, Argentina, and Uruguay. By 1913, most countries in Europe and the Western Hemisphere were on the gold standard. By the late 1930s, the gold standard had disappeared. Note that countries are shown with their current borders.

Source: Maps prepared by authors from information in Christopher M. Meissner, "A New World Order: Explaining the International Diffusion of the Classical Gold Standard, 1870–1913," *Journal of International Economics*, Vol. 66, No. 2, July 2005, Table 1, p. 391.

What happens in France as U.S. importers like Sally Sharp ship their gold to Paris? Gold flows into France, expanding that country's international reserves because gold is eventually exchanged for francs. The United States loses an equivalent amount of international reserves because dollars are given to the government in exchange for gold. An increase in a country's international reserves increases its monetary base, whereas a decrease in its international reserves lowers its monetary base. The monetary base rises in France and falls in the United States, putting upward pressure on the price level in France and downward pressure on the price level in the United States. French goods become more expensive relative to U.S. goods. Therefore, the relative demand for French goods falls, restoring the trade balance and causing the exchange rate to rise toward the official rate of $1 = FF4$.

Alternatively, if the relative demand for U.S. goods rises, market forces put upward pressure on the exchange rate. Gold then flows from France to the United States, reducing the French monetary base and increasing the U.S. monetary base. In this case, the accompanying increase in the U.S. price level relative to the French price level makes French goods more attractive, restoring the trade balance. The exchange rate moves back toward the fixed rate of $1 = FF4$. So, we can conclude that the gold standard had an automatic mechanism that would cause exchange rates to reflect the underlying gold content of countries' currencies. This automatic mechanism was called the *price-specie flow mechanism*.

One problem with the economic adjustment process under the gold standard was that countries with trade deficits and gold outflows experienced declines in price levels, or deflation. Periods of unexpected and pronounced deflation caused recessions. During the 1870s, 1880s, and 1890s, several recessions occurred in the United States that were made more severe by deflation. A falling price level raised the real value of households' and firms' nominal debts, leading to financial distress for many sectors of the economy.

Another consequence of fixed exchange rates under the gold standard was that countries had little control over their domestic monetary policies. The reason was that gold flows caused changes in the monetary base. As a result, countries faced unexpected inflation or deflation from international trade. Moreover, gold discoveries and production strongly influenced changes in the world money supply, increasing instability. For example, in the 1870s and 1880s, few gold discoveries and rapid economic growth contributed to falling prices. This deflation caused substantial political unrest among farmers in the U.S. Midwest and Great Plains states, as they saw the real interest rates on their mortgages rise. In the 1890s, on the other hand, the gold rushes in Alaska and what is now South Africa increased price levels around the world.

In theory, the gold standard required that all countries maintain their promise to convert currencies freely into gold at fixed exchange rates. In practice, England made the exchange rate regime's promise credible. The strength of the British economy, its frequent trade surpluses, and its large gold reserves made England the anchor of the international monetary and financial system. During World War I, the disruption of the international trading system led countries to abandon their promises to convert currency into gold. The gold standard had a brief revival during the period between the two world wars but finally collapsed in the 1930s, during the Great Depression.

Making the Connection

Did the Gold Standard Make the Great Depression Worse?

When the Great Depression began in 1929, governments came under pressure to abandon the gold standard in order to allow their central banks to pursue expansionary monetary policies. In 1931, Britain became the first major country to abandon the gold standard. A number of other countries also went off the gold standard that year. The United States remained on the gold standard until 1933, and a few countries, including France, Italy, and Belgium, stayed on even longer. By the late 1930s, the gold standard had collapsed.

The earlier a country went off the gold standard, the easier time it had fighting the Depression with expansionary monetary policies. As the figure shows, the countries that abandoned the gold standard before 1933 suffered an average decline in industrial production of only 3% between 1929 and 1934. The countries that stayed on the gold standard until 1933 or later suffered an average decline of more than 30%.

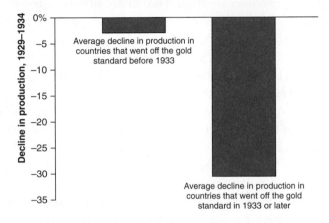

Why did countries that stayed on the gold standard suffer worse effects from the Great Depression? A key reason is that to remain on the gold standard, central banks often had to take actions that contracted production and employment rather than expanding them. For example, the United States experienced gold outflows during 1930 and 1931. The Fed attempted to stem the outflows by raising the discount rate because higher interest rates would make financial investments in the United States more attractive to foreign investors. Higher interest rates, though effective in stemming the gold outflow and keeping the United States on the gold standard, were the opposite of the lower interest rates needed to stimulate domestic spending. The United States did not begin to recover from the Depression until March 1933, the same month that it left the gold standard.

The devastating economic performance of the countries that stayed on the gold standard the longest during the 1930s is the key reason that policymakers did not attempt to bring back the classical gold standard in later years.

Sources: Ben Bernanke and Harold James, "The Gold Standard, Deflation, and Financial Crisis in the Great Depression: An International Comparison," in R. Glenn Hubbard, ed., *Financial Markets and*

Financial Crises, Chicago: University of Chicago Press, 1991; Barry Eichengreen, *Golden Fetters: The Gold Standard and the Great Depression 1919–1939*, New York: Oxford University Press, 1992; dates for abandoning the gold standard used in the figure from Melchior Palyi, *The Twilight of Gold, 1914–1936*, Chicago: Henry Regnery, 1972, Table IV-I, pp. 116–117; the change in production in the figure is the change in industrial production from League of Nations, *World Production and Prices, 1925–1934*, Geneva: League of Nations, 1935, Appendix II, Table 1, p. 133.

See related problem 4.7 at the end of the chapter.

Adapting Fixed Exchange Rates: The Bretton Woods System

Despite the gold standard's demise, many countries remained interested in the concept of fixed exchange rates. As World War II drew to a close, representatives of the United States, the United Kingdom, France, and other Allied governments gathered at Bretton Woods, New Hampshire, to design a new international monetary and financial system. The resulting agreement, known as the **Bretton Woods system**, lasted from 1945 until 1971. Framers of the agreement intended to reinstate a system of fixed exchange rates but wanted to permit smoother short-term economic adjustments than were possible under the gold standard. The United States agreed to convert U.S. dollars into gold at a price of $35 per ounce—but only in dealing with foreign central banks. U.S. citizens would not be able to redeem dollars for gold. The central banks of all other members of the system pledged to buy and sell their currencies at fixed rates against the dollar. By fixing their exchange rates against the dollar, these countries were fixing the exchange rates among their currencies as well. The United States was given a special role in the system because of its dominant position in the global economy at that time and because the country held much of the world's gold. Because central banks used dollar assets and gold as international reserves, the dollar was known as the *international reserve currency*.

Under the Bretton Woods system, exchange rates were supposed to adjust only when a country experienced fundamental disequilibrium—that is, persistent deficits or surpluses in its balance of payments at the fixed exchange rate. To help countries make a short-run economic adjustment to a balance-of-payments deficit or surplus while maintaining a fixed exchange rate, the Bretton Woods agreement created the **International Monetary Fund (IMF)**. Headquartered in Washington, DC, this multinational organization grew from 29 member countries in 1945 to 188 in 2012. In principle, the IMF was to administer the Bretton Woods system and to be a lender of last resort to ensure that short-term economic dislocations did not undermine the stability of the fixed exchange-rate system. In practice, the IMF—which survived the demise of the Bretton Woods system—also encourages domestic economic policies that are consistent with exchange-rate stability and gathers and standardizes international economic and financial data to use in monitoring member countries.

Although the IMF no longer attempts to foster fixed exchange rates (its core Bretton Woods system function), its activities as an international lender of last resort have grown. During the developing world debt crises of the 1980s, the IMF provided credit to such countries to help them repay their loans. IMF lending during the Mexican financial crisis of 1994–1995 and the East Asian financial crisis of 1997–1998 inspired major controversy over its role in the international financial system.

Bretton Woods system
An exchange rate system that lasted from 1945 to 1971, under which countries pledged to buy and sell their currencies at fixed rates against the dollar and the United States pledged to convert dollars into gold if foreign central banks requested it to.

International Monetary Fund (IMF) A multinational organization established in 1944 by the Bretton Woods agreement to administer a system of fixed exchange rates and to serve as a lender of last resort to countries undergoing balance-of-payments problems.

Advocates of IMF intervention point to the need for a lender of last resort in emerging-market financial crises. Critics of the IMF raise two counterarguments. The first is that the IMF encourages moral hazard, in the form of excessive risk taking, by bailing out foreign lenders. According to this view, the IMF's bailout of foreign lenders in the Mexican crisis encouraged risky lending to East Asian countries, precipitating that crisis. The second argument is that, in contrast to the IMF's treatment of foreign lenders, the institution's "austerity" programs in developing countries focus on reducing government spending and raising interest rates, which are macroeconomic policies that can lead to unemployment and political upheaval.

Fixed Exchange Rates Under Bretton Woods Central bank interventions in the foreign exchange market to buy and sell dollar assets maintained the fixed exchange rates of the Bretton Woods system. Exchange rates could vary by 1% above or below the fixed rate before countries were required to intervene to stabilize them. If a foreign currency appreciated relative to the dollar, the central bank of that country would sell its own currency for dollars, thereby driving the exchange rate back to the fixed rate. If a foreign currency depreciated relative to the dollar, the central bank would sell dollar assets from its international reserves and buy its own currency to push the exchange rate back toward the fixed rate.

In general, a central bank can maintain a fixed exchange rate as long as it is willing and able to buy and sell the amounts of its own currency that are necessary for exchange rate stabilization. When a foreign central bank buys its own currency, it sells dollars (international reserves). When a foreign central bank sells its own currency, it buys dollars. The result is an important asymmetry in central banks' adjustments in response to market pressures on the exchange rate. A country with a balance-of-payments surplus has no constraint on its ability to sell its own currency to buy dollars to maintain the exchange rate. However, a country with a balance-of-payments deficit has its ability to buy its own currency (to raise its value relative to the dollar) limited by the country's stock of international reserves. As a result, reserve outflows caused by balance-of-payments deficits created problems for central banks that were bound by the Bretton Woods system. When a country's stock of international reserves was exhausted, the central bank and the government would have to implement restrictive economic policies, such as increasing interest rates, to reduce imports and the trade deficit or abandon the policy of stabilizing the exchange rate against the dollar.

Devaluations and Revaluations Under Bretton Woods Under the Bretton Woods system, a country could defend its fixed exchange rate by buying or selling reserves or changing domestic economic policies, or it could petition the IMF to be allowed to change its exchange rate. When its currency was overvalued relative to the dollar, with agreement from the IMF, the country could **devalue** its currency—that is, lower the official value of its currency relative to the dollar. A country whose currency was undervalued relative to the dollar could **revalue** its currency—that is, raise the official value of its currency relative to the dollar.[2]

Devaluation The lowering of the official value of a country's currency relative to other currencies.

Revaluation The raising of the official value of a country's currency relative to other currencies.

---

[2]Recall that in a flexible exchange rate system, a falling value of the exchange rate is known as *depreciation* and a rising value of the exchange rate is known as *appreciation*.

In practice, countries didn't often pursue devaluations or revaluations. Under the Bretton Woods system, governments preferred to postpone devaluations rather than face political charges that their monetary policies were flawed. Revaluations were an even less popular choice. Domestic producers and their workers complained vigorously when the value of the currency was allowed to rise against the dollar because domestic goods became less competitive in world markets, reducing profits and employment. The political pressures against devaluations and revaluations meant governments changed their exchange rates only in response to severe imbalances in the foreign exchange market.

Speculative Attacks in the Bretton Woods System When investors came to believe that a government was unwilling or unable to maintain its exchange rate, they attempted to profit by selling a weak currency or buying a strong currency. These actions, known as *speculative attacks*, could force a devaluation or revaluation of the currency. Speculative attacks can produce international financial crises. Such an attack occurred in 1967, when the British pound was overvalued relative to the dollar. Figure 16.3 illustrates the speculative attack that took place against the pound. The intersection of the demand and supply for British pounds in exchange for dollars occurs at E_1, which is lower than the fixed exchange rate of £1 = $2.80. The result was a surplus of pounds in exchange for dollars. To defend the overvalued exchange rate, the Bank of England had to buy the surplus pounds equal to $Q_2 - Q_1$, using dollars from its international reserves.

As the Bank of England's international reserves shrank, currency traders knew that, at some point, the bank would have to abandon its stabilization efforts. Speculators responded by selling pounds, including pounds borrowed from banks, to the Bank of England at the fixed exchange rate of $2.80/£1, expecting the pound to fall in value

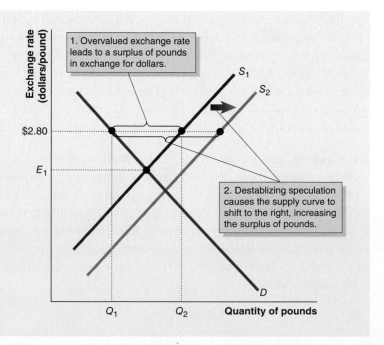

Figure 16.3

The Speculative Attack on the British Pound

The intersection of the demand and supply curves for British pounds in exchange for dollars occurred at E_1, which was below the fixed exchange rate of £1 = $2.80. The result was a surplus of pounds in exchange for dollars. To defend the overvalued exchange rate, the Bank of England had to buy the surplus pounds equal to $Q_2 - Q_1$, using dollars from its international reserves. Speculators became convinced that England would devalue the pound, which caused the supply of pounds to shift from S_1 to S_2, increasing the overvaluation.

against the dollar. When the pound did eventually fall in value, the speculators used dollars to buy back the now cheaper pounds, thereby earning a substantial profit. In terms of our graphical analysis, speculators were causing the supply of pounds to shift from S_1 to S_2, which caused the overvaluation of the pound to increase. This difference between the fixed and market exchange rates forced the Bank of England to buy even more pounds, until it ran out of dollars. On November 17, 1967, the Bank of England lost more than $1 billion of international reserves (on top of earlier losses of several billion dollars). On November 18, it devalued the pound by 14%.

Devaluations are forced by speculative attacks when a central bank is *unable* to defend the exchange rate, as in England's 1967 crisis. Revaluations, on the other hand, can be forced by speculative attacks when a central bank is *unwilling* to defend the exchange rate. A speculative attack on the undervalued deutsche mark in 1971 led to a revaluation of the mark against the dollar and hastened the demise of the Bretton Woods system.

The Speculative Attack on the Deutsche Mark and the Collapse of Bretton Woods By 1970, the U.S. balance-of-payments deficit had grown significantly. By the first quarter of 1971, the large balance-of-payments surpluses outside the United States were causing fear in international financial markets because many currencies were undervalued relative to the dollar. Worries were greatest in West Germany, as the Bundesbank (the German central bank) pursued policies to maintain a low inflation rate. The Bundesbank faced a dilemma. Because the German deutsche mark was undervalued against the dollar, if the Bundesbank defended the fixed exchange rate, it would have to sell marks and buy dollars in the foreign exchange market. By doing so, it would acquire international reserves, increasing the German monetary base and putting upward pressure on German prices. If Germany revalued the mark, it would avoid inflationary pressures but would break its promise under the Bretton Woods system and upset German firms that relied on exports to the United States.

The Bundesbank's dilemma set the stage for a speculative attack on the mark. In this case, speculators bought marks with dollars, expecting the mark to rise in value against the dollar. When the mark did rise, the speculators used the marks to buy back the now cheaper dollars, thereby earning a profit. By 1971, many investors were convinced that the Bundesbank would soon have to abandon the fixed exchange rate of $0.27 = DM1. On May 5, 1971, the Bundesbank purchased more than 1 billion U.S. dollars, expanding its monetary base by the same amount. Afraid that continued increases in the monetary base would spark inflation, the Bundesbank halted its intervention later that day. The mark began to *float* against the dollar, with its value being determined solely by the forces of demand and supply in the foreign exchange market.

The decision by the Bundesbank to abandon the fixed exchange rate against the dollar was a blow to the Bretton Woods system, but the system had even more fundamental problems. As U.S. inflation increased and U.S. balance-of-payments deficits mounted in the late 1960s, foreign central banks acquired large amounts of dollar-denominated assets. The Bretton Woods system was held together by the U.S. promise to exchange foreign central banks' dollars for gold at $35 per ounce. By 1971, however, the dollar assets that foreign central banks owned totaled more than three times the official U.S. gold holdings at the rate of $35 per ounce of gold. On August 15, 1971, the Nixon administration attempted to force revaluations of other currencies against the dollar. The United States suspended the convertibility of dollars into gold and imposed tariffs on imports that would be reduced only if a country revalued its exchange rate. This process of revaluations against the dollar was completed at the Smithsonian Conference in December 1971.

The exchange rate conditions that were agreed to at the Smithsonian Conference were not stable in the face of world events, however. In practice, many currencies began to float, although central banks intervened to prevent large fluctuations in exchange rates. At its January 1976 conference in Jamaica, the IMF formally agreed to allow currencies to float. At that conference, IMF members also agreed to eliminate gold's official role in the international monetary system.

In 1970, even before countries formally abandoned the Bretton Woods system, the IMF had begun issuing a paper substitute for gold. The IMF created these international reserves, known as *Special Drawing Rights* (*SDRs*), in its role as lender of last resort. The price of gold is now determined the same way that the prices of other commodities are determined—by the forces of demand and supply in the market.

To summarize, the Bretton Woods system was a fixed exchange-rate system with a lender of last resort to smooth out short-term economic adjustments in response to balance-of-payments deficits. The system eventually collapsed because the United States was not committed to price stability and because other countries were reluctant to revalue their currencies against the dollar, which led to strong market pressures on fixed exchange rates.

Central Bank Interventions After Bretton Woods

Flexible exchange rate system A system in which the foreign exchange value of a currency is determined in the foreign exchange market.

Since the demise of the Bretton Woods system, the United States has officially followed a **flexible exchange rate system**, in which the foreign exchange value of the dollar is determined in the foreign exchange market. Many other countries have followed the same course and allowed their exchange rates to float, or be determined by demand and supply. The Fed and foreign central banks have not, however, surrendered their right to intervene in the foreign exchange market when they believe that their currency is significantly undervalued or overvalued. For example, in 2012, the Bank of Japan intervened to buy U.S. dollars in exchange for yen in an attempt to lower the value of the yen against the dollar. The present international financial system is a **managed float regime** (also called a *dirty float regime*), in which central banks occasionally intervene to affect foreign exchange values. Therefore, international efforts to maintain exchange rates continue to affect domestic monetary policy.

Managed float regime An exchange rate system in which central banks occasionally intervene to affect foreign exchange values; also called a dirty float regime.

Policy Trade-Offs Central banks generally lose some control over the domestic money supply when they intervene in the foreign exchange market. To increase the exchange rate—that is, to make the domestic currency appreciate—a central bank must sell international reserves and buy the domestic currency, thereby reducing the domestic monetary base and money supply. To decrease the exchange rate, or make the domestic currency depreciate, a central bank must buy international reserves and sell the domestic currency, thereby increasing the domestic monetary base and money supply. So, a central bank often must decide between actions to achieve its goal for the domestic monetary base and interest rates and actions to achieve its goal for the exchange rate.

The Case of the U.S. Dollar Because of the traditional role of the dollar as an international reserve currency, U.S. monetary policy hasn't been severely hampered by foreign exchange market transactions. After the Bretton Woods system collapsed, the dollar retained its role as a reserve currency in the international monetary and financial system. During the 2000s, the euro and the Japanese yen increased in importance as reserve currencies. By 2012, though, the dollar still accounted for a majority of international reserves. Most economists believe that the U.S. dollar isn't likely to lose its position as the dominant reserve currency in the next decade.

Many industrial economies have high standards of living without the privilege of their currency being the reserve currency. Nonetheless, as the dollar has become less important as a reserve currency today than it was in 1962 or even 1992, many analysts believe that the United States has something to lose if the dollar is toppled from its reserve currency pedestal. Why?

First, U.S. households and firms might lose the advantage of being able to trade and borrow around the world in U.S. currency. This advantage translates into lower transactions costs and reduced exposure to exchange rate risk. Second, foreigners' willingness to hold U.S. dollar bills confers a windfall on U.S. citizens because foreigners are essentially providing an interest-free loan. Also, the dollar's reserve currency status makes foreign investors more willing to hold U.S. government bonds, lowering the government's borrowing costs. Finally, New York's leading international role as a financial capital might be jeopardized if the dollar ceased to be the reserve currency.

Fixed Exchange Rates in Europe

One benefit of fixed exchange rates is that they reduce the costs of uncertainty about exchange rates in international commercial and financial transactions. Because of the large volume of commercial and financial trading among European countries, the governments of many of these countries have sought to reduce the costs of exchange-rate fluctuations. Fixed exchange rates have also been used to constrain inflationary monetary policy. The theory of purchasing power parity indicates that a country's exchange rate will depreciate if it has a higher inflation rate than do its trading partners. So, when a government commits to a fixed exchange rate, it is also implicitly committing to restraining inflation.

The Exchange Rate Mechanism and European Monetary Union The countries that were members of the European Economic Community formed the *European Monetary System* in 1979. Eight European countries also agreed at that time to participate in an *exchange rate mechanism* (*ERM*) to limit fluctuations in the value of their currencies against each other. Specifically, the member countries promised to maintain the values of their currencies within a fixed range set in terms of a composite European currency unit called the ecu. Member countries agreed to maintain exchange rates within these limits while allowing the rates to float jointly against the U.S. dollar and other currencies. The anchor currency of the ERM was the German mark. Both France and the United Kingdom reduced their inflation rates by tying their currencies to the German mark.

The United Kingdom withdrew from the ERM in 1992, as a result of one of the most celebrated speculative attacks in the history of foreign exchange markets. Although linking the pound to the German mark forced the British government to take actions to reduce the inflation rate, the rate still remained well above the rate in Germany. With such different inflation rates, it would be difficult on purchasing power parity grounds for the pound to maintain a fixed exchange rate with the mark. In addition, as West Germany unified with the former East Germany, the German government kept interest rates high to attract the foreign investment needed to finance reconstruction in East Germany. These high interest rates attracted foreign investors to German securities, bidding up the value of the mark relative to the pound. Currency traders became convinced that the Bank of England would be unable to defend the exchange rate between the pound and the mark at the agreed-on level. Although the British government raised interest rates and insisted that it would defend the value of the pound, currency traders persisted in selling pounds for marks until on Black Wednesday, September 16, 1992, the British government abandoned the ERM and allowed the value of the pound to float. A notable winner among currency traders was George Soros, the Hungarian-born hedge fund manager. The financial press estimated that Soros had made more than $1 billion by betting against the pound. Some commentators called him "The Man Who Broke the Bank of England." Soros has argued, though, that his actions had little to do with the decision by the British government to abandon the ERM: "Markets move currencies, so what happened with the British pound would have happened whether I was born or not, so therefore I take no responsibility."[3]

As part of the 1992 single European market initiative, European Community (EC) countries drafted plans for the **European Monetary Union**, in which exchange rates would be fixed by using a common currency, the **euro**. A single currency would eliminate transactions costs of currency conversion and reduce exchange rate risk. In addition, the removal of high transactions costs in cross-border trades would increase efficiency in production by offering the advantages of economies of scale.

The European Monetary Union in Practice In 1989, a report issued by the EC recommended establishing a common central bank, the **European Central Bank (ECB)**, to conduct monetary policy and, eventually, to control a single currency. The ECB, which formally commenced operation in January 1999, is structured along the lines of the Federal Reserve System in the United States, with an Executive Board (similar to the Board of Governors) appointed by the European Council and governors from the individual countries in the union (comparable to Federal Reserve Bank presidents). Like the Fed, the ECB is independent of member governments. Executive Board members are appointed for nonrenewable eight-year terms to increase their political independence. The ECB's charter states that the ECB's main objective is price stability.

At Maastricht, the Netherlands, in December 1991, member countries agreed on a gradual approach to monetary union, with a goal of convergent monetary policies by the mid-1990s and completion of monetary union in Europe by January 1, 1999. To have a single currency and monetary policy required more convergence of domestic inflation rates and budget deficits than existed in the mid-1990s. By the time monetary union began in 1999, 11 countries met the conditions for participation with respect to inflation rates, interest rates, and budget deficits. The United Kingdom declined to participate. Figure 16.4 shows the 17 countries that in 2012 were using the euro as their common currency.

European Monetary Union A plan drafted as part of the 1992 single European market initiative, in which exchange rates were fixed and eventually a common currency was adopted.

euro The common currency of 17 European countries.

European Central Bank (ECB) The central bank of the European countries that have adopted the euro.

---

[3]Louise Story, "The Face of a Prophet," *New York Times*, April 11, 2008.

Figure 16.4

Countries Using the Euro

The 17 member countries of the European Union that had adopted the euro as their common currency as of December 2012 are shaded with red hatch marks. The members of the EU that have not adopted the euro are colored tan. Countries in white are not members of the EU.

As noted in the chapter opener, in its early years, the euro seemed quite successful. From the time the euro was introduced in January 2002 through the beginning of the financial crisis in 2007, most of Europe experienced a period of relative economic stability. With low interest rates, low inflation rates, and expanding production and employment, the advantages of the euro seemed obvious. Some of the lower-income European countries appeared to particularly prosper under the euro. The Spanish economy grew at an annual rate of 3.9% between 1999 and 2007. The unemployment rate in Spain dropped from nearly 20% in the mid-1990s to less than 8% in 2007. Ireland and Greece also experienced rapid growth during these years.

When the financial crisis of 2007–2009 hit and Europe entered a recession, the countries that were hardest hit could not pursue a more expansionary monetary policy than the ECB was willing to implement for the euro zone as a whole. These countries lacked the ability to revive their economies by depreciating their currencies and expanding their exports because they were committed to the euro, and most of their exports were to other euro-zone countries. During the years of the gold standard, countries had similarly been unable to run expansionary monetary policies and were unable to have their exchange rates depreciate. As we have seen, these drawbacks led one country after another to abandon the gold standard in the 1930s until the system collapsed.

Will the same thing that happened to the gold standard happen to the euro? In 2012, some economists thought that it might, particularly those who had been doubtful that adopting the euro had been a good idea in the first place. Ideally, the economies of countries using the same currency should be harmonized, as the individual states are in the United States. Although the economies of the states differ and some were hit harder than others by the 2007–2009 recession, there is free movement of workers and firms across state borders; federal legislation harmonizes some—but not all—labor and tax legislation; and the states share a common language and elect a common national government. The countries using the euro are much less harmonized in all these respects. Some steps have been taken to aid the free flow of workers and firms across national borders, to coordinate some aspects of labor and tax legislation, and so on. In fact, one argument in favor of the euro was that it would aid the harmonization of Europe's economies. But clearly the countries using the euro are much more diverse economically, politically, and culturally than are the states of the United States.

But are the countries of Europe so diverse that using a common currency seriously hinders their economies in dealing with a significant recession? The answer may depend in part on how quickly the countries most affected by the recession can return to higher growth and lower unemployment. It was several years into the Great Depression before most countries abandoned the gold standard. In addition, policymakers in Greece, Spain, Portugal, and Ireland—the countries that are perhaps most likely to abandon the euro—do not appear to see much gain from doing so. Abandoning the euro might allow these countries to increase their exports by depreciating their currencies and to spur recovery through expansionary monetary policies. But these actions would be at the expense of the long-term advantages these countries gain from the euro. So, while in late 2012 the euro was battered, it appeared likely to survive the crisis.

| **Making the Connection** | In Your Interest |

If You Were Greek, Would You Prefer the Euro or the Drachma?

If you lived in Greece, would you prefer that the government continue using the euro or abandon the euro and resume using the drachma, its former currency? Like other countries in southern Europe, Greece had experienced an apparently strong economy during the early years of using the euro. From 2002, when the euro was introduced, through 2007, real GDP in Greece grew at average annual rate of 4.2%. The unemployment rate declined from 10.7% in 2001 to 7.7% in 2008.

Beginning in 2008, however, real GDP in Greece began to decline and unemployment began to rise. Between 2007 and 2012, real GDP in Greece fell by more than 18% and the unemployment rate rose to depression levels of nearly 25%. In addition, the collapse in tax revenues led to a large government budget deficit and a national debt of more than 170% of GDP. Greece avoided defaulting on its debt only because of help from the "troika" made up of the European Commission, the European Central Bank (ECB), and the International Monetary Fund. The decision by the ECB to purchase

Greek government bonds was controversial because some economists believed it would increase moral hazard by making it possible for European countries to issue more debt than private investors were willing to buy.

Because the unemployment rate in Greece for younger workers was even higher than 25%, if you lived in Greece, it is likely that you would have difficulty finding a job as a new college graduate. But would your chances of finding a job and the chances of economic growth returning to Greece be higher if Greece continued using the euro or if it abandoned the euro for the drachma? As we have seen, countries using the euro cannot spur their exports by devaluing their currency. Not surprisingly, in 2008 Greece's current account deficit soared to nearly 15% of GDP.

Recall the expression for the real exchange rate:

$$e = E \times \left(\frac{P^{\text{Domestic}}}{P^{\text{Foreign}}} \right),$$

where:

$E =$ nominal exchange rate

$e =$ real exchange rate

$P^{\text{Domestic}} =$ domestic price level

$P^{\text{Foreign}} =$ foreign price level

With a fixed nominal exchange rate, a country can still lower its real exchange rate, thereby increasing the competitiveness of its goods and services, if its price level falls relative to the price levels of other countries. Because the inflation rates in France, Germany, and other euro countries have been low, Greece would have to experience *deflation* to lower its relative price level. This *internal devaluation* is difficult to achieve because wages and prices tend to exhibit downward rigidity, which means that, in practice, cutting wages and prices is difficult. In fact, attempting to reduce wages and prices led to significant political unrest in Greece.

Abandoning the euro would allow Greece to increase the competitiveness of its exports, but there would also be significant drawbacks. For example, many people in Greece believed that if the government left the euro, it would exchange euro bank deposits for drachmas at a rate of one for one. If the drachma then depreciated—as was widely expected—as someone living in Greece, you would suffer heavy losses on your bank deposits. In addition, the Greek government would likely default on its bonds, forcing it to pay for government spending exclusively with tax revenues. The result would be dramatic cuts in government spending, potentially further depressing the Greek economy.

In addition, foreign lenders to Greek banks and firms would likely object to being paid in drachmas, which could result in legal disputes and undermine the ability of Greek companies to borrow outside of Greece.

You and other people in Greece would probably be worse off in the short run if Greece left the euro. In the long run, abandoning the euro might make it easier for Greek firms to compete with foreign firms, which could help the economy. Uncertainty about the short-run and long-term consequences of abandoning the euro was a key reason that people in Greece and the Greek government appeared unwilling at the end of 2012 to return to using the drachma.

Sources: Jason Ng and Abhrajit Gangopadhyay, "Lagarde Says IMF Expects 'Real Fix' for Greece," Wall Street Journal, November 14, 2012; Paul Taylor, "Euro Here to Stay," *New York Times*, October 15, 2012; and International Monetary Fund, *World Economic Outlook Database*, October 2012.

See related problem 4.11 at the end of the chapter.

Currency Pegging

Pegging The decision by a country to keep the exchange rate fixed between its currency and another country's currency.

One way to maintain a fixed exchange rate is through pegging. With **pegging**, a country keeps its exchange rate fixed against another country's currency. It is not necessary for both countries in a currency peg to agree to it. For example, when in the 1990s, South Korea, Taiwan, Thailand, Indonesia, and other developing countries pegged their currencies to the U.S. dollar, the responsibility for maintaining the peg was entirely with the developing countries. Countries peg their currencies to gain the advantages of a fixed exchange rate: reduced exchange-rate risk, a check against inflation, and protection for firms that have taken out loans in foreign currencies. This last advantage was important to many Asian countries during the 1990s because some of their firms had begun taking out dollar-denominated loans from U.S. and foreign banks. So, for instance, in the absence of a currency peg, if the value of the Korean won declined against the dollar, a Korean firm with loans in dollars would find its interest and principal payments rising in terms of the won.

A peg, though, can run into the problem faced by countries under the Bretton Woods system: A currency's equilibrium exchange rate, as determined by demand and supply, may be significantly different than the pegged exchange rate. As a result, the pegged currency may become overvalued or undervalued with respect to the dollar. In the 1990s, a number of Asian countries with overvalued currencies were subject to speculative attacks. During the resulting *East Asian currency crisis*, these countries attempted to defend their pegs by buying domestic currency with dollars, reducing their monetary bases, and raising their domestic interest rates. Higher interest rates plunged their economies into recession and, in the end, were ineffective in defending their pegs, which these countries all eventually abandoned.

China and the Dollar Peg

In the late 2000s, there was considerable controversy over the policy of the Chinese government pegging its currency, the yuan, against the U.S. dollar. In 1978, China began to move away from central planning and toward a market system. An important part of Chinese economic policy was the decision in 1994 to peg the value of the yuan to the dollar at a fixed rate of 8.28 yuan to the dollar. Pegging against the dollar ensured that Chinese exporters would face stable dollar prices for the goods they sold in the United States. By the early 2000s, many economists argued that the yuan was undervalued against the dollar, possibly significantly so. Some U.S. firms claimed that the undervaluation of the yuan gave Chinese firms an unfair advantage in competing with U.S. firms.

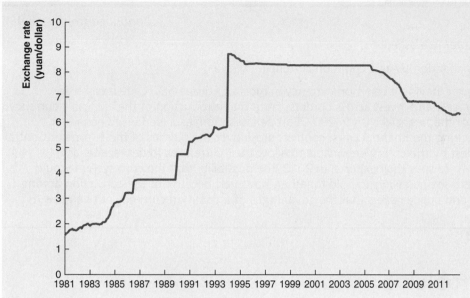

Figure 16.5

The Yuan–Dollar Exchange Rate

China began explicitly pegging the value of the yuan to the dollar in 1994. Between July 2005 and July 2008, China allowed the value of the yuan to rise against the dollar before returning to a hard peg at about 6.83 yuan to the dollar. In June 2010, the central bank of China announced that it would return to allowing the value of the yuan to rise against the dollar, which it did slowly through late 2012.

Source: Federal Reserve Bank of St. Louis.

In July 2005, the Chinese government announced that it would switch from pegging the yuan against the dollar to linking the value of the yuan to the average value of a basket of currencies—the dollar, the Japanese yen, the euro, the Korean won, and several other currencies. The immediate effect was a fairly small increase in value of the yuan from 8.28 to the dollar to 8.11 to the dollar. The Chinese central bank declared that it had switched from a peg to a managed floating exchange rate. Some economists and policymakers were skeptical, however, that much had actually changed because the initial increase in the value of the yuan had been small and because the Chinese central bank did not explain the details of how the yuan would be linked to the basket of other currencies.

Figure 16.5 shows that the value of the yuan did gradually rise against the dollar (that is, fewer yuan were required to buy one dollar) between July 2005 and July 2008, when the exchange rate stabilized at about 6.83 yuan to the dollar, indicating that China had apparently returned to a "hard peg." This change in policy led to renewed criticism from policymakers in the United States. In mid-2010, President Barack Obama argued that "market-determined exchange rates are essential to global economic activity." The Chinese central bank responded a few days later that it would return to allowing the value of the yuan to change based on movements in a basket of other currencies. In setting the value of the yuan each morning, the central bank said it would also pay attention to shifts in demand and supply in the foreign exchange markets. Through late 2012, the value of the yuan increased slowly against the dollar. But China continued to run large trade surpluses with the United States and the controversy over Chinese exchange-rate policies continued.

Answering the Key Question

Continued from page 487

At the beginning of this chapter, we asked:

"Should European countries abandon using a common currency?"

As we have seen in this chapter, having a common currency in most of Europe has made it easier for households and firms to buy, sell, and invest across borders. From the introduction of the euro as a currency in 2002 until the beginning of the financial crisis in 2007, European economies experienced economic growth with low inflation. During the financial crisis, conflicts arose over the policies of the European Central Bank. The countries hit hardest by the crisis were unable to allow their currencies to depreciate, as had happened in earlier recessions, to spur their exports. In 2012, the possibility that the euro system would collapse remained. The system seemed likely to hold together, however, because of the conviction among many European economists and policymakers that the advantages of a common currency outweighed its disadvantages.

Key Terms and Problems

Key Terms

Balance-of-payments account, p. 495

Bretton Woods system, p. 502

Capital controls, p. 494

Devaluation, p. 503

euro, p. 508

European Central Bank (ECB), p. 508

European Monetary Union, p. 508

Exchange rate regime, p. 498

Fixed exchange rate system, p. 498

Flexible exchange rate system, p. 506

Foreign exchange market intervention, p. 488

Gold standard, p. 498

International Monetary Fund (IMF), p. 502

International reserves, p. 488

Managed float regime, p. 506

Pegging, p. 512

Revaluation, p. 503

Sterilized foreign exchange intervention, p. 490

Unsterilized foreign exchange intervention, p. 490

16.1 **Foreign Exchange Intervention and the Monetary Base**
Analyze how the Fed's interventions in foreign exchange markets affect the U.S. monetary base.

Review Questions

1.1 What is the difference between a central bank carrying out a foreign exchange market intervention and carrying out a domestic open market operation?

1.2 If the Fed sells $2 billion of foreign assets, what happens to the Fed's holdings of international reserves and to the monetary base?

1.3 Does a purchase of foreign assets by the Fed have a greater effect, the same effect, or a smaller effect on the monetary base than an open market purchase of government bonds by the Fed? Briefly explain.

1.4 What is the difference between a sterilized foreign exchange intervention and an unsterilized foreign exchange intervention?

Problems and Applications

1.5 Allan Meltzer, an economist at Carnegie Mellon University, once argued:

> I have yet to see a study that shows that sterilized intervention, the most common type of intervention used by the Fed in the foreign exchange markets, has any effect on the value of the dollar at all.

  a. What is a "sterilized intervention"?

  b. How would the Fed carry out a sterilized intervention in the foreign exchange market?

  c. Why wouldn't a sterilized intervention have any effect on the value of the dollar?

  Source: Joel Kurtzman, "Fed vs. Treasury on Dollar's Value," *New York Times*, March 28, 1990.

1.6 Use T-accounts to show the effect on the Fed's balance sheet of the Fed selling $5 billion in Japanese government bonds, denominated in yen.

What happens to the Fed's international reserves and the monetary base? Is this a sterilized or an unsterilized foreign exchange intervention?

1.7 Use T-accounts to show the effect on the Fed's balance sheet of the Fed buying $2 billion in German government bonds, denominated in euros, and, at the same time, conducting an open market sale of $2 billion of U.S. Treasury securities. What happens to the monetary base? Is this a sterilized or an unsterilized foreign exchange intervention?

1.8 What effect does each of the following have on the U.S. monetary base?

  a. The Fed purchases $10 billion of foreign assets.

  b. The Fed sells $10 billion of foreign assets and purchases $10 billion of Treasury securities.

  c. The Fed conducts a sterilized foreign exchange intervention.

  d. The Fed sells $10 billion of foreign assets and sells $10 billion of Treasury securities.

16.2 ## Foreign Exchange Interventions and the Exchange Rate

Analyze how the Fed's interventions in foreign exchange markets affect the exchange rate.

Review Questions

2.1 To raise the foreign exchange rate, would a central bank buy or sell foreign assets? What would be the effect on the monetary base? What would be the effect on domestic interest rates?

2.2 How does a sterilized central bank intervention affect the demand curve and the supply curve for a country's currency?

2.3 What are capital controls, and why might a country impose them? What are the disadvantages of imposing capital controls?

Problems and Applications

2.4 On the foreign exchange market, who demands dollars—U.S. investors or foreign investors? Why does an increase in U.S. interest rates relative to Japanese interest rates increase the demand for dollars? An investor who holds

U.S. currency doesn't receive any interest, so why does the demand for dollars rise when U.S. interest rates rise?

2.5 Suppose the Bank of Japan sells $5 billion of U.S. Treasury securities. Use a graph of the demand and supply of yen in exchange for dollars to show the effect on the exchange rate between the yen and the dollar. Briefly explain what is happening in your graph. (Note that the exchange rate will be dollars per yen.)

2.6 [Related to Solved Problem 16.2 **on page 492**] In 2012, the Swiss National Bank (SNB) was intervening in foreign exchange markets to keep a "floor" of 1.2 Swiss francs = 1 euro in the exchange rate between the franc and the euro. An article in the *Wall Street Journal* reported: "Some exporters and traders had hoped the SNB would . . . raise the floor to 1.30 francs, which would mean intervention to strengthen the euro and weaken the franc, thereby helping the export trade."

a. Would raising the floor from 1.2 francs = €1 to 1.3 francs = €1 result in an appreciation of the Swiss franc against the euro or a depreciation? Briefly explain.

b. If the Swiss National Bank wanted to raise its floor exchange rate between the franc and the euro, what actions would it need to take? Use a graph of the demand for francs in exchange for euros to illustrate the effects of these actions.

c. The article cited here went on to state that the actions the SNB had taken to defend the

floor exchange rate between the franc and the euro had "led to an unprecedented surge in the central bank's foreign-currency reserves over the past two years." Would SNB be able to add to its foreign-currency reserves indefinitely? Briefly explain.

Source: Neil Maclucas, "Swiss Central Bank Keeps Euro-Franc Floor," *Wall Street Journal*, September 13, 2012.

2.7 Can a foreign exchange intervention by the Fed change the exchange rate if the Fed does not change its target for the federal funds rate? If the Fed wanted to carry out a foreign exchange intervention while leaving the target for the federal funds rate unchanged, what would the Federal Reserve System's account manager need to do to maintain the target federal funds rate?

16.3 The Balance of Payments
Understand how the balance of payments is calculated.

Review Questions

3.1 Distinguish between the types of transactions recorded in the current account and those recorded in the financial account. If a country runs a current account deficit, are its exports of goods and services larger or smaller than its imports of goods and services? Briefly explain.

3.2 Why must the current account balance plus the financial account balance equal zero?

3.3 Briefly explain in what sense a country can run a balance-of-payments surplus or a balance-of-payments deficit.

3.4 How do central banks use official reserve assets?

Problems and Applications

3.5 If the U.S. current account deficit is $400 billion, and if the statistical discrepancy is zero, what is the financial account balance? Does this financial account balance represent a net capital outflow or a net capital inflow?

3.6 Suppose that a U.S. firm buys 10 Volkswagen autos for $20,000 each, and the German company

uses the money to buy a $200,000 U.S. Treasury bond at a Treasury auction. How are these two transactions recorded in the balance-of-payments accounts for the United States?

3.7 Suppose that the U.S. government sells old warships worth $300 million to Japan, and Japan's government pays for them with its official holdings of dollar assets. How is this transaction recorded in the U.S. balance-of-payment accounts?

3.8 Briefly explain in what sense a country can run a balance of payments surplus or deficit. How would a country finance a balance of payments deficit in this sense? What important differences are there between how a U.S. balance-of-payments deficit can be financed and how other countries must finance their balance-of-payments deficits?

3.9 If a country imposes capital controls that result in its financial account balance being zero, would it be possible for the country to run a current account deficit? Briefly explain.

16.4 **Exchange Rate Regimes and the International Financial System**
Discuss the evolution of exchange rate regimes.

Review Questions

4.1 Briefly explain how the gold standard operated. What were the key differences between the gold standard and the Bretton Woods system?

4.2 Briefly answer each of the following questions about the gold standard:

a. Was it a fixed exchange-rate system or a flexible exchange-rate system?

b. Were countries able to pursue active monetary policies?

c. Did countries that ran trade deficits experience gold inflows or gold outflows?

d. How would a gold inflow affect a country's monetary base and its inflation rate?

e. During the Great Depression, how did the gold standard hinder economic recovery?

4.3 Under the Bretton Woods system, what were devaluations and revaluations? What is the difference between a devaluation and a depreciation? Why were countries hesitant to pursue a devaluation? Why were they even more hesitant to pursue a revaluation?

4.4 What is the euro zone? How do the countries of the euro zone benefit from using a single currency? What are the disadvantages to using a single currency?

4.5 What is pegging? What are the advantages of pegging? What are the disadvantages? Briefly discuss the controversy over China's pegging the value of the yuan.

Problems and Applications

4.6 Under a gold standard, is inflation possible? Consider both the case for an individual country and the case for the world as a whole.

4.7 [Related to the Making the Connection on page 501] In discussing the situation of countries leaving the gold standard, or "unilaterally devaluing" during the 1930s, Barry Eichengreen of the University of California, Berkeley, and Jeffrey Sachs of Columbia University argued: "In all cases of unilateral devaluation, currency depreciation increases output and employment in the devaluing country." Explain how leaving the gold standard in the 1930s would lead to an increase in a country's output and employment.

Source: Barry Eichengreen and Jeffrey Sachs, "Exchange Rates and Economic Recovery in the 1930s," *Journal of Economic History*, Vol. 45, No. 4, December 1985, p. 934.

4.8 Evaluate the following argument:

The United States did not really leave the gold standard in 1933. Under the Bretton Woods system, the United States stood ready to redeem U.S. currency for gold at a fixed price, and that is the basic requirement of the gold standard.

4.9 Why has support for a system of fixed exchange rates tended to be higher in Europe than in the United States?

4.10 [Related to the Chapter Opener on page 487] An article in the *Economist* magazine in late 2012 observed:

The euro was meant to buttress the single market, reducing transaction costs and removing the risk of competitive devaluation. Could it now destroy the single market instead?

a. How did the euro reduce transactions costs?

b. What is a "competitive devaluation"? Is not being able to devalue their currencies always a benefit to euro-zone countries? Briefly explain.

c. If countries abandon the euro and return to using their own currencies, how might this action "destroy" the single European market?

Source: "Coming Off the Rails," *Economist*, October 20, 2012.

4.11 [Related to the Making the Connection on page 510] In 2012, an article in the *New York Times* observed that: "The financial consequences of a Greek departure from the euro monetary union could be severe."

    a. What does the article mean by "a Greek departure from the euro monetary union"?

    b. Why might a Greek departure lead to severe financial consequences? Would only people in Greece feel the financial consequences? Briefly explain.

    Source: Mark Scott, "For Europe's Banks, Pinch of Debt Crisis Intensifies," *New York Times*, May 15, 2012.

4.12 In 2010, arguing that the Chinese yuan was overvalued versus the U.S. dollar, President Barack Obama said he wanted "to make sure our goods are not artificially inflated in price and their goods are not artificially deflated in price; that puts us at a huge competitive disadvantage."

    a. What does the value of the yuan have to do with U.S. goods being "artificially inflated in price" or Chinese goods being "artificially deflated in price"?

    b. Why would this "inflation" and "deflation" in prices put U.S. goods at a competitive disadvantage?

    Source: Edward Wong and Mark Landler, "China Rejects U.S. Complaints on Its Currency," *New York Times*, February 4, 2010.

4.13 In late 2012, an article in the *Wall Street Journal*, observed that: "The once-predictable Chinese yuan has become increasingly volatile, a development that . . . poses greater foreign-exchange risks for businesses and investors."

    a. Why was the yuan "once predictable"? Why had the yuan become more volatile?

    b. Why would the volatility of the yuan pose exchange-rate risks for businesses and investors?

    Source: Lingling Wei, "Staid Yuan Roams as China Lets Out Slack," *Wall Street Journal*, October 25, 2012.

Data Exercises

D16.1: [Recent movements in the yuan–dollar exchange rate] Go to the Web site of the Federal Reserve Bank of St. Louis (FRED) (research.stlouisfed.org/fred2/) and download and graph the data series for the yuan–dollar exchange rate (DEXCHUS) from July 2010 until the most recent day available. As this book went to press in December 2012, some economists speculated that the Chinese government would allow the value of the yuan to fluctuate more widely in response to market forces. Since July 2010, how has the exchange rate between the yuan and the dollar changed?

D16.2: [The current account and the business cycle] Go to the Web site of the Federal Reserve Bank of St. Louis (FRED) (research.stlouisfed.org/fred2/) and download and graph the data series for the U.S. current account balance (BOPBCA) from the first quarter of 1960 to the most recent quarter available. Go to the Web site of the National Bureau of Economic Research (nber.org) and find the dates for business cycle peaks and troughs. (The period between a business cycle peak and trough is a recession.) Describe how the current account balance moves just before, during, and just after a recession. Is the pattern the same across recessions?

CHAPTER 17

Monetary Theory I: The Aggregate Demand and Aggregate Supply Model

Learning Objectives

After studying this chapter, you should be able to:

17.1 Explain how the aggregate demand curve is derived (pages 521–525)

17.2 Explain how the aggregate supply curve is derived (pages 525–532)

17.3 Demonstrate macroeconomic equilibrium using the aggregate demand and aggregate supply model (pages 533–537)

17.4 Use the aggregate demand and aggregate supply model to show the effects of monetary policy (pages 537–544)

Why Was Unemployment So High for So Long?

Normally, after a recession is over real GDP and employment increase, and finding a job becomes easier. Typically, the deeper the recession, the stronger the recovery. The National Bureau of Economic Research's (NBER's) dating of business cycles is widely accepted. According to the NBER, what economists call "The Great Recession" began in December 2007 and ended in June 2009. It was the longest and deepest recession since the Great Depression of the 1930s. The unemployment rate at the end of the recession was already a very high 9.5% in June 2009 but rose to 10.0% by October 2009. Even in November 2012, more than three years after the end of the recession, the unemployment rate was still 7.7%, and it was much harder to find a job than it

should have been. Employment was still nearly 10 million jobs below its normal level.[1] A broader measure of the unemployment rate counts as unemployed some people who have become discouraged and stopped looking for work and people who are working part time because they can't find full-time jobs. This measure of the unemployment rate stood at 14.4% in November 2012. And the unemployed were staying unemployed for longer periods as well.

---

[1] In November 2012, the employment–population ratio was 58.7%. The same number of months after the end of the 2001 recession, the ratio was 62.7%. With a working-age population of 244,174,000, the difference in the employment–population ratios indicates a gap of 9.8 million jobs.

Continued on next page

Key Issue and Question

Issue: During the recovery from the financial crisis, the unemployment rate remained stubbornly high.

Question: What explains the high unemployment rates during the economic expansion that began in 2009?

Answered on page 544

In November 2012, 40.1% of the unemployed had been out of work for at least six months, compared with only 16.4% in June 2007, before the recession began.

Forecasts indicated that economic growth would not be fast enough to bring these high unemployment rates down anytime soon. The Federal Reserve forecast that the unemployment rate might not return to 6% until the end of 2015 or later. The forecasts of White House economists were also pessimistic, with the unemployment rate projected not to return to the full-employment rate of 5.3% until 2017—eight years after the recession ended. Some economists believed that even these gloomy forecasts might be optimistic. These economists had begun speaking of the "new normal," in which unemployment rates might be stuck at high levels for many years.

Why was the unemployment rate returning more slowly to full employment than during economic expansions prior to 2007? A number of factors seem responsible. An epic housing bubble had pulled labor, capital, and other resources into residential construction. When the bubble burst, more than 2 million construction jobs were lost. Some economists believed that it would take years for spending on residential construction to again reach its pre-bubble level. As a result, many people who had worked in this sector would need to find new occupations. Doing so might require workers to learn new skills or to move to other parts of the country. The situation was similar for people who worked in industries that depend on construction, such as mortgage lending, real estate appraisals, and manufacturing of furniture, appliances, and construction equipment.

Narayana Kocherlakota, president of the Federal Reserve Bank of Minneapolis, argued that during these years, the U.S. labor market was in the unusual situation of having high rates of unemployment in some industries, such as housing, while at the same time having many job openings in other industries, particularly in manufacturing and oil exploration, that required more skilled workers than were available. In other words, Kocherlakota believed that there was an unusually large mismatch between workers' skills and the available jobs. Without this mismatch, Kocherlakota argued, the unemployment rate would have been much closer to full employment by 2012. In addition, because housing prices had declined by 20% or more in many parts of the country, some people found that they owed more on their mortgages than their houses were worth, which made it difficult to sell their houses and move to areas where jobs were easier to find.

Finally, the U.S. economy in 2012 appeared headed toward what Fed Chairman Ben Bernanke called a "fiscal cliff." He was referring to a combination of significant increases in federal taxes and reductions in federal government spending scheduled to take effect in January 2013. By the fall of 2012, households and firms were already feeling the effects of the potential tax increases and spending cuts. When a firm considers expanding by building a new factory, store, or office and by hiring new employees, it looks not just at the present but also at the future. Expanding a business during a recession can turn into a financial disaster for a firm. Many firms were anticipating the fiscal cliff and decided it was not a good time to expand.

In 2012, as the Federal Reserve contemplated monetary policy, it was grappling with an unusually complicated set of problems.

Sources: U.S. Bureau of Labor Statistics, *Employment Situation Summary, October 2012*, October 5, 2012; U.S. Bureau of Economic Analysis; Narayana Kocherlakota, "Back Inside the FOMC," speech delivered in Missoula, Montana, September 8, 2010; and Ben S. Bernanke, *Semiannual Monetary Policy Report to the Congress*, July 17, 2012.

The causes and consequences of business cycles, such as the 2007–2009 recession and the following expansion, were not always a significant part of the study of economics. Modern macroeconomics began during the 1930s, as economists and policymakers struggled to understand why the Great Depression was so severe.

The U.S. economy has experienced business cycles dating back to at least the early nineteenth century. The business cycle is not uniform: Periods of expansion are not all the same length, nor are periods of recession. But every period of expansion in

U.S. history has been followed by a period of recession, and every period of recession has been followed by a period of expansion. Economists have developed macroeconomic models to analyze the business cycle. British economist John Maynard Keynes developed a particularly influential model in 1936, in response to the Great Depression.

In this chapter and the next, we explore *monetary theory*, which involves using macroeconomic models to explore the relationship between changes in the money supply and interest rates and changes in real GDP and the price level. We begin in this chapter with *the aggregate demand and aggregate supply (AD–AS) model*. This model captures some of the basic ideas first developed by Keynes in the 1930s.

The Aggregate Demand Curve

We start by looking at the relationship between the demand for goods and services and the price level. Economists analyze the demand for goods and services by households, firms, and the government in terms of aggregate expenditure. *Aggregate expenditure* on the economy's output of goods and services equals the sum of:

1. Spending by households on goods and services for consumption, C
2. Planned spending by firms on capital goods, such as factories, office buildings, and machine tools and by households on new homes, I
3. Local, state, and federal government purchases of goods and services (not including transfer payments—such as Social Security payments—to individuals), G
4. Net exports, which is spending by foreign firms and households on goods and services produced in the United States minus spending by U.S. firms and households on goods and services produced in other countries, NX

So, we can write that aggregate expenditure, AE, is:

$$AE = C + I + G + NX.$$

We can use the concept of aggregate expenditure to develop the **aggregate demand (*AD*) curve**, which shows the relationship between the price level and aggregate expenditure on goods and services by households, firms, and the government. In Figure 17.1, we show the aggregate demand curve using a graph with the price level, P, on the vertical axis, and aggregate output, Y, on the horizontal axis. In the following section, we derive the aggregate demand curve by analyzing the effect of a change in the price level on the components of aggregate expenditure.

The Money Market and the Aggregate Demand Curve

The shape and position of the *AD* curve are important in determining the equilibrium values of real GDP and the price level.

The *AD* curve is downward sloping because, if nothing else changes, an increase in the price level reduces aggregate expenditure on goods and services. We can understand why an increase in the price level has this effect by looking briefly at the *money market*.[2]

17.1

Learning Objective

Explain how the aggregate demand curve is derived.

Aggregate Demand (*AD*) Curve A curve that shows the relationship between the price level and aggregate expenditure on goods and services.

---

[2]Confusion alert: When economists refer to the "money market," they usually are referring to the market for bonds that mature in one year or less, such as Treasury bills. Here, though, we are using the phrase "money market" to refer to the analysis of money demand and money supply.

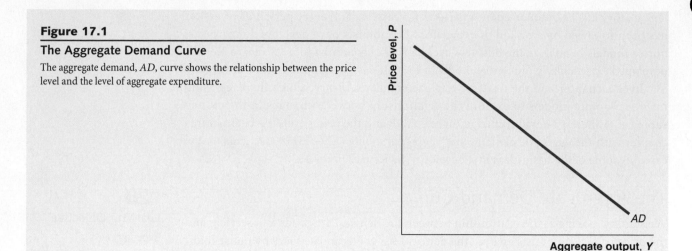

Figure 17.1

The Aggregate Demand Curve

The aggregate demand, *AD*, curve shows the relationship between the price level and the level of aggregate expenditure.

The money market involves the interaction between the demand for M1—currency plus checkable deposits—by households and firms and the supply of M1, as determined by the Federal Reserve. The analysis of the money market is sometimes called the *liquidity preference theory*, a term coined by Keynes.

The quantity of M1 that households and firms demand depends on the price level. One hundred years ago, when the price level was much lower, households and firms needed fewer dollars to conduct their buying and selling. As the price level increases, households and firms require a larger quantity of dollars. Economists capture this idea by assuming that households and firms demand, and the Federal Reserve supplies, **real money balances**, or *M/P*, where *M* is a monetary aggregate, such as M1, and *P* is a measure of the price level, such as the consumer price index or the GDP price deflator.

Panel (a) of Figure 17.2 illustrates the money market, using a graph with the short-term nominal interest rate, such as the interest rate on Treasury bills, on the vertical axis and the quantity of real money balances on the horizontal axis. The figure shows the demand for real money balances by households and firms as being downward sloping. We assume that the primary reason households and firms demand money is for what economists call the *transactions motive*—to hold money as a medium of exchange to facilitate buying and selling. However, households and firms face a trade-off between the convenience of holding money and the low—or zero—interest rate they receive on money. The higher the interest rate on short-term assets such as Treasury bills, the more households and firms give up when they hold large money balances. So, the short-term nominal interest rate is the *opportunity cost of holding money*. The higher the interest rate, the smaller the quantity of real balances households and firms want to hold. The lower the interest rate, the larger the quantity of real balances households and firms want to hold. Therefore, the demand for real balances is downward sloping. We show the supply of real balances as a vertical line because we assume that the Fed can perfectly control the level of M1. The behavior of banks and the public also affect the level of M1, but our simplification here does not significantly affect the analysis.

Real money balances
The value of money held by households and firms, adjusted for changes in the price level; *M/P*.

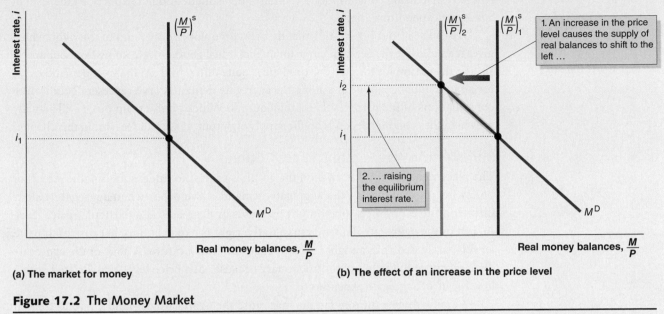

Figure 17.2 The Money Market

In panel (a), the demand for real balances is downward sloping because higher short-term interest rates increase the opportunity cost of holding money. The supply of real balances is a vertical line because we assume for simplicity that the Fed can control perfectly the level of M1.

In panel (b), we show that an increase in the price level causes the supply curve for real balances to shift from $(M/P)^s_1$ to $(M/P)^s_2$, thereby increasing the equilibrium interest rate from i_1 to i_2.

In panel (b) of Figure 17.2, we show the effect of an increase in the price level on the money market, assuming that the nominal money supply—the dollar value of currency plus checkable deposits—is held constant. The increase in the price level reduces the supply of real balances, shifting the supply curve to the left, from $(M/P)^s_1$ to $(M/P)^s_2$. After the supply curve has shifted, at the original equilibrium interest rate, i_1, the quantity of real balances demanded will be greater than the quantity supplied. Households and firms will attempt to restore their desired holdings of real balances by selling short-term assets, such as Treasury bills. This increased supply of Treasury bills will drive down their prices and increase interest rates on those bills. A rising short-term interest rate will cause households and firms to move up the demand curve for real balances until equilibrium is restored at interest rate i_2. We can conclude that an increase in the price level, holding all other things constant, will result in an increase in the interest rate.

An increase in the interest rate makes firms less willing to invest in plant and equipment, and gives consumers an incentive to save rather than to spend. If we include this behavior in our expression for AE, then C and I fall, and AE declines as P increases. There is also a change in net exports because of the effect of rising interest rates on the exchange rate. A higher domestic interest rate makes returns on domestic financial assets more attractive relative to those on foreign assets, which increases the demand for the domestic currency. The increased demand for the domestic currency raises the exchange rate, which increases imports and reduces exports, thereby reducing NX and AE.

Conversely, a decrease in the price level increases real money balances, leading to a drop in the interest rate in the money market. The lower interest rate reduces saving (thereby increasing consumption) and raises investment and net exports, so the level of aggregate expenditure rises.

We can see from Figure 17.1 that the *AD* curve slopes down and to the right, which gives it a slope like the demand curve for an individual good. But we know from our analysis that the reason for the *AD* curve's slope is quite different from that of a demand curve for an individual good. Points along the aggregate demand curve represent equilibrium combinations of the price level and total output. Which equilibrium point will actually prevail in the economy depends on the supply of output, as we will see later in this chapter.

Shifts of the Aggregate Demand Curve

The placement of the *AD* curve on the graph is crucial to understanding the effects of policy measures. Shifts of the aggregate demand curve occur when aggregate expenditure on the economy's total output increases or decreases at a particular price level. A shift of the aggregate demand curve to the right is expansionary because each price level is associated with a higher level of aggregate expenditure. A shift of the aggregate demand curve to the left is contractionary because each price level is associated with a lower level of aggregate expenditure.

We now review the key factors that cause the aggregate demand curve to shift. If the Fed increases the nominal money supply and, at least initially, the price level does not increase as much, real money balances rise. The interest rate then falls in the money market, causing consumption, *C*, investment, *I*, and net exports, *NX*, all to increase. As a result, aggregate expenditure increases, shifting the aggregate demand curve to the right. Conversely, if the Fed reduces the nominal money supply, real money balances fall in the short run. As a result, the equilibrium interest rate rises and consumption, investment, and net exports all decline. Aggregate expenditure falls, shifting the aggregate demand curve to the left.

Aggregate demand will also shift to the right if consumers decrease their saving and increase their consumption spending, *C*. A decline in saving might occur if consumers expect an increase in their future incomes. Many economists believe that increases in current income from tax cuts increase consumption. Firms increase planned investment, *I*, if they expect the future profitability of capital to rise or business taxes to fall. An increase in government purchases, *G*, directly adds to aggregate expenditure. An increase in foreign demand for U.S.-produced goods raises net exports, *NX*. Each change in *C*, *I*, *G*, or *NX* increases aggregate expenditure and shifts the *AD* curve to the right.

A decline in planned consumption or investment, in government purchases, or in net exports shifts the *AD* curve to the left. A decline in consumption can be caused by a decrease in expected future income or, possibly, less confidence about future economic conditions. During the 2007–2009 recession and its aftermath, households increased their saving and reduced their consumption, thereby reducing aggregate expenditure. Firms reduce planned investment if they expect the future profitability of capital to decline or business taxes to rise. There is also evidence that an increase in the level of uncertainty in the economy can lead firms to postpone, or cancel, investment projects. A drop in government purchases directly reduces aggregate expenditure, as does a decline in foreign demand for U.S.-produced goods. Table 17.1 summarizes the most important variables that shift the aggregate demand curve.

Table 17.1 Variables That Shift the Aggregate Demand Curve

An increase in . . .	shifts the *AD* curve . . .	because . . .
The nominal money supply		real money balances rise, and the interest rate falls.
expected future income		consumption rises.
government purchases		aggregate demand increases directly.
the expected future profitability of capital		investment rises.
income taxes and business taxes		investment declines.

The Aggregate Supply Curve

The second component of the *AD–AS* model is **aggregate supply**, the total quantity of output, or real GDP, that firms are willing to supply at a given price level. Firms differ in their reactions to changes in the price level in the short run and the long run. Therefore, we divide our analysis of aggregate supply according to the time horizon that firms face. Our initial goal is to construct a **short-run aggregate supply (*SRAS*) curve**, which shows the relationship between the price level and the quantity of aggregate output, or real GDP, that firms are willing to supply in the short run. We will then turn to the long-run aggregate supply curve.

Aggregate supply The total quantity of output, or GDP, that firms are willing to supply at a given price level.

Short-run aggregate supply (*SRAS*) curve A curve that shows the relationship in the short run between the price level and the quantity of aggregate output, or real GDP, supplied by firms.

17.2

Learning Objective

Explain how the aggregate supply curve is derived.

Economists are not in complete agreement about how firms respond in the short run to changes in the price level. Most economists believe that the aggregate quantity of output firms supply in the short run increases as the price level rises. And most economists also believe that, in the long run, changes in the price level have no effect on the aggregate quantity of output firms supply. But economists offer differing explanations of why the short-run aggregate supply curve is upward sloping.

Although the short-run aggregate supply curve may look like the supply curve facing an individual firm, it represents different behavior. The quantity of output that an individual firm is willing to supply depends on the price of its output relative to the prices of other goods and services. In contrast, the short-run aggregate supply curve relates the aggregate quantity of output supplied to the price level. We can briefly review the most widely accepted explanations for this relationship.

The Short-Run Aggregate Supply (*SRAS*) Curve

One explanation of why the *SRAS* curve is upward sloping is called the *new classical view* and was first proposed by Nobel Laureate Robert E. Lucas, Jr., of the University of Chicago. This approach is also sometimes called the *misperception theory* because it emphasizes the difficulty firms have in distinguishing relative increases in the prices of their products from general increases in the price level. For example, suppose that you are a toy manufacturer, and you see the price of toys increasing by 15%. If the price of toys has increased *relative* to other prices, then you can conclude that the demand for toys has risen and you should increase production. But if all prices in the economy are 15% higher, the relative price of toys is unchanged, and you are unlikely to increase your profits by producing more toys.

Of course, you are only one producer of many. Generalizing to include all producers in the economy, we can see why the misperception theory suggests a relationship between the quantity of aggregate output firms supply and the price level. Suppose that all prices in the economy rise by 15% but that relative prices don't change. If individual producers fail to recognize that relative prices haven't changed, aggregate output increases. This change in output occurs because producers think that some of the increase in prices represents increases in their products' relative prices, and they increase the quantity of their products supplied. According to the new classical view, firms that have perfect information about price changes would react by raising the quantity of toys supplied when prices of toys increased only if that increase differed from the expected increase in the general price level in the economy. If all producers expect the price level to increase by 10%, and as a toy manufacturer you see the price of toys increase by only 5%, you will *reduce* your toy production. If the price level actually increases by only 5% (when firms expected a 10% increase in the price level), firms will collectively cut output.

The new classical view suggests a positive relationship between the aggregate supply of goods and the difference between the actual and expected price level. If P is the actual price level and P^e is the expected price level, the relationship between aggregate output and the price level, according to the new classical view, is:

$$Y = Y^P + a(P - P^e),$$

where:

Y = real aggregate output, or real GDP

Y^P = *potential* GDP, or the level of real output produced when the economy is at full employment (Y^P is also sometimes called *full-employment GDP*)

a = a positive coefficient that indicates by how much output responds when the actual price level is different from the expected price level

The equation states that output supplied, Y, equals potential GDP, Y^P, when the actual price level and the expected price level are equal. When the actual price level is greater than the expected price level, firms increase output. When the actual price level is less than the expected price level, firms decrease output. As a result, output can be higher or lower than the full employment level in the short run—until firms can distinguish changes in relative prices from changes in the general price level. So, in the short run, for a particular expected price level, an increase in the actual price level raises the aggregate quantity of output supplied. Therefore, the *SRAS* curve is upward sloping.

An alternative explanation for why the *SRAS* curve is upward sloping comes from the argument of John Maynard Keynes and his followers that prices adjust slowly in the short run in response to changes in aggregate demand. That is, prices are *sticky* in the short run. In the most extreme view of price stickiness, we would observe a horizontal *SRAS* curve because prices would not adjust at all to increases or decreases in aggregate demand. Instead, firms would adjust their production levels to meet the new level of demand without changing their prices. Contemporary economists who follow Keynes's view of price stickiness have sought reasons for the failure of prices to adjust in the short run. Economists who embrace the *new Keynesian view* use characteristics of many real-world markets—long-term contracts and imperfect competition—to explain price behavior.

One form of rigidity arises from long-term nominal contracts for wages (between firms and workers) or prices for intermediate goods (between firms and their suppliers). Under a long-term nominal contract, a wage rate or price is set in advance in nominal terms for months or years. When contracts of this type exist, firms are not able to change prices easily in response to changes in demand because their costs of production are fixed. Many such long-term arrangements exist in the economy and not all contracts come up for renewal during a particular period because they are overlapping or staggered. So, only some wages and prices can be adjusted in the current period. In the long run, firms and workers will renegotiate contracts in response to changes in demand, but they can't renegotiate all contracts immediately.

New Keynesians also attribute price stickiness to differences in market structure and the price-setting decisions that take place in different types of markets. In markets for wheat or Treasury bills, the product is standardized, many traders interact, and prices adjust freely and quickly to shifts in demand and supply. In such *competitive markets*, the purchases and sales of individual traders are small relative to the total market volume. For example, a few wheat farmers can't raise their prices above those of other wheat farmers because no one would buy their wheat. However, many markets in the economy—such as the markets for high-fashion clothing, automobiles, and medical care—don't resemble the continuously adjusting price-taking markets for wheat or Treasury bills because their products are not standardized. Monopolistic competition results when products have individual characteristics and there are only a few sellers of each product. A seller who raises prices might see quantity demanded fall, but not to zero. In *monopolistically competitive markets*, sellers do not take prices as a given because they are price setters. New Keynesian economists argue that prices will adjust only gradually in monopolistically competitive markets when there are costs to changing prices. The costs of changing prices—sometimes called *menu costs*—include informing current and potential customers and changing prices in catalogues and on store shelves.

Why are menu costs potentially important in explaining movements in output and prices? Think again about a perfectly competitive market: When a seller of wheat charges a price that is slightly higher than other sellers charge, that seller will sell nothing at all. However, a monopolistically competitive firm (such as a clothing boutique) won't lose many of its customers if its prices are slightly higher than the market price. *If potential profits are small relative to the cost of changing prices, the firm won't change its price.*

Rather than adjust prices continually in the short run, a monopolistically competitive firm is likely to meet fluctuations in demand by selling more or less at the posted price. This strategy is reasonable for a monopolistically competitive firm because the product price is higher than the marginal cost—that is, the cost of producing an extra unit. So, the firm is happy to sell extra output when demand increases. As a result of responding to the level of demand without adjusting prices, the firm's output will rise and fall, depending on aggregate demand.

When firms have sticky prices, an increase in the price level will tend to increase these firms' profits in the short run and so will lead them to increase output. The short-run aggregate supply curve that is implied by the new Keynesian view is upward sloping, but the larger the proportion of firms in the economy with sticky prices, the flatter the *SRAS* curve will be. If all firms had sticky prices in the short run, the *SRAS* curve would be horizontal. Alternatively, if all firms had perfectly flexible prices in the short run, the *SRAS* curve would be vertical.

The Long-Run Aggregate Supply (*LRAS*) Curve

Long-run aggregate supply (*LRAS*) curve
A curve that shows the relationship in the long run between the price level and the quantity of aggregate output, or real GDP, supplied by firms.

The *SRAS* curve is upward sloping in both the new classical and new Keynesian explanations of aggregate supply, but this relationship doesn't hold in the long run. In the new classical view, firms eventually can distinguish changes in the relative prices of their products from changes in the price level. At that point, the actual and expected price levels are equal—that is, $P = P^e$. The new classical equation on page 526 indicates that when the actual price level equals the expected price level, current output, Y, equals potential GDP, Y^P. Therefore, the **long-run aggregate supply (*LRAS*) curve** is vertical at Y^P.

In the new Keynesian view, in the short run, many input costs are fixed, so firms can expand output without experiencing an increase in input cost that is proportional to the increase in the prices of their products. Over time, though, input costs increase in line with the price level, so in the long run both firms with flexible prices and firms with sticky prices adjust their prices in response to a change in demand. As with the new classical view, the *LRAS* curve is vertical at potential GDP, or $Y = Y^P$.

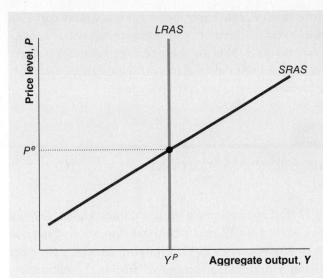

Figure 17.3

The Short-Run and Long-Run Aggregate Supply Curves

The *SRAS* curve is upward sloping because when the price level, *P*, exceeds the expected price level, P^e, the quantity of output supplied rises. In the long run, the actual and expected price levels are the same. Therefore, the *LRAS* curve is vertical at potential GDP, Y^P.

Figure 17.3 displays the short-run and long-run aggregate supply curves on the same graph. Note that the curves intersect at a price level equal to P^e.

Shifts in the Short-Run Aggregate Supply Curve

Shifts in aggregate supply can explain changes in output in the short run. There are three main reasons why the short-run aggregate supply curve shifts:

1. *Changes in labor costs.* Labor typically accounts for the majority of the costs of producing output. When output, *Y*, exceeds potential GDP, Y^P, the high volume of output produced raises the demand for labor. The higher labor demand, in turn, bids up wages, increasing firms' labor costs. As a result, the short-run aggregate supply curve will eventually shift to the left because at any given price level, firms will supply less output when their costs are higher. In the case when output falls below potential GDP, firms begin to lay off workers, and workers' wages decline. The resulting drop in production costs eventually shifts the short-run aggregate supply curve to the right.

2. *Changes in other input costs.* Unexpected changes in the price or availability of raw materials or in production technologies affect production costs and the short-run aggregate supply curve. Such changes are called **supply shocks** and include unexpected changes in technology, weather, or the prices of oil and other raw materials. Positive supply shocks, such as the development of labor-saving technologies or lower food prices due to good growing seasons, shift the short-run aggregate supply curve to the right. Negative supply shocks, such as an increase in the price of oil, shift the short-run aggregate supply curve to the left.

3. *Changes in the expected price level.* When workers bargain for wages, they compare their wages to the costs of goods and services that they buy. When workers expect the price level to rise, they will demand higher nominal wages to preserve their real wages. Similarly, firms make decisions about how much output to supply by comparing the price of their output to the expected prices of other goods and services. When the

Supply shock An unexpected change in production costs or in technology that causes the short-run aggregate supply curve to shift.

expected price level rises, firms raise prices to cover higher labor and other costs. An increase in the expected price level shifts the short-run aggregate supply curve to the left. A decline in the expected price level shifts the short-run aggregate supply curve to the right. This shift occurs because firms reduce prices as nominal wages and other costs fall, thereby supplying more output at every given price level.

Making the Connection

"Fracking" Transforms Energy Markets in the United States

From late 2008 until March 2012, the price of crude oil more than tripled, driving the price of gasoline well above $3.00 per gallon. In contrast, the price of natural gas decreased by over 50% from 2010 through 2012. Plunging natural gas prices are the result of the growing use of hydraulic fracturing (or "fracking") technology, which has allowed natural gas, as well as petroleum, to be extracted from shale rock formations. Natural gas has long been a source of energy for manufacturing products such as chemicals and fertilizers, while falling natural gas prices have caused U.S. manufacturers of aluminum, glass, and other products to switch away from coal and other fuels. But low-cost natural gas may prove to have its biggest effect on transportation markets. Firms in the long-haul trucking industry, which carries about three-quarters of the country's freight, have already began to switch from trucks fueled by diesel fuel to trucks fueled by much cheaper—and cleaner—natural gas. Companies such as Pilot Flying J have added natural gas tanks to their truck stops to accommodate the new trucks.

As a result of these developments in energy markets, the *SRAS* curve for the United States has shifted to the right. Economist Philip Verlager has predicted that the United States will eventually have the lowest energy costs of any country in the industrialized world, and Citigroup economists have estimated that the increase in production of oil and gas in the United States could result in over 3.5 million new jobs and substantially increase real GDP by 2020. Business executives are gradually being convinced that lower prices for natural gas will continue for decades. "We convinced ourselves that this is not a temporary thing," says Peter Cella, chief executive of Chevron Phillips. "This is a real, durable phenomenon, a potential competitive advantage for the United States." Geologists estimate that the supply of natural gas in the United States is sufficient to maintain current production for over a century. In November 2012, the International Energy Agency forecast that by 2030, the United States would be able to produce domestically all the energy it uses.

Using natural gas rather than coal to fuel manufacturing plants also yields benefits for the environment. Burning gas emits about one-half as much carbon dioxide as coal. Carbon emissions fell in the United States in the five years prior to 2012 by 450 million tons, more than in any other country. Ironically, emissions in the countries of the European Union rose over the same period, despite the commitment made in these countries to clean energy. Natural gas prices are much higher in Europe than in the United States; for example, three times as high in Germany and France. Consequently, firms responded to the price differences by burning coal. The price disparity is likely to persist because natural gas is more difficult and costly to transport than petroleum.

Despite the economic benefits of energy produced by hydraulic fracturing, the process has attracted critics. Fracking requires large amounts of energy and water and some people living close to production sites have complained of methane leaks. Some policymakers worry that the rush to take advantage of the new technology has overwhelmed the need to consider the short-term and long-term risks to the environment. The International Energy Agency has estimated that much of the potential adverse effects from fracking can be contained through careful monitoring, which would add about 7% to the cost of an average gas well.

Sources: Benoît Faucon and Sarah Kent, "IEA Pegs U.S. as Top Oil Producer by 2020," *Wall Street Journal*, November 12, 2012; Galina Hale and Fernanda Nechio, "Pricey Oil, Cheap Natural Gas, and Energy Costs," *FRBSF Economic Letter*, August 6, 2012; Ben Casselman and Russell Gold, "Cheap Natural Gas Gives Hope to the Rust Belt," *Wall Street Journal*, October 24, 2012; Jason Lange, "Analysis: Shale Energy Boom Dangles Prospect of Leap in Economic Growth," Reuters, May 24, 2012; "Fracking Great," *Economist*, June 2, 2012; and "Shale of the Century," *Economist*, June 2, 2012.

See related problem 2.10 at the end of the chapter.

Shifts in the Long-Run Aggregate Supply (*LRAS*) Curve

The long-run aggregate supply (*LRAS*) curve indicates the potential level of real output, or GDP, in the economy at a specific time. The *LRAS* curve shifts over time to reflect growth in potential GDP. Sources of this economic growth include (1) increases in capital and labor inputs and (2) increases in the growth of productivity, or output produced per unit of input.

Growth in inputs raises the economy's productive capacity. When firms invest in new plant and equipment—over and above just replacing old plant and equipment—they increase the capital stock available for production. Labor inputs increase when the population grows or more people participate in the labor force. Studies of output growth in the United States and other countries show that over long periods of time, productivity growth significantly influences the pace of output growth. Productivity growth occurs when firms can produce more output per unit of input, as, for instance, when better computers or more highly trained workers allow a firm to increase its output.

The principal sources of change in productivity growth are technological advances, worker training and education, government regulation of production, and changes in energy prices. The huge increases in oil prices in 1973 reduced productivity in heavy energy-using industries, such as trucking and plastics, and in the view of many economists, the increased oil prices led to a worldwide slowdown in productivity growth. Technological advances, as in communications technology and computers, raise productivity. Many economists believe that government environmental, health, and safety regulations reduce measured productivity growth because capital and labor inputs are devoted to these activities instead of to producing goods and services. These consequences of regulation do not necessarily mean that they are not in society's interest, however. For example, society must weigh the benefits of cleaner air or increased workplace safety against the potential costs of reduced output of goods and services.

Table 17.2 summarizes the most important variables that shift the short-run and long-run aggregate supply curves.

Table 17.2 Variables That Shift the Short-Run and Long-Run Aggregate Supply Curves

An increase in . . .	shifts the *SRAS* curve . . .	because . . .
labor costs		costs of production rise.
other input costs		costs of production rise.
the expected price level		wages and other costs of production rise

An increase in . . .	shifts the *LRAS* curve . . .	because . . .
capital and labor inputs		productive capacity rises.
productivity		efficiency of factors used to produce output rises.

Equilibrium in the Aggregate Demand and Aggregate Supply Model

17.3

Learning Objective

Demonstrate macroeconomic equilibrium using the aggregate demand and aggregate supply model.

Aggregate demand and short-run and long-run aggregate supply are the components of the *aggregate demand and aggregate supply (AD–AS) model* that we can use to determine the equilibrium level of output and the equilibrium price level in the economy. Because there is a difference in the behavior of firms in supplying output in the short run and the long run, we have two equilibrium values for output and the price level—the short-run equilibrium and the long-run equilibrium.

Short-Run Equilibrium

To determine output and the price level in the short run, we combine the aggregate demand (AD) curve and the short-run aggregate supply ($SRAS$) curve. Figure 17.4 shows these two curves.

The economy's short-run equilibrium occurs at the intersection, E_1, of the AD and $SRAS$ curves. No other point represents equilibrium. For example, point A lies on the AD curve, but at price level P_2, firms would supply more output than households and businesses would demand. The price level would fall to restore equilibrium at E_1. Point B lies on the $SRAS$ curve. However, at price level P_3, households and businesses would demand more output than firms would be willing to produce. The price level would rise to P_1 to equate the quantity of output demanded and the quantity of output supplied.

Long-Run Equilibrium

Our analysis of the economy's equilibrium in the short run suggests many possible combinations of output and the price level, depending on where the aggregate demand

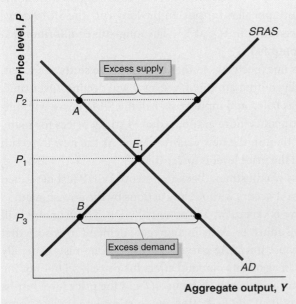

Figure 17.4

Short-Run Equilibrium

The economy's short-run equilibrium is represented by the intersection of the AD and $SRAS$ curves at E_1. The equilibrium price level is P_1. Higher price levels are associated with an excess supply of output (at point A, for example), and lower price levels are associated with excess demand for output (at point B, for example).

Figure 17.5

Adjustment to Long-Run Equilibrium

From an initial equilibrium at E_1, an increase in aggregate demand shifts the AD curve from AD_1 to AD_2, increasing output from Y^P to Y_2. Because Y_2 is greater than Y^P, prices rise, shifting the $SRAS$ curve from $SRAS_1$ to $SRAS_2$. The economy's new equilibrium is at E_3. Output has returned to Y^P, but the price level has risen to P_2. The $LRAS$ curve is vertical at Y^P, potential GDP. Shifts in the AD curve affect the level of output only in the short run. This outcome holds in both the new classical and new Keynesian views, although price adjustment is more rapid in the new classical view.

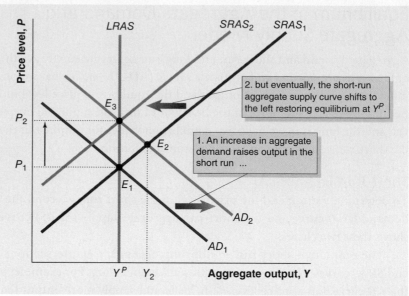

2. but eventually, the short-run aggregate supply curve shifts to the left restoring equilibrium at Y^P.

1. An increase in aggregate demand raises output in the short run ...

curve and the short-run aggregate supply curve intersect. However, in the long run, the price level adjusts to bring the economy into equilibrium at potential GDP, Y^P. So, the economy's long-run equilibrium occurs at the intersection of the AD, $SRAS$, and $LRAS$ curves. In Figure 17.5, the aggregate demand curve AD_1 and the short-run aggregate supply curve $SRAS_1$ intersect at Y^P, with a price level of P_1.

Now suppose that aggregate demand expands unexpectedly, shifting the aggregate demand curve to the right, from AD_1 to AD_2. Output and the price level both increase in the short run. The new short-run equilibrium, E_2, lies at the intersection of the AD_2 and $SRAS_1$ curves. But over time, as firms learn that the general price level has risen and as input costs rise, the $SRAS$ curve shifts to the left, from $SRAS_1$ to $SRAS_2$, because at the new price level, firms are willing to supply less output. In the long run, the $SRAS$ curve will have to shift far enough to intersect with AD_2 at Y^P. The long-run equilibrium is at point E_3, with a price level P_2 and output Y^P.

If aggregate demand contracts unexpectedly, so that the AD curve shifts to the left, the process will be reversed. Initially, output and the price level will decline. Over time, as firms learn that the price level has fallen and input costs fall, the $SRAS$ curve will shift to the right. This process of adjustment is more gradual (due to sticky prices for many firms) in the new Keynesian view than in the new classical view. At the new long-run equilibrium, output equals Y^P, and the price level is lower than P_1.

Economists refer to the process of adjustment back to potential GDP just described as an *automatic mechanism* because it occurs without any actions by the government.

In the long run, the $LRAS$ curve is vertical at Y^P, potential GDP. The economy will produce Y^P, and the price level will adjust to shifts in aggregate demand to ensure that the economy is in equilibrium. Because the $LRAS$ curve is vertical, economists generally agree that in the long run, changes in aggregate demand affect the price level but not the output level. This long-run relationship between shifts in AD and the price level results in **monetary neutrality**. For example, if the Fed attempts to stimulate the economy

Monetary neutrality The proposition that changes in the money supply have no effect on output in the long run because an increase (decrease) in the money supply raises (lowers) the price level in the long run but does not change the equilibrium level of output.

by increasing the money supply, in the short run both output and the price level will increase, but in the long run only the price level increases because the level of output returns to Y^P. Conversely, a decline in the nominal money supply lowers the price level in the long run but has no effect on output. So, we can conclude that *changes in the money supply have no effect on output in the long run*.

Economic Fluctuations in the United States

We can use the *AD–AS* model to explain past events and to predict future economic developments. Fluctuations in current output can be explained by shifts in the aggregate demand curve or the aggregate supply curve. In the following sections, we use *AD–AS* analysis to explain three episodes of economic fluctuations in the United States: (1) shocks to aggregate demand, 1964–1969; (2) supply shocks, negative during 1973–1975 and positive after 1995; and (3) a credit crunch shock to aggregate demand, 1990–1991. Then we use *AD–AS* analysis to predict consequences for output and prices of pro-investment tax reform.

Shocks to Aggregate Demand, 1964–1969 By 1964, U.S. participation in the conflict in Vietnam had grown to a major war effort, and real government purchases—principally for military equipment and personnel—had expanded by 9% since 1960. Those expenditures would increase by another 21% between 1964 and 1969. The Fed was concerned that the rise in aggregate demand caused by these increases in government purchases would increase money demand and the interest rate. To avoid an increase in the interest rate, the Fed pursued an expansionary monetary policy: The annual growth rate of M1 rose from 3.7% in 1963 to 7.7% in 1964.

The combination of fiscal and monetary expansions led to a series of shifts to the right of the aggregate demand curve. Rising aggregate demand caused output to exceed potential GDP in the mid-1960s, putting upward pressure on production costs and the price level. As we demonstrated in the analysis of short-run and long-run equilibrium with the *AD–AS* diagram, when output rises above potential GDP, eventually the *SRAS* curve shifts to the left, restoring the economy's full employment equilibrium at a higher price level. Because fiscal and monetary expansion continued for several years, *AD–AS* analysis indicates that output growth and inflation (the rate of change in the price level) should have risen from 1964 through 1969, and, in fact, that is what happened.

Supply Shocks, 1973–1975 and After 1995 By the early 1970s, many economists and policymakers believed that inflation tended to occur during periods when output was growing—a sensible conclusion when changes in the economy's equilibrium output and price level are driven by changes in aggregate demand. Then economists and policymakers in the United States and other industrialized countries were surprised by a period of rising inflation and *falling* output as a result of negative supply shocks in 1973 and 1974. In 1973, the Organization of the Petroleum Exporting Countries (OPEC) sharply reduced the supply of oil in the world oil market in an attempt to bring pressure on the United States and other countries supporting Israel in the 1973 Arab–Israeli conflict. Along with the quadrupling of world oil prices, poor crop harvests around the world caused food prices to rise significantly. In the United States, these two negative supply shocks were reinforced by the lifting of government wage and price controls that had been in effect since 1971. With the ending of these controls, firms raised prices, and workers pushed for higher wages to catch up with price and wage increases they had been unable to receive during the period of controls.

In *AD–AS* analysis, this set of negative supply shocks will shift the short-run aggregate supply curve to the left, raising the price level and reducing output. In fact, output fell in 1974 and 1975, while inflation rose. The combination of rising inflation with falling, or stagnating, output is called *stagflation*. Falling output and rising prices showed that aggregate supply shocks, as well as aggregate demand shocks, could change the economy's short-run equilibrium. A similar pattern occurred as a result of negative supply shocks caused by rising oil prices in the 1978–1980 period.

We can also examine favorable supply shocks, such as the acceleration in productivity growth experienced in the U.S. economy in the late 1990s and 2000s. Many economists believe that investment in information technology, particularly technology connected with the "new economy" of the Internet, explains this increase in productivity growth. This favorable supply shock can be illustrated using *AD–AS* analysis. Both the *SRAS* and *LRAS* curves shifted to the right, raising output and causing the price level to rise by less than it otherwise would have. Some economists feared that negative supply shocks associated with the September 11, 2001 terrorist attacks and Hurricane Katrina in 2005 would weaken productivity growth, but underlying productivity growth remained strong even during the recession of 2007–2009.

Credit Crunch and Aggregate Demand, 1990–1991 As we have discussed in previous chapters, a *credit crunch*, or a reduction in the ability or willingness of banks to lend, can cause a reduction in output. Many analysts believe that a credit crunch deepened the 1990–1991 recession. Recall that financial institutions, such as banks, are likely to be important suppliers of funds to borrowers who have few alternative sources of finance. Two events may have led to a credit crunch during this recession. First, more stringent bank regulation reduced banks' ability to lend. Second, declines in real estate values and the large debt burdens of many corporations reduced banks' willingness to lend to borrowers at any expected real interest rate. Because households and small and medium-sized businesses weren't able to replace bank credit with funds from other sources, spending for consumer durable goods and business plant and equipment fell.

In *AD–AS* analysis, the decline in spending translates into a reduction in aggregate expenditure, shifting the *AD* curve to the left. Over time, the drop in aggregate demand puts downward pressure on prices, shifting the *SRAS* curve to the right. In fact, output growth fell during the 1990–1991 recession, and inflation declined from 4.3% in 1989 to 2.9% in 1992.

Investment and the 2001 Recession The U.S. economic expansion that began in March 1991 ended exactly a decade later. The relatively brief 2001 recession lasted from March to November. The recession began as a result of a decline in business investment. In the late 1990s, firms had to replace computers and software that would have problems because of the year 2000; older computers stored the year as two digits, which would cause them to confuse 2000 with 1900. Many firms also invested heavily in information technology, as the spread of the Internet created many new business opportunities. However, some firms overestimated the profitability of establishing Web sites and investing in fiber-optic cables for rapid data transfer. As a result, the U.S. economy accumulated more capital than businesses desired when expectations of future profitability declined after 2000. The large decline in U.S. stock prices in 2000 and 2001 reflected this drop in expected future profitability. The actual capital stock being greater than the desired capital stock resulted in new business investment falling sharply. In *AD–AS* analysis, the decline in planned investment shifted the *AD* curve to the left, reducing both output growth and inflation during the recession.

The continued rapid pace of productivity growth during this period, leading to a rightward shift of the *SRAS* and *LRAS* curves, cushioned the decline in output that would otherwise have occurred as a result of the *AD* shift. The increase in aggregate supply also reinforced the downward pressure on the inflation rate as a result of the drop in aggregate demand. Indeed, in 2002 and 2003, some economists worried that the United States could experience deflation, a falling general price level, though that did not occur.

Are Investment Incentives Inflationary? In the late 1990s, many economists and policymakers urged Congress to consider tax reforms that would stimulate business investment. And in 2002, President George W. Bush proposed and won Congressional approval for investment incentives. Such reforms included (1) the introduction of expensing—in which businesses write off the purchase of new plant and equipment all at once, rather than gradually—and (2) cuts in dividend and capital gains taxes that reduced the cost of capital. Many economists argued that such reforms would significantly increase business investment demand and output of capital goods. Would they also increase inflation?

In *AD–AS* analysis, the stimulus to investment translates into an increase in aggregate demand, shifting the *AD* curve to the right. However, as the new plant and equipment are installed, the economy's capacity to produce increases, and the *SRAS* and *LRAS* curves shift to the right, reducing the inflationary pressure from pro-investment tax reform. Recent evidence suggests that the supply response is substantial and investment incentives are unlikely to be inflationary.

In September 2010, as the U.S. economy struggled to recover from the 2007–2009 recession, in an attempt to stimulate aggregate demand, President Barack Obama proposed, and Congress enacted, the Small Business Jobs Act of 2010, which allowed businesses to expense their spending on investment goods through the end of 2011.

The Effects of Monetary Policy

The **business cycle** refers to alternating periods of economic expansion and economic recession. In a business cycle, output grows during an expansion until the business cycle peak. Then output declines as the economy moves into a contraction or recession until the business cycle trough, when output begins to expand again. This pattern varies from several months to several years, and expansions and recessions vary in intensity. In the post–World War II period, the recessions of 1981–1982 and 2007–2009 were particularly severe.

When the economy moves into a recession, output declines and unemployment increases. These problems cause hardship for individuals and businesses. Most economists believe that increases in the money supply and decreases in interest rates can increase short-run output. It may be possible, then, for the Fed to use monetary policies that could stabilize the economy by reducing the severity of recessions and

17.4

Learning Objective
Use the aggregate demand and aggregate supply model to show the effects of monetary policy.

Business cycle
Alternating periods of economic expansion and economic recession.

Stabilization policy A monetary policy or fiscal policy intended to reduce the severity of the business cycle and stabilize the economy.

smoothing short-run fluctuations in output. Such a **stabilization policy** attempts to shift the *AD* curve by changing the money supply and interest rates. It is also possible for Congress and the president to pursue *fiscal policy* actions, such as changing the level of government purchases or taxes to stabilize the economy.

An Expansionary Monetary Policy

Suppose that the economy is hit by an *aggregate demand shock*, as happened in 2007, with the collapse of spending on new houses. Figure 17.6 illustrates the result. In panel (a), the economy starts at equilibrium at E_1, which is at the intersection of AD_1, $SRAS_1$, and $LRAS$. Output is at Y^P, and the price level is at P_1. As a result of the aggregate demand shock, the aggregate demand curve shifts from AD_1 to AD_2. The economy enters a recession at E_2, with output falling from Y^P to Y_2 and the price level falling from P_1 to P_2.

At this point, the Fed has to decide whether to implement an expansionary monetary policy. If the Fed does nothing, we know from our earlier analysis that the economy will eventually correct itself. At E_2, with output less than full employment, over time input costs and prices will fall, shifting the short-run aggregate supply curve to the right, from $SRAS_1$ to $SRAS_2$, and bringing the economy back to potential GDP at E_3. The economy eventually returns to potential GDP at price level, P_3, but the necessary

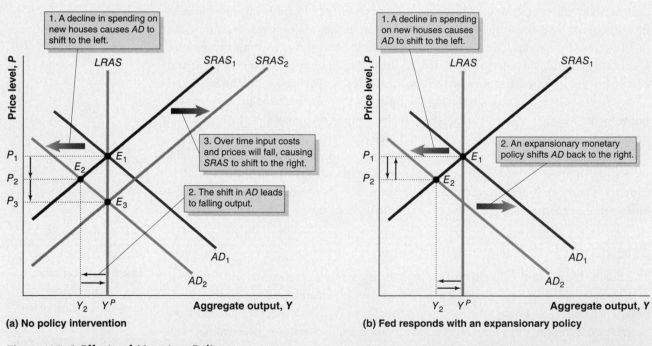

Figure 17.6 Effects of Monetary Policy

Panel (a) shows that from an initial full-employment equilibrium at E_1, an aggregate demand shock shifts the *AD* curve from AD_1 to AD_2, and output falls from Y^P to Y_2. At E_2, the economy is in a recession. Over time, the price level adjusts downward, restoring the economy's full employment equilibrium at E_3.

Panel (b) shows that from an initial full-employment equilibrium at E_1, an aggregate demand shock shifts the *AD* curve from AD_1 to AD_2. At E_2, the economy is in a recession. The Fed speeds recovery, using an expansionary monetary policy, which shifts the *AD* curve back from AD_2 to AD_1. Relative to the nonintervention case, the economy recovers more quickly back to full employment, but with a higher long-run price level.

adjustments to costs and prices may take years, during which time some workers suffer unemployment and some firms suffer losses.

Alternatively, as panel (b) of Figure 17.6 shows, the Fed could try to speed recovery by implementing an expansionary monetary policy. The Fed can implement an expansionary monetary policy by using open market operations to lower the target for the federal funds rate (see Chapter 15). An expansionary policy will shift the aggregate demand curve back to the right, from AD_2 to AD_1. The economy moves from recession at E_2 back to its initial full employment equilibrium at E_1. The economy returns to potential GDP more quickly than it would have if the Fed had followed the alternative of refraining from active policy. Stabilization policy, however, has a side effect: It leads to a higher price level than would exist if no action were taken.

During the 1960s, many economists encouraged the use of monetary and fiscal policies to smooth fluctuations in the economy. However, others doubted that attempts to *fine-tune* the economy would be effective, given the potentially long lags in formulating and implementing stabilization policies. Most economists today believe that because of these lags, policymakers can't hope to successfully counterbalance every economic fluctuation. Therefore, economists generally advocate that policymakers focus on long-run objectives such as low inflation or steady economic growth. Many economists argue that policymakers should restrict the use of activist policy to fighting major downturns in the economy. A major downturn is, of course, exactly what the U.S. economy experienced in 2007.

Solved Problem 17.4

Dealing with Shocks to Aggregate Demand and Aggregate Supply

Assume that the economy is initially in equilibrium at full employment. Then suppose that the economy is hit simultaneously with negative aggregate demand and aggregate supply shocks: There is a large increase in oil prices, and there is a sharp decline in consumption spending as households become pessimistic about their future incomes.

a. Draw an aggregate demand and aggregate supply graph to illustrate the initial equilibrium and the short-run equilibrium after the shocks.

Do we know with certainty whether the price level will be higher or lower in the new equilibrium?

b. Suppose that the Fed decides not to intervene with an expansionary monetary policy. Show how the economy will adjust back to its long-run equilibrium.

c. Now suppose that the Fed decides to intervene with an expansionary monetary policy. If the Fed's policy is successful, show how the economy adjusts back to its long-run equilibrium.

Solving the Problem

Step 1 **Review the chapter material.** This problem is about the Fed's implementing an expansionary monetary policy, so you may want to review the section "An Expansionary Monetary Policy," which begins on page 538.

Step 2 **Answer part (a) by drawing the appropriate graph and explaining whether we know if the price level will rise or fall.** A negative supply shock will cause the aggregate supply curve to shift to the left, from $SRAS_1$ to $SRAS_2$, and a negative demand shock will cause the aggregate demand curve to shift to the left, from AD_1 to AD_2. Your graph should look like this:

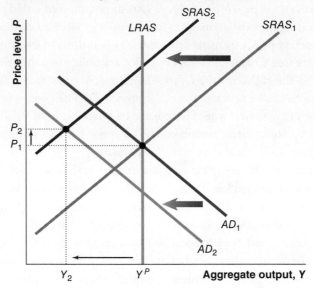

Note that as we have drawn the graph, the price level increases from P_1 to P_2, but it is possible that the AD curve will shift to the left by more than does the $SRAS$ curve. In that case, the price level will fall. So, we can't say with certainty whether the price level will rise or fall if the economy is hit by aggregate supply and aggregate demand shocks at the same time.

Step 3 **Answer part (b) by drawing the appropriate graph.** We start at the short-run equilibrium described in part (a), with output at Y_2 and the price level at P_2. With output at Y_2 being less than full employment, over time, prices and input costs will fall, shifting the short-run aggregate supply curve to the right, from $SRAS_2$ to $SRAS_3$, which will eventually bring the economy back to potential GDP, Y^P, at a lower price level, P_3.

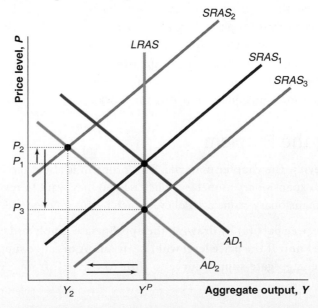

Step 4 **Answer part (c) by drawing the appropriate graph.** Starting again at the short-run equilibrium from part (a), an expansionary monetary policy will shift the aggregate demand curve from AD_2 to AD_3, restoring the economy to potential GDP, Y^P, at a higher price level, P_3.

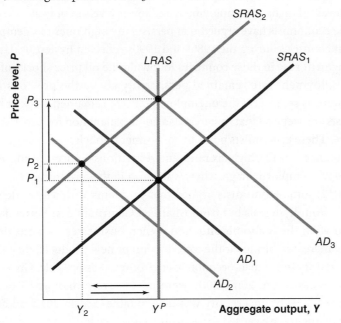

See related problem 4.7 at the end of the chapter.

Was Monetary Policy Ineffective During the 2007–2009 Recession?

As we saw in the chapter opener, in late 2012 the U.S. unemployment rate remained stubbornly high, and increases in real GDP were disappointingly modest. Do these facts indicate that monetary policy had failed? Not necessarily. Certainly, the Fed was unable to pull off a rapid and smooth return to full employment of the type illustrated in panel (b) of Figure 17.6 on page 538. Research has shown, though, that both in the United States and in other countries, recessions started by financial crises are almost always very severe (see Chapter 12). And the 2007–2009 recession was not caused simply by a temporary decline in aggregate demand. Instead, the declines in output in important industries may have resulted from structural changes in the economy and so were likely to be long-lived, perhaps even permanent. Therefore, expansionary monetary policy aimed at increasing aggregate demand would probably not succeed in re-employing workers who had lost their jobs in those industries. Many of those workers might need to be retrained for other jobs or to move to parts of the country where employment was increasing.

In other words, in 2012, many economists inside and outside the Fed were wondering whether prolonged levels of high unemployment were leading to long-lived reductions in aggregate supply. Some economists believe that large negative shifts in aggregate demand actually reduce the full employment level of output, a situation known as *hysteresis*. With hysteresis, the process of the economy automatically returning to equilibrium, as illustrated in panel (a) of Figure 17.6, breaks down. This breakdown occurs because if high rates of unemployment persist, more workers lose their skills—or are viewed by employers as lacking current skills—and therefore have difficulty being rehired. Furthermore, workers who are unemployed for long periods may become discouraged and drop out of the labor force permanently. These obstacles to locating new jobs lead to chronic levels of higher unemployment and lower levels of output.

Some economists have argued that persistently high rates of unemployment in many European countries during the 1980s and 1990s reflected hysteresis. Under this analysis, unemployment rose in those countries following the oil price shocks of the 1970s. When the unemployment rate remained persistently above the previous full employment level, hysteresis set in, and the unemployment rate remained stuck at high levels. Other economists are skeptical that hysteresis is a good explanation for persistent unemployment in Europe. These economists point to government policies, such as generous unemployment insurance benefits, high tax rates, and restrictions on firms hiring and firing workers, to explain why employment growth was sluggish in these countries.

In 2012, some economists argued that problems with aggregate supply may have arisen not from hysteresis but from what Fed Chairman Ben Bernanke called "unusual uncertainty" in the economic situation. When businesses are considering new capital spending, increased hiring, or the introduction of new products, they naturally prefer as little uncertainty in the macroeconomic environment as possible. Given that the financial crisis and recession of 2007–2009 were more severe than any since World War II, an increased level of uncertainty was unavoidable. But in 2012, additional sources of uncertainty might have caused some firms to produce less output and hire fewer workers than they would have otherwise. In 2010, Congress passed the Affordable Care Act, which overhauled the U.S. healthcare system. Owners of some small and medium-sized businesses were concerned that the act increased the cost of hiring workers because it required them either to provide the workers with health insurance or to pay a fine to the government. As we saw in the chapter opener, in 2012, many households and firms were concerned that tax increases and government spending cuts scheduled to begin in January 2013 might push the economy back into recession. Finally, as we have discussed in earlier chapters, many small to medium-sized businesses found that they were unable to secure bank loans to expand their businesses. Economists debated the extent to which these factors were restraining hiring and output growth.

So, the Fed found itself in a dilemma: Using conventional expansionary monetary policy to increase the rate of output growth would be effective only if the main problem facing the economy was insufficient aggregate demand, which a majority of economists and policymakers believed to be the case. If aggregate supply was the problem, however, conventional policy would be ineffective.

Making the Connection

Have Recent Years Been Like the 1930s?

During and after the recession of 2007–2009, economists and policymakers considered whether events from the Great Depression of the 1930s might provide insight into what was happening. The Depression had also involved a financial crisis, and it had persisted over more than a decade, a pattern that policymakers in 2012 were hoping not to repeat. We have seen that Ben Bernanke's academic studies of the bank panics of the early 1930s led him to take aggressive actions to save large financial firms during 2008.

One of the striking facts about the Depression was the high unemployment rate in the late 1930s. This high unemployment rate was in part due to the recession of 1937–1938, which the Fed had inadvertently helped cause through a series of increases in the required reserve ratio (see Chapter 14). Robert Gordon of Northwestern University has focused on the situation in the United States in 1939. Although estimates differ, Gordon believes that the unemployment rate that year was greater than 17% and that more than one-third of the unemployed had been without a job for more than a year. Despite the high unemployment rate, there was little indication of the falling wages and prices that would push the economy back to full employment by the process shown in panel (a) of Figure 17.6 on page 538. Some economists believe that the high unemployment of 1939 was due to problems with aggregate demand, while others believe it was due to problems with aggregate supply. Economists supporting the aggregate supply explanation point to: (1) the substantial increases in tax rates Congress had enacted during the 1930s; (2) the sharp increase in unionization, strikes, and labor unrest; and (3) what these economists see as the undermining of private property rights under President Franklin Roosevelt's New Deal. This debate echoes some of the points raised by economists in analyzing economic conditions in 2012.

Gordon disagrees with the aggregate supply arguments, holding instead that the United States was suffering from hysteresis brought on by insufficient aggregate demand. He argues that once Congress began to substantially increase spending on military goods in 1940 to prepare for the entry of the United States into World War II, aggregate output rapidly expanded, and unemployment declined. In other words, structural barriers to expanding output and employment disappeared once a sufficiently large increase in aggregate demand had taken place. Gordon's interpretation has been challenged, however. Economist Robert Higgs has argued that the high unemployment of the 1930s was caused by "regime uncertainty" due to New Deal policies. He argues that because the 1940–1945 increases in output were largely in the war material and munitions industries, and the decline in unemployment was due to the draft and the growth in employment in war industries, true prosperity did not return until the end of the war in 1945. The postwar prosperity was due to:

> the death of Roosevelt and the succession of Harry S Truman and his administration [which] completed the shift from a political regime investors perceived as full of uncertainty to one in which they felt much more confident about the security of their private property rights. . . . [I]nvestors set in motion the postwar investment boom that powered the economy's return to sustained prosperity notwithstanding the drastic reduction of federal government spending from its extraordinarily elevated war-time levels.

Higgs's argument has also been subject to criticism by economists who see the shift in policies from the Roosevelt to Truman administrations as being less dramatic than he does. Undoubtedly, economists will continue to explore the interesting parallels between the U.S. economy of the 1930s and the U.S. economy following the beginning of the financial crisis in 2007.

Sources: Robert J. Gordon, "Back to the Future: European Unemployment Today Viewed from America in 1939," *Brookings Papers on Economic Activity*, Vol. 19, No. 1, 1988, pp. 271–312; and Robert Higgs, *Depression, War, and Cold War: Challenging the Myths of Conflict and Prosperity*, Oakland, CA: Independent Institute, 2009.

See related problems 4.10 and 4.11 at the end of the chapter.

Answering the Key Question

Continued from page 519

At the beginning of this chapter, we asked:

"What explains the high unemployment rates during the economic expansion that began in 2009?"

As we have seen in this chapter, in late 2012, the unemployment rate remained at nearly 8%, which was unusually high for the post–World War II period. Economists disagreed about why the unemployment rate was so high. Some economists believed that high unemployment was the result of insufficient aggregate demand and suggested that production and employment could be expanded with conventional macroeconomic stabilization policies. Other economists, though, saw problems with aggregate supply, either because of potentially long-lived declines in the importance of some key industries, particularly residential construction, or because of increased economic uncertainty.

Key Terms and Problems

Key Terms

Aggregate demand (*AD*) curve, p. 521

Aggregate supply, p. 525

Business cycle, p. 537

Long-run aggregate supply (*LRAS*) curve, p. 528

Monetary neutrality, p. 534

Real money balances, p. 522

Short-run aggregate supply (*SRAS*) curve, p. 525

Stabilization policy, p. 538

Supply shock, p. 529

17.1 The Aggregate Demand Curve
Explain how the aggregate demand curve is derived.

Review Questions

1.1 Briefly describe each of the four components of aggregate expenditure.

1.2 Why is the *AD* curve downward sloping?

1.3 What is the primary reason that households and firms demand money? Why is the demand for real money balances downward sloping?

1.4 How does an increase in the interest rate affect each of the following types of aggregate expenditure?

a. Investment spending by firms on plant and equipment

b. Consumption spending by households

c. Net exports

Problems and Applications

1.5 Briefly explain whether each of the following shifts the aggregate demand curve to the right or to the left.

  a. The Federal Reserve sells $10 billion of U.S. Treasury securities.

  b. The federal government launches a massive program to rebuild the nation's highways.

  c. The federal government cuts the corporate profits tax.

  d. The foreign exchange value of the dollar rises.

  e. Firms become pessimistic about the future profitability of spending on factories and machinery.

1.6 Use a money market graph to explain the effect of a decrease in the price level on the equilibrium interest rate. How does the change in the interest rate affect planned investment spending, consumption spending, and net exports?

1.7 Use a money market graph to show the effect of an open market purchase of U.S. Treasury securities by the Federal Reserve. Use the results from your graph to explain why the aggregate demand curve shifts when the Fed purchases Treasury securities.

1.8 In the early to mid-2000s, stock prices and housing prices rose substantially. What effect would these increases in household wealth have on the saving rate and on consumption spending? How would the increase in stock prices and housing prices have affected aggregate demand?

1.9 Shortly before leaving her position as chair of the President's Council of Economic Advisers in the Obama administration, Christina Romer observed: "The only surefire ways for policymakers to substantially increase aggregate demand in the short run are for the government to spend more and tax less." Which policymakers was Romer referring to? Briefly explain why the government's spending more and taxing less increases aggregate demand.

Source: Deborah Solomon, "Romer: 'Spend More, Tax Less' to Boost Economy," *Wall Street Journal*, September 1, 2010.

17.2 The Aggregate Supply Curve
Explain how the aggregate supply curve is derived.

Review Questions

2.1 How do the slopes of the short-run aggregate supply curve and the long-run aggregate supply curve differ?

2.2 In the new classical view, why can't firms distinguish between increases in the general price level and increases in the relative prices of their products?

2.3 What is meant by the term *price stickiness* in the new Keynesian view? What explains price stickiness?

2.4 What factors shift the short-run aggregate supply curve? What factors shift the long-run aggregate supply curve?

Problems and Applications

2.5 Use the equation $Y = Y^P + a(P - P^e)$ to explain why in the new classical view, the short-run aggregate supply curve is positively sloped and the long-run aggregate supply curve is vertical.

2.6 Draw graphs to show the effect of each of the following on the short-run aggregate supply curve:

  a. A decrease in the expected price level

  b. A decrease in oil prices

  c. The development of personal computers that are 10 times faster than existing computers

  d. An increase in wages, resulting from output exceeding the full-employment level of output

  e. Severe winter storms that affect a large part of the United States

2.7 In a blog on the *Economist* web site, correspondent Matt Yglesias makes the following statement: "[We] need to note that rising oil prices represent both demand shocks and supply shocks to the American economy." Explain how increases in oil prices can cause shifts in both aggregate demand and aggregate supply.

Source: Matt Yglesias, "Oil: When the Supply Shocks Are Demand Shocks and the Demand Shocks Are Supply Shocks," *Economist*, February 26, 2012.

2.8 An article in the *Economist* magazine noted: "The economy's potential to supply goods and services [is] determined by such things as the labour force and capital stock, as well as inflation expectations." Do you agree with this list of determinants of potential GDP? Briefly explain.

Source: "Money's Muddled Message," *Economist*, May 19, 2009.

2.9 If the long-run aggregate supply curve shifts, does the short-run aggregate supply curve also have to shift? If the short-run aggregate supply curve shifts, does the long-run aggregate supply curve also have to shift? (Hint: Consider the factors that shift each curve and determine whether these factors also shift the other curve.)

2.10 [Related to the Making the Connection **on page 530**] Hydraulic fracturing has caused a dramatic reduction in the cost of producing natural gas and petroleum. Would you expect these cost reductions to have a greater effect on aggregate supply in the United States in the short run or in the long run? Briefly explain.

17.3 Equilibrium in the Aggregate Demand and Aggregate Supply Model
Demonstrate macroeconomic equilibrium using the aggregate demand and aggregate supply model.

Review Questions

3.1 In a graph illustrating the *AD–AS* model, where does short-run equilibrium occur, and where does long-run equilibrium occur? At what level of output does long-run equilibrium occur?

3.2 When the economy is in a short-run equilibrium, with output greater than potential GDP, what will happen to the short-run aggregate supply curve? Briefly explain.

3.3 Suppose that the economy is initially in equilibrium at potential GDP. If there is a decrease in aggregate demand, use an *AD–AS* graph to show the effects on the price level and the output level in the short run and in the long run.

3.4 Does monetary neutrality mean that changes in the money supply can never affect real GDP? Briefly explain.

Problems and Applications

3.5 Can the economy be in a short-run macroeconomic equilibrium without being in a long-run macroeconomic equilibrium? Can the economy be in a long-run macroeconomic equilibrium without being in a short-run macroeconomic equilibrium? Support your answer with an *AD–AS* graph.

3.6 An article in the *Economist* magazine observed: "Creating more inflation is harder than it sounds. . . . It requires aggregate demand to return to, and exceed, potential output." Use an *AD–AS* graph to show why aggregate demand being greater than potential GDP results in inflation. Is aggregate demand being greater than potential GDP the only way for inflation to occur in the *AD–AS* model? Briefly explain.

Source: "A Winding Path to Inflation," *Economist*, June 3, 2010.

3.7 Suppose that in Year 1 the price level equals 110 and the output level equals $14 trillion and that in Year 2 the price level equals 104 and the output level equals $13 trillion. In the *AD–AS* model, what shift in the aggregate demand curve or the aggregate supply curve would explain the movement in the price level and the output level that occurred from Year 1 to Year 2?

3.8 Assume that the economy is initially in equilibrium at potential GDP. Use an *AD–AS* graph to show the effect of an increase in government purchases on the price level and the output level in the short run and in the long run. Explain what is happening in your graph.

3.9 Assume that the economy is initially in equilibrium at potential GDP. Suppose that there is a decrease in income in Europe that causes a decrease in demand for U.S.-produced goods. Use an *AD–AS* graph to show the effect of the decline in income in Europe on output and the price level in the United States in the short run and in the long run.

3.10 In a blog entry on the Barron's Web site, the head of emerging markets research at the Japanese investment bank Nomura was quoted as saying the following about the Brazilian economy: "We think all this demand hitting a still inelastic aggregate supply will likely lead to a lot more inflation than growth."

a. Relying on the definition of "inelastic" that you learned in your principles of economics course, briefly explain what this person meant by "inelastic supply."

b. Why would an increase in aggregate demand cause more inflation than growth if aggregate supply is inelastic? Support your answer with an *AD–AS* graph.

Source: Reshma Kapadia, "UBS Recommends Near-term Caution In Global Equities; Credit Suisse Capitulates On MSCI China," blogs.barrons.com, August 30, 2012.

17.4 **The Effects of Monetary Policy**
Use the aggregate demand and aggregate supply model to show the effects of monetary policy.

Review Questions

4.1 Are all business cycles the same in length and severity?

4.2 Why might attempts to fine-tune the economy be ineffective? Instead of fine-tuning, what do economists generally advocate that policymakers do?

4.3 What policies might the Federal Reserve use to counteract an aggregate demand shock?

4.4 What is hysteresis, and what problems might it pose for an economy?

Problems and Applications

4.5 The Federal Reserve can use expansionary or contractionary policy to shift the aggregate demand curve. Use an *AD–AS* graph to show how monetary policy should be used to return output to potential GDP when:

a. the aggregate demand curve intersects the short-run aggregate supply curve to the left of potential GDP. Briefly explain how the Federal Reserve would carry out this policy.

b. the aggregate demand curve intersects the short-run aggregate supply curve to the right of potential GDP. Briefly explain how the Federal Reserve would carry out this policy.

4.6 Given that the economy can correct itself and return to potential GDP, why would the Federal Reserve pursue expansionary monetary policy following a negative aggregate demand shock? How could the Fed pursuing an expansionary monetary policy be preferable to the economy correcting itself? On the other hand, how could an expansionary monetary policy hurt the economy, given the lags in the impact of monetary policy actions?

4.7 [Related to the Solved Problem 17.4 on page 539] Assume that the economy is initially in equilibrium at potential GDP. Then suppose that the economy is hit simultaneously with a *positive* aggregate demand shock and a *negative* aggregate supply shock: There is a large increase in U.S. exports to Europe and a large increase in oil prices.

a. Use an *AD–AS* graph to illustrate the initial equilibrium and the short-run equilibrium after the shocks. Do we know with certainty whether in the new equilibrium the output level will be higher or lower than potential GDP?

b. Suppose that the Fed decides not to intervene with monetary policy. Show how the economy will adjust back to long-run equilibrium.

c. Now suppose that the Fed decides to intervene with monetary policy. If the Fed's policy is successful, show how the economy adjusts back to long-run equilibrium.

4.8 Normally we think of the factors that cause the *AD* curve to shift as different from the factors that cause the *LRAS* curve to shift. Is this still true in the case of hysteresis? Briefly explain.

4.9 [Related to the Chapter Opener on page 519] In a column in the *Wall Street Journal*, Michael Bordo, an economist at Rutgers University, argues that the slow recovery from the 2007–2009 recession:

> can largely be attributed to the unprecedented housing bust. . . . Another problem may be uncertainty over changes in fiscal and regulatory policy, or over structural change in the economy.

Discuss how each of these three factors may have slowed recovery from the recession.

Source: Michael Bordo, "Financial Recessions Don't Lead to Weak Recoveries," *Wall Street Journal*, September 27, 2012.

4.10 [Related to the Making the Connection on page 542] Writing in the *New York Times*, economist Tyler Cowen of George Mason University argued:

> In short, expansionary monetary policy and wartime orders from Europe, not the well-known policies of the New Deal, did the most to make the American economy climb out of the Depression.

Is Cowen's position more consistent with that of Robert Gordon or that of Robert Higgs? Briefly explain.

Source: Tyler Cowen, "The New Deal Didn't Always Work, Either," *New York Times*, November 21, 2008.

4.11 [Related to the Making the Connection on page 542] Economist Robert Gordon has written the following:

During 1939, more than any other year in the dismal Depression decade, the American economy exhibited every evidence of slipping into a low-employment trap. Prices were on a plateau, with no tendency to decline, despite high unemployment.

a. What does Gordon mean by a "low-employment trap"? (Hint: Think about Gordon's explanation for the high unemployment rate in 1939, as discussed in the *Making the Connection.*)

b. Why might the fact that prices were not declining despite high unemployment lead Gordon to conclude that the economy was in a low-employment trap?

Source: Robert J. Gordon, "Back to the Future: European Unemployment Today Viewed from America in 1939," *Brookings Papers on Economic Activity*, Vol. 19, No. 1, 1988, p. 272.

4.12 In April 2010, Christina Romer, who was then serving as chair of the President's Council of Economic Advisers, argued:

> The overwhelming weight of the evidence is that the current very high—and very disturbing—levels of overall and long-term unemployment are not a separate, structural problem, but largely a cyclical one.

Was Romer arguing that the high unemployment in 2010 was largely due to problems with aggregate demand or to problems with aggregate supply? Briefly explain.

Source: Sewell Chan, "Unemployment Is Tied to Big Drop in Demand," *New York Times*, April 17, 2010.

4.13 Writing in the *New York Times* in August 2012, Christina Romer, former chair of the President's Council of Economic Advisers, argued that: "The academic literature shows that monetary policy can be very effective at reducing unemployment in situations like ours."

a. What did Romer mean by "situations like ours"?

b. Are there situations in which monetary policy would be ineffective at reducing unemployment? Briefly explain.

Source: Christina Romer, "It's Time for the Fed to Lead the Fight," *New York Times*, June 9, 2012.

Data Exercises

D17.1: [**Showing movements in equilibrium real GDP and the price level**] Go to the Web site of the Federal Reserve Bank of St. Louis (FRED) (research.stlouisfed.org/fred2/) and find data on real GDP (GDPCA) and the GDP price deflator (USAGDPDEFAISMEI) for 1960, 1973, 1975, and 2007.

    a. In an *AD–AS* graph, using the actual values for real GDP and the GDP price deflator, show equilibrium for 1960 and for 2007. Assume that the economy was at equilibrium at potential GDP in both years. From 1960 to 2007, what happened to long-run aggregate supply? Given the change in the GDP implicit price deflator, did aggregate demand grow more or less than long-run aggregate supply?

    b. In an *AD–AS* graph, using the actual values for real GDP and the GDP price deflator, show equilibrium for 1973 and for 1975. Assume that the economy was in equilibrium at potential GDP in 1973 but in only a short-run equilibrium in 1975. Given the changes in real GDP and the GDP implicit price deflator, briefly explain what happened to short-run aggregate supply from 1973 to 1975.

D17.2: [**The effects of a positive supply shock**] Using data from the St. Louis Federal Reserve (http://research.stlouisfed.org/fred2/) FRED database, examine the experience of the U.S. economy during the 1990s. The U.S. economy experienced a supply shock with the spread of information communication technology and the Internet after 1995.

    a. Download monthly data on the Personal Consumption Expenditure price index (PCEPI) from 1981 to the present. Calculate the inflation rate from 1982 to 2007 as the percentage change in the Personal Consumption Expenditure price index from the same month in the previous year.

    b. Calculate the average inflation rate from 1982 to 1995 and the average inflation rate from 1995 to 2007.

    c. Are your calculations consistent with a positive supply shock after 1995? Briefly explain.

D17.3: [**Comparing business cycles across countries**] During the 2007–2009 period, shocks affected the United Kingdom in ways similar to the United States. As in the United States, oil prices were high, and housing prices had sharply escalated after 2000. The financial crisis in the United States also affected investment in the United Kingdom, both by limiting credit and increasing risk premiums. Using data from the St. Louis Federal Reserve (http://research.stlouisfed.org/fred2/) FRED database, examine the behavior of the U.K. economy since 2007.

    a. Download quarterly data for real GDP (GBRRGDPQDSNAQ) and the GDP deflator (GBRGDPDEFQISMEI) from 2006 to the present. Calculate the growth rate of real GDP as the percentage change from the same quarter in the previous year and calculate the inflation rate as the percentage change in the GDP deflator from the same quarter in the previous year. Download data on the unemployment rate (GBRURHARMMDSMEI) for the same time period.

    b. Download the three data series from 2007 to the present in the same graph. How similar do the data indicate that the experience of the United Kingdom was during these years compared with the experience of the United States?

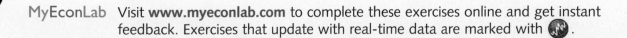

CHAPTER 18

Monetary Theory II: The *IS–MP* Model

Learning Objectives

After studying this chapter, you should be able to:

18.1 Understand what the *IS* curve is and how it is derived (pages 551–562)

18.2 Explain the significance of the *MP* curve and the Phillips curve (pages 562–570)

18.3 Use the *IS–MP* model to illustrate macroeconomic equilibrium (pages 570–579)

18.4 Discuss alternative channels of monetary policy (pages 579–581)

18.A Appendix: Use the *IS–LM* model to illustrate macroeconomic equilibrium (pages 588–591)

The Fed Forecasts the Economy

It was not good news in July 2012 when the Federal Reserve reported to Congress that it was lowering its forecasts for economic growth for the remainder of 2012. Earlier that year, the Fed had forecast that growth in real GDP for all of 2012 would be about 2.5%, but it lowered the forecast to 2.2%. In June 2011, the Fed had forecast growth of 3.5% for 2012. Although the differences in these forecasts may seem small, they were important. Economists estimate that real GDP has to grow at an annual rate of at least 2.5% to generate enough jobs to absorb each year's college graduates and other new job entrants. Growth slower than 2.5% for a prolonged period results in a rising unemployment rate.

Even a growth rate of 2.5%, while high enough to keep unemployment from increasing further, would not have been high enough to create the more than 9 million additional jobs necessary to bring employment back to normal levels. The severe recession of 2007–2009 had destroyed millions of jobs that a slowly growing economy was having trouble replacing.

Testifying before Congress, Federal Reserve Chairman Ben Bernanke cited a number of factors that were slowing economic growth. He noted problems in the housing market: "Many would-be buyers are deterred by worries about their own finances or about the economy more generally. Other prospective

Continued on next page

Key Issue and Question

Issue: By December 2008, the Fed had driven the target for the federal funds rate to near zero.

Question: In what circumstances is lowering the target for the federal funds rate unlikely to be effective in fighting a recession?

Answered on page 582

homebuyers cannot obtain mortgages due to tight lending standards, impaired creditworthiness, or because . . . they owe more than their homes are worth." He also argued that consumption spending was being held back because "households remain concerned about their employment and income prospects and their overall level of confidence remains relatively low." Bernanke also noted that: "Financial strains associated with the crisis in Europe . . . are weighing on both global and domestic economic activity." Finally, he argued that the "fiscal cliff"—increases in taxes and cuts in federal government spending scheduled to occur in early 2013—was increasing uncertainty, thereby reducing household and business spending.

The Fed was not alone in mid-2012 in reducing forecasts of economic growth. Many private forecasters also expected less growth for the remainder of 2012 and 2013 than they had anticipated earlier in the year. The Bank of England reduced its forecast of annual growth in real GDP in the United Kingdom during 2012 from a very weak 0.8% to zero, noting that slow growth in the rest of Europe would reduce British exports. The International Monetary Fund (IMF) reduced its forecast of growth of global real GDP from 3.5% to 3.3% for 2012 and to 3.6% from 3.9% for 2013. The IMF cited financial market problems and political uncertainty among the factors that were slowing growth.

In determining monetary policy, the Fed's forecasts of future economic growth are crucial. The Fed knows that changes in interest rates and the money supply affect the economy with a lag, so policies it implements today will not have their full effect on the economy for a year or more. Therefore, having some idea of the likely state of the economy in the future helps to guide policy today. In preparing its forecasts, the Fed, foreign central banks, and private forecasters usually rely on macroeconomic models. In this chapter, we explore a model that helps us analyze how Fed policies affect key macroeconomic variables.

Sources: Board of Governors of the Federal Reserve System, "Statement by Ben S. Bernanke Chairman Board of Governors of the Federal Reserve System before the Committee on Banking, Housing, and Urban Affairs, U.S. Senate," July 17, 2012; Board of Governors of the Federal Reserve System, "Monetary Policy Report to the Congress," July 17, 2012; Stephen Castle, "British Central Bank Cuts Growth Forecast," *New York Times*, August 8, 2012; and Annie Lowrey, "I.M.F. Lowers Its Forecast for Global Growth," *New York Times*, October 8, 2012.

In the previous chapter, we discussed the basic aggregate demand and aggregate supply (*AD–AS*) model. Although that model provides insights into how the price level and the level of real GDP are determined in the short run, it has some important shortcomings. First, the *AD–AS* model implicitly assumes that the full-employment level of real GDP remains constant when, in fact, it increases each year. Second, the model provides an explanation of the price level but not of *changes* in the price level—the inflation rate. Yet typically we are more interested in the inflation rate than we are in the price level. Finally, the model doesn't explicitly take into account how the Fed reacts to changing economic conditions. In this chapter, we develop a model that provides a more complete explanation of changes in real GDP, the inflation rate, and the interest rate.

The *IS* Curve

The *IS–MP model* is a more complete macroeconomic model than is the aggregate demand and aggregate supply (*AD–AS*) model.[1] We can use the *IS–MP* model to provide a more complete analysis of the effects of Federal Reserve policy. Note that "complete" is a relative term. To be useful, every model must simplify reality. The *IS–MP* model is

18.1

Learning Objective

Understand what the *IS* curve is and how it is derived.

---

[1]Economists love acronyms, even if they can sometimes be mysterious. In this case, *IS* stands for investment and saving, while *MP* stands for monetary policy. For a discussion of the historical origins of this model, see the *Making the Connection* on pages 571–572.

more complete than the *AD–AS* model and can answer questions that the *AD–AS* model cannot. But the *IS–MP* model is less complete than many other macroeconomic models, including some that the Fed uses to prepare its forecasts. Deciding whether a model is too simplified—or not simplified enough—depends on the context in which the model is being used. For our purposes, the *IS–MP* model is sufficiently complete to explain the key aspects of Federal Reserve policy.

The ***IS–MP*** **model** consists of three parts:

1. The ***IS*** **curve**, which represents equilibrium in the market for goods and services.
2. The ***MP*** **curve**, which represents Federal Reserve monetary policy.
3. The **Phillips curve**, which represents the short-run relationship between the output gap (which is the percentage difference between actual and potential real GDP) and the inflation rate.

We begin by analyzing the *IS* curve.

Equilibrium in the Goods Market

Economists think of *aggregate expenditure* on total goods and services, or real GDP, as being equal to the sum of consumption demand, *C*; demand for investment in business plant and equipment, business inventories, and housing, *I*; government purchases of goods and services, *G*; and net exports (or exports of goods and services minus imports of goods and services), *NX*. So, we can write that aggregate expenditure, *AE*, is:

$$AE = C + I + G + NX.$$

Recall that gross domestic product (GDP) is the market value of all final goods and services produced in a country during a period of time, typically one year. Nominal GDP is calculated using the current year's prices, while real GDP is calculated using the prices in a base year. Because real GDP gives a good measure of a country's output, corrected for changes in the price level, it is the measure of aggregate output that we will use in this chapter. The *goods market* includes trade in all final goods and services that the economy produces at a particular point in time—in other words, all goods that are included in real GDP. Equilibrium occurs in the goods market when the value of goods and services demanded—aggregate expenditure, *AE*—equals the value of goods and services produced—real GDP, *Y*. So, at equilibrium:

$$AE = Y.$$

What if aggregate expenditure is less than real GDP? In that case, some goods that were produced are not sold, and inventories of unsold goods will increase. For example, if General Motors produces and ships to dealers 250,000 cars in a particular month but sells only 225,000, inventories of cars on the lots of GM's dealers will rise by 25,000 cars. (Notice that because inventories are counted as part of investment, in this situation, *actual investment spending* will be greater than *planned investment spending*.) If the decline in demand is affecting not just automobiles but other goods as well, firms are likely to reduce production and lay off workers: Real GDP and employment will decline, and the economy will be in a recession.

If aggregate expenditure is greater than GDP, however, spending will be greater than production, and firms will sell more goods and services than they had expected.

IS–MP model A macroeconomic model that consists of an *IS* curve, which represents equilibrium in the goods market; an *MP* curve, which represents monetary policy; and a Phillips curve, which represents the short-run relationship between the output gap (which is the percentage difference between actual and potential real GDP) and the inflation rate.

IS curve A curve in the *IS–MP* model that shows the combinations of the real interest rate and aggregate output that represent equilibrium in the market for goods and services.

MP curve A curve in the *IS–MP* model that represents Federal Reserve monetary policy.

Phillips curve A curve that shows the short-run relationship between the output gap (or the unemployment rate) and the inflation rate.

If General Motors produces 250,000 cars but sells 300,000, then inventories of cars on dealers' lots will decline by 50,000 cars. (In this case, because firms are unexpectedly drawing down inventories, actual investment spending will be less than planned investment spending.) The dealers will be likely to increase their orders from GM's factories. If sales exceed production, not just for automobiles but for other goods as well, firms are likely to increase production and hire more workers: Real GDP and employment will increase, and the economy will be in an expansion.

Only when aggregate expenditure equals GDP will firms sell what they expected to sell. In that case, firms will experience no unexpected changes in their inventories, and they will not have an incentive to increase or decrease production. The goods market will be in equilibrium. Table 18.1 summarizes the relationship between aggregate expenditure and GDP.

Recall from your principles of economics course that using the *45°-line diagram* is one way to illustrate equilibrium in the goods market. The 45°-line diagram analysis is based on the simplifying assumption that of the four components of aggregate expenditure—*C*, *I*, *G*, and *NX*—changes in real GDP affect only *C*, consumption spending. To see why consumption depends on GDP, remember that when we measure the value of total production, we are at the same time measuring the value of total income. For example, when you buy a DVD at Best Buy for $10, the whole $10—leaving aside the sales tax you pay—becomes someone's income. Some of the $10 becomes wages for the person working the cash register, some becomes profit for Best Buy, some becomes wages for the workers who produced the DVD, and so on. If we add up the value of all the goods and services purchased, we have also added up all the current income produced during that period in the economy. (Sales taxes and some other relatively minor items cause there to be a difference between the value for GDP and the value for *national income*, as shown in the federal government's statistics. But this difference doesn't matter for our purposes.)

Studies have shown that households spend more when their current income is rising and spend less when their current income is falling.[2] The relationship between

Table 18.1 The Relationship between Aggregate Expenditure and GDP

If aggregate expenditure is . . .	then . . .	and . . .
equal to GDP	there are no unexpected changes in inventories	the goods market is in equilibrium.
less than GDP	inventories rise	GDP and employment decrease.
greater than GDP	inventories fall	GDP and employment increase.

---

[2]Many economists believe that consumption is better explained by a household's *permanent income* than by its current income. A household's permanent income is the level of income that it expects to receive over time. A household's current income might differ from its permanent income due to a temporary job loss, an illness, winning a lottery, having a year of particularly high or low investment income, and so forth. For our purposes, we can ignore this complication.

current consumption spending and current income, or GDP, is called the *consumption function*. Algebraically, we can write:

$$C = MPC \times Y,$$

where *MPC* stands for the marginal propensity to consume and is a number between zero and 1. If we look at the effect of changes in GDP on consumption, then $MPC = \Delta C / \Delta Y$, or the change in consumption divided by the change in GDP, or income. For instance, if the *MPC* is equal to 0.90, then households are spending $0.90 of every additional dollar they earn.

Because we are focusing on the effect of changes in GDP on aggregate expenditure, assuming that *I*, *G*, and *NX* don't depend on GDP is the same as assuming that their values are fixed. We can designate a variable with a bar over it as having a fixed value. So, we have the following expression for aggregate expenditure, substituting in the expression above for *C*:

$$AE = (MPC \times Y) + \bar{I} + \bar{G} + \overline{NX}.$$

Figure 18.1 shows equilibrium in the goods market using the 45°-line diagram. On the vertical axis, we measure total spending in the economy, or aggregate expenditure, *AE*. On the horizontal axis, we measure real GDP, or real total income, *Y*. The 45° line represents all points that are equal distances from the two axes, or in this case, all the points where $AE = Y$. Therefore, any point along the 45°-degree line is potentially a

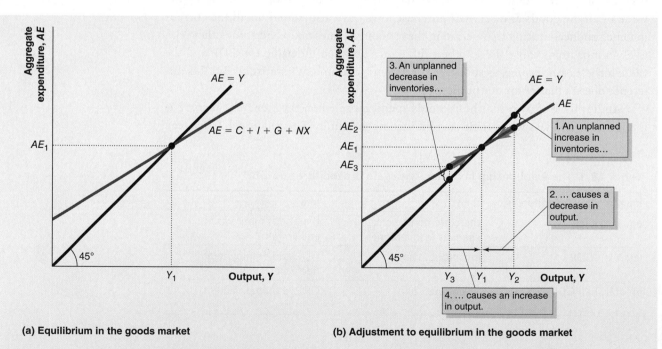

(a) Equilibrium in the goods market

(b) Adjustment to equilibrium in the goods market

Figure 18.1 Illustrating Equilibrium in the Goods Market

Panel (a) shows that equilibrium in the goods market occurs at output level Y_1, where the *AE* line crosses the 45° line. In panel (b), if the level of output is initially Y_2, aggregate expenditure is only AE_2. Rising inventories cause firms to cut production, and output will fall until equilibrium is reached at Y_1. If the output level is initially Y_3, aggregate expenditure is AE_3. Falling inventories cause firms to increase production, and output will increase until equilibrium is reached at Y_1.

point of equilibrium in the goods market. At any given time, though, there is just one equilibrium, which occurs at the point where the aggregate expenditure line crosses the 45° line. We draw the aggregate expenditure line as upward sloping because as GDP increases, consumption spending increases, while the other components of aggregate expenditure remain constant.

Panel (a) of Figure 18.1 shows that equilibrium in the goods market occurs at output level Y_1, where the AE line crosses the 45° line. Panel (b) shows why the goods market is not in equilibrium at other levels of output. For example, if the level of output is initially Y_2, aggregate expenditure is only AE_2. With spending less than production, there is an unexpected increase in inventories. Rising inventories cause firms to cut production, and output will fall until equilibrium is reached at Y_1. If the output level is initially Y_3, aggregate expenditure is AE_3. With spending greater than production, there is an unexpected decrease in inventories. Falling inventories cause firms to increase production, and output will increase until equilibrium is reached at Y_1.

Potential GDP and the Multiplier Effect

In Figure 18.1, Y_1 is the equilibrium level of GDP, but it is not necessarily the level policymakers want to achieve. The Fed's goal is to have equilibrium GDP close to **potential GDP**, which is the level of real GDP attained when all firms are producing at capacity. The capacity of a firm is *not* the maximum output the firm is capable of producing. Rather, it is the firm's production when operating on normal hours, using a workforce of normal size. At potential GDP, the economy achieves full employment, and cyclical unemployment is reduced to zero. So, potential GDP is sometimes called *full-employment GDP*. The level of potential GDP increases over time as the labor force grows, new factories and office buildings are built, new machinery and equipment are installed, and technological change takes place.

In Figure 18.2, we see what happens if the economy is initially in equilibrium at potential GDP, Y^P, and then aggregate expenditure falls. Assume that spending

Potential GDP The level of real GDP attained when all firms are producing at capacity.

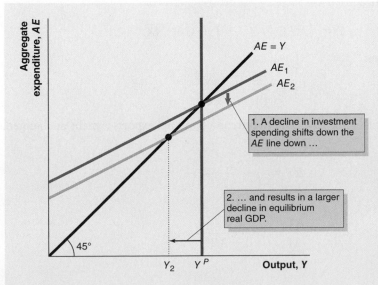

Aggregate expenditure, AE

$AE = Y$

AE_1

AE_2

1. A decline in investment spending shifts down the *AE* line down …

2. … and results in a larger decline in equilibrium real GDP.

45°

Y_2 Y^P Output, Y

Figure 18.2

The Multiplier Effect

The economy is initially in equilibrium at potential GDP, Y^P, and then the investment component, I, of aggregate expenditure falls. As a result, the aggregate expenditure line shifts down from AE_1 to AE_2. Output declines until a new equilibrium is reached at Y_2. The decline in output is greater than the decline in investment spending that caused it.

on residential construction declines, so the investment component, *I*, of aggregate expenditure falls. As a result, the aggregate expenditure line shifts down from AE_1 to AE_2. With spending now below production, there is an unintended increase in inventories. Firms respond to the inventory buildup by cutting production, and output declines until a new equilibrium is reached at Y_2. Note that the decline in output is greater than the decline in investment spending that caused it. In the context of this basic macroeconomic model, *autonomous expenditure* is expenditure that does not depend on the level of GDP. So, investment spending, government purchases, and net exports are all autonomous, while consumption spending is not. A decline in autonomous expenditure results initially in an equivalent decline in income, which then leads to an *induced* decline in consumption. For example, as spending on residential construction declines, homebuilders cut production, lay off workers, and cut their demand for construction materials. Falling incomes in the construction industry lead households to reduce their spending on cars, furniture, appliances, and other goods and services. As production declines in those industries, so does income, leading to further declines in consumption, and so on.

Multiplier effect The process by which a change in autonomous expenditure leads to a larger change in equilibrium GDP.

Multiplier The change in equilibrium GDP divided by a change in autonomous expenditure.

The series of induced changes in consumption spending that result from an initial change in autonomous expenditure is called the **multiplier effect**. The **multiplier** is the change in equilibrium GDP divided by a change in autonomous expenditure. In symbols, the multiplier for a change in investment spending is:

$$\text{Multiplier} = \frac{\Delta Y}{\Delta I}.$$

How large is the multiplier? It is quite large in our simple model. To see this, recall that our expression for aggregate expenditure is:

$$AE = (MPC \times Y) + \overline{I} + \overline{G} + \overline{NX},$$

and that at equilibrium:

$$Y = AE.$$

So, substituting, we have:

$$Y = (MPC \times Y) + \overline{I} + \overline{G} + \overline{NX},$$

or, rearranging terms:

$$Y = \frac{\overline{I} + \overline{G} + \overline{NX}}{(1 - MPC)}.$$

If investment changes, while government purchases and net exports remain unchanged, then we have:

$$\Delta Y = \frac{\Delta I}{(1 - MPC)},$$

or, rearranging terms:

$$\frac{\Delta Y}{\Delta I} = \frac{1}{(1 - MPC)}.$$

If, as we assumed earlier, *MPC* is equal to 0.9, the value of the multiplier equals:

$$\frac{\Delta Y}{\Delta I} = \frac{1}{(1 - 0.9)} = \frac{1}{0.1} = 10.$$

In other words, a decline in investment spending of $1 billion would lead to a decline in equilibrium real GDP of $10 billion. When multiplier analysis was first developed in the 1930s by John Maynard Keynes and his colleagues, they believed that a large multiplier effect helped to explain the severity of the Great Depression: With a large multiplier, a relatively small decline in investment spending could have led to the large declines in GDP experienced in the United States and Europe.[3]

Solved Problem 18.1

Calculating Equilibrium Real GDP

Use the following data to calculate the equilibrium level of real GDP and the value of the investment spending multiplier:

$$C = MPC \times Y = 0.8 \times Y$$
$$\bar{I} = \$1.6 \text{ trillion}$$
$$\bar{G} = \$1.3 \text{ trillion}$$
$$\overline{NX} = -\$0.4 \text{ trillion}$$

Solving the Problem

Step 1 **Review the chapter material.** This problem is about calculating equilibrium real GDP and the value of the multiplier, so you may want to review the section "Equilibrium in the Goods Market," which begins on page 552, and the section "Potential GDP and the Multiplier Effect," which begins on page 555.

Step 2 **Use the data to calculate equilibrium real GDP.** We know that at equilibrium, aggregate expenditure equals real GDP. The expression for aggregate expenditure is:

$$AE = (MPC \times Y) + \bar{I} + \bar{G} + \overline{NX}.$$

---

[3]Keynes thought that the value of the multiplier could be as large as 10. John Maynard Keynes, *The General Theory of Employment, Interest, and Money*, London: Macmillan, 1936, p. 51. Because macroeconomic statistics were not yet available in the 1930s, Keynes was unable to provide more than a rough estimate of the multiplier. He did note (p. 56) that Simon Kuznets's early estimates of investment and national income for the United States implied a multiplier of about 2.5. But Keynes thought the value of the marginal propensity to consume used in the calculation was "implausibly low," given the economic conditions in the United States during the 1930s.

So, at equilibrium:

$$Y = AE = (MPC \times Y) + \overline{I} + \overline{G} + \overline{NX}.$$

Substituting the values above gives us:

$$Y = 0.8Y + \$1.6 \text{ trillion} + \$1.3 \text{ trillion} + (-\$0.4 \text{ trillion})$$
$$Y = 0.8Y + \$2.5 \text{ trillion}$$
$$0.2Y = \$2.5 \text{ trillion}$$
$$Y = \frac{\$2.5 \text{ trillion}}{0.2} = \$12.5 \text{ trillion}$$

Step 3 **Calculate the value of the multiplier from the data given.** The expression for the investment spending multiplier is:

$$\frac{\Delta Y}{\Delta I} = \frac{1}{(1 - MPC)}.$$

With $MPC = 0.8$, the value of the multiplier is:

$$\frac{1}{(1 - 0.8)} = \frac{1}{0.2} = 5.$$

See related problem 1.6 at the end of the chapter.

Fiscal policy Changes in federal government purchases and taxes intended to achieve macroeconomic policy objectives.

Keynes and his followers believed in a large value for the multiplier, which led them to take an optimistic view of the effectiveness of fiscal policy. **Fiscal policy** refers to changes in federal government purchases and taxes intended to achieve macroeconomic policy objectives. Just as there is a multiplier for investment spending, there is a multiplier for government purchases:

$$\frac{\Delta Y}{\Delta G} = \frac{1}{(1 - MPC)}.$$

So, if the *MPC* is 0.9, the government purchases multiplier will also equal 10. In this case, if real GDP is $200 billion below its potential level, Congress and the president could bring real GDP back to potential GDP using fiscal policy by increasing government purchases by $20 billion (= $200 billion/10).

In fact, though, early estimates of the size of the multiplier turned out to be much too large. Our simple model—similar to those Keynes and his followers used in the 1930s—neglects several factors that cause the multiplier to be smaller than the value we have given here. These real-world complications include the effect that increases in GDP have on imports, the price level, interest rates, and individual income taxes.

In early 2009, the Obama administration proposed, and Congress passed, the American Recovery and Reinvestment Act, an $840 billion package of government spending increases and tax cuts that was by far the largest fiscal policy action in U.S. history. In proposing this policy action, White House economists estimated that the government purchases multiplier would have a value of 1.57, meaning that each

$1 billion increase in government purchases would increase equilibrium real GDP by $1.57 billion. This estimate is much smaller than the simple multiplier of 10 that we computed earlier. But some economists argued that even an estimate of 1.57 is too high. A few economists argued that the government purchases multiplier has a value of less than 1. Estimating an exact number for the multiplier is difficult because after Congress and the president engage in a fiscal policy action, many other things can happen in the economy that affect real GDP. So, isolating the effect of a change in government purchases is not an easy task, and the debate over the size of the multiplier will likely continue.

Constructing the *IS* Curve

As we have seen, normally the focus of Fed policy is establishing a target for the federal funds rate, with the expectation that changes in the federal funds rate will cause changes in other market interest rates (see Chapter 15). Therefore, we need to incorporate the effect of changes in interest rates into the model of the goods market.

Movements in the interest rate affect three components of aggregate expenditure: consumption, C; investment, I; and net exports, NX. We are interested in the real interest rate, which is the interest rate most relevant to the decisions of households and firms in this context. Recall that the real interest rate equals the nominal interest rate minus the expected inflation rate. An increase in the real interest rate makes firms less willing to invest in plant and equipment and makes households less likely to purchase new houses, so I declines. Similarly, an increase in the real interest rate gives consumers an incentive to save rather than to spend, so C declines. And a higher domestic real interest rate makes returns on domestic financial assets more attractive relative to those on foreign assets, increasing the demand for the domestic currency, thereby raising the exchange rate. The rise in the exchange rate increases imports and reduces exports, so NX declines. A decrease in the real interest rate will have the opposite effect—increasing I, C, and NX.

Panel (a) of Figure 18.3 uses the 45°-line diagram to show the effect of changes in the real interest rate on equilibrium in the goods market. With the real interest rate initially at r_1, the aggregate expenditure line is $AE(r_1)$, and the equilibrium level of output is Y_1 (point A). If the interest falls from r_1 to r_2, the aggregate expenditure line shifts up from $AE(r_1)$ to $AE(r_2)$, and the equilibrium level of output increases from Y_1 to Y_2 (point B). If the interest rate rises from r_1 to r_3, the aggregate expenditure line shifts down from $AE(r_1)$ to $AE(r_3)$, and the equilibrium level of output falls from Y_1 to Y_3 (point C).

In panel (b), we use the results from panel (a) to construct the *IS* curve, which shows the combinations of the real interest rate and aggregate output where the goods market is in equilibrium. We know that at every equilibrium point in the 45°-degree line diagram in panel (a), aggregate expenditure equals total output, or GDP. In panel (b), we plot these points in a graph that has the real interest rate on the vertical axis and the level of aggregate output on the horizontal axis. The points A, B, and C in panel (b) correspond to the points A, B, and C in panel (a). The *IS* curve is downward sloping because a higher interest rate causes a reduction in aggregate expenditure and a lower equilibrium level of output.

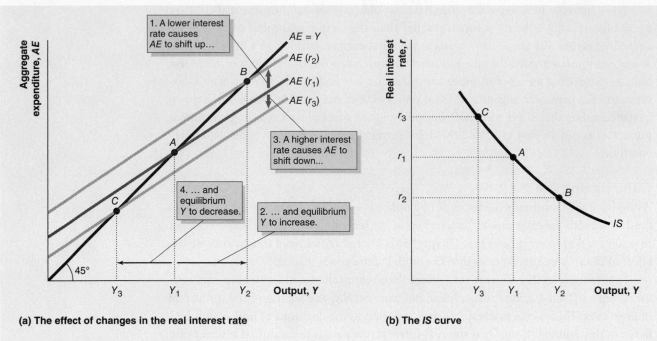

Figure 18.3 Deriving the *IS* Curve

Panel (a) uses the 45°-line diagram to show the effect of changes in the real interest rate on equilibrium in the goods market. With the real interest rate initially at r_1, the aggregate expenditure line is $AE(r_1)$, and the equilibrium level of output is Y_1 (point A). If the interest rate falls from r_1 to r_2, the aggregate expenditure line shifts up from $AE(r_1)$ to $AE(r_2)$, and the equilibrium level of output increases from Y_1 to Y_2 (point B).

If the interest rate rises from r_1 to r_3, the aggregate expenditure line shifts down from $AE(r_1)$ to $AE(r_3)$, and the equilibrium level of output falls from Y_1 to Y_3 (point C). In panel (b), we plot the points from panel (a) to form the *IS* curve. The points A, B, and C in panel (b) correspond to the points A, B, and C in panel (a).

The Output Gap

The *Taylor rule* offers one explanation of the Fed's selection of a target for the federal funds rate (see Chapter 15). With the Taylor rule, the Fed has a target for the federal funds rate and adjusts that target on the basis of changes in two variables: the inflation gap and the output gap. The *inflation gap* is the difference between the current inflation rate and a target rate, and the **output gap** is the percentage difference between real GDP and potential GDP. Figure 18.4 shows movements in the output gap from 1952 through the second quarter of 2012.

During recessions, the output gap is negative because real GDP is below potential GDP. During expansions, the output gap is positive once real GDP has risen above potential GDP. Figure 18.4 shows that the recessions of 1981–1982 and 2007–2009 were the most severe of the post–World War II era, as measured by the size of the output gap.

Because the Federal Reserve focuses on the output gap rather than on the level of real GDP, it would be useful to incorporate the output gap into our macroeconomic model. The graph of the *IS* curve shown in panel (b) of Figure 18.3 has the level of real GDP, rather than the output gap, on the horizontal axis. Can we replace the level of

Output gap The percentage difference between real GDP and potential GDP.

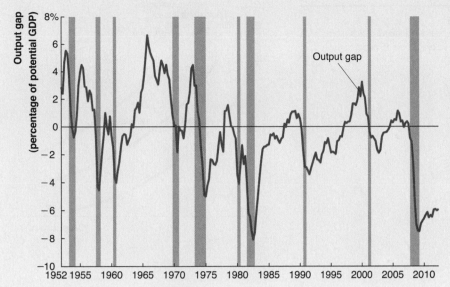

Figure 18.4

The Output Gap

The output gap is the percentage difference between real GDP and potential GDP. The output gap is negative during recessions because real GDP is below potential GDP.

Sources: Congressional Budget Office and U.S. Bureau of Economic Analysis.

real GDP with the output gap in the *IS* curve graph? Yes, we can, with the following qualification: We should think of changes in the real interest rate as affecting the level of investment, consumption, and net exports *relative to potential GDP*. For instance, when the real interest rate falls and *C*, *I*, and *NX* increase, the increase in aggregate expenditure will cause real GDP, *Y*, to increase relative to potential GDP, Y^P. In that case, when we graph the *IS* curve with the real interest rate on the vertical axis and the output gap on the horizontal axis, the *IS* curve is still downward sloping.

Figure 18.5 shows the *IS* curve graph with the output gap on the horizontal axis. We use the symbol $\widetilde{Y}$ to distinguish the output gap from real GDP, *Y*. As a reference, we have included a vertical line where $Y = Y^P$, which is also the point where the output

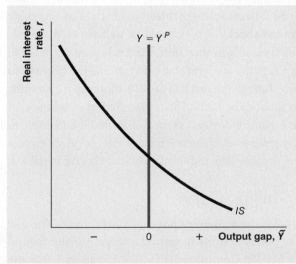

Figure 18.5

The *IS* Curve Using the Output Gap

This graph shows the *IS* curve with the output gap, rather than the level of real GDP, on the horizontal axis. Values to the left of zero on the horizontal axis represent negative values for the output gap—or periods of recession—and values to the right of zero on the horizontal axis represent positive values for the output gap—periods of expansion. The vertical line, $Y = Y^P$, is also the point where the output gap is zero.

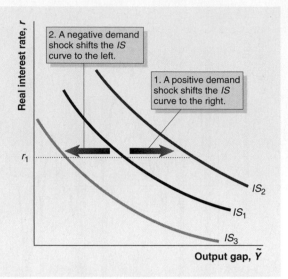

Figure 18.6

Shifts in the *IS* Curve

For any given level of the real interest rate, positive demand shocks shift the *IS* curve to the right, and negative demand shocks shift the *IS* curve to the left.

gap is zero. Normally, we draw graphs with the vertical axis beginning at a value of zero on the horizontal axis. In this case, though, our graphs are easier to understand if we move the vertical axis to the left, leaving zero in the middle of the horizontal axis. Note that values to the left of zero on the horizontal axis represent negative values for the output gap—or periods of recession—and values to the right of zero on the horizontal axis represent positive values for the output gap—periods of expansion.

Shifts of the *IS* Curve

We have derived the *IS* curve by looking at the effect of changes in the real interest rate on aggregate expenditure, holding constant all other factors that might affect the willingness of households, firms, and governments to spend. Therefore, an increase or a decrease in the real interest rate results in *a movement along the IS curve.* Changing other factors that affect aggregate expenditure will cause a *shift of the IS curve.* These other factors—apart from changes in the real interest rate—that lead to changes in aggregate expenditure are called **aggregate demand shocks**. For example, as we have seen, spending on residential construction declined rapidly in the United States beginning in 2006. This decline in a component of *I* was a *negative demand shock* that shifted the *IS* curve to the left. During late 2009 and continuing through the first half of 2012, more rapid economic growth in some U.S. trading partners than in the United States resulted in an increase in U.S. exports. This increase in *NX* was a *positive demand shock* that shifted the *IS* curve to the right. Figure 18.6 shows that for any given level of the real interest rate, positive demand shocks shift the *IS* curve to the right and negative demand shocks shift the *IS* curve to the left.

Aggregate demand shock A change in one of the components of aggregate expenditure that causes the *IS* curve to shift.

18.2

Learning Objective

Explain the significance of the *MP* curve and the Phillips curve.

The *MP* Curve and the Phillips Curve

The second piece of the *IS–MP* model is the monetary policy, or *MP*, curve. The *MP* curve represents the Fed's monetary policy actions in setting a target for the federal funds rate through the Federal Open Market Committee (FOMC). We assume that the

Fed chooses a target for the federal funds rate according to the Taylor rule. Recall the expression for the Taylor rule (see Chapter 15):

$$\text{Federal funds rate target} = \text{Current inflation rate} + \text{Equilibrium real} \\ \text{federal funds rate} + (1/2 \times \text{Inflation gap}) \\ + (1/2 \times \text{Output gap}).$$

The Taylor rule tells us that when the inflation rate rises above the Fed's target inflation rate of about 2%, as it did during late 2005 and early 2006, the FOMC will raise its target for the federal funds rate. And when the output gap is negative—that is, when real GDP is less than potential GDP, as it began to be in 2007—the FOMC will lower the target for the federal funds rate.

Although the FOMC can control the target for the federal funds rate, which is a short-term nominal interest rate, long-term real interest rates are more relevant in determining the level of aggregate expenditure. For instance, when people decide whether to buy a new house, they consider the real interest rate on 30-year mortgage loans, and when corporations borrow to finance new investment, they look at the real interest rate on long-term corporate bonds. However, short-term interest rates and long-term interest rates tend to rise and fall together. So, when the FOMC raises or lowers its target for the federal funds rate, long-term interest rates typically also rise or fall. Similarly, although the federal funds rate is a nominal interest rate, if expectations of future inflation remain stable, then by raising or lowering its target for the nominal federal funds rate, the FOMC is typically able to raise or lower the real rate.

The *MP* Curve

For the reasons described in the preceding section, we assume in the *IS–MP* model that the Fed is able to control the real interest rate by changing its target for the federal funds rate. Figure 18.7 shows the *MP* curve as a horizontal line at the real interest

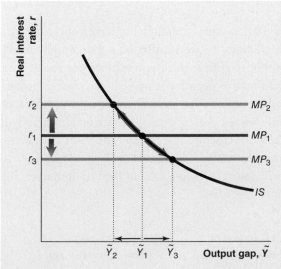

Figure 18.7

The *MP* Curve

The *MP* curve is a horizontal line at the real interest rate determined by the Fed. When the Fed increases the real interest rate from r_1 to r_2, the *MP* curve shifts up from MP_1 to MP_2, causing a movement up the *IS* curve, and the value of the output gap changes from $\widetilde{Y}_1$ to $\widetilde{Y}_2$. When the Fed decreases the real interest rate from r_1 to r_3, the *MP* curve shifts down from MP_1 to MP_3, causing a movement down the *IS* curve, and the value of the output gap changes from $\widetilde{Y}_1$ to $\widetilde{Y}_3$.

rate determined by the Fed because we assume that the Fed is able to keep the interest rate constant, despite increases or decreases in the output gap. When the Fed increases the real interest rate from r_1 to r_2, the *MP* curve shifts up from MP_1 to MP_2; consumption spending, investment spending, and net exports all decline, causing a movement up the *IS* curve; and the value of the output gap changes from $\widetilde{Y}_1$ to $\widetilde{Y}_2$ as real GDP falls relative to potential GDP. When the Fed decreases the real interest rate from r_1 to r_3, the *MP* curve shifts down from MP_1 to MP_3; consumption spending, investment spending, and net exports all increase, causing a movement down the *IS* curve; and the value of the output gap changes from $\widetilde{Y}_1$ to $\widetilde{Y}_3$ as real GDP increases relative to potential GDP.

The Phillips Curve

The Taylor rule indicates that the Fed typically increases the real interest rate when the inflation gap is positive—that is, when the current inflation rate is above the Fed's target inflation rate of 2%. Raising the real interest rate causes real GDP to decline relative to potential GDP. With real GDP below its potential level, firms operate below capacity, and the unemployment rate rises, which puts downward pressure on costs and prices, ultimately leading to a lower inflation rate. The Fed relies on *an inverse relationship between the inflation rate and the state of the economy*: When output and employment are increasing, the inflation rate tends to increase, and when output and employment are decreasing, the inflation rate tends to decrease.

The first economist to systematically analyze this inverse relationship was the New Zealand economist A.W. Phillips in 1958. Phillips plotted data on the inflation rate and the unemployment rate in the United Kingdom and drew a curve showing their average relationship. Since that time, a graph showing the short-run relationship between the unemployment rate and the inflation rate has been called a *Phillips curve*.[4] The graph in Figure 18.8 is similar to the one Phillips prepared. Each point on the Phillips curve represents a combination of the inflation rate and the unemployment rate that might be observed in a particular year. For example, point *A* represents the combination of a 4% unemployment rate and a 4% inflation rate in one year, and point *B* represents the combination of a 7% unemployment rate and a 1% inflation rate in another year.

Economists who have studied the Phillips curve relationship have concluded that rather than there being a single stable trade-off between inflation and unemployment, the position of the Phillips curve can shift over time in response to supply shocks and changes in expectations of the inflation rate. A negative supply shock, such as an unexpected increase in oil prices, can cause output to fall (and, therefore, unemployment to rise) at the same time that it causes upward pressure on the price level, which will increase the inflation rate (see Chapter 17). Unemployment and inflation both being higher means that the Phillips curve has shifted up. Changes in households' and firms' expectations about the inflation rate will also shift the position of the Phillips curve. For

---

[4]Phillips actually measured inflation by the percentage change in wages rather than by the percentage change in prices. Because wages and prices usually move roughly together, this difference is not important to our discussion.

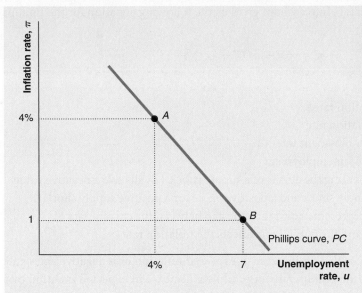

Figure 18.8

The Phillips Curve

The Phillips curve illustrates the short-run relationship between the unemployment rate and the inflation rate. Point *A* represents the combination of a 4% unemployment rate and a 4% inflation rate in one year. Point *B* represents the combination of a 7% unemployment rate and a 1% inflation rate in another year.

example, if workers and firms expect that the inflation rate will be 2% per year, but they experience an extended period of 4% inflation, they are likely to adjust their expectations of future inflation from 2% to 4%.

Expectations of inflation become embedded in the economy. For example, if workers believe that the future inflation rate will be 4%, rather than 2%, they know that unless their nominal wage increases by at least 4%, their real wage—their nominal wage divided by the price level—will decline. Similarly, the Fisher effect indicates that an increase in the expected inflation rate will cause an increase in nominal interest rates (see Chapter 4). As workers, firms, and investors adjust from expecting an inflation rate of 2% to expecting an inflation rate of 4%, at any given unemployment rate, the inflation rate will be 2% higher. In other words, the Phillips curve will have shifted up by 2%.

Finally, most economists believe that the best way to capture the effect of changes in the unemployment rate on the inflation rate is to look at the gap between the current unemployment rate and the unemployment rate when the economy is at full employment, which is called the *natural rate of unemployment*. The gap between the current rate of unemployment and the natural rate represents *cyclical unemployment* because it is unemployment caused by a business cycle recession raising the unemployment rate above its full employment level. When the current unemployment rate equals the natural rate, the inflation rate typically does not change, holding constant expectations of inflation and the effects of supply shocks. When the current unemployment rate is greater than the natural rate, there is slack in the labor market, so wage increases will be limited, as will firms' costs of production. So, the inflation rate will decrease. When the current unemployment rate is less than the natural rate of unemployment, labor market conditions will be tight, and wages are likely to increase, which pushes up firms' costs of production. So, the inflation rate will increase.

Taking all these factors into account gives us the following equation for the Phillips curve:

$$\pi = \pi^e - a(U - U^*) - s,$$

where:

π = the current inflation rate

π^e = the expected inflation rate

U = the current unemployment rate

U^* = the natural rate of unemployment

s = a variable representing the effects of a supply shock (s will have a negative value for a negative supply shock and a positive value for a positive supply shock).

a = a constant that represents how much the gap between the current rate of unemployment and the natural rate affects the inflation rate

The equation tells us that an increase in expected inflation or a negative aggregate supply shock will shift the Phillips curve up, while a decrease in expected inflation or a positive supply shock will shift the Phillips curve down.

What might cause the expected rate of inflation to change? Many economists believe that households and firms adjust their expectations of inflation if they experience persistent rates of actual inflation that are above the rates that they had expected. For example, inflation during the 1960s averaged about 2% per year but accelerated to 5% per year from 1970 to 1973 and 8.5% per year from 1974 to 1979. These persistently high rates of inflation led households and firms to revise upward their expectations of inflation, and the Phillips curve shifted up. Notice that once the Phillips curve has shifted up, the short-run trade-off between inflation and unemployment becomes worse. That is, every unemployment rate becomes associated with a higher inflation rate. Paul Volcker became Federal Reserve chairman in August 1979, with a mandate from President Jimmy Carter to bring down the inflation rate (see Chapter 15). When the economy experienced the severe recession of 1981–1982, the inflation rate declined sharply as the unemployment rate soared and firms experienced excess capacity. From 1983 to 1986, the inflation rate averaged 3.3% per year. Accordingly, households and firms lowered their expectations of future inflation, and the Phillips curve shifted down.

Figure 18.9 illustrates the Phillips curve shifting.

Okun's Law and an Output Gap Phillips Curve

The Phillips curve shows the short-run relationship between the inflation rate and the unemployment rate. We saw in Figure 18.7 on page 563 how we can use the *IS* curve and the *MP* curve to illustrate the Fed's use of monetary policy to affect the output gap. If we could show the relationship between the output gap and the inflation rate, we could integrate the Phillips curve into the *IS–MP* model. That would allow us to illustrate the effects of changes in the inflation rate on Fed policy and the effects of changes in Fed policy on the inflation rate. Fortunately, there is a straightforward way of modifying the Phillips curve to change it from a relationship between

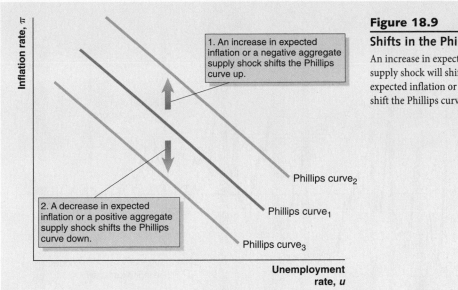

Figure 18.9

Shifts in the Phillips Curve

An increase in expected inflation or a negative aggregate supply shock will shift the Phillips curve up. A decrease in expected inflation or a positive aggregate supply shock will shift the Phillips curve down.

the inflation rate and the unemployment rate to a relationship between the inflation rate and the output gap.

Okun's law, named after Arthur Okun, who served as chairman of the President's Council of Economic Advisers in the 1960s, conveniently summarizes the relationship between the output gap, $\widetilde{Y}$ and the gap between the current and natural rates of unemployment, or cyclical unemployment:

$$\widetilde{Y} = -2 \times (U - U^*).$$

Figure 18.10 shows the actual rate of cyclical unemployment and the rate of cyclical unemployment calculated using Okun's law for the years since 1950. Because the values track so closely in most years, we can be confident that substituting the output gap, $\widetilde{Y}$, for cyclical unemployment, $(U - U^*)$, in our Phillips curve equation will capture the effect of changes in the output gap on the inflation rate:

$$\pi = \pi^e + b\widetilde{Y} - s.$$

The coefficient b in the equation represents the effect of changes in the output gap on the inflation rate.

Figure 18.11 shows our revised Phillips curve, *PC*, with the output gap on the horizontal axis and the inflation rate on the vertical axis. Notice that with the output gap version of the Phillips curve, the curve is upward sloping rather than downward sloping, as in Figure 18.8 on page 565. This change in slope occurs because inflation typically falls when the unemployment rate increases but rises when real GDP increases. When the output gap equals zero and there are no supply shocks, the actual inflation rate will equal the expected inflation rate.

Okun's law A statistical relationship discovered by Arthur Okun between the output gap and the cyclical rate of unemployment.

MyEconLab Real-time data

Figure 18.10

Using Okun's Law to Predict the Cyclical Unemployment Rate

Okun's law states that the output gap is equal to negative 2 times the gap between the current unemployment rate and the natural rate of unemployment. The graph shows that Okun's law does a good job of accounting for the cyclical unemployment rate.

Sources: Congressional Budget Office and U.S. Bureau of Economic Analysis.

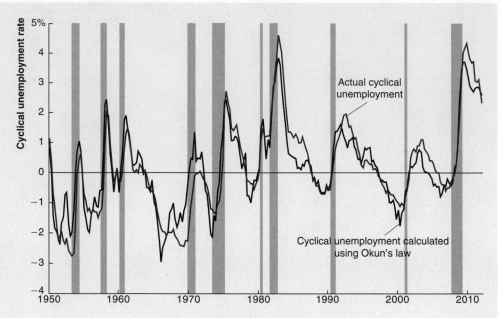

Figure 18.11

The Output Gap Version of the Phillips Curve

This Phillips curve differs from the one shown in Figure 18.8 by having the output gap, rather than the unemployment rate, on the horizontal axis. As a result, the Phillips curve is upward sloping rather than downward sloping. When the output gap equals zero and there are no supply shocks, the actual inflation rate will equal the expected inflation rate. An increase in expected inflation or a negative supply shock shifts the Phillips curve up, and a decrease in expected inflation or a positive supply shock shifts the Phillips curve down.

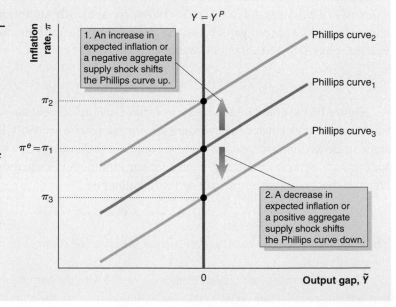

As with the original Phillips curve, an increase in expected inflation or a negative supply shock shifts the Phillips curve up, and a decrease in expected inflation or a positive supply shock shifts the Phillips curve down.

Did the Aftermath of the 2007–2009 Recession Break Okun's Law?

During 2009 and 2010, White House economists were criticized for their inaccurate predictions of the unemployment rate. In early 2009, Christina Romer, who was then chair of the President's Council of Economic Advisers, and Jared Bernstein, economic adviser to Vice President Joe Biden, predicted that if Congress passed President Barack Obama's stimulus program of higher federal government spending and tax cuts, unemployment would peak at about 8% in the third quarter of 2009 and then decline in the following quarters. Although Congress passed the stimulus program, the unemployment rate was 9.7% in the third quarter of 2009. It rose to 10.0% in the fourth quarter of 2009 and was still at 8.1% in the third quarter of 2012.

Romer and Bernstein were hardly alone in failing to forecast the severity of unemployment during 2009 and 2010. One reason for the faulty forecasts was that the decline in output was greater than expected, so, given Okun's law, the increase in the unemployment rate was also greater than expected. What explains the high levels of unemployment following the recession? Figure 18.10 shows that for the whole period since 1950, Okun's law does a good job of accounting for movements in the unemployment rate. The graph below, which covers just the period from the first quarter of 2007 through the third quarter of 2012, shows that Okun's law does not do as well in accounting for movements in the unemployment following the 2007–2009 recession.

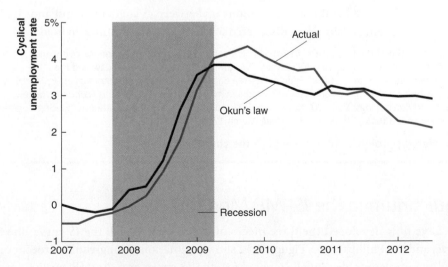

The graph shows that beginning in mid-2009 and continuing for nearly two years, Okun's law predicted a cyclical unemployment rate about 1 percentage point lower than the actual unemployment rate. Then, in the fourth quarter of 2011, the pattern reversed, with the actual unemployment rate dropping well below the level predicted by Okun's law. What explains the relatively poor performance of Okun's law during this period? Some economists have pointed to the behavior of labor productivity—the amount of output produced per worker—as the main explanation. When labor productivity increases, firms can produce either more output with a given number of workers or the same amount of output with fewer workers. From late 2009 through most of 2011, many firms appear to have taken the second option—maintaining their production levels with fewer workers—thereby leading to a higher level of unemployment than many economists had forecast.

But in the fourth quarter of 2011 and the first three quarters of 2012, cyclical unemployment as predicted by Okun's law was greater than the actual cyclical unemployment rate. Why did Okun's law shift from underpredicting the actual unemployment rate to overpredicting it? Some economists believe that because the 2007–2009 recession was so severe, many firms worried that they might be forced into bankruptcy. As a result, they took actions to cut their costs by laying off more workers than they ordinarily would have, given the extent of the decline in their sales. By late 2011, firms had become more optimistic about the economic expansion continuing and substantially increased their hiring. Okun's law also had difficulty accurately accounting for the unemployment rate following the severe recession of 1981–1982, raising the possibility that Okun's law may not be accurate during severe recessions.

Some economists argue that changes in the labor market may account for problems with Okun's law. For example, Robert Gordon of Northwestern University believes that a decline in unionization and a rise in temporary employment may have increased the willingness of firms to lay off workers when sales decline. If true, then the equation for Okun's law will have to be modified if it is to accurately predict changes in unemployment during recessions.

It's unclear whether the strong relationship between changes in output and changes in unemployment Arthur Okun discovered 50 years ago will continue to hold.

Sources: Christina Romer and Jared Bernstein, "The Job Impact of the American Recovery and Reinvestment Plan," January 10, 2009; Mary Daly and Bart Hobjin, "Okun's Law and the Unemployment Surprise of 2009," Federal Reserve Bank of San Francisco *Economic Letter*, March 8, 2009; Robert J. Gordon, "Okun's Law and Productivity Innovations," *American Economic Review: Papers and Proceedings,* Vol. 100, No. 2, May 2010, pp. 11–15; and Jon Hilsenrath, "Piecing Together the Job–Picture Puzzle," *Wall Street Journal*, March 12, 2012.

See related problem 2.10 at the end of the chapter.

18.3

Learning Objective

Use the *IS–MP* model to illustrate macroeconomic equilibrium.

Equilibrium in the *IS–MP* Model

We have now developed the three pieces of the *IS–MP* model: the *IS* curve, the *MP* curve, and the Phillips curve. Figure 18.12 shows a situation of long-run macroeconomic equilibrium using this model. In panel (a), the *IS* curve and the *MP* curve intersect where the output gap is zero and the real interest rate is at the Fed's target level. In panel (b), the Phillips curve shows that because the output gap is zero, the actual and expected inflation rates are equal.

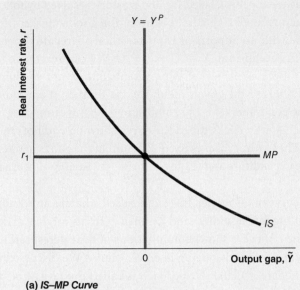

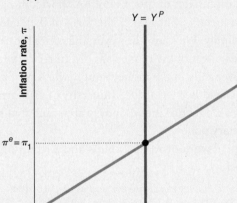

(a) *IS–MP Curve*

(b) Phillips curve

Figure 18.12

Equilibrium in the *IS–MP* Model

In panel (a), the *IS* curve and the *MP* curve intersect where the output gap is zero and the real interest rate is at the Fed's target level. In panel (b), the Phillips curve shows that because the output gap is zero, the actual and expected inflation rates are equal.

Making the Connection

Where Did the *IS–MP* Model Come From?

The macroeconomic model we have been discussing in this chapter has deep historical roots. British economist John Maynard Keynes developed the basic ideas behind the *IS* curve in his 1936 book *The General Theory of Employment, Interest, and Money*. Keynes was the first economist to discuss in detail the idea that total production would increase and decrease in response to fluctuations in aggregate expenditure. He believed that the collapse in aggregate expenditure beginning in 1929 caused the Great Depression.

Keynes did not explicitly draw the *IS* curve in *The General Theory*. The *IS* curve first appeared in an article written by John Hicks in 1937. Our discussion of the *IS* curve has left it something of a mystery as to why it is labeled *IS*. The mystery is solved by following Hicks's alternative approach to analyzing equilibrium in the goods market. If we look at a closed economy—one with no imports or exports—then aggregate expenditure equals $C + I + G$. And, in equilibrium, $Y = C + I + G$. We can rearrange this expression as $Y - C - G = I$. Because $Y - C - G$ represents output not consumed in the current period by households or the government, we can think of it as *national saving, S*. So, we can say that the goods market is in equilibrium when investment equals national saving, or $I = S$, which is why Hicks called the curve showing equilibrium in the goods market the *IS* curve. The two approaches to equilibrium in the goods market— (1) Total output $=$ Aggregate expenditure and (2) Investment $=$ Saving—are exactly equivalent.

Hicks did not use the *MP* curve in his model. Instead, he used what became known as the *LM* curve, with *LM* standing for "liquidity" and "money." (In his original article, Hicks labeled the curve *LL*.) The *LM* curve shows combinations of the interest rate and output that would result in the money market being in equilibrium. (We discussed the money market in the previous chapter.) Hicks's approach is called the *IS–LM model*. (See the appendix on pages 588–591 for a discussion of this model.) A shortcoming of the *IS–LM* model is that it assumes that monetary policy takes the form of the Federal Reserve's choosing a target for the money supply. We know, however, that since the early 1980s, the Fed has targeted the federal funds rate, not the money supply. In recent years, the Fed has paid very little attention to movements in the money supply when conducting short-term monetary policy. In 2000, David Romer of the University of California, Berkeley, suggested dropping the *LM* curve in favor of the *MP* curve approach that has become more standard for analyzing monetary policy.

You can find out more about the original work of A.W. Phillips and Arthur Okun by reading the articles in the source note below.

Sources: John Maynard Keynes, *The General Theory of Employment, Interest, and Money*, London: Macmillan, 1936; John R. Hicks, "Mr. Keynes and the 'Classics'; A Suggested Interpretation," *Econometrica*, Vol. 5, No. 2, April 1937, pp. 147–159; David Romer, "Keynesian Macroeconomics Without the *LM* Curve," *Journal of Economic Perspectives*, Vol. 14., No. 2, Spring 2000, pp. 149–169; A. W. Phillips, "The Relation Between Unemployment and the Rate of Change of Money Wage Rates in the United Kingdom, 1861–1957," *Economica*, Vol. 25, No. 100, November 1958, pp. 283–299; and Arthur M. Okun, "Potential GDP: Its Measurement and Significance," *Proceedings of the Business and Economic Statistics Section of the American Statistical Association*, 1962.

See related problems 3.5 and 3.6 at the end of the chapter.

Using Monetary Policy to Fight a Recession

Suppose that starting from the situation shown in Figure 18.12, the economy is hit by a demand shock, as happened, for example, in 2007 when spending on residential construction declined following the collapse of the housing bubble. Panel (a) of Figure 18.13 shows that the demand shock causes the *IS* curve to shift to the left, from IS_1 to IS_2. Real GDP falls below potential GDP, so the economy has a negative output gap at $\widetilde{Y}_1$ and moves into a recession. Panel (b) shows that a negative output gap causes a movement down the Phillips curve, lowering the inflation rate from π_1 to π_2. The Fed typically fights recessions by lowering its target for the federal funds rate. This action lowers the real interest rate, shifting the monetary policy curve from MP_1 to MP_2.

A lower real interest rate leads to increases in consumption spending, investment spending, and net exports, causing a movement down the *IS* curve. Real GDP returns to its potential level, so the output gap is again zero. In panel (b), the inflation rate rises from π_2 back to π_1.

Complications Fighting the Recession of 2007–2009

As we saw in earlier discussions of Fed policy during the 2007–2009 recession, a smooth transition back to potential GDP, as shown in Figure 18.13, did not occur. One reason is that even though we have been assuming in the *IS–MP* model that the Fed controls the real interest rate, in fact, the Fed is able to target the federal funds rate but typically does not attempt to directly affect other market interest rates. Normally, the Fed can rely on the long-term real interest declining when the federal funds rate declines and rising when the federal funds rate rises. However, the recession of 2007–2009 did not represent normal times.

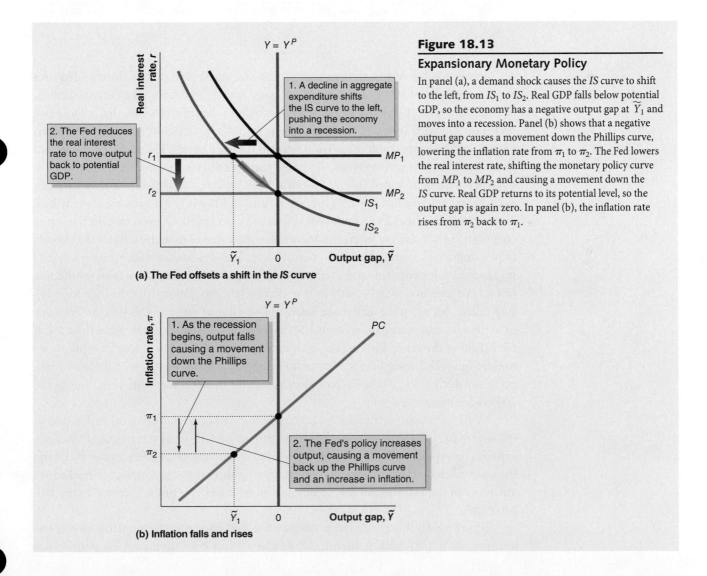

Figure 18.13

Expansionary Monetary Policy

In panel (a), a demand shock causes the *IS* curve to shift to the left, from IS_1 to IS_2. Real GDP falls below potential GDP, so the economy has a negative output gap at $\widetilde{Y}_1$ and moves into a recession. Panel (b) shows that a negative output gap causes a movement down the Phillips curve, lowering the inflation rate from π_1 to π_2. The Fed lowers the real interest rate, shifting the monetary policy curve from MP_1 to MP_2 and causing a movement down the *IS* curve. Real GDP returns to its potential level, so the output gap is again zero. In panel (b), the inflation rate rises from π_2 back to π_1.

Figure 18.14

An Increasing Risk Premium During the 2007–2009 Recession

During the financial crisis of 2007–2009, the default risk premium soared, raising interest rates on Baa-rated bonds relative to those on Aaa-rated bonds (the red line in the figure) and 10-year U.S. Treasury notes (the blue line in the figure).

Source: Federal Reserve Bank of St. Louis.

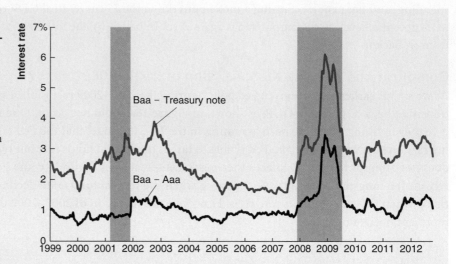

Recall that the default risk premium is the additional yield that an investor requires for holding a bond with some default risk (see Chapter 5). During the financial crisis, particularly after the failure of Lehman Brothers in September 2008, the default risk premium soared as investors feared that firms would have difficulty repaying their loans or making the coupon and principal payments on their bonds. Figure 18.14 shows two measures of how much investors increased the default risk premium they required to buy corporate bonds rated Baa by Moody's. The blue line shows the difference between the interest rate on Baa-rated corporate bonds and the interest rate on 10-year U.S. Treasury notes. The red line shows the difference between the interest rate on Baa-rated corporate bonds and the interest rate on Aaa-rated corporate bonds. Baa-rated bonds are an important source of funds to firms. Baa is Moody's lowest investment-grade rating, and the bonds of many more firms are able to qualify for that rating than for the Aaa rating. For instance, in 2012, only four nonfinancial corporations qualified for Moody's Aaa rating. So, when the difference between Baa interest rate and the 10-year Treasury note interest rate soared from about 1.5% before the financial crisis to more than 6% at the height of the crisis, there was a significant effect on the ability of many corporations to raise funds by issuing bonds. Note that Figure 18.14 shows that the increase in the risk premium during the 2007–2009 recession was much greater than the increase during the 2001 recession.

As we have seen, by the end of 2008, the Fed had caused the federal funds rate to fall nearly to zero, but the rise in the risk premium counteracted the effects of the Fed's expansionary policy. The Fed attempted to bring down long-term interest rates by taking the unusual step of directly buying both 10-year Treasury notes and mortgage-backed securities, but the Fed was not able to entirely offset the effects of the increase in the risk premium.

Figure 18.15 illustrates the problems the Fed had in implementing an expansionary monetary policy during 2008. The collapse in spending on residential

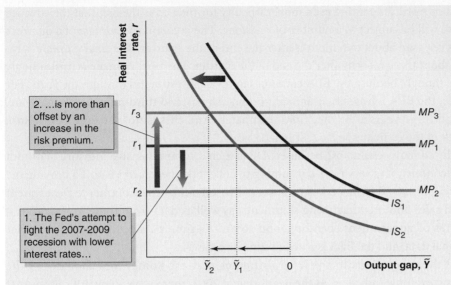

Figure 18.15

Expansionary Monetary Policy in the Face of a Rising Risk Premium

During the recession of 2007–2009, the collapse in spending on residential construction shifted the *IS* curve from IS_1 to IS_2, and real GDP fell below potential GDP at $\widetilde{Y}_1$. The Fed responded by lowering the real interest rate from r_1 to r_2, but the increase in the risk premium caused the real interest rate actually to increase to r_3, pushing the economy into a deeper recession at $\widetilde{Y}_2$.

construction shifted the *IS* curve from IS_1 to IS_2, and real GDP fell below potential GDP at $\widetilde{Y}_1$. The Fed responded by lowering the real interest rate from r_1 to r_2, which would in normal circumstances have been sufficient to bring the economy back to potential GDP. But the increase in the risk premium caused the real interest rate actually to increase to r_3, pushing the economy into a deeper recession at $\widetilde{Y}_2$. The economy started to recover in mid-2009 only after the risk premium began to decline to more normal levels. The Fed helped to reduce the risk premium by undertaking unconventional policies such as buying mortgage-backed securities issued by Fannie Mae and Freddie Mac.

Making the Connection

Trying to Hit a Moving Target: Forecasting with "Real-Time Data"

We saw at the beginning of the chapter that the Fed relies on forecasts from macroeconomic models to guide its policymaking. The Fed uses models similar to the *IS–MP* model we have developed in this chapter. To use these models to analyze the current state of the economy and to forecast future values of key economic variables such as real GDP and the inflation rate, the Fed relies on data gathered by a variety of federal government agencies.

One key piece of economic data is GDP, which is measured quarterly by the Bureau of Economic Analysis (BEA), part of the Department of Commerce. The *advance estimate* of a quarter's GDP is not released until about a month after the quarter has ended. This delay can be a problem for the Fed because it means that, for instance, the Fed will not receive an estimate of GDP for the period from January through March until the end of April. Presenting even more difficulty for the Fed is the fact that the advance estimate will be subject to a number of revisions. The *preliminary estimate* of a quarter's GDP is released about two months after the end of the quarter. The *final estimate* is released about three months after the end of the quarter. The final estimate is misleadingly named, though, because the BEA continues to revise its estimates through the years. For instance, the BEA releases first-annual, second-annual, and third-annual estimates one, two, and three years after the "final" estimates. And this is not the end: *Benchmark revisions* of the estimates will occur in later years.

Why so many estimates? Because GDP is such a comprehensive measure of output in the economy, it is very time-consuming to collect the necessary data. To provide the advance estimate, the BEA relies on surveys carried out by the Commerce Department of retail sales and manufacturing shipments, as well as data from trade organizations, estimates of government spending, and so on. As time passes, these groups gather additional data, and the BEA is able to refine its estimates.

Do these revisions to the GDP estimates matter? Sometimes they do, as the following example indicates. At the beginning of 2001, there were some indications that the U.S. economy might be headed for recession. The dot-com stock market bubble had burst the previous spring, wiping out trillions of dollars in stockholder wealth. Overbuilding of information technology also weighed on the economy. The advance estimate of the first quarter's GDP, though, showed a reasonably healthy increase in real GDP of 1.98% at an annual rate. Nothing for the Fed to be worried about? Well, as the graph below shows, that estimate was revised a number of times over the years, mostly downward. Currently, BEA data indicate that real GDP actually *declined* by 1.31% at an annual rate during the first quarter of 2001. This swing of more than 3 percentage points is a large difference—one that changes the picture of what happened during the first quarter of 2001 from one of an economy experiencing moderate growth to one of an economy suffering a significant decline. The National Bureau of Economic Research dates the recession of 2001 as having begun in March, but some economists believe it actually began at the end of 2000. The current BEA estimates of GDP provide some support for this view.

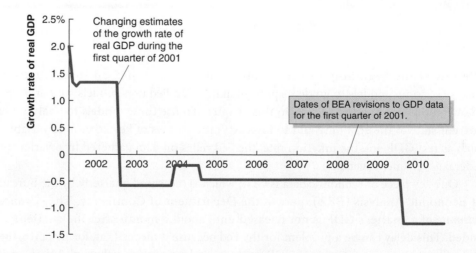

This example shows that in addition to the other problems the Fed faces in successfully conducting monetary policy, it must make its forecasts using data that may be subject to substantial revisions.

Sources: Federal Reserve Bank of Philadelphia, "Historical Data Files for the Real-Time Data Set," August 24, 2010; and Bruce T. Grimm and Teresa Weadock, "Gross Domestic Product: Revisions and Source Data," *Survey of Current Business*, Vol. 86, No. 2, February 2006, pp. 11–15.

See related problem 3.7 at the end of the chapter.

Solved Problem 18.3

Using Monetary Policy to Fight Inflation

Fed Chairman Paul Volcker took office in August 1979, with a mandate to bring down the inflation rate (see Chapter 15). Use the *IS–MP* model to analyze how the Fed can change expectations of inflation to permanently reduce the inflation rate. Be sure that your graphs include the *IS* curve, the *MP* curve, and the Phillips curve. Also be sure that your graphs show the initial effect of the Fed's policy on the output gap and the inflation rate. Finally, be sure to illustrate how the economy returns to long-run equilibrium at a lower inflation rate.

Solving the Problem

Step 1 Review the chapter material. This problem is about using the *IS–MP* model and the reasons for shifts in the Phillips curve, so you may want to review the section "The Phillips Curve," which beings on page 564, and the section "Equilibrium in the *IS–MP* Model," which begins on page 570.

Step 2 Describe the policy the Fed would use to reduce the inflation rate and illustrate your answer with a graph. To permanently reduce the inflation rate, the Fed needs to reduce the expected inflation rate. The expected inflation rate will decline if households and firms experience an inflation rate that is persistently lower than the inflation rate they had expected. The Phillips curve tells us that if real GDP falls below potential GDP, the inflation rate will decline. The Fed can cause a decline in real GDP by raising the real interest rate. Your graph should show the *MP* curve shifting up from MP_1 to MP_2, the new equilibrium output gap, $\widetilde{Y}_1$, and the reduction in the inflation rate from π_1 to π_2 along the Phillips curve.

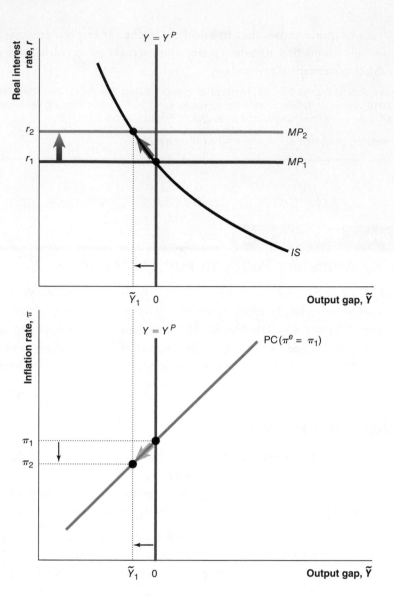

Step 3 **Show how after the Phillips curve shifts down, the Fed can return the economy to potential output at a lower inflation rate.** If the inflation persists at π_2, households will eventually lower their expectation of the inflation rate from π_1 to π_2. Once that happens, the Phillips curve will shift down and the Fed can lower the real interest rate from r_2 back to r_1, returning output to potential GDP.

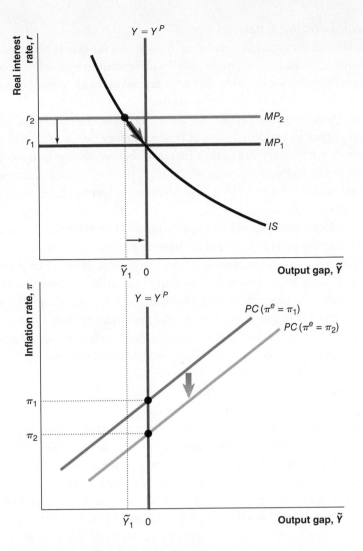

See related problem 3.8 at the end of the chapter.

Are Interest Rates All That Matter for Monetary Policy?

Economists refer to the ways in which monetary policy can affect output and prices as the *channels of monetary policy*. In the *IS–MP* model, monetary policy works through the channel of interest rates: Through open market operations, the Fed changes the real interest rate, which affects the components of aggregate expenditure, thereby changing the output gap and the inflation rate. Economists call this channel the *interest rate channel*. An underlying assumption in this approach is that borrowers are indifferent as to how or from whom they raise funds and regard alternative sources of funds as close substitutes. Bank loans play no special role in this channel.

18.4
Learning Objective
Discuss alternative channels of monetary policy.

The Bank Lending Channel

Bank lending channel
A description of how monetary policy influences the spending decisions of borrowers who depend on bank loans.

Households and many firms depend on bank loans for credit because they have few or no alternative sources of funds. The **bank lending channel** of monetary policy emphasizes the behavior of borrowers who depend on bank loans. In the bank lending channel, a change in banks' ability or willingness to lend affects the ability of bank-dependent borrowers to finance their spending plans. This channel's focus on bank loans also suggests a modified view of how monetary policy affects the economy. In this channel, a monetary expansion increases banks' ability to lend, and increases in loans to bank-dependent borrowers increase their spending. A monetary contraction decreases banks' ability to lend, and decreases in loans to bank-dependent borrowers reduce their spending.

In the interest rate channel, the Fed increases bank reserves through open market purchases, thereby decreasing the real interest rate and increasing output in the short run. This increase in output occurs because the decline in the federal funds rate leads to declines in other interest rates that are important to the spending decisions of households and firms. The predictions of the bank lending channel are similar to those of the interest rate channel in one respect: When the Fed expands bank reserves through open market purchases, the increase in bank reserves leads to lower loan interest rates. Many borrowers can choose between bank loans and borrowing from nonbank sources, so lower bank loan rates lead to lower interest rates in financial markets.

The bank lending channel holds further, however, that monetary policy affects the economy through the volume of bank lending to and spending by bank-dependent borrowers. In the bank lending channel, an expansionary monetary policy causes aggregate expenditure to increase for two reasons: (1) the increase in households' and firms' spending from the drop in interest rates, and (2) the increased availability of bank loans. In other words, if banks expand deposits by lowering interest rates on loans, the amounts that bank-dependent borrowers can borrow and spend increases at any real interest rate. Therefore, *in the bank lending channel, an expansionary monetary policy is not dependent for its effectiveness on a reduction in interest rates.* Similarly, a contractionary monetary policy is not dependent for its effectiveness on an increase in interest rates.

The Balance Sheet Channel: Monetary Policy and Net Worth

Balance sheet channel A description of how interest rate changes resulting from monetary policy affect borrowers' net worth and spending decisions.

Monetary policy may also affect the economy through its effects on firms' balance sheet positions. Economists have modeled this channel through the effects of monetary policy on the value of firms' assets and liabilities and on the liquidity of balance sheet positions—that is, the quantity of liquid assets that households and firms hold relative to their liabilities. According to these economists, the liquidity of balance sheet positions is a determinant of spending on business investment, housing, and consumer durable goods. The **balance sheet channel** describes the ways in which, by changing interest rates, monetary policy affects borrowers' net worth and spending decisions. We know that when the information costs of lending are great, high levels of net worth and liquidity help borrowers to carry out their planned spending.

How does monetary policy affect borrowers' balance sheets? Recall that information problems increase the gap between the costs of external and internal funds as a borrower's net worth falls. That is, a decline in a borrower's net worth increases the cost of raising funds for capital investment. Increases in interest rates in response to a contractionary monetary policy increase the amounts that borrowers with variable-rate loans pay on their debts and reduce the value of borrowers' net worth by reducing the present value of their assets. This fall in net worth raises the cost of external financing by more than the increase that is implied by higher interest rates, and it reduces firms' ability to invest in plant and equipment. The balance sheet channel emphasizes this effect. *Even if monetary policy has no effect on banks' ability to lend, the decline in borrowers' net worth following a monetary contraction reduces aggregate demand and output.* Moreover, the balance sheet channel implies that spending by low-net-worth firms is particularly likely to fall following a monetary contraction.

The balance sheet channel, like the interest rate channel and the bank lending channel, holds that expansionary policy initially decreases interest rates, increasing output, while contractionary policy initially increases interest rates, reducing output. The balance sheet channel emphasizes the link between households' and businesses' net worth and liquidity and their spending. In the presence of information costs, changes in net worth and liquidity may significantly affect the volume of lending and economic activity.

Most economists believe that accepting the significance of the bank lending or balance sheet channel does not require rejecting the interest rate channel's implication that monetary policy works through interest rates. Instead, the bank lending and balance sheet channels offer additional methods by which the financial system and monetary policy can affect the economy.

Table 18.2 summarizes the key points of these three channels of monetary policy.

Table 18.2 Channels of Monetary Policy

Channel	Focuses on . . .	Monetary expansion . . .	Monetary contraction . . .
Interest rate channel	interest rates.	lowers interest rates, causing aggregate expenditure to increase.	raises interest rates, causing aggregate expenditure to decrease.
Bank lending channel	bank loans.	increases banks' ability to lend to bank-dependent borrowers, causing aggregate expenditure to increase.	decreases banks' ability to lend to bank-dependent borrowers, causing aggregate expenditure to decrease.
Balance sheet channel	the link between the net worth and liquidity of households and firms and their spending.	increases net worth and liquidity, causing aggregate expenditure to increase.	decreases net worth and liquidity, causing aggregate expenditure to decrease.

Answering the Key Question

Continued from page 550

At the beginning of this chapter, we asked:

"In what circumstances is lowering the target for the federal funds rate unlikely to be effective in fighting a recession?"

As we have seen throughout this book, the recession of 2007–2009 was accompanied by a financial crisis that made the recession unusually severe. The Fed realized by the fall of 2008 that its normal policy of fighting recessions primarily by lowering its target for the federal funds rate was unlikely to be effective. The *IS–MP* model developed in this chapter provides one explanation of why normal monetary policy was ineffective. Although the Fed lowered the target for the federal funds rate nearly to zero, an increase in the risk premium demanded by investors caused a rise in the interest rates, such as the Baa bond rate, that many businesses pay, despite the Fed's efforts.

Key Terms and Problems

Key Terms

Aggregate demand shock, p. 562
Balance sheet channel, p. 580
Bank lending channel, p. 580
Fiscal policy, p. 558
IS curve, p. 552

IS–MP model, p. 552
MP curve, p. 552
Multiplier, p. 556
Multiplier effect, p. 556
Okun's law, p. 567

Output gap, p. 560
Phillips curve, p. 552
Potential GDP, p. 555

18.1 The *IS* Curve

Understand what the *IS* curve is and how it is derived.

Review Questions

1.1 Describe each of the three parts of the *IS–MP* model.

1.2 Draw a 45°-line diagram showing an equilibrium in the goods market. Label the equilibrium level of real GDP, Y_1. Now show on your graph the situation when real GDP is equal to Y_2, where Y_2 is greater than Y_1, and the situation when real GDP is equal to Y_3, where Y_3 is less than Y_1. Be sure that your graph shows the level of aggregate expenditure and the level of unintended changes in inventories at Y_1, Y_2, and Y_3. Briefly explain how real GDP adjusts to equilibrium if it is initially equal to Y_2 or Y_3.

1.3 What is the relationship between the *MPC* and the multiplier? Would a larger value for the *MPC* tend to increase or decrease the stability of the economy? Briefly explain.

1.4 Explain how the *IS* curve represents equilibrium in the goods market. Why is the *IS* curve downward sloping?

1.5 Give an example of a shock that could shift the *IS* curve to the left. Give an example of a shock that could shift the *IS* curve to the right.

Problems and Applications

1.6 [Related to Solved Problem 18.1 **on page 557**]
Use the following data to calculate the values of equilibrium output and the investment spending multiplier:

$$C = MPC \times Y = 0.75 \times Y$$
$$\bar{I} = \$2.3 \text{ trillion}$$
$$\bar{G} = \$1.7 \text{ trillion}$$
$$\overline{NX} = -\$0.5 \text{ trillion}$$

1.7 Briefly explain whether you agree with the following argument:

> Potential GDP is the level of real GDP attained when all firms are producing at capacity. Firms have the capacity to operate 24 hours per day if they have to, but they rarely do. Therefore, because firms can almost always produce much more output than they actually do, real GDP is almost always well below potential GDP.

1.8 Why does a change in the real interest rate shift the aggregate expenditure line in the 45°-line diagram but not shift the *IS* curve?

1.9 In each of the following situations, briefly explain whether the *IS* curve will shift and, if it does shift, in which direction it will shift:

a. Consumers become more optimistic about their future incomes.

b. The federal government cuts the corporate profit tax.

c. The real interest rate rises.

d. Firms become pessimistic about the future profitability of spending on new information technology.

1.10 How would the size of the multiplier affect the slope of the *IS* curve? (Hint: In the 45°-line diagram, how does the multiplier affect the change in the equilibrium level of real GDP for a given change in the real interest rate?)

1.11 If consumption spending becomes more sensitive to changes in the real interest rate, how will the slope of the *IS* curve be affected?

1.12 Some economists believe that during a recession, business demand for investment in factories, office buildings, and machinery becomes less sensitive to changes in the real interest rate. If these economists are correct, how might the slope of the *IS* curve be different during expansions than during recessions? Illustrate your answer by drawing an *IS* curve graph.

18.2 ## The *MP* Curve and the Phillips Curve
Explain the significance of the *MP* curve and the Phillips curve.

Review Questions

2.1 How can changes in the federal funds rate cause changes in long-term real interest rates?

2.2 Why is the *MP* curve a horizontal line? How is the Fed able to change the position of the *MP* curve?

2.3 When the Federal Reserve increases the real interest rate, is the result a movement up or down the *IS* curve, and does the value of the output gap increase or decrease?

2.4 What factors cause the Phillips curve to shift?

2.5 How can Okun's law be used to derive an output gap Phillips curve?

Problems and Applications

2.6 A columnist in the *Wall Street Journal* argues: "Whether you're a borrower or a saver, what matters isn't the nominal interest rate but the 'real,' post-inflation rate of return." Do you agree? Briefly explain.
Source: Brett Arends, "What Deflation Means for Your Wallet," *Wall Street Journal*, July 7, 2010.

2.7 An article in the *Economist* magazine observes: "When inflation rises, for instance, bondholders will expect a higher nominal interest rate on new debt." Briefly explain whether you agree with this statement.

Source: "The Maths Behind the Madness," *Economist*, October 17, 2012.

2.8 In a column in the *New York Times*, Harvard economist Edward Glaeser argues: "Theory and data both predict that the 1.2 percentage point drop in real interest rates that America experienced between 1996 and 2006 should cause a [housing] price increase of somewhat less than 10 percent."

a. How can the Fed cause the real interest rate to increase or decrease?

b. Why would a decline in real interest rates cause an increase in housing prices?

Source: Edward Glaeser, "Did Low Interest Rates Cause the Great Housing Convulsion?" *New York Times*, August 3, 2010.

2.9 In each of the following situations, briefly explain whether the short-run Phillips curve with the unemployment rate on the horizontal axis will shift, and if it does shift, in which direction it will shift:

a. The expected inflation rate decreases.

b. The actual inflation rate increases.

c. The price of oil substantially decreases.

d. Cyclical unemployment increases.

e. Favorable weather conditions result in bumper agricultural crops.

2.10 [Related to the Making the Connection **on page 569**] An article in the *Wall Street Journal* in 2012 discussing Okun's law observes: "The law has been unreliable lately. Under [Okun's law], it would take

growth between 4% and 5% to explain the improvements in unemployment in the past year—much more than the recovery has actually delivered."

a. What is Okun's law?

b. What explanations have economists offered for the unreliability of Okun's law after the 2007–2009 recession?

Source: Jon Hilsenrath, "Piecing Together the Job–Picture Puzzle," *Wall Street Journal*, March 12, 2012.

2.11 If households and firms change from expecting mild inflation to expecting mild deflation, how will the Phillips curve shift? Draw an output gap Phillips curve graph to illustrate your answer.

2.12 An article in the *Economist* magazine argues that the expected inflation rate in the United States followed "a steady downward trend" between December 2007 and May 2012.

a. Holding other factors constant, what would be the effect of this trend on the long-term real interest rate?

b. If the Fed had wanted to offset the effect you describe in part (a), what action could it have taken?

Source: "What's Inflation Telling Us about the Output Gap?" *Economist*, May 20, 2012.

2.13 Some economists have suggested that structural changes in the construction industry and the automobile industry in the mid- to late 2000s may have resulted in a new higher natural rate of unemployment. How would an increase in the natural rate of unemployment affect the short-run Phillips curve? Consider both the unemployment rate version of the Phillips curve and the output gap version of the Phillips curve.

18.3 ## Equilibrium in the *IS–MP* Model
Use the *IS–MP* model to illustrate macroeconomic equilibrium.

Review Questions

3.1 Draw graphs showing long-run macroeconomic equilibrium in the *IS–MP* model. One of your

graphs should show the output gap version of the Phillips curve. In long-run equilibrium, what does the output gap equal, and what is true about the actual and expected inflation rates?

MyEconLab Visit **www.myeconlab.com** to complete these exercises online and get instant feedback. Exercises that update with real-time data are marked with 🌐.

3.2 When the Federal Reserve lowers the real interest rate, what happens to the output gap and to the inflation rate?

3.3 What is the default risk premium, and why did it dramatically increase during the 2007–2009 recession? How did this increase affect the *MP* curve and the output gap?

Problems and Applications

3.4 Use the *IS–MP* model (including the output gap Phillips curve) to analyze how the Federal Reserve would respond to a large positive demand shock. Assume that the economy was in long-run macroeconomic equilibrium before the demand shock. Use a graph to show both the effect of the positive demand shock and how the Fed might respond.

3.5 [Related to the Making the Connection on page 571] John Maynard Keynes developed a model, later elaborated by John Hicks, in which total output is determined solely by total spending with little consideration of the supply (production) side of the economy. Why would Keynes and Hicks writing during the Great Depression be likely to develop a model of the economy that focused on total spending?

3.6 [Related to the Making the Connection on page 571] John Hicks, in his original macroeconomic model, the *IS–LM* model, developed the *LM* curve to show the combinations of the real interest rate and output that result in equilibrium in the money market. The *LM* curve assumes that monetary policy takes the form of the Federal Reserve choosing a target for the money supply. Why would David Romer in 2000 suggest dropping the traditional *LM* curve and replacing it with the *MP* curve?

3.7 [Related to the Making the Connection on page 575] Economists debate whether the Federal Reserve, Congress, and the president should attempt to "fine-tune" the economy—smooth almost every fluctuation in GDP or inflation—with stabilization policy, or, instead, should focus on long-run objectives, such as low inflation or steady economic growth, and restrict the use of activist policy to fighting major downturns in the economy. Does the reality that policymakers must rely on "real-time data" that is subject to revisions weaken or strengthen the argument against fine-tuning the economy with activist stabilization policy? Briefly explain.

3.8 [Related to Solved Problem 18.3 on page 577] Suppose the Fed is concerned that deflation will harm the economy over the long run. Use the *IS–MP* model (including the output gap Phillips curve) to analyze how the Federal Reserve would fight deflation.

a. Use an *IS–MP* model graph to show long-run macroeconomic equilibrium with a deflation rate of 2%.

b. If the Fed wants the economy to return to a long-run equilibrium with an inflation rate of 2%, how should it change its target for the federal funds rate? Show the effects of this change in the target for the federal funds rate on an *IS–MP* graph, including the Phillips curve. What happens to the output gap and to the inflation rate?

c. Use an *IS–MP* graph, including the Phillips curve, to illustrate how the economy returns to long-run equilibrium at the higher inflation rate.

3.9 [Related to the Chapter Opener on page 550] In testifying before Congress in mid-2012, Fed Chairman Ben Bernanke noted that the economic recovery "could be endangered by the confluence of tax increases and [government] spending reductions that will take effect early next year if no legislative action is taken."

a. Use an *IS–MP* graph to show the effects of tax increases and government spending reductions on the output gap. Briefly explain what your graph is showing.

b. In the same testimony, Bernanke referred to "the additional negative effects likely to result from public uncertainty about how these [taxing and government spending] matters will be resolved." What components of aggregate expenditure might be affected by an increase in uncertainty? Use an *IS–MP* graph to show the effects of uncertainty on the output gap. Briefly explain what your graph is showing.

Source: Board of Governors of the Federal Reserve System, "Statement by Ben S. Bernanke Chairman Board of Governors of the Federal Reserve System before the Committee on Banking, Housing, and Urban Affairs, U.S. Senate," July 17, 2012.

18.4 Are Interest Rates All That Matter for Monetary Policy?
Discuss alternative channels of monetary policy.

Review Questions

4.1 What do economists mean by the channels of monetary policy?

4.2 If monetary policy does not cause a change in interest rates, can it still affect the output gap and the inflation rate? Briefly explain.

Problems and Applications

4.3 When the Federal Reserve changes the real interest rate to affect the output gap and inflation rate, do the bank lending channel and the balance sheet channel reinforce or partially offset the effect of the change in the real interest rate? Briefly explain.

4.4 In the bank lending channel, an expansionary monetary policy is not dependent for its effectiveness on a reduction in interest rates, and a contractionary monetary policy is not dependent for its effectiveness on an increase in interest rates. How can an expansionary monetary policy be effective without reducing interest rates to stimulate spending, and how can a contractionary monetary policy be effective without increasing interest rates to slow down spending?

4.5 Would you expect the bank lending channel of monetary policy to have a larger or a smaller effect in emerging economies, such as Brazil or India, than in the United States? Briefly explain.

4.6 Over time, as the financial system expands and develops additional sources of financing for small to medium-sized firms, such as asset-backed securities, would the bank lending channel become more or less important? Briefly explain.

Data Exercises

D18.1: **[The Relationship between the federal funds rate and the long-term interest rate]** Go to the Web site of the Federal Reserve Bank of St. Louis (FRED) (http://research.stlouisfed.org/fred2/) and download to the same graph data from January 1984 to the most recent available month on the nominal federal funds rate (FEDFUNDS) and the nominal 10-year constant maturity U.S. Treasury security (GS10).

a. Is the relationship between the federal funds rate and the long-term nominal interest rate as strong as the relationship between the federal funds rate and other short-term nominal interest rates? Briefly explain. Hint: Think of the term-structure of interest rates.

b. Now add the monthly interest rate of the 30-year fixed rate mortgage (MORTG) to your graph. Is the relationship between the federal funds rate and the mortgage rate stronger or weaker than the relationship between the federal funds rate and the interest rate on 10-year U.S. Treasury notes? Briefly explain. In particular, comment on the behavior of mortgage interest rates during the first part of the 2007–2009 recession. Hint: Think of the risk-structure of interest rates.

D18.2: **[Analyzing the default risk premium]** Go to the Web site of the Federal Reserve Bank of St. Louis Federal Reserve (FRED) (http://research.stlouisfed.org/fred2/) and download data on the interest rate on AAA rated corporate bonds (AAA) and the interest rate on constant maturity 10-year U.S. Treasury notes (GS10) from January 1953 to the most recent available month.

a. Calculate the default-risk premium and plot the resulting data series on a graph.

b. You can find the dates of U.S. recessions at the website of the National Bureau of Economic Research (http://www.nber.org/cycles/cyclesmain.html). What happens to the default-risk premium during recessions? Holding everything else constant, what would you expect to happen to the *MP* curve during recessions?

c. What actions could the Fed take to offset the effect of the changes in the default-risk premium on the *MP* curve?

D18.3: **[Analyzing the real interest rate]** Go to the Web site of the Federal Reserve Bank of St. Louis Federal Reserve (FRED) (http://research.stlouisfed.org/fred2/) and download from January 2003 to the most recent available month data on the 10-year constant maturity U.S. Treasury notes (GS10) as a measure of the nominal interest rate and the 10-year U.S. Treasury inflation protected security (FII10) as a measure of the real interest rate.

a. The Fisher relationship tells us that the expected inflation rate is the nominal interest rate minus the real interest rate. Calculate the expected inflation rate over the next ten years using these data.

b. For January 2003 to the most recent available month, download data on Aaa corporate bonds (AAA). The Fisher relationship also tells us that the real interest rate equals the nominal interest rate minus the expected inflation rate. Calculate the real interest rate

for Aaa corporate bonds using your results from part (a). Plot the resulting data series on a graph.

c. What happened to the real interest rate from the beginning of the recession in December 2007 to August 2008? Does this movement in the real interest rate suggest that shifts in the *IS* curve or *MP* curve were most likely to have been responsible for the start of the recession? Briefly explain.

d. What happens to the real interest rate during the period from September 2008 to November 2008? Does this movement in the real interest rate suggest that shifts in the *IS* curve or *MP* curve were responsible for the worsening of the recession during the fall of 2008? Briefly explain.

D18.4: **[Testing the Phillips curve]** Go to the Web site of the Federal Reserve Bank of St. Louis (FRED) (research.stlouisfed.org/fred2/categories/22) and download annual unemployment data (UNRATE) for 1962 to the present (to convert the data from a monthly frequency to an annual frequency, click on Edit Graph and Frequency). Next, download the annual inflation rate measured using the consumer price index, or CPI (CPIAUCSL). (Once you have converted the data from a monthly frequency to an annual frequency, you can find the inflation rate by clicking on Units and selecting Percentage Change from Year Ago.) Briefly explain whether for each of the following periods, the relationship between the annual unemployment rate and the annual inflation rate is consistent with a movement along the short-run Phillips curve or with a shift in the Phillips curve. If the data are consistent with the Phillips curve having shifted, briefly explain whether the shift resulted from a negative shock or a positive shock.

a. 1966–1969

b. 1973–1975

c. 1992–1994

d. 2000–2002

Appendix

The *IS–LM* Model

18.A

Learning Objective

Use the *IS–LM* model to illustrate macroeconomic equilibrium.

IS–LM model A macroeconomic model of aggregate demand that assumes that the central bank targets the money supply.

LM curve A curve that shows the combinations of the interest rate and the output gap that result in equilibrium in the money market.

The *IS–MP* model that we developed in this chapter assumes that the Fed targets the federal funds rate and uses open market operations to adjust the level of reserves in the banking system in order to hit its target. We used the *IS–MP* model because the Fed and many other central banks today use as their monetary policy target a short-term bank lending rate, such as the federal funds rate.

At one time, though, some central banks targeted the money supply rather than a short-term interest rate. The **IS–LM model**, which we noted in the *Making the Connection* on pages 571–572 was first developed by British economist John Hicks in 1937, is similar to the *IS–MP* model. The difference is the *IS–LM* model assumes that the Fed is targeting the money supply rather than the federal funds rate.

Both the *IS–MP* and *IS–LM* models use the *IS* curve to show the negative relationship between the real interest rate and expenditure in the market for goods and services. The *IS–LM* model differs from the *IS–MP* model because it assumes that the Fed is targeting the level of the money stock and, so, substitutes an *LM* curve for the *MP* curve. The **LM curve** shows the combinations of the interest rate and the output gap that result in equilibrium in the money market.

Deriving the *LM* Curve

To derive the *LM* curve, we use the money market from the last chapter. In that chapter, we assumed that equilibrium in the money market determined the short-term nominal interest rate. Because equilibrium in the goods market, as shown by the *IS* curve, depends on the real interest rate, we will make the simplifying assumption that the expected inflation rate is constant so that a change in the nominal interest rate is equivalent to a change in the real interest rate. In addition, we will assume that movements in short-term rates result in corresponding movements in the long-term interest rates that are important for consumption and investment decisions. If these assumptions hold, then the equilibrium long-term real interest rate is determined in the money market.

To derive the *LM* curve, we consider what happens to the demand for real balances when the output gap, or the percentage difference between real GDP and potential GDP, increases. (Note that we are measuring output as the output gap rather than as the level of output, to be consistent with the *IS–MP* model.) In panel (a) of Figure 18A.1, the economy begins in equilibrium at point *A*. A change in the output gap from $\widetilde{Y}_1$ to $\widetilde{Y}_2$ causes the demand for real balances to shift from M_1^D to M_2^D. The demand for real balances increases as output increases because households and firms need larger money balances to finance the increased transactions that result from higher levels of output. As the demand for real balances increases, the real interest rate must increase from r_1 to r_2 in order to maintain equilibrium in the money market at point *B*. This analysis tells us that, *holding the supply of real balances constant*, higher levels of output are associated with higher levels of the real interest rate in the money market. Panel (b) of Figure 18A.1 plots

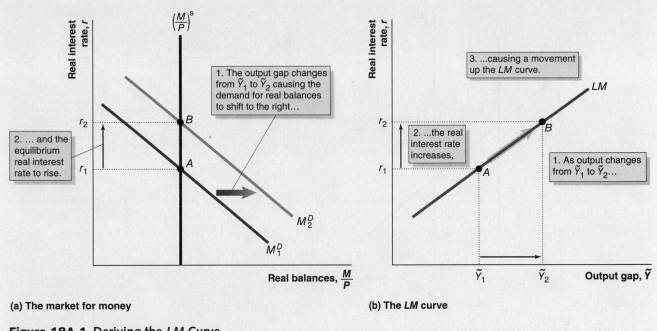

(a) The market for money

(b) The *LM* curve

Figure 18A.1 Deriving the *LM* Curve

In panel (a), the economy begins in equilibrium at point *A*. A change in the output gap from $\tilde{Y}_1$ to $\tilde{Y}_2$ causes the demand for real balances to shift from M_1^D to M_2^D. The real interest rate must increase from r_1 to r_2 in order to maintain equilibrium in the money market at point *B*.

Panel (b) plots the combinations of the interest rate and the output gap from the equilibrium points *A* and *B* in panel (a). The *LM* curve shows all the combinations of the real interest rate and the output gap that result in equilibrium in the money market.

the combinations of the interest rate and the output gap from the equilibrium points *A* and *B* in panel (a). If we continued to vary the level of output in panel (a), we would trace out the combinations shown on the *LM* curve in panel (b). In other words, the *LM* curve shows all the combinations of the real interest rate and the output gap that result in equilibrium in the money market.

Shifting the *LM* Curve

If factors that affect the demand or supply for real balances, other than output, change, then the *LM* curve will shift. For example, Figure 18A.2 shows the effect of an increase in the money supply on the *LM* curve. In panel (a), the money market begins in equilibrium at point *A*. The Fed then increases the supply of real balances from $(M/P)_1^S$ to $(M/P)_2^S$. The real interest rate falls from r_1 to r_2, and equilibrium in the money market is restored at point *B*. In panel (b), we show that the result of the increase in real money balances is to shift the *LM* curve to the right, from LM_1 to LM_2. Compared with point *A*—which corresponds to point *A* in panel (a)—at point *B*, the output gap remains the same, while the real interest rate is lower.

Monetary Policy in the *IS–LM* Model

In Figure 18A.3, we bring together the *IS* curve and the *LM* curve. Where the two curves cross, we have equilibrium in both the goods market and the money market. We can

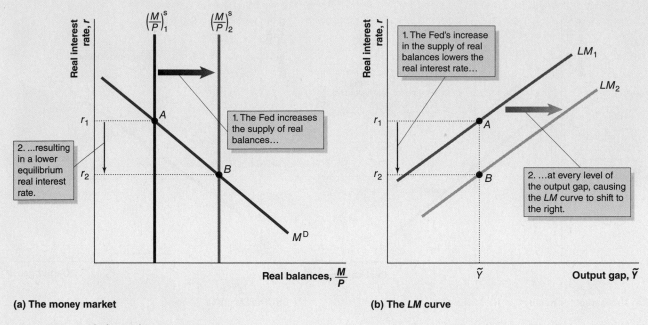

(a) The money market

(b) The *LM* curve

Figure 18A.2 Shifting the *LM* Curve

In panel (a), the money market begins in equilibrium at point *A*. The Fed then increases the supply of real balances from $(M/P)_1^S$ to $(M/P)_2^S$. The real interest rate falls from r_1 to r_2, and equilibrium in the money market is restored at point *B*. Panel (b) shows that the result of the increase in real money balances is to shift the *LM* curve to the right, from LM_1 to LM_2.

Figure 18A.3

Expansionary Monetary Policy

At the initial equilibrium at point *A*, real GDP is below potential real GDP. Increasing the supply of real balances shifts the *LM* curve to the right, from LM_1 to LM_2. Equilibrium will move to point *B* with real GDP at its potential level, while the real interest rate will fall from r_1 to r_2.

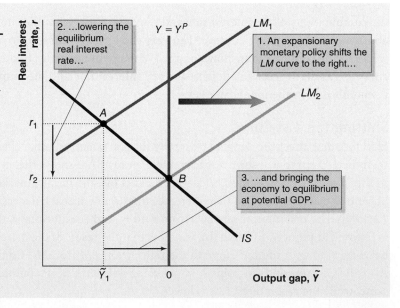

use this graph to illustrate the effects of the Fed conducting an expansionary monetary policy that consists of increasing the supply of real balances rather than decreasing the target for the federal funds rate. At the initial equilibrium at point A, real GDP is below potential real GDP at $\widetilde{Y}_1$. As we saw in Figure 18A.2, increasing the supply of real balances shifts the LM curve to the right. If the Fed increases real money balances sufficiently to shift the LM curve from LM_1 to LM_2, equilibrium will move to point B with real GDP at its potential level, while the real interest rate will fall from r_1 to r_2.

Key Terms

IS–LM model, p. 588
LM curve, p. 588

Glossary

Adaptive expectations The assumption that people make forecasts of future values of a variable using only past values of the variable. *(p. 171)*

Adverse selection The problem investors experience in distinguishing low-risk borrowers from high-risk borrowers before making an investment. *(p. 257)*

Aggregate demand (*AD*) curve A curve that shows the relationship between the price level and aggregate expenditure on goods and services. *(p. 521)*

Aggregate demand shock A change in one of the components of aggregate expenditure that causes the *IS* curve to shift. *(p. 562)*

Aggregate supply The total quantity of output, or GDP, that firms are willing to supply at a given price level. *(p. 525)*

Appreciation An increase in the value of a currency in exchange for another currency. *(p. 226)*

Asset Anything of value owned by a person or a firm; in particular, a financial claim. *(pp. 2 and 281)*

Asymmetric information The situation in which one party to an economic transaction has better information than does the other party. *(p. 257)*

Balance sheet A statement that shows an individual's or a firm's financial position on a particular day. *(p. 281)*

Balance sheet channel A description of how interest rate changes resulting from monetary policy affect borrowers' net worth and spending decisions. *(p. 580)*

Balance-of-payments account A measure of all flows of private and government funds between a domestic economy and all foreign countries. *(p. 495)*

Bank capital The difference between the value of a bank's assets and the value of its liabilities; also called shareholders' equity. *(p. 281)*

Bank lending channel A description of how monetary policy influences the spending decisions of borrowers who depend on bank loans. *(p. 580)*

Bank leverage The ratio of the value of a bank's assets to the value of its capital, the inverse of which (capital to assets) is called a bank's leverage ratio. *(p. 293)*

Bank panic The situation in which many banks simultaneously experience runs. *(p. 351)*

Bank reserves Bank deposits with the Fed plus vault cash. *(p. 419)*

Bank run The process by which depositors who have lost confidence in a bank simultaneously withdraw enough funds to force the bank to close. *(p. 351)*

Barter A system of exchange in which individuals trade goods and services directly for other goods and services. *(p. 25)*

Basel accord An international agreement about bank capital requirements. *(p. 376)*

Behavioral finance The application of concepts from behavioral economics to understand how people make choices in financial markets. *(p. 181)*

Board of Governors The governing board of the Federal Reserve System, consisting of seven members appointed by the president of the United States. *(p. 394)*

Bond A financial security issued by a corporation or a government that represents a promise to repay a fixed amount of money. *(p. 3)*

Bond rating A single statistic that summarizes a rating agency's view of the issuer's likely ability to make the required payments on its bonds. *(p. 126)*

Bretton Woods system An exchange rate system that lasted from 1945 to 1971, under which countries pledged to buy and sell their currencies at fixed rates against the dollar and the United States pledged to convert dollars into gold if foreign central banks requested it to. *(p. 502)*

Bubble A situation in which the price of an asset rises well above the asset's fundamental value. *(pp. 15 and 182)*

Business cycle Alternating periods of economic expansion and economic recession. *(p. 537)*

Call option A type of derivative contract that gives the buyer the right to buy the underlying asset at a set price during a set period of time. *(p. 203)*

Capital controls Government-imposed restrictions on foreign investors buying domestic assets or on domestic investors buying foreign assets. *(p. 494)*

Capital gain An increase in the market price of an asset. *(p. 68)*

Capital loss A decrease in the market price of an asset. *(p. 68)*

Check A promise to pay on demand money deposited with a bank or other financial institution. *(p. 30)*

Checkable deposits Accounts against which depositors can write checks. *(p. 282)*

Closed economy An economy in which households, firms, and governments do not borrow or lend internationally. *(p. 113)*

Collateral Assets that a borrower pledges to a lender that the lender may seize if the borrower defaults on the loan. *(p. 261)*

Commercial bank A financial firm that serves as a financial intermediary by taking in deposits and using them to make loans. *(p. 5)*

Commodity money A good used as money that has value independent of its use as money. *(p. 25)*

Compounding The process of earning interest on interest, as savings accumulate over time. *(p. 52)*

Contagion The process by which a run on one bank spreads to other banks resulting in a bank panic. *(p. 351)*

Contractual saving institution A financial intermediary such as a pension fund or an insurance company that receives payments from individuals as a result of a contract and uses the funds to make investments. *(p. 334)*

Corporation A legal form of business that provides owners with protection from losing more than their investment if the business fails. *(p. 158)*

Counterparty risk The risk that the counterparty—the person or firm on the other side of the transaction—will default. *(p. 193)*

Coupon bond A debt instrument that requires multiple payments of interest on a regular basis, such as semiannually or annually, and a payment of the face value at maturity. *(p. 59)*

Credit default swap A derivative that requires the seller to make payments to the buyer if the price of the underlying security declines in value; in effect, a type of insurance. *(p. 214)*

Credit rationing The restriction of credit by lenders such that borrowers cannot obtain the funds they desire at the given interest rate. *(pp. 260 and 295)*

Credit risk The risk that borrowers might default on their loans. *(p. 294)*

Credit-risk analysis The process that bank loan officers use to screen loan applicants. *(p. 294)*

Credit swap A contract in which interest-rate payments are exchanged, with the intention of reducing default risk. *(p. 214)*

Currency in circulation Paper money circulating outside of the Fed. *(p. 419)*

Currency in M1 Currency held by the nonbank public. *(p. 419)*

Currency swap A contract in which counterparties agree to exchange principal amounts denominated in different currencies. *(p. 213)*

Currency-to-deposit ratio (*C/D*) The nonbank public's holdings of currency, *C*, relative to their holdings of checkable deposits, *D*. *(p. 430)*

Debt instruments (also known as **credit market instruments** or **fixed-income assets**) Methods of financing debt, including simple loans, discount bonds, coupon bonds, and fixed payment loans. *(p. 58)*

Debt-deflation process The process first identified by Irving Fisher in which a cycle of falling asset prices and falling prices of goods and services can increase the severity of an economic downturn. *(p. 362)*

Default risk (or **credit risk**) The risk that a bond issuer will fail to make payments of interest or principal. *(p. 126)*

Deflation A sustained decline in the price level. *(p. 77)*

Depreciation A decrease in the value of a currency in exchange for another currency. *(p. 226)*

Derivative An asset, such as a futures contract or an option contract, that derives its economic value from an underlying asset, such as a stock or a bond. *(p. 191)*

Devaluation The lowering of the official value of a country's currency relative to other currencies. *(p. 503)*

Discount bond A debt instrument in which the borrower repays the amount of the loan in a single payment at maturity but receives less than the face value of the bond initially. *(p. 59)*

Discount loan A loan made by the Federal Reserve, typically to a commercial bank. *(p. 421)*

Discount policy The policy tool of setting the discount rate and the terms of discount lending. *(p. 452)*

Discount rate The interest rate the Federal Reserve charges on discount loans. *(p. 422)*

Discount window The means by which the Fed makes discount loans to banks, serving as the channel for meeting the liquidity needs of banks. *(p. 452)*

Discounting The process of finding the present value of funds that will be received in the future. *(p. 54)*

Disintermediation The exit of savers and borrowers from banks to financial markets. *(p. 374)*

Diversification The division of wealth among many different assets to reduce risk. *(pp. 13 and 93)*

Dividend A payment that a corporation makes to its shareholders, typically on a quarterly basis. *(pp. 3 and 159)*

Dividend yield The expected annual dividend divided by the current price of a stock. *(p. 166)*

Dual banking system The system in the United States in which banks are chartered by either a state government or the federal government. *(p. 299)*

Duration analysis An analysis of how sensitive a bank's capital is to changes in market interest rates. *(p. 297)*

Economic growth Increases in the economy's output of goods and services over time; a goal of monetary policy. *(p. 450)*

Economies of scale The reduction in average cost that results from an increase in the volume of a good or service produced. *(p. 257)*

Efficient markets hypothesis The application of rational expectations to financial markets; the hypothesis that the equilibrium price of a security is equal to its fundamental value. *(p. 172)*

E-money Digital cash people use to buy goods and services over the Internet; short for electronic money. *(p. 31)*

Equity A claim to part ownership of a firm; common stock issued by a corporation. *(p. 58)*

Euro The common currency of 17 European countries. *(p. 508)*

European Central Bank (ECB) The central bank of the European countries that have adopted the euro. *(p. 508)*

European Monetary Union A plan drafted as part of the 1992 single European market initiative, in which exchange rates were fixed and eventually a common currency was adopted. *(p. 508)*

Excess reserves Any reserves banks hold above those necessary to meet reserve requirements. *(pp. 285 and 419)*

Exchange rate regime A system for adjusting exchange rates and flows of goods and capital among countries. *(p. 498)*

Exchange-rate risk The risk that a firm will suffer losses because of fluctuations in exchange rates. *(p. 231)*

Expectations theory A theory of the term structure of interest rates which holds that the interest rate on a long-term bond is an average of the interest rates investors expect on short-term bonds over the lifetime of the long-term bond. *(p. 140)*

Expected return The rate of return expected on an asset during a future period. *(p. 89)*

Federal deposit insurance A government guarantee of deposit account balances up to $250,000. *(p. 283)*

Federal Deposit Insurance Corporation (FDIC) A federal government agency established by Congress in 1934 to insure deposits in commercial banks. *(p. 352)*

Federal funds rate The interest rate that banks charge each other on short-term loans; determined by the demand and supply for reserves in the federal funds market. *(pp. 11 and 452)*

Federal Open Market Committee (FOMC) The 12-member Federal Reserve committee that directs open market operations. *(p. 395)*

Federal Reserve The central bank of the United States; usually referred to as "the Fed." *(p. 11)*

Federal Reserve Bank A district bank of the Federal Reserve system that, among other activities, conducts discount lending. *(p. 390)*

Federal Reserve System The central bank of the United States. *(p. 389)*

Fiat money Money, such as paper currency, that has no value apart from its use as money. *(p. 28)*

Finance company A nonbank financial intermediary that raises money through sales of commercial paper and other securities and uses the funds to make small loans to households and firms. *(p. 333)*

Financial arbitrage The process of buying and selling securities to profit from price changes over a brief period of time. *(pp. 70 and 172)*

Financial asset An asset that represents a claim on someone else for a payment. *(p. 2)*

Financial crisis A significant disruption in the flow of funds from lenders to borrowers. *(pp. 15 and 350)*

Financial intermediary A financial firm, such as a bank, that borrows funds from savers and lends them to borrowers. *(p. 4)*

Financial liability A financial claim owed by a person or a firm. *(p. 4)*

Financial market A place or channel for buying or selling stocks, bonds, and other securities. *(p. 2)*

Fiscal policy Changes in federal government purchases and taxes intended to achieve macroeconomic policy objectives. *(p. 558)*

Fisher effect The assertion by Irving Fisher that the nominal interest rises or falls point-for-point with changes in the expected inflation rate. *(p. 107)*

Fixed exchange rate system A system in which exchange rates are set at levels determined and maintained by governments. *(p. 498)*

Fixed-payment loan A debt instrument that requires the borrower to make regular periodic payments of principal and interest to the lender. *(p. 60)*

Flexible exchange rate system A system in which the foreign exchange value of a currency is determined in the foreign exchange market. *(p. 506)*

Foreign exchange Units of foreign currency. *(p. 3)*

Foreign-exchange market An over-the-counter market where international currencies are traded. *(p. 230)*

Foreign exchange market intervention A deliberate action by a central bank to influence the exchange rate. *(p. 488)*

Forward contract An agreement to buy or sell an asset at an agreed-upon price at a future time. *(p. 193)*

Future value The value at some future time of an investment made today. *(p. 52)*

Futures contract A standardized contract to buy or sell a specified amount of a commodity or financial asset on a specific future date. *(p. 194)*

Gap analysis An analysis of the difference, or *gap*, between the dollar value of a bank's variable-rate assets and the dollar value of its variable-rate liabilities. *(p. 296)*

Gold standard A fixed exchange rate system under which currencies of participating countries are convertible into an agreed-upon amount of gold. *(p. 498)*

Gordon growth model A model that uses the current dividend paid, the expected growth rate of dividends, and the required return on equities to calculate the price of a stock. *(p. 169)*

Hedge To take action to reduce risk by, for example, purchasing a derivative contract that will increase in value when another asset in an investor's portfolio decreases in value. *(p. 191)*

Hedge fund A financial firm organized as a partnership of wealthy investors that make relatively high-risk, speculative investments. *(p. 330)*

Hyperinflation Extremely high rates of inflation, exceeding 50% per month. *(p. 39)*

Idiosyncratic (or unsystematic) risk Risk that pertains to a particular asset rather than to the market as a whole, as when the price of a particular firm's stock fluctuates because of the success or failure of a new product. *(p. 94)*

Information costs The costs that savers incur to determine the creditworthiness of borrowers and to monitor how they use the funds acquired. *(p. 256)*

Information Facts about borrowers and expectations of returns on financial assets. *(p. 13)*

Initial public offering (IPO) The first time a firm sells stock to the public. *(p. 315)*

Inside information Relevant information about a security that is not publicly available. *(p. 173)*

Insolvent The situation for a bank or another firm of having a negative net worth because the firm's assets have less value than its liabilities. *(p. 351)*

Insurance company A financial intermediary that specializes in writing contracts to protect policyholders from the risk of financial loss associated with particular events. *(p. 336)*

Interest rate The cost of borrowing funds (or the payment for lending funds), usually expressed as a percentage of the amount borrowed. *(p. 3)*

Interest-rate parity condition The proposition that differences in interest rates on similar bonds in different countries reflect expectations of future changes in exchange rates. *(p. 243)*

Interest-rate risk The risk that the price of a financial asset will fluctuate in response to changes in market interest rates. *(pp. 74 and 296)*

Interest-rate swap A contract under which counterparties agree to swap interest payments over a specified period on a fixed dollar amount, called the *notional principal*. *(p. 212)*

International Monetary Fund (IMF) A multinational organization established in 1944 by the Bretton Woods agreement to administer a system of fixed exchange rates and to serve as a lender of last resort to countries undergoing balance-of-payments problems. *(p. 502)*

International reserves Central bank assets that are denominated in a foreign currency and used in international transactions. *(p. 488)*

Investment banking Financial activities that involve underwriting new security issues and providing advice on mergers and acquisitions. *(p. 314)*

Investment institution A financial firm, such as a mutual fund or a hedge fund, that raises funds to invest in loans and securities. *(p. 327)*

IS curve A curve in the *IS–MP* model that shows the combinations of the real interest rate and aggregate output that represent equilibrium in the market for goods and services. *(p. 552)*

IS–LM model A macroeconomic model of aggregate demand that assumes that the central bank targets the money supply. *(p. 588)*

IS–MP model A macroeconomic model that consists of an *IS* curve, which represents equilibrium in the goods market; an *MP* curve, which represents monetary policy; and a Phillips curve, which represents the short-run relationship between the output gap (which is the percentage difference between actual and potential real GDP) and the inflation rate. *(p. 552)*

Large open economy An economy in which changes in the demand and supply for loanable funds are large enough to affect the world real interest rate. *(p. 115)*

Law of one price The fundamental economic idea that identical products should sell for the same price everywhere. *(p. 234)*

Legal tender The government designation that currency is accepted as payment of taxes and must be accepted by individuals and firms in payment of debts. *(p. 28)*

Lender of last resort A central bank that acts as the ultimate source of credit to the banking system, making loans to solvent banks against their good, but illiquid, loans. *(p. 352)*

Leverage A measure of how much debt an investor assumes in making an investment. *(p. 293)*

Liability Something that an individual or a firm owes, particularly a financial claim on an individual or a firm. *(p. 281)*

Limited liability A legal provision that shields owners of a corporation from losing more than they have invested in the firm. *(p. 158)*

Liquidity The ease with which an asset can be exchanged for money. *(p. 13)*

Liquidity premium theory (or **preferred habitat theory**) A theory of the term structure of interest rates that holds that the interest rate on a long-term bond is an average of the interest rates investors expect on short-term bonds over the lifetime of the long-term bond, plus a term premium that increases in value the longer the maturity of the bond. *(p. 147)*

Liquidity risk The possibility that a bank may not be able to meet its cash needs by selling assets or raising funds at a reasonable cost. *(p. 293)*

LM curve A curve that shows the combinations of the interest rate and the output gap that result in equilibrium in the money market. *(p. 588)*

Loan commitment An agreement by a bank to provide a borrower with a stated amount of funds during a specified period of time. *(p. 303)*

Loan sale A financial contract in which a bank agrees to sell the expected future returns from an underlying bank loan to a third party. *(p. 303)*

Long position In a futures contract, the right and obligation of the buyer to receive or buy the underlying asset on the specified future date. *(p. 195)*

Long-run aggregate supply (LRAS) curve A curve that shows the relationship in the long run between the price level and the quantity of aggregate output, or real GDP, supplied by firms. *(p. 528)*

M1 A narrow definition of the money supply: The sum of currency in circulation, checking account deposits, and holdings of traveler's checks. *(p. 32)*

M2 A broad definition of the money supply: all the assets that are included in M1, as well as time deposits with a value of less than $100,000, savings accounts, money market deposit accounts, and noninstitutional money market mutual fund shares. *(p. 33)*

Managed float regime An exchange rate system in which central banks occasionally intervene to affect foreign exchange values; also called a dirty float regime. *(p. 506)*

Margin requirement In the futures market, the minimum deposit that an exchange requires from the buyer and seller of a financial asset; reduces default risk. *(p. 202)*

Market (or **systematic**) **risk** Risk that is common to all assets of a certain type, such as the increases and decreases in stocks resulting from the business cycle. *(p. 94)*

Marking to market In the futures market, a daily settlement in which the exchange transfers funds from a buyer's account to a seller's account or vice versa, depending on changes in the price of the contract. *(p. 202)*

Medium of exchange Something that is generally accepted as payment for goods and services; a function of money. *(p. 27)*

Monetary aggregate A measure of the quantity of money that is broader than currency; M1 and M2 are monetary aggregates. *(p. 32)*

Monetary base (or **high-powered money**) The sum of bank reserves and currency in circulation. *(p. 417)*

Monetary neutrality The proposition that changes in the money supply have no effect on output in the long run because an increase (decrease) in the money supply raises (lowers) the price level in the long run but does not change the equilibrium level of output. *(p. 534)*

Monetary policy The actions the Federal Reserve takes to manage the money supply and interest rates to pursue macroeconomic policy objectives. *(p. 11)*

Money Anything that is generally accepted in payment for goods and services or to pay off debts. *(pp. 3 and 24)*

Money market mutual fund A mutual fund that invests exclusively in short-term assets, such as Treasury bills, negotiable certificates of deposit, and commercial paper. *(p. 328)*

Money supply The total quantity of money in the economy. *(p. 3)*

Moral hazard The risk that people will take actions after they have entered into a transaction that will make the other party worse off. *(p. 257)*

MP curve A curve in the *IS–MP* model that represents Federal Reserve monetary policy. *(p. 552)*

Multiple deposit creation Part of the money supply process in which an increase in bank reserves results in rounds of bank loans and creation of checkable deposits and an increase in the money supply that is a multiple of the initial increase in reserves. *(p. 427)*

Multiplier The change in equilibrium GDP divided by a change in autonomous expenditure. *(p. 556)*

Multiplier effect The process by which a change in autonomous expenditure leads to a larger change in equilibrium GDP. *(p. 556)*

Municipal bonds Bonds issued by state and local governments. *(p. 132)*

Mutual fund A financial intermediary that raises funds by selling shares to individual savers and invests the funds in a portfolio of stocks, bonds, mortgages, and money market securities. *(p. 327)*

National bank A federally chartered bank. *(p. 299)*

Net interest margin The difference between the interest a bank receives on its securities and loans and the interest it pays on deposits and debt, divided by the total value of its earning assets. *(p. 292)*

Net worth The difference between the value of a firm's assets and the value of its liabilities. *(p. 262)*

Nominal exchange rate The price of one currency in terms of another currency; also called the *exchange rate*. *(p. 225)*

Nominal interest rate An interest rate that is not adjusted for changes in purchasing power. *(p. 75)*

Off-balance-sheet activities Activities that do not affect a bank's balance sheet because they do not increase either the bank's assets or its liabilities. *(p. 302)*

Okun's law A statistical relationship discovered by Arthur Okun between the output gap and the cyclical rate of unemployment. *(p. 567)*

Open economy An economy in which households, firms, and governments borrow and lend internationally. *(p. 113)*

Open market operations The Federal Reserve's purchases and sales of securities, usually U.S. Treasury securities, in financial markets. *(pp. 420 and 451)*

Open market purchase The Federal Reserve's purchase of securities, usually U.S. Treasury securities. *(p. 420)*

Open market sale The Fed's sale of securities, usually Treasury securities. *(p. 420)*

Option A type of derivative contract in which the buyer has the right to buy or sell the underlying asset at a set price during a set period of time. *(p. 203)*

Option premium The price of an option. *(p. 206)*

Output gap The percentage difference between real GDP and potential GDP. *(p. 560)*

Over-the-counter market A market in which financial securities are bought and sold by dealers linked by computer. *(p. 159)*

Payments system The mechanism for conducting transactions in the economy. *(p. 29)*

Pegging The decision by a country to keep the exchange rate fixed between its currency and another country's currency. *(p. 512)*

Pension fund A financial intermediary that invests contributions of workers and firms in stocks, bonds, and mortgages to provide for pension benefit payments during workers' retirements. *(p. 334)*

Phillips curve A curve that shows the short-run relationship between the output gap (or the unemployment rate) and the inflation rate. *(p. 552)*

Political business cycle The theory that policymakers will urge the Fed to lower interest rates to stimulate the economy prior to an election. *(p. 403)*

Portfolio A collection of assets, such as stocks and bonds. *(p. 8)*

Potential GDP The level of real GDP attained when all firms are producing at capacity. *(p. 555)*

Present value The value today of funds that will be received in the future. *(p. 54)*

Primary credit Discount loans available to healthy banks experiencing temporary liquidity problems. *(p. 464)*

Primary market A financial market in which stocks, bonds, and other securities are sold for the first time. *(p. 9)*

Prime rate Formerly, the interest rate banks charged on six-month loans to high-quality borrowers; currently, an interest rate banks charge primarily to smaller borrowers. *(p. 295)*

Principal–agent problem The moral hazard problem of managers (the agents) pursuing their own interests rather than those of shareholders (the principals). *(p. 266)*

Principal–agent view A theory of central bank decision making that holds that officials maximize their personal well-being rather than that of the general public. *(p. 403)*

Private equity firm (or corporate restructuring firm) A firm that raises equity capital to acquire shares in other firms to reduce free-rider and moral hazard problems. *(p. 268)*

Public interest view A theory of central bank decision making that holds that officials act in the best interest of the public. *(p. 402)*

Publicly traded company A corporation that sells stock in the U.S. stock market; only 5,100 of the 5 million U.S. corporations are publicly traded companies. *(p. 159)*

Put option A type of derivative contract that gives the buyer the right to sell the underlying asset at a set price during a set period of time. *(p. 203)*

Quantitative easing A central bank policy that attempts to stimulate the economy by buying long-term securities. *(p. 463)*

Quantity theory of money A theory about the connection between money and prices that assumes that the velocity of money is constant. *(p. 36)*

Quota A limit a government imposes on the quantity of a good that can be imported. *(p. 237)*

Random walk The unpredictable movements in the price of a security. *(p. 174)*

Rate of return, *R* The return on a security as a percentage of the initial price; for a bond during a holding period of one year, the coupon payment plus the change in the price of a bond divided by the initial price. *(p. 73)*

Rational expectations The assumption that people make forecasts of future values of a variable using all available information; formally, the assumption that expectations equal optimal forecasts, using all available information. *(p. 171)*

Real exchange rate The rate at which goods and services in one country can be exchanged for goods and services in another country. *(p. 229)*

Real interest rate An interest rate that is adjusted for changes in purchasing power. *(p. 76)*

Real money balances The value of money held by households and firms, adjusted for changes in the price level; M/P. *(p. 522)*

Relationship banking The ability of banks to assess credit risks on the basis of private information about borrowers. *(p. 262)*

Required reserve ratio The percentage of checkable deposits that the Fed specifies that banks must hold as reserves. *(p. 419)*

Required reserves Reserves that the Fed requires banks to hold against demand deposit and NOW account balances. *(pp. 285 and 419)*

Required return on equities, r_E The expected return necessary to compensate for the risk of investing in stocks. *(p. 165)*

Reserve requirement The regulation requiring banks to hold a fraction of checkable deposits as vault cash or deposits with the Fed. *(p. 452)*

Reserves A bank asset consisting of vault cash plus bank deposits with the Federal Reserve. *(p. 285)*

Restrictive covenant A clause in a bond contract that places limits on the uses of funds that a borrower receives. *(p. 267)*

Return The total earnings from a security; for a bond during a holding period of one year, the coupon payment plus the change in the price of the bond. *(p. 73)*

Return on assets (ROA) The ratio of the value of a bank's after-tax profit to the value of its assets. *(p. 292)*

Return on equity (ROE) The ratio of the value of a bank's after-tax profit to the value of its capital. *(p. 292)*

Revaluation The raising of the official value of a country's currency relative to other currencies. *(p. 503)*

Risk The degree of uncertainty in the return on an asset. *(p. 90)*

Risk sharing A service the financial system provides that allows savers to spread and transfer risk. *(p. 13)*

Risk structure of interest rates The relationship among interest rates on bonds that have different characteristics but the same maturity. *(p. 125)*

Seasonal credit Discount loans to smaller banks in areas where agriculture or tourism is important. *(p. 465)*

Secondary credit Discount loans to banks that are not eligible for primary credit. *(p. 465)*

Secondary market A financial market in which investors buy and sell existing securities. *(p. 9)*

Securitization The process of converting loans and other financial assets that are not tradable into securities. *(p. 4)*

Security A financial asset that can be bought and sold in a financial market. *(p. 2)*

Segmented markets theory A theory of the term structure of interest rates that holds that the interest rate on a bond of a particular maturity is determined only by the demand and supply for bonds of that maturity. *(p. 146)*

Settlement date The date on which the delivery of a commodity or financial asset specified in a forward contract must take place. *(p. 193)*

Short position In a futures contract, the right and obligation of the seller to sell or deliver the underlying asset on the specified future date. *(p. 195)*

Short-run aggregate supply (SRAS) curve A curve that shows the relationship in the short run between the price level and the quantity of aggregate output, or real GDP, supplied by firms. *(p. 525)*

Simple deposit multiplier The ratio of the amount of deposits created by banks to the amount of new reserves. *(p. 427)*

Simple loan A debt instrument in which the borrower receives from the lender an amount called the principal and agrees to repay the lender the principal plus interest on a specific date when the loan matures. *(p. 58)*

Small open economy An economy in which the quantity of loanable funds supplied or demanded is too small to affect the world real interest rate. *(p. 114)*

Specialization A system in which individuals produce the goods or services for which they have relatively the best ability. *(p. 26)*

Speculate To place financial bets, as in buying or selling futures or option contracts, in an attempt to profit from movements in asset prices. *(p. 192)*

Spot price The price at which a commodity or financial asset can be sold at the current date. *(p. 193)*

Stabilization policy A monetary policy or fiscal policy intended to reduce the severity of the business cycle and stabilize the economy. *(p. 538)*

Standard of deferred payment The characteristic of money by which it facilitates exchange over time; a function of money. *(p. 27)*

Standby letter of credit A promise by a bank to lend funds, if necessary, to a seller of commercial paper at the time that the commercial paper matures. *(p. 302)*

Sterilized foreign exchange intervention A foreign exchange market intervention in which the central bank offsets the effect of the intervention on the monetary base. *(p. 490)*

Stock Financial securities that represent partial ownership of a firm; also called *equities*. *(p. 3)*

Stock exchange A physical location where stocks are bought and sold face-to-face on a trading floor. *(p. 159)*

Stock market index An average of stock prices that is used to measure the overall performance of the stock market. *(p. 161)*

Store of value The accumulation of wealth by holding dollars or other assets that can be used to buy goods and services in the future; a function of money. *(p. 27)*

Strike price (or exercise price) The price at which the buyer of an option has the right to buy or sell the underlying asset. *(p. 203)*

Supply shock An unexpected change in production costs or in technology that causes the short-run aggregate supply curve to shift. *(p. 529)*

Swap An agreement between two or more counterparties to exchange sets of cash flows over some future period. *(p. 212)*

Syndicate A group of investment banks that jointly underwrite a security issue. *(p. 315)*

Systemic risk Risk to the entire financial system rather than to individual firms or investors. *(p. 340)*

T-account An accounting tool used to show changes in balance sheet items. *(p. 289)*

Tariff A tax a government imposes on imports. *(p. 237)*

Taylor rule A monetary policy guideline developed by economist John Taylor for determining the target for the federal funds rate. *(p. 474)*

Term premium The additional interest investors require in order to be willing to buy a long-term bond rather than a comparable sequence of short-term bonds. *(p. 147)*

Term structure of interest rates The relationship among the interest rates on bonds that are otherwise similar but that have different maturities. *(p. 137)*

Theory of purchasing power parity (PPP) The theory that exchange rates move to equalize the purchasing power of different currencies. *(p. 235)*

Time value of money The way that the value of a payment changes depending on when the payment is received. *(p. 54)*

Too-big-to-fail policy A policy under which the federal government does not allow large financial firms to fail, for fear of damaging the financial system. *(p. 370)*

Transactions costs The cost of a trade or a financial transaction; for example, the brokerage commission charged for buying or selling a financial asset. *(pp. 25 and 256)*

Troubled Asset Relief Program (TARP) A government program under which the U.S. Treasury purchased stock in hundreds of banks to increase the banks' capital. *(p. 306)*

Underwriting An activity in which an investment bank guarantees to the issuing corporation the price of a new security and then resells the security for a profit. *(p. 315)*

Unit of account A way of measuring value in an economy in terms of money; a function of money. *(p. 27)*

Unsterilized foreign exchange intervention A foreign exchange market intervention in which the central bank does not offset the effect of the intervention on the monetary base. *(p. 490)*

Vault cash Cash on hand in a bank; includes currency in ATMs and deposits with other banks. *(pp. 285 and 419)*

Venture capital firm A firm that raises equity capital from investors to invest in startup firms. *(p. 268)*

Wall Street Reform and Consumer Protection Act (Dodd-Frank Act) Legislation passed during 2010 that was intended to reform regulation of the financial system. *(p. 398)*

Wealth The sum of the value of a person's assets minus the value of the person's liabilities. *(p. 28)*

Yield to maturity The interest rate that makes the present value of the payments from an asset equal to the asset's price today. *(p. 63)*

Index

Key Symbols and Abbreviations

$*$: Equilibrium value of a variable

Δ: Change in a variable

ΔD: Change in deposits

ΔR: Change in reserves

π: Current inflation rate

π^e: Expected inflation rate

a: A constant that represents how much the gap between the current rate of unemployment and the natural rate affects the inflation rate

AD: Aggregate demand

AD–AS model: Aggregate demand and aggregate supply model

AE: Aggregate expenditure

AS: Aggregate supply

B: Monetary base

B_{non}: Nonborrowed monetary base

BR: Borrowed reserves

C: Consumption spending

C: Coupon (on a bond)

C: Currency in circulation

C/D: Currency-to-deposit ratio

D: Checkable deposits

e: Real exchange rate

E: Nominal exchange rate

ER: Excess reserves

ER/D: Excess reserves-to-deposit ratio

FP: Fixed payments

FV: Future value

g: Constant growth rate of dividends in the Gordon growth model

G: Local, state, and federal government purchases

i: Nominal interest rate

i_{1t}: Interest rate at time t on a one-year bond

i_{nt}: Interest rate at time t on an n-year bond

i_D: Discount rate; interest rate the Federal Reserve charges on discount loans to banks

i_{ff}: Federal funds rate

i_{rb}: Interest rate paid by the Federal Reserve on banks' reserve deposits

I: Investment spending (on real physical capital)

IS curve: Equilibrium in the goods market

$LRAS$: Long-run aggregate supply

m: Money multiplier

M: Quantity of money

M1: Currency plus checkable deposits; narrow definition of the money supply

M2: Broad definition of the money supply

MP curve: Monetary policy

M/P: Real money balances

MPC: Marginal propensity to consume

n: Years

NX: Net exports

P: Price level

P^e: Expected price level

PPP: Theory of purchasing power parity

r: Real interest rate

R: Rate of return

R: Total reserves equals required reserves (RR) plus excess reserves (ER)

r_E: Required return on equities

ROA: Return on assets

ROE: Return on equity

rr_D: Required reserve ratio

RR: Required reserves

s: A variable representing the effects of a supply shock

$SRAS$: Short-run aggregate supply

U: Current unemployment rate

U^*: Natural rate of unemployment

V: Velocity of money

Y: Real aggregate output, or real GDP

Y^P: Potential GDP, sometimes referred to as *full-employment GDP*

Equations

Aggregate expenditure: $AE = C + I + G + NX$ — Chapter 17, page 521

Assets $=$ Liabilities $+$ Shareholders' equity — Chapter 10, page 281

Compounding: $PV \times (1 + i)^n = FV_n$ — Chapter 3, page 55

Consumption function: $C = MPC \times Y$ — Chapter 18, page 554

Currency in M1 $=$ Currency outstanding $-$ Vault cash — Chapter 14, page 419

Discounting: $PV = \dfrac{FV_n}{(1 + i)^n}$ — Chapter 3, page 55

Equation of exchange: $M \times V = P \times Y$ — Chapter 2, page 36